THE CAMBRIDGE ILLUSTRATED HISTORY OF
Warfare

THE CAMBRIDGE ILLUSTRATED HISTORY OF

Warfare

The Triumph of the West
Revised and Updated

Edited By

GEOFFREY PARKER

Andreas Dorpalen Professor of History at the Ohio State University

CAMBRIDGE
UNIVERSITY PRESS

CAMBRIDGE
UNIVERSITY PRESS

University Printing House, Cambridge CB2 8BS, United Kingdom

One Liberty Plaza, 20th Floor, New York, NY 10006, USA

477 Williamstown Road, Port Melbourne, VIC 3207, Australia

314–321, 3rd Floor, Plot 3, Splendor Forum, Jasola District Centre, New Delhi – 110025, India

79 Anson Road, #06–04/06, Singapore 079906

Cambridge University Press is part of the University of Cambridge.

It furthers the University's mission by disseminating knowledge in the pursuit of education, learning and research at the highest international levels of excellence.

www.cambridge.org
Information on this title: www.cambridge.org/9780521738064

First published 1995
First paperback edition 2000
Reprinted 2004 (twice), 2005
Revised and updated 2008
3rd printing 2020

Printed in Singapore by Markono Print Media Pte Ltd

A catalogue record for this publication is available from the British Library

ISBN 978-0-521-73806-4 Paperback

Contents

Preface   vii

INTRODUCTION: THE WESTERN WAY OF WAR   2
Geoffrey Parker

PART 1 THE AGE OF MASSED INFANTRY

1 Genesis of the Infantry 600–350 BC   12
Victor Davis Hanson

2 From Phalanx to Legion 350–250 BC   32
Victor Davis Hanson

3 The Roman Way of War 250 BC–AD 300   50
Victor Davis Hanson

PART 2 THE AGE OF STONE FORTIFICATIONS

4 On Roman Ramparts 300–1300   64
Bernard S. Bachrach

5 New Weapons, New Tactics 1300–1500   92
Christopher Allmand

6 The Gunpowder Revolution 1300–1500   106
Geoffrey Parker

PART 3 THE AGE OF GUNS AND SAILS

7 Ships of the Line 1500–1650   120
Geoffrey Parker

8 Conquest of the Americas 1500–1650   132
Patricia Seed

9 Dynastic War 1494–1660   146
Geoffrey Parker

10 States in Conflict 1661–1763   164
John A. Lynn

11 Nations in Arms 1763–1815   186
John A. Lynn

PART 4 THE AGE OF MECHANIZED WARFARE

12 The Industrialization of War 1815–71   216
Williamson A. Murray

13 *Towards World War 1871–1914*   242
Williamson A. Murray

14 *The West at War 1914–18*   266
Williamson A. Murray

15 *The World in Conflict 1919–41*   298
Williamson A. Murray

16 *The World at War 1941–45*   320
Williamson A. Murray

17 *The Post-War World 1945–2007*   340
Williamson A. Murray and Geoffrey Parker*

EPILOGUE: THE FUTURE OF WESTERN WARFARE   389
Geoffrey Parker

REFERENCE GUIDE

Chronology   407

Glossary   411

Bibliography   415

THE CONTRIBUTORS   423

NOTES   425

PICTURE ACKNOWLEDGEMENTS   429

INDEX   430

*Williamson Murray wrote the text down to page 363; Geoffrey Parker wrote the rest.

Preface

This work follows the format of other Cambridge Illustrated Histories in that pictures and text both seek to tell the same story in parallel. The authors have sought illustrations – sometimes clusters of illustrations – that clarify points of particular importance, so that readers can fully appreciate each of the key stages in the 'triumph of the west'.

We are fully aware that our approach, from our sub-title onwards, lays itself open to the charge of Eurocentrism; but we offer three defences. First, it would be impossible to provide adequate coverage in a single volume of the military history of all major cultures (some of them, like the Chinese way of war, stretching back even further than that of Europe). Second, merely to pay lip-service to the military and naval traditions of Africa, Asia, and the Americas, while devoting the lion's share of the attention to the West, would be unpardonable distortion. Finally, as explained in the Introduction, for good or ill over the past two centuries the western way of war has become dominant all over the world. In the nineteenth and twentieth centuries remarkably few states and cultures managed to resist western arms for long – and the few that did so usually succeeded by imitation or adaptation. The rise and development of this dominant tradition, together with the secret of its success, therefore seems worthy of examination and analysis.

The editor has accumulated many debts of gratitude. Since all the contributors to this volume wrote their drafts at the same time, a substantial amount of revising and rewriting was required to ensure that each chapter complemented, but did not duplicate, the others. First and foremost, therefore, I wish to thank my co-authors, who graciously accepted more editorial interference than any scholar should have to suffer and also provided me with invaluable assistance and encouragement. Next I am delighted to acknowledge the support of my editors at Cambridge University Press: Peter Richards first proposed the idea of this book to me, and without his advice and acumen it would never have been completed; Eric Crahan oversaw the expansion of the original text (which ended with the Gulf War of 1991) down to the present. I also thank Peter Pierson and Jon Sumida for drawing some errors in the original edition to my attention. Finally, we are all grateful to those who have offered suggestions and references: to Jon Sumida, who offered me some excellent advice at an early stage; to Michael Howard and Donald Kagan, who read the entire work in first draft; and to the many other colleagues whose assistance to individual contributors is acknowledged on pages 423–4 below.

Geoffrey Parker

Dedicated by the authors to
Michael Howard and William McNeill,
who set the standard to which we aspire.

Left: Serving a Perrott rifle gun,
Union army, American Civil War.

Page i: The trenches in World War I

Pages ii–iii: The use of the musket
and the pike, in Jacob de Gheyn's
Exercise of Arms, 1607.

INTRODUCTION *The Western Way of War*

Every culture develops its own way of war. Societies where land is plentiful but manpower scarce tend to favour a ritualized conflict in which only a few 'champions' actually fight but their fate decides that of everyone. The 'flower wars' of the Aztecs and the 'amok' combats of the Indonesian islanders caused relatively little bloodshed because they aimed to seize people rather than territory, to increase each warlord's available manpower rather than waste it in bloody battles. In China, too, strategy aimed to achieve victory without battle: according to the most revered military theorist, Sun-Tzu (writing in the fourth century BC), 'To subdue the enemy without fighting is the acme of skill' (although the rest of his book in fact deals with how to win by fighting). Many non-western military traditions have displayed great continuity over time: thus even in the 1960s anthropologists could study the wars of the highland peoples of Irian Jaya in Indonesia who still settled their disputes in the same ritualized way as their ancestors. By then, however, most other military cultures had been transformed by that of the West – of Europe and the former European colonies in the Americas.

The western way of war, which also boasts great antiquity, rests upon five principal foundations. First, the armed forces of the West have always placed heavy reliance on superior technology, usually to compensate for inferior numbers. That is not to say that the West enjoyed *universal* technological superiority – until the advent of musketry volleys and field artillery in the early seventeenth century, the recurved bow used by horse archers all over Asia proved far more effective than any western weaponry – but, with few exceptions, the horse archers of Asia did not directly threaten the West and, when they did, the threat was not sustained. Nor did all the advanced technology originate in the West: many vital innovations, including the stirrup and gunpowder, came from eastern adversaries.

Now military technology is usually the first to be borrowed by every society, because the penalty for failing to do so can be immediate and fatal; but the West seems to have been preternaturally receptive to new technology, whether from its own inventors or from outside. Technological innovation, and the equally vital ability to respond to it, soon became an established feature of western warfare. Indeed, since the Persian wars in the fifth century BC, few periods can be found during which the West proved unable to muster forces with a fighting potential superior to that of its immediate adversaries.

THE PRIMACY OF TECHNOLOGY AND DISCIPLINE

A 'technological edge', however, has rarely been sufficient in itself to ensure victory. As the Swiss military writer Antoine-Henri Jomini wrote in the early nineteenth century: 'The superiority of armament may increase the chances of success in war, but it does not of itself win battles.' Even in the twentieth century, the outcome of

Military innovation has always been a hallmark of the western way of war. World War I alone (1914–18) initiated soldiers into the use of camouflage, tank warfare, and aerial combat and reconnaissance. It also introduced them to a new and hideous kind of weapon: poison gas. But relatively effective counter-measures soon evolved, and the war dragged on. Here a German soldier wears a box respirator to carry food to his dug-out during a gas attack.

wars has been determined less by technology than by better war plans, the achievement of surprise, greater economic strength and, above all, superior discipline. Western military practice has always exalted discipline – rather than kinship, religion or patriotism – as the primary instrument that turns bands of men fighting as individuals into soldiers fighting as part of organized units. Naturally the other factors play their part: many military formations, even in the eighteenth century, came from the same area and served under their local leaders almost as an extended family; the 'Protestant cause' proved a potent rallying cry for much of the sixteenth and seventeenth centuries in northern Europe; and 'Your country needs you,' and similar slogans, have assisted recruiting down to our own days. Nevertheless, these elements have always been eclipsed in the West by the primacy of discipline, in the twin forms of drill and long-term service.

Even the hoplites of fifth-century Greece, who were farmers first and soldiers second, turned out so regularly for battle in their phalanxes that they perfected a high degree of combat effectiveness. For the critical element of discipline is the ability of a formation to stand fast in the face of the enemy, whether attacking or being attacked, without giving way to the natural impulses of fear and panic. Repeated group activities, whether directly related to combat (firing practice) or not (drill), all have the effect of creating artificial kinship groups – some of them, like the cohort, the company and the platoon, further reinforced by the creation of small fellowships within the unit in order to increase cohesion and therefore combat efficiency even further.

Once again, the crucial advantage lay in the ability to compensate for numerical inferiority, for whether defending Europe from invasion (as at Plataea in 479 BC, at the Lechfeld in AD 955 and at Vienna in AD 1683), or in subduing the Aztec, Inca and Mughal empires, the western forces have always been outnumbered by at least two to one and often by far more. Without superb discipline as well as advanced technology, these odds would have proved overwhelming. Even Alexander the Great and his 60,000 Greek and Macedonian troops could scarcely have destroyed the forces of the Persian empire in the fourth century BC without superior discipline, since his adversaries probably numbered more Greek soldiers (fighting with much the same equipment) in their own armies!

Discipline proved particularly important for western armies in another way because, with surprisingly few exceptions, their wars were normally won by infantry. The long reign of the hoplites and the legionaries was followed by a millennium in which men fighting on foot won most of the battles (and of course bore the brunt of the more numerous sieges). The rise of missile weapons – first bows and then firearms – only served to reinforce the trend. However, withstanding a full cavalry charge without flinching always required arduous training, strong unit cohesion, and superb self-control. The same was true of war at sea: whether resisting boarding parties on a galley or enduring a cannonade aboard a ship-of-the-line, discipline and training proved essential.

Only two civilizations have invented drill for their infantry: China and Europe. Moreover, both of them did so twice: in the fifth century BC, in North China and in Greece, and again in the late sixteenth century. Exponents of the second phase – Ch'i Chi-kuang in Imperial China and Maurice of Nassau in the Dutch Republic – explicitly sought to revive classical precedents, and in the West marching in step and standing on parade became a permanent part of military life (even when, as for one British Guardsman in 1970, the ordeal proved overwhelming).

The Peerlesse Macedon, chylde of triumphã victori
Presents his armes, his arte of warr, & fortie vnto thee

THE TACTIKS OF
ÆLIAN

Or art of embattailing an army
after y.e Grecian manner

Englished & illustrated w.th figures throughout
& notes vpon y.e Chapters of y.e ordinary
motions of y.e Phalange by J.B.

The exercise military of y.e English by y.e order
of that great Generall Maurice of
Nassau Prince of Orange &c
Gouernor & Generall of y.e
vnited Prouinces is added

London for Lawrence Lisle & are to be sold at
his Shoppe at y.e signe of the Tygers head
in Paules Churchyard   6 : 6 :

CONTINUITY OF THE WESTERN MILITARY TRADITION

Reinforcing these elements, and indeed refining them, is a remarkable continuity in military theory. The history of *Concerning Military Matters*, a compendium of Roman military practice first composed by Flavius Renatus Vegetius around the year AD 390 (and revised into its final form about fifty years later), offers perhaps the most remarkable example. In the early eighth century the Northumbrian scholar Bede, on the north-western fringe of the former Roman world, possessed a copy; in the ninth, the Carolingian ruler Lothar I commissioned an abridgement of the work to help him devise a successful strategy for resisting the Scandinavian invasions; while in 1147, when Count Geoffrey Plantagenet of Anjou was engaged in a siege, an incendiary device was constructed and used thanks to a reading of Vegetius, Translated into many vernacular languages (French, Italian, English, German, Spanish, and perhaps even Hebrew) between the end of the thirteenth and the beginning of the sixteenth centuries, the sustained popularity of *Concerning Military Matters* is further attested by the number of surviving medieval manuscripts, some of them reduced to pocket size for use in the field. Even in the middle of the eighteenth century, the young George Washington possessed and annotated his own copy.

Other classical works on military affairs also enjoyed continuing popularity and influence. In AD 1594 Maurice of Nassau and his cousins in the Netherlands devised the crucial innovation of volley fire for muskets after reading the account in Aelian's *Tactics* (written c.AD 100) of the techniques employed by the javelin- and sling-shot throwers of the Roman army, and spent the next decade introducing to their troops the drills practised by the legions. In the nineteenth century Napoleon III and Helmut von Moltke both translated the campaign histories of Julius Caesar, written almost 2,000 years earlier, while Count Alfred von Schlieffen and his successors in the Prussian general staff expressly modelled their strategy for destroying France in the 'next war' upon the stunningly successful tactic of encirclement attributed by Roman writers to Hannibal at the battle of Cannae in 216 BC. In AD 1914 it came within an ace of success. More recently still, General George C. Marshall argued that a soldier should begin his military education by reading Thucydides' *History of the Peloponnesian War*, written almost 2,500 years before.

These striking continuities derive from the fact that ancient theorists and modern practitioners of war shared not only a love of precedent, and a conviction that past examples could and should influence present practice, but also a willingness to accept ideas from all quarters. Religious and ideological constraints have seldom interfered with either the discussion or the conduct of war in the West. On the one hand, the 'laws of war' have (until the nineteenth century) been drawn in the most general terms and normally lacked any effective machinery of enforcement. On the other, from Plato's Academy down to the modern war colleges, censorship – both religious and secular – has been generally absent, allowing the full systematization of knowledge. Certain core ideas have therefore remained remarkably constant. These include not only the constant emphasis on the need for superior technology and discipline, but also a vision of war centred on winning a decisive victory that brought about the enemy's unconditional surrender. As Carl von Clausewitz put it in his early nineteenth-century treatise *On War*: 'The direct annihilation of the enemy's forces must always be the dominant consideration' because 'Destruction of the enemy forces is the overriding principle of war.' Other theorists, however, stressed an alternative strategy for achieving total victory, attrition, of which the military history of the West also offers abundant examples: Fabius Cunctator ('the Delayer') of Rome, whose reliance on time, the 'friction' of campaigning and the superior marshalling of resources eventually reversed the verdict of Cannae; the duke of Alba in the service of sixteenth-century Spain; even Ulysses S. Grant against Robert E. Lee during the last phase of the American Civil War (1864–65).

Yet the overall aim of western strategy, whether by battle, siege or attrition, almost always remained the total defeat and destruction of the enemy, and this contrasted starkly with the military practice of many other societies. Many classical writers commented on the utter ruthlessness of hoplites and legionaries, and in the early modern period the phrase *bellum romanum* acquired the sense of 'war without mercy' and became the standard military technique of Europeans abroad. Thus the Naragansetts of southern New England strongly disapproved of the western way of war: 'It was too furious,' one brave told an English captain in 1638, 'and [it] slays too many men.' The captain did not deny it: the Indians, he speculated, 'might fight seven years and not kill seven men.' In 1788, warfare in West Africa seemed much the same to European observers and the local warlords confirmed 'that the sole object of their wars was to procure slaves, as they could not obtain European goods without slaves, and they could not get slaves without fighting for them.' Clearly peoples who fought to enslave rather than to exterminate their enemies would, like the indigenous inhabitants of the Americas, Southeast Asia, and Siberia before them, prove ill-prepared to withstand the unfamiliar tactics of destruction employed against them by the Europeans.

THE CHALLENGE-AND-RESPONSE DYNAMIC

But the steady spread of western military power rested on far more than the triad of technology, discipline and an aggressive military tradition. Many other military cultures (such as those of China and Japan) also placed a high premium on technology and discipline, and the teachings of Sun Tzu strikingly anticipated many positions later developed by Clausewitz and Jomini. However, the West differed in two crucial respects: first, in its unique ability to change as well as to conserve its military practices as need arose; second, in its power to finance those changes.

Areas dominated by a single hegemonic power, such as Tokugawa Japan or Mughal India, faced relatively few life-threatening challenges and so military traditions changed slowly if at all; but in areas contested by multiple polities the

Opposite: When in 1616 John Bingham published an English translation of the *Tactics* of Aelian, written c.AD 100 and describing the drills of the Roman and Macedonian army, he added a section on the 'exercise military' recently developed by Maurice of Nassau, leader of the Dutch Republic. This was justified, since the military reforms of the Dutch army had been directly influenced by reading Aelian and other classical texts; less reasonable was the scene at the top of Bingham's frontispiece, in which Alexander the Great ('the peerlesse Macedon' on the right) is shown handing over his sword, and by implication his military genius and pre-eminence, to Maurice.

need for military innovation could become extremely strong. Admittedly, when the states remained relatively underdeveloped, with backward political and economic institutions and infrastructures, the tension between challenge and response seldom resulted in rapid and significant change. But where the major competing states were both numerous and institutionally strong, the challenge and response dynamic could become self-sustaining, with growth (in effect) begetting growth.

This mechanism has been compared to the biological model known as 'punctuated equilibrium', in which development proceeds by short bursts of rapid change interspersed with longer periods of slower, incremental alteration. Thus, in the fourteenth century, after a long period in which infantry had slowly but steadily increased in importance, Swiss pikemen and English archers suddenly and dramatically enhanced its role; then, after about a century of experiment, gunpowder artillery began in the 1430s to revolutionize siegecraft; and about a century after that, following constant (and extremely expensive) experiment, a new defensive technique known as the artillery fortress brought positional warfare back into balance. Each innovation broke the prevailing equilibrium and provoked a phase of rapid transformation and adjustment.

However, the ability to reproduce unfamiliar military techniques and strategies required more than changes in the art of war. Above all, a military system based on maintaining a technological edge is, by definition, expensive: *labour*-intensive systems, which rely for their impact upon concentrating an overwhelming number of men, may only require a society to mobilize its adult males – probably only for a brief period – equipped with traditional weapons (sometimes, as in the case of Japanese or early medieval European swords, weapons of considerable antiquity that could, like Excalibur, be re-used again and again). The financial burden of fighting may therefore be spread over a wide social group and even over several generations. A capital-intensive military system, by contrast, requires the stockpiling of a wide panoply of weapons that, although extremely expensive, may soon become outdated. Its attraction, however, lay precisely in the combination of high initial cost with low maintenance: thus Harlech castle, one of Edward I's magnificent fortifications in Wales, cost almost an entire year's revenue to build, but in 1294 its garrison of only thirty-seven soldiers successfully defended it against attack. The king's strategic vision anticipated that of the 'Manhattan Project', which spent millions of dollars on the production of nuclear devices which, delivered on two August mornings in 1945 by just two airplanes, precipitated the unconditional surrender of Imperial Japan and the millions of her troops still in arms all over southeast Asia.

After the introduction of gunpowder weapons and defences, the cost of each war proved significantly higher than that of the last, while the cost of military hardware rose to such a degree that only a centralized state could afford to buy. Creating the means to fund such an expensive form of warfare clearly served to enhance the power of the state in the West, with each change in the size or equipment of armed

The search for a 'wonder weapon' that might secure instant victory obsessed both sides in World War II. Germany developed a liquid-fuel ballistic missile, yet despite huge expenditure (prompted by unfounded fears that the Allies were pursuing similar research) the first 'Vengeance Weapon 2' (V-2 rocket) only struck London in September 1944. Shortly afterwards General Walter Dornberger (the project director) and Dr Wernher von Braun (the chief scientist) received from Hitler a telegram of congratulation and a Knight's Cross (which both of them wear in the photograph, taken at a celebratory dinner). However, the 3,000 or so rockets launched did little to stave off Germany's defeat.

forces requiring both new efforts to extract resources from the subject population and an expanded bureaucratic structure to handle them. Naturally, prolonged financial pressure often provoked opposition among those required to pay; but that, too, could lead to increased control – and therefore increased internal power – by the state over its subjects, making possible further military innovations and developments. This proved particularly true of wars waged to gain or extend hegemony, which required the steady transfer of centrally raised money and munitions to distant theatres, since this simultaneously promoted higher taxes, greater borrowing and increased integration. Military activity and state formation in the West therefore became inextricably linked: states made war but wars also made states. To use another biological analogy, one is reminded of the 'double helix' structure of the DNA molecule, with two complex spirals interacting at various discrete points.

The complexity of this image serves as a reminder that imitating the western way of war involved adaptation at many levels. Simply copying weapons picked up on the battlefield could never suffice; it also required the 'replication' of the whole social and economic structure that underpinned the capacity to innovate and respond swiftly. 'Westernizing war' depended upon the ability of warriors, traditionally one of the most conservative groups, to accept both the need for change and the need for instruction from 'inventors' from a different (and normally inferior) social background. It also presupposed an ability on the part of the state to mobilize resources rapidly, in large quantities, and often for long periods so that any technological inferiorities revealed in the course of a conflict could be remedied swiftly. Naturally, the less developed the economy, the less easily the cost of military preparedness could be absorbed – even within the West. Thus in 1904, France spent 36 per cent of her budget on the army whereas Germany spent only 20 per cent; however, in real terms this meant that France spent only thirty-eight million francs as against ninety-nine million for Germany. Thus France devoted twice as much of her budget in order to spend only half as much as her major rival. The continuation of this pattern for much of the next decade helps to explain why France found herself at such a disadvantage, especially in artillery, when war broke out in 1914.

However, the introduction of ingenious new taxes and other means of 'instant' wealth extraction proved far less important for feeding Mars than the development, from the sixteenth century onwards, of new techniques for mobilizing credit – such as national banks, banknotes, letters of credit and bonds – because few states ever manage to finance a major war out of current income. But creating and (even more) conserving an adequate credit base proved highly elusive. In the evocative phrase of the eighteenth-century English political economist, Charles Davenant:

> Of all beings that have existence only in the minds of men, nothing is more fantastical and nice than credit. It is never to be forced; it hangs upon mere opinion. It depends upon our passions of hope and fear; it comes many By

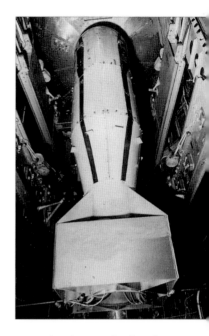

Atomic bombs were developed at great cost by the western Allies, largely because they feared that Germany had already begun nuclear research. Nevertheless no weapons became available until after Germany's defeat: only in July 1945 was an atomic bomb tested successfully. Two more were ready for use against Japan, along with test-unit replicas so that crews would know how to handle them (the photograph shows one of these in a B-29 aircraft bomb bay). Unlike Germany's V-2 rockets, this investment brought spectacular results – the first bomb fell on Hiroshima on 6 August 1945, the second on Nagasaki three days later, and Japan offered to surrender the following day.

times unsought for, and often goes away without reason; and when once lost, is hardly to be quite recovered.

Nevertheless, in eighteenth-century England at least, credit seemed to exist everywhere. Contemporaries estimated that two-thirds of all commercial transactions involved credit rather than cash and by 1782 the Bank of England alone handled bills of exchange worth a total of over £2 million annually – a stunning extension of the available monetary stock.

However, borrowing to finance wars depends not only upon the existence of extensive private credit, but also upon a convergence of interest between those who make money and those who make war, for public loans depend on finding borrowers willing to lend as well as taxpayers able to provide ultimate repayment. In England, tax revenues increased sixfold in the century following 1689. As an alarmed member of parliament exclaimed:

> Let any gentleman but look into the statute books lying upon our table, he will there see to what a vast bulk, to what a number of volumes, our statutes relating to taxes have swelled...It is monstrous, it is even frightful to look into the Indexes, where for several columns together we see nothing but Taxes, Taxes, Taxes.

And yet most Members, who paid the taxes themselves, accepted their necessity; and so did the majority of the political nation. By 1783, when the unsuccessful American War came to an end, Great Britain's national debt stood at £245 million, equivalent to more than twenty years' revenue; yet many of the loans had been contracted at just 3 per cent interest. 'Who pays and why' is as important, in the western way of war, as 'Who fights and why', and the ability to organize long-term credit (and therefore the existence of a secure and sophisticated capital market) to fund public borrowing in wartime represented a crucial 'secret weapon' of the West.

It also served to define which states could adopt the 'western way of war'. Mainly because of the cost of keeping abreast of changing technology and of maintaining the resources to deploy it effectively, relatively few states proved able to remain in the race for long. Some (like Denmark after 1660) proved too small or (like Poland after 1667) too fragmented; others (like Sweden, Switzerland or – with less success – Belgium) chose neutrality. Others still, particularly in regions with less developed economies, directed the energies of their armed forces towards containing and combating internal threats. Conversely, although not all western states proved able to fight in the western way, certain other countries did. Japan offers the classic example, thanks to the vital combination of discipline, doctrinal flexibility and a sophisticated financial structure which, in the sixteenth and again in the nineteenth century, permitted both the acquisition of expensive military technology and the equally expensive successive adaptations required in order to keep abreast if not ahead of all rivals.

THE DOMINANT MILITARY TRADITION

These various developments possessed a significance far beyond the region of their origin, because aggression – the 'export of violence' – played a central role in the 'rise of the West'. For most of the past 2,500 years, military and naval superiority rather than better resources, greater moral rectitude, irresistible commercial acumen or, until the nineteenth century, advanced economic organization under-pinned western expansion. This military edge meant that the West seldom suffered successful invasion itself. Armies from Asia and Africa rarely marched into Europe and many of the exceptions – Xerxes, Hannibal, Attila, the Arabs and the Turks – achieved only short-term success. None encompassed the total destruction of their foe. Conversely, western forces, although numerically inferior, not only defeated the Persian and Carthaginian invaders but managed to extirpate the states that sent them. Even the forces of Islam never succeeded in partitioning Europe into 'spheres of influence' in the western manner. On the other hand, however, time and again a favourable balance of military power critically advanced western expansion. As Jan Pieterzoon Coen, one of the founders of Dutch power in Indonesia, observed in 1614,

> Trade in Asia should be conducted and maintained under the protection and with the aid of our own weapons, and those weapons must be wielded with the profits gained by trade. So trade cannot be maintained without war, nor war without trade.

By 1650, a generation after these words were written, the West had already achieved military – and therefore economic – mastery in four separate areas: south, central and northeast America; Siberia; some coastal areas of sub-Saharan Africa; and much of the Philippines. In addition its ships sailed at will all over the seven seas and, in most of them, managed to regulate and in some cases to control the seaborne trade of commercial rivals.

By 1800 western states controlled some 35 per cent of the world's land surface; by 1914 they had increased that total to almost 85 per cent – acquiring 10 million square miles between 1878 and 1914 alone. Even in the twenty-first century, although the area under their direct control has shrunk dramatically, the ability of western armed forces to intervene directly and decisively by land and sea more or less wherever they choose serves to safeguard the economic interests of its compo-nent states and to perpetuate a favourable balance of global power. The military abilities that preserved the West at Salamis (480 BC) and the Lechfeld (AD 955), and expanded its dominance at Tenochtitlán (1519–21) and Plassey (1757), for better or worse still sustain its preponderant role in the world today. The rise of the West is inconceivable without them.

The Age of Massed Infantry Part 1

CHAPTER 1

Genesis of the Infantry

Overleaf: the Greek phalanx,
a scene from the Nereid
Monument (c.400 BC) at
Xanthus in Asia Minor.

At the beginning of the third millennium BC, the success of intensive, irrigated agriculture on the plains of Egypt and the Near East changed the culture of organized war-making, which had previously consisted of small skirmishes between rival groups of nomadic tribesmen. Hydraulic projects, improved agronomic techniques, and planned economies at Sumer, Ur, Babylon, Assur, Nimrud, and Egypt created the necessary capital to support armies, logistics, and fortifications.

Far more important, sophisticated agriculture instilled an overriding territorial impulse: growing but stationary populations sought ever more effective ways to defend and to acquire productive farmland. Furthermore, the Near East provided the ideal arena for large, mobile armies: warm weather during a long growing season, coupled with extensive plains, broken by accessible rivers. Rugged mountains, swamps, snow, ice, and sudden rain – the banes of large-scale and decisive military operations – were all but absent.

The agricultural surpluses of the Sumerians, Hittites, and Egyptians freed a sizeable minority of those peoples from the daily burden of producing food; they could instead fabricate metals for weapons and raise horses to draw war chariots. Yet complex warfare was not merely the consequence of new bronze metals, edged weapons, or increases in the numbers of ponies, dramatic as these new developments were. Just as important was a novel social and economic complexity centring around the 'palace', an institution that created underlords with specialized military, political, and religious responsibilities – precisely those disciplines prerequisite for war on any large scale. The Hittites, Egyptians, and Assyrians for the first time possessed the capability to muster enormous armies. They were able and willing to extinguish thousands of combatants in a single battle, obliterating entire cultures through the directives and sanction of powerful religious and political palace officials. Thus the early Assyrian ruler Tiglath-Pileser (c.1100 BC) in near epic terms bragged of his destruction of Hunusa:

Opposite: The mastery of
siegecraft displayed by the
early empires of the Near East
is well captured in this multifaceted Assyrian attack of
spearmen, swordsmen, and
archers depicted on the war
reliefs of Sargon II (721–
705 BC) at the palace of
Khorsabad in northern Iraq.

> Their fighting men I cast down in the midst of the hills, like a gust of wind. I cut off their heads like lambs; their blood I caused to flow in the valleys and on the high places of the mountains…That city I captured; their gods I carried away; I brought out their goods and their possessions, and I burned the city with fire. The three great walls of their city which were strongly built of burnt brick, and the whole of the city I laid waste, I destroyed, I turned into heaps and ruins and I sowed crops thereon.

Although Bronze Age and (later) Assyrian and Persian military forces constituted ferocious killing systems – usually unmatched in lethality throughout Greek, Roman, and even modern times – there were inherent limitations to the organization of these military societies. The reliance on the bow and the sling, the horse and the chariot, for example, required some expertise and so the creation of specialized military castes. The Near Eastern propensity for the construction – and destruction – of extensive fortifications also depleted resources to an astonishing degree. The familiar Biblical account of Joshua's destruction of Jericho provides some idea of the potential for carnage:

> …the people shouted with a great shout, and the wall fell down flat, so that the people went up into the city, every man straight before him, and they took the city. And they utterly destroyed all that was in the city, both man and woman, both young and old, and ox, and sheep, and ass, with the edge of the sword.

Most important, Bronze-Age societies were authoritarian and very narrowly hierarchical: the power to initiate, to manage, and to terminate wars lay in the hands of only the very privileged few. Often a single ruler might claim to have enslaved thousands. The death of a strong-man, subsequent fights over his royal succession, feuds between rival dynasts, could all provoke the mobilization – and annihilation or enslavement – of thousands, even when few economic or social advantages resulted for the majority of the combatants. In similar fashion, the loss or removal of those select few with the expertise and authority to conduct wars, often necessary wars, might severely curtail the military potential of an entire society and thus call into question its survival. No wonder that the capture, torture, or execution of a rival potentate, followed by the subsequent destruction of his fortress, appear so frequently in the dynastic annals, hieroglyphs, and stone reliefs of the Near East. There were no military rules, no common protocols of war in the ancient Near East that might have limited war to the combatants themselves and so moderated the destructive tendencies of these regimes.

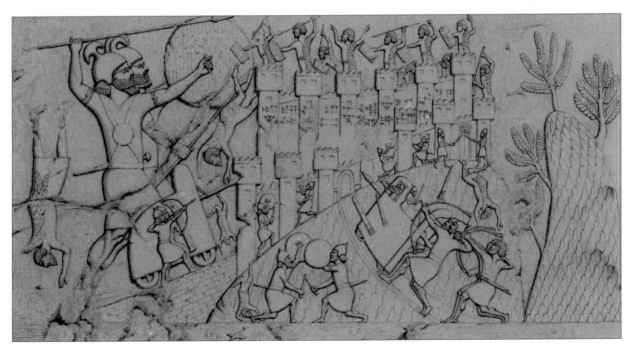

YEOMEN OF THE GREEK *POLIS*

One of the earliest extant hoplite panoply, found in the grave of an eighth-century warrior at Argos in the northern Peloponnese. Numerous bronze helmets, breastplates, greaves, swords, and spearheads survive from both individual graves and sanctuaries. However, wooden shields and spear shafts are nearly all lost and we know their form and function only from literature, art and the few bronze, leather, and iron fittings which have survived.

Warfare underwent a second transformation in Greece, again as a consequence of evolving agricultural practice. In the second and third millennia BC farming in Greece remained a bureaucratic enterprise along Near Eastern lines. Mycenean society on the Greek mainland (1600–1200 BC) was largely analogous to other Mediterranean and Asian palace monarchies – therefore offering very little chance for military experimentation, much less the dissemination of military planning and responsibility beyond the very few. But once warfare was 'liberated' – if we dare use that word in a context of organized slaughter – from centralized palatial control to the power of individuals, battle was left to evolve in a manner previously unknown. For the origins of western warfare, for the geneses of sophisticated metallurgy and technology, superior discipline, ingenuity in challenge and response, and the creation of a broad, shared military tradition among the majority of the population, one should look to the collapse of the Mycenean palaces on the Greek mainland and the ensuing Dark Ages (1100–800 BC).

There arose in the eighth century BC communities of equal property owners: the emerging culture of the Greek *polis* (city-state). With the *polis* began western military practice as we now recognize it – a practice at its birth largely at odds with moral fervour, immune from religious interference, and centred around decisive confrontation in pitched battle rather than the comfort of bellicose posturing and sheer numbers, or the expertise of engineers and logisticians. Early on, the Greeks quite chauvinistically recognized that their city-state constituted a unique institution, in sharp contrast to the palace-based cultures of past ages. The early Greek poet Phocylides confidently wrote, 'A small *polis* on a headland is superior to senseless Nineveh if its affairs are conducted in an orderly fashion.' Another sixth-century BC poet, Alcaeus, sounded a similar populist theme: 'Not finely roofed houses, nor the stones of well-built walls, nor even canals or dockyards make the *polis*, but rather men of the type able meet the challenge at hand.'

The earliest surviving image of a phalanx, on a mid- to late seventh-century BC Corinthian vase. The warrior-farmers of classical Greece (30–50 per cent of the adult male population in most city-states), are called hoplites after their shield – the circular 'hoplon'. The majority, but not all, lived on their land, usually a plot of about ten acres, often with only one slave in the household.

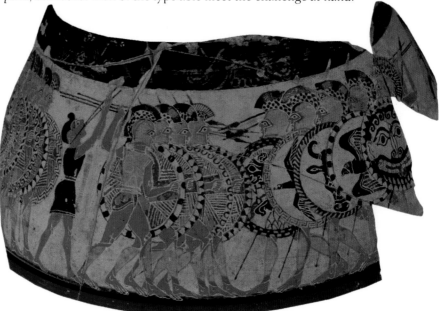

The key to the Greek cultural renaissance of the eighth and seventh centuries BC, to the move from the collective towards the individual, lay in a radical change in agricultural production, and concurrently in the manner of waging war. Under the pressure of population growth, the Greeks turned to family-operated, privately owned farms, where intensive practices ensured food surpluses, and yet allowed agricultural bounty to be free from bureaucratic interference at the top. In short, there was now to be no 'top'. Instead, to protect and empower this new group of rising farmers, there arose broad-based oligarchies and a cultural ethos of property egalitarianism among a privileged yeomanry. Farmers formed the voting citizenry of more than a thousand small city-states throughout the Greek-speaking world.

As hoplites neared the enemy in open formation (top), ranks closed and shields met to form a nearly solid wall of bronze and wood (below). Most phalanxes ranged from eight to sixteen men in depth. They resembled a series of rectangles, extending from a few hundred yards to a mile or two in length as armies grew in number to 10,000 or even 30,000 warriors.

In this climate of agrarianism appeared the 'hoplite' fighter or heavy infantryman. The fourth-century BC historian Xenophon (see page 29) stressed in his *Oeconomicus* just this connection between yeomanry and group fighting in the phalanx: 'Farming teaches one to help others. So, too, in fighting one's enemies, just as in working the earth, it is necessary to have the help of other people.' Small farmers alone, not leisured aristocrats, not hereditary monarchs, not hired thugs or cabals, in most regions of Greece in the seventh and sixth centuries BC increasingly made the laws, grew the food, and fought the wars of their cities.

For two centuries (700–500 BC), Greek warfare remained static, in the sense that hoplite battle followed extensive agrarian custom and contrived military protocol, deliberately limiting an entire conflict to a single afternoon's collision between columns of spearmen encased in bronze. When conflict arose – almost exclusively, before the fifth century BC, over disputed, often marginal, border territory – city-states agreed to decide the issue through one sudden collision of armoured columns. Each warrior-landowner purchased his own armour, which could weigh a punishing seventy-five pounds of wood and metal: greaves (bronze shin protectors), helmet, concave round shield, breastplate, double-pointed spear and short secondary sword.

Singly and in isolation the Greek agrarian hoplite presented a plodding, helpless target. He could easily be outmanoeuvred. He could be cut off, especially if he ventured onto rough terrain in mountain passes, or, worse, became caught in the open by horsemen or lightly clad missile troops. In a sense, therefore, the infantryman was intrinsically ill-suited to the natural relief and terrain of Greece. But most Greek farmers had no intention of fighting either alone, or far away from their favoured flat cropland, much less against mounted magnificoes or in the hills against their clear social inferiors, the landless skirmishers. Instead, arrayed in the packed ranks of the phalanx, they chose agricultural warfare on their own predominantly agrarian terms: farmers fighting farmers on farmland over farmland. The accumulation of raised shields across the armoured columns, the protruding spears of the first three ranks made the serried files of the phalanx invincible to either light-armed or mounted attack. 'It was a sight at once awesome and terrifying', remarked the first-century AD biographer Plutarch of the Spartan

Fashioned from a single sheet of bronze, the Corinthian helmet quickly replaced the early open-faced helmet (see page 14). Its expansive cheek and nose guards providing superior protection, it remained the standard hoplite headgear from the seventh to the mid-fifth centuries BC. Hoplite armour originated in the northern Peloponnese and was probably refined and codified by the early rulers of Argos and Corinth. As the superiority of hoplite arms became known, the shield and helmet were identified by most Greeks as the Argive and Corinthian respectively.

phalanx, drawing his description from centuries-old sources, 'as they marched in step to the pipe, leaving no gap in their line of battle and with no confusion in their hearts, calmly and cheerfully advancing into danger.'

Once Greek warfare was redefined solely as hoplite battle, both the affluent and the impoverished were relegated to secondary status on the battlefield – the growing yeoman class of independent property-owners had crafted fighting to reflect their own political and economic agenda. If the countryside was to be a patchwork of roughly similar farms worked by leather-clad yeomen, so, too, the phalanx was an analogous grid of identically armoured fighters. Just as intensive agriculture in Greece of the *polis* had swallowed the horse's domain of open range land, so too the hoplite now displaced the mounted fighter. Xenophon reflected the dominant hoplite ideology of the seventh to fifth centuries BC when he scoffed that 'only the weakest in strength and the least eager for glory' mounted horses.

'No one', Xenophon on another occasion reminded his 10,000 mercenary hoplites, 'has ever lost his life in battle from the bite or kick of a horse, but it is men who do whatever is done in battle.' In a very real sense, for a thousand years to come, in western warfare the cavalry grandee was ancillary to the infantry.

When Greek property-owners voted to march beyond their borders to fight, local hamlets and kin-groups quickly mustered into the ranks of their city-state's phalanx. The trek over the mountains, the fight, and the return home, usually required no more than a three-day excursion. Until the fifth century BC little attention was given to logistics. Fighting itself was equally economical. After the attackers provoked the enemy to march out – often by cutting down a few trees and vines – both sides squared off. 'Battle-leader' is a better term than 'general' for an officer, who was posted in the front rank, with responsibility only to lead by example, and thus to fight and to die in front of his men. The poet Archilochus remarked in the seventh-century BC , 'I don't like the towering captain with the spraddly length of leg, one who swaggers in his lovelocks and clean shaves beneath his chin. Give me instead a man short and squarely set upon his legs, a man full of heart, not to be shaken from the place he plants his feet.' After such a commander gave a brief harangue, and the seer sanctioned the pre-battle sacrifice of a ram or goat in front of the phalanx, the two columns would collide (in the words of the poet Tyrtaeus): 'toe to toe, shield against shield hard driven, crest against crest, and helmet on helmet'.

The key in this peculiar fighting was for the farmer-hoplite to make some gap in the enemy's line. Such a disruption would allow his armoured comrades to be pushed on through behind him, sowing disorder within the belligerents' interior, thus creating panic among the mass of enemy hoplites who could not hear, and scarcely see.

Military casualties in the classical age

The lethal effect of ancient weapons – the spear, sword, javelin, arrow, and sling – derived from their rapid rates of fire, their durability, and the ease with which they entered unprotected flesh. Until the late seventeenth century, for example, Near-Eastern archers were more deadly than European soldiers using firearms, and iron-tipped pikes were more likely to find and to penetrate their targets than early musketry.

Yet hoplite fatalities were usually only ten per cent of the total force assembled (fifteen per cent dead for the defeated, five per cent for the victors). The explanation rests with hoplite bronze armour. Favoured over stronger, heavier iron because of its greater malleability, ease in casting, and resistance to rust, bronze armour offered a quarter to half an inch of protection. The impact energy required to pierce breast-plates and helmets made of this material – when worn by a man who was still on his feet – was beyond all ancient weaponry.

If an infantryman could stay standing in battle (with twenty-pound shield, thirty- to forty-pound breastplate, and ten to twenty pounds in his helmet, greaves, sword, and spear, often a difficult task), he rarely risked any grave wound to the head or the chest. The great three-foot shield that he held above and in front of him often blunted a weapon's impact before it met metal. But casualties could result from attacks on exposed flesh, specifically the groin, and face, and to a lesser extent arms and legs. Both poetry and Greek vase-painting seem to concentrate on just those targets. The downward thrust of the spear could sever a major artery, bleeding the hoplite to death in seconds, or at least opening a gaping flesh wound in the limbs, with the spectre of sepsis and infection. Finally, repeated two-handed thrusts with a sword or the bronze butt-spike of a spear on a fallen warrior could tear through armour, as holes in surviving breastplates and helmets attest.

But the most significant cause of death was trampling. Most casualties on ancient battlefields probably resulted from com-pound fractures, as the skulls, chests, and limbs of fallen and stunned warriors were smashed underfoot by advancing and retreating infantry.

This fallen warrior depicted in stone on the pediment of the temple of Aphaia at Aegina (480 BC) reveals both the heroic and graphic nature of hoplite battle. Warriors were often stunned and wounded, only to be trampled beneath the feet of friend and foe alike. Notice the hoplite ideal that under no circumstances was the defeated and dying to abandon his shield, the physical and psychological linchpin to the solidarity of the phalanx.

Ancient authors emphasize the dust, the confusion, and the gore of the phalanx melee, and there is good reason to agree that a Greek battle of this era was a horrific scene, not an ordered pushing-match between squared columns. Indeed at the battle of Delium in 424 BC, during the Peloponnesian War, Thucydides says that the Athenians became 'confused in their encirclement, mistook and thus killed one another'. Later, in Sicily, 'they were thrown into disorder until they finally came into collision with each other in many places on the field, friends with friends, citizens with citizens, and not only terrified one another, but even began fighting and could be separated only with difficulty.'

SOLIDARITY AND DISCIPLINE

In the tumult of the hoplite battlefield, tactics and strategy meant nothing; solidarity and discipline were everything. Fighting aimed deliberately to eliminate entirely the need for reserves, articulation, stratagems and manoeuvre. Even in the fourth century BC, Xenophon could still rightly remark that 'Tactics form only a

Hoplite battles, such as the one portrayed here on a Corinthian vase of around 600 BC, were highly idealized. Infantrymen appeared not as cumbersome, bulky, or grubby, but 'heroically nude', revealing youthful and muscular physiques. Similarly, a small group of two or more hoplites side-by-side often represented the vast rows of the phalanx, a formation whose depth and width was difficult to capture with any degree of realism.

small part of army command.' Instead, in the heyday of the hoplite, an agrarian code prevailed that discouraged ruse or even individual heroics outside the ranks of the phalanx.

Under this system of open battle before the Peloponnesian War (431–404 BC), internecine fighting could be very frequent among the Greek city-states, but their defence expenditures remained small. Arms were the same in all camps, nearly uniform, and thus recyclable, as well as both durable and repairable. No rarefied officer corps existed. Battle fatalities in a single pitched battle were kept to around ten per cent of the respective armies, as extensive pursuit was impracticable and often discouraged. Military training and time lost to campaigning were similarly negligible. Pay, protracted sieges, and the extensive fortifications characteristic of later Greek warfare were still sporadic.

Historians sometimes seem reluctant to appreciate the consciously agrarian nature of this fighting: the astonishing degree to which farming protocol and the rural sociology of the *polis* defined warfare across the variegated landscape of the emerging Greek communities. Nevertheless, the Greeks themselves continually reinforced these practices through their literature, philosophy, vase-painting, sculpture, and public commemoration – all incessantly stressing the hoplite's bravery and cohesion, glorifying his arms and armour, and exalting his final battle sacrifice before the eyes of friends and family – all to the implicit diminution of the missile-men, the light-armed, and even the wealthier horsemen.

These warriors did not necessarily share the hoplite's peculiar notions of agrarian exclusivity. They were not committed, as the hoplite was, to preserving the existing structures of property ownership, landed control of voting councils and assemblies, and reliance on local produce. Rather than fight for all that, the poor and the elite preferred missile weaponry and

Lightly-armed bowmen and skirmishers were usually despised by hoplite farmers as the landless poor who could not afford bronze armour and had no stake in battles fought mostly over property. However, as the hoplite monopoly eroded, soldiers like this archer portrayed on a sixth-century Athenian plate by Epiktetos, became crucial to prevent surprise attacks, cavalry sorties, and raiding in rough terrain.

horses, ambush and pursuit, skirmishing and siegecraft – where military prowess was not simplistically predicated on an hour's exhibition of muscular strength and steely nerve.

But these non-hoplites formed a despised minority. In the first century AD the geographer Strabo claimed he had seen an inscription on an ancient pillar that forbade missiles altogether in early Greek warfare. Of his fatal wounding by a rare arrow, a Spartan hoplite made the famous complaint that 'death was of no concern, except that it was caused by a cowardly archer.' 'The Greeks of the past', wrote the historian Polybius nostalgically in the second century BC:

> did not even choose to defeat their adversaries through deceit, thinking instead that there was nothing glorious or even secure in military successes unless one side killed the enemy drawn up in open battle. Therefore, there was an agreement not to employ unseen weapons or missiles against one another, but they decided that only hand-to-hand fighting in massed column was the true arbiter of events. For that very reason, they made public announcements to each other about wars and battles in advance, when they would decide to enter them, and even concerning the places where they were to meet and draw up their lines.

In the classic age of hoplite battle, 700–431 BC, the overall material prosperity and steady cultural evolution of the Greek city-states stemmed in large part from the careful *restrictions* on fighting. Citizens sought no utopian (and hence doomed) effort to end warfare. Rather, they crafted rituals that allowed for frequent, inevitable conflict and battlefield heroics – all without real cost to the infrastructure of Greek society, which in the first two to three centuries of the *polis* remained emphatically agrarian. In sum, the culture of the Greek *polis*, in contrast to the ancient Near East, flourished precisely because organized killing and defence expenditure remained within 'reasonable' limits. The historian Thucydides, writing at the end of the fifth century BC, remarked of earlier times:

> There was no war by land, at least not by which any hegemony was acquired; there were many border contests, but of foreign expeditions designed for conquest there were none among the Greeks. Indeed, no subject city-states fell under the control of the great city-states, thus these Greek communities did not unite as equals for allied expeditions. Instead, fighting at this time consisted merely of local warring between rival neighbours.

The fifth century BC changed all that.

EAST MEETS WEST

Knowledge about Greek warfare before the Persian wars (490, 480–478 BC) is sketchy. It has to be pieced together from lyric and elegiac poetry, later speculation of historians, philosophers and antiquarians, and the physical remains of arms and armour. In contrast, the infantry and naval fighting of the fifth and fourth centuries

Persian cavalry meets Greek infantry in this impression made from an engraved gemstone of the fourth century BC. Unlike the lone figure depicted here, the Greeks in the Persian wars were arrayed in dense formation and wore bronze armour. Armed with spears that extended 8–9 feet, well practised in meeting shock assaults, and sharing a common language and culture, they were at an advantage over the Persian horsemen. These, mounted on little more than ponies, with neither stirrups nor armour, belonged to a polyglot force with weak leadership and poor tactics.

BC are well documented in the great histories of Herodotus, Thucydides, and Xenophon. And it is from Herodotus' history, for example, that the Persian invasions appear momentous, unlike anything in the past Greek experience of the prior two centuries.

A preliminary Persian probe of 490 BC under an expansion-minded King Darius I, was decisively checked by the Athenians at Marathon, where the Persians unwisely staked the outcome on a single infantry clash upon the enclosed Attic seaside plain. The Greeks' victory there set a pattern of East–West confrontation that remained virtually unaltered for the next three centuries: if at any time, at any locale, or in any number, eastern infantry were foolish enough to charge the disciplined ranks of western armoured pikemen, they inevitably crumbled. And yet, despite the later glorification and exaltation of the heroic 'Marathon men' in Athenian literature, their victory merely postponed the Eastern onslaught for a decade. When the Persians returned in 480 BC under Darius' son and heir, Xerxes, the military situation was entirely altered, the challenge unique, the invaders far more sophisticated and better prepared. As the contemporary dramatist Aeschylus put it, the Easterners sought no single pitched battle, but rather they now planned 'to yoke Hellas in servitude'.

Xerxes' assault on Greece in 480 BC was no expeditionary brigade, but a veritable travelling polyglot city of thousands, slowly inching its way southward into Greece, gobbling up city-states by capitulation or accommodation as it progressed.

Accompanied by a prodigious fleet, the Persians had no intention of fighting a single infantry battle. Indeed, they scoffed at the so-called 'laws of the Greeks', which restricted Hellenic warfare to a single land battle. 'These Greeks', mused Mardonius the Persian general, 'are accustomed to wage their wars amongst each other in the most senseless way, for as soon as they declare war on each other they

The Greek victories

In 499 BC Athens and Eretria gave support to Greek-speaking cities of Asia Minor in revolt against Persian rule, provoking the Persian king Darius I to send expeditionary forces into mainland Greece.

The Persians landed at Marathon, and could not advance by road to Athens, for the Athenians and their allies, holding the high ground, blocked the way. The Persians instead planned to send a strike-force against Athens by sea – with most of their cavalry and some infantry. The bulk of the Persian infantry attacked the Greeks to prevent them from returning to the defence of their city.

The outnumbered Greeks left their centre thin in order to match their line in length to the Persians', but they kept their wings deep. When they came within range of the archers in the advancing Persian line, the Greeks charged. They overwhelmed the Persian wings, made up mainly of conscripts, who fled towards their camp.

Instead of pursuing them, the Greek wings turned on the Persian centre, which crumbled. Only 192 Athenians died, but the Persians lost about 6,400: many drowned in the escape to the ships. Seven ships were captured. The Athenians marched back to their city in time to prevent the Persian strike-force from landing.

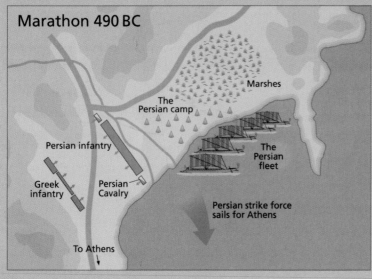

Marathon 490 BC

Marshes

The Persian camp

Persian infantry

The Persian fleet

Greek infantry

Persian Cavalry

Persian strike force sails for Athens

To Athens

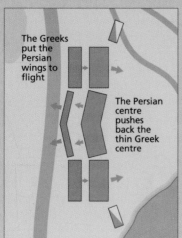

The Greeks put the Persian wings to flight

The Persian centre pushes back the thin Greek centre

The Greek wings attack the centre

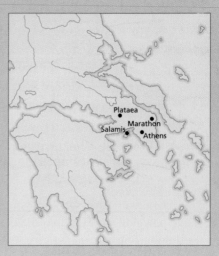

Plataea

Marathon

Salamis

Athens

seek out the fairest and most level ground, and then go down there to do battle on it. Consequently, even the winner leaves with extreme losses; I need not mention the conquered since they are annihilated. Clearly since they all speak Greek, they should rather exchange heralds and negotiators and thereby settle differences by any means rather than battle.' The Persians, by contrast, came bent on outright

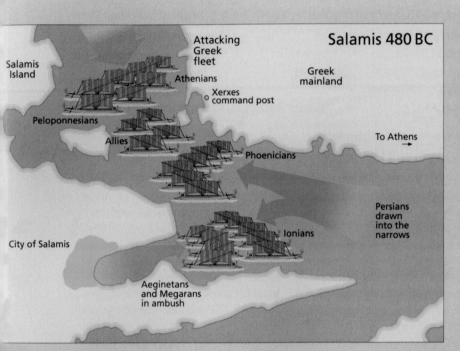

Salamis 480 BC

Without their fleet, the invaders were cut off, but the Persian general Mardonius, occupying Thessaly, brought at least 25,000 Asian infantry and 5,000 Asian cavalry south in the spring. His Greek allies, notably Thebes, supplied an additional 13,000 infantry and 5,000 horsemen. An army of more than 40,000 hoplites, supported by 70,000 light-armed troops, confronted them at Plataea.

After several days in which each side manoeuvred for position and harassed supply lines, Mardonius made an all-out assault. The gains of his cavalry in the early stages of the battle could not be sustained by his foot-soldiers, overwhelmed by heavy Spartan infantry. Only 3,000 of Mardonius' command survived the rout.

Ten years later Darius' son Xerxes led a second Persian invasion, one which needed to dispose of an allied Greek fleet by now at sea under the leadership of Themistocles of Athens. The Persians found the Greek fleet enclosed in narrow straits at the Athenian island of Salamis. By night they blocked the entrances of both the eastern and western channels. Next day, as the main Persian force advanced into the neck of the eastern strait, the combined navies of Athens, her Peloponnesian allies, and Aegina and Megara, cities of the Saronic Gulf, attacked vigorously and broke the advancing line. In the confines of the straits, the Persians could not take advantage of their superior numbers. They retreated after several hours of fighting and the loss of 200 ships. The Greeks had lost only 40.

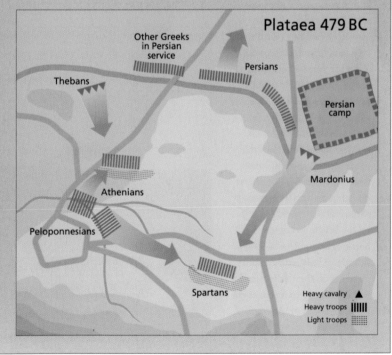

Plataea 479 BC

Heavy cavalry ▲
Heavy troops ▐▐▐▐▌
Light troops ▒▒▒▒

conquest, and their challenge was clear to the Greek city-states: numbers, sailors, tactics, fortification, evacuation, trickery, subterfuge, and generalship were all needed, and quickly. Overnight they entered the mainstream practice of Greek warfare.

An advance Spartan contingent was mowed down in glorious annihilation defending the high frontier pass up north at Thermopylae (480 BC), its king Leonidas decapitated, his head impaled on a pole. An Athenian-led fleet shadowed the approaching eastern ships, as Xerxes made his way through central Greece and on into a deserted Athens. In this new world of total war, some Greeks were forced not merely to redefine their traditional way of fighting, but to change their concept of the city-state itself. Not a mere physical entity of buildings, an acropolis, and the surrounding fields of its farmers, the *polis* (the city-state) was, after all, 'people'.

The cost of naval power

The Greek trireme (seen here in a twentieth-century reconstruction, the *Olympias*) was powered by three vertical banks of about 170 rowers. It was light and fast, achieving short bursts of about ten knots. Triremes equipped with a bronze ram, and piloted by veterans, could generate real force as they ploughed into an enemy line. With their own oars raised, they could shear off those of an enemy vessel, then quickly turn to ram its sides and rear. The ships hugged the coast, for their simple sails and weak rudders made them unstable in strong and shifting winds. Crews ate and slept on shore, dragging up the flat-bottomed ships and their tackle to dry on the beach. Every naval battle of antiquity was fought in sight of land, with infantry cheering on their sailors and standing ready to rescue them from the water or slay men from capsized enemy ships.

Military ships brought extraordinary advantages to the very few Greek city states, for example, Athens, Corinth, Syracuse, and Corcyra, wealthy and innovative enough to master their use. Triremes could transport and disembark hoplites behind enemy lines, and attack or protect trade as the situation required. Rich but defenceless communities across the water, especially in the late fifth and fourth centuries BC, were raided, plundered, and sometimes conquered, their wealth extracted in the form of annual tribute. Yet social, financial, and technological considerations ensured that naval forces were subservient to infantry throughout all of Greek warfare. In most Greek city-states, landed citizenry composed the prestigious ranks of the phalanx. The poor, relegated to skirmishing and missile-firing, remained on the peripheries.

However, when extensive navies were developed in the fifth century BC, freemen

People were all that mattered: the native-born residents of all classes who could be saved through evacuation to return as avengers on either land or sea. Landed conservatives at Athens calling on farmers for a single hoplite conflict of the old style to protect the city proper and the agrarian prestige of the countryside were not merely misguided, but nearly lunatic as well. The Athenians therefore left their *polis* to the invader's torch, evacuating to nearby free territory, relying on the 'wooden walls' of their ships to defeat the Persians off the adjacent island of Salamis. Whatever the later complaints of reactionary Athenian philosophers that sea-power was unheroic (the anti-democrat Plato, a century after Salamis, felt the Athenian victory there had made Greeks 'worse' as a people), all Greeks knew that the destruction of Xerxes' armada at Salamis had ruined the morale of the Persians and set the stage for a final fight at Plataea the next spring.

without property were recruited to row merchant vessels and triremes. The crews were often highly trained, dependable, and courageous, as the stunning Greek victory over the Persians at Salamis and the Greek dismantling of the overseas Persian empire in the following decades attest. By the late fifth century BC Athens had more than 40,000 rowers in a fleet of more than 200 triremes. The poor of Athens gained enormous influence and steady pay from this naval expansion, and they expected to be better represented in the politics of the city-state. This tension at Athens evolved into radical democracy. The abolition of the property qualification guaranteed civic participation for the *thetes*, or landless sailors, an extension of the franchise bitterly represented by philosophical conservatives such as Plato and Aristotle, who saw the legacy of the Greek naval victory over the Persians at Salamis as the beginning of demagoguery, cultural degeneracy, and erosion of infantry morale.

Greek fleets were enormously expensive, and not at all subject to the agrarian constraints on landed expenditures. Pay, constant upkeep of the ships, and the construction of dockyards demanded that a Greek navy justify its existence by scouring out new sources of income. However, commercial activity was antithetical to the original agrarian geneses of the *polis*, and few states could stand the burden of a navy. After the long tribulations and heavy expenditures of the Peloponnesian war and the dismantling of the Athenian empire few Greek *poleis* resurrected large fleets. The arming of ships, unlike citizen armies, required state spending, and represented the intrusion of government into a traditional private, civilian domain.

Themistocles engineered the construction of the Athenian fleet on the eve of the Persian invasion and convinced the reluctant Greeks to gamble all their ships in a decisive battle within the narrows between Salamis and the mainland. While his promotion of the landless navy was popular neither with most hoplites nor with the city's aristocrats, most Athenians came to realize that he had saved democracy, altered the course of Athenian society, and laid the foundations for its maritime empire.

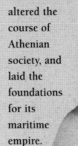

Pericles is portrayed wearing the hoplite Corinthian helmet; but, in fact, no Athenian did more to shift power away from the agrarian infantry to the urban navy. His strategy of forced evacuation into Athens in the first years of the Peloponnesian War made it clear that the city's hopes would rest on its naval forces at Piraeus, and not on a single glorious showdown with the Spartan invaders on the plain of Athens.

Suddenly, without their fleet, the haughty Persian invaders in the spring of 479 BC found themselves cut off. They were in an increasingly untenable position, as hoplites from all over central and southern Greece flocked to form a grand army of last resistance near the small village of Plataea on the Athenian-Boeotian border. Spartan discipline and, in the words of the playwright Aeschylus, the power of 'the Dorian spear' that 'poured blood in unmeasurable sacrifice', backed by Athenian enthusiasm and the sheer mass of Greek infantry (never again would classical Greece field a force approaching 70,000 combatants) broke the Persian army, and then slaughtered the fleeing survivors.

AFTERMATH OF THE PERSIAN WARS

In the aftermath of the Persian invasion and defeat, as is common after any great social and cultural upheaval, a conscious return to normality occurred in Greek warfare. Once more we hear for a time of a series of infantry 'wars' over borders among the city-states decided in the old way: traditional one-hour stand-offs at the battles of Dipaea (471 BC), Tanagra and Oinophyta (457 BC), and Coroneia (447 BC). But stones were thrown into the hoplite pond by the Persian experience, as the multifarious lessons of the victories over Xerxes rippled slowly throughout Greek city-states. Chief among the new realities were two phenomena that help explain the sharp break with the *polis* warfare of the past.

First, the victory left two city-states, Sparta and Athens, alone prestigious and pre-eminent. Both were unusually powerful, atypical – and antithetical – Greek city-states, which could afford to ignore the old rules of agrarian warfare. Supported by nearly 200,000 helots, or indentured servants, who worked the farms of Messenia and Laconia, the Spartans fielded professional hoplites, year-round infantry not subject to the normal restrictions that free agriculture placed on yeomanry in infantry battle. The Spartan King Agesilaus once asked his allied Peloponnesian army to stand up by profession – potters, smiths, carpenters, builders, and all the others. At last only the minority of his Spartiates remained seated, those few who did nothing other than make war. 'You see, men', Agesilaus scoffed, 'how many more soldiers we send out to fight than you do.' Plutarch records that the Spartans could boast: 'Not by caring for the fields, but rather by caring for ourselves did we come to own those fields.'

Nor were the increasingly democratic Athenians comfortable to carry on simply with the traditional artificial collision between oligarchical, armoured farmers. In the wake of the Persian withdrawal (479 BC), Athens' fleet continued to increase. Nurtured on the tribute of vassal states in the Aegean, Athenian triremes were not mothballed, but became instead a 'benign' police force of sorts for her Greek subject allies overseas. Like the Spartans, imperial Athens too saw little need to limit warfare to a single summer afternoon, or indeed, given the success of her evacuation before Xerxes and subsequent naval response, to risk at all her infantry in defence of the farmland of Attica.

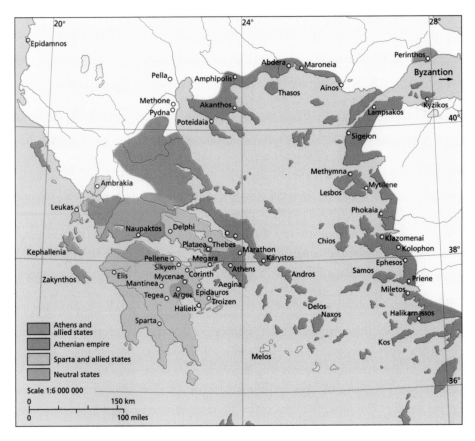

On the eve of the Peloponnesian War, Athens possessed an enormous maritime empire and important allies, ensuring her of a formidable navy, plentiful manpower, and rich sources of capital. Yet Sparta and Thebes fielded the best hoplites in the Greek world and could hem Athens in from the north and south. Stalemate was assured until Athens exhausted herself in failed interventions in Boeotia, the Peloponnese, and Sicily, allowing Sparta to acquire a competent navy which whittled away at her weakened overseas empire.

Second, the success of the non-hoplite forces in the Persian wars left a marked impression on the Greeks. Ships, light-armed troops, and cavalry had been present in a variety of theatres and terrains, underscoring how vulnerable and how inadequate the hoplite phalanx might become before any adversary who was (wisely) unwilling to face it in a single pitched battle.

The problem for the Greek *polis* was not merely fielding such diverse contingents, but rather coping with the inevitable social challenges that the use of such forces posed. Give rowers, skirmishers, or cavalry, military importance and the old agrarian exclusivity of the *polis* – the very fabric and ideology of the Greek city-state – was compromised. Farmers with heavy armour and spear no longer warranted privileged social and political status. As Aristotle once observed in his *Politics*, 'In a *polis*, the ones who fight have the supreme power, and those who possess the armament are the citizens.'

The ensuing Peloponnesian War between Athens and Sparta was not decided in an afternoon, nor even in the space of a summer or two. The killing dragged on for twenty-seven years. It is easy to see why. Abandoning her countryside to Spartan invaders, Athens refused pitched battle with the crack hoplites of Sparta. Of the hoplite farmers who were obliged to trek into the city walls, Thucydides movingly remarked, 'Most Athenians still lived on their farms with their families and households, and were consequently not at all inclined to move now, especially as

Thucydides, aristocratic landowner, general, and historian, more than anyone else of his generation, saw that the Peloponnesian War had forever ended the traditional protocols of Greek warfare.

they had only just restored their establishments after the Persian invasion. Deep was their discontent and unhappiness at leaving behind their homes.'

Instead Athens, once besieged, increasingly imported food and material into her port at Piraeus, all the while sending out her magnificent fleet to stabilize her maritime empire and to prevent Peloponnesian infiltrations. Sparta, for her part, found the old strategy of ravaging cropland discomfitingly ineffective: her hoplites in Attica could neither draw the Athenian army out nor reduce the city economically. Consequently, both belligerents turned to a variety of secondary theatres throughout the Aegean world and Asia Minor. In these latter proxy wars between 421 and 404 BC, Athens ironically used her hoplites in combined maritime operations, whereas Sparta and her allies in time developed a competent fleet. During the entire course of the Peloponnesian War there were not more than three or four battles of the old style. Mercenaries, light-armed skirmishers, sailors, and siege engineers filled the void. All were expensive, and – disastrously for both sides – all apparently were incapable in themselves of ending an engagement decisively through the destruction or humiliation of an enemy's forces in the field.

Strategy became prominent, as the Athenians made inconsequential probes into Spartan territory and, most tragically, lost an entire expedition of forty thousand men a thousand miles distant in repeated defeats before Syracuse in Sicily (415–413 BC). Thucydides summarized that novel Greek experience of outright military extermination. 'The Athenians', he wrote, 'were beaten in all areas and altogether; all that they suffered was great; they were annihilated, as the saying goes, with a total annihilation, their fleet, their army – everything was annihilated, and few out of many returned home.' Sparta, for her part, more pragmatically, systematically garrisoned Attica to encourage desertions and local disruptions in commerce, all the while applying steady pressure to pry away tribute-paying Athenian allies in the Aegean, the life-blood of the city's capital and military reserves.

No wonder that, after nearly three decades, at war's end in 404 BC Athens was left bankrupt, exhausted, and demoralized. But Sparta and her allies were in no position to assume lasting hegemony of Greece. In the detritus of the Peloponnesian War, agrarian fighting of the old *polis* was ended, as warfare now meant expansion of conflict onto a variety of costly and deadly new horizons.

INTO THE FOURTH CENTURY

Fondness for the collision of infantry columns was not entirely forgotten in the next century. Despite attempts by modern scholars to detect tactical evolution in fourth-century BC hoplite phalanxes – reserves, feints, manoeuvre – crashes between columns in themselves really changed little, as the reactionary battles between hoplite dinosaurs at Nemea (394 BC), Coroneia (394 BC), Leuctra (371 BC), and Mantineia (362 BC) attest. Indeed, even a hoplite at Leuctra (371 BC), supposedly the most revolutionary of fourth-century BC battles, would have felt at home – in armament, fighting practice, and spirit – among the ranks of his ancestors battling three hundred years earlier at Hysiae (669 BC). And of the horrific old-style struggle between Spartan and Theban hoplites at the second battle of Coroneia, the contemporary witness Xenophon (see below) dryly concluded of its predictability, 'They collided, pushed, fought, killed, and died.' What was transformed, and transformed very radically, was not battle, but war. Fighting now consisted of

Xenophon: the beginnings of strategic theory

The superiority of western military practice derives in part from its tradition of free speech, unbridled investigation, and continual controversy, relatively free from state censorship or religious stricture. The legacy of independent military science begins in Greece

Agrarian hoplite thinking from the seventh to the fifth centuries BC had tended to stifle military innovation completely, but during the latter part of the fifth century warfare became more complicated, and the 'science' of killing soldiers in their thousands came into the mainstream of the Greek intellectual tradition. Erosion of the old agrarian city-state in the aftermath of the Peloponnesian War allowed a variety of new forces and technologies to emerge – all free from sanctimonious agricultural stricture. Logistics, encampment, siegecraft and the permanent occupation and administration of captured land became part of Greek warfare.

Greek intellectual fervour in the late fifth century was dominated by philosophers and rhetoricians who were singularly pedagogical and utilitarian, seeking concretely to apply dialectic, language, and induction to practical topics: agriculture, medicine, natural science, politics – and, of course, war. Military affairs became a category of this systematized and rational approach to learning.

Xenophon (428–354 BC) offers the best example of battlefield experience mixed with philosophical training. In some sense, he stands as the founder of the military intellectual tradition in the West. Veteran of a wide variety of campaigns and a follower of Socrates, xenophon wrote handbooks such as *The Cavalry Commander* and *On Horsemanship*, and he discussed generalship, tactics, and strategy in his *Memorabilia, Oeconomicus,* and *Education of Cyrus.*

The moral element is present throughout his work; criticism of current Greek warmaking is implicit; original and sometimes radical innovation advised. Xenophon himself was not widely read by the general public, but his work suggests that the topics he discusses were the rage in the fourth-century BC both for city-state leaders and for professional mercenary captains.

Xenophon's contemporary, the pragmatic Aeneas the Tactician (c.360 BC), also left his mark. His *military Preparations*, which according to tradition formed a vast work, is lost; but an extant chapter, *How to Survive Under Siege*, covers everything from the mundane (passwords, reveille, codes, tunneling, fire-signals) to the broader questions of how to employ mercenaries effectively, how to conduct sorties, and how to make and carry out plans of evacuation.

Unfortunately, almost all the later Greek military thinkers are mere names. Their numerous pragmatic treatments of phalanx tactics, ballistics, fortification, and siegecraft are now lost. However, they founded a vibrant body of practical, hands-on military research.

More pedantic writers on military theory followed during the Roman and medieval periods. For many, the Greek texts and Latin translations of Greek texts to which they had access were their closest, personal experience of military planning and organization, and it is only in their scholarly tomes that any trace of most of the original Greek work now survives.

Few Greeks lived as full a life as Xenophon (428–354 BC). Pupil of Socrates, leader of the mercenary 10,000, historian, biographer, philosopher, and novelist, he was the first western military scientist as well. His treatises were unique combinations of practical speculation. They stand in stark contrast to many of the more dry and pedantic handbooks of the centuries to follow.

skirmishing, garrisoning high passes, mercenary raiding, marine assaults, sieges, and counter-fortifications. Plunder and the search for captives reflected new economic realities, as war came to be a source of state capital, a line item on state budgets. And this confusion was as it should be, for once Greece re-entered the main fabric of Mediterranean history in the fifth and fourth centuries BC, its wonderful absurdity, the city-state – dominated by an exclusive trinity: small-holder food-producer/

Gods and heroes as citizen warriors

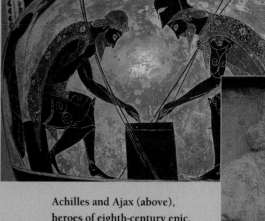

With a face like a hoplite's helmet, the Little Owl (*Athene noctua* – seen here on a fifth-century cup) was regarded as a feathered incarnation of Athena, protectress of fortifications, encampments and towns, and goddess of wisdom. Opposite she is portrayed in human form, bearing a hoplon shield with menacing imagery, and wearing a necklace of snakes poised to strike.

The exclusivity of hoplite warfare was re-inforced within Greek society through an array of symbols, images, and rhetorical flourishes. Nearly every Greek temple, for example, cloaked mythical fighting in ex-pressions of contemporary phalanx warfare. Pedimental sculpture, friezes, and dedicat-ory statues were all media in which infantry-men appeared in the guise of demi-gods or Olympian deities. The same is true of Greek ceramic art: only rarely were archers or rowers depicted on vases. Nearly all port-rayals of epic heroes were translated into conventional hoplitic imagery, albeit with occasional licence to heroic nudity. Markets and stores similarly might offer sweeping panoramas such as the victory of Marathon, where the shopper was re-minded of the prominent role of Athenian infantry.

Hoplites reappeared at panhellenic sanctuaries such as Olympia, Delphi, Isthmia, and Nemea; there the great majority of votive offerings comprised captured infan-try arms and armour. Even a walk through the Greek countryside could present trophies of past battles, prominent displays in stone of captured hop-lite weapons. Almost all funeral orations foc-used on the infantry dead. Even at Athens, the most democratic and maritime of the city-

Achilles and Ajax (above), heroes of eighth-century epic, appear on a sixth-century vase as contemporary hoplite warriors. A frieze (right) in the treasury of the Syphnians at Delphi shows Apollo, Artemis, and Ares fighting against stumbling and dying giants, as if, far from being distant legends, they were all familiar to the sixth-century warriors in the phalanx.

states, orators through metaphor and ex-plicit allusion often transformed the fallen warriors of the city-state – horsemen, skirmishers, rowers – into martyred hoplites. Drama and comedy also depicted battle scenarios with phalanx and hoplite, often disparaging all other modes of fighting.

The result was a veritable saturation of pictorial and verbal images that bombarded the Greek citizen each time he shopped, hoplite infantryman/maker of laws – was shown to be a *closed* system. It had no will to assimilate non-landed wealth, gifted foreigners, and those who fought outside the agrarian phalanx. The genie was now out of the bottle: western warfare, created as a protective mechanism for their agrarian city-state, had entered a new, far more sophisticated, far more lethal phase, one divorced from social constraint, but still fuelled by the Greek genius for innovation and response.

sacrificed, glanced at public monuments, picked up fine wares, went to the assembly, or sat in the theatre, reminding him constantly, continuously, that it was the phalanx, not the cavalry, not the fleet, not the rag-tag skirmisher, that preserved the Greek city-state. Consequently, for nearly three centuries, the peculiar 'rules' of hoplite warfare, and its accompanying agrarian agenda, went largely unchallenged by the citizens of the Greek *polis*, landed and landless alike.

CHAPTER 2

From Phalanx to Legion

The waning Greek city-states attempted valiantly – but more often tragically – to incorporate new methods of fighting, even though they were antithetical to the old amateur hoplite battle and the traditional etiquette of agrarian warfare. Nostalgia about the old ways continued, but political leaders were forced to confront the new military realities. 'Nothing', the orator Demosthenes warned his fourth-century BC audience of complacent Athenians, 'has been more revolutionized and improved than the art of war. I know that in the old times', he continued, 'the Spartans, like everyone else, would devote four or five months in the summer to invading and ravaging the enemy's territory with hoplites and citizen militia, and then would go home again. And they were so old-fashioned – or such good citizens – that they never used money to buy advantage from anyone, but their fighting was fair and open.'

Social status was now largely divorced from the battlefield. Wealthy, middling, and poor Greeks could all ride horses, throw javelins, or wield spears, either as hired killers or as reluctant militiamen. The exclusive equation of farmer and infantryman disappeared. Xenophon complained in his *Ways and Means* that at Athens the phalanx was losing esteem by recruiting the city's resident aliens into the ranks of the infantry, 'The *polis* also would be helped', he advised, 'if our citizens served alongside one other, and no longer found themselves mixed together with Lydians, Phrygians, Syrians, and barbarians of every type, who form a large portion of our resident alien population.'

The plain of Mantineia, site of one of the last true hoplite battles (362 BC), was inhabited by two minor rivals, Tegea and Mantineia, but its ideal terrain and its strategic location between mutually hostile powers, Argos and Sparta, made it the focus of several great battles of antiquity.

The chief problem in this expansive, brave new world of fourth-century BC Greek warfare was its cost. Torsion catapults, mercenary skirmishers, permanent navies, skilled archers, slingers, and stone-throwers, the ability to confront all sorts of military challenges at any time, required capital. Yet, paradoxically, the move towards year-round confrontation in all theatres of the Mediterranean also ensured that the vital sources of Greek military revenue – commerce, agriculture, and calm in the countryside – would be continually disrupted.

WAR BECOMES TOO EXPENSIVE

Many city states, then, found themselves in a dilemma: they could neither endure provocation and plundering of their territory, nor afford the necessary permanent force to ensure tranquillity. Xenophon saw that the complex warfare between the squabbling city-states had become too expensive for most *polis* treasuries, and so belligerency sometimes demanded a pragmatic, rather than a heroic, posture: 'Someone might ask me', he speculated, 'that even if a *polis* is wronged, should she then remain at peace with the aggressor? No, of course not. But I do say that we should have better luck against an enemy, if we first of all provoke no one by doing wrong ourselves.'

Few hoplite militias after the indecisive battle of Mantineia (362 BC, between Thebes and Sparta) fought decisive pitched engagements – and even then phalanx collision no longer determined the outcome of wars. Indeed, the last hoplite standoff, between the Spartans and
the Thebans at Mantineia,
solved

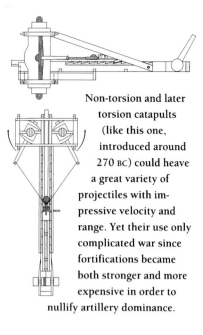

Non-torsion and later torsion catapults (like this one, introduced around 270 BC) could heave a great variety of projectiles with impressive velocity and range. Yet their use only complicated war since fortifications became both stronger and more expensive in order to nullify artillery dominance.

Opposite: Over five miles of fortifications at Messene in the Peloponnese were built around 370 BC to protect the newly freed city from its traditional enemy, the Spartans. Often such enormous circuits included undeveloped land where refugees could find both housing and space for their livestock. The sophisticated design and aggregate capital invested gave the defenders a sense of smug security, and precluded any idea that the Messenians would venture beyond their impressive walls to meet an invader in the field.

nothing: Xenophon claimed in the last pages of his history of Greece that after the battle 'neither side turned out to be any better off, to have any additional territory, any additional *polis*, or any more influence. In fact, even more confusion and disorder occurred in Greece after the battle than before'. After all, once stripped of its surrounding and protective agrarian protocol, by itself the phalanx was tactically problematic: a clumsy instrument of pursuit, poorly adapted to destroy the increasingly multifarious forces in the field. If it could no longer achieve decisive results, other forces hired by the state could.

So the old set-piece battle was replaced by the daring and braggadocio of mercenary captains and itinerant condottieri, buccaneers who ignored the protocol of the old Greek city-states. Isocrates, a fourth-century BC Athenian orator, complained that his compatriots no longer selected military commanders from among their amateur politicians, but turned instead to shady professionals: 'The men whose advice we follow in areas of the greatest importance we do not elect to be our generals, as if we distrusted their intelligence. But those whose advice no one would want either for his own business or for that of the *polis*, these we now send into the field with unchecked authority.' Employing alliance, counter-alliance, subterfuge, and plotting, the major players – Athens, Sparta, Thebes, Argos, Corinth, Thessaly, and Sicily – used all forces at their disposal to maintain an exhausting, but nevertheless rough balance of power for the first half of the fourth century BC, all while apprehensively eyeing the new threat of Macedon to the north.

THE PHALANX REINVENTED

Unfortunately for the Greek city-states, Philip II of Macedon was no mere hoplite battle-leader of the old style. Much less was he simply a crafty, underpowered brigand, who could carve out or extort a few years' hegemony over Greek communities. Instead, meticulously, insidiously, for more than twenty years (359–338 BC) Philip crafted a grand new army, supplied, led, and organized quite differently from anything in past Greek practice.

To his phalanx (see page 36) of grim, professional 'foot-companions' (*pezetairoi*) – 'the biggest and strongest of all the Macedonians', according to a contemporary commentatary – Philip added the 'companion cavalry' (*hetairoi*), an elite body of aristocratic horsemen, heavily armoured on strong mounts. Another contingent of infantry, with perhaps less armour, the 'shield bearers' (hypaspists), occupied the centre of the Macedonian line, beside the phalanx. The hypaspists were usually the first infantry forces to follow behind the cavalry onslaught, thereby providing a crucial link between the initial mounted attack and the subsequent follow-up by the phalanx proper. Professional corps of light infantry, slingers, archers, and javelin men rounded out the composite army group, supplying both preliminary bombardment and crucial reserve support.

These Macedonian contingents were not a fragmentation of forces, but rather a diversification and sophistication in arms: they were a symphony, not a cacophony,

Inside the Macedonian phalanx

Macedonian shields were less than two feet in diameter, about a foot smaller than the hoplite version, and hung from the neck. This allowed infantrymen to hold a massive pike with both hands, and crowd closer to each other. Usually, each soldier in rank had three feet in which to manoeuvre. Standard column depth was usually either eight or sixteen shields. The hoplite's cumbersome equipment put a high price on mutual protection, but Macedonians opted strictly for offence. The key to staying alive was not their equipment (reduced in size and weight considerably), nor comrades to their right. Rather, safety lay in the vast array of spears that kept any enemy from breaking into the ranks. The Macedonian phalanx was a more vulnerable formation than its Greek predecessor, but it had far more offensive power.

The first five rows of pikes all reached targets in the initial collision, their wall of jostling spears harpooning attackers, and – like bristles – bouncing back the pressure of the enemy advance. Men in the middle and rear, too, kept busy, warding off arrows with raised pikes, stabbing the enemy wounded on the ground with their butt-spikes, pushing on with their shoulders into the men ahead. Accidental casualties from a swarm of bobbing spear-butts in the faces of the men behind must have been severe. And at the front of the killing, as Livy saw when he wrote that each Roman was targeted by ten pikes, the 'demand' of the crowded spearheads was greater than the 'supply' of available enemy targets, so it became crucial for each Macedonian pikeman to keep his weapon level, jabbing back and forth to occupy critical empty space should an attacker try to find a wedge between the tips. Exhaustion came in minutes, given the weight of the pike and

the pressure of the pushing ranks. Few soldiers had any idea whom or how many – if any – of their opponents they had in fact speared. Success was gauged simply by motion forward, defeat felt through stasis and paralysis reverberating in a growing panic back through the ranks.

If a row of pikes went down, if enemy swordsmen were catapulted into the interior, or, worse, crashed in from the naked sides of the phalanx, disaster was immediate, death assured. The secondary dagger – as ridiculously small as the pike was absurdly big – offered little protection for the Macedonian. And the pike itself was, of course, impossible to wield against the face of an immediate intruder. But for the phalangite to throw the spear down, to run unheroically to the rear, would only open the breach even wider; while ignominious flight was impossible anyway given the compression of bodies.

Once inside the columns, enemy swordsmen carved at the bellies, groins, and limbs of stunned and trapped phalangites with abandon, until the entire mass of the phalanx simply disintegrated, men frozen, trying to hold their pikes firm as they were in fact disembowelled. The phalangite often had little warning of his approaching extermination. After all, his sense of battle depended primarily on touch, feel, pressure, as well as shouts and rumour, for a sea of dust, blood, and whirling bodies soon blinded the interior and prevented accurate vision or acoustics.

Yet if brave men could just keep their pikes intact as a group, spear-tips wall-like in unison, whilst their comrades to the rear pushed them on, then the butchery was all on the other side. Indeed, once phalanx momentum was achieved and the pikes began their advance, nothing could withstand the terrifying force of oncoming Greek iron.

Imagine the enemy unfortunates simply shredded by repeated stabbing. The chief problem for the victorious executioners was to keep spearheads free of the debris of ruined enemy equipment and the weight of mutilated corpses. No wonder, for this horrific phalanx-killing, that it was not sleek youth, not elegant muscle, that a commander sought, but stout, grubby old veterans, with the nerve and experience not to flinch from the task at hand.

of professionally equipped men. The phalanx was thoroughly rehabilitated by Philip, and it gained fresh importance; but with him the evolution away from its agrarian roots accelerated. The fourth-century BC Athenian general Iphicrates had foreseen these multifaceted military innovations when, in typically Greek fashion, he compared the new army to a human organism: light-armed troops as hands, the cavalry as feet, the infantry phalanx proper as chest and breast-plate, and the general as head.

Philip's contribution to the history of western warfare was as much organizational as tactical. At first, the equipment and tactics of his Macedonian phalanx did not differ considerably from the traditional hoplite columns of the Greek city-states. The spear (sarissa), for example, was retained, but it was lengthened from eight to nearly fourteen feet. It now required both hands for adequate control and handling. The round shield shrank, as greaves, most breastplates, and heavy head-gear were replaced with leather or composite materials, or abandoned.

But the central idea of the fighting mass remained predominant. Writing in the Roman era, the military theorist Onasander remarked of the Macedonian phalanx that 'the advancing formations appear more dangerous through the splendour of their equipment, and that terrible sight frightens the very souls of the enemy.' Indeed, integrated with, and protected by, such variegated forces, Philip's phalanx of pike-men was both more lethal and more versatile than the traditional hoplite columns. Now the first five, not merely the initial three, ranks could strike at the enemy. The second-century BC Greek historian Polybius knew that infantry who faced such a 'storm of spears' might have as many as ten iron points concentrated on each man. 'Nothing', Polybius simply concluded, 'can stand up to the phalanx. The Roman by himself with his sword can neither slash down nor break through the ten spears that all at once press against him.' The men of the Macedonian phalanx, after all, could turn their attention exclusively to thrusting their dreadful spears, without the cumbersome weight of the old hoplite panoply, or the need to protect with an enormous shield their immediate comrades on the right. Offence, pikes, and motion forward, now counted for everything; defence, large shields, and worry over covering neighbours meant little.

The Macedonians aimed at advance and annexation, not the preservation of their borders. Used with great precision and power, the new Macedonian phalanx usually delivered a knock-out blow, once the target had been sighted and then left vulnerable by the work of cavalry and ancillary contingents. Hammer-like cavalry attacks battered the enemy back onto the clumsy mile-long anvil of the spear-bristling phalanx (although this infantry mass, as the Greek historian Polybius explained, always had to be careful to stay on 'clear ground, free of ditches, ravines, trees, ridges, and water courses, all of which can stop and break up such a formation'). Such co-ordination between infantry and horsemen was an entirely new development in the history of western warfare, far beyond the tactical capacity or vision of even the most militarily innovative fourth-century BC Greeks.

A Macedonian infantryman, perhaps even a general, around 300 BC. With his light leather armour, he was less encumbered than a hoplite. He could march further and manoeuvre a more deadly weapon – his pike – in the phalanx. The Macedonian front ranks used the spear end (right) for impaling attackers, and pushing back the enemy line. Ranks behind used the butt end (far right) for stabbing the enemy wounded as they advanced over them.

A small ivory bust of Philip II of Macedon from his funerary regalia at the Royal Tomb of Vergina, in Northern Greece (late fourth century BC). Scholars increasingly trace much of his son Alexander's military success to the earlier tactical, strategic, and logistical reforms of Philip.

MACEDONIAN MASTERY

Philip also brought to western warfare an entirely new ideology of battle. True, the actual stand-up fighting still involved frontal assaults and so continued to be every bit as gallant as in the old Greek phalanxes of the past. The running collision of massed infantry, the spear-tip to the face of the enemy, were still the preferred creed of any Macedonian phalangite who lined up in column. But war-making had become much more than personal courage, nerve, and physical strength.

Nor did the grim-faced Macedonians just kill for territorial gain. Rather, battle was designed predominantly as an instrument of ambitious state policy. Philip's destructive mechanism for conquest and annexation was a radical source of social unrest and cultural upheaval, not a conservative Greek institution to preserve the existing agrarian community. His men, too, were a completely different breed from the hoplites of the past. In his comedy *Philip*, the playwright Mnesimachus (c.350 BC) makes his characteristic Macedonian phalangites boast:

> Do you know against what type of men you'll have to fight?
> We dine on sharpened swords,
> and drink down blazing torches as our wine.
> Then for dessert they bring us broken Cretan darts

On 2 August 338 BC, Philip II marched north and met the allied Greeks in the small plain of Chaeroneia in northern Greece. Philip attacked the Athenians and then back-pedaled. The Athenians swarmed after him, but left an enormous gap in their centre. On cue, Alexander drove through the hole and encircled the Theban right. Philip then resumed his attack on the Athenians, who panicked when they found their own right trapped. Chaeronea saw the end of the hoplite phalanx, the destruction of the Sacred Band, and the futility of the resistance of Demosthenes, who fled the battle in shame back to Athens.

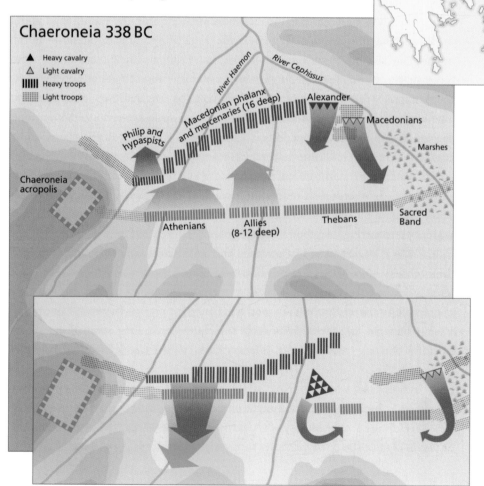

and splintered pike shafts. Our pillows are shields
and breastplates, and beside our feet lie bows and slings.
We crown ourselves with catapult garlands.

Philip's known hostility towards independent city-states composed of yeoman hoplites explains his exaggerated portrayal in the conservative fourth-century BC oratory of the Greek *polis*. Demosthenes described him as a limping, one-eyed monster 'so fond of danger…that in order to make his empire greater, he has been wounded in every part of his body whilst fighting his enemies' – a terrible superman who would fight at any time, in any and all manners. Demosthenes warned the Athenians:

> You hear that Philip marches unchecked not because he leads a phalanx of hoplites, but rather because he is accompanied by skirmishers, cavalry, archers, mercenaries, and similar troops. When relying on these forces, he attacks a people that is at odds with itself, and when through distrust no one goes forth to fight for his country, he next brings up his artillery and lays siege. I need hardly tell you that Philip makes no difference between summer and winter, and has no season set apart for inaction.

At Chaeroneia (338 BC) Philip and his eighteen-year-old son Alexander shattered the phalanx of the Thebans and Athenians, and with it they broke the national resistance of Greece. Beware of attributing the causes of that watershed victory to superior Macedonian technology, skill, or tactical innovation alone: it was the panic and collapse of the advancing, wild-eyed Athenians on the left that fatally weakened the cohesion of the Greek line. The Athenian infantry nearly swarmed through the ranks of the Macedonians, as their allied Thebans across the plain on the right wing held out stubbornly against the attack of the young mounted Alexander.

In contrast, Macedonian discipline, superb integration of horse and infantry-man, complete battlefield command and control of all contingents – rather than the lengths of their pikes or Philip's feigned withdrawal – explain the Northerners' triumph. In the battle's aftermath the Thebans lay annihilated on the field. The elite corps, their 'Sacred Band' of 150 pairs of homosexual lovers, had gone down like some magnificent wounded stag, later to be interred under the stone lion (right), which still stands beside the modern roadway. Of the slain Athenians at Chaeroneia, the last generation of free hoplite infantry, a poignant epitaph recorded:

> Time, the all-surveying deity of all kinds of affairs
> Be a messenger to all men of our sufferings
> How striving to save the sacred land of Greece
> We died on the famed plains of Boeotia.

In commemoration of the heroic stand of the Sacred Band at Chaeronea, after the battle Philip allowed a proud lion to be erected where their corpses, brought from across the battlefield, were interred. Modern excavators have unearthed remains of 245 bodies beneath the stone monument.

WEST MEETS EAST

From the experience of the battles of Marathon and Plataea (see pages 21–6), the Greeks had known that Persia was vulnerable. In 401 BC, the gallant '10,000', a Greek mercenary force hired by Cyrus II to reclaim the throne of Persia, discovered the same, though forced to retreat after the death of their employer at the battle of Cunaxa. The Spartans sent to drive the Persians out of Asia Minor in the 390s BC found that Greek infantry could experience little difficulty in breaking apart any infantry corps the Persians might field. Ironically, the chief worry for a Greek expeditionary army in the East was facing the ubiquitous Persian-bought, mercenary hoplites from their own country. For example, on his return from a visit to Asia (367 BC), Antiochus, the ambassador of a Greek city-state, scoffed that he had seen the Persian king's, 'bakers, cooks, wine-pourers, and door-keepers in vast numbers, but as for men of the type who could fight with Greeks, he had looked carefully, but could not find any.'

On the 'Alexander sarcophagus' of the late fourth century BC Alexander plunges into the Persian ranks. The mounted king with lion skin on head strikes a heroic pose, reflecting Alexander's contrived efforts to see himself as a Greek demi-god incarnate.

Conquest in the East, then, had been in the mind of some Greeks for generations. After all, the enormous wealth of the Persian empire was especially tempting to Greek politicians, given their own growing economic difficulties, and the accelerating erosion of imperial control across the Aegean in Asia. But the trick had always been to give up the old idea of a hoplite militia, devising in its place a logistical system and a loyal, unified army from all Greek city-states, a social and military amalgam that could be supplied over the great distances, whilst confronting a variety of enemy troops, on any terrain. For just that reason, the fourth-century BC Spartan king, Agesilaus, was supposed to have deplored the continual infighting of the Greeks while their enemy, the Persians, remained unattacked: 'If we are to continue to destroy those Greeks we find at fault, we had better be careful that we still have enough men to conqueror the Barbarians.'

After the assassination of Philip (336 BC), the twenty-year-old Alexander began his deceased father's planned Persian invasion with a victory at the Granicus River near the Hellespont (334 BC). No 'typical' Alexandrian battle exists; no exact blueprint explains the young general's tactical victories. But in his first savage onslaught at the Granicus, Alexander established a pattern that was to distinguish his next three major battle triumphs: at Issus (333 BC), Gaugamela (331 BC), and the Hydaspes (326 BC).

The pattern consisted of: (1) brilliant adaptation to local, often unfavourable, terrain (all his battles were fought on or near rivers); (2) generalship, by several frightful examples of personal – always nearly fatal – courage at the head of the companion cavalry; (3) stunning cavalry charges focused on a concentrated spot in the enemy line that aimed to turn the dazed enemy onto the spears of the advancing phalanx; (4) the assignment of specialized units for initial feints or to fill in sudden trouble-spots; and (5) the subsequent pursuit or destruction of enemy forces in the field, reflecting Alexander's impulse to eliminate, not merely to defeat, hostile armies.

At the Granicus, for example, Alexander shrugged off the ostensible disadvantage in crossing the swollen stream, once he discovered that the Persians had unwisely placed light cavalry in front of their Greek mercenary phalanx. He focused on the left-centre of their line for his main strike. To prevent the enemy from massing at just that point of attack, Alexander dispatched an initial – sacrificial – Macedonian cavalry charge further to the left of the Persian line, where the enemy instinctively, mistakenly, sent reinforcements. Suddenly, Alexander himself emerged out of the Granicus, driving on an oblique onslaught of heavy horsemen. The enemy cavalry reeled, then slowly gave way in the ferocious melee. Plutarch relates that in the hand-to-hand fighting Alexander nearly perished, his gaudy shield and white plume drawing the fire of numerous missiles. A javelin caught in his breastplate; a battle-axe nearly cleaved his helmet.

Immediately, the Macedonian phalanx and hypaspists came on, ploughing into the water, clambering up the banks, demolishing – as pike-carrying columns historically do – the confused enemy cavalry. With the Persian cavalry front shattered, the enemy Greek phalanx in the rear was quickly encircled by the left and right wing of the victorious Macedonian horse. It only remained to channel the doomed Hellenic mercenaries into the advancing infantry. The entire mass of hired Greeks either perished or surrendered. Less than 200 Macedonians fell; perhaps 10,000 Persians and Greek mercenaries died. No wonder Alexander's Macedonians – nobles, peasants, and thugs alike – would follow a commander like this deep into the rich interior of Asia.

Yet dramatic as these battlefield masterpieces were, decisive as his 'battle strategy' of seeking out enemy forces rather than mere territory was, major pitched confrontation still totalled no more than a week's work out of nearly 3,600 days of constant campaigning. And so it is wise to remember as well the less heralded sieges, marches, and skirmishes, operations that were equally a part of the Macedonians' remarkable decade-long destruction of Asian civilization. The personal courage of Alexander, including his magnificent – nearly suicidal – dives into the enemy line is rather deceptive: far from being a hothead, he was a calculating, master logistician. With an uncanny skill at recruiting innovative engineers, efficient quartermasters, and sound strategists, Alexander essentially invented the main disciplines of western military organization, and so systematically, methodically, dismantled the empire to the east.

Macedonians, unlike earlier Greeks or contemporary Persians, usually carried their own provisions and equipment. There was no long baggage train of wagons, women, and livestock. 'When Philip organized his first army', wrote Frontinus, the Roman military compiler, 400 years later, 'he ordered that no one was to use a wagon. The horsemen he allowed one servant each, but for the infantry he permitted for every ten men one attendant only, who was charged with carrying milling equipment and ropes. When the army went out during the summer, each man was ordered to carry thirty days' provisions on his back.' Usually, local officials

At the battle of the Granicus (334 BC) Alexander opened the attack with his light-armed troops on the right wing. As the Persians shifted to meet the attack, Alexander caught them in disorder, and his cavalry routed the entire line. The mercenary Greeks in Persian service were left in the rear to be butchered by the Macedonian phalanx and encircling cavalry.

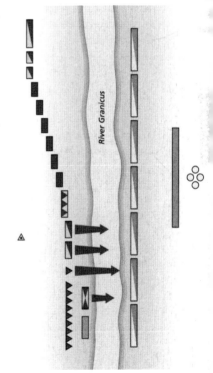

Persian cavalry   ▲ Companion cavalry
Greek mercenaries   Light cavalry
○ Persian satraps   Hypaspists
Archers   Phalanx
Javelin-men   ▲ Alexander

were forced to supply caches of food in advance, allowing Alexander's sleek army to hop from one depot to another. 'Philip', wrote the military rhetorician Polyaenus of the Roman era, 'made the Macedonians march 300 stadia [about 34 miles], bearing their arms, and carrying as well helmets, greaves, spears, provisions, and their daily utensils.' Without reconnaissance and promised food, there was simply no campaign. The enormous apparatus of travelling markets was inimical to the Macedonian's prime directive of speed, rapid onslaught, and decisive quick blows. In short, the Macedonian army travelled in exactly the same manner in which it attacked.

This same logistical organization of war was, ironically, also applied to sedentary operations; bureaucratization was clearly evident in the Macedonian mastery of *poliorcetics* or '*polis*-enclosure'. Alexander stormed three great cities: Halicarnassus (334 BC), Tyre (332 BC), and Gaza (332 BC). All these citadels were thought to be nearly impregnable; all were reduced by engineering mastery, patience, and use of missile-troops, naval contingents, and innovative artillery. Likewise, he conducted a number of smaller raiding and punishment expeditions against irregular contingents of mountaineers and mounted rebels in the mountains of Bactria, Scythia, and Afghanistan. In these campaigns, he organized a series of frontier forts from which heavier armed Macedonian cavalry could sortie out, holding the insurrection at bay until Alexander, through cash and promises of allegiance, could buy off rebellious

Ships of the Hellenistic age

The steady trend to larger, heavier ships reached its climax with the bizarre 400-foot vessel built for Ptolemy IV of Egypt (221–203 BC) drawn here in just one of several reconstructions that modern scholars have attempted. Three thousand rowers and 3,000–4,000 soldiers manned the 3,217-ton monster, which rose over 80 feet above the water. Such indulgences were unseaworthy and more matters of imperial prestige than real military assets.

In the Hellenistic period, ostentation and gigantism dominated the design of military equipment, and ships as well grew to enormous size. By the late fourth century BC quinqueremes (ships with five banks of oars) were common, and we even hear of seven-, eight-, all the way up to forty-oared ships, where two or three banks of rowers might be made up of anywhere from two to ten men sharing an oar.

These frightening, and thus prestigious, dreadnoughts were almost worthless in combined operations, and valuable only for massive sea battles in enclosed harbours or for attacking the seaward side of peninsular fortifications.

Almost simultaneous with this move to enormous battleships, a far more effective trend developed in exactly the opposite direction. Lighter craft manned by pairs of only fifty oarsmen or fewer, the so-called 'sharks' and 'one-and-a-halfs' (ships relying on both sail and oarsmen, with a portion of the crew doubling as infantry boarders), proved far more versatile in pursuing the Mediterranean's pirates and in protecting merchant ships.

Centres of seaborne commerce, such as the island of Rhodes, effectively mastered hybrid designs that allowed oarsmen to become marines as occasion demanded. In the general stalemate of the Hellenistic period before the coming of Rome, small island polities could thus protect themselves from pirates and would-be tyrants by their versatile fleets, and so they often carved out lucrative autonomies.

satraps on the fringe of the Persian empire. Such versatility, although reminiscent of the march of the desperate Ten Thousand through Persia seventy-five years earlier (see page 40), was beyond the resources and imagination of any Greek *polis* of the previous two centuries.

THE MONSTER ARMIES

When Alexander died, an exhausted alcoholic of 33, in 323 BC, the lands he had inherited and conquered were divided among the senior Macedonian commanders in the field and back at home in Greece. Very quickly the old-guard generals, Perdiccas, Craterus, and Eumenes, were eliminated and instead spheres of influence were tentatively allotted to the other surviving underlings: Antipater controlled Macedonia and Greece; Ptolemy received Egypt; Antigonus occupied Asia Minor; Seleucus inherited Mesopotamia and the East as far as India; Lysimachus retained Thrace and the lands around the Black Sea. Seleucus' subsequent victory at Ipsus (301 BC) over Antigonus proved that no lesser individual would inherit Alexander's legacy and so, for the next century and a half, rival Macedonian dynasts fought a series of inconclusive wars throughout the Greek and Asiatic world in futile attempts to reconstitute Alexander's brief empire.

The traditional Greek disdain for mercenary service is well captured by this third-century BC statuette in terra-cotta of a grubby hired killer, replete with theatrical masque and enormous pack. We should imagine him as an exaggerated version of a Hellenistic phalangite.

For the military historian the battles of the 'Successors' exercise an undeniable fascination: pikes lengthen to more than 20 feet, elephants make routine appearances, enormous and garish siege-engines assault cities. The treasures and other capital that flowed from the disruption of Persian hegemony made an arms race inevitable. Once unlimited money was devoted to war-making, and the technical and philosophical genius of the Greeks was applied to the new military science, organized killing became a Greek art form in itself. Throughout the Hellenistic period, continual technological sophistication refined both fortification and artillery, while ongoing debate redefined the proper role of the phalanx. In both cases, tradition always yielded to innovation. When Antigonus Gonatas (320–239 BC), for example, was asked how one should attack the enemy, he simply gave the utilitarian reply, 'In any way that seems useful.'

Nothing could ever match the sheer terror of a Macedonian phalanx. The Roman general Aemilius Paulus, who faced phalangites at Pydna in 168 BC, was left with a life-long image of terror: 'He considered the formidable appearance of their front, bristling with arms, and was taken with fear and alarm,' says Plutarch: 'nothing he had ever seen before was its equal. Much later he often used to recall that sight and his own reaction to it.' Nor could any enemy neglect the wide arsenal – heavy and light cavalry, light infantry, skirmishers, slingers, bowmen, and elephants – that megalomaniac Hellenistic commanders theoretically might bring onto the battlefield. Nevertheless, there were inherent weaknesses in Hellenistic military practice on both a tactical and a strategic level.

By the third century BC, most phalangites were exclusively hired mercenaries. Gone was any vestigial sense of agrarian solidarity and elan of the old Greek armies.

King Pyrrhus of the Epirus (d.272 BC), for example, reportedly told his officers, 'You pick out the big men; I will make them brave.' But unlike the lean forces of Philip and Alexander of even a few decades past, these much larger hired forces of the Successors required enormous non-combatant support: baggage carriers, engineers, wives, children, slaves, and markets. Such logistical and social dependence was often only haphazard and inefficiently organized. This relative sloppiness limited both the range and strategic options of large Hellenistic armies, as the occupation and control of conquered ground was increasingly a question only of cash, not of national interest, courage, or the patriotism of local citizenry. Much less was there to be lasting loyalty to either an idea or a man.

More important, the phalanx itself had grown unwieldy when heavy pikes approached twenty or more feet in length – an armchair tactician's fascinating nightmare. But the tradition of cavalry symphony under Alexander was neglected at just the period when cumbersome Macedonian infantry needed even greater integration; its flanks more, not less, protection by horsemen.

The open order of legionaries (top) allowed them to throw their javelins into a concentrated spot, then advance on the wounded and confused phalangites (bottom) with sword and shield. Their fluid order allowed the Romans to focus or disperse their attacks, while the phalanx was committed to a static wall of defence regardless of enemy manoeuvres.

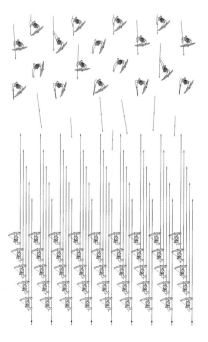

Elephants and local mercenary cavalry were not the answer, as the successor generals simplistically tried to match the lost genius of Alexander with bought manpower and brute force of arms. Increased power without grace simply made the phalanx more vulnerable than ever: 'The Macedonian formation' wrote Polybius 'is sometimes of little use, and at others of none whatsoever, since a phalangite is unable to operate either in smaller units or by himself – while the Roman formation is especially well rounded.'

LEGIONARY GENESIS

The emerging Roman way of war thus stood in stark contrast to the chaos of the Hellenistic military style. On a tactical level, the parochial Romans for centuries on the Italian peninsula had incorporated the old Etruscan phalanx, an institution itself borrowed from the Greeks. Indeed, throughout its later history Rome retained a fascination with the phalanx, at times under duress bunching its legions together to seek the greater thrust of massed columns. But mobility and fluidity, not naked force, and the short sword, not the pike, gave new-found lethality to Roman infantry. In comparing legion with phalanx, Polybius simply concluded: 'The Roman legionary is adaptable to any place at any time and for any purpose'.

It is difficult to talk in any meaningful way of the 'Roman army'. After all, the Roman military evolved steadily over nearly a millennium, from an instrument of republican government in the fourth century BC to authoritarian imperialism eight centuries later; from a nucleus of Italian yeomanry to hired professionals drawn from the entire Mediterranean. The genesis of the legion, however, occurred in Italy during the fourth and third centuries BC. The limitations of the Roman phalanx were ever more apparent as Rome slowly expanded through the Italian peninsula, finding a need to adapt its forces to a wide variety of different armies to its north, east, and south.

As an example of the scope of Roman campaigning, and the wide-ranging experiences of her legionaries, Livy reports the often quoted example of the Roman citizen-soldier Spurius Ligustinus. In his thirty-two-year career in the army (200–168 BC), the fifty-year-old recruit, father of eight, fought against Macedonian phalanxes in Greece, battled in Spain, returned to Greece to fight the Aetolians, then was back on duty in Italy, and then off again to Spain. 'On four occasions within a few years', Spurius claimed in Livy's highly rhetorical account, 'I was chief centurion. Thirty-four times I was commended for bravery by my commanders; I received six civic crowns (for saving the life of a fellow soldier).'

The columnar formation of the Roman phalanx was gradually broken up into smaller tactical units, called maniples ('handfuls'). In line with this new move to quickness and fluidity, Roman infantrymen abandoned the spear and large round shield in favour of the curved, rectangular *scutum*, the throwing-javelin (*pilum*), and the short, double-edged thrusting sword (*gladius*) – 'excellent for thrusting, both of its edges cutting effectively, as the blade is very strong and firm', said Polybius. By the second century BC when the Romans met the Hellenistic Greeks, a legion of men like Spurius was composed of about 4,200 infantry and 300 cavalry, divided into three successive lines of ten maniples,

The *gladius*, the Romans' short thrusting sword, wielded here by legionaries sculpted on a sarcophagus. When powered by a skilled legionary in a slashing or hacking attack, it generated great force. Under normal conditions, such blows could not quite penetrate iron or bronze armour. But limbs could always be severed with astonishing ease. Livy, for example, records how the Macedonians were devastated in an early cavalry encounter with Roman swordsmen. Accustomed to the puncture wounds of the Greek pike, they were physically and psychologically broken by the far more lethal Roman sword. Livy suggests it was a bloodbath: 'bodies maimed by the Spanish sword, arms cut off along with the shoulder, heads separated from bodies, with the entire neck cut away, insides laid bare and other disgusting sights'.

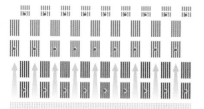

The Roman battle system.
1 The *velites*, or light-armed skirmishers, attempt to probe and confuse the enemy before retreating back through their own lines of *hastati*, *principes*, and *triarii*.

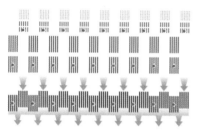

2 The rear centuries of first-line *hastati* now step up to form one solid mass. The *hastati* hurl their *pila* and advance to crash into the enemy with shields raised and swords drawn.

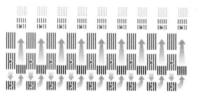

3 The *hastati* break apart once more into individual centuries and pass through the advancing second-line *principes* on their way to the rear, always retreating through gaps in the *principes* in order to maintain a solid line at the front.

Velites		Hastati	
Triari		Posterior century	
Principes		Prior century	

each maniple separated from its like counterpart by about the width of its own formation. So the ten independent maniples of each line – at least before they crashed against the enemy – had free space on both sides, as well as to the front and rear. On an organizational level, Roman infantry were recruited into the legion by 'centuries', groups of about sixty to seventy Italian farmers led by a skilled centurion. Two centuries fought together in a maniple, one stacked behind the other. In conventional Roman battlefield order (*triplex acies*), imagine three successive lines of stacked infantry rectangles, a mile- or two-long checkerboard (*quincunx*), each maniple positioned in the gap of the line ahead.

After initial skirmishing between light-armed troops and horsemen (*velites*), the first line of ten maniples, the so-called *hastati* (anachronistically called 'spearmen'), approached to within about fifty to a hundred yards of the enemy, then ran and flung their javelins when about thirty yards distant. With sword and shield, the *hastati* followed their missiles and banged into the stunned enemy line, searching for pockets of collapsed men whom their *pila* had just wounded or disarmed. The initial aerial barrage of *pila* achieved about the same terror as the traditional collision of hoplite spears, but the shorter *gladius* allowed the pikeless legionary far greater manoeuvrability to get inside the enemy formation with his sword, and to carve at exposed limbs. At this point, the second line of Roman swordsmen, the *principes* ('leaders'), followed up. They either pushed their advancing *hastati* on through the opponents' line, or – if the enemy proved formidable – served as a separate reserve, a second wave, battering the enemy with a fresh assault of more slashing and thrusting blades, as the exhausted first line of *hastati* retreated back through the gaps in their own advancing maniples.

This second line of *principes*, the most rugged and skilled swordsmen of the legion, usually broke the enemy's cohesion. But failing that, the third and last manipular row, the *triarii* ('third-liners'), were waiting to the rear on their knees, covering with shields, spears extended. Rock-like, these ten maniples were on the look-out for any wavering of the first two lines, giving rise to the dire proverb 'matters have come down to the *triarii*'. If the legion was in real trouble, desperate maniples of defeated and dejected *hastati* and *principes* could separate from each other to filter back through these protective rectangles of *triarii* to the palisaded camp – 'a resting-place for the victor, a refuge for the loser'. More often, however, given the frequency of Roman legionary success, in the swell of victory, the *triarii* also advanced cautiously, and applied the *coup de grâce* to any battlefield stragglers or crumbling formations, the enemy now 'seeing with the greatest terror that a new line suddenly had risen up with increased numbers'. As with the phalanx, auxiliary cavalry and light-armed allies covered the flanks.

AN ARMY FOR ALL SEASONS

Obviously, the key to the legion's early success was co-ordination and adaptability, all made possible by reserves and the sheer diversity of forces. *Pila* gave Roman infantry an offensive reach unknown to a phalanx, its deadly shower of javelins superior in lethality to the slinger's projectiles or the archer's arrows. Once inside the stunned enemy mass, the *gladius* could make short work of phalangites, and the tall, ovoid *scutum* was handy for pushing in the manner of the phalanx, if maniples – once bunched together at impact – needed group thrusting power to break the solid enemy line. Spearmen to the rear prevented collapse. In a pinch, they could overwhelm confused and disorganized opposition.

On a tactical level, time and space were well under control in the hands of subordinate officers, military men of education and training who could co-ordinate the waves of their three assaulting lines, arranging the thirty maniples of each legion to achieve either greater density or flexibility along the line as the situation required. And with so many smaller and mobile units, real articulation became possible. Holding actions in the middle, flank attack, feints, retreats, and encirclements were all tactical options. At the most extreme, all maniples of the legion could coalesce horizontally, their three lines joined vertically as well, the legion now forming an enormous quasi-phalanx to achieve greater striking power through accumulated, pushing shields. Flat, unbroken terrain was not, as in the case of the phalanx, so absolutely crucial to legion cohesion, since maniples could just as easily create distance between one another, in order to advance around obstacles. Indeed, rough ground that might thwart a clumsier enemy column was often welcomed. Consequently, the great variety of Roman weaponry and potential formations facilitated prompt response against tactical challenges of almost any armed enemy.

Only two environments proved lethal to a Roman legion. First, under *no* circumstance must it become caught on narrow, flat terrain so that it might find itself – as happened at Cannae (see pages 48–9) – trapped and squeezed between flanking enemy pincers. In these natural or man-made valleys and canyons, maniples had no chance to flow independently, but rather tended to conglomerate. And with no room to the side, individual legionaries lost their open space and the crucial ability to use their swords with advantage. Instead, like underpowered phalangites, they were funnelled *en masse* against columns of heavier enemy spearmen, legionaries waiting in line as it were, helpless to prevent their predictable annihilation at the fore.

Just as fatal was the situation of nearly the opposite degree: unending and open treeless plains. With no real heavy cavalry and unreliable light horse, Roman legions might then become swallowed up by the sheer expanse of the terrain, harassed and goaded endlessly by mounted nomads and archers, who could not be caught, much less targeted by the maniples. Under those conditions – Crassus at Carrhae (53 BC) provides a good example – extinction by endless aerial bombardment was slower than pulverization before a column, but just as ineluctable.

The legion, then, represented the perfect culmination of existing western military prowess. Drawing on an early Greek battle tradition of shock and decisive

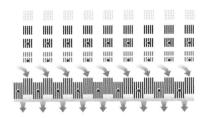

4 Rear centuries of the *principes*, in similar fashion to the prior manoeuvre of the *hastati*, now step up to join their own comrades ahead, forming a solid front the instant the *hastati* have departed. Thus the legions have brought in a fresh wave of fighters without any reprieve for the enemy.

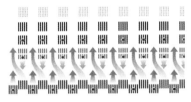

5 Should the second-line *principes* tire, they too in turn pass through the advancing *triarii* spearmen, who now coalesce into yet a third line and ensure that the fighting continues without let-up. The enemy has been exposed to an unceasing attack of javelin, sword, and spear wielded by three fresh lines of legionaries.

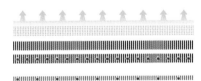

6 The *triarii* now finish off the enemy, protect a gradual withdrawal, or begin the three-phase cycle again, should the enemy prove especially stubborn. Notice that the centuries can be bunched together or thinned according to the nature of the opposing forces.

confrontation, coupled with the Macedonian legacy of integration and diversity of force, the pragmatic Romans achieved a marvellous balance between power and grace. With the aid of their unmatched and elaborate governmental organization, and the capital of an expanding market economy, Romans surrounded the legionary with a rich infrastructure of war-making – roads, camps, hospitals, arms and

The Battle of Cannae 216 BC

For two millennia, no battle has exerted such a narcotic spell on western military thinking as Cannae, the Carthaginians' most devastating victory during Hannibal's invasion of Italy (218–203 BC). Century after century military theorists and military planners who want to understand how it is possible to encircle and destroy entire armies have studied this battle intently. The fascination with Cannae lies in the annihilation of the enemy through a single hammer-like stroke. It was accomplished by the masterful diversity of Hannibal's tactics, his deft use of incongruous light-armed soldiers, horsemen, missile troops, and infantry from all over the Mediterranean world, and by his daring decision to weaken the centre of his outnumbered army, so that his wings might then lengthen and swallow the stunned Romans.

After a series of disastrous and cumulative defeats at Ticinus (218 BC), Trebia (218 BC), and Trasimene (217 BC), the Roman senate desperately searched for ways to extinguish Hannibal before northern and western Europeans and local Italians – flocked to his army. But the Romans now faced an anomaly in their military experience, an authentic tactical genius whose use of ambush, ruse, and simple battlefield articulation could nullify in a single afternoon all Rome's numerical and organizational superiority. Worse, Hannibal had little respect for legionary repute, but instead was one of the few foreigners in the entire history of the ancient world who actually welcomed a frontal assault against western armies. Hannibal wanted to break Roman legions outright in the field, as part of his plan to discredit the notion of Roman military invincibility and so systematically uncouple the Italian allies.

On the morning of the battle, the Romans unwisely – and uncharacteristically – sought to stack their maniples deep, almost phalanx-like, on the narrow plain of Cannae, hoping on this occasion that the sheer force of their enormous army

(80,000 men) might simply drive through the Carthaginian centre. Shell-shocked after a string of defeats, Roman commanders gambled that this time overwhelming force could not be finessed by mere military profundity. In short, Cannae was an abject reversal of the usual military paradigm of the ancient world: now a western army outnumbered its foe, relying on unintelligently deployed, but savage power – the non-western enemy in contrast seeking protection for its outnumbered forces by co-ordination and strategy.

Hannibal adapted his battle plan brilliantly – and precisely – to facilitate the brutishness of Roman tactics. He and his brother Mago stationed themselves with suspect Gauls and Spaniards right at the acme of the Roman attack, hoping their presence could steady their unreliable troops long enough to

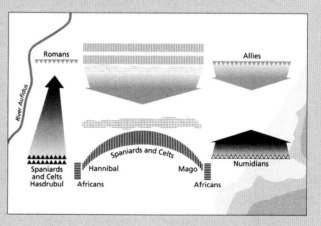

conduct a gradual withdrawal, to backpedal slowly, sucking in the oncoming Roman weight. The key for Hannibal and his allies was to survive long enough to allow the Carthaginian infantry on the wings, and cavalry streaking to rear and sides, to enclose the enormous legionary mass, thereby deflating its forward pressure before it blew away the core of their army.

Charges by Hannibal's horsemen at the flanks and at the back, a barrage of missiles from all sides, and the sheer confusion of seeing enemies in all directions stalled the Roman advance just in time. The planned envelopment was soon completed, as Hannibal's thin wall of North African and European irregulars held tight a surging throng of Roman armour, support services, pensions, salaries, medical corps, officers – and so crafted warfare as an enormous bureaucratic enterprise, its legions designed, if need be, to cope with challenges far beyond the boundaries of Italy. That their creation lasted for half a millenium is a testament to the vision and imagination of the last generation of the Roman republic.

infantry. With the Romans' forward assault nullified – legionary cohesion collapsed into terror. Eighty thousand men were surrounded, a trapped, but formidable and extremely well-armed beast, itself larger than nearly all the cities of the time in Italy. Most, hemmed in by their own comrades, were unable even to get at the enemy to use their weapons.

For the rest of that August day Cannae became an abject slaughter, a battlefield Armageddon unrivalled until the twentieth century. The destruction of some 50,000 snared Italians in a single afternoon – more than 100 men killed each minute – was in itself a vast problem in the logistics of killing. Our written sources (Appian, Livy, Plutarch, and Polybius) depicted the long afternoon as horrific butchery. Never had so many Romans – consuls, ex-consuls, quaestors, tribunes (after the battle Hannibal would collect their gold rings by the bushel) – been trapped on the battlefield with no chance of escape.

In the dust of thousands of shod feet on the summer plain, in the continual shower of missiles on the stationary target, with thousands of plumed legionary heads bobbing in the strong summer winds, no wonder Appian recorded that the Romans simply 'could not see the enemy'. Nor could they hear amid the wild shrieking of wounded men within and the cacophony of dozens of strange dialects without.

To have any notion of what it was like for the Romans, we must examine briefly the postmortem accounts of the battle. Livy says that corpses were discovered 'with their heads buried in the earth. Apparently they had dug holes for themselves and

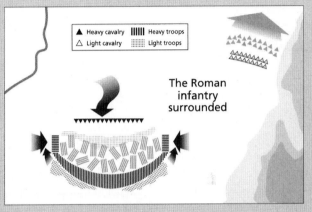

The Roman infantry surrounded

Heavy cavalry | Heavy troops
Light cavalry | Light troops

then, by smothering their mouths in the dirt, had choked themselves to death.' Yet, he also records examples of extraordinary Roman courage, of a Numidian who had been brought alive out of the pile from beneath a dead Roman legionary, his ears and nose gnawed away by the raging Roman infantryman who had lost the use of everything but his teeth – and his will to resist. Hannibal, in the ancient tradition of victorious military commanders, grandly inspected the battlefield dead. He was said to have been shocked at the sheer carnage – even as he gave his surviving troops free rein to loot the corpses and execute the wounded. (The August heat made it imperative to strip promptly the bloated bodies and dispose quickly of the stinking flesh.)

All this, however, was an eerie premonition of Hannibal's own impending catastrophe. Fourteen years later at Zama (202 BC), another young military prodigy, this time a Roman, Scipio, would create a ring of his own around the Carthaginians, manned by the Roman orphans of Cannae, and kill 20,000 Carthaginians in the process.

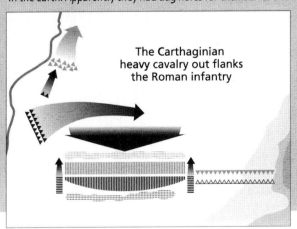

The Carthaginian heavy cavalry out flanks the Roman infantry

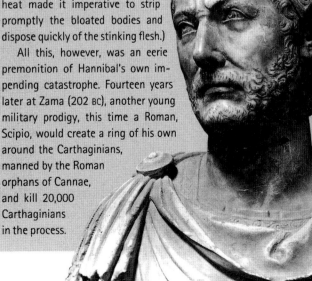

Hanniba

| CHAPTER 3 | *The Roman Way of War* |

Incredibly enough, in the third century BC, Rome expanded simultaneously eastwards against the Greeks and Macedonians and west and south against Carthage, the great commercial and military power that had grown out of a Phoenician colony in present-day Tunisia. The three Punic wars (264–241 BC, for Sicily; 218–201 BC, for Italy and Spain; and 149–146 BC, for Carthage itself) were a struggle for the central Mediterranean which culminated in the abject destruction of Carthage. Throughout these conflicts, superior Roman military organization and infrastructure repeatedly demonstrated that the smallholders who made up the legions – as long as they fought in or near Italy – could overcome poor generalship and poor tactics, winning wars even when they lost major battles.

THE EMERGENCE OF A MEDITERRANEAN ARMY

By the late second and early first century BC, however, the Roman military faced a dilemma: overseas expansion was outstripping traditional military capability. Near-constant fighting to the north and west against the Germanic tribes (the Cimbri and Ambrones, 113–102 BC), to the south against the African Jugurtha in Numidia (112–106 BC), and to the east against Mithridates of the Black Sea region (96–82 BC) demanded either restructuring of the republican legions or the cessation of further such intervention altogether. Roman campaigning now typically spanned the entire Mediterranean and the whole year, with little chance for legionaries to return home and farm after a series of summer battles. Garrisoning walls, forts, harbours, and entire frontiers required permanent, professional troops who could master skills beyond those of mere battlefield combat, such as construction, siegecraft, and local policing. The historian Tacitus later remarked of legionary activity on the German frontier in the early first century AD: 'They complained about the difficulty of the work, and particularly about building ramparts, digging ditches, foraging, collecting lumber and firewood, and all the other camp tasks that are either necessary or else invented to keep the men busy.'

Often, the legions would be called on to create real infrastructure in the provinces from virtually nothing. Of their later activity as permanent garrison troops in Egypt, an anonymous Roman historian of the fourth century AD observed: 'There are still to be viewed in very many parts of the Egyptian cities, public works of the emperor Probus [AD 276–82], which he had constructed by military labour...He built bridges, temples, porticoes, and basilicas, all by the labour of the soldiers, and he dredged many river-mouths, drained a large number of marshes and converted this into good agricultural land.' If Roman soldiers were to take on the combined roles of professional killers, construction workers, and occupational guards, they needed a much higher degree of training and organization. In short, by the late republican era the whole centuries-long tradition of amateur Roman

Opposite: **The successors of Alexander often fielded troops which were organized and equipped increasingly along Roman lines. This second-century BC tomb painting from western Asia Minor portrays an Anatolian mercenary with bronze helmet, scale armour, and *thureos* shield in the service of Ptolemy VI of Egypt, and reflects the general Mediterranean trend to emulate wherever possible superior Roman weaponry and organization.**

yeoman farmers providing their own arms and armour, organized by region, and led by local officers, had become completely inadequate. Native smallholders suffered enormously in the third and second centuries BC during the extended military absences from their farms, and yet continual overseas Roman annexation – the fruit of the legionaries' own labours – led to massive importation into Italy of non-landed capital such as slaves, cash, food, and luxury items. This plunder usually accrued to the already affluent Roman senatorial and equestrian elites, men who increasingly invested their profits in larger, more specialized, and often absentee estates: prestigious Italian manors now worked by slave gangs and managed by bailiffs.

In this circular, cause-and-effect relationship, the rise of corporate agriculture (*latifundia*), financed by expropriated foreign capital, led to a gradual depopulation of the Italian countryside – the very recruitment ground of the old Roman army whose manpower had secured overseas lucre in the first place. Appian, a Roman historian of the second century AD, gave a rhetorical, but accurate, portrayal of the dilemma of the late republic. The wealthy, he claimed:

> were obtaining possession of the greater part of the undistributed lands. Emboldened by the lapse of time to believe that they would never be dispossessed, absorbing any adjacent strips and their poor neighbours' allotments, partly by purchase under persuasion, partly by force, they came to cultivate vast tracts instead of single estates, using slaves as workers and herdsmen, lest free labourers be recruited into the army. At the same time, the ownership of slaves brought them great gain from the number of their offspring, who in turn multiplied because they were exempt from military service. So, certain powerful men became extremely rich and the group of servile workers grew throughout the country, all the while the Italian people dwindled in numbers and strength, being oppressed by poverty, taxes, and military service. And if any small farmers had respite from such evils, they spent their time in idleness, because the land was held by the rich, who employed slaves as their cultivators instead of free men.

This paradox somewhat resembled that facing the mature Greek city-states of the fourth century BC, when a high profile in the Mediterranean had exposed the limitations of the conventional Greek idea of restricting citizenship to its local farmers, of constructing war solely around a dominant infantry of landed yeomanry. True, the move to a professional legion and a cosmopolitan nation of assimilated peoples was a prerequisite for the sophisticated economic and military conduct of Roman imperialism; but it predictably also spelled the end of the old insular Roman agricultural state, the fountainhead of all Roman military and civic tradition. And in an even larger sense, this socio-military predicament has plagued the West repeatedly ever since: the success of dynamic armies abroad calls into question – and sometimes undermines – the ideological and political premises of the established social order at home.

The final transition in the Roman military from yeoman infantryman to professional legionary is well illustrated by the career of the Roman general Gaius Marius (157–86 BC). During the pursuit of Jugurtha (107–105 BC) in North Africa, Marius apparently bypassed the property qualification for Roman infantry service and, in a quest for greater manpower, equipped his legions at state expense. He also gradually normalized a sixteen-year, rather than an indefinite, term of service. Now military recruitment of Roman citizens, as in the Hellenistic army, was to be largely separated from status or wealth. This ensured a much larger pool of potential

The rise of the cohort

Two centuries make one
maniple of the front line

After Marius's reform, the cohort, not the maniple, served as the chief tactical and administrative unit of the legion. Some idea of the Roman army's new organizational flexibility can be seen from the battle plan of Julius Caesar's early army in Gaul (58 BC). Four legions (about 20,000 men) formed the corps of the army, flanked by 2,000 Spanish and Gallic cavalry on the wings, and 2,000–3,000 light-armed skirmishers and missile troops in the front. Legions drew up alongside one another, each arranged in the now familiar *triplex acies* formation. Four front-line cohorts of centuries eight men deep were followed by two consecutive lines of three cohorts each, with their centuries six men deep. Thus two eighty-man centuries stacked back-to-back formed a maniple, and three such maniples constituted each cohort of the legion. All cohorts were armed identically with *pila*, *gladius*, and *scutum* as the old *triarii* essentially disappeared as a unique corps. Commanders now dealt with ten uniform and quite large companies (480 men to a cohort), which could be arranged

in the familiar three-line order or formed in any manner a commander felt necessary given the terrain and nature of the enemy.

Two smaller centuries make
one maniple of line 2 or 3

Three maniples make one
cohort of the front line

One legion of three lines of ten cohorts

Three maniples make one
cohort of line 2 or 3

Cavalry   Four legions   Cavalry

Skirmishers, slingers, archers

soldiers, an army that could look exclusively to the 'government' for both its livelihood and its retirement. Consequently, a professional legionary ostensibly welcomed, rather than disdained, continued 'work' overseas in the legions. Vegetius remarked that recruits now needed only 'keen eyes, an erect head, broad chest, muscular shoulders, strong arms, long fingers, modest belly, thin buttocks, and tough, not fat, calves'.

But Marius also set a dangerous precedent in curtailing the agrarian tradition of Roman amateur militias. Professional armies – as subsequent centuries attest – could easily transfer their 'state' allegiance to the particular general who led them, who distributed their pay, who provided their equipment, who allowed them to plunder, and (above all) who pledged them retirement benefits. Demobilization during peace soon did not mean a return to agricultural work for growing hordes of Romans, but instead no work at all and the spectre of urban unemployment and sure impoverishment. Instead of a shared rural background, much less a belief in protecting the territory of Italy, the common bond in the legions became simply the job itself – and the accompanying baser desires for cash, glory, and adventure. The emperor Severus Alexander (AD 222–35) supposedly summed up later Roman legionary ideology: 'One should not fear the soldier provided he is properly clothed and well armed, and has a stout pair of boots, a full belly, and something in his money belt.'

No one changed the face of the Roman army more radically than Gaius Marius (157–86 BC). He ended the property qualification, reorganized the legion around the cohort, improved logistics and training, and professionalized the army into a permanent force loyal more to its general than to the state. While such radical changes facilitated the Roman absorption of the Mediterranean, they also created enormous burdens of taxation, continual military interference into politics, and a sizable body of dangerous mercenary soldiers – military and political crises that were never solved and led eventually to the decline of Roman society itself.

To meet new military challenges in various terrains and local environments, Marius also inaugurated a series of overdue (in the strictly military sense) logistical and tactical reforms. Cohorts (usually formed of about 480 men, three times larger than the maniple of about 160) gradually evolved as the fundamental tactical unit of the legion, which was thus largely now to be defined as ten cohorts of 4,800 soldiers. In the past, a cohort had been not much more than a loosely defined administrative organization of three distinct maniples, each drawn from the three lines of the *triplex acies*. After Marius's reforms, however, each cohort became in some sense a mini-legion in its own right, a real fighting formation, not a mere rubric for recruitment and record-keeping. Its three maniples coalesced one behind another, or side by side, and so fought as a single mass: the old first-line *hastati*, the second-row *principes*, and the rearward *triarii* each giving up one maniple to be integrated together into the new cohort. In turn, individual cohorts, not maniples, now reconstituted the new *triplex acies*, four in front, three in the middle and three to the rear.

With this newly constructed cohort, the ten (rather than the previous thirty) tactical segments of the legions were both more powerful and more versatile. They were better able to concentrate on specific points in the enemy line. Legionary reformation ensured greater flexibility, and so a Roman general did not necessarily need to follow the standard triple (and predictable) sequence of assault throughout the entire legion, but instead could diversify his attack, by directing cohorts to the wings and rear where they could proceed with a phased charge on their own. And

Given the flexibility and organization of the legions, and the dynamic nature of her new mercantile classes, Rome found success in nearly every theatre during the second and first centuries BC and the first century AD. Military mastery over the more civilized and older regimes to the east and south was matched by relentless colonization and exploitation to the west and north among the more barbaric peoples of a largely unexplored Europe.

legionary commanders could now have much more confidence that such independently operating corps would not, as in the case of the older and smaller maniples, be isolated and overwhelmed at one stroke.

In line with this growing military sophistication, Marius tried to standardize in every respect the newly professional legions. Men (now dubbed 'Marius's mules') were to carry their own equipment and arms. Like Philip's Macedonian phalangites more than two centuries earlier, legionaries marched several miles daily, independent of auxiliary food and baggage support. More important still, the skirmishers (the *velites*: the Roman poor armed with a rag-tag assortment of light armament), were given standard gear and brought into the formal apparatus of the legion; any non-legionary light and missile troops, when needed, were now to be composed exclusively of allies. In this move towards cohesion and uniformity, the third-rank *triarii* also gave up their *hasta* (lance) and were issued the standard sword (*gladius*) and javelin (*pilum*). The latter weapon took on increased military efficacy when Marius had one of the rivets connecting its iron head to the shaft replaced by a wooden pin. Now the javelin simply broke or was unusable once it hit either the ground or its target, preventing enemy troops from picking it up and hurling it back. The first-century AD historian Valerius Maximus credits Marius with introducing uniform methods of weapon handling and technique:

> No general before him had done this, but he summoned the masters of the gladiators from Gaius Aurelius Scaurus' school and introduced to our legions a more accurate way of parrying and inflicting blows. He consequently produced a combination of courage and skill in such a way that the one reinforced the other, with courage supplementing skill with all its zeal, and skill teaching courage how to safeguard itself.

In a more symbolic gesture, though one emblematic of the entire transformation of the Roman army, Marius reconstituted the legionary standards, uniformly giving primacy to the martial eagle (*aquila*), abolishing the old agricultural banners of the wolf, horse, boar and minotaur – confirming, in other words, the mercenary rather than the agrarian nature of the new legions.

THE RISE OF THE HIRED ARMIES

Sulla, a junior officer under Marius in the war against Jugurtha, combined with his old mentor (and now bitter rival) in bringing to an end the so-called Social War (90–89 BC) against Rome's allied Italian states (the *socii*), who now received formal rights of Roman citizenship, with equal opportunity to join the Roman army. The prestige of that successful campaign, and the growing practice of allotting the newly professional legions to an individual general for foreign commands, gave Sulla enormous influence and an army of thousands loyal not to the senate, but to his own person. From 88 BC until his death in 78 BC, Sulla systematically devastated much of Greece and Asia Minor and, with six legions, marched on Rome itself in order to destroy popular domestic opposition to traditional aristocratic interests.

Consequently, thanks to both Marius and Sulla, by the seventies of the first century BC the Roman army had become both entirely professional and firmly embedded within domestic politics. This dangerous combination would remain mostly unchanged for the next 500 years. Both the military advantages and predictable drawbacks of such a transformation emerged in a series of subsequent challenges to Roman rule by rebellious legions under Sertorius in Spain (80–72 BC). Slave uprisings led by Spartacus (73–71 BC) and the activities of freelance pirates (67 BC) called for extraordinary measures, as did renewed assaults by Mithridates in Asia (74–63 BC), and the final conquest of Gaul (58–51 BC).

In each theatre, Roman military prowess – essentially the professionalism and training of the legions – overcame numerical superiority, tactical cunning, and a wide array of difficult terrains. Only Crassus's unfortunate and unwise move against

Troops embark on a ship in a scene from Trajan's column. Before the 260s BC, Rome had little experience of naval warfare. When she did build a navy, it was not to master the complicated techniques of man-oeuvre and ramming in the Greek tradition. Her galleys were platforms for seaborne infantry. She copied the Greek and Phoenician tradition of banked oared ships and applied innovations of her own. The corvus (raven), a twenty-four-foot hooked derrick, could be raised, swivelled, and lowered by pulleys. It allowed Roman infantry to run across to the snagged enemy boats with ease. Later, there were fortified towers and a harpoon-grapnel, fired from a catapult on a galley to grab and reel in enemy ships. Roman naval success centred on building galleys in enorm-ous number and organizing competent rowing crews.

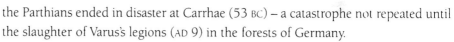

the Parthians ended in disaster at Carrhae (53 BC) – a catastrophe not repeated until the slaughter of Varus's legions (AD 9) in the forests of Germany.

In the near-constant fighting of the first century BC, whether Roman soldiers battled against trained gladiators, rebel legionaries, seaborne mercenaries, eastern phalangites, or northern European tribal irregulars, the result was almost always the same: eventual battlefield victory, slaughter of enemy combatants, absolute elimination of gifted adversaries. Yet paradoxically, the prestige and plunder that accrued from the skill and constancy of the Roman soldier in these decades did not enhance the republican government, much less the individual legionary himself. Instead, generals like Metellus, Lucullus, Pompey, Julius Caesar, and Crassus used their provincial commands to extort state capital, which in turn subsidized their growing private armies, and thus ensured their own further consolidation of personal power.

The relative success of each of these grandees depended solely on his own degree of military acumen and his relative daring in subverting entirely any vestigial republican notion of public service, which might check military command and the appropriation of foreign capital. Thus three centuries of continual Roman military advancement culminated in the first century BC with a military apparatus that steam-rollered both foreign and domestic opposition. After gobbling up most of the Mediterranean, the legions proceeded to devour the very constitution that had spawned them.

The two decades that followed Caesar's crossing of the Rubicon in 49 BC saw legion pitted against legion in almost continuous fighting. It is difficult to detect qualitative military superiority among the respective armies of Caesar, Pompey, and their successors; although the veterans of Caesar's harsh campaigns in Gaul (58–51 BC) perhaps proved the most seasoned (if not the most spirited). His battle-hardened corps of staff officers and legionaries contributed mightily to the string of infantry victories at Pharsalus in Greece (48 BC, over Pompey), Zela in Anatolia (site of Caesar's famous claim: 'Came, Saw, Conquered' in 47 BC, when he overcame Pharnaces, son of Mithridates), Thapsus in Tunisia (46 BC, over generals who had followed the now-dead Pompey), and Munda (45 BC, in Spain, where he destroyed the last resistance of Pompey's partisans). Yet Caesar's victory proved only temporary: after the dictator's assassination in 44 BC the killing continued in a renewed round of fighting between the next generation of Pompey's surviving offspring and Caesar's heir and eventual winner, Octavian, who assumed the title Augustus Caesar in 27 BC, the first Roman emperor.

Military success in the civil wars usually centred on logistics, recruitment and political propaganda, and thus ultimately hinged on control of the largest reservoir of capital. In this sense, Octavian, more than any other contemporary usurper, realized the importance of the psychological element, the value of championing traditional (and mostly lost) Roman values in Italy in an effort to depict his adversaries as enemies of the Roman order and thuggish collaborators with foreign dynasts attempting to undermine the Italian state. The result was that eventually the Roman aristocracy, and especially the recently enriched commercial interests, welcomed Octavian's steady pragmatism and so lent him their support. His partisans saw correctly that, of the entire confused pantheon of would-be tyrants, Octavian was the most successful and single-minded in his effort to consolidate financial support, muster armies, and end the last vestiges of republicanism.

THE BUREAUCRACY OF WAR

On his accession to imperial power, the newly proclaimed Augustus was beset with an array of military problems that went far beyond the slaughter and financial exhaustion of two decades of war. The fractious Roman army needed to be regrouped under a central command and paid regularly through state funds. But throughout the preceding century, generals had found that surrendering their legionary commands to the government meant an end to their ambitions and often exile or proscription. Therefore, in a series of complex legislative manoeuvres, Augustus nominally gave power to a newly constituted, hand-picked senate from which he in turn received consulships, tribunal power, and provincial command. The legions now swore personal fealty to Augustus himself, and therein ostensibly expressed their loyalty to the Roman state. Thus the military–political problem abated, but it was never really solved: future buccaneers would still battle their way to Rome, gain governmental 'authorization', and then get their hands on state treasuries to pay their troops for support, ratified by the personal oaths of legionaries in the ranks.

The historian Dio Cassius (c. AD 230) described the ultimate and logical development of the new system. On the death of the emperor Pertinax in AD 193:

> there ensued a most disgraceful business and one unworthy of Rome. For just as if it had been in some market or auction room, both the city and the entire empire were auctioned off. The sellers were the ones who had killed their emperor, and the would-be buyers were Sulpicianus and Julianus who gradually raised their bids to 20,000 sesterces per soldier...Sulpicianus would have been the first to name the figure 20,000, had not Julianus raised his bid no longer by a small amount, but by 5,000 at one time, shouting it in a loud voice, and also indicating the amount with his fingers. So the soldiers, captivated by the extravagant bid and at the same time fearing that Sulpicianus might avenge Pertinax – an idea Julianus put into their heads – received Julianus and declared him emperor.

The exorbitant cost of bribing the legions, continues Dio Cassius, meant that 'it was impossible to give them their pay in full in addition to the donatives they were receiving – and impossible not to give it.'

Under Augustus, the enormous resources of the Roman principate and its ever masterful system of judicial and civil administration ensured a quick return to an overwhelming military presence after the devastation of the civil wars. For the next

Opposite: Sulla (d.79 BC, top), Pompey (d.48 BC, centre) and Caesar (d.44 BC, bottom) all shared a cynical contempt for republican government and an overriding confidence in their own ability to deploy legions loyal to themselves alone. While all three contributed to continual legionary evolution in equipment, tactics, and strategy, and proved capable administrators of their military gains, they became the models for generations of later provincial buccaneers, who would hire mercenary legions, ignore imperial directives, and drive on Rome to claim their due. More Romans died by or in the legions of these three grandees than were lost in the entire history of Roman warmaking abroad.

Augustus Caesar (63 BC–
AD 14), the adopted son of
Julius Caesar, ended any hopes
of a restored republic and
became the first Roman
emperor (27 BC–AD 14). The
statue of the commander-in-
chief of the legions, still
standing in the Roman forum,
captures the majesty of the
imperial presence and the
indistinguishable association
between military and political
affairs. After Augustus all
heads of the Roman state
calibrated their power,
prestige, and wealth by the
degree of control they
exercised over the army.

two centuries the army deployed roughly twenty-five to thirty legions, some 125,000–150,000 legionaries, on constant garrison duty in the provinces, supported by perhaps another 350,000–375,000 cavalry, light-armed troops, and infantry irregulars, totalling perhaps a half million paid soldiers under arms. From Scotland to Syria they dressed alike, marched in the same way, and defended similar walls.

However all this created a new, difficult, and ambiguous role for the enormous Roman imperial army, a problem quite separate from the legions' propensity to meddle in politics. Expansion was stopped in the north at the Rhine and the Danube, in the east with the annexation of Judaea (AD 6) and agreements with Parthia, and in the west with the pacification of Spain and Gaul, and an uneasy presence in Britain. The formal incorporation of Egypt as an imperial province secured the coast of northern Africa. Consequently, the legions, especially in the east, turned from the aggressive warriors of the past three centuries into an enormous – and very expensive – police force. At Antioch, for example, the Roman rhetorician Fronto complained that the legionaries now 'spent their time applauding actors, and were more often in the nearest tavern than in the ranks. Horses were shaggy from neglect, but every hair was plucked from their riders, a rare sight was a soldier with a hairy arm or leg.' The inevitable entropy that set in when troops were in the barracks, rather than on the move, undermined morale, as the legionaries, often with unofficial but numerous dependants, immersed them-selves in local administration and frequent extortion. Hadrian reportedly once concluded of this legionary dilemma simply that 'inactivity is fatal'. And letters from imperial soldiers sometimes reflected more the social than the bellicose aspects of Roman military service in the provinces:

> Julianus Apollinarius to his father Sabenus, 26 March [AD 107]: Things are going well for me here, thanks to Sarapis. I got here quite safely, and although others the whole day long are gathering stones and are engaged on other tasks, I so far have suffered none of this. I asked Claudius Severus, the governor, to appoint me as a clerk on the governor's staff.

LEGIONS ON THE FRONTIER

Because of the vast size of the empire, regionalism also soon set in: the Roman professional army was as a whole multicultural, but more and more provincial legions might never see Italy or any other area of the empire. Thus, they recruited men and officers from local residents and sought stability within their own immediate domain. This practice explains why later revolutionary insurrection usually originated on the frontier, and why the Romans for centuries remained reluctant to create a large central reserve that could marshal the empire's entire resources against a single flash-point.

Nevertheless, despite the increasing bureaucratization of daily garrison routine and the politicization of the army, despite the spectre of killing other Romans at a moment's notice, and despite the increasing obsession with pay and retirement, most of the legions themselves continued somehow to fight superbly on the battlefield during the first three centuries of the empire. Josephus, the Jewish-Roman historian of the early first century AD, in a famous and often quoted observation, remarked of Roman battlefield superiority,

> If one looks at the Roman military, it is seen that the Empire came into their hands as the result of their valour, not as a gift of fortune. For they do not wait for the outbreak of war to practise with weapons nor do they sit idle in peace mobilizing themselves only in time of need. Instead, they seem to have been born with weapons in their hands; never do they take a break from training or wait for emergencies to arise...One would not be incorrect in saying that their manoeuvres are like bloodless battles, and their battles bloody manoeuvres.

Nearly four hundred years later, Vegetius, the fifth-century author of a manual on Roman military institutions, still saw such training and organization at the root of Roman battle success: 'Victory was granted not by mere numbers and innate courage, but by skill and training. We see that the Roman people owed the conquest of the world to no other cause than military training, discipline in their camps, and practice in warfare.'

How did such skilled forces meet the challenges on the vast Roman frontier? What was the empire's strategy of defence, and the imperial policy towards client states and peoples on or at the border during the nearly five centuries of Roman defence until the fifth century AD? Some historians have seen constant preparedness against foreign attack as an overreaction: simply men and material substituting for a sophisticated and flexible military strategy. Others even interpret the half millennium of border service as one huge phony 'cold war', the existence of massive armies on the frontier no more than the exploitative arm of the Roman economy, the means to draw capital from foreign barbarians into the empire, while justifying their own increasing militarization of Latinized society.

Although there may never have been a formal Roman 'war college' of strategic planners, the threat of invasion was nevertheless real, the provisions for imperial defence intricate, and the deployment of soldiers and bases sophisticated. From the end of the first century AD onwards, a succession of Roman emperors *were* military strategists and increasingly *did* seek to envision one vast, but static, circuit of Roman civilization, within which all would possess citizenship and follow Roman custom and practice. The strategy of the Julio-Claudian emperors (27 BC–AD 68) – acquiring client kings and taking punitive offensive action into hostile territory – gave way, beginning with Vespasian (AD 69–79), to a more entrenched defence, a policy of avoiding expeditionary campaigning, one characterized more by permanent fortifications — walls, camps, and forts. And after Diocletian (AD 284 –305) instituted a programme of frontier construction, more mobile reserves finally appeared. Under Constantine and his successors, frontier ground could be ceded

At one of the farthest frontiers of an already overstretched empire, Hadrian's wall zig-zags across seventy-three and a half miles of northern England, a lasting testimony to the Romans' uneasy occupation of Britain. Built after 120 AD on the orders of the Emperor Hadrian, the fortification protected Roman settlements against Celtic tribesmen to the north. The wall was garrisoned and kept in repair until the late fourth century.

and re-acquired, as defence in depth, rather than adherence to a single – and increasingly expensive – line in the sand, made more and more sense.

In short, despite the interference by the legions in Roman politics, and despite the vast territory to be covered, the enormous taxes to be raised, the growing corruption and disorder inherent within permanent military garrisoning, the imperial legions for nearly five centuries managed to preserve the tradition of rigid

The Roman infrastructure of war

Opposite: Tending wounded legionaries at a forward dressing station. Behind, other legionaries wait their turn to go into battle in a scene from Trajan's column in Rome. The Romans, unlike other cultures, saw nothing shameful in portraying their own battle casualties graphically. The treated wounded seen here were not an admission of weakness, but confirmation of Rome's superior organization and concern for its men in the field.

Rome inherited the Greek genius for technology, military innovation and response, as well as the notion of decisive and heroic assault, and then applied to it standardization and bureaucratization through constant training and rigid discipline. There had been, for example, no standard depth to a Hellenistic phalanx, no uniform chain of command, no regulation for recruitment, length of service, and retirement among the Greeks. Much less was there a system of military decorations, punishments, and rationale for military advancement through the ranks.

In contrast, in the Roman army, legions were generally kept at steady strength. Recruitment followed careful procedures governing civic and social status, health, height, and weight. Centurions, tribunes, and quaestors knew their precise role and limits of military responsibility.

Whether a Roman army fought on the Danube or in North Africa, its camp would be constructed about the same, the legionaries armed in roughly uniform arms and armour. Rations, mail service, sanitation — all the apparently inconsequential and often forgotten aspects of military life — were also carefully systematized and therefore usually ample. Roman roads facilitated the easy transportation of even large armies; local port garrisons and a merchant marine assisted in lengthy sea transport. Consequently, both planners at Rome and commanders in the field had precise knowledge of the time, the expense, and the effort required for moving the legions throughout the provinces.

Such a vast supporting infrastructure naturally resulted in increased military efficacy. Most legionaries were better fed, better housed, better armed and indeed healthier, than almost all enemy troops, giving the legions qualitatively superior manpower at the instant of collision with almost any enemy in the Mediterranean world. Such an omnipresent military foundation ensured that mere numbers of combatants were not paramount, as Caesar's remarkable victories over the numerically dominant armies he met in Gaul attest.

The psychological element proved crucial. Roman infantrymen always knew exactly the standard Roman sequence of battle, knew which troops were ahead of them, which to the rear, knew how they would attack, knew what advance or retreat meant to the overall outcome of the battle. In addition, most Roman soldiers took for granted what and when they would eat, where they would sleep, and how they would be cared for should they fall sick, be wounded, or die. The frightening look of naked Germans, the harsh snows of the northern frontier, the peculiar armament of African cavalry could not startle Roman armies, so confident were individual legionaries that their Roman way of war had prepared them in advance for all exigencies.

On a strategic level, bureaucratization also meant that individual setbacks rarely spelled theatre catastrophe. The bloodbath at Cannae (216 BC), the destruction of Varus in Germany (AD 9), even Crassus' disaster at Carrhae (53 BC), neither caused a collective discipline and sterling technology so characteristic of Graeco-Roman battlefield superiority. Even in the eighth century the army of the East Roman (or Byzantine) empire, although now using the Greek language, still employed the commands and signals created to control 'Marius's mules' almost a thousand years before; while, in the West, Rome's military legacy would prevail for a further eight hundred years.

loss of nerve nor extinguished Roman battle strength. Instead, in the wake of horrific defeat, Roman war machinery instantly swung into operation, calling for new levies, gearing up armouries, reassigning trained veteran centurions to oversee new conscripts. Such efficiency almost always ensured that lapses in generalship – and there were many in the Roman army, given the political nature of such appointments – were not necessarily fatal. Almost as if by automation, the centurion-based legions needed little direction from the top to feed and house themselves, to march in formation, to line up for battle.

Unfortunately, as the empire spread in the second and first centuries BC, lines of communication thinned and defence responsibilities grew, so that this infrastructure became nearly insupportable by the first century AD, and finally unsustainable by the third and fourth. Roman military systemization also became increasingly problematic once Italian manpower alone was unable to fill the ranks. Non-Latin speakers were gradually recruited, and local practices applied to meet various regional needs throughout the Empire, resulting in an insidious, steady balkanization of the legions as a whole. Veterans needed cash and land when they retired. But on the cessation of Roman expansion in the early Empire, land became a finite commodity, one increasingly scarce after centuries of retirement grants to superannuated troops. Road construction and upkeep were also expensive. Standing armies of professional legionaries, along with engineers, auxiliaries, and support personnel, demanded increased salaries to meet growing inflation.

By the second and third centuries AD, the price of Roman defence was increased taxation levied on an already hard-pressed and diminishing rural populace. By the fourth and fifth centuries AD, the peasantry was completely exhausted, and the source of funding thus finally ran dry. And so the once vast Roman machinery of war slowly ground to a halt, its visible infrastructure still intact, but its lifeblood of capital and manpower drained for good.

The Age of Stone Fortifications PART 2

CHAPTER 4

On Roman Ramparts

Overleaf: The walls of
Constantinople, built by the
Roman emperor Theodosius in
the fifth century AD.

From the reign of the emperor Diocletian (AD 285–305) until the development of
firearms in the fourteenth century, the essentials of military organization, strategy,
and tactics in Europe display a startling continuity. This reflects in part the enduring dominance of Roman military topography – the surviving infrastructure of
fortified cities, fortresses, ports, and roads created in the third to fifth centuries.
After the gradual dissolution of imperial power in the western half of the empire
during the fifth century, those responsible for military decision-making in Rome's
successor states had neither the inclination nor the resources to eliminate Roman
walls. Like Byzantine emperors in the East, the Romano-German rulers differed
little from the later Roman emperors in the means they used to control and make
effective use of these assets. Continuity also reflects the unchallenged superiority
of ancient military science, which decision-makers could find in books such as
Vegetius's *Concerning Military Matters* (see page 4) and the substantial contact
between the West and Byzantium which stimulated the exchange and study of
ancient military techniques.

THE PRIMACY OF THE SIEGE

The biblical city of Naher is
here represented as a fortified
small town, in the late antique
artistic tradition, from a
biblical manuscript probably
illustrated in Alexandria
during the fifth century.

Late Roman grand strategy revolved around holding the urban centres of administration, religious organization, manufacture, and population, which had been
fortified or rebuilt in the wake of the invasions and civil wars of the third century.
This network of self-sustaining fortifications – the earliest example of a defence-in-
depth strategy in the West – served two purposes. First, each stronghold sheltered
mobile field forces which could threaten an invader's movement and lines of supply.
Second, if an enemy chose to lay siege to one of the defended towns, it could
become an anvil against which the main field army could crush the invader. The
quality of the Roman fortifications – and their strategic locations – made their
capture very difficult. Large armies were required, well-supplied not only with siege
machines but also with the means to maintain them while deployed in static
encampments for months.

Attila's failed invasion of Gaul in 451 provides an excellent example of the
success of Rome's defence-in-depth strategy. For several months the Huns and their
allies exhausted their resources in attacking fortified cities, enjoying only limited
success despite the absence of a Roman relief force. Then, while Attila besieged the
city of Orléans, the Roman general Aetius approached with an army raised largely
in Gaul. The Huns withdrew with the Romans in pursuit. At Châlons, half way
across Gaul, Attila decided to stand and fight. The Hunnic army was defeated. It
retreated, without making any territorial conquests, much poorer in both men and
treasure than when the campaign began.

This pattern of siege, relief (most sieges failed with or without a relief force), and either a battle or more likely a phased withdrawal by the besieging force, dominated western warfare for a thousand years. The siege became by far the most common form of military encounter and the techniques and tactics of both defence and offence became widely disseminated. Flavius Merobaudes, a fifth-century Roman general and writer of Frankish origin, noted that the Visigoths had learned a great deal about the conduct of war during the two generations following their flight from their homeland beyond the Danube in 376. According to Merobaudes, the 'Teutons' whom Caesar had fought possessed only a 'crude command of warfare and were inexperienced in its developed art', but the Visigoths were no longer 'a race from a barbarian land'. They were 'enemies equal [to the Romans] in war' who had acquired the ability to defend the fortified towns of the Roman empire, and the citadels within them. Indeed, he claimed, they had even learned something of the art of constructing fortifications as well.

Increasing the size of the imperial army enabled the later Roman emperors to defend the massive stone fortifications that dotted the landscape, while maintaining a reserve of troops to meet any major invasion. Far more men served under arms during the later Roman empire than in the days of Julius Caesar and Augustus. By AD 300 Diocletian commanded a regular army that numbered over 435,000 men and the combined forces for both the eastern and western divisions reached a peak of perhaps 645,000 around 430. In addition to 'Roman' military personnel, the various groups of Germans and other settlers within the western empire could also muster large military forces. For example, the Visigoths, who were established in Aquitaine by the imperial government, could mobilize some 20,000–25,000 men; so could the Ostrogoths who came to dominate Italy under their king, Theodoric the Great (who also served as Roman governor of the region), the Vandals in north Africa, and the various Frankish rulers in Gaul whose combined forces matched those of the Visigoths in strength. Field armies were also quite large. For example, the emperor Julian led an army of some 65,000 men on the Persian campaign of 357; Valens at the battle of Adrianople in 378 commanded a force of 30,000–40,000 men; and Aetius's army at Châlons, which was raised largely in Gaul, numbered between 40,000 and 50,000 men.

The important north Italian city of Aquileia, located east of Venice, as depicted in the Peutinger Table, a road map of the later Roman empire, probably executed during the fourth century AD. Drawings such as these were highly stylized and bear little resemblance to the actual defences when they can be checked against the archaeological data. Rather, the drawings emphasize the need of contemporaries to represent all settlements of note as being fortified.

LATE ROMAN MILITARY ORGANIZATION

The later Roman empire saw two major developments in military organization. While the army became integrated into the non-military institutions of society, largely as soldier-farmers but also as soldier-townsmen, the civilian population gradually became militarized. The 'domestication' of the military was well in train by the late fourth century when the anonymous author of the *Historia Augusta* quoted an edict issued by the emperor Severus Alexander (AD 222–35):

> The lands taken from the enemy were presented to the leaders and soldiers of the auxiliary troops, with the provision that they should continue to belong to them

only if their heirs entered military service, and that they should never belong to civilians, for he [the emperor] said that men serve with greater enthusiasm if they are defending their own lands…He added to these lands, of course, both animals and slaves, so that the soldiers would be able to cultivate what they had been given.

Roman drills for medieval horsemen

DOMESTICI EQUITES

The manuscript *Notitia Dignitatum* reproduces the only surviving 'order of battle' for the later Roman empire (c.430). All units are represented by shield insignia. Those of the commander of the imperial household cavalry are shown here. The shields of soldiers in the unit probably bore the same design; such insignia presaged medieval usage.

Although siege warfare had enjoyed primacy in the later Roman empire, field forces were not neglected. Horsemen with lances were trained to dismount rapidly, so that they could fight on foot as 'pikemen', and to vault into the saddle when the time came to fight on horseback. The infantry carried less body armour than the legionaries of earlier days and could deploy more rapidly. Major battles of the later fourth and fifth centuries illustrate the flexibility of late Roman battle tactics – for example, Mursa (in 351, fought against Magnentius, who had usurped the imperial title from the emperor Constans), where lancers dismounted to fight on foot, or Châlons (451, against the Huns), where imperial infantry fought in concert with allied Visigothic and Alan horsemen. Ammianus Marcellinus, a professional soldier and the leading Roman historian of his day, paid tribute to this flexibility in his description of the emperor Constantius (d.361): 'He was especially able in riding, in hurling the javelin and in the use of the bow. In addition, he was very knowledgeable with regard to all the tactics and armament of foot-soldiers.'

Throughout the early middle ages, troop training programmes provide considerable insight into prevailing tactics. In both East and West, revised versions of Vegetius's *Concerning Military Matters*, based upon the earliest surviving revision which was done at Constantinople in AD 450, abounded. Although he focused on the training of infantry (he believed that the mounted arm needed little reform), Vegetius did devote special attention to the need for tactical flexibility among mounted troops. This flexibility was pursued throughout the middle ages and ultimately it became institutionalized in the 'dragoon', a term which originally, in the sixteenth century, applied to a mounted soldier trained to fight on foot.

The following passage was copied and edited by Rabanus Maurus, a cleric and scholar at the court of the Carolingian king Lothair II, who provided an epitome of Vegetius's work which included only those things which were of importance 'in modern times'. Rabanus selected, among other chapters, a key element in the training regime for cavalry recruits:

Wooden horses are placed during the winter under a roof and in summer in a field. The recruits at first try to mount unarmed, then they mount carrying shields and swords, and finally with very large pole weapons. And this practice was so thorough that they were forced to learn how to jump on and off their horses not only from the right but from the left and from the rear and in addition they learned to jump on and off their horses even with an unsheathed sword.

Mounted troops also trained to fight on horseback and no less importantly trained their horses for combat. These training exercises of the early middle ages anticipate the spectacle of the tournament. Nithard, a grandson of Charlemagne, described a particularly impressive (but hardly isolated) practice session carried out near Verdun in 842:

For purposes of training, games were often arranged in the following manner.

Soldiers became more like farmers, and civilians more like soldiers: in an act of 406, the emperor Honorius ordered that, 'Slaves shall offer themselves for war...Of course, we especially encourage the slaves belonging to men who are in the imperial armed service, and also the slaves of allies and of free foreigners, because it is clear that these slaves are making war alongside their owners.'

Left: A horseman, probably German, armed with spear, sword, and shield (embossed with a design that may have indicated his unit), appears on this crude imitation of a Roman stele of about AD 700, found near Magdeburg in Germany. His Roman-style helmet resembles imitations found in Swedish graves of the sixth and seventh centuries.

Above: Before the effective use of stirrups, there was a limited value to charging the enemy on horseback with a couched lance – the rider could do little more than press his thighs against the side of his mount (above left) to avoid being thrown from the saddle by the impact when his lance struck. Stirrups reached western Europe at least by AD 700, but they had no discernible military impact for some two centuries. The rider's foot and leg were turned away from the flank of the horse (above right), stirrup leather cutting across the shin. The toes pointed down. The leg was thrust forward against the stirrup and away from the horse.

Fighting men would be deployed in a place where they could be observed. The entire group...divided into two units of equal size. They charged forward from both sides and came towards each other at full speed. Then [before contact was made] one side turned its back and under the protection of their shields pretended to be trying to escape. Then those who had been engaged in the feigned retreat counter-attacked and the pursuers simulated flight. Then both kings [Louis the German and Charles the Bald] and all of the young men, raising a great yell, charged forward brandishing their spear shafts. Now one group feigned retreat and then the other. It was a spectacle worthy of being seen as much because of its nobility as because of its discipline.

A generation later even free civilians who lacked any regular connection with the military were called up for local defence. In 440, neither Roman citizens nor the members of guilds living in a city could be compelled to undertake regular military service in the field. However, emperor Valentinian ordered that even these relatively privileged groups were liable for militia service, 'defending the walls and the gates of the city when necessity demanded'. Conscription as traditionally practised had by then ended in the western half of the Roman empire – presumably because sufficient forces could be recruited on a voluntary basis. Even in the eastern half of the empire, armies comprised volunteers mustered for specific field operations, the personal armed followings of the generals, and foreigners recruited from beyond the frontiers as mercenaries (federates).

This major shift in imperial policy came about not only through the militarization of the civilian population but also by recruitment from outside the empire. Various groups from beyond – often far beyond – the imperial frontiers were encouraged to settle within the western part of the empire: Germans, Alans (a nomadic people from south Russia between the Don and the Dnieper), Sarmatians (a semi-nomadic or perhaps pastoral people from south Russia) and others provided military services in Britain, Gaul, Italy, and Spain during the later fourth and fifth centuries. Normally, imperial officials provided these immigrants with homesteads and one third of the tax revenues, usually in places that had been deserted by their owners. Thus, for example, Pactus Drepanius, a late fourth-century court poet, praised Theodosius I for his treaty of 383 which settled the Visigoths in Thrace because 'You received into your service Goths to provide soldiers for your army...and cultivators for the land.'

A more select group of fighting men served in the armed followings of the great men – high imperial officials, such as dukes and counts, as well as magnates with no specific governmental position. Although from time to time the imperial government strove to limit those who might employ such an army, personal armed followings became ubiquitous in late Roman and medieval society. The men who served in these units, whether in direct attendance upon their leader or in some form of encampment, were ostensibly professional fighting men, in contrast to the farmer-soldiers and urban militiamen who served on a part-time basis.

ROMANO-GERMAN ARMIES

The Roman army in the West did not simply pack and leave when the formal organs of imperial conscription ceased to function in the middle of the fifth century. Indeed, early in the sixth century units identifiable by their uniforms and banners as 'Roman' still operated in the region west of Orléans, for example, under local political leadership. But the rank and file of the erstwhile imperial military establishment, as well as the greater part of the fighting forces of the so-called 'barbarian' peoples, became absorbed into the military organization of the Romano-German kingdoms and over time the vast majority of their descendants – like those

Agilulf, king of the Lombards (590–615), flanked by soldiers equipped in a strikingly Roman style. The Lombards were a Germanic people driven south into Italy by the Avars. They dominated the northern third of the peninsula for over 200 years, relying heavily on Roman principles of military organization to hold the Roman-built walled cities that dotted their territory. The Lombard kingdom ended with Charlemagne's successful siege of their capital, Pavia, in 774.

of the indigenous rural population, whether free or unfree – became farmer-soldiers. The Visigothic kings of Spain, for example, called up laymen and clergy, regardless of either social or legal status, for military service whenever they organized a major campaign, and also used slaves extensively in these efforts. Roman settlers proved particularly important in the manning and commanding of Visigothic and Vandal naval operations, forming a crucial part of (for example) the Vandal expedition from north Africa that culminated in the sack of Rome in 455.

Elsewhere, for offensive purposes, a select group of both rural and urban inhabitants – the 'select levy' – was required to perform military service beyond the demands of local defence in order to participate in extended offensive military operations. These soldiers, drawn from towns and villages, comprised the rank and file of field armies. In the regular campaign armies of the Romano-German successor states, they served alongside the personal armed followers of the magnates, and especially those of the king. In Merovingian Gaul, and no doubt elsewhere, adult males also had to serve in a general levy for the defence of the region in which they lived. This service was a 'public duty' from which neither the poor nor even the unfree dependents of ecclesiastical establishments enjoyed exemption, while the able-bodied inhabitants of the walled cities and fortified towns were required to man the defences, just as had been the case under imperial rule.

Any attempt to estimate the militarized rural population leaves much room for speculation since it depends in large part upon calculating the size of the able-bodied adult male population living in the countryside. Thus, between one and two million males of fifteen to fifty-five years of age probably lived in sixth-century Gaul and were available for some type of service under arms. More accurate estimates can be advanced for the urban militias, however. For example, approximately 100 walled towns can be identified in Gaul, with fortified perimeters averaging some 1,500 yards. Given the available technology, it required one man to defend approximately four feet of wall, and thus simply to defend the towns – let alone other smaller fortified centres – required an aggregate urban militia force in Gaul of approximately 100,000 men. The great difficulties experienced by besieging forces in capturing the massively fortified cities of the former western empire indicates that urban militias were kept up to strength and in good fighting form.

Field armies could on occasion be large. For example, when in 585 King Guntram of Burgundy (561–92) set in motion both the standing army of his realm as well as almost all of his select militia in order to crush the usurper Gundovald, his army probably reached 20,000 men. A generation earlier, the Ostrogothic kings in Italy frequently deployed forces in excess of 10,000 against the forces of the Byzantine empire in a war that lasted for more than two decades, while the Vandals in north Africa could on very short notice put 15,000 men into the field.

The Byzantines, by contrast, controlled much larger areas which on the whole were more densely populated than the Romano-German kingdoms. Thus, the army of 52,000 which the eastern emperor Anastasius mustered for a war against Persia

Seal ring of Childeric of the Merovingian dynasty, king of the Franks and imperial military commander of the region around Tournai (in modern Belgium), who is depicted wearing Roman armour. The seal was used to validate documents that the king could not read but which required a sign of his authority in order to have legal status; he could, however, understand the text when it was read to him aloud in Latin. With imperial sanction Childeric's son Clovis (481–511) created a kingdom encompassing all of Gaul, except for the southeast, and received the title 'consul' from the East Roman emperor Anastasius.

in 503 was surely consistent in order of magnitude with those led by his predecessors and, despite the plague epidemics which struck the empire intermittetly during the next generation, the combined field armies of the emperor Justinian (527–65) probably approached the 170,000 men available for the defence of the same area a century before. For example, during the 530s and 540s, Belisarius and Narses, two of Byzantium's most successful generals, commanded a series of armies averaging about 20,000 men. In the seventh century the reforms carried out in the wake of the Muslim invasions left the emperor with a field army based in and around Constantinople of about 25,000 men.

FROM JUSTINIAN TO CHARLEMAGNE

The Romano-German kingdoms established in Gaul, Italy, Spain, North Africa, and Britain during the fifth century engaged in intermittent warfare, prompting the Byzantine emperor Justinian to attempt to reassert direct imperial control over the western half of the empire. Byzantine plans for the reconquest of the West focused upon the fortified cities and towns of Africa, Italy, and Spain. It was assumed at Constantinople that the Roman populations in these regions, far outnumbering their Vandal, Ostrogothic, and Visigothic rulers, would prefer to be reintegrated into the empire and would fight for the privilege. It was believed that the urban militias, composed in large part of 'Romans', would overpower, where necessary, the German garrisons stationed within the walls and turn over their cities to the Byzantine armies as they approached. Deprived of their military infrastructure, and cut off from their sources of supply, the forces which remained loyal to the German rulers would thus ostensibly become 'strangers' in their own kingdoms and would either have to fight the Byzantines in the open field or make some sort of accommodation.

At first Byzantium's strategy seemed to work well: when Belisarius defeated the Vandals at the battle of Tricameron (535) both king and kingdom fell into imperial hands and it proved unnecessary to mount elaborate sieges in order to reduce the many fortified cities of North Africa. By contrast, the effort to impose direct imperial control in Italy involved a war of sieges during which, over twenty years, the Byzantines captured the major cities of Italy. However, gaining possession of the cities was not in the end sufficient. Narses, Belisarius's successor, found it necessary to defeat the Ostrogothic army in a series of battles culminating in the Byzantine victory at Taginae in 552 where the greater part of the enemy force was annihilated. Thereafter Byzantine military efforts turned eastward to the Persian empire, which finally fell in 628.

This century of warfare by Byzantium in both the West and the East, although successful, weakened the empire dramatically and thus facilitated the Muslim conquest of much of the eastern Roman empire during the seventh and early eighth centuries. The military map of western civilization was radically redrawn. The Byzantine state was irreparably weakened by the loss of its most

The East Roman emperor Justinian I and his most successful general Belisarius gaze down from a mosaic in the great church of Ravenna, the imperial headquarters in sixth-century Italy. Justinian's grand strategy, put into effect by Belisarius, stabilized the imperial frontier against the Persians and 'reconquered' much of the West. However, Justinian became worried about Belisarius's loyalty and recalled him to the East.

populous and richest provinces: Syria, the Holy Land, and Egypt. It also lost North Africa and most of Italy, where the fruits of Justinian's reconquest soon dwindled to a few strategic locations in Italy. In addition, the Visigothic kingdom in Spain was destroyed in 711 and replaced by a Muslim state, while southern Gaul was ravaged until the Carolingians, during the later eighth and early ninth centuries, extended their rule into Aquitaine. They then pushed beyond the Elbe, conquered the Lombard kingdom of northern Italy, and advanced into Spain as far as Barcelona.

Western warfare for most of the seventh and early eighth centuries remained largely local. However, the Frankish leaders Charles Martel (d.742), Pepin (d.768), and Charlemagne (d.814) resuscitated central control of the military system in the West. From time to time they and their successors tinkered with various aspects of it in order better to sustain lengthy operations far from home. The county (the *civitas* of the Roman empire, not unlike the *polis* of classical Greece) continued under the military and civil administration of a count, and various formulae were developed by the central government to ensure sufficient forces. The select levies provided the rank and file of Carolingian armies for offensive operations. Rich men owning twelve estates or more were required to muster with horse and armour. Men

The territory of the East Roman empire at its maximum extent under Justinian in 565, compared with the the Islamic empire at the time of its furthest penetration into western Europe (732), and with the Carolingian empire at its peak in 840.

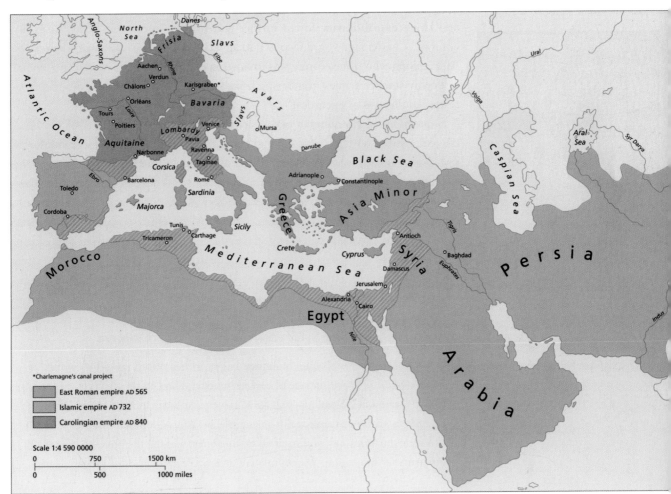

*Charlemagne's canal project

- East Roman empire AD 565
- Islamic empire AD 732
- Carolingian empire AD 840

Scale 1:4 590 0000

0   750   1500 km
0   500   1000 miles

Charlemagne (742–814), king of the Franks from 768 and crowned emperor of the Romans by the pope on Christmas Day 800, extended the borders of the Frankish state eastward across the Elbe and Danube and south into Italy and Spain. The empire remained unified under his son, Louis the Pious (d.840), but the central government that Charlemagne had restored to the West gradually disintegrated following the division of the realm into three parts by his grandsons in the treaty of Verdun (843).

owning five estates generally owed service on campaign, but with less armament. Someone living close to the theatre of operations could be called up with only three or four manors; while landholders possessing as little as a half an estate were formed into partnerships with a total wealth of five estates and ordered to provide a soldier for the select levy.

Like their Merovingian predecessors, the Carolingians required all free men to take an oath of fidelity to the king and to be registered on the rolls of the county in which they lived. This was done not only to identify those eligible for service in the local defence forces and the select levy but also to gain direct central control of the many thousands of highly professionalized fighting men who served in the personal armed followings of the lay and secular magnates. When it became clear, around 750, that many local leaders recruited unfree men for their retinues, the oath was demanded of all followers who had been honoured with 'vassal' status.

Charlemagne ruled a much larger area than the Byzantine state, now truncated by the Muslim conquests, and he could muster for simultaneous major campaigns perhaps 150,000 men, of whom at least 35,000 were heavily armed mounted troops. Individual armies of 35,000 to 40,000, though hardly common, were not unknown. Charles Martel, Pepin, and Charlemagne, progressively projected larger and larger expeditionary forces further and further from their home bases. By contrast, Charlemagne's grandsons Lothair I, Louis the German, and Charles the Bald, among whom the empire was divided in 843 by the treaty of Verdun, tended to deploy smaller armies numbering from 8,000 to 10,000 men in comparatively restricted theatres of operation.

Strategy in the Carolingian period centred on holding the cities already within the realm and acquiring those of neighbours. Thus Pepin I's conquest of Aquitaine rested on his capture of Bourges in 762 and his adversaries' recognition of the effectiveness of his siege train. The Lombard kingdom fell to Charlemagne when Pavia surrendered after a lengthy siege in 774; and the Spanish march was established with the fall of Barcelona, after an investment lasting almost two years, in 801. Since fortified cities and their surrounding counties constituted the principal prizes, campaign strategy, and to a lesser extent battle tactics, recognized the need to minimize the destruction. The strategic implications of these aims emerge clearly from Gregory of Tours' account of a putative conversation between the Gallo-Roman magnate Aridius and the Merovingian king Clovis (d.511) while the latter was laying siege to the massively fortified city of Avignon:

> O king, if the glory of your highness deigns to hear from me a few words of humble advice…it will be useful to you in general and to the districts through which you intend to pass. Why…do you keep this army in the field when your enemy sits in this exceptionally strong place? You depopulate the fields, you consume the meadows, you hack down the vines, you fell the olive trees, and all the fruits of this region you completely destroy. Yet you do not prevail against

Medieval techniques of siege warfare

Siege warfare dominated military life, and medieval soldiers placed a high premium on its technology. The stone-throwing 'engine' most commonly used throughout late antiquity and the early middle ages for the defence of fortifications against a besieging force was the heavy onager, a type of one-armed catapult weighing some two tons, which could hurl an 8-pound stone 500 yards. Heavier machines threw heavier loads even further – however, the most likely type to be transported in the baggage train of a besieging force was the light version of the onager. This engine, weighing no more than about 1,000 pounds, the maximum carrying capacity for vehicles of the period, could hurl a 3- or 4-pound stone about 100 yards, once unloaded from its transport vehicle and placed on solid level ground. Heavier machines of this type had to be constructed on the site of the siege or assembled from parts brought along in the baggage train.

Battering rams were not any less important to a besieging army than stone-throwing machines. The *Mappae Clavicula*, a technical treatise written in the eighth century, described the type of battering ram in use from late antiquity until the eleventh century in the following terms:

> Make the three front feet five cubits long, the middle ones four cubits, and the rear one three cubits. And there should be wheels one and one half spans high, and four inches thick. Make them round and make a hole in the centre; cut columns, and insert them four inches deep into the wheels. Cover the wheel and make a joint on top and fix it tightly with a wedge. Bind the rams and wind ropes around them. Shield with leather, and cover on top with pieces of felt, and over the felt, put pieces of leather; and over the leather four inches of sand, and over the sand, wool, so that the sand cannot move, and on top more pieces of leather. The columns themselves should have hinges such that when it walks you may turn it where you wish.

This preoccupation with protecting the ram against incendiary devices was thoroughly justified, since several formulae for the production of incendiaries existed in the West. The authors of the *Mappae Clavicula* themselves identified one which was particularly suited for destruction of the roof of a battering ram. However, by far the most famous incendiary agent of the middle ages was 'Greek fire' (see pages 78–9), probably made from some combination of petroleum and resin. The Byzantines used it with great effect against Arab ships during the siege of Constantinople in the 670s.

The technology of siege warfare was not monopolized by Rome's successor states. In 451, for example, battering rams employed by the forces of Attila the Hun came near to breaking through the wall of Orléans, while in 626 the Avars from the Danube basin not only used battering rams when they besieged Constantinople, but built wooden towers, to assault the top of the walls.

Technological continuity: although this battering ram (left) with its protective 'house' has been drawn from a relief on the arch of Septimius Severus (AD 203) the picture also fits the description quoted in the text from the eighth-century handbook of technology, the *Mappae Clavicula*.

The onager (above), uses torsion through twisted rope or hair to supply power. This siege weapon also demonstrates the technological continuity between the siege engines of the ancient world and the middle ages. The onager was the basic light artillery piece during the greater part of the middle ages.

your enemy. Rather send an envoy to him and impose on him a yearly tribute that he will pay to you so that this region may be saved. You will be lord and the tribute will be paid perpetually.

The advice given by Aridius neatly encapsulates the differences between 'barbarian' warfare and the teachings of ancient military science. His advice echoed the views

Medieval military earthworks

The early eighth-century historian Bede believed Hadrian's wall in northern England and the Antonine wall in southern Scotland had been built during the early fifth century, the first without any aid from Rome. His confidence in the ability of early medieval rulers to undertake and accomplish such major projects probably stemmed in part from his knowledge of the Danewirke (pictured below right) completed in 737. The sophisticated logistics which could be mounted for early medieval military construction projects are perhaps best illustrated, however, by Charlemagne's efforts in 793 to build a canal connecting the Rhine and Danube rivers.

Charlemagne's waterway would have made it possible to deploy military forces from the North Sea to the Black Sea and to supply them by water. (Throughout the middle ages, water transport was the fastest and most efficient way of conveying large amounts of equipment and supplies over long distances.) It would have given Charlemagne not only the upper hand in the Balkans but also the capacity to project his power around the coast of the Black Sea to the gates of Constantinople.

Although Charlemagne's Rhine-Danube project ultimately failed, and the linking of the North Sea to the Black Sea by a continuous water route was not to be realized until 1846, the

Offa's Dyke (above). Offa (d.796), a contemporary of Charlemagne, was king of Mercia. The dyke lies between England and Wales, stretching almost 150 miles northwards from the Severn estuary. Its earthen ramparts rise about twenty-five feet from ground level, fronted by a ditch about six feet deep. The wall and ditch complex averages about sixty feet in width. In the eighth century, at least some parts of the rampart were topped by a stone wall, others probably by a wooden palisade.

The Danevirke, probably known to Offa, was once an enormous earthen rampart that cut off the Jutland peninsula in Denmark from the mainland. The first and most impressive phase of this earthwork was completed in about 737. It was probably started about a decade earlier.

of Alexander the Great, who told his army as they entered Asia that 'they ought not destroy what they were fighting to possess.'

NEW WALLS, OLD FOUNDATIONS

In the turbulent dissolution of the Carolingian empire, the roots of western Europe's emerging nation-states lay exposed to attack. The treaty of Verdun between

emperor's strategic vision, logistic infrastructure, and skilled resources to sustain such a monumental task command respect. Written sources, as well as archaeological, topographical, geodetic, and hydrographic research, indicate that, during a period of about ten weeks in the autumn of 793, Charlemagne set a minimum of 6,000 workers to dig a carefully laid out trench – Roman surveying manuals and other valuable technical handbooks of the ancient world were available throughout the middle ages. It was to connect the Rezat, a navigable affluent of the Regnitz-Main-Rhine river network, with the Altmühl, an affluent of the Danube in the neighbourhood of Weissenburg about equidistant (45 miles) from the old Roman cities of Regensburg to the east and Augsburg to the south.

The remains indicate that the entire project was to be about a mile long, more than ninety feet wide and up to twenty feet deep in the centre of the channel. The workers were expected to move just over one million cubic yards of earth at a rate of 0.4 cubic yards per manhour. Modern estimates, which may be too high, suggest that the work-site had to be supplied with some 1,200-1,500 tons of grain, about 1,000-1,200 oxen and 2,000 to 3,000 pigs to provide approximately 4,000 calories per day for each worker over the course of the ten week period of labour.

The 6,000 workers constituted only part of the resources which had to be mobilized for the project. For example, 1,500 tons of grain would fill thirty wagon loads drawn by sixty oxen. Each ox required fifty pounds of fodder per day. A herd of 1,000 oxen on the hoof and of 3,000 pigs had to be levied through the tax system and these herds had to be driven to the work site, corralled, and fed until ready for use. Field kitchens had to be established and staffed with butchers, cooks, bakers, and other support personnel. Wood cutters were needed not only to bring in fuel for the cooking fires but also for lumber to shore up the sides of the canal. This lumber had to be prepared for use by carpenters. Smiths were needed to keep the tools in repair and they too needed either wood or charcoal for their fires. The wood-cutters and carpenters were

also no doubt required to build huts for the workers and outbuildings for the kitchens and smithies. Even the 6,000 largely unskilled labourers had to be spared that autumn from work on the harvest; and even where slaves or serfs were used, a system had to be in place for taking these workers from their usual obligations and detailing them for public service.

In the end, the canal project did not fail for lack of workers or supplies but because the autumn of 793 was exceptionally rainy, undermining the sides of the canal and making it often difficult if not impossible to dig. It nevertheless offers a glimpse of Carolingian grand strategy in action.

Charlemagne's canal project today provides a village pond for Grabben, Germany.

The Lindisfarne stone shows seven Viking warriors on a raid. The stone is from Lindisfarne island (off the coast of Northumberland, northern England), where Viking raiders are recorded as early as 793. The Vikings were the most successful fighting men in Europe for much of the ninth, tenth and into the eleventh centuries, from Ireland in the west to Kiev in the east. They were vigorously recruited by the Byzantines. Like the Anglo-Saxons, the Vikings used horses for transportation but not for combat.

Charlemagne's grandsons in 843 created the base for France and Germany, along with an indefensible middle kingdom stretching from Frisia to Rome over which its neighbours to the east and west would fight for a thousand years. England was forged in the crucible of the Viking invasions, and the various kingdoms on the Iberian peninsula gradually coalesced in a haphazard series of campaigns against the Muslims. Only Italy remained a mere geographical expression.

The western European states, as well as Byzantium, stood on the defensive. This created a wide variety of organizational problems. A society in offensive mode could muster its troops each year for the campaigning season and then send them home when operations had been completed. In a defensive mode, by contrast, highly trained mobile troops needed to be mustered and ready to respond at all times. The means had to be found to maintain a constant state of readiness, and the economic advantages of a successful offensive posture were not available. Resourceful leaders, however, found the means to spread the burdens and to build afresh on old defensive foundations. They refurbished Roman fortifications – and Roman ideas about defence – until the costs of a siege became prohibitive.

THE ENGLISH RESPONSE

Alfred the Great of Wessex defended his realm against the Vikings with forces structured like those of the earlier Romano-German kingdoms (see page 69). A general levy manned local defence, while a select levy provided the rank and file of field armies, serving alongside an elite drawn from the retinues of military magnates, the nobles. Alfred solved the problem of constant readiness for defence by dividing his select levies into two sections: one in the field, prepared for a rapid response to enemy attacks, and the second at home. These forces rotated regularly.

He apparently mobilized the personal armed followings of the magnates according to a similar pattern. Alfred also established a quota of paid garrison troops in each of the thirty-three burgs established for the defence of Wessex. These men served alongside the local inhabitants who were detailed to defend the town or stronghold in which they lived and shared responsibility for keeping the walls in repair. In addition, local defence in rural areas continued to be sustained by the members of the general levy and of the select levy who were not on active service with the king.

This continuation of Romano-German military organization was common all over the medieval West. The general population in arms provided the manpower for local defence; a selection of the more highly militarized civilian population formed the rank and file of the government's expeditionary forces; and the elite troops came largely from the personal armed followings of the more important lay and secular magnates, including the kings and their highest nobility. In great empires and small states, these basic units of military organization remained constant down to the thirteenth century and sometimes beyond. Even the city-states of early Renaissance Italy had a select levy of fighting men for offensive operations and called upon able-bodied men to defend the state in a general levy; in Florence the upper limit stood at seventy years of age. City authorities mobilized men not only from within the urban precincts, but also from the countryside.

Alfred augmented his naval forces, by building special warships, in order to resist the Vikings on the sea as well as on land. Ships with sixty oars were the norm. He also accomplished considerable building, rebuilding, and repair of fortifications. A document called the *Burghal Hidage*, drawn up in England at some point between 899 (when Alfred died) and 914 lists thirty-three fortifications. It provides a glimpse of the sophistication of Anglo-Saxon military administration. The perimeter defences of the thirty-three fortifications were measured or surveyed. Then income-producing landed resources were listed and assessed so that the returns from one 'hide' of land – the amount of land required to support a family – went to maintain each member of the garrison. Each member in turn was required to defend and keep in repair one quarter-pole (4.25 feet) of the wall. The high quality of this administrative work is illustrated, for example, at the old Roman city of Winchester where 2,400 hides were allocated for the support of the garrison required to defend a perimeter wall that measured 9,954 feet. The margin of error in providing the resources to sustain a force of 2,400 fighting men was less than one per cent. The *Burghal Hidage* also suggests that the men who orchestrated Anglo-Saxon military policy possessed a well-developed sense of strategy. This can best be illustrated on the ground itself. No burg was more than twenty miles – a day's march – from at least one other burg. Thus, relief forces and columns of supplies enjoyed the advantage of a defended line of march, since no unit en route from one burg to another had to encamp in the open at night where it might be surprised by an enemy attack. In addition, units from one burg could be rapidly deployed to relieve forces at another nearby burg that came under siege.

King Henry the Fowler of Germany (d.936) also strove to build a coherent system of fortifications, endowed with regular garrisons and efficient supply based on service by landholders and a tax on their produce. His endeavours bear more than a passing resemblance to those made slightly earlier in Anglo-Saxon England. According to the chronicler Widukind, Henry provided for the garrisoning of fortifications in Saxony by choosing:

> One from every nine farmer-soldiers and requiring that they live in burgs in order to build small dwelling places [within the fortifications] for the other eight members of the unit and in order to receive a third part of their produce and keep it in the burg. The eight men were to sow and to harvest the grain [from the land] of the ninth man [stationed in the burg].

Both the German and the English systems probably owed much to the Roman principle of defence in depth (see page 64), known from earlier unrecorded imitations of this model, from surviving records, or from its uninterrupted use in Byzantium.

THE BYZANTINE RESPONSE

The eastern Roman empire had to defend itself against Arabs, Persians, Kurds, Turks, and Khazars from the east. Its security, especially the security of its capital at Constantinople, depended, in large part, upon the effectiveness of the fleet. The Byzantine navy was successful for four centuries in maintaining the empire's interests not only in the Mediterranean but also in the Black Sea and on the Danube. The standard Byzantine warship was the dromon, with two banks of rowers: 100

Greek fire in action from a Byzantine warship. Medieval painting differs from modern photography in that it emphasized key values rather than realism: thus, few rowers are shown here, and the focus both in terms of the centrality of composition and in the very bright colour is the Greek fire itself. The syphon is also emphasized as extending significantly beyond the prow of the ship in order to show how the fire is kept from blowing back onto one's own craft. The sail demonstrates that the ship could be used on the open sea.

men, two men to a bench. The bow of each dromon carried a syphon-like device that produced a spray of Greek fire at enemy ships. Hand-held weapons also sprayed Greek fire. Surviving descriptions of many devices are vague. One shot a package of small arrows which broke apart before reaching the enemy, perhaps like a modern cluster bomb. Breakable containers, probably clay jugs, containing incendiaries were thrown onto the enemy ships. The 100 oarsmen on the dromon were also soldiers, expected to fight. The fifty men on the benches below deck had no armour but those above wore the finest, as did the 'marines' on deck.

In 911 and 949 the Byzantine fleet carried out substantial amphibious operations against the Muslim forces holding Crete, and finally regained the island in 961. In the eleventh century numerous attacks were launched against Muslim Sicily. In these operations the Byzantines demonstrated a consummate ability to ship horses over relatively long distances and land them in battle-ready condition. Towards the middle of the eleventh century, the Normans in southern Italy also learned their secrets of horse transport and ultimately passed this information along to Duke William, whose successful invasion of England in 1066 was made possible by horse transports of Byzantine design.

The Byzantines continually strove to improve their naval technology. For example, they pioneered skeletal construction of ships. Protecting military secrets was a high priority and their intelligence and counter-intelligence were well organized. Due in part at least to the effectiveness of Byzantine security, the Muslims always lagged behind their Christian neighbours. The nomad horsemen of Arabia lacked a naval tradition and so they used Christians, some of whom converted to Islam, to build and man their ships. Some of the most important Muslim naval commanders, such as Leo of Tripoli and Damian of Tarsus, were deserters from the Byzantine empire. However, by the second half of the eleventh century the fleet was in relative decline as the Italian city-states, particularly Venice, began to build more and more ships with better designs.

In 1204 the crusaders sacked Constantinople, the Byzantine capital, in order to loot its great treasures and to make the Byzantine empire part of the West by ending the schism between the pope and the patriarch. They established a Roman Christian in Constantinople as head of the eastern church, and installed a westerner as emperor.

SMALL STATES, SMALL ARMIES

Truncation of the eastern Roman empire through Muslim conquest, and fragmentation of the Carolingian empire into a great many states, meant that the size of armies mustered for offensive operations in both East and West fell far below those fielded by the later Roman emperors and by Charlemagne. Nevertheless, by the middle of the ninth century Byzantium was again able to support a regular army of some 120,000 men, with a field army of about 25,000 men and the provincial army of 95,000 distributed in twenty themes (military districts) throughout the empire. A population base of some eight million sustained this force.

The small states which emerged in the western half of the erstwhile Carolingian empire in the tenth and eleventh centuries had to make do with smaller expeditionary forces. This diminution in the size of field armies, however, did not necessarily result from a noteworthy decline in the number of soldiers: rather, rulers proved unable to exercise effective command over the various magnates who administered the counties and were responsible for bringing their contingents to the muster. Likewise, the townsmen who manned the walls of their cities and the militarized rural population do not appear to have substantially decreased in number, but some population redistribution must have occurred in the period of the Viking invasions.

The great quadrangular tower at Loches in southern Touraine (France) was begun by Geoffrey Greymantle, count of the Angevins (960–87), and completed by his son, Fulk Nerra, around 1030. This stronghold served as the anchor for the defences of the southeastern quadrant of the Angevin heartland and as a base for expansion beyond.

In England during the later ninth and tenth centuries, foreign invasions and civil wars also took their toll upon the military. However, soldiers were not lacking. Alfred the Great's burgs were garrisoned by 28,000 paid troops in addition to the local militiamen, while the five-hide system of military recruitment for the select levy provided a further 20,000 well-trained troops for campaigns. In addition to these forces, the Anglo-Saxon kings could draw upon their own personal armed followings and those of their magnates for offensive operations. At the battle of Hastings, King Harold mustered some 8,000 soldiers, mostly of the select levy, but this constituted only a fragment of the Anglo-Saxon troops available for campaigning.

Across the Channel, Hugh Capet of France (d.996) could raise a force of 6,000 men, both infantry and cavalry, from the small nucleus of territories around Paris under his direct control, while one of his more successful magnates, Count Fulk Nerra of Anjou (987–1040), could also muster a force of about 6,000

Fulk Nerra's net of stone castles

Fulk Nerra (987–1040), count of the Angevins, built a state which dominated the west of France and served as the base upon which his descendants, Geoffrey Plantagenet (d.1151) and Henry II (d.1189), built an empire that stretched from the Pyrenees in the south to Scotland in the north.

Fulk's frontiers were defended by a chain of stone castles – an innovation at that time – situated about twenty miles apart. Within these borders, Fulk either built or took control of more than twenty additional strongholds which created a defence in depth. Raiders in search of booty no longer enjoyed easy entrance and exit from the Angevin heartland.

Although men stationed in towers could not block roads or fords by massive fire power, like defenders of an eighteenth century fortress, archers and crossbowmen could still force detours and take a toll among raiders careless enough to come within range. More importantly, mounted forces from the stronghold could be deployed as far as twenty miles beyond the walls to harass the enemy, and these horsemen could obtain supplies and camp securely at night at nearby fortifications. Fulk's strongholds could not have stopped an invasion, if one had occurred, but they would have severely impeded it. Invaders who stopped to capture a fortification would give Fulk the time to gather a large army to repel them, while each stronghold the enemy bypassed left a base behind their lines with a protected mobile force able to harass the march and cut off supplies and communications. Any invader who chose to detail separate units to besiege each stronghold that posed a danger risked reducing the size of the main force and abandoning the deployed units to sustain themselves in hostile territory.

The Angevin heartland under Fulk Nerra bristled with fortified towns and strongholds. The count divided his flat territories into 'valleys' by the systematic siting of fortifications which controlled the direction of movement through the countryside and dominated the waterways. Since enemy forces had to move through these valleys, Fulk could muster his field armies and choose where and when to fight.

men for offensive operations. In 1067, the city of Angers alone provided about 1,000 men for the select levy, while the walls of the town required some 1,500 urban militiamen for its defence. Duke William of Normandy, Fulk's younger contemporary, managed to gather a force of about 14,000 men, including mercenaries and some 2,000 to 3,000 mounted troops, for his invasion of England in 1066.

The Battle of Hastings 1066

On the death of the English king Edward the Confessor in January 1066, Harold Godwinson, Earl of Wessex, who had been Edward's right-hand man, was hurriedly crowned. If Edward's kinsman, Duke William of Normandy, were to make good his own claim to the throne, an invasion of England had to be launched before the campaigning season came to an end and the new monarch was firmly established. In early 1066, however, William had no fleet, and no experience in, nor technology for, the transport of large numbers of war horses in battle-ready condition across the Channel. He had insufficient trained manpower within Normandy. However, William solved all of these problems and met Harold in the longest major battle in medieval history (nine hours), winning by a combination of Norman firepower and brief – but fatal – lapses in Anglo-Saxon discipline.

William garnered support from the great Norman magnates and recruited specialists from Norman enclaves in southern Italy and Sicily to design horse transports. He recruited his partly mercenary army largely from other areas of northern and western France. By the beginning of August, his army and ships lay ready at Dives-sur-Mer. Sophisticated logistics sustained the encampment, which included some 14,000 men and between 2,000 and 3,000 war horses, for more than a month. When the Anglo-Saxon war fleet returned to the Thames estuary for refitting, he sailed across the Channel to Pevensey, the old Roman port of Anderita, where proper disembarkation facilities existed for the horses, and landed unopposed. William dispatched his fleet carrying his foot soldiers and supplies to Hastings – the mounted troops travelled overland.

Fortuitously, Harold was preoccupied at York, 190 miles from London, with a Viking invasion which he decisively defeated, with great losses, just five days before learning of the Norman landing. He ordered the mobilization of his southern levies and hurried to London with those of his professional troops who remained fit for service. His strategy was to blockade the invaders on the Hastings peninsula. By the time Harold reached Hastings a force of some 8,000 men was gathered, the vast majority local levies called up from the area between London and Hastings. They had been instructed to

muster about seven miles north-northwest of Hastings, at a place now called Battle. Perhaps 1,000 or so of Harold's troops were highly trained professional fighting men and the personal armed followings of his brothers and other important Anglo-Saxon magnates.

Of the 14,000 men William had gathered at Saint Valéry, probably only 10,000 were with him as the day for battle drew near, between 2,000–3,000 of them heavily armed horsemen. About 1,000 men had been left to garrison the fortifications at Pevensey and another 1,000 were needed to garrison the defences at Hastings. Though William had a noteworthy contingent of archers and crossbowmen, the Anglo-Saxons were seriously lacking in 'fire power' – the ability to inflict damage upon the enemy at a distance.

William could not permit himself to be blockaded. He had to provoke Harold to engage as soon as possible, and so he harried the parts of Sussex where a substantial portion of Harold's own estates were located. Since Harold was not eager to engage William, he took up an extremely strong defensive position on a ridge some 880 yards in length, rising in places 275 feet above the marshy plain below. He deployed his militiamen in a deep phalanx, placing the professionals in the front ranks to stiffen both the line and morale. William could thus have his battle, but first he would have to march his army at dawn some seven miles, establish a base camp

Across the Rhine, by the middle of the tenth century the German kings commanded the service of some 15,000 heavily armed mounted troops, a force proportionally consistent, in light of economic and demographic growth, with the territory's obligations under Charlemagne. At the battle of the Lechfeld in 955, against the Magyars, Otto the Great's force of 8,000 to 10,000 constituted only a part

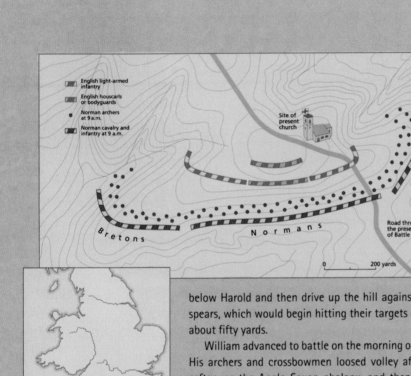

The keep at Hedingham castle, Essex, built between 1130 and 1152, is similar in all essentials to the great quadrangular stone towers built by Fulk Nerra more than a century earlier (see page 80). Usually these keeps were strengthened, first with ditches and outer earthworks, then with wooden outworks and finally (by the later eleventh and twelfth centuries) with increasingly elaborate stone curtain walls. However, no set or uniform design existed for a medieval keep: terrain, resources and purpose all affected where to place a keep or tower, how high to build it, and what kind of other defensive elements to provide.

Opposite: 'King Harold is killed' (*Harold rex interfectus est*), reads this scene from the Bayeux tapestry. Tradition holds that Harold is the man on the left, hit by an arrow in the eye, not the man on the right, struck down by a Norman horseman. It is a fitting tradition: William won with a combination of arms, especially firepower, well deployed. The Norman horse was at an advantage only when Anglo-Saxon infantry broke ranks.

below Harold and then drive up the hill against showers of spears, which would begin hitting their targets at a range of about fifty yards.

William advanced to battle on the morning of 14 October. His archers and crossbowmen loosed volley after volley to soften up the Anglo-Saxon phalanx, and then a combined force of foot and horse attacked the Anglo-Saxon lines. These held like a stone wall. A pattern of combined attacks covered by barrages of arrows and bolts was repeated into the afternoon, when William decided to try a feigned retreat on his left flank with his Breton horsemen, experts in this tactic. The ruse worked, and a portion of the right flank of the Anglo-Saxon line broke in hot pursuit of the 'fleeing' Bretons. At a prearranged signal these horsemen wheeled their mounts and easily rode down the scattered foot soldiers, outmatched on open ground and tired from their pursuit. A second feigned retreat, now by William's right, had the same effect. The Anglo-Saxon phalanx was weakened and morale undermined as Harold's brothers, his two ablest commanders, died.

Towards dusk, William's forces were gaining ground on the ridge in vigorous hand-to-hand combat when Harold was seriously wounded. With Harold's position in the centre of the line overrun, the king himself finally hacked down, and the standard thrown to the ground (the normal signal for retreat), the Anglo-Saxon phalanx finally broke, and a rout followed.

of the campaign forces available in the German kingdom: at the same time another major army raised largely in Saxony attacked the Slavs. For his unsuccessful Italian invasion in 982, Otto II probably led an army that exceeded 20,000 men and included some 10,000 heavily armed horsemen.

Between 1096 and 1099 an army recruited throughout much of western Europe for the First Crusade, led by Bishop Adhémar of Le Puy, the papal legate, and estimated at some 60,000 men, marched into the Middle East. This force was thus double the order of magnitude of those raised by Charlemagne, and its logistic range was considerably greater because various Christian naval powers, including both Byzantium and Genoa provided supplies. Along the route from Constantinople to the Holy Land, the crusaders, often aided by specialized Byzantine units – from lightly armed horsemen to engineers and naval personnel – defeated several large Muslim armies. The First Crusade arguably constituted the most complex and difficult campaign conducted by a western army during the middle ages. The siege and capture of great fortified cities such as Antioch (1098) and Jerusalem (1099) constituted the key victories in the First Crusade, making possible the foundation of the Crusader kingdoms in Palestine and Syria. The Crusaders worked diligently to protect these states with a defence in depth based on castles which could be used as bases for offensive operations against enemy territory and supply lines.

INFANTRY AGAINST CAVALRY

It is difficult to find medieval battles where men fighting on horseback formed the tactically dominant element. In most campaigns, men on foot far outnumbered those with horses: ratios of 5:1 or 6:1 seem to have been normal in the West, while the Byzantines operated closer to 4:1. Moreover, in the majority of the most significant medieval battles most and sometimes all of those with horses dismounted and fought on foot. Mounted attacks, especially when unsupported by archers, crossbowmen, or other troops fighting on foot, rarely succeeded.

Foot soldiers who stood their ground could not only repel a mounted charge but, if the charge were poorly executed, also destroy the attacking force. However, disaster could arise when foot soldiers failed to follow orders. The feigned retreat by mounted troops often served to lure an emplaced force on foot from its position in an undisciplined manner, and thus permit the horsemen to wheel and counter-attack, engaging individual foot soldiers in open terrain. The feigned retreats executed by William the Conqueror's forces at Hastings were undoubtedly of great importance to his ultimate victory. Such tactics could also be used effectively against mounted troops as at Cap Colonna in 982 where a force of lightly armed Muslim horsemen decoyed Emperor Otto II's heavy cavalry into a lengthy pursuit. It ended in the ambush of the Christian forces, after their horses had been worn down, chased in flank attacks by a pre-positioned reserve.

The quality of infantry training could be very uneven. Abbot Regino of Prüm's condemnation of the local levy of his part of the Rhineland in 882 is often cited:

Staying in the saddle. In the eleventh century, a man wielding a lance on horseback stood in the stirrups (top), which he used as a platform from which to launch his attack. In the twelfth century (bottom), he sat in the saddle, legs thrust forward against the stirrups, his back resting against the wrap-around cantle of the saddle. The shock of an enemy's lance attack drove him into the cantle, instead of sending him over the horse's rump. By the end of the middle ages riders in a joust were outfitted more like drivers in a demolition derby than as soldiers who could function effectively in battle. Battle armour was much less elaborate and less protective, enabling the mounted soldier to fight effectively either on horseback or on foot.

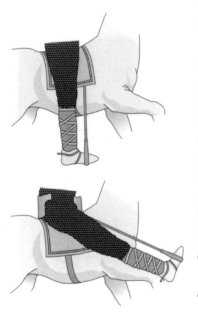

There approached an innumerable multitude of men on foot, banded together from the fields and the villas into one mass…When the Northmen understood that [the weakness of] this ignoble crowd was not so much that it was lacking in defensive armour as that it was lacking in military discipline, they rushed upon them with a shout, and cut them down in so great a slaughter, that they did not seem to be slaying men but dumb animals.

At the other end of the scale, in 955, the spectacular victory won by Otto the Great over the Magyars at the battle of the Lechfeld near Augsburg revealed remarkable discipline. The vast majority of Otto's men fought on foot and thus their victory over mounted archers seems even more remarkable.

Contemporary observers identify by their approval and disapproval what might be considered 'the medieval doctrine' of mounted combat. William the Conqueror followed established doctrine at Hastings when he refused to permit his mounted troops to charge head on against an emplaced enemy until he had softened them up with barrages of arrows and attacks by his foot soldiers. Indeed, against an entrenched enemy, the only real option was for horsemen to dismount and fight on foot.

Commanders of mounted troops often found themselves in difficulty when they ignored established doctrine and charged emplaced enemies without support or in

Unarmoured infantry mixes together with dismounted lightly armed horsemen (the men with kite-shaped shields and swords) in this twelfth-century manuscript illustration from Angers, France. The commander of the unit is the heavily armed dismounted horseman on the left. (Note that he, like the other dismounted horsemen, have removed their spurs in order to fight on foot: a wise precaution.) Mixed units of this type – called *phalanxes* in contemporary documents – fought in battles throughout the middle ages.

a frontal assault. Charlemagne's biographer Einhard describes a disaster that took place in the Süntal mountains in 782 when the Franks attacked their Saxon foes:

> Not as though they were intending to attack a prepared battle line but as if they were chasing down fugitives from behind and gathering up booty. The Saxons stood in their battle line in front of their encampment and each and every one of them [the Franks] rode at them as fast as possible. Once the fighting began the attackers were surrounded by the Saxons and almost all of the Franks were killed.

Cavalry doctrine also called for mounted troops to be deployed against the enemy in flank attacks. At Dorylaeum on the First Crusade in 1097, when one half of the army was attacked by the Muslims, the horsemen dismounted and fought on foot. The other half of the army rode to the rescue and attacked on the flank. The enemy was crushed between hammer and anvil as though the battle strategy had been worked out in advance. A planned surprise attack of this kind was executed in 933 at Riade by Henry the Fowler of Germany against a Magyar force of mounted archers. He used a decoy force of lightly armed horsemen to lure the enemy into position; then his heavily armed cavalry using sword and lance made contact before the mounted archers could launch more than one volley of arrows.

Some medieval texts suggest that cavalry played a far more important role on the battlefield than the facts warrant. Thus, Anna Comnena, daughter of the Byzantine emperor Alexius, writes that the charge of the Frankish horsemen was so vigorous it could break through the walls of Babylon. She says her father's experience of fighting heavily armed Norman horsemen convinced him that cavalry charges were irresistible. More notoriously, medieval romances portray the mounted knight as

Château Gaillard (below) was built at great expense (£44,000) by Richard I of England in the 1190s. On cliffs above the Seine near Rouen, this key position in the defences for Normandy fell to king Philip II Augustus of France after a lengthy siege in 1204. Normandy, English since 1066, became French. From the twelfth century on, sieges became more expensive to mount and more uncertain of success, as castle designs improved and towns were better fortified. The siege of Château Gaillard was one of the few to result in substantial territorial gains.

dominating warfare. In fact, Alexius easily nullified the advantages enjoyed by the Norman horsemen. Their frontal assaults were rendered useless by caltrops (iron balls with protruding spikes, scattered on the ground) and other simple devices. And the romances are no more accurate.

Medieval military decision-makers and fighting men knew the realities. They invested vast resources in building and keeping in repair city walls and fortresses, artillery, sophisticated siege towers, and battering rams, all manned by footsoldiers. Great effort was dedicated to the proper training and recruitment of local militia and the common footsoldier. The most frequently copied, translated, and consulted secular prose work of the early middle ages was Vegetius's *Concerning Military Matters*, a handbook for infantry training which devoted very little attention to cavalry (see page 66).

STRONGPOINTS UNDER SIEGE

Many of the fortifications built in western Europe after the dissolution of the Carolingian empire were put together by local magnates to protect a small region from their enemies. These constructions were of limited military importance, even though they were extremely numerous: there are 400 in County Wexford, Ireland, alone, and so many upon the central Spanish plateau that they gave their name to a major state, Castile. Networked fortifications were the ones that mattered. The defence-in-depth strategy developed by Alfred in Wessex, Henry the Fowler in Germany, and Fulk Nerra in Anjou remained fundamental throughout the middle ages. It is also seen, for example, in William the Conqueror's disposition of many scores of strongholds throughout England after 1066 and in the assertion of control by the Capet dynasty over the Ile de France during the twelfth century.

Thanks to so much building, siege warfare continued to dominate military activity and great battles in the field remained few by comparison, except when fought between besiegers and a relief army. However, despite striking developments in artillery, with

the introduction first of the traction trebuchet and then with the invention of counter-weight technology (which far surpassed ancient machines in power and operational efficiency), sieges from the twelfth century onwards generally proved less successful and more costly. The art of defence, as evidenced by increasingly elaborately articulated fortifications, more than kept pace with the technology. The growing political strength of the major states, such as France and England, also made it less likely that a successful siege would bring down a dynasty.

Strenuous training and high levels of unit cohesion were essential. A crew of fifty sappers digging a mine only a hundred yards in length at a depth of thirty feet beneath the walls of a city required levels of expertise, training, and cohesion which rivalled those of submariners liable to depth charge attack by an enemy destroyer. The combat team operating a battering ram under enemy fire, or a catapult crew keeping their weapon in operation day and night, certainly required the same training and unit cohesion as modern tank or mortar crews. Even the dozen men assigned to carry each forty-five foot long scaling ladder across a hundred-yard killing ground, place and secure it against the wall, and then climb it in a prescribed order while under withering enemy fire required far more than 'dumb courage'.

During the two centuries following the First Crusade the armies of many western states increased. This reflected growth in Europe's population and wealth as well as the expansion of a few states and the elimination or absorption of a great many others. In England, for example, monarchs in the late twelfth century could raise some 20,000 mounted troops, while at the battle of Bouvines in 1214 the opposing armies may have reached a combined total of 40,000 men. Towards the end of the thirteenth century, Edward I (d.1307) mustered some 25,000 infantry and 5,000 horsemen on a recurring basis for his wars in Wales and Scotland; and French royal forces probably reached the same order of magnitude, with the south of the kingdom alone able to provide Philip the Fair (d.1314) with 20,000 men.

The military forces available to the Italian city-states in the thirteenth century, both for defensive operations and for offensive efforts against nearby adversaries, seem immense. Milan, perhaps with some exaggeration by its propagandists, is said to have been able to raise 10,000 cavalry and 40,000 infantry from the 200,000 people dwelling in the city itself – that is, one quarter of the total urban population – with another 30,000 men drawn from its 600 dependent communities. The figures for Florence appear more realistic, with 2,000 horsemen and 15,000 infantry drawn from a total population of 400,000.

THE MYTH OF THE MOUNTED KNIGHT

There was a romantic time not long ago when it was generally believed that medieval warfare consisted of undisciplined fief-holding warriors, irrationally driven by their chivalric ethic, fighting an individualistic style of combat dominated by battles between single knights who engaged in mounted shock combat. This view is false.

Extending the city walls

In the late twelfth century cities in the West began the lengthy, laborious and expensive process of increasing the perimeter of their defensive walls. These programmes, which could be completed only with great expenditure of both material and human resources, indicate the immense importance which contemporary military thinkers, like their predecessors, attributed to the fortress city.

In England, the number of fortified towns doubled to around 200, most of their new walls measuring six feet in width and twenty to thirty feet high. Many of them deliberately included uninhabited areas to accommodate refugees and to allow for future growth, to allow cultivation and grazing within the walls, and to provide some shelter to the town centre from bombardment. Some new fortifications became very large indeed: at York, for example, they extended for more than two miles.

When an old Roman city with a circuit wall of 2,000 yards received a new wall of 4,000 yards, the defensive perimeter merely doubled, but the area enclosed quadrupled from 250,000 square yards to 1,000,000. Demands made upon the urban militia in turn doubled, but four times as many people could now live in the space they defended.

Besieging forces were thus thwarted in two ways by the newly extended walls. The increase in the physical object to be overcome greatly increased the numbers of troops required for an effective siege. But the percentage of the protected population now required for defence now fell.

Substantial numbers of city and town dwellers throughout western Europe were demilitarized as a result, just when the population as a whole was rapidly increasing.

Older, inner, ramparts (right) at Carcassonne in southern France stand on foundations left by the Romans and the Visigoths, who lost the town to the Moors in the eighth century. The outer circuit (left) was added in the reign of the French king Louis IX (1214–70). Carcassonne was a strongpoint on the frontier with Roussillon, which did not become French until 1659.

Three basic reasons account for the discrepancy between the medieval military record and such flawed interpretations. First, the fief has played a very important role in European property law (in contrast to its relative unimportance in military affairs) and thus has rightly garnered considerable attention from scholars who focus upon legal and institutional history. Second, most fief-holders in western Europe were nobles, and they have left a substantial 'parchment trail' of documents to be studied. Finally, and most important in creating a highly misleading picture of the medieval military in all its aspects, the romantic epics known as the *chansons de geste* portrayed the mounted knight as dominating medieval warfare and more particularly the battlefields of Europe – much as the 'Westerns' of the American cinema show the cowboy conquering the frontier with his six-gun. Neither image is true. Medieval literary entertainment and medieval games popularized and magnified the importance of the man on horseback, and their posterity has for too long accepted fiction and play as reality.

The willingness of those men in the middle ages, who saw themselves as the military elite, to propagate the myth that they were the essential feature of a

medieval army through song and story, and even through the patronage of 'historians' and artists, is noteworthy. Nevertheless, the 'feudal host' of 'knights' serving their lords for forty days in return for fiefs was, in general, of relatively little importance in medieval military organization. The limitations imposed upon the formulation of strategy and the prosecution of extended campaigns by term of service lasting less than two months undermined whatever value feudal rulers may have envisioned in such a system. Thus it is not surprising that references to the 'feudal host' appear more frequently in the works of modern writers than in the medieval sources. Furthermore, the training of militias for local defence, together with the support of levies of foot soldiers and substantial numbers of archers and crossbowmen for offensive military operations throughout medieval Europe, clearly indicate the importance accorded to such units by those who formulated military policy or grand strategy. Finally, the training of mounted troops to fight on foot and the dominance of siege warfare provide more than a subtle hint regarding the multifaceted nature of medieval warfare in which sieges dominated and the knight of romantic literature was but one figure in a very complex equation.

Mounted troops were of minor importance in a siege, but the bias of both patrons and artists is illustrated here by devotion of the greatest attention to the horsemen. This is shown not only by the amount of space allotted but by their out-of-scale, excessive size. Both space and grandeur are ways in which medieval artists, following western tradition, illustrate importance. Nevertheless, an air of 'realism' is provided by accurate depictions of weapons and other equipment. (From William of Tyre's manuscript *History* of the crusading kingdoms, written and illustrated c.1280.)

CHAPTER 5   *New Weapons, New Tactics*

A German knight of c.1377 wears a breastplate covered by a *jupon*, a closely fitting layered outer garment, with a skirt. Much of his protective wear is chain mail, but since this proved so vulnerable to the arrow, plate armour came to be used with increasing frequency during the second half of the fourteenth century.

Although men had fought on foot throughout the Middle Ages, in the course of the thirteenth century infantry began to assume an increasingly significant role in western warfare. The crossbow, albeit condemned by the Church, appeared in action with greater frequency, posing a considerable threat to the mounted warrior and his horse; the longbow, which could discharge arrows at the rate of about ten a minute (in contrast to the much slower rate of two bolts from the crossbow), could penetrate chain-mail armour with ease. The gradual introduction of plate armour from around 1250, to reinforce chain mail, reflects the recognized need to respond to the development of the bow which would continue to influence the way war was fought for a century and a half.

Self-protection against the 'new' missile was necessary; but it inevitably turned the cavalry into a much heavier and less flexible 'fighting machine'. It also made war more expensive. For reasons that were largely economic, the nobleman, who traditionally formed the basis of the feudal cavalry, found it increasingly difficult to support his military role and fulfil the obligation to fight which arose from his status and his allegiance because estate revenues, diminishing at the very time when the costs of war were rising, affected both his ability and his willingness to fight.

Political factors also influenced combat in the West. The last centuries of the middle ages saw a widespread growth in the ambition of societies to govern themselves and to throw off their dependence on others. In the early fourteenth century the communes of Flanders moved against the feudal domination of the crown of France; in Scotland, the 'imperial' power of the king of England met with fierce resistance in the War of Independence; while in Switzerland, several cantons rose against Austrian overlordship. Towards the end of the same century the Portuguese confirmed their independence on the battlefield at Aljubarrota (1385), while the next century saw successful wars in Bohemia against German domination. These conflicts, pursued with great intensity, involved armies drawn increasingly from the general population concerned.

PIKES AND BOWS

In Flanders, economic and political control was passing to the townsmen who now formed the backbone of the armies with which they sought their independence. In Scotland, Robert Bruce (Robert I) fought his war against England with what was essentially a 'popular' army, using guerrilla tactics incompatible with the war of the mounted horseman associated with aristocracy. In Switzerland (like Scotland, a largely mountainous country unsuitable for the use of heavy cavalry) the ordinary foot soldier had more of a future than the mounted unit, especially when used as part of an aggressive tactic. Furthermore, weapons in keeping with the much more modest social background of such armies came into play. The spear, the halberd, the pike, the club, and the axe were relatively cheap to produce; the halberd, in particular, with its hook capable of pulling a cavalryman off his horse, proved to be a suitably 'democratic' weapon. Above all, the longbow, a cheap and 'popular' weapon could, when drawn vertically over the shoulder, project arrows much further and with greater accuracy than the small bow, held and drawn horizontally, had ever done. Used *en masse*, the longbow became a weapon of very great effectiveness. The English also learned to develop its potential to the full in conjunction with mounted men-at-arms (using the lance and sword) and, increasingly, with those same men-at-arms fighting on foot alongside the archers. The tactic possessed great advantages. It preserved some continuity with the past, in that it gave the man-at-arms (a person of a certain social standing) a new, indeed vital, role to play in war, including the leadership of those around him; and it also helped to create and develop a bond among the different elements in the army which, in its turn, contributed towards its success.

When Edward I of England invaded Wales in the final quarter of the thirteenth century, he did so at the head of armies which included ten or fifteen foot soldiers to every cavalry man, with the aim of using mounted men-at-arms in conjunction with archers and crossbowmen in set battles. The system worked, both against the Welsh and, very soon afterwards, against the Scots. Archers and cavalry now combined to provide a new tactical system: arrows disrupted the enemy before the cavalry moved in against him. In the company of (and reinforced by) the man-at-arms, the archer could now stand his ground; he had less reason than his predecessors to flee before the menace of advancing cavalry.

Events in the early years of the fourteenth century underlined the vulnerability of unsupported cavalry. In July 1302 an army of Flemings, drawn from local militias and burgher forces, using pike and spear, routed an army of French knights (killing almost 1,000 of them) at Courtrai near the French border. Although this defeat of cavalry with unusually heavy losses was important, it served only as a portent: before long the French cavalry had defeated the Flemings at Mons-en-Pévèle (1304) and at Cassel (1328), and the Flemish communes would suffer crushing humiliation at Roosebeek in 1382.

Yet Courtrai was more than a freak victory. In June 1314, at Bannockburn near Stirling, Edward II of England, although accompanied by an army of more than 21,000 infantry, allowed the Scots, well led by Robert Bruce and in a state of good morale, to defeat his cavalry, the English infantry playing only a minor role in the battle. In this decisive encounter

> [the Scots] issued from the woods in three battalions on foot, boldly holding their course direct for the English army, which had been under arms all night, with their horses bitted. The English, who were not accustomed to fight on foot, mounted with much alarm; whereas the Scots had taken the example of the Flemings who earlier at Courtrai had, on foot, defeated the forces of France. The aforesaid Scots

The funeral effigy of Matthew Swetenham from Northamptonshire in England, who died in 1416, shows the full panoply of plate armour, from the helmet and neck guards, through the articulated protection for arms, hips, and legs, to the encased feet.

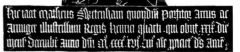

One of the great military leaders of the later middle ages, John Hawkwood, born the son of a tanner near Colchester in England, fought with his mercenary company for various Italian states from 1360 until 1377, when he entered the service of Florence. In return for an annual salary of 250,000 florins he served the city faithfully until his death in 1394, and in 1436 this funeral monument by Paolo Uccello, Florence's foremost artist, was placed in the cathedral to honour the memory of its chief protector.

came all in a line in schiltrons [clusters of spearmen] and attacked the English formations, which were jammed together and could do nothing against them because their horses were impaled on the pikes. The men at the English rear recoiled into the ravine of the Bannockburn, each falling over the others.

The same point was underlined in 1315 when a force of knights and footmen serving Leopold of Austria was defeated at Morgarten by mountaineers drawn from Schwyz and Uri in Switzerland, while in 1319, at Dithmarschen in Saxony, peasants scored another victory over the knights.

The success achieved by the Scottish, Swiss, and Saxon militias represented the development of a new tactic: the aggressive rush by massed infantry who, by making the best use of a site, caught the knights unawares in a confined space. The future lay increasingly with those able and willing to fight in mass or large groups, a style which would prove successful both in attack and defence.

Yet these developments did not prevail everywhere. In Italy, mounted knights achieved a brief period of dominance, and until 1450 large bodies of even highly trained infantry seldom challenged their supremacy on the field. Between 1320 and 1360, for example, about 700 cavalry leaders (most of them Germans) are known to have been active in Italy, leading 'free companies' of veteran troops, at first as temporary associations to extort booty from civilian populations but later as permanent military formations which spent most of their time in the pay of one or other of the numerous Italian states. The 'Great Company' led by the Provençal knight Montréal d'Albarno (called by the Italians Fra Moriale) in the 1350s numbered about 10,000 fighting men and 20,000 camp followers; its 'reign of terror' only ended with the arrival of the White Company, consisting of some 6,000 veterans of the wars in France invited into Italy by the marquis of Montferrat. In a battle at the bridge of Canturino, west of Milan, the White Company (so called because its members wore more plate armour, kept brightly burnished by their pages, than was then customary in Italy) defeated its rival in 1363 and soon, led by Sir John Hawkwood, passed into the service first of Pisa, then of the papacy, and finally of Florence – which Hawkwood served as captain-general until his death in 1394. State service did not preclude extortion and booty, however: thus the republic of Siena suffered thirty-seven visitations from free companies between 1342 and 1399, the city fathers often deciding that appeasing the experienced professionals would prove less costly and disruptive than mobilizing to fight them.

THE HUNDRED YEARS WAR

In the Hundred Years War (1337–1453) – the dominant conflict of the period because of its length, and a war of conquest for the English but a war of self-defence and self-assertion for the French – the battles at Crécy (1346) and Poitiers (1356) demonstrated French determination to maintain tactics that relied heavily on the shock which they hoped their cavalry would achieve. As the defenders, the English

The battle of Poitiers (1356) was one of a series of spectacular victories won by the English invaders of France, who relied on archers and dismounted men-at-arms, against the mounted knights of the French. The archers are confident; the cavalry, with horses which are clearly very vulnerable to arrows, are not – some, already wounded, have begun to retreat. In the rout that followed, the French king himself and one of his sons fell prisoner to the English.

mostly dismounted to absorb the attack when it came, and in the ensuing hand-to-hand fighting the men on foot enjoyed a considerable advantage. Likewise at Agincourt (1415) the English king, Henry V, facing a numerically superior enemy, waited for the French to attack him. Once again, many of the advancing cavalry and infantry were brought down by arrows (clouds of them, we are told by an eyewitness) before they could even reach the English line.

If the defenders were well-trained, well-armed, and well-disciplined, it proved increasingly difficult for attackers to defeat them. Having absorbed an assault already much weakened by the massive use of arrows, a defending army stood ready to take the initiative against a demoralized enemy, cavalry being on hand to pursue those who might flee the battlefield.

Yet, while the Hundred Years War witnessed some important battles, the main tactic of English aggression in the fourteenth century remained the raid – or *chevauchée* – carried into French territory by relatively small armies sometimes only two or three thousand strong. The principal aim was to weaken the enemy's morale and his ability to pay taxes, and to break his resolve to resist through a form of war whose prime targets were population, economy, and social infrastructure rather than armies. In the words of the Italian poet Petrarch (born in 1309):

In my youth the…English were taken to be the meekest of the barbarians. Today they are a fiercely bellicose nation. They have overturned the ancient military glory of the French by victories so numerous that they, who once were inferior to the wretched Scots, have reduced the entire kingdom of France by fire and sword to such a state that I, who had traversed it lately on business, had to force myself to believe that it was the same country I had seen before. Outside the walls of towns there was not, as it were, one building left standing.

In such a war of intimidation great sophistication of armour and weaponry were not required; nor were the traditional virtues and skills of the military aristocracy. The horse used on such raids could be small and of cheap breed, while the common soldier was as good as his social superior at setting fire to a village or to a farmer's barn. They moved fast – sometimes, as on the great raid from Aquitaine led by the Black Prince in 1355, covering ten miles a day – with the troops spread out in parallel columns in order to devastate as much enemy territory as possible, hoping either to force the French to fight (and lose) or to flee and lay the kingdom open to further devastation. In 1346 (at Crécy) and 1356 (at Poitiers) the English achieved the former, in 1355 (the Carcassone raid) and 1359 (the Rheims campaign) the latter. And in 1360, thanks to his strategic flexibility, the treaty of Brétigny conferred upon Edward III in full sovereignty territories comprising one-third of France, together with a huge ransom for King John, taken prisoner at Poitiers.

SIEGES AND ARTILLERY

Damaging as it proved both to the French economy and to the reputation of France's nobility, however, this style of war could scarcely force a total surrender. Consequently, in 1415 the English turned to a war of conquest in the hope, partially fulfilled by 1420, that such a method might bring overall victory. The new objective required the use of other, older methods, in particular the siege, since capture of a castle or fortified town could lead to the military control of the country round about, and sometimes even to a measure of political and administrative control. If Henry V's victory at Agincourt stands out, so did his successful sieges of Harfleur, Falaise, Cherbourg, and Rouen, which gave the English control of Normandy and the ability to extend their territorial ambition further.

The siege was a slow and relatively undramatic way of making progress. It demanded specialists, in particular miners and men who would work the artillery – the traditional trebuchet and other tension and leverage weapons, still in use in the early fifteenth century, alongside (if not always in conjunction with) the new gunpowder artillery (see Chapter 6). The new weapons certainly enlivened a siege: as contemporary descriptions testify, life became much more dangerous for the defenders. Walled towns in France greatly increased in number during the fourteenth century in order to deter those who rode out on *chevauchées*. To the attacker with artillery, however, they constituted a sitting target, provided he could approach close enough to bring them within effective range. Range was crucial: it often gave the besiegers, with larger artillery pieces, the advantage over the defenders whose cannon were frequently smaller. To the besieged facing an army

Opposite: The Hussites of Bohemia defended their independence in the early fifteenth century with *wagenburgen*, mobile fortresses made mainly out of farm carts, their very ordinariness and cheapness emphasizing the humble origins of the peasants who formed the army. Some wagons sheltered infantry who fired crossbows and handguns or hurled stones; others carried field artillery and spare weapons. Although intended mainly for defensive purposes, in particular against cavalry, *wagenburgen* also proved successful in an offensive capacity.

well provided with artillery, it was not a question of whether, but of how long, they could hold out. In the mid-fifteenth century, as contemporary evidence makes clear, it was the threat posed by his artillery that enabled King Charles VII of France to recover in a few months those fortified places which, a generation earlier, had withstood the English for far longer. The cannon caused fear as well as destruction.

THE HUSSITES AND THE SWISS

The increased use of artillery and the need to build defences added considerably to the cost of war. But not all innovations proved exorbitantly expensive. For example, total disregard for cavalry and cheapness characterized the army and style of fighting adopted by the Bohemian Hussites in their war of independence during the first quarter of the fifteenth century. Motivated by nationalism, religion, and social egalitarianism, the followers of John Huss, executed for heresy in 1415, sought to establish a state which reflected their radical political, social, and religious ideas. In so doing they introduced innovative methods of waging war which would prove influential for a long time. Under John Zizka, a leader of military genius, they developed a style of fighting peculiar to themselves. New, for example, was the use of the *wagenburgen*, or mobile wagon fortresses made up of carts, to create what was at first a defensive unit to be used against cavalry attacks but which later came to be employed offensively – almost like a tank – to break up and dislodge the enemy and drive him back, as Zizka did when he and his army were all but encircled at Kutná Hora, in Bohemia, in December 1421.

Zizka owed his fame and his success at least in part to his resourcefulness: the wagon was essentially a peasant's instrument, as were the flail (manufactured in large numbers for war) and the pike which his supporters used. But the Hussite army was successful for other reasons, not least because it was among the very first to make use of artillery in the field, the wagons being used to convey cannon from place to place. Elsewhere, heavy cannon and mortars travelled from one place to another laid on four-wheeled carts: at the point of use, they were taken down and set up on frames ready for firing. Not until the mid-fifteenth century – surprisingly late – do sources mention carriages borne on only two wheels, with 'trunnions' (stumps mounted on either side of the barrel to pivot the angle at which the gun should be set). The degree of mobility and greater speed of action thus achieved gave the artillery an increasingly integral role in tactical warfare, especially against slow-moving targets such as troops trying to scale fieldworks or advance in close formation over difficult terrain. Nevertheless, the slow rate of fire and the danger of explosion meant that gunpowder artillery, at least in numbers, constituted a weapon whose day had yet to come.

By contrast, the Swiss forces which served in both French and Burgundian armies in the second half of the fifteenth century consisted largely of pikemen and handgunners. Their tactical style favoured collective aggression, thanks to the high proportion of the population with military experience and the general absence of social differentiation. Faced with a siege, the Swiss normally opted for rapid action, such as the storming of defences; and they seldom took prisoners (the common practice among aristocratic societies where the lure of capturing rich prisoners acted as an incentive in war). Furthermore, their habit of challenging the enemy to battle stood in broad contrast to the widely accepted practice of avoiding battle (and thus the consequences of defeat). Hardly surprisingly, then, the Swiss became popular as mercenaries, prepared by training and tradition to face the cavalry charge which, at the close of the fifteenth century, was still the most dangerous manoeuvre to be used against them.

THE SURVIVAL OF CAVALRY

For it would be wrong to say that the day of the cavalry was over. Although few areas were as dominated by mounted forces as Italy, the fifteenth-century French army included many mounted men, heavy cavalry as well as infantry on light horses, while the rival army of the dukes of Burgundy also incorporated heavy cavalry. This situation reflected a number of factors. One was the survival of the traditional social order, feudalism, in France and Burgundy; the mounted warrior, perhaps a knight or a member of the nobility, mirrored the persistent influence of

This depiction of the battle of Shrewsbury (21 July 1403) between the armies of Henry IV of England and the rebel Percy family, vividly conveys the combined strength and energy of cavalry horses and their riders. The picture – made in the 1490s – underlines the fact that cavalry, better protected with plate armour, continued to play a vital role in the outcome of many battles throughout the fifteenth century.

that order. Burgundy, too, preserved the influential chivalric tradition which had been deliberately fostered and encouraged during the long reign of Duke Philip the Good (1419–67). The second half of the fifteenth century witnessed the beginning of a revival of the battle, of which there had been relatively few during the previous hundred years, thanks to the new territorial ambitions of the French crown (now recovered from the long war with England). In this regard the Franco-Burgundian wars, involving the active participation of the Swiss, are particularly instructive with regard to how war was fought, and with what forces, in the third quarter of the fifteenth century. With the protection of both horse and rider now better assured through the development of increasingly sophisticated plate armour (which meant that the rider could dispense with a shield), cavalry staged something of a comeback. While cannon and, in particular, portable firearms were being used on an increasing scale, their rate of fire was still slow. The battles of Charles the Bold, duke of Burgundy (1467–77), at Grandson (March 1476), Morat (June 1476), and, finally, Nancy (January 1477), all testify to the practical use of cavalry: whether used for attack or defence, a fifteenth-century army was unlikely to achieve a decisive victory on the field of battle without it, particularly if the enemy lacked effective artillery.

THE LATE MEDIEVAL ARMY

This, then, was a period of change caused not merely by technical factors but, more importantly, by social, political, and economic realities. Duke Charles of Burgundy may not have been the Alexander or the Caesar with whom he compared himself, yet he was imaginative and experienced enough to recognize the necessity of including a variety of weapons, both traditional and new, in his armies. That of 1472, the product of major reforms introduced in the previous year, consisted of heavy cavalry (some 15 per cent), archers supplied with mounts for transport (some 50 per cent), pikemen (some 15 per cent), handgunners (10 per cent) and foot archers (10 per cent). Although only approximate, such figures underline the importance of the horse in battle. Its role must be neither ignored nor forgotten.

Nevertheless, the armies of Charles the Bold, and others, remained dominated by infantry. In fourteenth-century England the normal ratio in recruiting cavalry (men-at-arms) and infantry was 1:2. Under Henry V, in the early fifteenth century, the figure was normally 1:3, rising as high as 1:10 in the 1440s when recruiting became very difficult. Significantly, the change to greater numbers of infantry took place far more slowly in France than in England: as late as the beginning of the fifteenth century the ratio stood at two men-at-arms to one foot soldier, changing to 1:2 and then to 1:5 or 1:6 in the 1440s and 1450s when the English were expelled first from Normandy and finally from Aquitaine. In Spain, the army that reconquered Granada a generation later consisted of one cavalry trooper to every three or four infantrymen. Only in a country such as Bohemia, where the wars arose from socio-religious factors, did the ratio differ significantly. The army sent by the Holy

- ← Charles the Bold's artillery
- • Charles the Bold's archers
- ■ Charles the Bold's infantry
- ▦ Charles the Bold's cavalry
- ⚉ Hedges

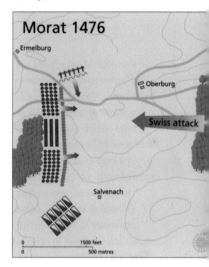

At the battle of Morat in June 1476 Charles the Bold, duke of Burgundy, drew up his army in a complex formation in which infantry alternated with formations of archers, protected by a hedge, with his cavalry on the right wing and entrenched artillery on the left. In all, he may have commanded between 15,000 and 20,000 men. However, in the event, the impetuous advance of three Swiss pike columns, at a time when the duke had allowed the bulk of his troops to return to camp, broke through the Burgundian defences.

Roman Emperor Sigismund against the Hussites in 1422 totalled 1,656 horsemen and 31,000 infantry, a ratio of 1:19.

Armies naturally varied greatly in size, depending on circumstances, military objectives, and the availability of money. At the end of the thirteenth century many armies manned by those obliged to give military service were large. In 1298 Edward I of England had with him almost 30,000 men (in a ratio of one cavalryman to about eight infantry) on his expedition into Scotland. In the late summer of 1340 Philip VI of France may have had at his disposal, in all theatres, as many as 100,000 men, either paid directly or financed by his cities and nobles, while his adversaries, Edward III of England and his allies, maintained perhaps 50,000. These, however, probably constituted the largest military establishments of the later middle ages. The development of paid armies, coupled with the adverse effects of the Black Death after 1348, soon brought down army sizes. The average French army towards the end of the fourteenth century comprised some 5,000 men, although Henry V had about twice that number with him in 1417, and the Venetian army in about 1430 might have numbered some 7,000 men.

MEDIEVAL WARFARE AT SEA

Hostilities did not take place on land alone. The long conflict between England and France saw a growing appreciation of the role of the sea in war. In order to fight on the mainland of Europe, the English had to take to the sea to transport personnel and horses (in their thousands), as well as all forms of armaments, provisions, and equipment. Ships had to be found for this purpose, and to secure these when they were needed (a need that might last for months) merchant fleets were plundered through commandeering carried out by royal officers. The system was slow, and caused much resentment among the communities of merchants and fishermen whose activities suffered from the military needs of the kingdom. Meanwhile, in France, late in the thirteenth century, King Philip IV caused a shipyard, the Clos des Galées, to be built at Rouen on the river Seine. The intention was to give the French crown the opportunity to construct ships of its own (ships which could be brought quickly into service), as well as to provide facilities for their repair.

In June 1340, in the first (and perhaps the bloodiest) battle of the Hundred Years War, Edward III led a powerful expeditionary force across the Channel to the Flemish port of Sluys. There he found the French fleet drawn up before the port, determined to impede his landing. In the words of the chronicler Jean Froissart, 'This battle of which I am speaking was very foul and very horrible, because battles and assaults on the sea are both harder fought and more cruel than those on land, for one cannot flee or retreat.' As the English chronicler, Geoffrey Le Baker, wrote:

> An iron cloud of bolts from crossbows, and arrows from bows, fell upon [the French] bringing death to thousands. Then those who wished, or were daring enough, came to blows at close quarters with spears, pikes, and swords; stones,

thrown from the ships' castles, also killed many. In brief, this was without a doubt an important and terrible battle which a coward would not have dared to observe even from afar off.

Contemporary estimates of the French losses varied from 20,000 to 55,000 (and modern ones from 16,000 to 18,000), including both commanders, together with most of their ships. The defeat at Sluys dealt a heavy blow to French pretensions to exercise any control over the seas.

Henry V also appreciated the importance of maintaining naval mastery, maintaining his military ambitions in France with a fleet of some thirty-nine vessels,

Sea battles in the fifteenth century were dominated by close in-fighting with missiles. In this incident in 1416, a French soldier in the crow's nest is transfixed by an arrow as he prepares to hurl a boulder onto the crossbowmen and archers on the decks below, who are defending Richard, Earl of Warwick, captain of English-held Calais, during a crossing to England. Note the two small cannon poking over the side of the ship on the left, and the absence of gun-ports through which heavier pieces could be fired.

some accumulated by inheritance, capture or purchase, others built at the new shipyard which he established at Southampton (see page 123).

The typical high-sided vessel of northern waters needed port facilities (or at least a quayside) to discharge its cargo and its men; but galleys, shallow-keeled and propelled by either sails or oars, could make a landing on a beach. Castile and Genoa were the main suppliers of such ships throughout the middle ages, and their importance can be judged by the diplomatic efforts made by both England and France to secure their support during the Hundred Years War. Thus, on a calm day in the summer of 1372, a Castilian galley fleet destroyed an English squadron off La Rochelle on the Bay of Biscay; and the ships either sunk or taken in the mouth of the river Seine on 15 August 1416 by an English squadron included a number of Genoese vessels which had assisted the French in a land and sea blockade of the town of Harfleur, won by the English in the previous year.

War on land and war at sea coalesced in such blockades. In 1346–47 the English had forced the surrender of Calais through a long siege on land sustained by a blockade at sea, gaining a valuable bridgehead on the European continent (held until 1558). Ports, and the control of ports, were essential both for the defence of a long coast line (such as that of France) and for purposes of attack. Ports were the places where fleets tended to gather, and where they could be destroyed, so that naval actions normally took place near the coast, in shallow waters, rather than out

Among the books commissioned by Charles the Bold, duke of Burgundy (1467–77), was a new translation into French of *The Deeds of Alexander the Great*, the great military leader whom Charles admired so much. Here the Macedonians try to land in Scythia, despite the fire of three breach-loading cannon (supplied with balls, 'chambers' containing powder, and an apparatus for elevating the barrel). The ship also has three cannon on deck, while some handguns may be seen in the aft castle. However, the chief missile weapons on both sides are bows.

at sea. Ports situated on estuaries also controlled access to rivers. The capture of Harfleur in 1415 gave the English the chance to ship men, artillery, and siege engines up the Seine to Rouen for the long blockade which led to the capture of that city four years later. Rivers proved particularly useful in conveying cannon and other heavy equipment within a country. Access to rivers, as the English understood, would have to be gained and maintained from the sea. A measure of 'control' over the sea was something which, by the fifteenth century, was becoming increasingly important. It could not be achieved, however, without some sort of navy, among whose tasks would be included the protection of a country's legitimate trading interests.

THE STATE AND WAR

As Jean de Bueil wrote in his military treatise of 1466, *Le Jouvencel*, 'All empires and all lordships find their origin in war', and the later middle ages were no exception. But state-formation, like state-preservation, depended upon maintaining access to soldiers. Already in 1300 this could mean hiring mercenaries, usually for short-term service. The growing Italian city-states did this, while the great kingdoms of northern Europe, England, and France, remained largely dependent on their traditional social system to provide the men needed for war. But the decline of feudal obligation to serve in war, the prolongation of conflicts, and the unwillingness of men pressed by economic necessity to fight for anything other than financial reward led inevitably to the practice of paying all troops for their military service.

The increasingly widespread development of this practice from the late thirteenth century onwards had certain important consequences. Since huge sums of money were involved, only the central authority (the king, the prince, the 'state') possessed the ability to provide funds which could not be raised except through taxation, thereby sharing responsibility for making war between those who fought and those who paid. As a consequence the ruler, as the paymaster, became the employer, making terms with those who served him through a military contract, known variously as the 'indenture' (England), the *lettre de retenue* (France), and the *condotta* (Italy).

The indenture was a document of both practical and symbolic importance. It presupposed the right of a society's leaders to decide on war and peace. Equally, it claimed the explicit right to appoint men to lead armies in time of war. (How these should be chosen and on what principles, was another question.) Finally it gave the right to insist on standards which would lead to efficiency: those receiving pay had the obligation to train, to serve out their length of agreed service (desertion became a crime of importance), and to be properly provided with arms according to their position in the army, as agreed in the contract. The need to apply discipline, which owed much to Roman tradition as well as to the revival of the Aristotelian idea that any society should be ready to defend itself, lay at the root of such thinking. For some, the jousts or combats between two opponents, usually mounted, and the tournaments in which team skills were practised, seemed appropriate. Yet the need for others to practise was also clearly recognized. In England the Assize of Arms (1181) and the Statute of Winchester (1285) initiated a series of measures, inspired by the crown, emphasizing the obligation of able-bodied male adults to prepare themselves for war. The following centuries witnessed the renewal of such measures all over Europe. Regular archery practice was demanded in England in 1363; the Scots were urged to renounce football and golf for the same end in 1456; while in 1473 those serving in the Burgundian army received orders to prepare themselves both for individual combat and for fighting in formation. Discipline was also enforced through the system of regular inspection known as 'muster and review' which, largely based on English practice, developed during the Hundred Years War. Here the emphasis lay not only on the counting of numbers (in order to prevent unit leaders from seeking money to pay soldiers who had deserted or, worse, never served) but on ensuring that minimum standards of dress and armament were maintained. In this way, two requirements were met: the contractor knew that he was receiving value for money, while at the same time the standards of military efficiency were maintained.

The ruler could expect certain things of those whom he employed to fight, but he likewise had obligations towards them, two of which possessed particular importance. One was to provide the army with the weapons, equipment (including expensive cannon), and provisions which it would need on campaign. This required not only money; military organization and administration had to be developed so that armies could be supplied properly and regularly with these material requirements. The second was to provide pay, normally in cash, for the army. This was often even more difficult to achieve and caused frequent indiscipline among soldiers who, unrewarded, might turn on 'soft' targets in attempts to make up what was owed to them. Such activity alienated civilian populations (and potential 'political' support) and earned the criticism of commentators who, in these years, became increasingly aware of the plight of the victims of action of this kind. Perhaps more important still, such undisciplined behaviour quickly led to a decline in military efficiency and effectiveness. No wonder, then, that the need for armies to act in orderly fashion was well understood, and the supposed strict discipline of the Roman army became widely admired. English, French, Bohemian, Swiss, and Burgundian commanders issued ordinances aimed at controlling soldiers' activities, while the development of the military office of constable reflected realization of the need to establish order within an army.

THE EXAMPLE OF THE ANCIENTS

The thinking behind such developments went back a long way. The classical (in particular the Roman) tradition in the waging of war was well known and its chief lessons understood. A man such as Duke Charles the Bold of Burgundy was much aware of the successes of the great soldiers of history; he had tapestries of Alexander and Hannibal hung in the great hall of his palace in Brussels, while 'he took pleasure in the deeds of Julius Caesar, of Pompey, of Hannibal, of Alexander the Great, and of other great and famous men whom he wished to follow and imitate.' Likewise he had a translation of Caesar's *De Bello Gallico* made for him. In this respect, history was useful for its didactic value. Equally so were the military authors of ancient times. The literature favoured by the military aristocracy of the fifteenth century was not that of the traditional chivalric background but, rather, one based upon a growing appreciation of the military values of Rome (in particular) and of what these had to offer. Although copies of the *Stratagemata* of Sextus Julius Frontinus circulated widely, Vegetius's *Concerning Military Matters* remained, a millennium after it was written, the most cited work on the military art to be bequeathed by the ancient world (see page 4). His teaching, in diluted form, was also handed down in works such as the *Siete Partidas* of King Alfonso X of Castile and the *De Regimine Principum* of Giles of Rome, both written in the second half of the thirteenth century, and, more than a century later, in *Les Faits d'Armes et de Chevalerie* of Christine de Pisan, which formed the basis of the *Fayttes of Armes and of Chyvalrye* which William Caxton compiled and printed in England in 1490. In this way the ideas of the classical tradition became more diffused than ever in the new age.

It was to that same tradition that men looked for inspiration in creating a permanent army. Founded upon the practice of providing a king or prince with a personal bodyguard, it soon grew into something bigger. It also developed from the practice of calling upon a largely, but not solely, indigenous force (shades of the tradition of the 'citizen' army of the ancient world) which was being developed in the kingdom of Naples, as well as in the republic of Venice and in Milan, by the middle years of the fifteenth century. Particular military needs and the growing reluctance to rely solely on costly mercenaries both lay behind such advances in organization. In France, the foundations of the permanent army had been laid through the creation of the *Compagnies d'Ordonnance* by Charles VII in 1445; his successor, Louis XI, greatly increased the number of soldiers in royal pay after 1470, by which time his arch-rival, Duke Charles of Burgundy, was doing much the same. The final stage in the Christian reconquest of Spain – the recovery of Moorish Granada in 1492 – was only achieved by maintaining up to 80,000 men through ten hard-fought annual campaigns.

The spread of mass-produced gunpowder weapons, however, swiftly transformed the nature of warfare in the West. Although Charles the Bold would have had little difficulty in understanding the military world of his great-grandfather, Philip the Bold, who had fought at Poitiers in 1356, thanks to the gunpowder revolution he would have been totally baffled by that of his great-grandson, the emperor Charles V, who in 1552 maintained an army of perhaps 150,000 men fighting in five separate theatres on land as well as in the Mediterranean and in the North Atlantic.

CHAPTER 6

The Gunpowder Revolution

In Robert Barret's military treatise of 1598, *The Theory and Practice of Modern Wars*, 'a gentleman' pointed out to 'a captain' that Englishmen in the past had performed wonders with longbows rather than firearms; to which the captain witheringly replied, 'Sir, then was then, and now is now. The wars are much altered since the fiery weapons first came up.' Most professional soldiers of the day agreed. According to Sir Roger Williams, another English veteran writing in 1590: 'We must confess Alexander, Caesar, Scipio and Hannibal, to be the worthiest and most famous warriors that ever were; notwithstanding, assure yourself…they would never have…conquered countries so easily, had they been fortified as Germany, France, and the Low Countries, with others, have been since their days.'

Such recognition of innovation and change was unusual in an age which prided itself on classical precedents and continuity, but the facts were unanswerable. The introduction of 'the fiery weapons', especially artillery, and of new systems of fortifications, had revolutionized the conduct of war.

THE RISE OF THE 'FIERY WEAPONS'

The correct formula for making gunpowder – from saltpeter, sulphur, and charcoal – was first discovered in China, perhaps as early as the ninth century AD; and by the twelfth century Sung armies used both metal bombards and grenades. The new technology gradually spread westwards until by the early fourteenth century several Arabic and European sources mention iron artillery and the first known illustration of a bombard in Europe (dated 1327, right) bears a striking resemblance to the earliest picture from China (dated 1128, left).

It is significant that the first western pictures of guns showed them in action against wooden castle gates, because for at least another century gunpowder weapons in Europe were used mainly against 'soft' targets such as gateways or houses. According to a contemporary chronicle, when the English laid siege to Berwick-upon-Tweed (then just over the Scottish border) in 1333:

> They made many assaults with guns and with other [siege] engines to the town, wherewith they destroyed many a fair house; and churches also were beaten down unto the earth, with great stones that pitilessly came out of [the] guns and of other [siege] engines. And nonetheless the Scots kept well the town…[so that the English] might not come therein…[But they] abided there so long, till those that were in the town failed victuals; and also they were so weary of waking that they knew not what to do.

This account makes clear, on the one hand, that early artillery was used in just the same way as traditional siege engines, such as catapults and trebuchets, to lob missiles into the town in order to damage houses and churches (rather than to

The earliest representation of a gunpowder weapon, discovered in 1985 among a group of figures carved in high-relief on the walls of a Chinese cave temple, dates from 1128. The sculpture could not have been done by anyone who had used a gun-powder weapon, because it would have been much too hot to hold while in use. However, its appearance alongside bows, battle-axes, and swords indicates that by the early twelfth century gunpowder artillery already formed a regular part of the Chinese way of war.

batter down walls); and, on the other, that its impact remained limited – although it may have made the defenders 'weary' by keeping them awake, the town still had to be starved out.

Stone-throwing trebuchets and other 'engines' continued to play their part in sieges well into the fifteenth century. Christine de Pisan's 1409 treatise on military practice considered them to be as essential as iron guns for a successful siege; and they saw action in France on several occasions during the 1420s. But ten years later the bombard at last came into its own. During the second phase of the Hundred Years War in France (see page 96), at a siege in 1430 big guns did 'so much damage to the walls of the castle that the garrison capitulated'; at another in 1433 artillery 'pointed against the gates and walls...damaged them greatly, breaches being made in diverse parts'; while at a third in 1437 gunfire left 'a great part of the walls...thrown to the ground so that [the town] was in no way defensible.'

Although fortresses could still resist if topography placed them beyond the range of the guns, or if the besiegers' artillery proved inadequate, from the 1430s onwards the cannon deployed by the major states of western Europe could successfully reduce most traditional vertical defences to rubble within a matter of days. Harfleur, which had resisted a siege for six weeks in 1415, and for six months in 1440, fell to Charles VII of France in December 1449 after only seventeen days thanks to the damage inflicted by the sixteen bombards founded specially for the task. And Harfleur was just one of over seventy English strongholds in Normandy to be regained by the French between May 1449 and August 1450. Not all were subdued by

The earliest known depiction of gunpowder artillery in Europe dates from 1327 and shows a knight gingerly igniting the charge with a red-hot poker. The design is remarkably similar to the Chinese gun of 1128, depicted opposite, and the weapon (known as a 'bombard') shoots an arrow at a gate. (From the manuscript treatise of Walter de Milamete, *De Nobilitatibus, sapientiis et prudentiis regum*, dated 1326–27).

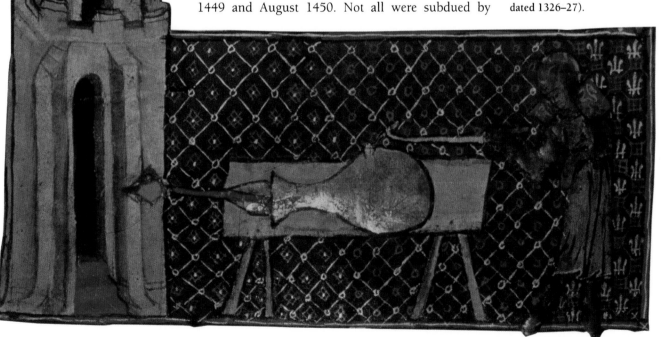

bombardment – some of them were abandoned because they were deemed indefensible while a surprising number fell through treachery – but most surrendered because the French siege train made further resistance impossible. The rapid conquest of Brittany by France and of Granada by Castile, both in the 1480s, were likewise achieved largely by the superior firepower of the victors' cannon.

These striking successes reflected important technological innovations. Early artillery had a limited range, for in order to make an impact firing horizontally the guns needed to be placed close up; yet if they came too near they could be captured or damaged by an enemy sortie. Even in the sixteenth century experts considered less than 100 yards too close to be safe yet more than 300 yards too distant to be effective. The short-barreled gun of the 1320s portrayed on page 107 clearly lacked the power to penetrate reinforced walls even at 100 yards, and the same remained true in the early fifteenth century when the ratio of barrel length to shot size still rarely exceeded 1.5:1. By 1430, however, the ratio had doubled to 3:1, which increased not only accuracy but also muzzle velocity and therefore range. Both of the latter were further enhanced by the discovery at about the same time that, on the one hand, gunpowder prepared in small granules ('corned' powder) was far more effective (some contemporaries reckoned three times more effective) than before; and that, on the other hand, iron or lead projectiles did far more damage to a target than stone shot. Finally, improvements in metallurgy made it possible to cast guns of unprecedented size and impact: among the surviving examples from the earlier fifteenth century, the smallest bombard fired a 5-inch shot and the largest discharged a ball 30 inches in diameter weighing more than 1,500 pounds.

Nevertheless, these monsters were still manufactured in much the same way as a beer barrel, with forged iron staves kept in place by hoops, and this could easily

cause disaster. Thus a large Burgundian piece used against the Turks in 1445 blew up when it was fired too often – first it burst two hoops and at the next round two more hoops and a stave – while in 1460 James II of Scotland died when he stood too close to a gun whose staves exploded when it fired. But other pieces in the Scottish king's siege train, such as 'Mons Meg', proved more durable and effective.

Although casting in bronze rather than iron reduced the weight of big guns significantly, nevertheless only large calibre weapons proved truly effective against reinforced walls. Even two centuries later, just after the outbreak of a major rebellion in 1641, the governors of Ireland saw clearly that:

> Besides the walled towns revolted, there will be very many castles to be gained by no other means than battery; and if we have no other ordnance than culverins the service will be much the more difficult…by reason of the many shots that culverins are forced to make before they can make a breach, whereas cannon clears and rents the walls at first and leaves them so shaken as a few shots afterwards from the culverin breaks down all that the cannon has shaken.

But moving such massive guns to their designated target required a safe route, which usually involved securing the protection of either an army or a navy. In effect this meant that, until the defeat of the enemy's main forces, heavy artillery could only be used either against seaports, as at Constantinople in 1453, or as part of a major campaign in which the field army and the siege train moved together at a snail's pace.

For this reason, artillery seldom played a decisive role in medieval battles, being fired at first rather to intimidate than to harm the enemy: at Crécy (1346) for example, according to a contemporary, the English 'fired off some cannons they had brought to the battle in order to frighten the Genoese [crossbowmen]'. A century later, however, the range of artillery exceeded that of archers, while improvements in design – above all the combination of trunnions with two-wheeled carriages – made it possible to aim individual pieces relatively rapidly (see page 97).

The first known reference to special hand-held firearms in Europe dates from 1364, when an inventory of the arsenal at Perugia in Italy recorded '500 bombards, one span long, which are held in the hand: very handsome and able to pierce any armour'. The earliest illustrations, from around 1400, still show a miniature 'bombard' mounted on a wooden firing frame, and hand-held weapons only seem to have been fired from the chest or the shoulder around 1450. However, for some time portable firearms remained just one weapon among many, far outnumbered in action by bows, crossbows, partisans, and pikes. Even Duke Charles the Bold of Burgundy, who fully appreciated the importance of missile weapons in battle, still trusted in the 1470s to archers rather than to gunners (see page 99). Although it took far less time to train men to fire an arquebus than to pull a bow, so that far more infantry could be mobilized, another century elapsed before firearms became the arbiter of battle in Europe.

Opposite: 'Mons Meg', a bombard cast for the duke of Burgundy in 1449 and later shipped to Scotland, measured 15 feet, weighed 15 tons and fired an 18-inch granite ball. With its aid a number of important strongholds fell, although getting the gun into action could present problems. In 1497, for example, even though 100 workmen and a team of oxen accompanied 'Mons' as she set off from Edinburgh on campaign, she broke down just outside the city and it took three days to repair the carriage. As a rule, bombards, cannon and culverins (a gun able to fire a smaller ball for a longer distance) could only be brought to their target when water transport was available.

Opposite: Field artillery already played an important part in European battles when Diebold Schilling of Bern in Switzerland composed and illustrated his *Chronicle* in 1483. In the foreground two soldiers Jay aside swords to use a primitive elevating device on field pieces balanced on the axle of a two-wheeled carriage. Behind them, other guns are mounted on special carts around the bear standard of Canton Bern, preparing to repel the cavalry massing on the right.

A hand-held gun – half way between a small bombard and a musket – as illustrated by Conrad Kyeser of Eichstätt in Germany. Kyeser composed the first illustrated manual of military technology in 1402 and called it *Bellisfortis*. He began with the weapons of war described by Vegetius, a thousand years earlier, before dealing with those of his own day.

By then, gunpowder had already transformed siege warfare. 'Great towns that once could have held out for a year against all foes but hunger now fell within a month,' noted one chronicler about the artillery that secured the rapid conquest of the Moorish kingdom of Granada in southern Spain during the 1480s. 'When brought up to the walls they were set up with unbelievable rapidity. With only the briefest interval between shots they fired so rapidly and powerfully that they could do in a few hours what in Italy used to take days,' echoed a contemporary historian, describing the guns which the French introduced into Italy after 1494. According to the military commentator Niccolò Machiavelli, writing in 1519, 'No wall exists, however thick, that artillery cannot destroy in a few days.'

The defenders' problem after the gunpowder revolution, therefore, was how to keep the enemy's heavy guns at bay and, failing that, how to limit the damage they could do. By the 1360s many fortified places had installed cannon of their own in order to pick off or keep out of range those of the enemy: Bologna in central Italy had 35 artillery pieces on its walls in 1381; Mechelen in the Netherlands increased its arsenal by an average of fourteen cannon per year between 1372 and 1382; while Dijon in Burgundy possessed thirteen cannon in 1417 and ninety-two in 1445. The 1360s also saw the appearance of gunports (sometimes merely an enlargement of existing arrow-slits), particularly in towers and gatehouses where they could harass an enemy attack. Somewhat later, new towers were added to existing fortifications in order to increase such flanking fire, while both towers and walls were reinforced and thickened so as to withstand the weight and the recoil of the heavy guns placed upon them and to absorb the impact of incoming shots. But these measures, since they remained within the framework of the traditional vertical defences, could only delay the deadly onset of an artillery barrage; they could not avert it.

The Italian architect and humanist, Leon Battista Alberti, first divined the correct response to the bombard. His essay *On the Art of Building*, composed in the 1440s, argued that defensive fortifications would be more effective if 'built in uneven lines, like the teeth of a saw', and speculated that a star-shaped configuration might be best because it would provide interlocking fields of fire. Several other Italian military writers later in the century also argued for polygonal, angled defences; but at first few rulers paid heed and these treatises long remained unpublished. In the last decades of the century, however, although most new fortifications continued to be built according to the traditional vertical design, a few fortresses in central Italy included huge angled bastions at regular intervals in order both to keep away the enemy's artillery and to produce a lethal flanking fire on any attempt at assault. Then, in 1515, the papal port of Civitavecchia received a full circuit of quadrilateral bastions in order to create a complete defensive system of supporting fields of fire. The 'artillery fortress' was born.

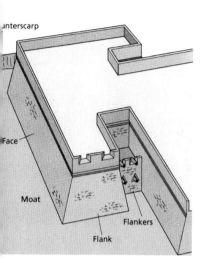

The bastion formed the dominant feature of the new style of defensive fortifications that developed in early modern Europe. Built squat and solid, behind a wide moat, two of its sides pointed outwards and carried heavy artillery to keep besiegers at bay, while the other two – the flanks – stood at right angles to the main wall and bristled with lethal anti-personnel weapons.

ITALIAN STYLE DEFENCE

Contemporaries immediately recognized the bastion system – known in Italy as the 'modern style' (*alla moderna*) and elsewhere as 'the Italian style' (*trace italienne*) – as the only fully effective defence against the gunpowder revolution. In the succinct phrase of the military architect Francesco Laparelli: 'It is impossible to defend a place against an army with artillery without bastions', while the French military expert Raymond de Beccarie, lord of Fourquevaux, held that only fortifications constructed since the year 1510 presented a serious obstacle to a well-armed aggressor:

> Because those fortified before that date cannot be called strong, seeing that the art of making bastions came to light only a short while ago. But those which have received ramparts since then, or in our own day, must (provided they were constructed at leisure and not in haste) be held extremely difficult to capture.

The distinction between speedy and systematic construction was important because building a 'modern' defensive system represented a major undertaking – indeed perhaps the greatest engineering venture of the age. Thus the pentagonal citadel at Antwerp, commissioned in 1567, involved the removal of 650,000 cubic yards of earth and the construction of 221,000 cubic yards of masonry at the record speed of 6,000 cubic yards per month – but even so it took over three years to complete. Clearly such a lengthy venture, especially when applied to an entire city, could only be undertaken in anticipation of a threat, not in response to one.

Niccolò Machiavelli, writing in 1526, perceived three distinct ways of turning a town into an artillery fortress. Two involved starting from scratch: tearing down the existing walls and either building a new defensive system beyond them, so as to include all suburbs and all points (such as neighbouring high ground) from which an enemy might threaten; or else building a smaller circuit than before, abandoning (and levelling) all areas deemed indefensible. However, both these methods involved colossal expense: thus the papacy abandoned its scheme to surround Rome with a belt of eighteen powerful bastions in 1542 when the bills for constructing just the first one came in; and in the 1590s the Venetians resolved to reduce the size of their projected fortress at Palmanova from twelve bastions to nine in order to economize. But creating an artillery fortress also involved high social costs for it affected, by definition, far larger areas than before – particularly the suburbs lying just beyond the medieval walls which often included important buildings such as hospitals, religious houses, and industrial plant (mills and furnaces).

Machiavelli's report of 1526 therefore admitted a third technique of installing modern fortifications which, although inferior to the others, proved both far quicker and far cheaper: a drastic modification of the existing defences, reducing the height and increasing the depth of the existing walls, redesigning the towers and gateways into bastions, and creating an escarpment to give a proper field of fire.

Of course earthen ramparts, when unprotected by brick or stone, would not last for long (contemporary estimates ranged from four years, with minimal maintenance, up to ten) before the weather eroded them. But they proved relatively fast and cheap to erect; they could absorb incoming fire effectively; and, with enough determined defenders, they could defy even the largest armies of the day. Thus in 1552 the city of Metz in Lorraine (eastern France) managed to resist a siege mounted by 55,000 men – probably the largest western field army of the century – despite its lack of a full 'modern' defensive system. The French had taken the city in May, but five months later the huge force assembled by the emperor Charles V arrived to recapture it. Nevertheless the 5,800-man French garrison worked day and night to strengthen the existing fortifications, erecting 'boulevards' (sixteen feet thick in places), with 'flanks' on either side of them, at precisely the most vulnerable places, and backing all walls with ramparts of earth and bales of wool. And so when, on 27 November, having fired over 7,000 rounds against a sector of the curtain wall, the besiegers finally brought some seventy feet of it crashing down, they still dared not launch an assault because it proved impossible to silence the guns on the flanks.

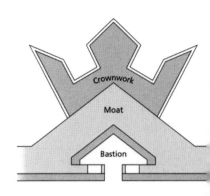

As artillery ranges improved, further fortifications – crownworks (above), ravelins and hornworks (below), were added in order to improve the bastion's defensive capacity.

Later in the century, as both the power of artillery and the techniques of siege-craft improved, such *ad hoc* additions to medieval defences became inadequate. Only the angled bastion offered security, and so the artillery fortress invented in central Italy steadily spread all over Europe. By 1550 the new style predominated in the Italian peninsula and along the Franco-Netherlands and the Habsburg-Ottoman borders. The years between 1529 and 1572 saw the construction of some twenty-six miles of bastioned defences in the Netherlands alone: four citadels, twelve entirely new circuits of walls, and eighteen substantially new circuits. By 1610 fifty artillery fortresses studded France's 600-mile land frontier between Calais and Toulon, while others defended strategic sectors of Germany, England, Ireland, Denmark, Poland, and Russia, as well as colonial outposts such as Havana and Cartagena in the Caribbean, Mombasa, Diu, and Malacca around the Indian Ocean, and Manila, Macao, and Callao on the shores of the Pacific.

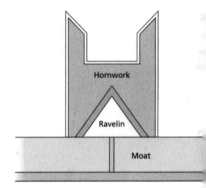

The impact of these developments made itself felt in several ways. First, sieges now took far longer. Gone were the days when seventy and more strongpoints could be wrested from an enemy in a couple of campaigning seasons (see page 107) for, wherever bastions existed, one or at most two fortresses now represented the maximum attainable gain. The capture of each stronghold defended by the *trace italienne* required months if not years. Indeed, laying siege to an artillery fortress could prove almost as arduous as constructing one: a chain of siegeworks had to be built and manned until either the defenders surrendered through starvation or, alternatively, trenches could be advanced far enough to permit either close-range bombardment of the walls or else the sinking of gunpowder mines under a bastion.

However, taking an artillery fortress did not merely take longer; it also involved far more troops. On the one hand, manning the siegeworks required a larger besieging army: Sébastien le Prestre de Vauban, the leading military engineer of the seventeenth century, considered a ratio of ten besiegers to every defender, with a minimum of 20,000 men, essential for success. On the other hand, offensive action represented only one aspect of each campaign, for it was also necessary to defend one's own territory against possible enemy aggression, both by maintaining adequate garrisons and by keeping a potential relief army in reserve.

At one level, the *trace italienne* proved labour efficient: Szigeth in Hungary, defended by a complete circuit of modern walls, successfully defied the Turks in 1566 with a garrison of only 800 men. But with multiple fortresses to defend, even relatively small garrisons could – cumulatively – tie down between 40 and 50 per cent of each state's forces. For its 1640 campaign, the high command of the Spanish Army of Flanders planned to man 208 separate places in the South Netherlands, accounting for 33,399 soldiers at a time when the total strength envisaged for the army stood at only 77,000. Somewhat later, Louis XIV of France also found it prudent to commit almost half his army to manning the bastions of his realm's 'iron frontier': 166,000 men in 221 strongholds in 1688, rising to 173,000 men in 297 fortresses in 1705.

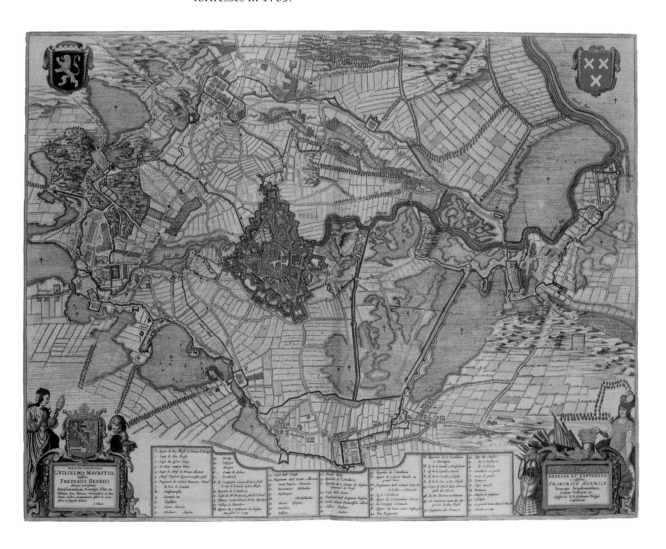

Naturally, effective defence called for more than men alone; it also required guns and ammunition. In the 1440s, the French army had needed only 20 tons of powder and forty qualified gunners for its artillery, but by 1500 the equivalent figures were 100 tons and 100 gunners, and, by 1540, 500 tons and 275 gunners.

The diffusion and multiplication of military resources – both human and material – on this scale created critical new strategic problems. The nineteenth-century German military theorist Carl von Clausewitz, in his influential work *On War*, borrowed from physics the concept of a 'centre of gravity' to explain what seemed to him the essential aim of strategy: 'A theatre of war, be it large or small, and the forces stationed there, no matter what their size, represent the sort of unity in which a single centre of gravity can be identified. That is the place where the decision should be reached.'

Clausewitz drew upon his direct experience of the spectacular French victories of the period 1792–1812 (see Chapter 11), and his extensive reading of military history, to conclude that: 'For Alexander, Gustavus Adolphus, Charles XII, and Frederick the Great, the centre of gravity was their army. If their army had been destroyed, they would all have gone down in history as failures.' But his analysis ignored the fact that the army of Gustavus Adolphus did in fact meet with a major defeat, at Nördlingen in 1634 (two years after the king's death at the indecisive battle of Lützen), and yet this did not lead Sweden to 'fail'. On the contrary, when the war eventually ended with the Peace of Westphalia in 1648, Sweden achieved all her major war aims: extensive territorial gains, adequate guarantees for her future security, and a substantial war indemnity.

The contradiction between the defeat at Nördlingen and the gains at Westphalia stemmed from Sweden's control of numerous artillery fortresses which held steady even after the defeat of the main army. In 1648 the Swedish forces in Germany still numbered 70,000 troops, of whom almost half garrisoned 127 strategically located strongpoints: they thus presented no 'centre of gravity' that an adversary could destroy with a single blow. Other theatres of war dominated by the *trace italienne* in the sixteenth and seventeenth centuries proved equally resistant to the knock-out blows advocated by Clausewitz. The problem was memorably summarized by Don Luis de Requeséns, commander of the Spanish forces striving to suppress the Dutch Revolt. 'There would not be time or money enough in the world,' he warned his master, Philip II, in 1574, 'to reduce by force the twenty-four towns which have rebelled in Holland if we are to spend as long in reducing each one of them as we have taken over similar ones so far.' Or again, slightly later:

Many towns and a battle have been won, each of them a success enough in itself to bring peace and even to win an entire new kingdom elsewhere; but here they have been to no avail…I believe that God for my sins has chosen to show me so many times the Promised Land here, as he did to Moses, but that someone else is to be the Joshua who will enter therein.

Opposite: The siege of a major artillery fortress constituted one of the greatest engineering projects of the age. When the Dutch laid siege to the heavily fortified town of Breda in the Spanish Netherlands in 1637, some 5,000 pioneers dug a double line of earth walls, protected by redoubts, in order to protect the besiegers from attack either by the defenders or by a relief army. After six months of blockade, and after 23,000 cannon balls had been fired at the town, the exhausted Spanish garrison surrendered.

But no Spanish Joshua appeared: instead, the artillery fortresses of Holland and Zeeland defied all of Philip II's efforts at reconquest until his treasury declared bankruptcy in 1575 and his army mutinied and abandoned its posts in 1576. A pattern of warfare in which sieges eclipsed battles in importance and wars eternalized themselves prevailed throughout much of Europe until the eighteenth century.

The proliferation of artillery fortresses enhanced the cost of war in two crucial respects: by increasing the longevity (and decreasing the gains) of each military operation, and by driving up the number of troops and the amount of equipment required to fight wars. Spain's expenditure on war escalated five-fold during the later sixteenth century, an experience shared by other smaller states: in 1565 England's chief minister petulantly complained about 'the uncertainty of the charge of the war, as at this day it is seen that all wars are treble more chargeable than they were wont to be'.

However, the rapidly spiralling burden of war in the sixteenth century stemmed from more than just technology. First, the 'price revolution' of the period increased the cost of everything – whether or not it had to do with war. Foodstuffs, for example, cost on average 4 per cent more each year, and the price of clothes, weapons and other equipment rose accordingly.

This relentless price inflation was, however, associated with a dramatic and sustained expansion in economic activity. Between 1450 and 1580, the population of western Europe almost doubled, steadily augmenting domestic demand so that land cultivation, agricultural output, industrial production, and trade all burgeoned. This in turn made additional resources (whether raised through loans, taxes, or both) available to the states to support war. To be sure, as in the middle ages, many items of military expenditure were offloaded. Above all, towns often had to pay for their own defence. Thus the city of Antwerp financed its splendid new walls (with nine bastions and five monumental gateways), completed between 1542 and 1557, and later its citadel, entirely from loans secured by local taxes on property and foodstuffs (the 'fortification fund' thus created had still not been paid off two centuries later!). Moreover the recurring costs of local defence also normally fell upon individual communities – standard responsibilities included maintaining and manning the walls, as well as lodging and feeding the garrison – so that between 50 and 75 per cent of many municipal budgets went on defence.

However, a fortuitous political development during the period forced most states in western Europe to commit an unprecedented share of their resources to defence, leading to heavy taxation, heavier borrowing, and (ultimately) constitutional crisis if not revolution. The marriage of Maximilian of Habsburg to Mary of Burgundy (the heiress of Duke Charles the Bold) in 1477 began the rapid rise of a minor south German dynasty to European prominence: through a series of further judicious unions and unexpected deaths, their grandson Charles V became first ruler of the Burgundian Netherlands (1506), then king of Spain and Spanish Italy (1516), and

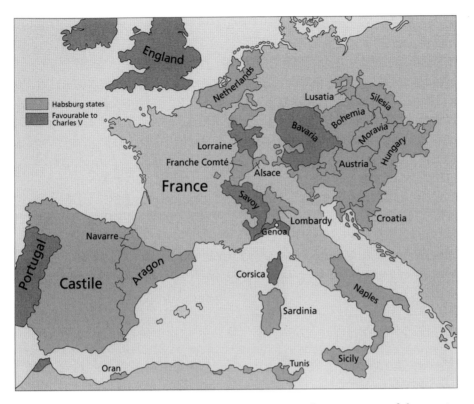

Habsburg states
Favourable to Charles V

England
Netherlands
Lusatia
Silesia
Bohemia
Bavaria
Moravia
Lorraine
Hungary
Franche Comté
Austria
Alsace
France
Croatia
Savoy
Lombardy
Genoa
Navarre
Corsica
Naples
Portugal
Castile
Aragon
Sardinia
Oran
Tunis
Sicily

Western Europe after the gunpowder revolution. Emperor Charles V (1519–58) succeeded to four separate inheritances, one from each of his grandparents. From Ferdinand of Aragon he acquired Sicily, Naples, Sardinia and Aragon, adding Lombardy and Tunis (1535). The legacy of Ferdinand's wife Isabella included Castile, Granada, and the West Indies, to which Charles added Mexico (1519–22) and Peru (1532–34). Mary of Burgundy provided most of the Netherlands, Charles annexing more provinces in the northeast. Her husband Maximilian of Habsburg bequeathed him Austria and Alsace, and helped to secure his election as Holy Roman emperor in 1519, while Charles's brother Ferdinand added Hungary, Bohemia, Moravia, Lusatia and Silesia in 1526. Habsburg territories now surrounded France or – as one Spanish minister put it – 'The heart of the Spanish empire is France.'

finally Holy Roman Emperor (1519). France, once the most powerful state in western Europe, now felt encircled by the territories of a single ruler and for over a century successive French monarchs struggled to break the perceived Habsburg stranglehold. They gradually realized that this could not be achieved by fighting in only one or two theatres at a time. Thus in the autumn of 1552, while Charles V besieged Metz in Lorraine, Henry II maintained one army of observation in Champagne, in case Metz needed to be relieved; another on the northern frontier, where in December it seized Hesdin (thus forcing the emperor to abandon the siege of Metz); and a third in Italy, at first in defence of Parma and then to garrison the rebellious republic of Siena. France thus fought on three fronts at once – four, if one counts the garrisons on other frontiers and the forces occupying Savoy; five if one counts the French navy, operating off the Italian coast in conjunction with the Turks. The French state had never before intervened simultaneously in so many different theatres (although she repeatedly did so in the future).

The combination of the gunpowder revolution, strong price inflation, and Habsburg hegemony in Europe had created a new and costly mould for major international conflicts. The principal motive for fighting remained dynastic rivalry; but, whereas the various conflicts of the middle ages often took place in isolation, after 1500 they frequently became linked. Moreover the simultaneous development of new technology in naval warfare extended hostilities to the high seas, as well as to parts of the Americas, Africa, and Asia, so that henceforth the major European powers also had to maintain expensive navies.

The Age of Guns and Sails PART 3

CHAPTER 7

Ships of the Line

A Chinese war junk encountered by Peter Mundy in 1637 when his English ship tried to force a passage up the Pearl River to Canton. However, although large, well-painted, and provided with two gun decks and gunports, it carried only small guns. Mundy and his shipmates feared far more the Chinese fireships, armed with gunpowder, batteries of rockets with hooks attached to catch masts and rigging, and grapnels under water to catch the cables of enemy vessels as they passed by.

Naval warfare in the West has been dominated for the last three centuries by large warships ('capital ships'), using heavy artillery as their principal weapon, often drawn up in a single line of battle so that their big guns could fire broadsides. The rival fleets at Jutland in 1916, in the age of steam (see pages 282–3), deployed in much the same way as the sailing warships of the Anglo-Dutch wars (fought in much the same location) in the mid-seventeenth century.

It is hard, however, to date with confidence the emergence of this dominant and durable tactic. For example, much uncertainty surrounds the first effective use of gunpowder artillery at sea. Some surviving Chinese bronze and cast-iron naval guns date from the fourteenth century, but all are relatively small. The inscription on a gun dating from the year 1372 reads:

Left naval guard squadron, Chin division, no 42. Fire-barrel with large bowl-shaped muzzle, weight 26 catties. Cast on a fortunate day in the twelfth month of the fifth year of the Hung-Wu reign by the Imperial Foundry Office.

The number '42' proves that a regular programme of naval gun-casting existed during the reign of the first Ming emperor (Hung-Wu, 1368–98), but weapons with a total length of 1 foot 5 inches and weighing barely 35 pounds could only harm people; they could not sink ships. Even in the seventeenth century Chinese war junks still deployed only anti-personnel weapons. A large imperial warship sketched off Canton in 1637 by the English traveller Peter Mundy (left) showed 'doores [i.e. gunports] in their broadsides', but noted that the guns were only light cast-iron pieces weighing 'near 4 or 5 hundredweight each', with a calibre of about 1 inch and firing a ball of about 1 pound. Such weapons could do no structural harm to other ships. According to Mundy, the junks could not carry heavier guns because they were 'so weakly plancked and timbred'.

GUNPOWDER AND GALLEYS

The earliest references to the shipboard use of heavy artillery comes not from China but from Europe. Jean Froissart's chronicle of the Hundred Years War mentions that in the 1340s some Spanish vessels carried 'everything necessary for their defence' such as 'crossbows, iron cannon, and culverins' (a culverin was a gun able to fire a smaller ball for a longer distance), and in due course such armament became standard. Thus a century later, according to the records of the ordnance office of the dukes of Burgundy, each galley in the ducal fleet carried (at least in theory) five heavy guns 4 feet long, 'each firing a [stone] shot of 4 inches diameter' and 'each [was] provided with three chambers, each chamber capable of being used for all guns', together with two lighter pieces also supplied with interchangeable chambers.

Overleaf: In Quiberon Bay in Brittany on 20 November 1759 British warships under Admiral Edward Hawke cornered a French fleet attempting to invade Scotland and attacked under full sail, despite 45-mile-an-hour winds.

Now the galley – long, shallow, and propelled primarily by oars – had already served for centuries as the premier warship in European waters. But the introduction of heavy artillery precipitated major design changes: the ram gave way to a special artillery platform at the prow carrying one heavy cannon in the centre flanked by some lighter pieces. The largest Spanish galley in 1506, for example, carried a 'bombard of iron' weighing about 4 tons as a centreline gun, together with two others half its size and one more weighing just over a ton. These weapons all fired stone projectiles but by the 1530s bronze ordnance, throwing metal shot, had replaced them: a centreline cannon, flanked by either two or four other heavy pieces and a number of lighter anti-personnel weapons, became standard. The centreline guns aboard galleys were unquestionably the most powerful gunpowder weapons afloat: although 50-pounders predominated, some Venetian galleys in the mid-sixteenth century carried 60-pounder (7-inch calibre) and even 100- and 120-pounder weapons. The detailed records of the Republic's test-firing programme, as well as contemporary chronicles, suggest that these cannon possessed an effective range of up to 1,000 yards and a maximum range of 2 miles. From the 1540s, an even more powerful oared fighting ship appeared: the galeass, propelled by sails as well as by oars, carried eight or more heavy guns (divided between the poop and the prow) together with an appropriate complement of lighter, anti-personnel weapons. The Neapolitan galeass *San Lorenzo*, which sailed with the Spanish Armada in 1588, boasted some fifty guns, including ten cannon and culverins.

In the 1550s, the design of Mediterranean galleys changed again as vessels propelled by banks of three oars, each pulled by one man, gave way to others in which three or more men worked a single enormous oar. This development permitted a modest increase in the size of galleys, and a substantial rise in the number of oarsmen – from a total of 144 to 180 or even 200 per galley – and in the complement of fighting personnel. Some vessels now carried 400 men, a population larger than that of many European villages, so that (as one seventeenth-century galley captain commented) 'When every man is at his post, only heads can be seen from prow to stern.' This numerical increase produced two further consequences. First, adding more men significantly reduced the provisions per man that could be carried. The situation proved particularly serious with water: since each man consumed at least half a gallon a day, each galley now needed to cram 200 gallons of water into its limited storage space for each day at sea. Every increase in the ship's company thus reduced the distance at which a vessel could operate away from its home base. Second, even though the cost of maintaining each galley tripled between 1520 and 1590, the increasing ability of European states to mobilize resources for war led to ever-larger galley fleets. Charles V had fought his Mediterranean campaigns with under 100 galleys, but his son Philip II of Spain mobilized almost 200.

Taken together, these four developments – galleys that were larger, more heavily manned, more powerfully gunned, and

The gun-deck of a sixteenth-century Spanish galley often carried a 50-pounder cannon flanked by two 10-pounders, with a stubby stone-thrower to the right and a lighter piece to the left. The upper deck contained an assortment of breach-loading weapons. Note that the galley's 'beak', normally a pointed ram, has been sawn off, to allow the main centreline piece to depress fully and fire directly into the enemy vessel as it made contact, as the Christians did at the battle of Lepanto (1571).

more numerous – transformed the nature of naval warfare under oars. On the one hand, the effective range of the major fleets became severely curtailed; on the other, the number of ports and anchorages capable of serving as effective bases dwindled. Galley warfare in the Mediterranean turned increasingly into a series of huge frontal assaults on heavily fortified positions (Djerba 1560; Malta 1565; Cyprus 1570–71; Tunis 1573–74) while the rare major battles (Prevesa 1538; Lepanto 1571)

The Battle of Lepanto 1571

The battle of Lepanto on 7 October 1571 (below) was both the largest European engagement of the sixteenth century, involving perhaps 170,000 men, and the first major battle at sea to be decided by firepower. The 208 galleys and six galeasses of the Christian navy mounted some 1,815 pieces of artillery, as against only 750 on the 230 Turkish galleys, and their impact proved devastating. Shortly before the battle, Don John of Austria (commander-in-chief of the Christian forces) asked a senior adviser about the best moment to discharge his ships' artillery. 'Fire when you are so close to the enemy that you are covered with his blood,' came the chilling response; 'The sound of the galleys colliding and of the artillery discharging should occur at the same time.' As a result, after the Christian assault, broken and sinking ships 'lay scattered over about eight miles of water. The sea was entirely covered, not just with masts, spars, oars, and broken wood, but with an innumerable quantity of corpses that turned the water as red as blood.' In all, the Ottoman fleet lost some 200 galleys, together with their artillery, stores, and some 30,000 men. In addition, the resounding defeat sparked off several risings in Greece and Albania which seemed, for a time, to herald the collapse of Ottoman rule in the entire Balkan peninsula. It appeared to be one of the decisive battles of the century.

But it was not. Galleys could be built with relative ease, and the Mediterranean coasts under Ottoman control boasted numerous boat-builders with the necessary experience, shipyards, and stocks of raw material to start work immediately on replacing the vessels lost at Lepanto. Some reserve galleys may also have been ready in the imperial arsenals of Sinop and Istanbul, where (in any case) a massive building programme began as soon as news of the defeat arrived. By April 1572, a mere six months after the defeat, some 200 galleys and five galeasses stood ready for service.

occurred at or near the major fleet anchorages. By 1600, except for coastal defence and for piracy, in most of Europe the galley had fallen into disuse because the cost of maintaining a force of oared fighting vessels capable of achieving major strategic goals had grown prohibitively high. Galley fleets continued to operate only in the Baltic, where the small rocky islands fringing the coasts complicated navigation by sail: the Russians used galleys to raid the Swedish coast in 1719–21, and the Swedes destroyed most of the Russian navy at Svensksund in 1790 thanks to the imaginative use of heavily gunned galleys. Elsewhere, however, they collapsed under the burden of their own weight.

THE CAPITAL SHIP

The origins of the capital ship, which replaced the galley as Europe's premier warship, lie in the fifteenth century. The medieval shipwrights of the Atlantic ports specialized in producing sailing vessels built 'clinker' style, with caulked overlapping planking around a simple shell. Some were very large and could be adapted to military use. Thus Henry V of England (1413–22) possessed several great warships of traditional design: one, the *Gracedieu* of 1418, built with two layers of planking and (probably) two masts, measured perhaps 80 feet from stem to stern, weighed 1,400 tons and carried four cannon (albeit all of them small and fired from the upper deck). Soon afterwards, however, starting in Spain and Portugal, shipwrights along Europe's Atlantic seaboard began to build their vessels around a complete skeleton, with ribs and braces, fitting the planks 'carvel' style, without any overlap. The added strength conferred by this technique made possible a more complex rig: now three and sometimes four masts carried a variety of sails, some square to provide motive power and some triangular to assist lateral movement. By 1500 the 'full-rigged ship' – one of the greatest technological inventions of medieval Europe – had become the most important sailing vessel in the Atlantic. With its great holds, it served the needs of the burgeoning European economy; with its

The Mediterranean in the sixteenth century became a naval battleground between Christians (in the north and west) and Muslims (to the south and east). Gradually, isolated outposts fell – Peñón de Vélez to Spain, Rhodes and Cyprus to the Turks – and the strategic bases in the central Mediterranean came under more frequent attack. Tunis, for example, changed hands four times: captured by the Christians in 1535 and 1573, retaken by the Turks in 1570 and 1574. But then peace broke out: first the Venetians (1573) and then Spain (1577) concluded an armistice with the Turks and the great galley fleets gave way to smaller pirate squadrons.

superb sailing qualities, it facilitated voyages of discovery and overseas colonization; with its powerful construction, capable of absorbing the recoil of outgoing gunfire as well as the impact of incoming rounds, it opened the way for the ship-smashing broadside.

The broadside, however, also required the invention of hinged gunports in the hull, for heavy artillery could only be safely deployed along the sides of a ship's lower decks. Although visual evidence reveals the existence of gunports as early as the 1470s, the first true sailing warship capable of firing broadsides seems to have been the 1,000-ton *Great Michael*, launched in Scotland in 1511, which carried twelve cannon on each side as well as three 'grete basilisks' at the bow and stern and some 300 smaller pieces. She served as the flagship of a Scottish navy of at least eleven vessels. The fleet scarcely survived the death of its creator, King James IV, in 1513 – the *Great Michael* was sold to France the following year to save money (her running costs alone absorbed 10 per cent of the total state income!). However it endured long enough to provoke Henry VIII of England to commence a rival and longer-lasting programme of naval construction. The *Great Harry*, launched a year after the Scottish flagship and possibly built in imitation of her, also displaced 1,000 tons and carried forty-three heavy and 141 light guns, with a combined weight of 100 tons (the largest piece, of 12-inch calibre, measured 18 feet). When Henry died in 1547, having defeated a major French invasion force in the Solent two years

The Armadas of 1588 and 1688

In 1688, just a century after the Spanish Armada of 130 vessels and 30,000 men set forth on its disastrous attempt to invade England, a Dutch Armada under the command of Prince William of Orange, with some 463 vessels and 40,000 men, succeeded. The contrasts between the two enterprises could hardly have been greater: the Spaniards had taken almost three years to prepare their expedition, the Dutch took just three months; the former tied down almost all the naval resources of its creator, the latter absorbed only a fraction; the first never managed to land its assault troops, the second captured London and established a new government within a month and William of Orange became William III of England, Scotland, and Ireland. His success, however, provoked a declaration of war by Louis XIV of France that plunged Britain, the Dutch Republic, and France into a war that lasted, with one brief intermission, until 1713 (see page 174).

Left: the formation to be adopted by the Dutch fleet, as sketched by William III's leading adviser, Hans Willem Bentinck.

previously, his navy consisted of fifty-three well-armed warships with a total displacement of some 10,000 tons.

This fleet, like that of James IV of Scotland, also proved too expensive to last. By 1555 it had dwindled to only thirty vessels, and the capital ships had declined from twelve to three. By 1588, however, although the Royal Navy still included only thirty-four fighting ships, eighteen of them exceeded 300 tons and the total displacement of the fleet exceeded 12,000 tons. All vessels were mobilized in that year against the Armada sent by Philip II against England, and the surviving Spanish accounts remarked on the constant artillery barrage maintained by the queen's ships: some claimed that the English seemed able to fire four or five rounds in the time it took the Armada to fire once, while veterans of Lepanto considered that, in comparison, the cannonading they experienced in the Channel and the North Sea in 1588 was twenty times more furious.

This is surprising, because the technique of long range naval battery, like the full-rigged ship, originated in Spain and Portugal. The *Instructions* provided in 1500 by the king of Portugal to the commander of a fleet dispatched to the Indian Ocean specified that, when he met any hostile ships, 'you are not to come to close quarters with them if you can avoid it, but only with your artillery are you to compel them to strike sail...so that this war may be waged with greater safety, and so that less loss may result to the people of your ships.' The precision of these orders suggests that they were not new in 1500. In any case they came into immediate use, with Portuguese fleets overseas deployed in line ahead to engage their enemies, firing one broadside and then putting about in order to return and discharge the other (see page 130). But the Portuguese failed to maintain their technological edge in naval warfare. In his treatise of 1555, *The Art of War at Sea*, Fernando Oliveira recognized that 'at sea we fight at a distance, as if from walls or fortresses, and we seldom come close enough to fight hand-to-hand.' He too recommended the single line ahead as the ideal combat formation, but he advised captains to carry heavy weapons only at the prow, like a galley, with lighter pieces, mostly muzzle-loaders, on the broadsides. 'Do not place heavy artillery on small ships,' he warned, 'because the recoil will pull them apart.' Even in 1588, the armament aboard the Portuguese galleons that led the Spanish Armada remained relatively light: although each vessel carried up to fifty guns, most appear to have been 14-pounders or less. By this time all the galleons of the English navy carried three or four 30-pounders, as well as a broadside of twenty 17- and 14-pounders. So the Royal Navy could fire heavier guns, as well as fire them more often. Although English gunfire sank only one Armada ship outright in 1588, several others suffered such damage from artillery bombardment that they failed to survive the journey back to Spain. Even the flagship, the 1,000-ton Portuguese galleon *San Martín*, only made it home thanks to two great hawsers tied around her damaged sides.

English operational records for 1588 have been lost, precluding greater precision on the navy's achievement against the Armada. However the surviving documents

This four-masted Portuguese warship, with a broadside of twenty-four guns and two 'stern-chasers', formed the frontispiece to the *True History and Description of a Journey to America* by the German traveller Hans Staden in 1557. The crew sets the sails, while the pilots make observations of the sun (with a sextant) and the moon (with a backstaff.) These and other capital ships protected the rich trading vessels that sailed between Portugal and her overseas empire in Brazil, Africa, and Asia.

The *Mary Rose*, one of Henry VIII of England's warships, pictured in 1545. The large number of guns carried proves that the importance of artillery at sea had been fully appreciated by this time; however, the importance of keeping the lower gunports closed in rough seas had not – for while moving down the Solent later that year to thwart a French invasion, the *Mary Rose* heeled over, flooded, and sank.

for the 1596 raid on Cadiz carried out by sixteen galleons of the Royal Navy, the cutting edge of a fleet of over 120 English and Dutch vessels, shed more light. Thus the 400-ton *Dreadnought* carried thirty-five guns, of which seventeen fired heavy calibre ammunition. She left England with 576 iron roundshot for these seventeen guns and fired 353 (or 61 per cent) of them. Meanwhile the 500-ton *Rainbow* carried twenty-six guns, of which no less than twenty-five fired heavy calibre ammunition. She left England with 670 iron roundshot for these weapons and fired 392 (or 58 per cent) of them. Now discharging almost 400 heavy calibre rounds per ship in a single campaign – many of them on a single day (21 June 1596) when, according to a contemporary account, 'infinite store of shot was spent between our ships, the town and galleys, much to their damage and nothing to our loss' – marked an entirely new style of naval warfare.

The Armada campaign and the Cadiz raid had significant consequences. First, they revealed Spain's weakness at sea, leading on the one hand to more aggressive and confident English attacks on the possessions of Philip II and, on the other, to the creation, for the first time, of a Spanish High Seas fleet to parry the new threat. Second it encouraged others to try their luck against the demonstrated vulnerability of Philip II's global empire. The Dutch, like the Spaniards, began to build a proper navy. At first their ships were intended primarily for coastal defence and remained relatively small, but from 1596 larger vessels capable of carrying war to the enemy were laid down. By 1621 the Dutch navy included nine capital ships of 500 tons or more.

A naval arms race now began, with all the major Atlantic powers vying to produce more and bigger warships. The 1,200-ton *Prince Royal*, launched in England in 1610, was probably the largest warship in the world; she was certainly the most heavily armed, with fifty-five guns weighing just over 83 tons. The same was true of the 1,500-ton *Sovereign of the Seas*, launched in 1637, with 104 guns weighing over 153 tons. Measuring 127 feet long by 43 feet wide, she was in fact only one-third smaller than the *Victory* (measuring 170 by 53 feet), the British flagship at Trafalgar in 1805. These warships, and dozens more like them, all exceeded the size of the average country house and carried more artillery than many fortresses of the day.

THE LINE OF BATTLE

However, seventeenth-century capital ships carried less than half the sail of an equivalent vessel of the Nelsonian era, making them unwieldy to handle (the more so since the steering wheel did not replace the tiller until the early eighteenth century); and it was in part their cumbersome character that made fighting in a single line ahead so attractive. Precisely the same tactic laid down for the Portuguese fleet in Asia in 1500 was echoed in the 'Instructions for the better ordering of the fleet in fighting' issued to the English navy in the North Sea in 1653:

> As soon as they see the *General* [the flagship] engage…then each squadron shall take the best advantage they can to engage with the enemy next unto them; and in order thereunto the ships of every squadron shall endeavour to keep in line with the chief.

The Dutch already favoured the same tactic, and so the battles of the Anglo-Dutch Wars (1652–54, 1665–67, and 1672–74) saw two giant fleets of capital ships, strung out in a single line for 5 miles or more, locked in a deadly artillery duel that could last for days. The three naval battles fought in the North Sea during the summer of 1673 between the Dutch and English fleets, for example, each involved between 130 and 150 capital ships – now known as 'ships of the line' – with a combined firepower of between 9,000 and 10,000 guns.

The keel of the *Sovereign of the Seas*, the first three-deck warship ever built, was laid down in January 1636 in the presence of Charles I of England, and she was launched twenty months later, at a total cost of over £40,000 (half of it for the wages of the men who built her). Her principal architect, Phineas Pett, had intended her to carry ninety guns, but King Charles over-rode him and increased the total to 102, making her the largest warship of her day.

St James's Day Fight, 25 July 1666, took place off the coast of Kent and pitted eighty-nine English warships against a Dutch fleet of eighty-eight. The two navies deployed in a line stretching over 9 miles and exchanged broadsides at close range for the entire day, the thunder of the guns rattling windows 50 miles inland. Nevertheless, only two Dutch and one English vessel were lost and, though the action clearly favoured the English, they managed to blockade the Dutch coast for only a short time. The following year, in view of their inability to win a decisive victory, the two sides made peace.

Although these ships bristled with artillery, cannon balls alone rarely sank them. Even a 32-pound shot, usually the heaviest fired by a ship of the line, did not make much of a hole as it pierced a ship. The oak splinters that exploded from the point of entry wounded and killed the crew, but left the structural integrity of the ship largely intact. Captains most commonly struck their colours only when fire threatened to destroy their vessel, when casualties among the crew reached unacceptable levels, or when the ship could no longer manoeuvre.

The naval arms race therefore continued. By 1688, the Dutch navy numbered 102 warships (including sixty-nine ships of the line), the English 173 (including 100 ships of the line), and the French 221 (including ninety-three ships of the line). Almost all the capital ships were two- or three-deckers carrying between fifty and 100 heavy guns – indeed their basic similarity gave rise to a common ruse: flying false colours in order to deceive enemy shipping – and they proved fairly evenly matched. Thus although William III's daring descent on England in November 1688 (see page 124) took the French by surprise, Louis XIV's navy secured command of the Channel the following year, permitting a major invasion of Ireland, and in 1690 it defeated the combined Anglo-Dutch battlefleet off Beachy Head (a headland on the Sussex coast).

As with Lepanto, however, a single naval victory did not suffice if the vanquished retained formidable strength at sea. In the words of the defeated English admiral in 1690: 'Most men were in fear that the French would invade, but I was always of another opinion, for I always said that whilst we had a fleet in being, they would not make the attempt.' He was right, and after Beachy Head England's 'fleet in being' steadily increased in size: from 173 ships with 6,930 guns and a total displacement of almost 102,000 tons in 1688 to 323 ships with 9,912 guns and a total displacement of 160,000 tons by the end of the century. Of the new vessels, seventy-one were ships of the line.

Few, however, were 'first rates': the huge men-of-war, burdened with 90–100 guns, proved too expensive to build and too unwieldy to operate except in a flat calm. Gradually, the weight of guns relative to the hull size declined, and rigging steadily improved thanks to the addition of more sails, of reef points for shortening sail, and of foot ropes to allow sailors a more secure hold on the yards. In the eighteenth century the French, who had developed a more scientific school of ship design (in which each dockyard had a 'construction council' consisting of senior serving officers and chief shipwrights), pioneered two new influential warship designs: the two-decked seventy-four-gun capital ship, the most versatile and seaworthy of all ships of the line, from 1719; and the lighter frigate, with twenty-six guns deployed on a single deck, from 1744. Other naval powers soon followed suit, so that the 'seventy-four' and the frigate became standard; but French warships continued throughout the eighteenth century to include innovations that revealed their builders to be in the forefront of naval design and construction – so much so that British admirals sometimes converted French prizes into their flagships!

COUNTING THE COST

The cost of the naval arms race proved crippling, however. The expense of building a capital ship, which stood at only £2,500 in 1588, had soared to £13,000 a century later; by then, with over 4,000 workers, the naval dockyards formed by far the largest industrial enterprise in Britain. Moreover, while less than 16,000 men manned the fleet that defeated the Spanish Armada in 1588, Cromwell's navy in the 1650s included up to 30,000 and William III's in the 1690s numbered 45,000. Where were these men found? Only the merchant fleet could supply the trained sailors necessary to man a navy in wartime, and so an important relationship existed between the size of the merchant marine and the battle fleet. Here England reaped the benefits of her island status, which meant that all foreign trade must by definition be seaborne, for even when half the crews aboard her warships were 'pressed' men, taken into state service by force, most of them were used to managing ships at sea. Finding a suitable and sufficient officer corps to command the ships proved somewhat more difficult, but gradually the permanence of the naval establishment began to attract men of substance to serve as professional officers.

England's navy consumed £1.5 million during the war against Spain between 1585 and 1604, £9 million during the period 1648–60, and almost £19 million during William III's War (1689–97). No other European state could match this level of spending, for the simple reason that all except England were continental powers obliged to maintain a large land army. This did not mean that the French and the Dutch could no longer compete at sea – on a number of occasions in the later seventeenth century, and again around 1780, they did (with some success); but so long as England could count on continental allies to threaten its enemies by land, they could not destroy England's supremacy at sea.

EUROPE'S FIRST SEABORNE EMPIRES

The naval arms race in the North Atlantic thus culminated in a costly stalemate in home waters. It had, however, created fleets capable of pursuing strategic objectives far from home. Once again, the Portuguese showed the way. In 1502, for example, a squadron of five small caravels (small warships), three large carracks (larger, armed merchant vessels), and ten other craft met with an Indian fleet of some twenty large and sixty small ships off the Malabar coast. The Indians, encouraged by their numerical superiority, closed for battle, whereupon the Portuguese commander

> ordered the caravels to come one astern of the other in a line and to run under all the sail they could carry, firing their guns whenever they could, and he did the same with the carracks to their rear. Each of the caravels carried thirty men, with four heavy guns below, and above six falconets and ten light pieces placed on the quarter deck and in the bows…The carracks carried six guns on each side, with two smaller ones at the poop and the prow, and eight falconets and many smaller guns.

As they sailed among the Malabar fleet, each vessel fired its broadside and 'made haste to load again, loading the guns with bags of powder which they had measured out ready for this purpose so that they could load again very rapidly.' Then, 'having passed through, they turned about' and did the same again. According to this account, their big guns aimed at the waterline while the smaller ones concentrated on the masts, the rigging, and the people thronging the deck. Several enemy vessels sank, others suffered extensive damage, and the loss of life was appalling. But the Portuguese emerged more or less unscathed for, although the Indian ships 'fired the many guns that they carried, they were all small' and did no structural damage; moreover the Europeans kept mainly below the decks, so that neither bullets nor arrows harmed them. The shattered remnants of the Malabar fleet fled.

Opposite: The caravel (top) proved to be the ideal vessel for exploration and coastal trade. It could manoeuvre inshore and sail close to the wind. It could also carry large cargoes (or crews) in relation to its size and, as in this example drawn by a Dutch observer in 1564, an impressive gun battery. The Spaniards and Portuguese, however, also constructed far larger trading vessels: the carracks (such as the one opposite below, in a painting of c.1540). These ships – some of them, at 2,000 tons, the largest wooden ships ever built – possessed vast holds for cargo, with gunports cut in the lower deck for heavy artillery. In the words of the Portuguese poet Camoës, the caravels and carracks 'sailed the oceans that none had sailed before' and opened the way for European conquests overseas.

Other naval encounters between the Portuguese and their adversaries resulted in similar victories, making possible the creation of a chain of forts and trading posts around the shores of the Indian Ocean and into the China Sea, and the regulation of most seaborne commerce in south Asian waters. The Europeans had taken with them the adage, proven time after time in the Middle Ages, that they could not have trade without war or war without trade.

Perhaps, however, the naval gun and the line of battle made the acquisition of empire too easy. In the words of a disillusioned Portuguese writer in the later seventeenth century:

> From the Cape of Good Hope onwards, we were unwilling to leave anything outside our control. We were anxious to lay bur hands on everything in that huge stretch of over 5,000 leagues from Sofala to Japan. And what was worse...we set about this without calculating our strength, or thinking that...this conquest could not last for ever.

In the 1590s, both English and Dutch fleets entered the Indian Ocean and began to challenge Portuguese control of trade. In 1602, for example, the fleet sent by the Dutch East India Company comprised fourteen ships, of which nine exceeded 400 tons, while the fleet sent in 1603 included the 900-ton capital ship *Dordrecht*, armed with six 24-pounder and eighteen 8- or 9-pounder guns. Between 1602 and 1619 the Company had established fortresses and major trading posts in thirteen places, and sent out 246 ships to Asia; by contrast only seventy-nine Portuguese vessels, albeit some of them very large, reached their destination in India. Only forty-three returned.

The balance of power in the Americas did not tip so far against the Iberian powers – but, then, the Iberians had managed to establish their power there far more effectively. Within a generation of Columbus's fortuitous Caribbean landfall in 1492, by a combination of force, treachery, and luck, a small number of Spaniards had established effective control over 750,000 square miles of the New World, an area four times as large as the peninsula of the Old World from which they came, and over a population of some twenty million souls, seven times that of Spain. In addition, and equally remarkably, thanks to the superior sailing qualities and arma- ment of their vessels, they had turned the ocean connecting southern Europe with the Caribbean into a Spanish lake. The next generation of invaders and explorers did almost as well: the frontiers of European occupation were steadily advanced, even though the native population contained within them inexorably declined, and in the wake of Magellan's circumnavigation of the globe in 1519–22, the Pacific too became a Spanish lake. It seems ironic that, just as the West faced its most serious challenge by land for several centuries (in the shape of the Ottoman Turks), by sea it commenced a period of unprecedented expansion, for the sixteenth century was not only an era of military and naval revolution: it was also the golden age of the conquistador.

CHAPTER 8

The Conquest of the Americas

'They bear no arms, nor know thereof; for I showed them swords and they grasped them by the blade and cut themselves through ignorance. They have no iron.' Thus wrote Christopher Columbus of the first natives he encountered in the New World on 12 October 1492. Arriving in the Bahamas on board one of three lightly armed ships widely used in voyages of exploration, Columbus reached a part of the world unknown to the ancients.

While wrong about so many things, about this Columbus was right: the native peoples of the New World used no iron. Most indigenous Americans employed only stone age technologies, encountering iron weapons and even iron tools for the first time only after Columbus's arrival. In their previous voyages of exploration to Africa and Asia Europeans had encountered people who, like themselves, used iron weapons and tools. When the natives on San Salvador in 1492 'cut themselves through ignorance' they showed themselves to be completely unfamiliar with the sharp cutting edge that only iron can hold. This iron edge would be central to the conquest, for iron (sometimes in its purer form, as steel) formed the principal component of powerful swords, knives, daggers, and lances, and a crucial element in crossbows, all of which could be used to inflict deadly injury; it was also the central component of firearms, the arquebus and the cannon. Finally it constituted the key element of the defensive devices, helmets and cuirasses (metal vests and shoulder protectors), by which Europeans would shield themselves from native weapons.

According to Columbus, the natives carried bows of the same size as those used in Europe, but with longer arrows made of a cane or a reed of sharp wood, sometimes with a fish's tooth at the end. Indeed, hunting and fishing tools throughout the Americas comprised rods, bones, or teeth; hence iron hooks for hunting and fishing, iron tips for arrows, iron hatchets for cutting timber and iron knives for carving soon became the most sought after trade-goods everywhere in the Americas since they made hunting and fishing for food so much easier than before. Seventeenth-century Mohawks near Albany, New York, even nicknamed Europeans 'the iron-workers' for this reason. But iron tips for arrows, and iron knives for carving or hatchets for wood cutting could also be used as weapons, eventually changing for ever the way that natives fought wars in the Americas.

At first the Caribbean peoples Columbus met showed greater interest in those weapons most like their own, particularly the iron-reinforced crossbow that shot arrows further and penetrated a target more deeply than conventional bows and arrows. But the advantages of the unfamiliar steel swords were not so immediately apparent. Upon seeing the Tainos' interest in the crossbow, Columbus drew his sword from the scabbard and showed it to them, saying that it was as powerful as the crossbow. And these two – the sword and crossbow – would be the only weapons used in the Europeans' first military encounters in the Caribbean.

Aztec warriors armed with bronze-tipped arrows and obsidian-rimmed wooden clubs confront steel-helmeted and armed Spaniards in this scene from the history of the conquest of Mexico compiled in the 1580s by the Dominican friar, Diego Durán.

CANNON: MAKING AN IMPRESSION

The most impressive tools of war that the westerners brought with them to the New World were their latest technological inventions – their arquebuses, and more importantly their cannon: cast iron and bronze weapons that had already begun to change the shape of European warfare. Europeans throughout the Americas were anxious to show off their newest and most powerful weapons to the peoples of the New World, who were suitably impressed. After ordering the firing of a Turkish bow on Santo Domingo on 26 December 1492, Columbus ordered two gunpowder weapons, a large cannon and a spingard (forerunner of the arquebus), to be fired and 'when the king [chief] saw the effect of their force and what they penetrated he was astonished. And when his people heard the shots they all fell to the ground.' The natives then gave Columbus a large mask decorated with considerable quantities of gold.

The bombardment of Tenochtitlán

Cannon were useful in shows of strength during the conquest of the New World, but they were not usually needed in the fighting. The most famous exception was the siege of Tenochtitlán, the Aztec capital at the heart of present-day Mexico City.

The Spaniards reached the capital on 8 November 1519, and immediately seized the Aztec leader Montezuma as a hostage. Nearly six months later they massacred a group of native lords at a dinner and provoked an explosive response. Despite their cannon and arquebuses, and tens of thousands of native allies, Spanish soldiers suffered their greatest defeat and heaviest casualties in the first fifty years of conquest. Hundreds of them were killed – perhaps as many as 450 Spaniards, along with 4,000 of their Indian allies – and the remainder had to retreat from the capital on 1 July 1520. To avenge the defeat Cortés returned and adopted standard European tactics of siege warfare.

Tenochtitlán was an island in the middle of a lake, tethered to the mainland by three causeways. After militarily severing the capital from its lakefront allies, and then stationing three armies of 200 Spaniard and 25,000 Indian troops at the entrance to each causeway, Cortés managed to isolate the city. He then attacked the city's aqueduct and destroyed its fresh water supply. With the city thus isolated, mounting his artillery on each of thirteen brigantines specially constructed to carry the weight of men and armament, Cortés began to bombard the city in mid-May 1521. But while he handily dominated the water around the city, and captured the three causeways, he could not force its surrender, on one occasion barely escaping capture and execution himself. He was forced to land his cannon and destroy the city building by building, stone by stone. When the siege ended three months later, not a single building remained intact. A new city had to be constructed on the site of the old.

Cortés trains his cannon and crossbows on Tenochtitlán (top, from brigantines on the lake; bottom on land, building by building). This episode produced epic laments and poetry written down in the Nahua language, years and sometimes decades after the event, portraying in moving terms the devastation and the human costs of the siege for civilians. It also produced numerous triumphalist accounts from the victorious Spaniards.

While not every conqueror received gold for demonstrating his weapons, countless Europeans ordered their cannon to be fired in order to impress the natives with their military capabilities. In 1536, on his second voyage up the Saint Lawrence, Jacques Cartier had a dozen small shipboard artillery pieces fired into woods opposite the ships. The Algonkian were, according to Cartier, 'so much astonished as if the heavens had fallen upon them and began to howl and to shriek in such a very loud manner that one would have thought hell had emptied itself there.'

Cases of mistaken identification also occurred. Thus on 29 August 1564 a lightning bolt hit near the French settlement on the Florida coast causing a fire that consumed over 500 acres. As soon as the fire had burned itself out, six Indians went to the leader of the French expedition. After presenting him with several baskets full of grain, pumpkins, and raisins the Timucua chief said that 'he found the cannon shot that I had fired towards his settlement very strange. It had caused an infinity of green prairies to burn…and he thought he would see his home on fire.' Realizing that the Timucua had seen the giant flash of lightning and believed that it had come from a cannon rather than being an act of nature the French commander, Laudonnière, in his own words 'dissembled'. He told the leader that he had fired the cannon to indicate his displeasure and that he had spared the Indians homes even though he could have just as easily ordered their destruction. He had fired the weapon 'in order for him to recognize my power'. For similar reasons, Hernán Cortés in Mexico ordered a demonstration of cannon fire before a native scribe who drew his impressions on bark paper to be carried to the emperor Montezuma. Indians throughout the Americas had no trouble recognizing the degree of destruction possible with cannon.

STONE AND BRONZE WEAPONS

Nevertheless, the ability of the Aztecs and their allies not merely to halt, but occasionally to defeat and inflict substantial casualties on Spanish troops suggest not only a powerful and highly motivated fighting force, but also effective weapons. In three regions the indigenous technologies had moved from the stone age into the first metal age (the bronze): the central Andean highlands, a northern spur of the Andes (present-day Colombia), and highland Mexico. Of the three bronze-age peoples only those of highland Mexico had developed significant military uses for metal. The copper-tipped arrows and javelins the Spaniards first encountered among the Tlaxcalans so impressed Cortés that he ordered surrounding villages to make

Armed native warriors allied with the Spaniards head into battle in this detail from the anonymous mid-sixteenth-century indigenous drawing of the conquest called the Lienzo de Tlaxcala (the 'Tlaxcala canvas'). The men carry shields and flat oak clubs 2 feet 8 inches long, inset with obsidian. Less-experienced soldiers wear plain cotton armour and a loincloth (left) while more experienced and higher ranking warriors wear elaborate feathered tunics over the cotton armour (right). The feathered headdresses indicate rank. Despite fighting alongside the Spaniards, these troops used only the traditional native weapons and gear.

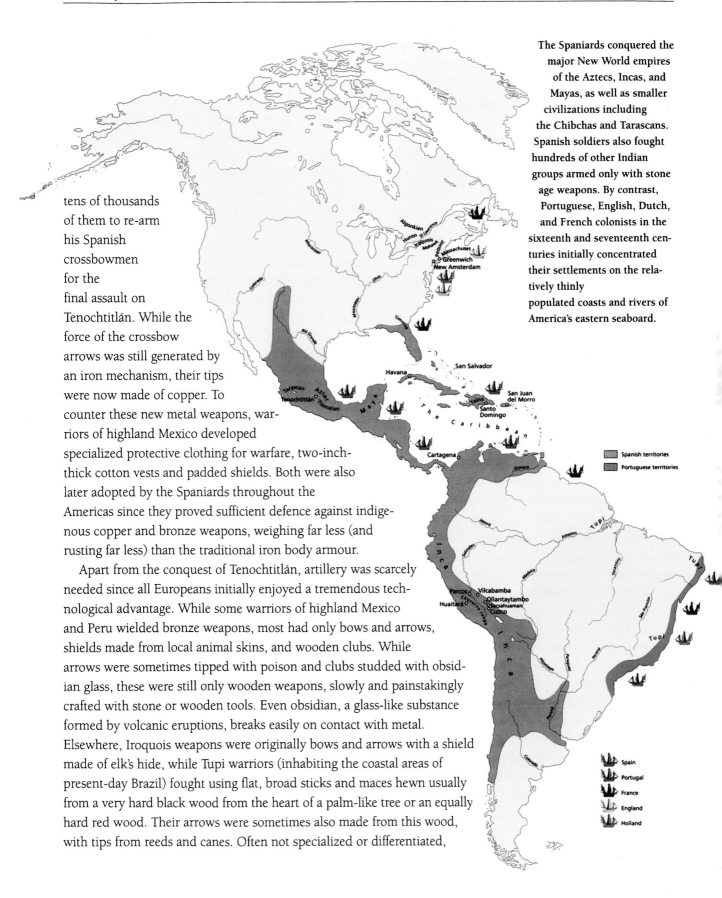

The Spaniards conquered the major New World empires of the Aztecs, Incas, and Mayas, as well as smaller civilizations including the Chibchas and Tarascans. Spanish soldiers also fought hundreds of other Indian groups armed only with stone age weapons. By contrast, Portuguese, English, Dutch, and French colonists in the sixteenth and seventeenth centuries initially concentrated their settlements on the relatively thinly populated coasts and rivers of America's eastern seaboard.

tens of thousands of them to re-arm his Spanish crossbowmen for the final assault on Tenochtitlán. While the force of the crossbow arrows was still generated by an iron mechanism, their tips were now made of copper. To counter these new metal weapons, warriors of highland Mexico developed specialized protective clothing for warfare, two-inch-thick cotton vests and padded shields. Both were also later adopted by the Spaniards throughout the Americas since they proved sufficient defence against indigenous copper and bronze weapons, weighing far less (and rusting far less) than the traditional iron body armour.

Apart from the conquest of Tenochtitlán, artillery was scarcely needed since all Europeans initially enjoyed a tremendous technological advantage. While some warriors of highland Mexico and Peru wielded bronze weapons, most had only bows and arrows, shields made from local animal skins, and wooden clubs. While arrows were sometimes tipped with poison and clubs studded with obsidian glass, these were still only wooden weapons, slowly and painstakingly crafted with stone or wooden tools. Even obsidian, a glass-like substance formed by volcanic eruptions, breaks easily on contact with metal. Elsewhere, Iroquois weapons were originally bows and arrows with a shield made of elk's hide, while Tupi warriors (inhabiting the coastal areas of present-day Brazil) fought using flat, broad sticks and maces hewn usually from a very hard black wood from the heart of a palm-like tree or an equally hard red wood. Their arrows were sometimes also made from this wood, with tips from reeds and canes. Often not specialized or differentiated, offensive indigenous weapons remained ordinary hunting tools. In time of war, shields and sometimes helmets were added, necessary for self-defence when fighting a human rather than an animal adversary.

The types of weapons that most natives used – together with their lack of protective clothing or armour – suggest, as do many of the early European narratives, that their warfare often aimed either to wound the enemy or else to render him temporarily unconscious in order to be able to capture him. Moreover, among most native societies of the New World, warfare aimed either at revenge or at the replacement of lost labour. If the former, captives were ritually beaten or devoured; if the latter, they were commonly enslaved or even adopted by the other tribe. In either case, enemies were frequently known, even by name, and indigenous battles often targeted specific members of rival tribes. By contrast, European warfare was far less personalized: indigenous enemies were rarely known to the Europeans and appeared more frequently as categories rather than persons with identities. The differences in the manner of carrying out warfare – killing rather than capturing – and the enormous technological advantage of iron weapons made European attacks on indigenous peoples seem particularly brutal.

THE CONQUEST OF THE INCAS

However, the two biggest empires in the Americas – the Incas centred in Peru, and the Triple Alliance led by the Aztecs on the central plateau of Mexico – possessed more specialized warriors and weapons. Of the two, the Incas had less deadly metal weapons, using clubs with semi-circular bronze ends that lacked a sharp edge and bent easily when striking iron. Nevertheless, although largely dependent upon stone weapons, the Incas made excellent use of these technologies in combination with the strategic advantages offered by their region. Residing in a mountainous terrain that yielded little wood, the Incas' most effective weapons were stones, rolled down hills or hurled from slingshots. But while the stones that Inca warriors hurled could kill as well as stun, Spanish iron helmets and mail or iron vests normally deflected the missiles of stone and rendered them incapable of deadly harm. How ineffective stone age weapons proved against iron age ones can be seen in the Inca siege of Cuzco in 1536 where 190 soldiers wearing steel helmets and vests defeated 200,000 people armed with stones. The lone Spanish casualty was a soldier who failed to wear his helmet. Gonzalo Pizarro claimed to have cut off the hands of two hundred Inca warriors with his steel-edged sword in a single afternoon during the battle for Cuzco. The Incas could do nothing comparable against the Spaniards except occasionally fell their horses by using a local lasso – three stones twirled on a string (a technique still used to round up cattle on the Argentine pampas). But they could rarely get close enough to follow up the advantage.

While stone-age weapons afforded little help against slashing steel swords in pitched battle, the dizzyingly vertical terrain of the Andes sometimes provided Inca fighters with a tactical advantage which they soon learned to use. Exploiting their

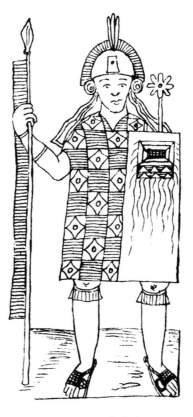

Two Inca warriors drawn by Guaman Poma de Ayala, descended from a scribe who served the last Inca rulers in the early seventeenth century. The drawing on the left shows traditional stone throwing tactics: stones were launched from slings that were first twirled overhead to gain speed and force. The figure on the right shows an Inca soldier carrying a spear and a mace with stone or bronze head. The star-shaped mace was a classic weapon in Inca hand-to-hand fighting.

topographical advantage to lure Spaniards into narrow passes provided the Incas with their only opportunities to inflict heavy casualties. Unlike most of the rest of the Americas, Inca warriors historically fought to kill rather than merely capture and so, after blockading the exit of a pass and occupying the high ground above the Spanish soldiers, the Incas rolled huge stone boulders down into the pass, killing and maiming both horses and men. Three such attacks occurred in 1536. Seventy Spanish soldiers under Gonzalo de Tapia were trapped and nearly all killed near Huaitará; fifty-seven out of sixty men under Diego Pizarro were killed near Parcos; and a further thirty under Morgovejo de Quiñones suffered a similar fate descending the Chocorvo range to the coast. After that, Spanish soldiers travelled far more cautiously through mountain passes.

In addition to inflicting casualties, the Incas' effective use of the Andes' vertiginous terrain forced Spanish troops to fight differently than elsewhere in the Americas. During the first major battles near Cuzco (1536–37), a major contingent of Incas occupied two nearly inaccessible stone fortresses: Sacsahuaman above Cuzco and mountaintop Ollantaytambo. Artillery would have been forced to fire at such a steep angle that the recoil of the cannon might have shot the cannon back down the slope. In the siege of Sacsahuaman the Pizarro brothers therefore had to employ traditional siege techniques, scaling the walls with ladders.

While the Incas exploited their steep terrain to stage two major rebellions against the Spaniards, however, the odds were ultimately against them. Both uprisings were defeated by a substantial inflow of men and material from throughout the Americas and Spain. Over a thousand men, hundreds of horses, and thousands of weapons poured into Peru in 1536 and 1537. By November 1539, the second great Inca rebellion was over. Even so a final victory in this terrain eluded the Spaniards for decades. It was forty years after the capture of Atahualpa on the plains of Cajamarca in 1532 before the last Inca military leader, Tupac Amaru, was killed. He held out by using the tactical advantage of a nearly inaccessible location: Vilcabamba, his last stronghold, could only be reached by crossing through

The Inca hillside fortress-temple of Ollantaytambo, located north of Cuzco, provided easy access to both the Andes and the Amazon basin. It served as the base of the Inca leader Manco, and stones hurled from the fortress at the mounted Spaniards successfully prevented its capture in 1536. The steeply angled hillside also prevented Spaniards from deploying their cannon. However, Manco abandoned the fortress for an even more inaccessible location, following his half-brother's defection to Spanish forces, and the site fell into ruin.

mountain passes 12,000 feet above sea level and then descending across narrow rope bridges into Amazonian rain forest.

STRATEGIC ALLIANCES

While iron-based weapons gave the Europeans a decisive technological edge in the New World, even in difficult terrain, part of the reason for their successes was strategic: they also successfully exploited native conflicts. Arriving at first in

relatively small groups, not massive armies, skill in acquiring alliances with natives or in deploying traditional hatreds for their own ends proved critical. From the outset the Spanish, French, and Portuguese invaders vigorously pursued policies of allying themselves with one group of indigenous peoples or another. The Portuguese and Spaniards did so by design, searching for traditional enemies who might be looking for new allies. Cortés joined with the Tlaxcalans – who hated the Aztecs – in order to gain needed warriors and supplies for the attack on Tenochtitlán. Diego de Almagro, one of the leaders of the Spanish forces, managed to force Manco Inca to withdraw from the steep hillside of Ollantaytambo late in 1537 by persuading Manco's brother Paullu and his followers to defect to the Spanish side and reveal his brother's strengths and weaknesses. The Pizarro brothers and Almagro could always find an Inca leader with some claim to rule who, in return for substantial privileges and honours within Spanish society, would ensure that the Inca empire would remain divided and some portion of it loyal to Spain.

The Portuguese also made effective use of local alliances, joining with the Tupi to fight the Ayamores in Brazil; while the French under Champlain allied successfully with the Algonkians and Hurons in Canada only to find themselves embroiled in fighting the Iroquois. Even the Dutch and English, who initially resisted 'entangling alliances' with native peoples, found eventually that they could not survive without utilizing native rivalries and relying upon such alliances for support.

But indigenous enemies were not the only ones Europeans had to fight in the Americas. Spanish troops – even at the height of the conquests of Mexico and Peru – were also busy fighting and killing each other. In the middle of the campaign against Tenochtitlán in 1520, Cortés had to retrace his steps in order to launch an attack against 900 Spanish troops sent to unseat him. The hatreds between the principal leaders of the conquest of Peru (the Pizarro brothers and Almagro) were legendary – erupting in a civil war in which they (or their followers) killed each other in the midst of major Inca uprisings. Fellow soldiers were more than willing to resort to arms against each other in battles over control of military leadership and economic rewards. However, even these squabbles failed to break the European stranglehold. Had the natives known how to exploit those divisions and rivalries as successfully as the Spaniards exploited their own, the outcome would have been in greater doubt.

THE IRON EDGE

Beyond Peru's mountainous terrain and Mexico's copper-tipped arrows and javelins, the only other potent danger Europeans encountered came from poison darts and arrows. Most widely used by inhabitants of the Caribbean and the eastern seaboard of South America, poison darts were principally used to paralyse large game or fish. Wars had customarily been fought with clubs but, after the arrival of

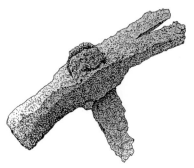

the technologically superior Europeans, poison darts and arrows were turned against human prey. For protection, the Portuguese turned to the cotton-padded armour that they had begun to adopt in Africa during the 1440s in response to warriors who fired poisoned arrows. After 1548 every Portuguese settler in America was required to own a layer of cotton padding, preferably covered by a leather cuirass vest, and owners of sugar mills were required to store at least twenty of these on their property. Thus both Spanish and Portuguese troops in the Americas would adopt cotton vests: the Spaniards having learned it from the Tlaxcalans, the Portuguese seventy years before from the Africans.

Enemies at war the world over learn quickly from each other. Just as the Portuguese and Spaniards had learned from their enemies, so the New World peoples learned from theirs. Throughout the Americas all kinds of iron technology were speedily adapted: iron tools for hunting and fishing obtained from Europeans were rapidly taken up everywhere they were introduced; iron hinges changed the construction of Iroquois longhouses and altered their patterns of hunting. In 1492 Columbus may have found that the natives were 'very naive about weapons', but they would not remain naive for long. Eighteen months after Pizarro captured the Inca prince Atahualpa, a warrior under his successor had acquired a Spanish sword, axe, helmet, and shield and used them to defend the fortress above Cuzco. Within approximately fifty years, the natives of the New World both mastered and acquired sufficient numbers of iron and steel weapons to mount an effective response; unfortunately for them, by then it was too late.

This fifty-year interval before natives acquired both stockpiles and mastery of iron weapons accounts for the relatively few fatalities suffered by the Spaniards in their early conquests, since all their major victories occurred before the indigenous peoples became proficient with the deadly iron weapons. And whenever Europeans made war on natives throughout the Americas, for the first fifty years the pattern resembled the early years of the Spanish conquest: the occasional surprise attack with heavier losses, but more commonly few European deaths against heavy indigenous casualties. Jean de Forest, a French Huguenot fighting in Guyana in 1624, reported 'more than 120 enemy [Indian] dead and more wounded. Among ourselves there was one death and fifty injured.' Similar results characterized the Pequot War in New England (1638–39) where Indian casualties were high at the final engagement – 400 to 500 – whereas the Europeans suffered no fatalities and few wounded. Likewise a Dutch attack by 140 men on an Indian village at Greenwich, Connecticut, in February 1644 killed 500 to 700 Indians, but resulted in no fatalities among the Dutch soldiers and only fifteen wounded.

But even in the seventeenth century, the possession of iron conferred only an initial advantage in the New World. By the 1670s, Massachusetts Indians were able to manufacture shot and build tools to repair muskets. The nomadic Mapuche of southern Chile adopted both the horse and the pike and proved able to hold off well-armed Spanish troops for decades. Once equipped with iron age technology,

Opposite: Within about fifty years of their first contact with Europeans, American Indians created ingenious stone tools both to repair captured weapons and to provide them with ammunition. Shown are half of a stone mould (top), used to make six lead shot for European guns, and a stone claw hammer (bottom), used to repair muskets. Both come from Massachusetts, from Sutton and from Burr's Hill burial ground respectively.

indigenous peoples became far better able to defend themselves, and the contest between the natives and the Europeans much less one-sided. Once the European edge was gone, fatalities increased dramatically – 3,000 English casualties in King Philip's war with the Indians 1675–76 – and the ability to conquer large inland empires vanished along with it.

Of all the New World powers, the Spaniards exploited the iron edge to its limit – using their swords, crossbows and muskets, as well as their helmets and vests to conquer indigenous societies rapidly, before iron weapons could fall into their hands. The Spaniards also managed to keep control of their vast conquests by continuing to maintain a monopoly of iron weapons. While both English and Dutch authorities eventually issued laws forbidding any trade in arms with the natives, once they realized the dangers to themselves, their fellow countrymen were often more eager to make a profit by trading prohibited weapons than to participate in a ban. But Spanish soldiers and settlers came from a different cultural background. Bearing arms, which in this case meant iron weapons, was traditionally associated with aristocratic privilege: keeping arms out of Indians' hands was thus in part a matter of maintaining social distinction. Moreover, Spanish officials were following a practice originally pursued by the Muslims in the Iberian peninsula – prohibiting the ownership of iron weapons by conquered peoples. In the middle ages, defeated Jews and Christians had been forbidden to own iron weapons, including knives. Reconquering Spaniards imposed the same restrictions upon the defeated Moors as had been imposed upon them: no iron weapons, and restrictions on ownership of iron tools, such as knives, that might be used as weapons. Shortly after 1492 such conditions were imposed upon the Moors of Granada. Hence widespread co-operation with a ban on iron weapons or potential weapons made both social and strategic sense. By the end of Spanish colonial rule in the early nineteenth century, laws still forbade the ownership and use of firearms by Indians.

Historically and culturally, therefore, the Spaniards were ready to exploit the technological advantages of iron. But other European powers were not similarly prepared. Over a hundred years after the Spaniards had so successfully overthrown major empires in the New World, Dutch officials initially considered it more important to keep horses out of Indian hands than either guns or iron weapons. The first Dutch colonists in New York could sell Indians iron-based weapons, even guns, but they could not either let Indians ride or teach them to ride horses without losing all their property and wages, and being permanently expelled from the colony. Only later did Dutch officials realize that it was iron-based weapons rather than horses that were crucial, and tried to ban them instead. But by then it was too late: the natives were already armed, often by the Dutch themselves.

Portuguese traders had initially provided the Brazilian natives with iron hatchets and knives since it made their task of felling Brazilwood trees so much faster and more efficient. But nearly twenty years after the start of settlement, the colonists realized their mistake. The first governor-general was given draconian powers to

Opposite: Horses added deadly speed and power to the impact of lances upon the more lightly armoured Indian troops. On level, even terrain, mounted Spaniards could break through Indian lines; in the mountains they made possible lightning forays into the countryside to forage for food.

halt the further sale of arms as well as of heavy knives to the natives. Where the penalty was once excommunication, it now became death – with an incentive for mutual spying, for those who denounced someone for selling arms to the natives would receive half of their estate.

HORSES

A final subsidiary advantage enjoyed by the Europeans was the use of domesticated animals for warfare, particularly horses. The domestic animals of the New World were few – wild beasts such as bears were occasionally kept in pens and fattened until eaten, and llamas and vicuñas (bad-tempered relatives of the legendarily bad-tempered camel) served principally as pack animals. While less crucial to the initial European victories than iron, the speed of the European horse in attack, combined with the iron-sharp points on lances and swords, increased the force with which the blows from iron weapons were delivered. But there were difficulties. Although initially men mounted on horseback were perceived as a single, frightening being, that original shock soon wore off. Cavalry charges were most effective in regions of vast open plains; but most of Central and South America was mountainous terrain, and a great deal of the rest was rain forest and swamp. Neither environment lent itself to mounted action. Only in the Andes region, much of it covered with well-maintained roads, could horsemen travel fast, bringing a vanguard of troops that could both strike and retreat quickly. And during the Inca siege of Cuzco (1536–37) when the Spanish conquest of Peru hung in the balance, it was lightning horseback raids for food in the surrounding regions that kept the Spaniards alive until strategic manipulation of leadership rivalries within the Inca forces, and a massive inflow of Spanish arms, lifted the siege. Such cavalry raids were successful in part because the Incas had neither cavalry nor anti-cavalry weapons to counter them. In the Andes sometimes as many as one-third of the troops were mounted – as opposed to at most 10 per cent of Cortés's army. Much later, horses and cavalry tactics would become important on the plains of Chile, Argentina and, eventually, North America. Like other areas of the world in the sixteenth century, with the exception of the Andes, it was principally infantry and infantry weapons – arquebuses, crossbows, swords and occasionally field artillery – that constituted the key to success.

DISEASE

A final unwitting weapon brought by the Europeans that contributed to their victories were epidemic diseases previously unknown on the American continent: smallpox, measles, typhoid, typhus, influenza. These diseases demonstrated an organizational weakness in the large-scale indigenous militaries in the New World. Shortly before Pizarro arrived in Peru, for example, an epidemic swept the Inca capital killing the heir apparent and reopening succession struggles. The result was an empire divided against itself, and at first far more concerned with its own conflicts than with a handful of foreigners. Among the Aztecs of Tenochtitlán a decade before, the first devastating epidemic of smallpox hit after Cortés's retreat, and functioned as a kind of Trojan horse. In addition to debilitating the population, including the warriors, it also illuminated succession problems in military leadership. Lacking any tradition of replacing slain leaders on the battlefield (since the Aztecs fought wars principally to capture, not to kill) major epidemics left wholly unexpected power vacuums in the military command structure. The resulting confusion over replacements (and replacement strategies) limited the ability of even this major military machine to regroup effectively and counterattack.

FORTIFIED POSITIONS

Once entrenched in the New World after their initial victories, the Europeans engaged in long-term low-intensity warfare with the indigenous populations. The native peoples of America successfully appropriated European technology (knives, swords, firearms, and horses) and adapted them to their own tactical and strategic traditions (ambush, hit-and-run raids, night attacks); and in this they proved as successful at keeping European advances slow and difficult as in any other place on the globe.

In both North and South America, therefore, the Europeans adopted defensive strategies against long-term warfare by building fortified settlements. In areas of Spanish conquest where policies forbidding arming indigenous peoples operated effectively, the settlers needed no such fortifications: only on the northern frontiers were such defensive techniques necessary. Elsewhere in the Americas, however, some form of fortification was needed for protection against native enemies. The French initially constructed forts in Brazil, Florida, and Canada; the Portuguese required agricultural settlements to have military features. Each sugar mill owner had to build a fortified house complete with an outside rampart and watch tower. By contrast, in New England, village sites were initially selected a safe distance away from indigenous habitation (and the possibility of surprise attack). Hence their settlements were less heavily armed and equipped. Arquebuses and muskets were their weapons. In Virginia, however, where European settlements lay somewhat closer to native ones, towns often boasted wooden walls as protection against indigenous weapons.

But indigenous enemies were not the only ones against whom defensive fortifications proved necessary. Just as Spanish soldiers had squabbled among themselves over the conquests of Peru and Mexico, so the various European groups soon fell out. The riches captured by Spaniards and the opportunity offered by new lands led every major European power to attempt to conquer the Americas. Arriving in disputed or potentially disputed territory, the first step of new arrivals was to fortify themselves against the other Westerners already established on the continent. After 1550 this included the construction of the newest European fortifications – broad walls and earth fortifications to withstand cannon blasts. In 1607 the first permanent English settlers under George Percy erected a fort which was 'triangle-wise, having three Bulwarks at every corner like a half moon, and four or five pieces of artillery mounted in them.' The initial action of the French Huguenots in Florida was to construct a bastioned citadel because they were aware of its importance in contemporary warfare. These fortifications were not designed for defence against natives: rather the location and the European-style fortifications grew up where the most likely targets or aggressors were other Europeans.

Since assaults by artillery-bearing European ships were bound to come from the sea, all New World coastal fortifications were carefully constructed against seaward attacks. The Dutch constructed defences on Manhattan island designed to catch ships travelling up the East River in cross fire. The Spanish city of Santo Domingo on the Caribbean island of Hispaniola took advantage of the massive cliffs to mount cannon that would prevent a direct landing on the beaches. However, since the indigenous peoples of the island had been exterminated, the Spaniards left the rear of the fort open and in 1585 Francis Drake followed the simple expedient (there and elsewhere) of landing out of range of the artillery and attacking from behind the fortress. He then sacked and looted the city.

After Drake's devastating raid in the Caribbean in 1585–86, military engineers built and refurbished fortifications around the coasts of Spanish America to prevent such assaults in the future. Massive walls were henceforth carefully constructed around the cities. These Spanish fortifications still exist throughout the Caribbean: the walls at San Juan del Morro in Puerto Rico, at Havana (Cuba), and at Cartagena (Colombia) can still be admired today. But there is a more famous fort that can no longer be seen: the palisade and breastwork wall erected to strengthen one side of the Dutch fort at the southern tip of Manhattan island. The passageway or street across the breastworks was named for the ramparts or wall. The most famous street in the United States, synonymous with American capitalism – Wall Street – is named for the ramparts, the pre-eminent symbol of the western way of war, constructed by the Dutch in 1652 to maintain their foothold on the American continent.

Fort Amsterdam (on the right in this seventeenth-century view – where New York City's Battery Park lies today) dominated the navigable approaches to New Amsterdam. Fortifications were constructed on coasts throughout the Americas to protect Europeans against other cannon-firing Europeans. The strongest walls of the fort usually lay towards the sea, where European attacks were most likely to originate. However, colonists also had to prepare for attack by land, and the street that eventually became the most famous financial centre in the world takes its name from the wall seen as a vertical line in the centre of the drawing, dividing the Dutch settlement from the rest of Manhattan island.

CHAPTER 9 — # *Dynastic War*

The revolution in fortress design, the greater reliance on firepower in battle, and the increases in army size during the century 1530–1630 (see chapter 6) transformed the western way of war. On the one hand, hostilities now affected more people (both directly, as the number of soldiers grew, and indirectly, as the impact of war on society augmented); on the other, sieges far outnumbered battles. According to the experienced French soldier Blaise de Monluc, writing in the mid-sixteenth century, siegecraft constituted 'the most difficult and the most important' aspect of warfare; while in the words of Roger Boyle, earl of Orrery, a century later: 'Battles do not now decide national quarrels, and expose countries to the pillage of the conquerors as formerly. For we make war more like foxes than like lions and you will have twenty sieges for one battle.'

THE RISE OF PROFESSIONAL ARMIES

In addition, wars now occurred more often, lasted far longer, and involved far more men. The sixteenth and seventeenth centuries saw more belligerence than almost any other period of European history, registering a grand total of only ten years of total peace across the continent. During the sixteenth century, Spain and France were almost constantly at war; while during the seventeenth, the Ottoman empire, the Austrian Habsburgs and Sweden were at war for two years out of every three,

Spain for three years out of every four, and Poland and Russia for four years out of every five.

'This,' as the Italian poet Fulvio Testi wrote in 1641, 'is the century of the soldier.' Certainly, every state maintained far more of them. Charles the Bold of Burgundy had created an army in the Netherlands which scarcely numbered 15,000 men in the 1470s but a century later his descendant Philip II supported 86,000 there. In 1640 the Spanish army in the Low Countries still exceeded 88,000 troops. The same trend occurred almost everywhere else, and in the course of the seventeenth century, between ten and twelve million Europeans became soldiers. Most of these armies consisted overwhelmingly of infantry: when Francis I of France invaded Italy in 1525, the 32,000-man French army included only 6,000 cavalry; and when France went to war against the Habsburgs in 1635, orders went out to raise 132,000 infantry but only 12,400 cavalry.

In wars dominated by sieges and skirmishes, in which the principal military targets comprised fortified cities rather than field armies, recruiting infantry rather than cavalry made perfect sense. Whether in the trenches or on the ramparts, foot soldiers – and especially musketeers – were at a premium, whereas horses seemed more vulnerable to gunfire than their armoured riders (many men lost several mounts in a single engagement). Financially, too, the shift brought advantages since many footsoldiers could be recruited, equipped, and maintained for the same outlay as a single trooper and his chargers. But the transition also generated serious problems.

Most serious, the administrative system responsible for the new larger armies and the increased areas of operation remained relatively static, while the military bureaucracy (like other departments of state) suffered from overlapping jurisdictions, gross irresponsibility, and disabling conflicts between rival groups of administrators. Moreover, governments knowingly recruited far more troops at the beginning of each campaigning season than they could pay or even feed. This combination of insufficient control and inadequate resources produced serious problems of discipline. Cavalry normally came from the elite of society, its members trained for combat since childhood, and so might be expected to tolerate great hardships; but infantry, drafted at short notice and sometimes unwillingly from civilian roles, often took poorly to the military and expressed their disapproval either through desertion or mutiny. Two solutions were widely adopted: resort to foreign professional soldiers, hired under contract; and a programme of discipline and training for native recruits. The first predominated in the sixteenth century, only gradually giving way to the second.

The use of mercenaries became common in the middle ages, with entire military formations hiring themselves out to any state that would pay them, and the practice continued in the early modern period. Swiss and south German military entrepreneurs, in particular, maintained cadres of trained troops who could be mobilized at short notice. At the first sign of trouble, governments issued a contract to an

Opposite: At the battle of Pavia in northern Italy (1525), the troops of the Habsburg emperor Charles V defeated those of Francis I of France largely through their imaginative use of hand-held firearms. Here a phalanx of men with arquebuses, dressed in white for ease of identification, repels a cavalry charge while pike squares clash in the background. The French suffered eight times as many casualties as the imperial army, and their king was taken captive.

entrepreneur of proven ability, specifying the number of troops to be raised and armed, the wages to be paid, and the place and date of the first muster. Sometimes, in anticipation of danger (or simply to prevent the troops from being recruited by another warlord), a 'retainer' (*Wartgelt* in German: waiting money) would be paid until either full mobilization took place or else the crisis passed; but, mostly, entrepreneurs were expected to produce their men 'on demand'.

The system worked because able and willing entrepreneurs abounded. Thus the German knight, Götz von Berlichingen (1480–1562), specialized in fighting feuds – either his own or (in return for one third of the gains) on behalf of others – and his memoirs, entitled *My Feuds and Disputes*, listed thirty of them, fought with the bands he recruited (numbering up to 150 men) all over western Germany. Noble contemporaries able to command greater resources could recruit larger forces than Götz – a regiment, perhaps even two or three – and by the early seventeenth century a few proved able to mobilize an entire army. During the Thirty Years War

Military medicine and care for veterans

Knowledge of how the human body worked was rudimentary in the sixteenth century, but soldiers could at least take comfort in the fact that army doctors and surgeons were the most experienced medical practitioners available. New techniques such as amputation were developed to deal with limbs crushed in combat or by stone or metal shot from gunpowder weapons. In this woodcut (left) from Hans von Gersdorff's *Manual of Military Surgery* (1517), the first illustrated treatise on surgery ever published, one patient (standing right) holds the bound off stump of a successfully amputated hand, while another loses his right leg. Pressed back in a chair, wounded leg crossed over good and gripping his knee for support, the patient is blindfolded to shield him from what is going on.

The surgeon's tools varied little between the sixteenth and nineteenth centuries: saws, a brace-and-bit, and a large number of instruments long, sharp, and thin. An incision with a knife and a few strokes of the saw were enough: a tub underneath caught the blood. To stop the bleeding and prevent infection, most doctors believed the only solution – despite the agonizing

pain and shock it caused the patient in the era before anaesthetics – was to cauterize (burn) the flesh around the amputation. Only in the sixteenth century was it found that if the wound was painted with thick animal fat it healed just as well and much less painfully.

If the patient avoided death from his injuries, shock, or infection, and was wealthy enough to afford them, artificial limbs were available. A whole series of designs (below)

(1618–48) at least 100 military entrepreneurs operated at any one time in Germany, increasing to perhaps 300 in the 1630s. Albert of Wallenstein recruited an army of some 25,000 men for the Holy Roman Emperor on two separate occasions (in 1625 and 1631–32); while Bernard of Saxe-Weimar brought his personal army of 18,000 men into French service in 1635. By the time of Bernard's death in 1639, foreign troops raised abroad by entrepreneurs made up 20 per cent of the French army (which numbered roughly 125,000 men); while in 1648, at the end of the Thirty Years War, the 60,000-man army maintained by Sweden in Germany included only 18,000 Swedes.

The great advantage of hiring mercenaries was, of course, that they already knew how to use their weapons and how to fight in formation. Foreign mercenaries, as a French military writer observed in the 1540s, were 'those whom one trusts more than anyone and without whom we would not have the courage to undertake the least thing.' Nevertheless, they could prove unreliable at critical moments, refusing

A mercenary from Alexander Hamilton's regiment of Scots and Irish infantry, 800 men strong, hired to fight for Gustavus Adolphus of Sweden in 1631. In the course of the Thirty Years War (1618–48), some 25,000 Scots – almost 10 per cent of the kingdom's adult male population – went abroad to serve as soldiers, mostly in the service of Protestant states. The unusual appearance of these troops aroused considerable interest: this contemporary print, made in Nuremberg shortly after they arrived in Germany, provides the first known illustration of Highland ('Irish') dress.

for false legs was developed by the foremost military doctor of the later sixteenth century, Ambroise Paré, to alleviate the disabilities of amputees.

Combat injuries often needed to be dealt with on or near the field of battle. Military hospitals were few and far between, and only Spain tried to care properly for her wounded soldiers. Her armies were served by teams of trained doctors and surgeons, and the forces continuously at war in the Netherlands between 1572 and 1659 were provided with the first military hospital in Europe, at Mechelen in Brabant (now Malines, Belgium). This eventually had 330 beds and a staff of between sixty and a hundred, ranging from the chief doctor to the women who did the laundry. Soldiers were treated, with remarkable success, for everything from dysentery and malaria, through psychological disorders and battle trauma, to severe combat injuries. Treatment was free but one *real* of each soldier's basic monthly wage of thirty *reales* was kept back to be put towards the cost of running the hospital. Infectious diseases were as much of a problem as injuries, and syphilis was so common – affecting about a quarter of the Spanish soldiers in the Netherlands at any one time – that the Mechelen hospital received a government grant specifically to treat it.

No other country cared for its wounded soldiers so well. England's Queen Elizabeth I had a markedly different way with her troops, and after the defeat of the Spanish Armada in 1588 refused all requests to provide veterans with money. Eventually disability pensions were paid. As the Act of Parliament of 1593 authorizing them belatedly decreed, 'It is agreeable with Christian charity, policy, and the honour of our nation that such as have since the 25th day of May 1588 adventured their lives and lost their limbs or disabled their bodies, or shall hereafter adventure their lives, lose their limbs or disable their bodies in the defence and service of her majesty and the state, should at their return be relieved and rewarded to the end [that] they may reap the fruit of their good deserving, and others may be encouraged to perform the like endeavours.' Despite the Act's fine sentiments, however, for five years previously those crippled in the Armada action had been left to starve to death or beg in Channel ports. The belated pensions benefited only the survivors.

The number of enemy colours captured often served to measure the scale of a victory and soon became treasured trophies. For example the States-General of the Netherlands, the paramount authority of the Dutch Republic, met in a hall decorated with scores of regimental and company colours won in action from the Spanish Army of Flanders in the course of the Dutch struggle for independence (1568–1648). One (upper left) displays the Pillars of Hercules, the personal emblem of the emperor Charles V; some depict the royal arms of Habsburg Spain; most bear the St Andrew's cross of the dukes of Burgundy (from whom the Habsburgs inherited the Netherlands).

to fight if they were led too far afield, if they found compatriots among the forces ranged against them, or (above all) if their pay fell into arrears. Moreover, their edge of experience soon crumbled as hostilities continued, since not only did their numbers diminish through casualties but the calibre of the native levies improved with the passage of time.

Several developments assisted the growing professionalism of local recruits. Most governments introduced prophylactics against fear such as uniforms, martial music, and permanent regiments with their own focuses of loyalties. Thus in 1534 Charles V organized a permanent regiment of Spaniards (called a *tercio*) in three of his Italian possessions: Naples, Sicily, and Lombardy. Each boasted its own insignia and colours, its own chaplains and law officers, as well as its own musical and medical support teams (the former outnumbering the latter by twenty-five to three!), with the express intention of stimulating the same enduring martial traditions and fierce unit loyalties as the legions of the Roman empire. The ploy succeeded. When the *tercio* of Lombardy, then serving in the Netherlands, was dissolved in 1589 for insubordination, and the officers ceremonially destroyed their badges of rank and tore up their colours 'which, since they no longer represented His Majesty the King, no longer demanded the veneration and care in which they had been held,' the whole Spanish army felt stunned because the *tercio* enjoyed the reputation of being 'the father of the other regiments and the seminary of the best soldiers who have been seen in Europe in our time'.

INSIGNIA, UNIFORMS, AND EQUIPMENT

Other states soon followed the Habsburgs' lead and created their own semi-permanent regiments, proud of their corporate insignia. By the later sixteenth century, most military commentators measured the outcome of an encounter not by the numbers slain but by the number of colours that changed hands. However, as yet no effort was made to regulate dress. Some felt that uniforms resembled a servant's livery and so might 'remove the spirit and fire which is necessary in a soldier.' Others cited the example of Don Fernando Alvarez de Toledo, third duke of Alba and perhaps the most famous general of the sixteenth century, 'who whenever he was on active service clothed his entire person in bright blue,' and held that 10,000 soldiers refulgently attired in contrasting colours would look more dangerous than 20,000 all dressed in black 'as if they were townsmen and shopkeepers'.

However, no army in Alba's day possessed the ability to clothe 20,000 men all in one colour, let alone in a single style, for mass production of uniform apparel was impossible. Furthermore, even if men began a campaign in clothes of the same colour and design, few would still be wearing them at the end. Robert Monro, colonel of a Scottish regiment serving in Germany, marched (by his own reckoning) a total of 3,000 miles between 1629 and 1633. During the English civil wars, between April and November 1644 King Charles I travelled almost 1,000 miles with his army; while in the three years following September 1642 his nephew and principal commander, Prince Rupert of the Rhine, changed his army's location 152 times, marched all night on nine occasions, slept out in the open seven nights, and fought eleven battles and sixty-two skirmishes.

In such conditions it did not take long to ruin coats, boots, and breeches – as an English soldier who fought in the Netherlands discovered one night in 1633:

> I had nothing to keep me from the cold, wet ground but a little bundle of wet dried
> flax…And so with my boots full of water, and wrapped up in my wet cloak, I lay
> as round as a hedgehog, and at peep of day looked like a drowned rat.

Men wearing worn-out or damaged clothes like these needed to replace them from any and all available sources – from fallen comrades, from civilians (whether by purchase or plunder), even from the enemy. Thus in 1651 orders went out that a regiment of Scottish lifeguards 'might all of them have coats of one colour'; but when a supply ship bearing replacement uniforms for their English adversaries was blown off course and captured, the Scots gladly made use of them!

It was therefore imperative for commanders to issue distinguishing marks to their harlequin troops – usually a coloured sash, a ribbon, or a plume. Thus the soldiers of the Habsburgs, whether Spanish or Austrian, always wore a red token, while those of France wore blue, those of Sweden wore yellow, and those of the Dutch Republic wore orange. When the troops of more than one army combined, some additional common denominator was needed: at the battle of Breitenfeld (1631) the allied Saxons and Swedes all plucked a leafy branch or fern from a forest

A bedraggled group of soldiers from the Spanish Army of Flanders at the siege of Aire-sur-la-Lys in northern France in 1641, portrayed by Pieter Snaeyers, an artist in Antwerp (Belgium) who specialized in 'realistic' war paintings. Although the siegeworks and tents in the background seem neat and orderly, the troops – although well-armed – are not. All wear clothes whose only common denominator, at the end of the campaigning season, is an advanced state of decay.

In the Provincial Armoury at Graz, Austria, almost 4,000 helmets – and as many muskets with their powder flasks and other accessories, as well as pistols, swords, breastplates, and other pieces of military equipment – still stand ready to equip troops in case of a sudden attack. The wars of the seventeenth century inflated the demand for military artefacts to such levels that mass-production became both more economical and more efficient.

through which they passed on their way to the battle and placed the token in their hats, while at Marston Moor (1644) the united Parliamentary and Scottish troops received orders to wear something white about their person. But the situation soon changed. When in 1645 the commander-in-chief of the imperial armies placed an order with Austrian clothiers to supply outfits for 600 of his men, he attached a sample of the exact material and specified the colour to be copied. He also sent samples of powder-horns and cartridge belts to be manufactured en masse by local suppliers. Once permanent regiments existed, creating a constant and predictable demand, uniform dress at last became possible.

The same process affected the supply of weapons. Although exact standardization mattered relatively little with sword or bow, it was essential for the effective use of firearms. Roger Boyle complained that his musketeers in Ireland during the 1640s almost lost one battle because the shot supplied proved too large for the weapons available, so that some men 'were forced to gnaw off much of the lead [while] others cut their bullets, in which much time was lost [and] the bullets flew a less way.' Part of the problem, as with clothes, was the need to ensure that replacements as well as initial supplies all corresponded to a single standard; and again, as with clothes, the need for replacements could be high. Sir Ralph Hopton, a royalist commander in the English Civil War, complained petulantly in 1643 that 'It is inconceivable what these fellows were always doing with their arms; they appear to be expended as fast as their ammunition.' He soon had cause for further complaint when a cargo of 1,000 muskets imported from France for his troops was found to contain 'three or four score sundry bores – some pistol bores, some carbine bores, some little fowling pieces, and all the old trash that can be rapt together.' Clearly this situation could not be tolerated and gradually, as in other wars of the period, a steady and substantial demand led to the production and distribution of standardized arms.

FROM SQUARES TO LINES

But firearms, whether standardized or not, could not be used to maximum effect without drastic changes in the method of deploying infantry in action. Pictures of sixteenth-century battles, as well as surviving muster rolls, clearly show a transition. Compact infantry formations composed largely of pikemen fighting in 'squares' (not unlike a Greek phalanx), with a few files of marksmen milling about the periphery until it came to the 'push of pike', gave way to linear formations composed largely of musketeers protected by a few files of pikemen. The change sounds simple, but it transformed the life of the infantryman.

At the battle of Fornovo in July 1495, for example, some 10,000 soldiers (plus some 6,000 camp followers) under the personal command of Charles VIII of France, forced their way past an Italian army at least twice as large, drawn up in a defile on the Taro River. Over half of each army consisted of mounted knights. The action commenced at around 8 a.m. with an artillery duel, cut short when rain dampened the powder, and continued about two hours later with Italian cavalry delivering charges in two places. Both failed, mainly because the rain turned the Taro into a raging torrent and the surrounding terrain into a slippery morass ill-suited to mounted manoeuvres. As the Italian horse fell back, the French advanced in close order, giving no quarter and killing everyone they found in their path. The fallen knights lay imprisoned and helpless in their armour as the victors moved around the battlefield, breaking their visors with hatchets and either splitting their heads open or cutting their throats: those who later visited the battlefield noted that most corpses had a stab wound in the throat or the face. Perhaps 3,000 Italian and 200 French soldiers perished, and Charles VIII led his troops back to France in safety.

Apart from the larger numbers involved, and the enhanced role of the infantry, most battles of the earlier sixteenth century resembled Fornovo. At Marignano (1515), Mühlberg (1547), and St Quentin (1557) the outcome was decided relatively swiftly; firepower played little part in the outcome; and each man chose his adversaries more or less at will. Even though at Bicocca (1522) and Pavia (1525) infantry firepower played a key role in defeating Swiss pike formations, broken ground and field fortifications provided essential support: the use of firearms in the field remained in its infancy throughout the first half of the sixteenth century.

The major war of the succeeding period – the conflict that ravaged and eventually partitioned the Netherlands between 1568 and 1648 – included scarcely any battles. Instead, the commanders of the government's forces, beginning with the duke of Alba, adopted a 'steamroller strategy' towards the rebels, led by the prince of Orange, and sought to outmanoeuvre them without resort to battle. In the words of a theatre commander, Don Sancho de Londoño:

> The duke [of Alba] has laboured specifically to avoid fighting a battle, despite pressure from those who forget that victory is a gift of Fortune, which can favour the Bad as well as the Good. If Orange were a powerful monarch who could maintain a mighty army for longer, I would be in favour of fighting a battle; but since it is certain that shortage of money will cause his forces to crumble, and that he will not then be able to regroup, I am against it.

But time was of the essence: unless the enemy could be defeated within a single campaign, serious problems developed. Thus in 1572, Orange mounted a major invasion of the Netherlands which aroused widespread popular support; and despite a successful campaign that recaptured either by force or by fear nine-tenths of the area in rebellion, by the end of the year twenty-four fortified towns in the maritime provinces of Holland and Zealand remained in revolt. As Alba bitterly complained, although he commanded some 60,000 men, 'a sufficient number to conquer many kingdoms, it does not suffice here' – for many recaptured towns had required garrisons; Alba's campaign army had declined to a mere 12,000 men (not enough to lay siege to one town, let alone to twenty-four); and, after nine months of continuous service in the field without pay, the morale of those men verged on mutiny. Worst of all, the cost of Alba's huge military machine far exceeded the income of his master, Philip II – an income that had to support many other enterprises (including a full-scale naval offensive against the Turks in the Mediterranean) besides the war in Holland. Not surprisingly, in July 1573 the Spanish infantry, which had been in constant action for fifteen months, mutinied for their unpaid wages (totalling two whole years). The Dutch Revolt continued.

THE RISE OF THE MUSKET

One of Alba's most important innovations in response to this style of attritional warfare was to increase the firepower of his troops. In the 1550s, in Italy, he had added to each company a number of men equipped with muskets, a weapon so heavy that it could only be fired using a forked rest but delivering a ball with such force that (according to the English military writer Humphrey Barwick) it could penetrate plate armour at 200 yards (although most weapons probably did little damage beyond 80 yards). The musket thus offered great advantages both in skirmishing and, even more, in the trench warfare around besieged towns that dominated the Low Countries' wars. Alba therefore further enhanced the firepower of his infantry by adding to each *tercio* two companies armed entirely with firearms: in 1571 a muster of the Spanish *tercios* in the Netherlands, with a total strength of 7,509 men, revealed 450 officers, 596 musketeers, 1,505 men armed with the lighter arquebus, and the rest with pikes – a ratio of two 'shot' to every five pikes. However, just thirty years later, in 1601, a muster of the Spanish *tercios* in the Netherlands, with a total strength of 6,001 men, revealed 646 officers, 1,237 musketeers, 2,117 men with arquebuses, and the rest with pikes – a ratio of three 'shot' to every pike.

This dramatic shift in weaponry accompanied equally dramatic changes in tactics. Several Spanish commanders experimented with tactical systems designed to make optimum use of firepower, but none worked as well as the innovations of Maurice of Nassau, son of the prince of Orange defeated by Alba in 1568, who during the 1590s began to introduce his troops to 'exercises' – forming and reforming ranks, drilling, and parading – in the manner advocated by Roman writers. It was while reading Aelian's *Tactics* in 1594 that Maurice's cousin, William Louis of Nassau, realized that rotating ranks of musketeers could replicate the continuous hail of fire achieved by the javelin and sling-shot throwers of the legions. This device overcame the basic weakness of the muzzle-loading musket – its slow rate of fire – because an infantry formation deployed in a series of ranks, the first firing together and then retiring to reload while the others did the same, would produce a continuous hail of lethal fire.

The development of volley fire had a critical impact upon battle tactics. To begin with, armies now had to spread out during battle, both to maximize the effect of outgoing fire and to minimize the target for incoming missiles. This achieved a significant 'economy of scale', because the linear deployment of troops placed far more soldiers in a position to kill enemy troops.

This, too, had important consequences. First, changing a pike square perhaps fifty deep into a musketry line ten deep (or less) inevitably exposed far more men to the terror of face-to-face combat, calling for superior courage, proficiency, and discipline in each individual soldier. Second, it placed great emphasis on the ability of entire tactical units to perform the motions necessary for volley-firing both swiftly and in unison.

The solution to both problems was, of course, practice: troops had to be trained to fire, countermarch, load, and manoeuvre all together. The counts of Nassau therefore divided their army into far smaller formations – companies shrank from 250 men with eleven officers to 120 men with twelve officers; regiments of 2,000 and more gave way to battalions of 580 – and taught them to drill. Another of Maurice's cousins, Count John of Nassau, developed a crucial new tool of military training – the drill book – and in 1616 opened the first true military academy in Europe, the *Schola Militaris*, at his capital of Siegen in western Germany, to educate young gentlemen in the art of war. Training took six months, with arms, armour, maps, relief models, and other instructional aids provided by the school. The first director, Johan Jakob von Wallhausen, published several manuals of warfare, all of them explicitly based on Dutch practice (the only system taught at Siegen).

The Nassau 'exercises' rapidly spread over Europe – especially Protestant Europe – thanks to the innumerable foreigners who came to serve in the Dutch army, the various authors of military treatises who described (and sometimes illustrated) them, and the supply of Dutch military instructors to friendly foreign states (Count John himself paid a brief visit to Sweden). Their fame also spread across the Atlantic. The Virginia Company in London actively recruited Englishmen in the Dutch army and appointed those who accepted their terms to positions of command: every governor of Virginia between 1610 and 1621 had served as an officer under Maurice of Nassau. Many leaders of other English colonies had also fought for the Dutch, including Miles Standish, who began drilling his forces in the Dutch fashion as soon as they disembarked from the *Mayflower* at Plymouth; John Winthrop, who entrusted each of Massachusetts Bay's four militia companies to the veterans of the Dutch army whom he had persuaded to join him; and Thomas Dudley, who organized the defenses of the Puritans on Providence Island in the Caribbean. In the first half of the seventeenth century, settlers throughout English America took their orders from veterans of the Dutch army.

The full value of the Nassau family's military reformation remained unrealized in the Netherlands, however, since the Dutch army seldom exposed itself to the supreme test of battle. Admittedly Maurice and his cousins showed great interest in combat tactics – Count William Louis wrote a treatise on the battle of Cannae in 216 BC (see pages 48–9) and the linear battle order was partially designed to imitate Hannibal's outflanking manoeuvre – but the ambiguous outcome of their two pitched encounters (at Turnhout in 1597 and at Nieuwpoort in 1600) suggests that the formula for total victory had not entirely been mastered. Even the early battles of the Thirty Years War (1618–48) resembled those of the previous century fairly closely, with large phalanxes of infantry and cavalry arranged in a chess-board pattern. In 1631, however, King Gustavus Adolphus of Sweden demonstrated the full potential of volley fire and

Opposite: The *Exercise of Arms*, a volume of prints engraved and published in 1607 by Jacob de Gheyn of Amsterdam, represented an entirely new concept in military education: the drill book. A numbered sequence of pictures showed each of thirty-two distinct positions for the pike (starting with 'pick it up'), twenty-five for the arquebus and thirty-two for the musket (ending with 'fire'), to enable instructors to make their soldiers drill in unison. The basic idea (and the preliminary drawings) were developed by Count John of Nassau-Siegen (1561–1623) for use in the Dutch army, and de Gheyn's work quickly appeared in Danish, German, French, and English editions.

linear formations. In the first place, thanks to constant drill and practice, in the course of the 1620s he improved reloading speeds among his musketeers to the point where only six ranks (instead of the ten required in the Dutch army) could maintain an effective continuous barrage. So strongly did the king feel about the matter that he even gave personal demonstrations to freshly recruited units of how to fire a musket standing, kneeling, even lying down. Second, Swedish firepower was greatly increased by the addition of field artillery. Whereas the Dutch army at Turnhout had deployed a mere four field guns, and at Nieuwpoort only eight, Gustavus Adolphus took eighty with him when he invaded Germany in 1630. All guns belonged to one of only three calibres (24-, 12-, and 3-pounders) and some came supplied with cartridges already attached, for speedier loading. The 3-pounders could therefore fire up to twenty rounds an hour – not much slower than a musketeer. Finally, Gustavus also trained his cavalry to charge home with swords drawn, rather than to skirmish with pistols and carbines (as most German horsemen preferred to do).

THE BATTLE OF BREITENFELD

The battle of Breitenfeld, fought just outside Leipzig on 17 September 1631, convincingly demonstrated the superiority of the new military system. A veteran army in the service of the Holy Roman Emperor, numbering 10,000 horse and 21,400

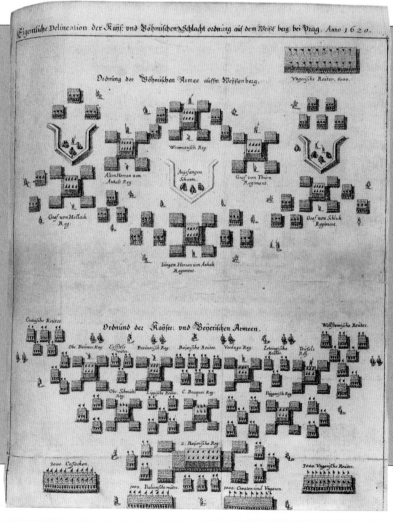

From pike to musket

The military innovations pioneered by the Dutch in the first decade of the seventeenth century did not immediately pass into practice. Battles such as White Mountain (1620, diagrammed left), fought between the Bohemians and a combined Habsburg – Bavarian army, saw huge phalanxes of pikemen pushing at each other, with relatively few musketeers and little artillery support. However at the battle of Jankow in 1645 (opposite), fought between the Habsburgs and the Swedes, the two sides deployed in thinner, longer lines, with more field artillery and more musketeers. While White Mountain was decided by cavalry and 'push of pike', Jankow was won by firepower. Both battles proved important: the first abruptly terminated the revolt of Bohemia which began the Thirty Years War; the second forced the Habsburgs to begin serious negotiations with the victorious Swedish forces and opened the way to a final settlement to the war.

foot and commanded by an experienced and previously successful general (Count Tilly), deployed in squares thirty deep and fifty wide, supported by twenty-seven field guns. The Swedes and their Protestant allies, however, boasted fifty-one heavy guns, while every Swedish regiment included a battery of four light field pieces. Their 28,000 foot stood in six ranks, covered by 13,000 cavalry. In the event, the German troops fighting with Gustavus broke after the first hour, but the Swedish reserve marched across in perfect order and took their places. In the second hour's fighting, almost 8,000 imperialist troops died (most of them killed by Swedish gun-fire) and a further 9,000 fell prisoner or else deserted; still more fell in the headlong retreat that followed. In all, two-thirds of the imperial army, 120 of its regimental and company standards, and all of its guns were lost. Tilly, the defeated commander, lost his nerve and moped about his headquarters, 'Wholly perplexed and seemingly cast down, wholly irresolute in council, not knowing how to save himself, abandoning one proposal after another, deciding nothing, seeing only great difficulties and dangers.' With no enemy army to stand in their way, in the course of the next six months almost all of Germany fell to Gustavus and his allies, and in 1632 the Swedish king directed the operations of six separate armies totalling 183,000 men.

The contrast with Fornovo (see page 152) was clear. Breitenfeld, although fought between armies of unequal size, lasted far longer (about seven hours), and

Silver medallion of 1613 showing Maurice of Nassau wearing the Order of the Garter, found in the 1622 ruins of Martin's Hundred, Virginia, owned by Sir George Yardley, Governor of Virginia, who had earlier served in Maurice's army.

the outcome was decided by infantry, discipline, and firepower: the Swedish musketeers formed the decisive element, sometimes firing a lethal 'double salvo', with the men crammed into just three lines – one rank kneeling, the second crouching, the third upright – in order to 'pour as much lead into your enemy's bosom at one time [as possible]...and thereby you do them more mischief...for one long and continuated crack of thunder is more terrible and dreadful to mortals than ten interrupted and several ones.' Consequently, far more men died at Breitenfeld, partly because gunfire is more murderous than sword and pike thrust, since gunshots wounds could more easily smash a bone or rupture a vital organ, creating wounds that (given the limited medical knowledge of the age) would prove fatal.

The tactical and strategic impact of Breitenfeld proved immense. Other armies hastened to copy the Swedish system: at Lützen, the following year, the imperialist army led by Wallenstein possessed sufficient firepower and flexibility to hold the field. Gustavus himself died in a furious but indecisive charge. Within a short time all major armies in western Europe fought in long thin lines, dominated by musketeers.

BIG BATTLES AND SMALL WARS

And yet few of these spectacular battles proved 'decisive': like the much-studied Cannae, most of them brought the campaign to a victorious conclusion, but they did not win the war. Breitenfeld was offset by Lützen and, in 1634, by a major Habsburg victory over the main Swedish army at Nördlingen. The battles of Jankow and Allerheim in 1645, although they destroyed the armed forces of the emperor and his Catholic allies, weakening their negotiating position, were followed by three more years of ceaseless hostilities before peace finally ended the Thirty Years War.

Most military actions of the early modern period involved relatively few troops; many of them also involved civilians. Sebastian Vrancx of Antwerp portrayed an imaginary – but all too familiar – scene in his painting of 1616: the attack on a wagon train by a group of soldiers intent on plunder. Men are shot; women stripped; possessions looted. Note that most of the soldiers wear a red distinguishing mark (such as a plume or a sash), indicating that they served the Habsburgs.

The problem was partly military and partly political. On the one hand, maintaining large armies in the field year after year, as well as the need to garrison all strategic defences, placed an intolerable strain on every state. Transporting the vital artillery alone posed major logistical problems. The emperor Charles V's military advisers in the 1550s calculated that moving just one large siege gun required thirty-nine horses, plus 156 more for a week's supply of powder and shot; a century later, their successors reckoned that 1,849 pair of oxen and 753 vehicles would be required to move and serve a train of ten siege guns and ten mortars. Feeding the oxen and the other draught animals, along with the cavalry's mounts (and replacements), presented another headache, because 20,000 horses required ninety tons of fodder (or 400 acres of grazing) each and every day.

Victualling the troops presented even more of a headache because, as Cardinal Richelieu noted, 'One finds in the history books that many more armies perished through lack of food and lack of order than through enemy action.' An army of 30,000 men, properly fed, required daily 45,000 lbs (20 tons) of bread – that is, over 100,000 lbs of flour plus the ovens to bake it – and 30,000 lbs of meat (equivalent to 1,500 sheep or 150 bullocks). Moreover, although the livestock could be transported 'on the hoof' until required, a week's supply of flour and its ovens required 250 carts and a corresponding number of draught animals. Then came the camp followers, whose numbers could sometimes equal and occasionally exceed the total of combatants. When the Spanish army laid siege to Bergen-op-Zoom in the Netherlands in 1622, the Calvinist pastors in the beleaguered town virtuously recorded that 'such a long tail on such a small body never was seen:…such a small army with so many carts, baggage horse, nags, sutlers, lackeys, women, children, and a rabble which numbered far more than the army itself.'

Not surprisingly, therefore, field armies remained relatively small. To take a single example, in November 1632, when Gustavus Adolphus directed the activities of 183,000 soldiers, 62,000 were scattered over northern Germany in ninety-eight garrisons; 34,000 guarded Sweden, Finland, and the Baltic provinces; and 66,000 more operated as quasi-autonomous, regional forces in the Holy Roman Empire. The king therefore fought and died at Lützen at the head of a mere 20,000 men.

'War' in 1632, as in every other year of hostilities in early modern Europe, meant skirmishes and surprises far more than it meant full-scale sieges and battles, and the verdict of the latter could swiftly be offset by the debilitating drain of the former, prolonging the conflict. Thus, during the civil wars in England and Wales, between 1642 and 1648 over 600 engagements occurred. However, only nine encounters involved the death of more than 1,000 men: the rest of the 80,000 or so fatal casualties of the wars fell in comparatively minor hostilities – almost half of them in engagements where fewer than 250 died. In addition, of course, many soldiers either perished or left the service through disease or accident. 'We bury more toes and fingers than we do men,' lamented one royalist officer.

But politics proved equally important in eternalizing war. Above all, many of the issues for which early modern wars were fought defied any easy solution. In the sixteenth century, wars tended to be fought for dynastic rights (Charles VIII of France invaded Italy in 1494, for example, in order to assert his claim to the kingdom of Naples) whereas in the seventeenth they more often concerned the control of adjacent territory. Increasingly, rulers seem to have pursued a more pragmatic approach to asserting their rights – fighting only for lands and titles that represented genuine strategic or economic benefits – and even took to occupying by force convenient lands to which they had no claim (the Swedes lacked any title at all to Pomerania and Mecklenburg, which they demanded as part of any peace settlement: they merely insisted that possession of the duchies had become essential to Sweden's national security and kept on fighting until everyone else agreed).

However, dynastic pretension also made way between 1530 and 1650 for a far more potent ideological justification for waging war: religion. Not that the two were mutually exclusive. Robert Monro, a Scotsman who served first Denmark and then Sweden during the Thirty Years War (and wrote the first regimental history in English: *Monro His Expedition with the Worthy Scots Regiment Called Mackays*, London 1637) gave as his principal reasons for fighting the defence of the Protestant faith and the claims and honour of Elizabeth Stuart, his king's sister, who had been deprived of her lands and titles by the Holy Roman Emperor. 'The Protestant cause' mobilized many: it justified England's decision to assist the Dutch Republic after 1585, as well as the intervention of Denmark and Sweden in the Thirty Years War. An apparent threat to the Catholic faith proved equally powerful among the rulers of Spain and Italy. In 1591, one of Philip II of Spain's ministers became so exasperated by his master's support for deserving Catholic causes everywhere, plunging his country into war with France and England as well as the Dutch, that he chided the king:

> If God had intended Your Majesty to heal all the lame who come to you for cure, He would have given you the power to do so; and if He had wished to oblige Your Majesty to remedy all the troubles of the world, He would have given you the money and the strength to do so.

The king, however, did not listen and Spain's war with France continued until 1598, with England until 1604, and with the Dutch until 1609 (only to resume again in 1621).

RELIGION AND THE LAWS OF WAR

The religious overtones of many early modern conflicts seem to have caused not only greater longevity but also an increase in brutality. Admittedly this was also an age when warfare was dominated by sieges, which in all ages have tended towards savagery; but many soldiers seem to have displayed an unusual harshness towards

The etiquette of atrocity

A certain amount of brutality is probably inevitable in all conflicts, given that the business of the military in war is killing people and breaking things. Moreover, many 'atrocities' take place in certain circumstances that have produced similar results in almost all societies, above all when the sudden collapse of an enemy force turns one army into a cowardly crowd and the other into a murderous mob. This happens most often after an adversary is completely broken in battle, for whereas in close combat, in the midst of a press of men, it might be difficult to deal deadly blows, it is very different when the victors can ride down individual fugitives. Carnage occurred even more frequently when a town was taken by storm. Sieges have always been treated as 'total war', because soldiers who seek a civilian shelter and civilians who militarize their homes by accepting a garrison in effect present an undifferentiated target to the besiegers.

Military and civilian personnel and property could be hard to distinguish during the battery, the assault, and the sack that normally followed a successful storm. Moreover, the catharsis of passing through the breach and emerging unscathed has spurred many victors on to indiscriminate violence.

Some conflicts, however, seem to have been waged with greater brutality than others. Wars fought against rebels, or against followers of a different religious creed, normally involved far more savagery – or so it seemed to contemporaries. An English booklet of 1638, entitled *The Lamentations of Germany*, provided a long and harrowing report on the misery created by the Thirty Years War, divided into chapters with titles such as 'Of tortures and torments', 'Of rape and ravishing', and 'Of bloodshed and killing' – all accompanied by chilling illustrations (right) to emphasize man's inhumanity in time of war.

Images from *The Lamentations of Germany*, 1638

their foes because they believed they were punishing the enemies of God. Thus the Catholic army commanded by Count Tilly in 1631, shortly before meeting its nemesis at Breitenfeld, sacked Protestant Magdeburg in a three-day orgy of killing – ranked by other Protestants at the time as a 'memorable catastrophe' similar to the fall of Troy or Noah's flood, but justified by Catholics as the chastening of unbelievers enjoined in the Old Testament.

The rhetoric of churchmen at this time did little to encourage restraint. A sermon preached in 1645 to the soldiers of the English Parliament just before they stormed Basing House, the stronghold of a Catholic peer, for example, condemned those within as 'open enemies of God', 'bloody papists', and 'vermin', calling for their extermination. Here, as on other occasions, military chaplains acted almost as political commissars, maintaining ideological fervour and repressing any sense of pity among their troops. Small wonder, then, that few of the defeated defenders of Basing House received quarter.

More remarkably, in the age of religious wars the same blinkered intransigence also affected strategic decisions. Thus in 1571, when his plan for an invasion of England in support of a Catholic rising began to unravel because of the arrest of the chief conspirators, Philip II of Spain nevertheless insisted upon going ahead:

> I am so keen to achieve the consummation of this enterprise, I am so attached to it in my heart, and I am so convinced that God our Saviour must embrace it as His own cause, that I cannot be dissuaded. Nor can I accept or believe the contrary.

The king only agreed to cancel the project two months later. Likewise in 1586, when Philip II decided to sanction Spanish intervention in France in support of the Catholic party, he noted:

> Truly, I have only agreed to this because it seems to be the only way available to remedy the religious state of that kingdom. It may well mean that we shall encounter other difficulties arising from what we are doing, but the cause of religion is the most important thing of all.

Similar statements from this period abound: most rulers equated their own interests, and those of the lands they ruled with God (as Philip II once put it to a dispirited subordinate: 'You are engaged in God's service and in mine – which is the same thing'); and most nations regarded themselves as the new 'Chosen People', granted a direct warrant by God to resist and defeat those who did not share their ideology.

The confessional ferment unleashed by the Reformation intensified diplomatic intercourse as well as war: co-religionists exchanged ambassadors, visited each other's capitals and signed mutual defence pacts. Periods of relative peace, such as the decade before 1618 (rather like the years before 1914), saw frenzied attempts to create international alignments that would guarantee support in case of attack; while, in wartime, governments sought to counter the effects of military defeat by enlisting further allies against their temporarily victorious foes. As an experienced ambassador observed in 1619, just as the Thirty Years War got under way: 'The wars of mankind today are not limited to a trial of natural strength, like a bull-fight, nor even to mere battles. Rather they depend on losing or gaining friends and allies.' But on what criteria should these 'friends and allies' be chosen? It was here that the polarization of Europe into separate religious camps between the 1530s and the 1640s proved so destabilizing, for confessional and political advantage seldom coincided, creating a seemingly endless cycle of uncontrollable conflict.

By the mid-seventeenth century many observers feared that war had brought Europe perilously close to self-destruction. 'Oh come on!' ran one of the hymns written by the German pastor Paul Gerhardt, 'Wake up, wake up you hard world, open your eyes before terror comes upon you in swift sudden surprise.' A desperate entry in a Swabian peasant family's Bible from 1647 reads: 'We live like animals, eating bark and grass. No one could imagine that anything like this could happen to us. Many people say that there is no God.' A little later in England, writing a few months after the end of the Civil War, John Locke regretted 'all those flames that have made such havoc and desolation in Europe and have not been quenched but with the blood of so many millions.'

Political leaders, as well as writers, artists, and ordinary people, began to feel revulsion towards the excesses of the preceding period and harboured a fervent hope that it should never happen again. As in the aftermath of World War I, the slaughter had been so great, the spectre of chaos so terrifying, that 'no more war' attitudes became current. Some have detected in these sentiments a climate favourable to the development of absolute states, for certainly political elites throughout western Europe recognized that armies needed to be better controlled, and that this control should be exercised by the state. They also acknowledged that paying heavy taxes to a monarch who (although he might claim absolute power) lay subject to certain restraints, was preferable to providing endless contributions to a mercenary army subject to none.

Political elites in the West also began to favour a measure of 'deconfessionalization' in order to reduce the risk of conflicts spiralling out of control. Of course religion continued to influence war and politics – for example it helped William III to unseat the Catholic James II in 1688, while fear of Louis XIV's anti-Protestant policies after 1685 certainly played a part in unifying his northern enemies. But after the 1640s religion, like dynastic interest, ceased to dominate international relations. Thus Calvinist William's staunchest ally in the wars against Louis XIV was the Catholic Prince Eugene of Savoy, who served the no less Catholic Austrian Habsburgs; while in the Great Northern War (1700–21), Lutheran Sweden eventually collapsed before a coalition of Lutheran Denmark, Calvinist Brandenburg, Catholic Poland, and Orthodox Russia. In the later seventeenth century, although wars continued to be fought in much the same way, they were waged for very different causes and with a far greater degree of state control.

Groß Europiſch Kriegs Balet/getantzet durch die Könige vnd Potentaten Fürſten vnd Reſpublicken/ auff dem Saal der betrübten Chriſtenheit.

'The Great European War Ballet', a satirical print of 1647–48, shows rulers trying to move in concert at the peace conference convened to end the Thirty Years War, as angels scatter olive branches and apples of discord before them. On the right, the infant Louis XIV holds hands with the prince of Orange (leader of the Dutch Republic), the king of Portugal and a Swedish general (Gustavus Adolphus lies sleeping beside them); they move almost in step with the emperor and his allies on the left. Meanwhile the neutral Swiss, in the foreground, seek their own advantage.

CHAPTER 10   *States in Conflict*

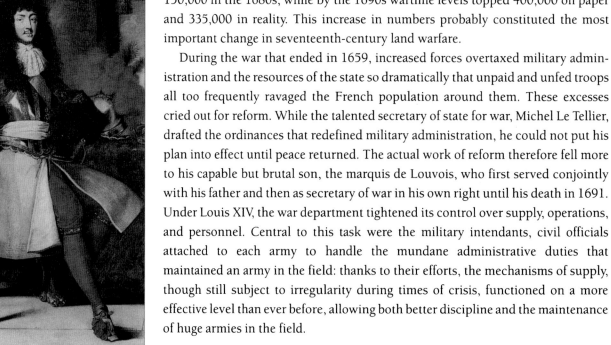

Pitau's portrait of Louis XIV at age thirty-two shows the proud and imperious young monarch as he prepared to magnify his glory by attacking the Dutch in 1672. He had yet to suffer defeat, yet to see his kingdom exhausted by war and his ambitions thwarted by a coalition of his enemies.

With her victory over Spain in 1659, France seized the high ground as the pre-eminent land power in Europe and transformed the face of Mars. The Bourbons expanded wartime forces, improved military administration, and created a powerful standing army, and in doing so set a new pattern for Europe. Prussia and Russia imported this design and found that it required governmental as well as military reform. Through warfare, these two new powers carved out a place beside the other European states. At sea the British dominated, shouldering aside the Spanish, Dutch, and French to expand British colonial holdings. Finally, western powers put warfare on a truly global stage in the Seven Years War, as they contested dominion in Europe, America, and India. The period from 1661 to 1763 provided a historical theatre for the ambitions of powerful statesmen who both refashioned their military instruments and wielded them in a series of wars for glory and empire.

THE GRAND MONARCH IN ARMS

France, more than any other state, provided the paradigm for western armies early in this period. The French army grew to unprecedented size during the reign of Louis XIV (1643–1715), who came to the throne as a boy but only assumed full authority in 1661. During the long war with Spain, 1635–59, actual army size peaked at about 125,000 men. Such numbers doubled the size of the army maintained by the preceding generation, but growth did not end there. Peacetime forces, which had remained in the range of 10,000–20,000 since 1500, reached 150,000 in the 1680s, while by the 1690s wartime levels topped 400,000 on paper and 335,000 in reality. This increase in numbers probably constituted the most important change in seventeenth-century land warfare.

During the war that ended in 1659, increased forces overtaxed military administration and the resources of the state so dramatically that unpaid and unfed troops all too frequently ravaged the French population around them. These excesses cried out for reform. While the talented secretary of state for war, Michel Le Tellier, drafted the ordinances that redefined military administration, he could not put his plan into effect until peace returned. The actual work of reform therefore fell more to his capable but brutal son, the marquis de Louvois, who first served conjointly with his father and then as secretary of war in his own right until his death in 1691. Under Louis XIV, the war department tightened its control over supply, operations, and personnel. Central to this task were the military intendants, civil officials attached to each army to handle the mundane administrative duties that maintained an army in the field: thanks to their efforts, the mechanisms of supply, though still subject to irregularity during times of crisis, functioned on a more effective level than ever before, allowing both better discipline and the maintenance of huge armies in the field.

To accomplish this reformation, Louis and Louvois tamed the officer corps. Before Louvois' administration, officers had enjoyed surprising independence but, with the backing of the king, Louvois circumscribed their judgements and actions. He insisted that officers attend their troops rather than lounging at court, and he exerted much greater control over the financial abuses they committed. Moreover, in 1675 the *ordre de tableau* (Table of Ranks) firmly established that seniority, not birth and status, would determine rank.

The single greatest failure of French military institutions as a whole was not strictly military: Louis XIV never overhauled the way in which the monarchy financed war, so that the kind of low-cost, long-term credit mobilized by the English and the Dutch proved beyond his means. Jean-Baptiste Colbert, Louis' finance minister between 1661 and 1683, tried to put French fiscal policy on a more rational basis, but Louis' lust for war undercut his efforts. In November 1671 Colbert, who had resolutely opposed the king's plan to launch a surprise invasion of the Dutch Republic, made a final attempt to dissuade his master: during an interview Colbert claimed that he could not see how to finance the proposed war. 'Think

Bread for the soldiers of France

These passages from François Nodot (one of the contractors who supplied food to Louis XIV's troops) in his *Le munitionnaire des armées de France* (*The Supply Contractor of the Armies of France*, Paris, 1697) illustrate the regularity and rationality achieved in French logistics by the 1690s. Here he discusses the transport of bread in specially designed caissons, or coffers, mounted on wagons, and grouped in *équipages*, or company-sized transportation units.

> France, where good order reigns during wartime as well as during peace... today has this advantage over its enemies, that its troops are well served for their subsistence; other nations... do not enjoy the use of caissons, a practice regularly established by the French, nor do other nations have well-placed magazines stocked with everything that is necessary to allow their armies to subsist...
>
> The secretary of state for war sets the number of *équipages* according to that of the troops who are to go on campaign: ordinarily one creates four times as many *équipages* as would be necessary to carry subsistence for one day, since food is often furnished only every four days to the troops...that is to say [at the most, bread stays] four days in the soldiers' haversacks, and four days in the caissons.
>
> Each *équipage* is of 100 horses; there are four of them for each caisson, driven by a teamster, thus there are 25 caissons for each *équipage*...
>
> The caisson is in the shape of a great chest, the cover of which is raised a bit in the centre...so that the rain flows off... The caisson will be 8 feet 4 inches long...3 feet 4 inches high from the bottom to the crest of the cover, [tapering from] 2 feet 5 inches at the bottom [to] 2 feet 9 inches wide at the top...The tops will be covered with waxed cloth...The caisson will be painted with at least two coats of red oil paint.

An army of 60,000 troops could include 40,000 horses, each of which daily consumed about fifty pounds of green fodder. The mountain of forage required by such a force had to be found locally, and the endless task of supplying an army's horses consumed a great deal of time and manpower. Cavalrymen spent more hours wielding scythes than swords. In this engraving by N. Guérard, c.1696, soldiers cut, bale, and load bundles of fodder weighing as much as two hundred pounds. Forage parties often included thousands of men commanded by a lieutenant general.

about it' the king retorted icily. 'If you can't do it, there will always be somebody who can.' Colbert agonized for a week (during which his voluminous correspondence came to a total halt) but then capitulated and developed a fiscal policy based on expensive short-term credit secured by mortgaging future revenues.

However, Louis resorted as much as he could to other financial means besides taxation and credit. In two notable ways, war could partially pay for itself. First, troops holding foreign territory demanded that the occupied population hand over 'contributions': *ad hoc* payments in money and in kind. At times the French rationalized the exaction of contributions to such a degree that they seemed more like regular taxation than pillage, yet the threat of violence remained central. As Louis XIV himself once mused in 1691, 'It is terrible to be obliged to burn villages in order to bring people to pay contributions, but since neither menace nor sweetness makes them pay, it is necessary to continue to use these rigours.'

Second, Louis also made eager French aristocrats pay for the right to command regiments or companies of their own. It was necessary for aspirants to purchase commissions as colonels or captains, but the purchase price was just the first in a series of expenses. Colonels often paid the costs of creating their regiments and, in addition, should food, equipment, or pay not arrive, or should the amount allotted for recruitment bounties prove insufficient, commanders were expected to draw on their own resources to make good the shortfall.

BATTLE AND SIEGE

The army of Louis XIV experienced no great tactical revolution, merely a continuation of earlier trends. Between 1660 and 1715 infantry formations continued to become thinner and longer in a steady progression, reducing from a battle order six deep at the beginning of this period down to four or even three. Pikemen, who had composed a third of an infantry battalion in 1660, made up only a fifth of it, at the most, by 1700. The matchlock musket, dominant in 1660, gradually disappeared in the French army until entirely replaced by the handier – but more expensive –

flintlock musket in 1699. In 1703 the French also abandoned the pike altogether, in favour of the socket bayonet which at the end of a flintlock musket sufficed to make it an effective short pike as well as a firearm. The adoption of the flintlock and bayonet brought with it no radical transformation of tactics, however, just one more step in a direction long followed. Cavalry and artillery enjoyed modest advances too. Cavalry regiments added picked companies of carabiniers (troopers armed with rifled carbines) while Louis multiplied the number of his dragoon regiments (mounted soldiers trained to fight both on horseback and on foot). French artillerists standardized cannon and increased the number of mortars used in siege warfare. The disposition of a field army for battle also remained much as it had evolved by 1660, with the entire force deployed in two or three lines, infantry in the centre, cavalry on the wings, and artillery parceled out across the front.

Louis XIV spent a great deal of time with his armies, until advancing age limited his activities. While he never commanded at a single battle in the open field, the king attended many major sieges. Siege warfare suited contemporary strategic and tactical parameters, and it also appealed to Louis' taste for detail and control. This painting by Jean-Baptiste Martin portrays the king, in red cape, at the siege of Namur in 1692, successfully directed by Vauban. In 1695, however, the allies retook the fortress.

Sébastien Le Prestre de Vauban's portrait by the court painter Hyacinthe Rigaud reveals the great engineer's character. It is the face of a strong and surprisingly sensitive man who, appalled by the human cost of war, proposed his systematic method of taking fortresses in order to 'burn gunpowder and spill less blood'. Vauban was also brave. At the siege of Lille in 1667 he was struck by a musket ball in his left cheek, a scar he bore through life, and took such risks that Louis eventually forbade him to enter the siege trenches.

Operations in the field became more and more dependent upon supplies brought up from the rear, even though the green, or fresh, fodder used to feed horses during the campaign season still had to be gathered in the immediate area occupied by an army, because it would have been too heavy to haul overland. However, the standard daily ration of 1.5 pounds of bread distributed to each man on campaign could be and was carted: bread was too important an item to be left to chance, since troops left unfed or unpaid in the seventeenth century deserted, marauded, or mutinied. Since the only guarantee against such fates was regular supply, armies were bound by their commissaries – not because generals were unimaginative, but because they justifiably feared the consequences if they outran their supplies.

The dependence on regular supply added to the importance of fortresses which served as magazines, guarded lines of communication, and shielded resource areas from the imposition of contributions by the enemy. Louis' pre-eminent military engineer, Sébastien Le Prestre de Vauban, improved both the design of fortresses and the techniques used to attack them. His monuments of military architecture can be seen today in the *plans en relief*, models once displayed in the Hall of Mirrors at Versailles and still preserved in the Musée de l'Armée in Paris. Not only did he design individual forts, but he arrayed them in the *pré carré*, a double line of fortresses that buttressed the vulnerable northeast frontier of France. As a result, in the second half of the seventeenth century, warfare in and around France revolved around sieges, not battles. As the German military writer Johann Behr stated in 1677, 'Field battles are in comparison scarcely a topic of conversation…Indeed… the whole art of war seems to come down to shrewd attacks and artful fortifications.'

Louis XIV fought his first wars in the name of glory, which he sought through military victory and territorial conquest. Not long after assuming power in 1661, Louis asserted flimsy claims based on the inheritance of his Spanish wife and ordered his armies to invade the Spanish Netherlands in 1667. Although he thought that the Dutch and English would allow his assault on their traditional enemy, instead they joined with Sweden to force Louis to stop this 'War of Devolution' in 1668. Louis regarded this as betrayal, and accused the Dutch of 'ingratitude, bad faith, and insupportable vanity.'

It comes as little surprise that Louis directed his next war against the Dutch Republic itself, so as to eliminate their opposition to his conquest of the Spanish Netherlands in the future. He bought English support by secret payments to Charles II, and attacked the isolated Dutch in May 1672. At first, French forces under command of the prince de Condé and Henri de la Tour d'Auvergne, vicomte de Turenne, met with success; however, ten days after the French crossed the Rhine on 12 June, the resolute Dutch cut the dikes and stalled Louis' armies. Alarmed by Louis' appetite for conquest, Spain, the Empire, and Brandenburg rallied to the Dutch, while England made a separate peace in 1674. In the face of such opposition, Louis withdrew his forces from Dutch territory, only to continue fighting on other fronts. Nevertheless, the treaty of Nijmegen that ended the Dutch

War in 1678 gave Louis impressive new lands, particularly Franche Comté, so he had won some glory.

In fact, Louis' policies had changed by 1678. In 1675 Turenne died and Condé retired, and with the passing of these bellicose generals, Louis listened to the more cautious Louvois and his protégé Vauban. The king became obsessed with protecting what was his, and this meant shoring up his frontiers. As Clausewitz later observed, 'It had become almost a question of honour for Louis XIV to defend the frontiers of the kingdom from any threat, however insignificant.' To seal off his German frontier, in 1681 he seized Strasbourg, and in 1684 he took Luxembourg. But if Louis regarded these land grabs, christened 'Reunions,' as defensive, Europe understandably viewed them as naked aggression.

The fortress of Neuf Brisach, shown here in model form, represents Vauban's most advanced style of fortification, his 'third' system, which employed artillery towers at each point of the octagonal design. Because this fortress, begun in 1698, is situated on flat marshy ground on the banks of the Rhine it is absolutely regular in shape. Vauban would have taken advantage of natural obstacles had there been any.

HABSBURG VICTORIES

As Louis buttressed his Rhine frontier in the 1680s, the potential foe that he feared most was neither the Spaniards nor the Dutch, but the Austrian Habsburgs, whose power grew as they began to push back the Turks. On their southeastern border, the Habsburgs had duelled with the Ottoman Turks for generations, but the climax came when the Ottoman Empire launched its final major assault on the West, in

1678–83. The Turks' first target was Ukraine, but in 1681 they gave up their claims to that area. Instead, when a rebellion threatened the Habsburg hold on Hungary two years later, the Turks marched into Austria with a large army of about 90,000 men. The Habsburg field army of 33,000 withdrew before them, leaving a garrison of 12,000 in Vienna, and the Turks laid siege to the city in mid-July.

The engineer Georg Rimpler had reinforced Vienna's walls and bastions in anticipation of a siege, and the defenders had a marked superiority in artillery – 312 cannon to 112 – but the odds were still against them. Using mines more than artillery, the Turks concentrated their attack on two bastions. The long siege wore down the garrison until only 4,000 troops remained by September, when mines destroyed the main bastion and the Turks seemed poised to storm the city. However, signal rockets illuminated the sky over the Vienna woods on the night of 7–8 September, a sign that a relief army had arrived. King Jan Sobieski of Poland had brought a Polish army of 21,000 troops south from Warsaw, a journey of 220 miles, in only fifteen days – a rapid march indeed. With the Poles and several German contingents, the Christian field army now totalled 68,000

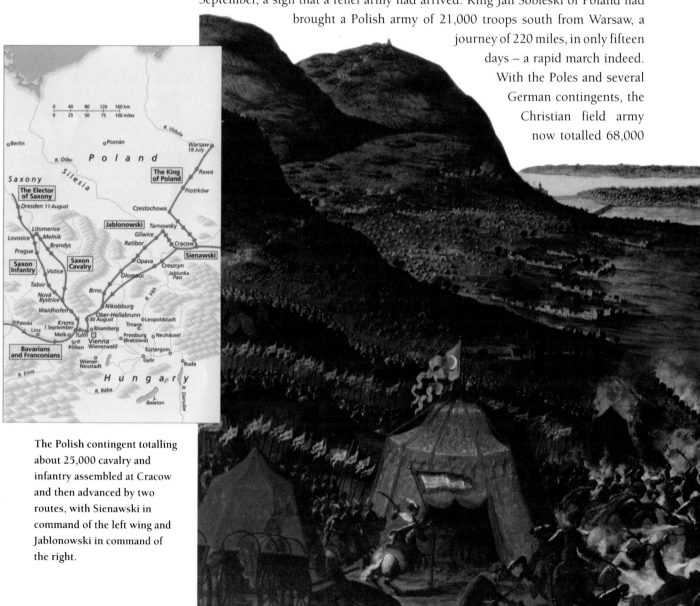

The Polish contingent totalling about 25,000 cavalry and infantry assembled at Cracow and then advanced by two routes, with Sienawski in command of the left wing and Jablonowski in command of the right.

– large enough to take on the Turks. On 12 September this force charged out of the Vienna woods, 'like a herd of maddened swine' according to the Ottoman commander, and destroyed the Turkish host. Austrian forces pursued the retreating Ottomans, expelling them from Hungary, and an Austrian victory at Mohacs (1687) drove the Turks east of the Danube.

Certainly, the surge of the Habsburg forces against the Ottomans constituted one aspect of the growing western military domination of the globe. It was almost another great crusade. Still Louis XIV feared that with the Ottoman threat in decline and Austrian armies advancing, the emperor would turn his increased resources against Christian France, and in this he was right. Habsburg victories won for them more territory, population, and resources so that, even stripped of the Spanish holdings that had once benefited Charles V, and devoid of much of the old imperial authority since the peace of Westphalia, the Austrian Habsburgs stood poised to reassert their status as major players in European affairs.

Actually, by the late seventeenth century, Europe had split into two primary power systems: France, England, Spain, and the Dutch Netherlands in the west and Austria, Brandenburg-Prussia, Sweden and Russia in the east. On the whole, these two systems compartmentalized European international relations. However, they were linked by diplomacy and interest at times. Austria more than any other power exerted her influence both in the east and the west.

The relief of Vienna (left), 12 September 1683. After a two-month siege, the relief army commanded by King John Sobieski of Poland in person, charged down upon the Turkish camp. Christian lancers pouring in from the left bear crosses on their pennants; Turkish cavalry can be identified by their turbans. The lack of defences around the Turkish camp contributed to their defeat. A contemporary engraving (below) details the Turkish siege trenches which concentrated on only a small section between two bastions of Vienna's walls. To the left is the Löwel Bastion and to the right is the Burg Bastion; between them lie the remains of the Burg Ravelin, an outwork advanced from the main walls.

PETER THE GREAT

The other state to benefit from the faltering Ottoman Empire, Russia, underwent a military and political transformation under Peter I, the Great (1689–1725). Imperial Russia, long isolated in the east, had already begun to play a role in the struggles of central Europe and to reform its forces along western lines before Peter's accession to the throne, but he accelerated and accentuated both trends to such a degree that his accomplishments can truly be called revolutionary. Reshaped by Peter's work, Russia replaced Sweden as the most significant military force in the north and began a course of expansion.

Traditional Russian forces consisted of cavalry composed primarily of petty nobles, the Middle Service Class, who enjoyed land holdings and fought as horse archers. Along with this force served a body of infantry known as the Streltsy, created in 1550 and armed with muskets and halberds. Both kinds of traditional troops had once been potent, but could no longer match Russia's foes. The Middle Service Class cavalry were mounted poorly and carried obsolete weapons, while the Streltsy suffered from poor leadership and had become more interested in their peacetime trades than in their wartime duties. In the seventeenth-century the tsars therefore recruited foreign mercenaries to stiffen their armies. At first entire foreign regiments fought for the tsar, but by mid-century the pattern shifted to hiring only individual foreign officers to train and lead Russian-born troops. These foreign officers imported the military models pioneered in the West, creating Russian 'new formation regiments' in imitation of western armies. The Thirteen Years War (1654–67) against Poland confirmed the triumph of gunpowder weapons, and in the last years of this struggle the Russians created a strong base of new formation regiments; however, with the return of peace, the tsar discharged his western-style units in the interests of economy, and traditional forces still constituted the vast majority of the Russian army when Peter came to the throne.

Even as a boy, Peter displayed a taste for western military styles and organized two regiments of youths that he drilled and commanded. After the young Peter acceded to his troubled throne in 1689, he seemed more concerned with this small army than with the more mundane duties of government. However, his military expeditions against the Crimean Tatars in 1695 and 1696 both spurred his ambition for conquest and heightened his resolve to westernize his army and his state. In 1697–98 he journeyed through western Europe, learning what he could and paying special attention to military and naval matters.

Peter next took on Sweden in the Great Northern War (1700–21). During the first year of the war, he led an army of 40,000 troops to besiege Narva, where he met defeat at the hands of a mere 8,000 Swedes under Charles XII (1697–1718), and this humiliation drove Peter to overhaul his army completely. After 1705 he instituted a system of conscription, which yielded 337,000 men by 1713. Peter not only increased the size of his army but also re-equipped his entire infantry with modern flintlock muskets and socket bayonets, trained it in western tactics, and

Opposite: Peter the Great's enthusiasm for the West extended even to matters of style and appearance. Therefore, this 1717 portrait by J. M. Nattier shows the Tsar in the pose and armour of a western European monarch. (Compare it with the image of Louis XIV nearly fifty years earlier on page 164.) Peter imported military and government reforms from the West, but he imposed them on his people in the brutal manner of a Russian autocrat.

hardened it through constant, though limited, military engagements. At first he continued to rely upon mercenary officers hired from abroad, but he also forced Russian men of land and wealth into the army to supply a corps of capable native-born officers. An edict of 1725 stipulated that foreigners could make up no more than one third of all officer cadres.

Peter did even more for the Russian navy. At the start of his reign no navy existed and Russians showed little interest in going to sea. The Tsar accomplished miracles, building naval yards, establishing ports – St Petersburg being only the most famous – and even creating an academy for naval officers. By the end of the Great Northern War, his Baltic fleet alone numbered 124 Russian-built sailing vessels, in addition to ships captured from the Swedes. Peter also constructed hundreds of shallow-draft galleys for use in the Baltic and the Black Sea. While he imported western experts to design and command vessels, he also trained Russians who would eventually fill these roles themselves. All this Peter accomplished without the benefit of a merchant fleet to supply skilled sailors and seasoned captains, as was the case in Britain, the Dutch Republic, and France.

The course of reform initiated by Peter demonstrated what other countries would later also discover: that it was impossible to westernize the tools of war without transforming government and society as well. Peter overhauled government administration to supply the resources needed by his army and created a poll tax that, along with other fiscal devices, doubled state revenue. He also promoted education for the landed classes in order to produce a more effective officer corps, and rationalized the pattern of the social elite in the Table of Ranks of 1722. Peter even ordered his aristocracy to cut off their beards and adopt western styles of dress. Nor was the economy immune from his actions: to supply his troops with weapons, Peter expanded an already productive metals industry, while he also encouraged other forms of manufacture, including the woollens industry, to make his army self-sufficient. It is true that Peter's actions were so revolutionary that they generated a reaction that eliminated some reforms after his death; but he still succeeded in launching Russia as a major western power with formidable armed forces.

By 1708–09 he was ready to contest Charles XII on far better terms, and the rash Swedish king gave Peter his chance by advancing deep into Ukraine during 1708. In the autumn, Peter mauled a Swedish force sent to reinforce Charles, who could not properly supply his army during the winter of 1708–09, and it dwindled. In the spring of 1709, the already overwrought Swedes besieged Poltava. With new confidence in his army Peter resolved to 'seek our luck in combat with the enemy' and closed in to relieve the siege. Once near the Swedes, the Russians erected an impressive series of redoubts and entrenched their camp. Charles decided to attack before things became worse; therefore, early in the morning of 8 July Charles led 25,000 troops against Peter's camp, but in the first phase of the battle the Russian redoubts broke up their advance and inflicted serious losses. Then Peter's army of 45,000 sallied forth from its entrenched camp. In the ensuing struggle the numerous Russian cannon cut swathes through Swedish ranks, and when the Russians advanced, the Swedes bolted for the rear. At the battle itself and in the abortive retreat the Russians killed or captured nearly the entire Swedish army; their performance clearly announced Russia's arrival as a major military power. The war would drag on an additional twelve years, and Peter would continue his course of reform, but Europe had already seen the eclipse of one great power, Sweden, by another, Russia.

THE GREAT WARS OF LOUIS XIV

While Peter pursued his work of reform, Louis XIV engaged in his last two conflicts, the War of the League of Augsburg (1688–97) and the War of the Spanish Succession (1701–14). These long and costly struggles encompassed both the old and new worlds, since each European contest projected its image on North America, the first as King William's War and the second as Queen Anne's War. However, since the south Asian subcontinent remained relatively unaffected, these struggles lacked the truly global character of those of the mid-eighteenth century.

In 1688, Louis demanded permanent guarantees that no one would challenge the lands he had annexed during the Reunions and, failing to receive such assurances, he launched upon what he believed would be a short war against the Habsburg empire. In October his troops seized the fortress of Philippsburg, the last bridgehead on the Rhine that threatened Alsace. Next, his troops devastated the Palatinate in order to safeguard France from any attack across the Rhine by denying supplies to an enemy approaching the river. But French aggression and cruelty galvanized Europe into a new league against Louis; this Grand Alliance included the Habsburg empire, the Dutch Republic, Spain, Savoy, Brandenburg, and Great Britain (now ruled by the Dutch leader, William III).

Faced by such a mighty coalition, Louis mustered the largest army of his reign. Led by the able marshal Luxembourg in the field and directed by Vauban in siege warfare, the French won a series of victories with few outright defeats. The size of

John Churchill, duke of Marlborough (1650–1722), repeatedly humbled the armies of Louis XIV. This image from a tapestry at the magnificent house built for him by a grateful nation, Blenheim Palace, shows him at the moment of his greatest triumph: at Blenheim in 1704. The greatest general of his age, Marlborough never lost a battle or a campaign during the eleven years of the War of the Spanish Succession (1702–13), during which he held supreme command of the British and Allied army. His career involved thirty sieges, most of them successful, and four great battles.

The Battle of Blenheim 1704

In 1704, the French, together with their Bavarian allies, marched into the heart of Germany to drive the Austrian Habsburgs out of the war. In a remarkable march, the duke of Marlborough rushed south from the Netherlands with 21,000 troops to assist the Austrians. By arranging with local authorities to supply him en route, he covered 250 miles in five weeks during May and June. He even provided new shoes to his footsore troops at Heidelberg. By the time of his arrival, his army had grown to 40,000.

Once on the Danube he combined with an Austrian army led by Prince Eugene of Savoy, and on 13 August they faced 56,000 Franco-Bavarian troops at Blenheim. Marlborough and Eugene commanded 52,000. Marlborough, on the left squared off against a French army commanded by Tallard, while Eugene on the right faced Marsin and the Elector of Bavaria with a Franco-Bavarian force.

Marlborough seized the offensive by attacking the villages of Blenheim on his left and Oberglau on his right. His army suffered high casualties, but by drawing off French troops to each flank, Marlborough weakened Tallard's centre. At the crucial moment, he smashed through, precipitating the disintegration and destruction of the Franco-Bavarian forces, which suffered 38,600 killed, wounded, and captured for a loss of 12,000 killed and wounded among the forces

commanded by Marlborough and Eugene. A contemporary British memoirist, Captain Robert Parker, wrote of Louis' shock at learning of Blenheim: '[I]t being the first blow of any fatal consequence, his armies had received, during his long reign. And he said in passion, he had often heard of armies being beaten, but never of one taken.' Louis XIV would threaten the heart of Germany no more.

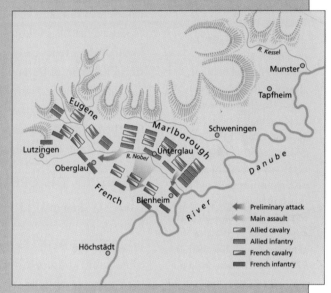

armies engaged in battle increased considerably: at the Battle of Neerwinden on 29 July 1693, 80,000 French troops under Luxembourg defeated 50,000 allies under William III. Despite such victories, however, this war so consumed Louis' resources and undermined his credit that he concluded a peace of exhaustion at Ryswick, where he gave up much that he had gained since 1678.

Europe might now have enjoyed peace but for the complications of the Spanish succession. The sickly and impotent King Carlos II died in 1700 without issue. Both French and Habsburg candidates vied for the throne, and attempts to hammer out a compromise partition failed when Carlos bequeathed all his domains to the French candidate, Louis' grandson, Philip of Anjou. The War of the Spanish Succession broke out in 1701, and while the French began resolutely enough, the strains caused by the previous conflict soon showed. They fought much like a tired and bruised boxer, hoping simply to stay on his feet until the bell. Again a powerful coalition faced off against France, now fighting with Spain as an ally. During this war, the English produced one of their greatest captains, the duke of Marlborough, who was ably seconded by Eugene of Savoy in command of the Imperial forces. In 1704 they triumphed at Blenheim, the most notable battle of the war.

French fortunes did not improve after Blenheim. If anything, 1706 brought even worst disasters: Marlborough defeated the French at the battle of Ramillies and thus won the Spanish Netherlands for the allies, while south of the Alps, Eugene routed another French army at Turin and thus drove them from Italy. For the French defeat followed defeat, and Louis XIV seemed unable to find a winning general until he placed Marshal Claude de Villars in command of his main forces in 1709. Although Marlborough and Eugene, again working in concert, drove Villars from the battlefield of Malplaquet on 11 September, it proved a Pyrrhic victory since the French retired in good order, ready to fight again. Both sides mustered as many as 90,000 troops that day, and the killed and wounded totalled over 30,000, making it the bloodiest battle of Louis' wars. The French held on until 1712 when, with Marlborough relieved of command for political reasons, Villars met and defeated the allied army at Denain. This French victory prepared the way for a final French offensive in the Spanish Netherlands which resulted in the peace treaties of 1713 and 1714 that maintained French borders and preserved the Spanish crown for the Bourbon dynasty. France was at last secure all along her southern frontier, although, in North America, the British took Acadia from the French forever.

FREDERICK THE GREAT

Louis XIV died in 1715, and with him died an era. He had fought for glory and for high stakes; but between 1715 and 1789 states fought for discrete advantages more than for hegemony. Never has war been based so much on rational economic calculation. Military historians describe this period as an age of limited warfare; and with some exception, this label holds true. This is not to say that states had not fought for economic gain before – certainly the Dutch and the increasingly commercial English had struggled over wealth and commercial advantage in the seventeenth century – but during the eighteenth century, economic conceptions lay at the heart of political plans across Europe. Those notions can be summed up in the term 'mercantilism', which posited a finite wealth in the world, stressed the need for economic self-sufficiency, and insisted on the desirability of selling to your rivals without purchasing as much in return, so as to accumulate treasure and fill up the war chest.

By this formula, for one state to gain, another must lose; it was a zero-sum game in which warfare was a fair means to an end. Of course, if a state fought for limited goals, it made little sense for that state to ruin itself in the process, so that limited goals called forth limited efforts. Thus, France and England struggled over the sugar islands of the Caribbean, the fur-rich trade of Canada, and the jewelled spoils of India, while on the continent of Europe the king of Prussia dreamed of stimulating new manufactures to make his domains self-sufficient and of seizing the province of Silesia to make them richer and stronger.

The Prussia of Frederick II, the Great (1740–86), was the newest and the most unlikely of Europe's major powers. It was very much the product of policies

Opposite: Frederick the Great of Prussia, seen here at the battle of Hohenlinden (1745), was more a great practitioner than a great innovator. He triumphed by raising a basically limited military system to its highest point, rather than by breaking the bonds of that system. His army benefited from the efforts of a dedicated aristocratic officer corps and from ruthless discipline over rank and file that contained many foreigners. Yet the system also depended on Frederick's genius and, after his death in 1786, the Prussians could not match their previous success and embarked on a course that led to their crushing defeat by Napoleon at Jena in 1806.

followed by its talented ruling family, the Hohenzollerns. When Elector Frederick William of Brandenburg (1640–88) came to power, his domains of Brandenburg, East Prussia, and assorted small parcels scattered across northern Germany lacked political integration; only the accidents of inheritance and succession had placed them all in his hands. Each territory boasted its own institutions and privileges, and none felt constrained to provide for the defence of any other. Yet the weakness of the elector's lands brought them calamity. Fortune had placed them between the warring parties of the Thirty Years War – Sweden to the north and Habsburg Austria to the south – and Brandenburg suffered severe devastation by campaign armies and forces of occupation from 1630 onwards. Frederick William resolved that only a considerable army of his own would allow him to defend his inheritance. But to establish and support a single army from the resources of his fragmented domains, he would have to forge those separate and distinct domains into a single polity. Prussia was thus a state created to support an army. Through both argument and naked military force, Frederick William wrung concessions from his territories that allowed him to collect taxes from each to support a single army and to recruit that force in all his lands. To gain such privileges in East Prussia he even besieged Königsberg, his own capital there.

His successors carried on the work. Frederick (1688–1713) won the title of Frederick I, king *in* Prussia, from the Emperor in exchange for allying with him against Louis XIV. The 'in' soon turned to 'of,' and the Hohenzollerns were accepted as true European monarchs. Frederick I showed an un-Prussian interest in luxury and display, but his son Frederick William I (1713–40) returned to more Spartan ways and, by rigorous economies and strenuous efforts, doubled the army he inherited into a force of 80,000, a standing army fully half the size of the French, even though the Prussian population numbered only 2.5 million (against over 20 million in France). The son of Frederick William I, Frederick the Great, almost immediately invested this asset so painstakingly created by his ancestors in a bid to seize the rich duchy of Silesia and thus make Prussia a German power to rival the Habsburgs.

Frederick and his army epitomized the style of warfare that had emerged in the seventeenth century. At base, this style built on the assumption that the common soldier could be trained but not trusted: whether a volunteer or a product of the rudimentary conscription schemes of the late seventeenth and eighteenth century, the soldier was regarded as a potential deserter. According to the count of St Germain, French secretary of state for war in 1775–77: 'In the present state of things, armies can only be composed of the slime of the nation and of all that is useless to society.' Such men had to be employed in formations that allowed close control and constant supervision, emphasizing heavy infantry and cavalry tactics that marshalled men in straight lines in the open field. Commanders disdained the tactics of the skirmisher, seeking his own cover, and fighting on his own initiative, as dangerous and ineffective. Given the chance to take cover away, from the watchful eyes of officer and sergeant, what would keep the soldier from deserting? Harsh discipline and constant practice alone allowed manoeuvre in the brittle line of battle, now thinner than before as infantry exploited volley fire by standing only three men deep with hardly any interval between ranks. Fear was essential to the smooth operation of Frederician tactics; as the king himself asserted, 'An army is composed for the most part of idle and inactive men. Unless the general keeps a constant eye over them…this machine…will soon disintegrate.' And '[the soldier] must be more afraid of his officers than of the dangers to which he is exposed.' Given the limitations of this system, Frederick raised it to its peak. He inherited the best drilled infantry in Europe, and when his cavalry failed to match the standards of his infantry, by ruthless training he whipped it into shape as well.

The key to making this system function was the Prussian officer corps, the most professional in Europe. Frederick compelled his young aristocrats to serve as officers, and once they joined the army only debility or death could release them. French officers acted as fairly independent aristocrats and spent much of their time away from their regiments, but Prussian officers stayed with their units, because they, not their sergeants, supervised training and administration. Prussian officers also led from the front. In order to honour his officers, Frederick also carefully crafted a social hierarchy in which soldiers dominated; even a mere lieutenant or captain took precedence over a senior civilian official.

With his magnificent army, Frederick seized the Habsburg province of Silesia in the War of the Austrian Succession (1740–48). As Emperor Charles VI (1711–40) neared death, he struck many bargains to ensure the succession of his daughter, Maria Theresa. All of them fell through, and she had to fight off ambitious neighbours, including Bavaria, Saxony, France, and Prussia. In the war that ensued, Frederick won Silesia but also the undying enmity of Maria Theresa. His goals and gains had been limited, but her hatred was not.

WEALTH, MIGHT, AND COLONIAL CONQUEST

The struggle between Frederick and Maria Theresa also pitted the French against the British, with the former supporting Prussia and the latter backing the beleaguered empress. One of the constants of international politics after 1688 was the rivalry between France and Great Britain, locked in a series of conflicts sometimes termed a second Hundred Years War. During the middle decades of the eighteenth century, French and British forces clashed around the globe in commercial and military battles for high stakes.

Conflict across the seas proved to be an unequal contest, however, owing to British naval pre-eminence. Great Britain enjoyed a key advantage over France for, try as she might to maintain a navy, France remained essentially a land power requiring a large continental army. In long and costly wars of attrition, the French could not afford to maintain both a great army and a powerful navy. Yet command of the sea allowed the British to win the economic struggles of the eighteenth century, since the ruler of the seas also ruled overseas commerce. In the eighteenth

Sepoys and the conquest of India

For Europeans to control areas of India beyond the range of their broadside-firing vessels, they had to develop and exploit the potential of Asian populations to use western military practices. It was not just a question of placing European weapons in Indian hands; in fact, Europeans enjoyed precious little technological superiority when they left their ships. Native princes had long employed muskets, and their armouries bristled with cannon. The key lay not in the possession of modern arms, but in their disciplined use. In 1749, John Grant, a British officer serving in India, reported that the armies of Indian rulers were hardly armies at all, 'having no regularity or Discipline amongst them.' Such European critics may have been too willing to overlook the military value of native forces, but they make clear that Indian forces were fundamentally different from western armies.

Geography limited the manpower resources commanded by Europeans in India, since importing large bodies of troops from Europe was impossible. Hiring local bands or contracting local alliances enhanced numbers, but the core of European forces could not equal the princely armies in size.

The French seem to have been the first to solve this problem by adding Indian troops trained strictly in western ways – discipline and drill that allowed tightly controlled and cohesive manoeuvre under fire. In 1746 Joseph Dupleix, governor of French India, joined 700 sepoys to his force of 300 Europeans to defeat the Nawab of the Carnatic. Stringer Lawrence, who arrived to command the army of the English East India Company in 1748, adopted the same innovation.

Henceforth, East India Company sepoys served under the immediate command of Indian officers, and a sepoy battalion had few European officers. By 1766 this number had increased to eight, five of whom bore the title of sergeant major, which may reflect the emphasis placed on drill.

Robert Clive, Lawrence's eager protégé, won his battles with very small armies, usually outnumbered ten to one by his Indian foes. He triumphed as much by diplomacy as by military action. But when the Company gained Bengal, its rich reserves of wealth and manpower changed the balance of power on the subcontinent. Already in 1767, Hydar Ali of Mysore faced an army of 800 Europeans and 5,000 sepoys. By 1782 the East India Company maintained an army of 115,000 men, 90 per cent of them sepoys, mostly from Bengal. Now the British could hope to dominate India by force of arms, aided by their talent at subterfuge and diplomacy.

These sepoys of the Madras army in 1825 wear European uniforms better suited to cold climates than to the heat of south India. The only concession to indigenous dress is their turban-shaped headgear. Their clothing is the outward symbol of a deeper transformation – the creation of a disciplined European-style soldier on the south Asian subcontinent.

century, the British followed a set pattern in European warfare, committing only a small army to fight on the Continent, turning her commercial wealth into subsidies for continental allies instead, and using her naval advantage to control the waters around Europe and to win the struggle for colonies and maritime trade.

In turn, colonial power further increased Britain's financial strength. If money be the sinews of war, Britain possessed a strength none could match. At the heart of her ability to conduct successful wars lay the state's ability to raise the necessary funds rationally, through long-term credit at low interest rates. The most apparent evidence of this capacity was the Bank of England, founded in 1694; but the real sources of strength were more basic – commerce and politics. Parliament controlled government finances, and Parliament represented the very classes of men made wealthy by land and commerce who financed the state and its wars. Whereas kings were famous for reneging on their debts, Parliament would not defraud its own. And since it honoured its debts meticulously, terms were reasonable, interest was low, and investments even flowed in from abroad. By contrast, an absolute monarch like Louis XIV refused to abdicate his power over taxes and finance, and thus could not command the confidence of creditors as could Parliament. At base, Britain's military and naval strength grew out of her political system as much as it did from her commercial wealth or the bravery of her sailors and soldiers.

The British used their naval and financial strength to become the great colonial power of the age, replacing the Spanish, Dutch, and French. In South America and the Caribbean, a declining Spain granted increasing commercial privileges to Britain; in India and North America, the major theatres of eighteenth-century colonial warfare, France put up a desperate but unsuccessful fight to retain her hard-won colonies.

India contained strong local states with advanced cultures, long military traditions, and large populations, so that any European power hoping to dominate the subcontinent had to ally with local rulers in order to expel European competitors and to take advantage of local conflicts in order to divide and conquer indigenous rulers. European warfare in India must, therefore, be placed in the context not only of western struggles, but also of Indian wars and rivalries. British success in India would be as much a victory of local diplomacy as a feat of arms.

The Europeans had long enjoyed a great advantage at sea, where their broadside-firing warships dominated the waves, particularly when the Dutch, English and French replaced the Portuguese as the pre-eminent European traders. But power at sea did not easily convert into power on land and, in any case, at first the European trading companies in India interested themselves in commerce, not conquest. The directors of the English East India Company calculated success on the basis of profit and loss, and insisted in 1677, 'Our business is trade not war.' However, successful trade required trading stations on shore, and the security of those stations required modern fortifications and soldiers to defend them. Eventually, Europeans fought to dominate territory as well as commerce, and the English East India Company profited from tribute in addition to trade. In order to fight both local rulers and European foes, westerners had to create their own armies in India. Since shipping European soldiers to India proved too difficult and expensive, sepoys – hired Indian troops armed and trained in European fashion (see page 179) – provided the answer. Once adequately trained and led, sepoys proved their worth against both native Indian and European troops. While not the first to employ them, the English East India Company ultimately enjoyed the greatest success with sepoys.

The wars between the French and English East India companies began in earnest in 1744 with the First Carnatic War (1744–48) and, once begun, drew in regular European military and naval forces. In 1746, the able French governor, Joseph Dupleix, aided by a French fleet, besieged and took the main British base at Madras. However, even though a British siege of the French base at Pondichery failed, the treaty of Aix-la-Chapelle handed Madras back to the British. The Second Carnatic War (1749–54) followed close on the heels of the first, as the French and British embroiled themselves in local Indian conflicts. Again Dupleix displayed his talents at diplomacy and war, and French-backed aspirants established themselves as Nawabs of the Carnatic, making the French the virtual rulers of southeast India. So the opening round went to the French, but their success would not endure.

European warfare in America during the eighteenth century was quite different. While both the British and the French made much use of native Americans as allies, they played only a secondary role in the fighting. This helped to render indecisive the struggle between the Europeans for control of the Americas. Thus the French lost Acadia to Britain in the War of the Spanish Succession, although they maintained their hold along the St Lawrence and the Mississippi. The next conflict, King George's War (1743–48) – the American phase of the War of the Austrian Succession – saw British and colonial forces from New England take the French fortress of Louisbourg on Cape Breton Island in 1745. However, the same treaty of Aix-la-Chapelle that handed Madras back to Britain also returned all conquests in the New World to their original owners, and the contest over Canada had yet to be resolved.

The campaigns waged against the native Americans proved far more decisive, however. Technology, disease and increasing numbers (by 1700 at least one million people of European descent lived in the Americas) gave the settlers great advantages (see chapter 8). By the eighteenth century, only along the frontier fringes of

Opposite: This elephant armour, part of the spoils from Clive's victory at Plassey in 1757, typifies traditional Indian military tactics. The elephant's bulk and weight constituted the real threat, as mahouts drove their huge mounts forward literally to crush their opponents. However, such traditional methods of war met defeat at the hands of modern European technology and tactics. Indian capacity to adopt European military methods produced the sepoy, but it also created forces among native powers, the Marathas, for example, that could fight in western fashion against the British. The British finally prevailed not only because they relied on artillery rather than war elephants, but because they mastered Indian politics.

European settlements could the native Americans hold their own – and not for long even there. The fights were bitter and the conduct of war brutal on both sides, but the result was a foregone conclusion. So long as the French and British battled between themselves, the natives could find allies on one side or the other, but the elimination of New France in 1763 (see pages 184–5) closed this option. The independence of the United States hurt the native Americans even more, since the British had in some degree respected Indian lands west of the Appalachian Mountains whereas the new state was from its inception hostile to native populations. The Declaration of Independence itself condemned the native Americans as, 'merciless Indian Savages, whose known rule of warfare, is an undistinguished destruction of all ages, sexes and conditions.' With attitudes such as this, the hounding of native tribes by the United States during its first century of existence comes as little surprise.

THE SEVEN YEARS WAR

This age of mercantilist warfare reached its climax in the Seven Years War (1756–63), a truly global conflict with enduring consequences in Europe, North America, and South Asia. In Europe, Frederick, now allied with the British, sought only to keep Silesia; his goal was limited, and it would have suited him to tailor the effort to the intent. However, Maria Theresa resolved to punish Frederick at almost any cost for his 'theft' of Silesia and, with Russia and France as allies, she came close to crushing the Prussian monarch. This forced him to commit an unlimited effort to his limited cause.

The year 1757 witnessed Frederick's greatest feats of arms. A major French offensive against him met with disaster on 5 November at Rossbach, where Frederick destroyed a Franco-German army twice the size of his own. But while he dealt with his enemy to the west, the Austrians invaded Silesia, so just one week later his troops left Leipzig and covered the nearly 200 miles to Parchwitz in sixteen days. From Parchwitz he advanced with 36,000 troops toward the Austrian army of about 80,000 led by Charles of Lorraine. When Charles learned that Frederick was on the march close by, he assumed a defensive position around the town of Leuthen, but wooded hills masked his five-mile-long line running north to south. On the morning of 5 December Frederick marched toward the Austrian position; then, using the hills to hide his columns, he veered south and concentrated his smaller army against the left flank of the Austrian line. His men moved so rapidly and deployed from marching column into line of battle with such precision that they caught the Austrian flank completely off guard. With strong artillery support, Frederick's troops ploughed into the Austrian flank at about 1 p.m. and then drove north, rolling up the opposition. Some of his musketeers fired off 180 rounds. By the end of the day, the Austrians had lost 10,000 killed and wounded and 21,000 prisoners, a total casualty list roughly equal to the size of Frederick's entire army. Napoleon said of this engagement: 'The battle of Leuthen is a masterpiece of

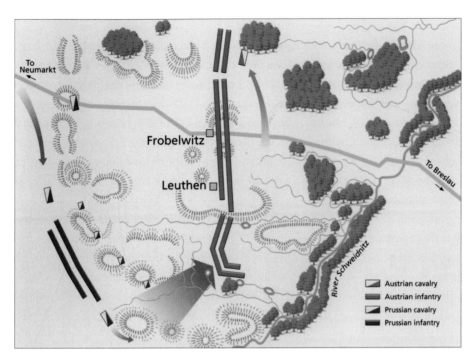

At the Battle of Leuthen, Frederick of Prussia won his greatest victory by breaking one of the supposed rules of war and exposing his army to flank attack as it marched across the front of the Austrian army. He expertly masked his movement behind a wooded ridge and drew the Austrians' attention to their right flank with a feint, while he marched to overwhelm their left.

movements, manoeuvres, and resolution. Alone it is sufficient to immortalize Frederick, and place him in the rank of the greatest generals.'

Rossbach and Leuthen may have rescued Prussia, but the war dragged on for six more years. Beginning in the late 1740s and continuing until the Seven Years War, Frederick's enemies improved their weapons, tactics, and administration. Thus the Russian Infantry Code of 1755 openly aped Prussian tactics; her artillery improved speed and accuracy by adopting better guns and holding prolonged exercises; and the adoption of a better supply system helped to reduce the army's baggage train, making it more mobile and less like an oriental host. Of even greater significance, Austria reformed her armed forces after her defeat in the War of the Austrian Succession: the infantry adopted a standard drill manual; training and equipment improved; a military academy opened at Wiener Neustadt; the artillery underwent extensive overhaul, including redesigned cannon which equalled or exceeded Prussian standards; the officer corps was opened to commoners; and a general staff was established in 1758. Eventually, the leading Austrian commander, Marshal Leopold von Daun, realized (in the words of one of his aides-de-camp) that the king of Prussia 'always launches his attack against one of the two wings of the army he attacks, [so] it is necessary simply to plan a suitable response.' And so, eventually overmatched by the resources and ingenuity of his powerful enemies despite his genius in the field, Frederick very nearly met destruction. By the end of 1761, he could see no escape and retreated to Berlin where he sank into despair, but the death of his inveterate foe, Elizabeth of Russia, in January 1762 saved him, since her successor, Peter III, favoured the Prussians. Prussia emerged from the war exhausted but intact.

British forces leave their ships on the St Lawrence and scale the cliffs to fight on the Plains of Abraham outside Quebec. Both sides risked much. Wolfe felt compelled to attack immediately because winter approached, but his efforts would have failed had the French been able to remain behind their walls. Montcalm, however, had to chance a battle in the open because he lacked supplies to withstand a long siege.

For France, linked in an unusual alliance with her traditional enemy, Habsburg Austria, the European phase of the Seven Years War was an odd struggle fought without much determination and without much success. But if the French had little to lose or win on the Continent, Louis XV (1715–74) played for high stakes overseas. In North America, the long-standing animosity between French and British led to a final confrontation, the French and Indian War (1754–63). With the arrival of a British force under generals Jeffrey Amherst and James Wolfe before Louisbourg in June 1758, British victory was not far away. After taking that fortress, Wolfe attacked Quebec.

With 9,000 British regulars and 500 colonials, Wolfe landed at the Île d'Orléans, just downstream from Quebec on 26–27 June and began a duel of three months with the French governor Marquis Louis Joseph de Montcalm. Wolfe tried several avenues of attack, only to be parried by Montcalm. By September, with winter approaching, the commander of the British fleet worried about getting his ships back down the St Lawrence before it froze and so Wolfe and his brigadiers resorted

A View of the Taking of QUEBEC September 13th 1759.
Shewing the manner of debarking the English Forces, & of the resolute scrambling of the light Infantry, up a Woody Precipice to dislodge the Captains post, which defended a small entrenched path, through which the Troops were to pass. Also a view of the signal Victory obtained over the French regulars, Canadians and Indians, which produced the surrender of Quebec.

Vüe de la Prise de QUEBEC le 13 Septembre 1759.
Qui Represente le debarquement des Troupes Angloises, & L'Intrepidité de L'Infanterie Legere en escaladant un Precipice Boiseux, pour deloger le poste du Capitaine qui defendoit un Sentier retranché par où les Troupes devoient passer. C'Aussi la vüe de la Victoire Signalée Remportée sur les François, Canadiens & Indiens, qui obligea la Ville à Capituler.

to a dangerous gambit, ascending a narrow trail leading up the cliffs from the river to the Plains of Abraham, just to the southwest of the city. So rugged was this path that the French though it impassable and left it lightly guarded. Through a combination of skill and luck the British accomplished this feat on the night of 12–13 September 1759. The next morning Wolfe marshalled 4,800 troops on the plain.

Montcalm now decided to offer battle with 4,500 troops, since Quebec held only two days' provisions and could hardly withstand a siege. After both armies arrayed for battle, the French advanced at 10 a.m. Wolfe, who had ordered his troops to lie down in order to spare them from French skirmishers, now commanded his men to rise and march forward. At a range of 40 yards they poured volley after volley into the French, who broke. The disciplined fire of the British decided the brief battle in fifteen minutes. The British pursued as the French withdrew into the city. In the fighting, Wolfe was hit three times, the last ball ending his life; Montcalm also died that evening from a gunshot wound received during the French retreat. Lacking supplies, the French surrendered Quebec on 18 September and, after provisioning the town, the Royal Navy withdrew. In spring 1760, the French besieged Quebec, but the timely arrival of another British squadron in the St Lawrence saved the garrison and won Canada for the British. They now held all of North America, from Georgia to Newfoundland to the Illinois country along the Mississippi.

Meanwhile, in India, the English East India Company ousted the French *Compagnie des Indes*. Just as in North America, the war in India had its own momentum, only partially dependent on European events. In 1756, the Nawab of Bengal seized the British trading base at Calcutta, condemning survivors to the infamous cramped prison known as 'the Black Hole'. Early the next year, Robert Clive retook the town, and then drove inland with 1,100 European troops and 2,100 sepoys to defeat the Nawab's army of 50,000 men at Plassey on 23 June. Clive won the battle that day more because the Nawab's allies and generals deserted him than because of superior fighting on the part of Clive's army. In 1760 the French surrendered Pondichery, and although the treaty of Paris returned it to them, they never regained their overall position. Finally, a Company army under Hector Munro defeated another Indian force at Buxar on 23 October 1764. This hard-fought battle won for the East India Company the rich provinces of Bengal, Bihar, and Orissa, the fulcrum from which it would lever itself into control of the subcontinent. The Company now formed a great sepoy army, recruited among the large population under its control and paid from the princely revenues taken as tribute by the Company from native populations.

To a large degree, the Seven Years War epitomized an age, an age in which military necessities shaped governments and war determined the fate of states in Europe, while spreading and defining western dominion across the globe. After 1763, however, the nature of European conflict would change: wars of dynastic states would give way to wars of nations fought with more intense commitment and with new military instruments.

CHAPTER 11   *Nations in Arms*

Between 1763 and 1815 revolution and war changed the face and the heart of the Western world. In 1763, at the end of the Seven Years War, the British settlements along the Atlantic coast of North America were still colonies, dependent upon Britain. Across the sea in France, a monarchy that could trace its roots back over eight hundred years ruled over a privileged aristocratic society, while serfs still worked the fields of their lords. The American and French Revolutions not only stand out as paramount events in the history of those two countries, but went on to influence every corner of the western world. The revolutionary tide that began in the United States eventually swept through Latin America as well. The transformation of French society that followed the fall of the Bastille to a Parisian crowd in 1789 changed not only France but Europe for ever.

Warfare too was transformed. The French Revolution realized the ideal of the nation in arms, and so nationalism added its force to the western emphasis on discipline. Common soldiers were now expected to display the same kind of commitment once reserved only to officers, and the new loyalties of the rank and file influenced tactics, logistics, and strategy. Eventually, Napoleon demonstrated the potential implicit in the new form of warfare and thus altered the conduct of military operations forever.

At the battle of Princeton, portrayed in this primitive painting, Washington scored a victory over some 2,000 British troops on 3 January 1777. This, combined with his defeat of 1,400 Hessians at Trenton a week before, gave heart to the revolutionaries. During this war, the American cause often benefited from small-scale triumphs that had political or morale effects far in excess of the numbers involved.

REVOLUTIONARY WAR IN AMERICA

Revolution came first to America. After driving the French from Canada and the lands west of the Mississippi by 1763, the British authorities attempted to place greater burdens upon, and exert greater control over, the Atlantic colonies. The process of demand, resistance, and repression finally led to war in April 1775 when the British governor of Massachusetts dispatched troops to seize arms and ammunition stored by the colonials at Concord, and the local militia resisted. The War of American Independence that began that day with 'the shot heard round the world' was a small-scale conflict by European standards; significant actions often involved no more than a few battalions. Both sides, but particularly the rebel Americans, committed militia to battle, often with disappointing results, but in addition to militia the Americans fashioned a force of regulars, or 'Continentals'. Skirmishers and sharpshooters mattered in the war, albeit not as much as legend would have it, and key battles were fought very much in traditional European style. Yet even though the number of troops remained small and their style of fighting essentially traditional, nonetheless the war decided great issues. Moreover, in their battle to win independence, American patriots upheld the ideal of a people's government defended by a people's army fourteen years before the outbreak of the French Revolution.

Soon after the fighting around Lexington and Concord, a force of 15,000 colonials besieged Boston, garrisoned by 7,000 British troops. The American Continental Congress chose George Washington to command the forces encircling the city, and history would justify their confidence in this Virginian planter and veteran of the Seven Years War – a man of great judgement and political virtue. At the battle of Bunker Hill (actually fought on Breeds Hill), on 17 June 1775, 1,500 entrenched colonials beat back two assaults by superior numbers of British, only to succumb when ammunition ran out. While a British victory, this battle gave the Revolutionary soldiers confidence that they could stand up to the redcoats.

After abandoning Boston in March 1776, the British directed their efforts to taking New York. Expecting that this would be the next flash point, Washington had already marched his army there, planning to resist by entrenching his troops, the tactic that had shown such promise at Bunker hill; but British forces under the command of Sir William Howe outmanoeuvred and outfought the Americans on Long Island, forcing Washington to abandon the city on 12 September and to retreat across New Jersey and into Pennsylvania, vigorously pursued by the British. 'The chain [of garrisons], I own, is rather extensive', General Howe presciently admitted on 20 December, but only a miracle seemed likely to save Washington's bedraggled army. Christmas Day brought it. Crossing the Delaware River with 2,400 men, Washington overwhelmed a surprised garrison of Hessians in British pay at Trenton the next morning. Nine days later he defeated a British detachment at Princeton. Small triumphs though they were, the battles of Trenton and Princeton gave back some measure of confidence to his bruised army.

General George Washington at Trenton, where he surprised and defeated the Hessian garrison on 26 December 1776. Washington was a wise man of character. While he could be daring when opportunity presented itself, he realized that in this war of attrition his primary task was to keep his small army together through the difficult times. Unlike other generals who commanded armies in revolutionary eras, he refused to use his troops in a bid for political power. When he became president in 1789, ballots not bayonets put him in office.

The fighting around New York taught Washington that he could probably not match the British in open battle. It also showed him that he did not have to; he need only keep his army in being, restrict the area controlled by the British, and wait for the right opportunity. Apart from a futile attempt to derail the British assault on Philadelphia in 1777, Washington generally avoided battle and conducted a war of attrition. And while his troops suffered terribly, most infamously during the winter of 1777–78 at Valley Forge, he somehow managed to keep his meagre forces together, and in that achievement lay the seeds of victory.

All this time Washington tried to transform his troops into an army capable of disciplined combat in the European style, an effort assisted by Augustus von Steuben, an officer with experience in the army of Frederick the Great. Von Steuben fashioned a new and simplified drill for Washington's army and taught it effectively, so by 1779 Washington's regulars came to rival the British in battlefield drill; but there were never enough of them.

After the British drove Washington from New York, the main fighting shifted to other fronts. Howe conceived an ambitious strategy for the 1777 campaign 'in order, if possible, to finish the war in one year by an extensive and rigorous exertion of His Majesty's armies'. Ten thousand men were to capture Providence and then (if possible) Boston; 10,000 more were to move up the Hudson from New York to Albany; while a further 8,000 would defend New Jersey and threaten Philadelphia. Another column of British, Iroquois, and loyalists would advance down the Mohawk Valley. Finally, a force from Canada, following first Lake Champlain and then the Hudson, would march south towards the army advancing northwards from New York. New England would thus be split off from the rest of the rebellious states.

It was a good plan, but it depended for success upon the arrival of 15,000 reinforcements (which Howe ingeniously suggested might be raised in Russia as well as in Germany and Britain) and an artillery battalion. However the government in London absolutely refused to commit further resources, so in April 1777 Howe decided to abandon his ambitious strategy – 'My hopes of terminating the war this year are vanished,' he complained – and instead concentrate his forces in an attack on Philadelphia.

Nevertheless, the army from Canada set forth for the Hudson under the command of General John Burgoyne. At first his campaign went well, but as the summer wore on he moved more slowly and suffered supply problems. Howe, as he had warned London (and Canada), moved with his main forces against Philadelphia and sent only a small army of 4,000 under Sir Henry Clinton in a half-hearted effort to link up with Burgoyne. After minor victories, Clinton turned back. Finally at the end of a long tether, Burgoyne met stiffening resistance, and in two battles near Saratoga, an army under General Horatio Gates defeated Burgoyne, who surrendered his troops on 17 October. Heartened by this American victory, France entered the war in February 1778 and two years later 6,000 French soldiers, who would do much to win the last great battle of the war, arrived at Newport, Rhode Island.

THE WAR IN THE SOUTH

The years 1778–81 remained relatively quiet in the north. In June 1778, Clinton, who replaced Howe in command, withdrew from Philadelphia to New York. Washington resumed his waiting game, and the action moved south. With the exception of an unsuccessful attempt by Clinton to seize Charleston, South Carolina, in 1776, the southern states had witnessed relatively little fighting before the redcoats took Savannah, Georgia, in December 1778. The next fall, a major French and American expedition tried to retake Savannah, but failed. In 1780 Clinton undertook another siege of Charleston, which fell in May. He then sailed back to New York but left an army of 8,000 behind to conquer the rest of the south. At the head of this force, Charles Cornwallis smashed an army under Gates at the battle of Camden, South Carolina, on 16 August 1780. Having defeated the victor of Saratoga, Cornwallis expected to win the war, but this was not to be the case.

The agent of this reversal of fortune, Nathanael Greene, took command of 3,000 Continentals and militia at Charlotte, North Carolina, to face Cornwallis's army of 4,000 regulars. In an amazing campaign, during which Greene won not a single battle, he so wore down the British that Cornwallis abandoned the Carolinas and led his army to Virginia by May 1781. In Virginia he sparred with another American force under the command of the marquis de Lafayette but, unable to bring him to battle, Cornwallis withdrew to Yorktown with 7,000 troops. Cornwallis had failed at being the cat; he was about to become the mouse.

Learning that Cornwallis had taken refuge at Yorktown, Washington sprang into action and rapidly marched his army south, accompanied by the newly arrived French troops under Jean-Baptiste Rochambeau. Meanwhile, at the battle of the Virginia Capes on 5–9 September, a French fleet stood off a British force, which

Three commanders who freed the Carolinas from British control, Nathanael Greene (left), Daniel Morgan (centre), and Andrew Pickens (right). Greene, a Rhode Islander, served as Washington's quartermaster general before being sent south to rescue the situation in the Carolinas. Greene was a talented amateur who recognized that he could defeat the British by running as well as by fighting. Morgan came out of retirement to serve as Greene's lieutenant and won the key tactical victory at the Cowpens. Pickens commanded militia guerrillas who harassed the British and hampered their ability to maintain themselves in the hostile countryside.

Nathanael Greene's South Carolina campaign

The Napoleonic battle of annihilation was not the only style of fighting to prove decisive in the period 1763-1815. In contrast, American General Nathanael Greene combined regular forces with guerrilla bands to exhaust and defeat an enemy army in a way that foreshadowed the tactics of twentieth-century wars of national liberation.

When Greene, a self-taught soldier, arrived in the south in December 1780, the British had essentially destroyed the American army in the Carolinas. Greene assembled a small army in South Carolina with the intention of working in conjunction with the established partisan bands to wear down Cornwallis.

Greene opened the campaign by splitting his small army of 3,000 troops, and Daniel Morgan in command of 1,000 of them smashed a British force at the battle of the Cowpens. The bait was set, and Cornwallis rose to take it. He rushed to the Cowpens where he burned his stores in order to free his column from impediment in their pursuit of the brash Americans. When news that Cornwallis had destroyed his own supplies reached Greene, he proclaimed 'Then, he is ours!' Greene realized that partisan bands nipping at Cornwallis's army would keep it from supplying itself on the march: his men would have only what was on their backs, and that would not be enough. So Greene ran fast and hard to the River Dan, Virginia, and safety; Cornwallis obliged by following. It was all Greene's men could do to keep out of the grasp of Cornwallis, but they won the race. In the chase, Cornwallis lost 500 of his 2,500 men to hunger and exhaustion.

After a brief pause, Greene re-crossed the Dan, pursuing Cornwallis to Guilford Courthouse, where Greene offered Cornwallis the battle he had always wanted. Greene knew that he could win even if he lost, and while Cornwallis gained the day, he lost an additional 530 casualties. With his battered survivors he now felt compelled to retreat to Cape Fear. From there he abandoned the Carolinas and marched to his rendezvous with defeat at Yorktown. Greene lost two more battles against other British forces, but again the victors suffered so much that they withdrew into Charleston and left the rest of the Carolinas to Greene. Greene commented:

> There are few generals that has run oftener, or more lustily than I have done...But I have taken care not to run too far and commonly have run as fast forward as backward, to convince our Enemy that we were like a Crab, that could run either way.

One hundred and fifty years later Mao Tse Tung echoed Greene's tactics, 'enemy advances, we retreat; enemy halts, we harass; enemy tires, we attack; enemy retreats, we pursue.'

---

sailed back to New York, sealing Cornwallis's fate. By late September 9,000 American and 7,800 French troops surrounded Cornwallis's 7,000 soldiers; the formal siege works were directed by French engineers under the command of Washington. Without hope of relief, Cornwallis surrendered on 19 October. This victory ended the major campaigns of the war in North America, and negotiations for peace soon began that resulted in the Treaty of Paris (1783), recognizing the independence of the United States of America.

NEW IDEAS, NEW WEAPONS

American victory gave France a sweet taste of revenge. Moreover, the French part in beating their British rivals to some extent legitimized the reform movement that had improved the French army after the humiliation of the Seven Years War.

At the heart of this movement lay a tactical debate between proponents of columns and lines. The supporters of deep column formations, the *ordre profond*, based their conclusions on time-honoured notions that the French were better at spirited assault than at stolid defence. No less an authority than Voltaire agreed 'that the French nation attacks with the greatest impetuosity and that it is extremely

At the battle of the Cowpens on 17 January 1781, General Daniel Morgan won the Americans' most brilliant tactical victory of the war, although the battle was on a small scale with only about a thousand soldiers on each side. Morgan understood the abilities and limitations of the troops under his command: asking his militia to do no more than they could accomplish, he relied upon his Continentals to anchor the line. In this painting, at the critical moment of the battle, Maryland and Delaware Continentals repulse the attack by British infantry.

difficult to resist its shock.' Advocates of line tactics, the *ordre mince*, took heart from the success of Frederick the Great, however, and for a time French drill books aped the Prussians. Recognizing the advantages of the two basic formations, Count Jacques de Guibert published his *Essai général de tactique* in 1772. His solution was to use both in battle, in what can be called the *ordre mixte*. The tactical controversy finally produced the drill manual of August 1791 which did not force any single solution, but offered a menu of formations and evolutions that could be served up according to a commander's taste.

As the French engaged in a war of words over the best tactics for heavy infantry, they also experimented with greater numbers of light infantry. Owing to the fear of desertion, at mid-century few commanders employed open order infantry which sought cover and targets at will (see page 178). However, all major European armies returned to the use of light infantry on a limited basis during the second half of the eighteenth century. Combat in the New World during the Seven Years War and the War of American Independence exerted only a tangential influence on this movement, but nevertheless by 1789 French infantry regiments included a light company, and the army boasted twelve entire battalions of *chasseurs à pied*.

This development was not tied to any improved technology, such as the rifle, since the French continued to arm their light infantry with smooth-bore muskets; however, if infantry weapons did not change much, artillery did. The Gribeauval system, adopted in 1774, significantly improved French cannon. Jean Vacquette de Gribeauval, who rose to supreme command of French artillery after the Seven Years War, changed the manufacture of guns: instead of casting the bore into cannon as before, cannon were now cast solid and then bored out, a process that resulted in much closer tolerances, permitting greater range with smaller powder charges. The Gribeauval system also brought in shorter, lighter and, therefore, more mobile field pieces. Along with the new materiel went improved training for artillery officers.

As well as proposing tactical and technological improvements, reformers spoke of a new kind of soldier and even of a new kind of society. Guibert wrote in his *Essai:*

> Imagine that there arose in Europe a people who united austere virtues with a national militia and a fixed plan of expansion, who did not lose sight of their system, who, knowing how to make war cheaply and to live by their victories, were not reduced to putting their arms aside because of financial calculations. One would see this people subjugate its neighbours, and overturn feeble constitutions like the wind bends over fragile reeds.

Others, including that influential intellectual Montesquieu, heaped similar praise upon the ideal of the citizen soldier.

Yet this does not mean that the reformers were revolutionaries; on the contrary, the reform movement as a whole exhibited profound social conservatism. A dominant theme was the demand for a strongly professional but exclusively aristocratic officer corps. As Maurice de Saxe claimed, 'Truly the only good officers are the poor gentlemen who have nothing but their sword and their cape,' and reformers condemned the purchase of commissions because it benefited rich aristocratic dilettantes of only recent noble origins and wealthy non-nobles. As a response to this criticism, the French began to phase out the purchase of commissions in 1776. The French also improved the professional education of officers by founding new cadet schools after 1750; however, admission to them soon required aristocratic status. As the crowning effort of this brand of reform, the Ségur law of 1781 denied a direct commission to any aspirant who could not demonstrate four generations of nobility in his paternal line. So while the French army made important changes before 1789, some of them were such that the Revolution could only reject them and fashion its own unique military institutions.

CITIZEN SOLDIERS OF THE FRENCH REVOLUTION

The Revolution that struck France in July 1789 shook the army almost as much as it shook the monarchy. When Louis XVI (1774–93) tried to use his soldiers against the crowds during the first year of the Revolution, the troops proved ineffective, reluctant, even rebellious. The year 1790 witnessed a series of revolutionary mutinies among regiments all over France, the worst breaking out at Nancy in Lorraine. Later, after the king tried to flee France in June 1791, mass resignations eviscerated the officer corps. The army of the *ancien régime* dissolved; France would need a very different force when war came again, as it did in April 1792.

The army first reconstituted its ranks through voluntary enlistments. As early as the summer of 1791 the government ordered the expansion of the line army; however, the revolutionaries did not want to rely exclusively upon it, since they saw it as a potential political threat. Therefore, at the same time, Paris issued a call for 100,000 volunteers to come from the recently-formed citizen militia, the National Guard. These Volunteers of 1791 grouped in their own battalions were later joined by the Volunteers of 1792, called up in July of that year. Yet by 1793 volunteerism could not fill the massive manpower needs of the war, so in August the revolutionary government decreed the *levée en masse*, or the total levy of the French people, something even more extreme than universal conscription:

> Young men will go to battle; married men will forge arms and transport supplies; women will make tents, uniforms, and serve in the hospitals; children will pick rags; old men will have themselves carried to public squares, to inspire the courage of the warriors, and to preach the hatred of kings and the unity of the Republic.

By the summer of 1794 the revolutionary army listed a million men on its rolls, of whom 750,000 were present under arms – a great force which, in terms of social class, occupation, and geographical origin, accurately reflected French society. It was the nation in arms composed of the best young men that France could offer.

To lead these troops the French created a radically new officer corps. The flight of officers from the old royal army left so many vacancies that they could only be

The disdain of the combat soldiers for the officials (Representatives on Mission) sent to supervise at the front and to ensure the political reliability of French officers stands out in this ironic lithograph by Raffet, whose father had been a soldier in the revolutionary army. The cold and ragged French soldiers stand waist high in water while the Representative boasts: 'The enemy does not suspect that we are here. It is seven o'clock—we will surprise him tomorrow at four in the morning.'

filled by rapidly promoting non-commissioned officers into the commissioned ranks. Volunteer battalions elected their own officers. Some officers rose with meteoric speed but, on the whole, the officer corps became more and more professional, as seniority and talent determined promotion. Before the Revolution, aristocrats constituted about 85 per cent of army officers, but by the summer of 1794 they composed under 3 per cent. Yet even though the officer corps did not represent the old privileged classes, the revolutionary government never really trusted its commanders. In order to monitor them, Paris dispatched the famous 'Representatives on Mission' and the less well known but far more numerous commissars. At the front, these agents scrutinized the actions and sentiments of officers; to earn their disapproval could mean the guillotine. In order to insure proper opinions among the rank and file, the revolutionary government also engaged in a campaign of political education, distributing millions of copies of official bulletins, radical newspapers, and even patriotic song-sheets to the troops.

With the 1791 drill book as a guide, this citizen army evolved an effective tactical system, although the new levies may never have mastered the minutiae of parade ground drill. Battalions still stood in line to mass firepower, but they also exploited the advantages of the battalion attack column, a new formation which stood twelve ranks deep and about sixty men across. This compact formation manoeuvred adroitly, deployed into line easily, and charged the enemy rapidly. In front of the main line, the French dispersed crowds of skirmishers to unsettle the enemy in preparation for assault. The greatest advantage enjoyed by revolutionary infantry

François Kellermann, riding the white horse on the right, commanded at Valmy, the battle that turned back the Prussian invasion of 1792. The commander of the invading army, the duke of Brunswick, expected the French to turn and run when they came face to face with the Prussians, then regarded as the finest soldiers in Europe. But as the Prussians attacked, Kellermann led his troops in a thundering cry of 'Vive la nation!' Later that day, seeing the firm defiance of the French, Brunswick told his generals, 'We shall not fight here today.' There would be no advance on Paris.

lay not in any one element, but in its flexible combination of tactics that could match the style of fighting to terrain and circumstance.

French cavalrymen exercised only a minor influence on the battlefield, since they were few in number and deficient in ability for the first several years of the war, but artillery proved invaluable. The French devoted more and more of their resources to horse artillery, mobile guns pulled by larger teams of horses and served by crewmen who were mounted in order to keep up with the guns. Such batteries could gallop forward, unlimber, fire, limber again, and dash off to the next critical position to provide powerful support for the infantry.

THE REVOLUTION ON THE BATTLEFIELD

When war began in April 1792, the half-trained troops of the French army met repeated disasters, particularly on the key northeast frontier. After a succession of unsuccessful generals, Charles Dumouriez finally assumed command there, with François Kellermann leading the army just to the south. In the late summer, an invasion by Prussian and Austrian troops under the command of the duke of Brunswick – who five years earlier had carried out a strikingly successful invasion of the Dutch Republic – pierced the French frontier at Longwy, took Verdun, and threatened to march all the way to Paris. Dumouriez manoeuvred brilliantly to frustrate Brunswick's plans, and at Valmy on 20 September Kellermann with 36,000 troops stood off Brunswick with 30,000–34,000. Valmy was little more than an artillery duel, but when the French gunners had the best of it and Kellermann's infantry stood firm, Brunswick called off his attacks. This unspectacular victory secured the Revolution. The great German poet Goethe witnessed the battle and prophesied to his comrades that evening: 'From this place and from this day forth commences a new era in the world's history, and you were there at its birth.' After Valmy, the French army went over to the offensive, winning triumphs in the Austrian Netherlands and along the Rhine before the end of the year.

However, 1793 began badly for the French. Dumouriez lost the Austrian Netherlands to a counter-offensive; but, instead of advancing, the allies, who now included the British, stopped to lay siege to frontier fortresses, Vauban's legacy to the Revolution. Defeat, coupled with the outbreak of a counter-revolutionary rebellion in the Vendée, shook the revolutionary government, which now created the dictatorial Committee of Public Safety and ruthlessly mobilized for war. Lazare Carnot, an experienced military engineer who came to be hailed as the 'Organizer of Victory,' stepped forward as the Committee's most able military authority. More than any other individual he drove war production, logistics, and strategy.

By the autumn of 1793 the French had stabilized the front in the north. Meanwhile, on the shores of the Mediterranean, owing to the effective use of artillery commanded by young Napoleon Bonaparte, the French successfully retook Toulon, previously seized by the British. Again the revolutionary armies surged forward. On 17–18 May 1794 around Tourcoing a French army of 60,000 defeated an encircling

The duke of Brunswick (above) who led the invasion intended to halt the course of the French Revolution, was no reactionary himself. He enjoyed such a high reputation as both a soldier and a liberal that early in 1792 the French minister of war considered offering him command of French forces.

Charles Dumouriez (below) deserves more credit than he generally receives for the French victory at Valmy. His energetic and brilliant manoeuvre seized the Argonne passes, blocked Brunswick's path, and forced battle on Brunswick at a time and place advantageous to the French.

manoeuvre by six columns totalling 73,000 Austrian, British and Hanoverian troops. This French victory paved the way for the better-known triumph at Fleurus on 26 June, when 75,000 French troops fought a successful defensive action against 52,000 troops under the prince of Saxe-Coburg. Marshal Nicolas Soult later said that it was the most desperate fighting he had ever seen. After Fleurus, the Austrians abandoned the Netherlands. Victories continued: the French forced the allies back across the Rhine, met success in Savoy and, early in 1795, conquered the Dutch Republic (restyling it the 'Batavian Republic').

After this last success, however, the war bogged down in Germany, partly because treason by a French general placed the Republic's invasion plans in the hands of the enemy. In Italy the French held on to the coast around Genoa but made little progress.

The army's first victories of 1792 and later triumphs in 1794 carried the Revolution beyond the borders of France. But if the tactical abilities of French troops raised the possibility of sparking sympathetic revolutions among oppressed peoples across Europe, the behaviour of those troops in occupied territories turned populations against their liberators. Poorly supported by an inefficient and corrupt supply service, French soldiers turned to pillage in order to survive. It was not what they wanted to do; it is what they had to do. In 1795 the Directory replaced earlier revolutionary regimes, and it became increasingly corrupt as it neglected the army while lining the pockets of war profiteers. However, the Parisian government would eventually pay for its neglect of the army. At the height of revolutionary fervour, soldiers had been treated as heroes; but as time passed the army began to see itself as neglected and victimized. Casualties and desertion drastically reduced the number of troops – from 750,000 men in the summer of 1794, to about 480,000 a year later and about 400,000 in 1796, little larger than it had been under Louis XIV. With good cause, the army believed that it represented the highest ideals of the Revolution: sacrifice for the common good, careers open to talent, and fraternity among equals. In contrast, the Directory seemed to have abandoned not only the army but the Revolution itself. Such a disaffected army could eventually be turned against that government, and Napoleon Bonaparte came to realize this.

BONAPARTE'S TOOLS OF WAR

On 27 March 1796 the 26-year-old general took command of the Army of Italy, a rag-tag force clinging to the Mediterranean coast between the French border and Genoa. Bonaparte promised them food and fame, even if he put little stock in Revolutionary ideals.

> Soldiers! You are hungry and naked; the government owes you much but can give you nothing. The patience and courage which you have displayed among these rocks are admirable; but they bring you no glory – not a glimmer falls upon you. I will lead you into the most fertile plains on earth. Rich provinces, opulent

towns, all shall be at your disposal; there you will find honour, glory and riches. Soldiers of Italy! Will you be lacking in courage or endurance?

In this, his first great campaign, Bonaparte faced and defeated combined Piedmontese and Austrian forces through a series of brilliant manoeuvres and hard fighting. He first split the Piedmontese from the Austrians by beating both in turn and driving them back on their diverging lines of communication. Then he pounced on the Piedmontese, forcing them out of the war on 28 April. Bonaparte next outmanoeuvred and outfought his Austrian opponent, Beaulieu, forcing him to abandon Lombardy to the French. Bonaparte's success, only six weeks after taking command, was truly astounding. Driving the Austrians from the rest of northern Italy took longer, since they held on to Mantua and repeatedly sent armies to relieve that beleaguered fortress. However, he defeated each in turn, and on 18 April 1797 the Austrians agreed to an armistice, later formalized as the Treaty of Campo Formio.

In 1798, the victorious Bonaparte led an expedition against Egypt, since he believed that control of Egypt would open the door to India – a romantic notion at best. After avoiding Admiral Horatio Nelson, who prowled the Mediterranean, Bonaparte landed his army of almost 40,000 men near Alexandria on 1–3 July and stormed the city. On 21 July he destroyed a large Mameluke army at the battle of the Pyramids. However, all of this counted for naught, because at the battle of the Nile on 1 August Nelson smashed the French fleet – only two of the thirteen ships of the line escaped – and marooned Bonaparte's army. Bonaparte put a brave face on the disaster by campaigning into Syria, but after failing to take Acre he was forced to turn back. Taking what glory he could from his Egyptian expedition, the frustrated but ambitious general deserted his army, boarded a frigate, and landed at Toulon on 9 October.

When he arrived in France, Bonaparte converted his military credit into political capital and, with the support of troops around Paris, overthrew the Directory on 9–10 November. Proclaimed First Consul, Bonaparte now ruled France, but he soon marched off to drive back the Austrians who had reconquered much of northern Italy during his Egyptian gambit. At Marengo on 14 June 1800 he won a narrow victory and this, combined with Jean Moreau's triumph at Hohenlinden on 3 December, compelled Austria to accept French terms once more. The British too signed a treaty with the French in 1802, and France was at peace. In 1804, Bonaparte assumed even greater office by crowning himself Emperor Napoleon.

Why had Napoleon won so many battles and risen to such heights in such a short period? There is no question that he inherited the legacy of the revolutionary army, including a dedicated soldiery, an officer corps based on talent, generals proven in battle, and a flexible tactical system superior to those of France's enemies. Napoleonic troops were no longer the revolutionaries of 1793–94, but they were still Frenchmen, sons of their nation, dedicated to it, and inspired by its leader. The

This unfinished portrait of Napoleon Bonaparte by Jacques-Louis David now hangs in the Louvre. It shows the young and lean general who conquered northern Italy in the 1796 campaign. Born on the island of Corsica in 1769, Napoleon first cast himself as a Corsican patriot, but became disillusioned and threw his lot in with revolutionary France. While he earned a high reputation in 1793 at the siege of Toulon, his military career was soon compromised by his association with the radical revolutionary Maximilien Robespierre, and Bonaparte spend some time under arrest. In 1795, he regained favour when he brutally suppressed a riot by turning cannon on the crowd in the famous 'whiff of grapeshot.'

Jourdan law of 1798 established a new system of universal conscription that required all young men to register, and each year the government set a quota of conscripts to be drawn from those eligible for the draft. This new conscription law provided the soldiers for Napoleon's army – more than two million by 1815 – and served as the model for conscription laws throughout western and central Europe.

Napoleon continued and refined a method of warfare suitable to his army. Often he simply adapted what he found, such as his tactical emphasis on a form of the *ordre mixte* that combined battalions in column and line. In addition, he benefited from the resurgence of French cavalry, which had slowly re-established itself in the late 1790s. He also appreciated the importance of artillery and increased its numbers.

Beyond this, he improved the organizational structure of the revolutionary army. In 1792 and 1793 the French had pioneered the use of the combat division, combining infantry, cavalry, and artillery to create a small army of a few thousand men which could operate either independently or in conjunction with other divisions. Before he undertook his 1805 campaign, Napoleon extended this organizational concept by combining divisions into corps, which varied a great deal in size, from less than 10,000 to nearly 30,000. The corps functioned even better than divisions as independent formations co-ordinated with other corps under the supreme command of Napoleon. Corps organization eased problems of command and supply. The new field forces that Napoleon committed to battle were simply too large to be controlled effectively by one man, and by subdividing his army into corps, Napoleon enhanced command and control (although nothing could entirely

In this romantic vision of the Battle of Friedland, 1807, jubilant galloping cuirassiers, heavy armoured cavalry, salute Napoleon as they charge past. Behind the emperor stand infantry of his Imperial Guard in white breeches and waistcoats and tall bearskin headgear. This painting displays some of the visual majesty of Napoleonic battle that captured the popular imagination. Colourful uniforms, dramatic action, and great victories constituted only part of reality: never-ending casualty lists were another consequence of Napoleon's limitless ambition.

eliminate confusion from the battlefield). Corps also improved logistics, since several corps operating along separate lines of advance could supply themselves more easily than could a single large army operating along a single route.

Nevertheless, Napoleonic mobility demanded a more flexible and improvised supply system. Commanders of the *ancien régime* tied themselves to cumbrous supply lines out of fear that hungry troops would either desert or mutiny; the soldiers of the French Revolution, by contrast, were expected to forage for their food if need be, yet still retain their integrity as fighting units. Living off the country made rapid movement possible at key times on campaign, but it proved no panacea because, although foraging could maintain an army on the move through rich country, it could not sustain an army stopped for long in one place or one that had to move through poor or denuded terrain (as Napoleon would find in Russia).

No analysis of his success can avoid Napoleon's genius. A superb master of tactics and operations, he aimed not simply at defeating an enemy army, but at destroying it. His classic manner of accomplishing this was through a *manoeuvre sur les derrières*, designed to threaten the flank and rear of an opponent. He held the attention of his enemy with part of his own army while directing another element, usually a corps, to march around the enemy's flank. This could turn a field defeat into annihilation, because Napoleon's army now commanded the enemy's line of retreat. When possible, an active pursuit finished off the work completed in battle, as when Napoleon bagged nearly the entire Prussian army after its defeat at Jena-Auerstadt in 1806.

THE GRANDE ARMÉE

Napoleon displayed his genius to best effect in his masterpiece, the campaign of 1805. France and Britain went to war again in May 1803, but at first the two opponents could not really come to grips; the French encamped at Boulogne and threatened an invasion that never came. But when the Austrians and Russians joined Britain to form the Third Coalition in 1805, Napoleon put aside any invasion plans and moved against Austria with all haste in August.

The *Grande Armée* that Napoleon shifted down to the Rhine now totalled about 210,000 troops. He left an additional 50,000 troops in his Kingdom of Italy under Marshal André Masséna. Against this latter force, the Austrians concentrated their main effort, with 95,000 men under Archduke Charles. This meant that the Austrians could station only about 72,000 troops at Ulm and 22,000 in the Tyrol, linking Ulm with Italy.

Unlike his previous campaigns against the Austrians, this time Napoleon intended to march directly down the Danube. In the manoeuvre warfare now practised by the French, fortresses had lost the dominant role they had enjoyed in the seventeenth century, but Napoleon could still not advance down the Danube with Ulm threatening the rear of his army. Living by foraging, the *Grande Armée* crossed the Rhine on 26 September and rapidly swung down to the east of Ulm, cutting the Austrians off from their lines of communications, and bagged nearly the entire Austrian force. Next, Napoleon moved on Vienna. Russian troops committed to the war provided the main opposition to his advance but, in spite of their efforts, Napoleon occupied the Austrian capital by 14 November.

Yet Vienna too was not his ultimate goal, since he knew that only by defeating the main forces of the enemy could he drive Austria out of the war. This needed to be done soon, because the Prussians threatened too to enter the war (and this would have made Napoleon's task far more difficult). So Napoleon conspired to force battle on the combined Austrian and Russian army hovering north of Vienna. He lured the allies forward by feigning disorder and by assuming what appeared to be an exposed position. Tsar Alexander and his general Mikhail Kutusov in command of the allied force took the bait, but even this was not enough for Napoleon's plans. He also had to entice the allies to attack him in such a way that they would expose themselves to destruction. He did this by presenting what appeared to be a weak right flank to Kutusov at Austerlitz on 2 December. The Russian obligingly sent the bulk of his army on a lateral manoeuvre to envelop the French, but the flank that appeared so weak had been reinforced by the arrival of Davout's corps which made a forced march during the night to arrive on the battlefield. Through heroic combat, Louis Nicholas Davout stopped the head of the oncoming Russian columns. Meanwhile, Kutusov had weakened his centre by drawing troops from it for his flanking manoeuvre. This is what Napoleon had hoped for and, at the proper moment, he hurled Soult's large corps into the Russian centre, shattering it, and then wheeling right to come down on the rear of the Russian flanking columns. The

One soldier's experience of supply by foraging

Essential to Napoleon's ability to destroy opposing armies was the French soldier's capacity to outmarch anyone else in Europe. The Emperor recognized that speed gained him time, and repeatedly stressed that 'The loss of time is irreplaceable in war.' As his grumbling troops, his *grognards*, were said to boast, 'The Emperor has found a new way to make war: he uses only our legs and not our bayonets.' But this was also an army that marched on its stomach, and rapid marches required a style of logistics that did not slow the pace.

In contrast to the commanders of the old royal army, Napoleon professed contempt for formal supply arrangements and called upon his troops to forage on the march. At no time did he exploit more brilliantly the mobility allowed by living off the country than in his grand *manoeuvre sur les derrières* against Ulm in September and October 1805, when his troops covered an average of sixteen to nineteen miles per day without impairing their military effectiveness.

The testimony of one of his *grognards* puts it best. Corporal Jean-Pierre Blaise wrote home to his family after taking part in this historic march:

The Emperor reviewed us [at Boulogne] on 25 August 1805. We learned that day with joy that we were going to leave the coast...to make war in Germany...[W]e were certain that led by the Emperor we would march to victory...I have nothing to say worth your attention concerning our route up to the Rhine, which we crossed, without seeing the enemy on 26 September...We left the enemy on the right in order to cross the Rhine at Mannheim; on the twenty-fifth, cartridges were given to each man and we were ordered to leave all unnecessary possessions at the depot at Frankenthal, so that we would be burdened with as little as possible...The rapidity of our march not permitting food supplies to follow us, we often lacked bread, despite all the care that our general in chief, Davout, gave to it; and when we did receive it, it was so bad that it could not be eaten. Yet we were all the more able to do without bread because we were in the midst of the best season for potatoes in a country where they are very good. How many times did we ruin the hopes of the villagers! We stole the product of a year's work. However, we were, so to speak, forced to do so. We might have been able to dispense with pillaging the fruits of which there was a great quantity; I have never seen so many apples in the country we crossed up to Neuburg. But the soldiers also ate many of these, however without this causing any sickness.

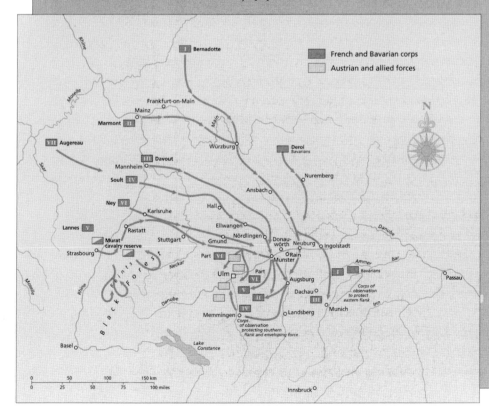

In 1805, the *Grande Armée* pivoted from the Rhine to the Danube in a huge *manoeuvre sur les derrières* that cut off Ulm from its lines of communication and retreat. Napoleon froze the Austrians in place by feinting a direct advance through the Black Forest with Murat's cavalry and Lannes' corps. French cavalry threw up a screen that hid the movements of the *Grande Armée*, which, aided by a corps-sized force of Bavarian allies, swung down behind Ulm, crossed the Danube, and surrounded the unfortunate fortress.

centre and left wing of the Allied army dissolved. Only the Russian right was able to withdraw in good order. Two days later the Austrians surrendered. No Napoleonic victory changed the map of Europe more than did Austerlitz for, as a result of it, in 1806 the Holy Roman Empire, a creation of the tenth century, ceased to exist, and the Habsburg ruler now simply styled himself emperor of Austria.

Austerlitz alone would have gained Napoleon fame as one of the greatest commanders of all time, yet despite his undeniable genius he ultimately met defeat. Four reasons explain his downfall: strategic greed, increasing local resentment towards French occupation, marked improvements and reforms among the armies that faced him, and the continued opposition of the world's dominant naval and commercial power, Britain. For all his tactical and operational abilities, Napoleon fell victim to a fatal strategic flaw: he neither knew what was enough nor when to stop. As such, he was doomed to fail sooner or later. In the narrow sense of knowing how to defeat one opponent at a time on campaign, Napoleon showed great talent: he devised campaigns in 1805, 1806, and 1807 which effectively imposed peace first upon Austria, then Prussia, and finally Russia. But Napoleon never seems to

Marshal Davout (below) played a key role in Napoleon's scheme at Austerlitz, for the Emperor expected him to hold the Russian flanking attack with his small corps. Davout would prove to be one of the greatest marshals both at Austerlitz and Auerstadt. Napoleon (right) shown in repose on the evening before Austerlitz, would often formulate his plans at night, after messengers had arrived to report the status and position of his corps. In the background a staff officer transcribes orders while Napoleon's Egyptian Mameluke servant rests in the foreground.

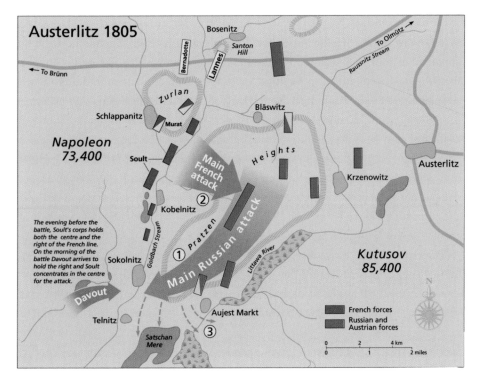

Austerlitz 1805

Napoleon 73,400

Kutusov 85,400

The evening before the battle, Soult's corps holds both the centre and the right of the French line. On the morning of the battle Davout arrives to hold the right and Soult concentrates in the centre for the attack.

French forces

Russian and Austrian forces

At Austerlitz, Napoleon drew the Russians into a battle they would have done better to avoid, and he tempted them to attack the right of his army, thus weakening the Russian centre for a French assault. The battle can be seen in three phases. (1) The Russians try to envelop the French right flank with the bulk of their forces, but the French under Davout stall the assault. (2) Napoleon hurls Soult's corps in an attack against the now weakened Russian centre, and after furious combat the French break the Russian line. (3) The French who have triumphed in the centre swing south to shatter the Russian left wing around the Satschan Mere.

have had a final goal that would satisfy him and guarantee a lasting stability to Europe. In contrast, Frederick the Great said after he had seized Silesia, the object of his ambition, 'Henceforth I would not attack a cat except to defend myself.' In a very real sense, the Seven Years War (see page 182) was forced upon Frederick; he would have preferred continued peace. Napoleon by contrast, seemed to be all ambition and very little restraint.

As part of his grand vision of victory against his long-standing enemy, Napoleon tried to organize the entire European continent in an economic war against Britain. In fact, the British had blockaded French ports since 1803; now Napoleon retaliated with his Continental System, designed to exclude all British goods from Europe. He first fashioned the System in the Berlin Decree of 1806 and then expanded it to include Russian participation by the Treaty of Tilsit the next year. While this was certainly not the first instance when one power exerted economic pressure during wartime in hopes of defeating its enemy, it was the grandest to date. However, Napoleon did not combine all the continental European states in a single free trade zone, but instead rigged tariffs to benefit France; consequently the Continental System represented French domination more than simply a common front against the British. With time, the exclusion of British goods was modified by various exceptions and a strong black market trade. Nevertheless, extension or preservation of the Continental System served as a *casus belli* as early as 1807 when the French invaded Portugal; moreover, when in December 1810 Tsar Alexander pulled away from Napoleon by declaring Russian ports open to neutral shipping carrying British goods, war between the two emperors became virtually inevitable.

Marshal Soult delivered the fatal blow to the Russians at Austerlitz, when his large corps drove into the Russian centre. His division commanders would complain, however, that Soult absented himself from the worst of the fighting. He had already amassed so much wealth and prestige that he was no longer eager to risk his life.

Francisco de Goya captured the outrage and fury of the Spaniards in his series of etchings, *The Disasters of War*. Here a peasant hacks at French soldiers who have raped his country. Goya recorded the fires of the 'people's war' in Spain that Napoleon never succeeded in extinguishing.

SPANISH ULCER AND RUSSIAN HAEMORRHAGE

When he set up his brother Joseph as king of Spain in 1808, Napoleon opened a constant lesion which drained French blood and resources for five years. The first British expedition landed in Portugal in 1808 and held on there, although it was pushed out of Spain. From his base in Portugal, Arthur Wellesley moved his forces into Spain again in mid-1809, only to be driven back once again. However, Wellesley, now Viscount Wellington, conducted a masterly defence of Portugal in 1810, exhausting the French army which stalled and starved before the fortified lines of Torres Vedras outside Lisbon. In 1812 Wellington took the offensive again and, although his forces suffered some setbacks, achieved great success in 1813. At the climactic battle of Vitoria on 21 June, Wellington with 80,000 men defeated an army of 65,000 commanded by Joseph Bonaparte.

Throughout the Peninsular War Spanish guerrillas terrorized the French and limited their ability to live off the country. The French staff officer Pelet described how guerrillas 'attempted to destroy us in detail, falling upon small detachments, massacring sick and isolated men, destroying convoys, and kidnapping messengers.' Just like the partisans during the War of American Independence, Spanish partisans confronted their enemies with a dilemma. The presence of British, Portuguese, and Spanish regular forces prohibited the French from dispersing to fight the guerrillas; but when the French did not disperse they found it difficult either to deal with guerrilla bands or to supply themselves by foraging. If the role of guerrillas was similar in Spain and in America, however, the brutal intensity of the Spanish war set it apart. Spanish guerrillas gave no quarter to Frenchmen who fell into their grasp, and French troops countered with brutal reprisals.

While the 'Spanish ulcer' slowly bled France, she suffered a massive haemorrhage in Russia. When he invaded Russia in June 1812, Napoleon massed a combined army of over 600,000 French and allied troops, but by the most generous estimate he returned with only 93,000 in December. He undertook this invasion, the greatest Napoleonic catastrophe, in the hopes of forcing the independent Russians back into the French orbit and of reasserting his faltering Continental System. The Russians realized that their strengths lay in a stout army and in the ability to trade space for time, so after the French won indecisive battles at Smolensk and Valutino, General Kutusov refused Napoleon the great battle he desired until Borodino, just 60 miles from Moscow, on 7 September. Napoleon addressed his troops that day: 'Soldiers! Here is the battle you have so long desired! Henceforth, victory depends on you; we have need of it.' In fact, it was the Emperor who desired and needed battle, but he did not make the best of his opportunity; he simply hurled his corps directly at the Russian position, and while he eventually won the day, he did so at great cost. With a total butcher's bill of 68,000 killed and wounded, Borodino produced the greatest blood-letting of the Napoleonic wars to date.

After the battle Kutusov simply stayed a tempting step ahead of Napoleon, and the French entered Moscow on 14 September. Rather than defend their capital, the Russians burned it, so Napoleon succeeded only in conquering its ashes and, failing to bring the Russians to terms, began his withdrawal a month later. With its logistics in a shambles and incapable of living off the barren winter landscape, Napoleon's massive army disintegrated in a retreat which ended in a desperate crossing of the Berezina River at the end of November. His losses in Spain and Russia, coupled with his continued unwillingness to pare down his strategic goals, doomed his attempts to hold on to Germany in 1813 and then to save his throne in 1814. But in these last campaigns the third factor also came into play: the improved abilities of his enemies.

Napoleon had benefited from the transition from dynastic to national warfare. The French Revolution had realized the ideal of the citizen soldier, committed to the cause and the people for which he fought. Napoleon exploited the nationalism of his own troops, but was taken aback when French conquest kindled opposing national sentiments in those peoples he had subjugated or humiliated. Spanish resentment against the French spawned the most bitter and brutal fighting of the Napoleonic wars. Russian resistance in 1812 proved to be unrelenting as well and, once pushed back into Germany, Napoleon faced a German uprising.

The German armies that fought to overturn French dominance over central Europe in 1813–14 were now motivated both by resentment, even hatred, towards the French and by an early form of German nationalism. In other ways as well, they were tougher opponents. German military reformers had imposed institutional and tactical changes since the humiliations of 1805–09. Moreover, Napoleon had taught Europe a new style of warfare, and, unfortunately for him, his enemies were excellent students.

Thus the vanquished Archduke Charles spearheaded a reform of the Austrian army after 1805. He tried to create as national a force as he could in the multi-national Austrian domains. In 1808 the Austrians created a *Landwehr*, or popular militia which eventually produced 240,000 troops, although these were best suited to rear echelon duties. Charles also borrowed the corps system of organization from the French. The new drill book incorporated skirmishing tactics, and light infantry battalions appeared on the army list. He also laboured to improve cavalry and, especially, artillery. However the new army had not yet time to gel before the Austrians took on Napoleon in 1809. And while they handed the emperor a set-back at the battle of Aspern-Essling on 21–22 May 1809, Napoleon defeated them once again at Wagram on 5–6 July.

A more profound and effective series of reforms transformed the Prussian army after the defeat at Jena-Auerstadt in 1806. The leading reformer, Gerhard von Scharnhorst, wished to create an army which could benefit from the dedication of the common soldier. He wrote, 'We shall be victorious when one learns to appeal, like the Jacobins, to the spirit of the people.' This would require more than simply military action and so, on 9 October 1807, the Prussian government issued an Edict of Emancipation to eliminate serfdom, much as the French had done in their Revolution. Scharnhorst also insisted upon a professional, educated officer class open to all without regard to aristocratic status. In 1808 an order redefined the officer corps as one based on talent and not on birth:

> From the whole nation, therefore, all individuals who possess these qualities can lay title to the highest positions of honour in the military establishment. All social preference which has hitherto existed is herewith terminated in the military establishment and everyone, without regard for his background has the same duties and the same rights.

To instruct this more inclusive officer corps, Prussian reformers established institutions for officer education superior to any others found in Europe, including a war college to train staff officers. Scharnhorst also laid the foundations of the Prussian General Staff that would become such an influence in nineteenth century warfare.

Prussian reform aimed at creating a people's army. The Treaty of Tilsit (1807) limited the regular army to only 42,000 men; however, the Prussians did what they could to circumvent these restrictions, creating a trained reserve of 33,600 additional men. Once war became likely with France in 1813, the Prussians expanded

The cuirass (below), worn at the battle of Waterloo by François-Antoine Fauveau, bears witness to the inadequacy of the breastplates worn by the charging cavalrymen (right) against cannon fire. There is something particularly symbolic about Fauveau's fate, for his life exactly spanned the Revolutionary and Napoleonic wars. Born in 1792, Fauveau died, his chest crushed, on the field of Waterloo at the same fatal moment that brought down the empire.

the regular army and created new forces. *Jäger*, volunteer riflemen of largely middle-class origins, displayed their patriotism; royal decrees called up the *Landwehr*, a militia of all men aged between seventeen and forty not enrolled in other forms of military service; the *Landsturm* (composed of all other men) served as a last line of defence. By August 1813, Prussia's fighting forces had climbed to 280,000 troops.

WATERLOO

Napoleon's foes in 1813 adopted his own operational principles and turned them against their creator. His enemies became more aggressive, and they sought not to defeat him but to destroy his major forces. The niceties of eighteenth-century combat and manoeuvre became a thing of the past. The allies struggled not to be defeated in detail as they had so often been before, but to unite for battle and march to the sound of guns. In 1813 at the climactic battle of Leipzig, the combined armies of Austria, Prussia, Russia, and Sweden, totalling 340,000 allied soldiers, defeated Napoleon's army of nearly 200,000 and ended his dominion in Germany. Napoleon showed something of his old brilliance in the defensive campaign of 1814, although he was assailed by Wellington's army – fresh from its victories in the Peninsular War – in the south while several armies in the east and north converged upon Paris. But when Napoleon manoeuvred to threaten Prussian and

The duke of Wellington, shown here in a portrait by Sir Thomas Lawrence, mastered the soldier's trade in India. Napoleon at first dismissed Wellington as a 'sepoy general', but soon came to respect him. In Portugal and Spain Wellington fought a series of campaigns that drove the French from Iberia, 1809–13. Wellington next invaded France, in 1814, reaching Toulouse before Napoleon abdicated. In 1815 he commanded British and allied forces at Waterloo.

At Waterloo, the French repeatedly fought without sufficient co-ordination between infantry, cavalry, and artillery. In his heroic canvas (left), Henri Philippoteaux portrayed the ill-fated charge by French cuirassiers against British infantry squares. At about 4 p.m. Ney ordered this attack which quickly got out of hand as additional unsupported French cavalry joined the fray.

Austrian lines of communication in order to force a withdrawal in late March, they demonstrated that they had mastered the essentials of Napoleonic warfare by ignoring the threat and marching on Paris. With the allies in Paris, Napoleon abdicated.

Vanquished, the unhappy emperor retired to exile on the island of Elba, but soon conspired to retake his throne. On 1 March 1815 he landed at Cannes to begin the ill-starred Hundred Days. The outcome was never really in doubt: European governments knew him too well to trust his pledge that he only wished to rule France in peace, and once the fighting commenced, his opponents had learned his art of war too well to fall victim to it. At Waterloo, Wellington and Blücher joined forces to defeat him once again on 18 June, and even had Napoleon won that day, he would surely have fallen before the massive armies of Austria and Russia, which had already put 450,000 troops in the field between them to finish the job.

In any case, it is doubtful whether France could have continued to field armies on the same scale. Of the two million Frenchmen who served in Napoleon's armies between 1806 and 1814, almost 15,000 officers were killed or wounded, 90,000 enlisted men died in battle and a further 300,000 in hospital, while no less than 625,000 others were recorded as either 'prisoners' or 'disappeared' when the conscription lists were closed in 1814. Of the dead, 84,000 met their end in Spain and Portugal, 171,000 in Russia, and 181,000 in Germany. In all, the wars of Napoleon killed 20 per cent – one in five – of all Frenchmen born between 1790 and 1795 (compared with the 25 per cent, or one in four, Frenchmen born between 1891 and 1895 killed in World War I).

The opposite side of the coin to French defeat was British victory. Britain had opposed France from 1793 to the final exile of Napoleon on St Helena, with only a brief respite in 1802–03. Britain remained the mistress of the seas throughout, and her naval pre-eminence won for her commercial and colonial wealth that allowed her to bankroll the continental wars against Napoleon.

While France had enjoyed a brief naval renaissance during the War of American Independence, her own Revolution hurt her navy badly. Revolutionary enthusiasm could not accomplish at sea what it could on land. Skilled aristocratic naval captains lost through emigration or purged by revolutionary action could not be replaced with the same facility as could infantry officers. Moreover ideals of liberty, equality, and fraternity were probably less congenial to the duties and discipline of life at sea than they were to life in the camps.

THE NELSON TOUCH

While the French periodically confronted the British on the seas during the wars of the French Revolution, it was to little avail. Admiral Richard Howe won the first major naval action of this long era of warfare on 29 May–1 June 1794, the battle of the Glorious First of June, when he defeated a fleet of French escort vessels, although the merchant vessels they were escorting managed to slip safely into the

French port of Brest. The next major action saw the French try and fail to land 13,000 troops at Bantry Bay (in southwest Ireland) in 1796; but this effort came to nothing, as much because of bad weather as because of British fleet action. The Royal Navy tangled with some of France's new allies in 1797. In February a British fleet under Admiral John Jervis, with Commodore Horatio Nelson as one of his subordinates, smashed a Spanish fleet at the battle of Cape St Vincent; while Admiral Adam Duncan ended Dutch naval competition with Britain for good at the battle of Camperdown on 11 October. But mutinies aboard British ships rivalled these victories in importance; during the spring and summer, the home fleet mutinied at Spithead and the Nore. In the first case the navy accommodated the mutineers, and in the second it suppressed them, but as a result of this turmoil life at sea for the common sailor improved.

The year 1798 proved to be particularly decisive, as the British dealt with two French amphibious operations. The French succeeded in landing a small force in Ireland, but it was soon captured by the British, and this led to still one more British victory over a French fleet sent to reinforce the effort. Meanwhile, in the Mediterranean, Nelson utterly destroyed the French fleet at the battle of the Nile (see page 197).

Nelson and Britain's other admirals transformed the character of naval combat in less than a decade. The standard naval tactic of the eighteenth century had been the line ahead which required that a fleet fight as a unit, with one ship of the line after the other discharging its broadside in neat procession. This tactic put a premium on order and stressed maximum control by a fleet admiral over his subordinates; however, time and again line ahead tactics resulted in indecisive battles during which both sides battered each other but won or lost little advantage. Fighting instructions insisted that commanders rigidly apply the line ahead, and at times they seemed more intent on doing so than on defeating the enemy. This seems to have been the case for the unfortunate Admiral John Byng, who was shot after a court martial found him guilty of having failed to do his utmost in a losing fight off Minorca in 1756.

In contrast to the line ahead, mêlée tactics turned a fleet action into a series of ship-to-ship battles by breaking up the enemy's formation. This meant sacrificing the order of the attacking fleet and relying on the skill and initiative of individual captains. Ideally there was some method to the mayhem of the mêlée, as the attacking fleet attempted to turn superior numbers or position to advantage before hurling itself upon its enemy.

Historians have long criticized the dead hand of line ahead tactics and praised the mêlée as Nelson applied it, particularly at his masterpiece, Trafalgar. But mêlée tactics only held the promise of victory to the fleet with the better captains and crews, since so much depended on the superiority of one fleet's ships over the other's. By the late eighteenth century, the British simply outstripped their Continental rivals in the quality of captains and crews; they needed little else to win

Horatio Lord Nelson, shown opposite, became England's most famous admiral. Entering service in the Royal Navy as a midshipman at the age of 12, he rose very fast, reaching the rank of captain at 21. His daring tactics changed naval warfare. His portrait testifies to his personal bravery, for the limp right sleeve of his coat betrays the loss of his arm in battle in 1797. Three years earlier he lost the sight of his right eye fighting in Corsica. There is little surprise in the fact that he died on the deck of his flagship, *Victory*, shot through by a musket ball at the battle of Trafalgar.

but a chance to get at their foes. Nelson recognized this and brought the matter to a head, but he was neither the only nor the first British admiral to do so. Howe imposed a mêlée on the French at the Glorious First of June in 1794, as did Jervis at Cape St Vincent in 1797.

At Trafalgar, Nelson relied upon mêlée tactics to his great renown. During that campaign in 1805 Nelson consulted regularly with his captains until that 'band of brothers' understood his goals and methods. He reported one of the conferences with his captains:

> [W]hen I came to explain to them the 'Nelson Touch', it was like an electric shock. Some shed tears, all approved…and from Admirals downwards, it was repeated – 'It must succeed, if ever they will allow us to get at them! You are, my Lord, surrounded by friends whom you inspire with confidence.'

Nelson could rely on his captains' abilities, and those of British tars in the rigging and at the guns, to win a great battle if brought head to head with the French. After what seemed like a wild goose chase to the West Indies in search of the French fleet, he finally encountered the combined French and Spanish fleet under Pierre Villeneuve off Cape Trafalgar on 21 October, as it tried to regain the safety of Cadiz. Nelson instructed his captains that he intended to attack in two divisions, led by himself and Cuthbert Collingwood. At 11:48 am, just as the two fleets were about to collide, Nelson ordered the signal: 'England expects that every man will do his duty.' The two British divisions then broke through the enemy line, Nelson toward the van of the allies and Collingwood about midway through their line. When the *Victory*, Nelson's flagship, smashed through the enemy fleet, it became ensnared with a French '74', the *Redoutable*. Musket fire from the *Redoutable* brought down many of the *Victory*'s crew and mortally wounded Nelson. But as the dying admiral had planned, once the British had broken the allied line a huge mêlée resulted which yielded victory. British seamanship enabled Nelson's ships to outmanoeuvre the allies and concentrate superior gunpower against isolated allied vessels. At the end of the day the British had sunk one enemy ship and captured seventeen others.

While the British continued a wary watch to seaward after 1805 and continued to augment their fleet, never again did the French contest British naval mastery in blue water fleet action. The British did conduct a series of amphibious operations against various French islands, Copenhagen, and Antwerp, not to mention Washington and New Orleans in the War of 1812 against the new United States. The most successful amphibious operation of the war, however, was the British effort in the Iberian Peninsula, 1808–13 (see page 204). Obviously without command of the sea, the greatest British land campaign of the war would have been inconceivable.

Clarkson Stanfield's painting of the battle of Trafalgar catches the action as Nelson's *Victory*, centre right, takes on the *Redoutable*, immediately to the left, and the *Bucentaire*, to the right with its stern to the viewer. At the far left, Collingwood's *Royal Sovereign* pierces the French–Spanish line at another point. On the extreme right is the *Santissima Trinidad*, the world's largest ship of the line with 130 guns. The key to Nelson's tactical style was to break into the enemy line of battle and fight in a pell-mell fashion, ship to ship. This view of the battle portrays the deadly and seemingly chaotic combat typical of the 'Nelson touch'.

BRITANNIA: MISTRESS OF COMMERCE AND EMPIRE

However, perhaps the major advantages won by the exercise of British naval power were colonial and commercial. With France eliminated as a naval power and Spain reduced to impotence – and often on the 'wrong side' of the struggle – Britain enjoyed a virtually free hand overseas and in world trade. Over the course of the war, the British deprived the French of much of their colonial empire. (In addition, Napoleon wisely jettisoned Louisiana, the last French holding in North America and one he could not defend, by selling it to the United States.) The British swept the seas of French merchant vessels, and all the French could do in reprisal was to build powerful raiders capable of operating independently against British commerce, seizing or destroying what ships they could. Other states that opposed Britain also put their colonies and trade at risk. Thus in 1795 the British seized the Dutch Cape Colony, restored it in the Treaty of Amiens (1802), but then retook it in 1806, this time not to relinquish it again until the twentieth century.

The most important colonial acquisitions garnered by the British during the long struggle with France came not in the Americas or Africa but in India. As was the case before, warfare in India followed its own logic and timetable. Once possessed of the large sepoy armies that the conquest of Bengal had made possible (see page 179), the British East India company took on two major opponents, Mysore and the Marathas, in a series of conflicts that lasted from 1766 to 1805. The south Indian state of Mysore confronted the British East India Company's new military power in four wars. In the first, 1766–69, Haider Ali fought the Company's armies effectively, but he fared worse in the second, 1780–83, although aided by a French naval squadron operating in the Indian Ocean. The Third Mysore War, 1789–92, was the most important of the struggles, and although the British experienced great difficulties in dealing with the Mysore light cavalry, they triumphed by enlisting the aid of Maratha light horse. In order to buy peace, Haider Ali's successor, Tippoo Sultan, ceded his most lucrative and populous territories to the Company, so he could not put up effective resistance in a final struggle in 1799, when he died fighting to defend his capital. In this brief war, Arthur Wellesley, the future duke of Wellington, saw his first action.

Wellesley played a key role in the next colonial drama, as the East India Company took advantage of civil war among the Marathas to challenge their erstwhile allies in the Second Maratha War, 1803–05. Although weakened by internal dissension, the Marathas put up a good fight; Wellesley later stated that his victory at Assaye on 23 September 1803 was the hardest-fought battle of his entire career. Victories against Mysore and the Marathas won the East India Company control over the Deccan to match its mastery of Bengal. During these conflicts, the East India Company accomplished its goals as much by learning the value of native Indian methods of warfare and by exploiting the political weaknesses of its Indian enemies as it did by deploying the superior fighting qualities of Company armies.

In the commercial and colonial phases of her struggle with Revolutionary and Napoleonic France, Britain rose as a colossus over world trade. She took full advantage of the first stages of the Industrial Revolution that magnified Britain's traditional commercial prowess. While the Industrial Revolution had yet to transform the weapons actually employed on the battlefield, it influenced the course of war by adding to Britain's coffers during her struggle with France. The eighteenth century produced a number of basic inventions that would eventually transform the textile industry, and these were linked to improvements in water and steam power. Between 1740 and 1806 British iron production grew from 17,000 tons to 260,000 tons and by 1813, the year of Vitoria, there were 3,000 power looms in use in Britain. It was production and trade that gave her the riches to finance her own efforts against Napoleon and to offer subsidies to the continental states that braved the French in the field.

The British possessed the most rational and effective system of war finance in Europe. To pay the costs of his armies and wars, Napoleon pillaged Europe – a method that, even when it produced adequate funds, alienated subject peoples and reluctant allies, thus preparing the way for his downfall. In contrast, Britain based her capacity to produce the sinews of war upon her government and credit institutions and upon her commerce. The Bank of England repeatedly proved its ability to mobilize credit at low rates, and Parliament built up an admirable record of paying off its debts. As workshop and entrepot for the world, particularly in the midst of war, Britain benefited from levies on trade that no other state could match – although, to be sure, tax rates also soared to foot the bill.

Britain's wealth allowed her to subsidize coalition after coalition against the French. Major opponents of Napoleonic France could count on payments, but it would be incorrect to argue that Britain carried the greatest burden of the effort. When in 1805 Britain promised support to members of the Third Coalition, she pledged to pay £1,250,000 pounds annually for every 100,000 men raised, but this sum would, according to Austrian estimates, pay only a quarter of the cost of Austria's war effort. The subsidies thus seem to have functioned as incentive as well as actual aid. Britain also supplied arms to her allies: for example, in 1813 the bulk of the weapons that re-equipped the Prussian Army came from England. Ultimately Napoleon could not carry the war to Britain, guarded as she was by her navy, while the British could find continental allies to carry the war to France; so that, unless Napoleon agreed to limitations on his empire that the commercial giant could accept, he could not escape frustration and failure.

The American and French Revolutions changed the nature of warfare forever. Before these revolutions, international conflict had been a dynastic affair between kings and princes, although the Dutch and the British cases modified this picture to some degree. When revolution or reform transformed a population from subjects to citizens by giving them more of a stake in society and more of a say in government, those citizens saw the struggles of the state as their own. As such, wars became contests between nations in arms.

Radical changes in government, society, and (consequently) motivation did not sweep through all of the western world at the same moment, or even in the same decade. In the late eighteenth century, their revolutions and representative institutions put the United States and France in the lead of this trend. Even earlier the British too had developed their own sense of identity and brand of nationalism based on their insular history and the triumph of Parliament over the monarchy in the seventeenth century. While nationalism may only have permeated the masses in Italy and Germany later in the nineteenth century, by 1813 the concept had taken hold among the literate elites and had become a factor in policy and war. The future would see all Europe engulfed in strong currents of nationalism with unforeseen and bloody results.

CHAPTER 12   # The Industrialization of War

The settlement of twenty-five years of war between the European powers in 1815 represented no easy task. But the victors agreed that they possessed certain interests in common; in particular they aimed to control the nationalistic emotions that had swept Europe. Perhaps even more critical to European peace, however, was the general exhaustion: none were willing to resort to war to settle territorial disputes or to consider hegemonic ambitions. Although the industrial revolution occurring in Britain before and during the revolutionary and Napoleonic wars had provided the British with unheard of wealth and economic power, they were content to maintain a balance of power on the continent while controlling the world's commerce.

The victors also agreed to grant the French an easy peace; they restored the Bourbon monarchy and the frontiers of 1792. The settlement in eastern Europe and 'the Germanies', however, proved more difficult than the problem of what to do with defeated France, for the impact of French conquest had so disturbed the fabric of German life that no settlement could possibly have turned the clock in central Europe back to 1789. Moreover, the Russians had considerable ambitions in eastern Europe, particularly with regard to Poland.

In the end the statesmen hammered out an acceptable settlement. The Russians received virtually all of Poland; in return the Prussians received territories along the Rhine on the French frontier, in order to prevent a resurgent France from moving into western Germany. These acquisitions conferred two important advantages upon Prussia: first, by trading most of its Polish lands for German territories, it became a state with a relatively homogenous population; equally important, it gained control of an obscure river valley, the Ruhr, which was to become the second great centre of the industrial revolution.

The Paris–St Germain line, 1837. Railways transformed economic structures throughout Europe, but only the Prussians perceived the military implications. They developed railroads in accordance with strategic as well as economic needs. Consequently, in the 1860s they could deploy and support larger forces on their frontiers more quickly than any potential opponents.

By accommodating the interests of all the major powers, the Congress of Vienna proved to be one of the most successful negotiated treaties in the history of western civilization. It did possess a number of weaknesses – the growing threat of nationalism being the most obvious – but on the whole the Congress provided the major powers with a rationale for upholding the balance of power among themselves, reinforced by memories of the catastrophic wars of 1792 to 1815 (which helped dampen down the ambitious, until another generation had come to power).

After 1815 Europe therefore settled into an unprecedented period of peaceful development. There were, of course, political difficulties. In 1830 a revolution in France tumbled the Bourbon monarchy for good, although the result only led to a dynastic change, while rioting in Brussels provoked partition of the Low Countries. In 1848 a more serious challenge to order occurred with trouble again starting in France. But this time it did not stop at the French frontier; instead it spread to central Europe. The system of control created by the Congress of Vienna, which aimed at throttling nationalism throughout the Habsburg and German lands,

Overleaf: Staff officers watch a display of British air power in 1913.

collapsed in a matter of weeks. In the end, only Russian intervention helped to crush rebel Hungarian nationalists and keep the Habsburg monarchy together.

In Prussia, the conservatives initially did little better against the revolutionary forces, but an assembly of representatives in Frankfurt proved incapable of putting together a new German state in the revolutionary situation. After a desperate struggle, the conservatives regained control of the situation. The Prussian king refused the offer of the Frankfurt assembly for the crown of a new German state with the derisory comment that he would not accept a crown from the gutter. Even though it failed in the most general of terms, however, the revolution of 1848 underlined the depths of nationalism underlying the European equilibrium.

THE CRIMEAN WAR

Russia's success both in avoiding revolution in 1848 and in putting down Hungarian nationalists encouraged the Tsar to pursue a more aggressive policy in the Balkans. The Ottoman Empire was already a decrepit, weak state, incapable of adapting to the industrial and technological challenge of the West; yet, it possessed an almost inexhaustible capacity to survive its disasters. The Russians hoped to take advantage of Ottoman weaknesses; the British and French demurred. They could not allow Russia to pick up the pieces from Turkey's collapse and the British, in particular, wished to prevent the Russians from gaining direct access to the Mediterranean.

In 1854, a Russian army crossed the Danube and invaded Ottoman territory; the British and French declared war and sent armies to Constantinople to defend the Turks. Even before fighting could occur south of the Danube, the Austrians stepped in and displayed astonishing ingratitude for Russia's aid in 1849: they demanded that the Tsar withdraw his forces from Ottoman territory.

The Crimea. Although France and Britain attacked targets in the Baltic, and mounted minor operations in the Arctic and the Pacific to facilitate a complete blockade of Russia, the Crimea remained their primary objective. Their steamships moved a substantial army to the peninsula and supported it there; the Russians, however, lacked railways reaching to the area and thus had difficulty supplying their forces. The allies landed in September 1854 with the intention of taking Sebastopol, the principal base of Russia's Black Sea fleet, before winter set in; but they failed to take into account the sophistication of the city's defences and the siege lasted a year.

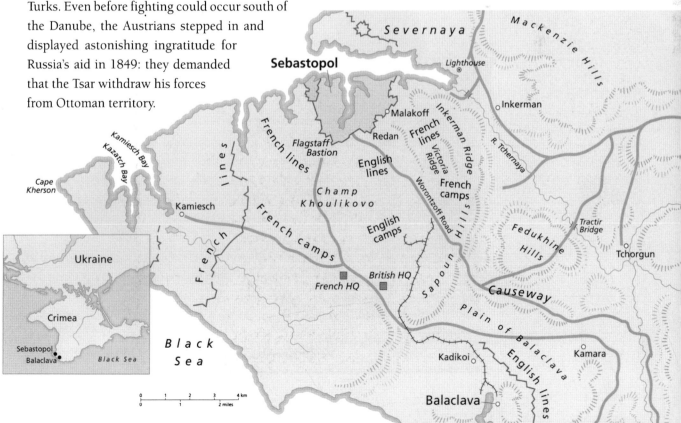

The Russians complied, thereby removing the *casus belli*, but British and French leaders determined to teach Russia a lesson. The result was the Crimean War.

In some respects the conflict represents a crucial watershed in the history of war; in others it was a throwback to the 'limited wars' of the eighteenth century. For the first time, the fighting saw the direct impact of science and technology on the battlefield. The invention of the 'minié' bullet for rifled muskets (muskets with spiral groves cut into the barrel) allowed infantrymen to reach out and hit opponents at ranges of upwards of 300 yards. (This lead bullet was hollowed at the bottom, which allowed the explosive charge to push out the flanges and make a tight enough fit that the rifling imparted spin and direction. It thus tripled the musket's killing range.) Of equal importance was the appearance of steamships in navies: the British and French could transport and supply their forces in Turkey and the Crimea with remarkable ease. Finally, the telegraph allowed governments in Paris and London to communicate with commanders in the field; moreover, newspaper correspondents got their stories to their editors in a matter of days rather than weeks. But despite technological advances, the governments waging the war never mobilized popular enthusiasm and nationalism for a total war. Rather,

the Crimean War remained a conflict fought over obscure issues, none essential to the participants' survival.

With the Russian withdrawal north of the Danube, Anglo-French commanders determined to invade the Crimea and attack the Russian naval base at Sebastopol. In September 1854 the allied fleet landed Anglo-French troops haphazardly on the Crimean coast; luckily no Russians opposed them. The combined army then marched south towards Sebastopol. On the way, they encountered a Russian army on the heights overlooking the Alma river. A British attack on the left overwhelmed the defenders; well-aimed fire from rifled muskets slaughtered the Russians, massed in columns, well before the advancing 'thin red line' came within range of enemy muskets. Victory at Alma reflected superior allied technology rather than training or discipline.

The allies then marched on Sebastopol. An immediate assault might have taken the port, but the French were cautious, and preparations for a siege allowed the Russians to complete their defences. Before winter terminated military operations, the Russians made two attempts to break through to the besieged garrison. At Balaclava, through a muddle of conflicting conceptions and misunderstandings,

Roll Call', an oil painting by Lady Butler. Although the Russian army lost some 500,000 men in the Crimea, the allies also suffered heavy casualties because their supply system broke down amid the harsh winter conditions along the Black Sea. Uniforms were inadequate; rations, when available, proved inedible; an incompetent medical system further exacerbated the misery. But unlike previous wars, the British reading public was kept informed of conditions by newspapers which maintained reporters on the scene who sent their copy to London by telegraph.

British cavalry attacked Russian artillery positions at the end of a long valley. It was all gloriously hopeless, and the 'Charge of the Light Brigade' added to the long list of heroic British failures. Nevertheless, by day's end the allies still remained between the Russians and Sebastopol. A second attempt to relieve the port was no more successful: at the battle of Inkerman, the rifled muskets of the allied troops completely dominated the battlefield and the Russians suffered 12,000 casualties, the allies only 3,000.

Then winter settled over the region, and the British army was not prepared. Its supply system broke down: conditions in the front lines and hospitals were soon appalling; some commanders wintered in their yachts. But for nations possessing representative governments, the time when senior officers could ignore the plight of common soldiers had passed. British correspondents reported the dreadful conditions under which the army was suffering, and the public outcry resulted in substantial reforms that began the process of modernizing the British army.

In the short term, however, the Crimean winter ruined the British forces, and the French and the Piedmontese had to bear the bulk of the fighting in 1855. The Russians made further attempts to relieve Sebastopol, but again technology told against them. In their last relief attempt, in mid-August, the Russians suffered over 8,000 casualties, the allies fewer than 2,000. On 8 September the French stormed the fortress at Malakoff. For the first time in history, the officers leading the assault columns synchronized watches. The attack succeeded, making further defence of the port impossible.

In the end, the Crimean War had little impact. It only temporarily halted Russian ambitions in the Balkans and put off to another century Turkey's collapse. Nevertheless, advances in weaponry that had marked the war's conduct at the tactical level underlined that technology and science were now crucial to battlefield success. The side that recognized and utilized such changes in its military forces would enjoy an important advantage over its opponents.

THE AMERICAN CIVIL WAR

The American Civil War ranks as the most important conflict of the nineteenth century because, for the first time, opposing governments harnessed the popular enthusiasm of the French Revolution to the industrial technology that was sweeping the West. From the first, the contending sides staked out positions that brooked no compromise: for the North there would be no peace without restoration of union; for the South there would be no peace without independence. Yet both sides initially underestimated their opponent's political will. Most southerners believed that a few quick successes against the cowardly Yankees would guarantee victory, while most northerners believed that the South's population opposed secession and a few victories would lead to the collapse of the secessionist conspiracy.

The North certainly enjoyed significant advantages. Its population numbered nearly 25 million, while the South had barely 9 million people (of whom 3 million

General Winfield Scott Hancock's division commanders and staff pause for reflection. By 1864 the Union army had evolved a highly effective staff and command system, consisting of regular and volunteer officers who had learned their trade on the battlefield. These men may have displayed a certain casualness towards the niceties of military dress, but they provided driving, competent leadership.

were slaves). Nearly all major industrial concerns and the majority of the nation's railways lay in the North. Moreover the Federal government controlled the navy and the army, as well as the bulk of the nation's bureaucratic machinery. But the South possessed other advantages, beginning with geography. The distance from central Georgia to northern Virginia is approximately the distance from East Prussia to Moscow; the distance from Baton Rouge in Louisiana to Richmond exceeds the distance from the Franco-German border to the eastern frontier of Poland. Exacerbating the challenge posed in launching military operations against the South was the fact that primeval wilderness covered many portions of the region, particularly in the west. While the eastern theatre lay relatively close to centres of northern industrial power, the starting point for the Union's western armies, Cairo, Illinois, was over a thousand miles from the North's industrial heart. Without railways and steamships, the North could not have brought its economic potential to bear and probably would have lost the war. The South also possessed the advantage that it did not have to 'win': it would achieve its aims by merely thwarting northern military efforts.

Both sides faced daunting problems in creating effective military forces out of nothing. The regular army was little more than a constabulary designed to overawe Indians; none of its officers had received the training or preparation to lead large armies. As with much of American military history, the Civil War was the story of military improvisation and learning on the battlefield. If the officers knew little about war, the politicians knew nothing; Abraham Lincoln was desperate enough to have the Library of Congress send over to the White House the classic works of military history. In the end, he proved an eminently successful wartime strategist and political leader, but almost entirely due to native intuition and guile – not to any serious intellectual preparation.

The first problem confronting both sides was gathering, training, and supplying large military forces. Ironically, the South again enjoyed an important advantage. Since it possessed no regular army, those who resigned their Federal commissions to fight for the Confederacy were spread throughout the various state militia regiments, where their experience provided a modicum of basic knowledge. In the North, however, the regular army remained in existence and refused to part with its officers for training volunteer regiments.

The armies themselves retained a fundamentally civilian character. Photographs of even the Army of the Potomac, supposedly the most 'spit-and-polish' of Civil War armies, suggest a general casualness towards the niceties of uniform. When properly led, however, these troops endured sacrifices that few units in American military history have equalled. The performance of the 1st Minnesota regiment at Gettysburg is a case in point. On 2 July 1863, it sustained over 80 per cent casualties; yet its few survivors were back in the line receiving Pickett's charge on the next afternoon.

The war's opening year, 1861, displayed Lincoln's extraordinary political talents: the North's successes in that year stand in stark contrast to mistakes in southern policy. The crucial strategic issue was who would control the border states. In Maryland a policy of direct military intervention by federal authorities overawed secessionists in Annapolis. In Missouri, local politicians and soldiers loyal to the Union seized control of the state and drove off rebel supporters, although in the back country a vicious guerrilla war began. The prize was Kentucky, where the state legislature and populace remained loyal but the governor favoured secession. In the impasse the state declared neutrality, but southern troops invaded and forced the pro-Unionists in the state to support the North.

Beside losing the border states, southern leaders made the mistake of embargoing cotton shipments to pressure European states into intervening in the conflict. Such hopes proved illusory: substantial portions of British and French populations were pro-union, while Britain always confronted the problem of how to defend Canada from a northern invasion. In the end, the cotton embargo robbed the South of substantial earnings and the opportunity to import sizeable amounts of weapons and ammunition while the federal blockade was still in its infancy.

THE WAR IN THE EAST

Military action in 1861 underlined how ill-prepared both sides were for war. Under pressure to 'thrash the rebs' and facing the fact that most ninety-day volunteer regiments would soon return home, the federal high command marched its forces out of Washington to Manassas. The resulting battle of Bull Run, with everything from heroism to comedy – a number of congressmen brought ladies out to watch the spectacle – saw southern troops win a closely fought struggle. After fighting with considerable heroism, the Union army collapsed in late afternoon before a rebel counter-attack in a panic that did not stop until the troops got to Washington.

Defeat at Bull Run underlined how idle had been Union hopes that a single victory could end the Civil War. Lincoln recognized the need for long-term enlistments and appointed a bright young general to command the army, George McClellan. 'Little Mac', as his troops affectionately called him, was a great trainer and self-propagandizer. However, his talents went no further. He rated himself as the successor to Napoleon and referred to Lincoln as 'that ape', but displayed little capacity on the battlefield to provide either leadership or guidance. He was a man afraid of the unknown; consequently, he consistently estimated his opponents as possessing numbers that were impossibly larger. Almost anything served to excuse inaction.

Despite political pressure to use the army he was training, McClellan refused to launch a major military operation for the rest of 1861. In 1862 he planned to move his Army of the Potomac up the James river against Richmond, now the Confederate capital; in spring McClellan made his move and achieved general surprise. Admittedly, he failed to receive all of the troops he requested for the attack, since Lincoln wished to protect Washington from the Confederates and kept one corps back. Nevertheless, McClellan enjoyed considerable superiority over his opponents. The advance on the James peninsula was a slow, tortuous movement in which

The bloodiest day in American military history occurred at the battle of Antietam, 17 September 1862, where 20,000 Americans were killed or maimed. At 'Bloody Lane', (shown in this fragment of an unrestored painting by Captain James Hope, who served as a scout and topographical engineer for the Vermont Infantry at Antietam), a major Union attack lapped a strong Confederate position along a sunken road. The result was a slaughter pen as Union troops firing the length of the trench massacred their opponents.

outnumbered Confederates consistently baffled the over-cautious Union commander. By the end of May McClellan was at the gates of Richmond and preparing for an extended siege. But the Confederates were also ready. Under the inspired leadership of General Robert E. Lee, they launched a series of savage counterattacks which drove McClellan and his army back to their supply ships. Not all the Confederate attacks were successful – the battle of Malvern Hill was a disaster – but Lee achieved a complete dominance over his opponent, a dominance from which the Army of the Potomac never fully recovered.

McClellan's ineptitude, rudeness, and arrogance eventually led Lincoln to remove him as the army's overall commander before the James peninsula expedition had ended. Now defeats in front of Richmond pushed Lincoln to appoint a new commander in Northern Virginia, John Pope, a successful and aggressive general from the west. Upon taking command, Pope announced to his new troops that soldiers in the west had never been accustomed to display their backs to the enemy; he soon antagonized his corps and division commanders as well. The result was another disastrous defeat at the Second Battle of Bull Run, where Lee used his subordinates, Thomas 'Stonewall' Jackson and James Longstreet, to confuse and eventually smash Pope's forces. With McClellan straggling back from the James peninsula and Pope in general disarray, Lee invaded the North. The Army of Northern Virginia marched into Maryland, while Jackson destroyed a Federal force at Harper's Ferry, Virginia.

Threatened by Lee's move, Lincoln reappointed McClellan as commander of the Army of the Potomac. Fortunately for the Union, Lee's plans for the campaign fell into Union hands, but even then, McClellan moved with an excruciating caution that allowed the Confederates to concentrate their forces at the last moment. The

USS *Cairo*, Mississippi River, 1862. One of the crucial advantages enjoyed by the Union forces throughout the war in the west was the large fleet of steamboats – some equipped with artillery others serving as transports – which allowed effective exploitation of the vast river systems that flowed into the Mississippi River from the states of Tennessee, Kentucky, Alabama, and Mississippi.

result was Antietam, the bloodiest single day in American military history, with the combined casualties well over 20,000. McClellan launched three great attacks on a thin line of Confederates; each came within a whisker of success, but the Confederates held and McClellan refused to commit his reserves despite the fact that the enemy was on the brink of collapse. McClellan claimed victory, though at best he had gained a draw. Nevertheless, Lincoln seized the opportunity of a battlefield 'success' to issue the Emancipation Proclamation; as of 1 January 1863 the slaves would be free in all territories that remained in rebellion. Lincoln's proclamation represented a direct attack on the social structure and culture of the South; few illusions remained about what would be required to win the war.

McClellan, who strongly objected to freeing the slaves, talked loudly about how he had saved the North, but he displayed no inclination to confront Lee again. Disgusted, Lincoln fired 'Little Mac' for good and appointed Ambrose Burnside commander of the Army of the Potomac. Burnside proved more aggressive but even less competent. In December he launched his troops against an impregnable southern position at Fredricksburg; the ensuing slaughter led to his replacement.

THE WAR IN THE WEST

Events in the west in 1862 proved more propitious for the Union. In early 1862 an obscure Union general, Ulysses S. Grant moved against the two forts guarding the entrances to the Cumberland and Tennessee rivers, Forts Henry and Donelson. Their seizure opened up the two rivers, secured Kentucky for the Union, and allowed Union gun boats to proceed up the Tennessee all the way to Mussell Shoals in Alabama where they cut the only east–west railroad in the Confederacy.

Grant's army then moved up the Tennessee to Shiloh, where in April he busily engaged in training his troops, while awaiting arrival of General Carlos Buell's army. General Albert Sydney Johnston's Confederate army arrived first and caught Grant by surprise. For a time it seemed that the Confederates might drive Grant's army into the Tennessee, but night and Buell arrived in time after a day of slaughter. On the second day, Grant and Buell drove the Confederates entirely off the field, and the North gained its second significant victory of the war.

The two days at Shiloh saw terrible casualties on both sides. Infantry formations, using rifled muskets, stood their ground and blasted away at each other. Napoleonic tactics proved incapable of accommodating the technological advances of the day. The results were to be repeated on numerous occasions in 1862, but the heavy losses at Shiloh did Grant's reputation considerable harm; public opinion in the North still had no idea of how costly the war would prove. Still Shiloh underlined the extent of southern resistance to the Union. As Grant commented in his memoirs:

> Up to the battle of Shiloh, I, as well as thousands of other citizens, believed that the rebellion against the Government would collapse suddenly and soon, if a decisive victory could be gained over any of its armies. Donelson and Henry were such victories…But when Confederate armies were collected which not only attempted to hold a line further south…but assumed the offensive and made such a gallant effort to regain what had been lost, then, indeed, I gave up all idea of saving the Union except by complete conquest.

After Shiloh and Antietam the defence resorted increasingly to building protected emplacements or digging trenches, while the attackers confronted the problem of crossing the killing zone – a problem that offered no solution until the end of World War I.

Union victory at Shiloh opened the way for an advance on Corinth, Mississippi, and perhaps the opening of the great river. The US navy had already seized New Orleans, and Confederate positions along the river were open to attack. But the

Confederate trenches at Petersburg (1865). By the last years of the war (1864 and 1865) both armies had become highly skilled at entrenching themselves. Lee's defensive system at Petersburg – which protected the Confederate capital at Richmond – was comprehensive, well-sited, and mutually supporting. Chevaux-de-frise (the sets of pointed metal stakes in the photograph) played the role that barbed wire would play in World War I, making such defences almost impregnable to direct attack.

Union commander in the west, General Henry Halleck, assumed direct command of Grant's and Buell's armies. Halleck's advance on Corinth made McClellan's moves look like blitzkrieg, and the remainder of 1862 saw Union efforts in the west fragment. In Tennessee and Kentucky the Confederates counter-attacked and almost reached the Ohio river before their advance collapsed. Along the Mississippi, Grant began his advance on Vicksburg, the key to control of the river, but substantial failures dogged his opening moves.

CHANCELLORSVILLE AND GETTYSBURG

The campaigning in the east in 1863 saw few changes in the balance between the contenders. In the east General Joseph Hooker, like McClellan, a man with an enormous regard for himself, took over from Burnside at the beginning of the year. In his appointment letter to Hooker, Lincoln specifically noted rumours circulating in Washington that the new commander had declaimed on the need for a military dictatorship. Lincoln dryly reminded the general that the prime requirement for such a coup was success on the battlefield. 'What I ask now of you is military success,' Lincoln observed, 'and I will risk the dictatorship.'

In early May 1863 Hooker moved against the Army of Northern Virginia, and for one of the rare times in the Civil War, a northern commander caught Lee by surprise. But on the far side of the Wilderness (an area of virgin forest in central Virginia), Hooker froze. Lee recovered, divided his army, and sent 'Stonewall' Jackson on a march that hit Hooker's flank at Chancellorsville with devastating effect. Only evening saved the entire Union right from collapse. The greatest impact of the flank attack, however, was on the mind of the Union commander: as Lincoln

Joshua Chamberlain, Brevet Major General, US Volunteers

By the time of the battle of Gettysburg, Joshua Chamberlain, former professor of rhetoric at Bowdoin College, had served in the army for less than a year. Appointed second-in-command of the 20th Maine, Chamberlain and his fellow Mainers had enlisted in summer 1862. They received their baptism of fire four months later at Antietam (the worst day for casualties in American military history). In June 1863 Chamberlain became the 20th's commander; on the second day at Gettysburg his brigade was rushed into the line to defend the crucial position of Little Round Top on the left of the Union line. In late afternoon a massive southern attack threatened to engulf Little Round Top. Intense fighting used up virtually all of the 20th's ammunition; with the enemy coming on again, Chamberlain ordered his men to fix bayonets and charge the enemy. This action broke the Confederate attack and saved the Army of the Potomac from defeat.

For his bravery and skill, Chamberlain received the Medal of Honor, and by the end of the war he was a brevet major general. Grant considered him the finest combat brigade commander in the Army of the Potomac and picked him to receive the southern surrender at Appomattox.

Chamberlain returned to Maine to become the state's governor and president of Bowdoin. He died in 1914 of the effects of a wound he had received in 1864.

noted, from that point on Hooker acted like a duck hit on the head by a board. Despite the fact that his corps commanders wanted to remain on the field and continue the fight, Hooker ordered a retreat.

The crucial question confronting the southern leadership was what to do next. Lee argued for an invasion of the North in pursuit of a decisive victory to end the war; others argued that Lee's victory at Chancellorsville should allow the South to stand on the defensive in the east, while reinforcing the west, where Grant had just trapped a Confederate army in Vicksburg. There, the South confronted the possible loss of both the Mississippi river and a major army. Thanks to his prestige, Lee won the argument: in mid-June the Army of Northern Virginia began its march towards Pennsylvania.

The Army of the Potomac and its new commander, General George Meade, known as 'old snapping turtle' to his staff, set out in pursuit. In a classic encounter battle, fought on ground that neither side chose, a titanic three-day struggle occurred at the little college town of Gettysburg. The Confederates won the first day handily and drove three Union corps pell-mell back through the town. The second day was a draw, but barely. Only the courage and toughness of Colonel Joshua Chamberlain, the commander of the 20th Maine – who, when outnumbered three to one and out of ammunition, ordered his men to fix bayonets and charge – saved the Union left flank. On the third day, Lee launched a massive corps attack on the Union centre. Union soldiers chanted 'Fredricksburg, Fredricksburg', as the Confederates emerged from the woods to begin a mile and a half walk up the slope towards Cemetery ridge. The result was a slaughter of General George Pickett's attacking force, as decisive as the one that had occurred below Mayre's Heights at Fredricksburg six months before. With his army shattered and almost out of ammunition, Lee withdrew.

Gettysburg was more than a tactical defeat for the Confederacy. By invading Pennsylvania Lee set the stage for catastrophic defeat in the west, a defeat that lost the Confederates control of the Mississippi and opened up Tennessee to Union invasion. In fact, his pursuit of a decisive victory accorded with neither the tactical realities of the war nor the South's strategic situation, given the crisis at Vicksburg. The rest of the year in the east saw desultory fighting. Lee sent Longstreet's corps out west and was hardly in a position to wage aggressive operations, while Meade recognized Lee's competence and proved unwilling to involve his forces in a war of manoeuvre against so talented an opponent.

GRANT TAKES CHARGE

In 1863 the weight of the war shifted west. After a dismal winter trying to get through the swamps north of Vicksburg Grant began his spring campaign with a stunning move: in May, he sailed his army down the Mississippi past Vicksburg and thereby cut his lines of communications to the north. Then, in perhaps the most impressive campaign of manoeuvre in the war, he separated the two southern

Ulysses S. Grant (1822–85).
Grant had failed at every
career he had chosen before
1861 – officer, farmer, and
store owner – but he displayed
extraordinary powers of
decision, was a shrewd judge
of men, and had sufficient
humility to learn from his own
mistakes as well as those of
others. His writing possessed a
clarity that was to make his
memoirs one of the literary
triumphs of the nineteenth
century. He was also the only
general in the Civil War who
came to have a clear
understanding of the larger
political and strategic issues –
skills that later helped him win
the presidency for two terms
(1869–77).

armies in the region and shut one up in Vicksburg. Thus began a major siege that culminated in the surrender of the city and its Confederate army on 4 July 1863 and opened up the Mississippi. Grant then suggested to his superiors that his army move against the crucial port of Mobile, but Halleck, jealous of his subordinate, demurred and divided Grant's forces among other commands.

As a result, the Union advance into central Tennessee under General Rosecrans lacked support from other operations in the west. Rosecrans, however, was up against one of the least capable southern commanders of the war, General Braxton Bragg. By late August, Rosecrans had manoeuvred Bragg out of Tennessee; but in Georgia the Confederates, reinforced by Longstreet's corps from the Army of Northern Virginia, counter-attacked. At the battle of Chickamauga, Longstreet's attack on the second day pushed through a gap in the centre of the Union line – a hole caused by the incompetence of staff officers and Rosecrans's inability to get along with his subordinates. The result was a great southern victory, although Bragg bungled the pursuit. The survivors of the Union defeat made their way back to Chattanooga, where the Confederates besieged them.

Lincoln responded with vigour. He gave Grant command of the entire western theatre and ordered deployment of two corps from the Army of the Potomac to reinforce the west. The Union logistical system moved 25,000 men with all their horses and artillery 1,200 miles in less than two weeks. Grant, displaying his usual aplomb, concentrated Union forces on Chattanooga. First, he opened up supply lines to the city, where troops were already on short rations.

Once communications were open, Grant attacked Bragg. Flanking attacks had some success, but did not dislodge the defenders from positions overlooking the city. Grant then ordered General George Thomas, who had saved Rosecrans's army from complete collapse at Chickamauga, to launch a probe against Confederate positions overlooking Chattanooga. The probe turned into a full scale assault that succeeded in the face of seemingly impossible odds.

Grant's successes restored the situation in the west. The Union now controlled the Mississippi river; moreover, its forces had driven through Tennessee to the gates of Georgia, the economic heart of the South. The contrast between Union successes in the west and failures in the east were marked. At this point, Lincoln, recognizing Grant's worth, appointed him Commander-in-Chief of all Union forces; Congress added to his honours by making him a Lieutenant General. Grant now assumed control of Union operational strategy to end the destructive war that had already lasted three years.

In 1862 Lincoln had suggested to McClellan that it might be good strategy for the North to pressure the South by offensive operations in all theatres. In letters to his wife McClellan expressed contempt for such an approach. But Lincoln had been right; the North with its superior resources and manpower could break the South by pressuring it concurrently from different directions. That was precisely what Grant intended to do. As he told his subordinate commanders: 'It is my design, if the enemy keep quiet and allow me to take the initiative…to work all parts of the army together, and somewhat toward a common centre.' In the east the Army of the Potomac would attack the Army of Northern Virginia, while the Army of the James struck south of Richmond to cut Lee off from supplies. Another Union army would move down the Shenandoah and deny the South the agricultural riches of that region. In the west, Sherman would move against General Joe Johnston's Army of Tennessee, while Banks moved against Mobile and forced Johnston to divide his forces.

Had these pieces moved in the fashion that Grant directed, the Civil War would have ended in 1864, but Banks went up the Red river instead of against Mobile; Siegel proved a dismal failure; and (in Grant's words) Butler got his army 'corked' in the James peninsula. Thus, everything fell on the backs of Sherman and Grant. Part of the problem was the fact that the subordinate players – Banks, Butler, and Siegel – were political generals without the competence to play their parts properly. But Grant never complained about their lack of performance or blamed them for the failure to achieve victory in 1864 for, alone among the North's senior generals, he recognized their political importance to Lincoln's bid for re-election in November 1864.

Grant placed himself with the Army of the Potomac. He recognized the lack of drive in both the army and its commander: while he admired Meade for his honesty and integrity, Grant also recognized Meade's sense of inferiority against Lee. Throughout the rest of the war Grant remained with the Army of the Potomac and assumed responsibility for its actions as it grappled with Lee. But the army and officer corps that McClellan had trained proved as flawed a military instrument as their former commander. No army in American military history has had a more dismal record; no US army has suffered more nobly in the pursuit of victory; and no army has missed more chances in its operations. Not until the Battle of Five Forks in April 1865 did it finally win a battle while on the offensive.

THE DEFEAT OF THE SOUTH

The Army of the Potomac fought its spring and summer battles of 1864 at an appallingly high cost to itself and the nation. In the horrific battle of the Wilderness, it barely survived a savage Confederate flank attack. Then, by a swift shift to the left, Grant attempted to outflank the Confederates and place his forces in a position where Lee would have to attack. But by the narrowest of margins the Confederates reached Spottsylvania Courthouse. A second terrible killing battle ensued as, protected by entrenchments, the Confederates took a heavy toll of attacking Federal troops. Bad luck continued to dog the Army of the Potomac. To encourage his troops General John Sedgwick, one of the more competent corps commanders, stood on an earthwork and announced that the Confederates could not hit an elephant at that distance; a rebel sharpshooter put a bullet through Sedgwick's head.

After a week of savage killing that bled both armies white, Grant again shifted south; at North Anna and Cold Harbor he launched direct assaults on Lee's

The defeat of the South. The Union strategy that evolved over the war's course had four basic elements: a blockade of the coast; the capture of Richmond; the opening of the Mississippi; and bringing the war to the South's economy and population. It was the last approach that finally broke the Confederates' will.

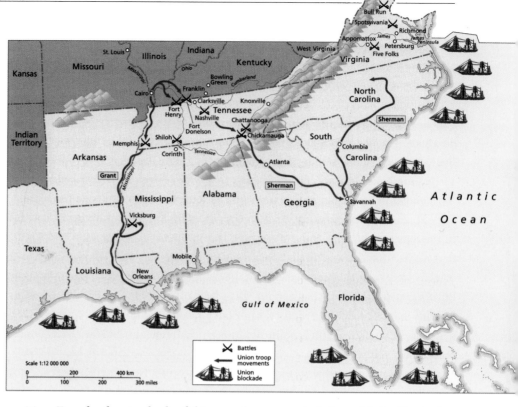

position. Even by the standards of this war, these were dark days. A brigadier in the Army of the Potomac wrote to his wife: 'For thirty days it has been one funeral procession past me, and it has been too much.' Grant then slipped around Lee to the James river. There, he placed his army in position to capture Petersburg and break the southern lines of supply. Had Petersburg fallen, Lee would have had to abandon Virginia and Richmond and retreat to North Carolina. But once again the Army of the Potomac's corps commanders missed the opportunity, and Lee got sufficient troops to Petersburg to man its defences. By this time both armies were exhausted, incapable of further offensive operations – although Grant had at least succeeded in his objective of drawing Lee's sting: the Army of Northern Virginia was no longer capable of offensive warfare.

So everything came down to what Sherman could achieve against Johnston. Sherman began his offensive against Atlanta in early May. The two armies fenced and, although he manoeuvred Johnston out of one position after another, he failed to achieve significant military success. By July, Johnston had retreated to defensive works in front of Atlanta. At that point the Confederate government, frustrated by retreat, replaced Johnston with a corps commander, General John Bell Hood. Hood had been a brilliant divisional commander under 'Stonewall' Jackson; he had also proven his bravery on many battlefields and had lost both an arm and a leg in battle. But Hood had also been a divisive and argumentative corps commander, and he proved to be as bad a choice for senior command as Bragg had been.

Hood's explanation for the troubles confronting the Confederacy in 1864 was that southern troops had lost the offensive edge they had enjoyed in 1862. As army commander in front of Atlanta, he determined to regain that offensive spirit. Over the course of the next month, he launched three savage attacks on Sherman, but experienced Union soldiers destroyed each strike, inflicted horrendous casualties on the attackers, and eventually forced Hood to abandon Atlanta. To the end, he blamed his failure on a lack of offensive spirit in his troops; he entirely missed the fact that the face of battle had changed in fundamental ways. Nevertheless, the casualties suffered by his attacks underlined that the South was still willing to suffer terrible losses in pursuit of independence.

Sherman's capture of Atlanta was crucial to Lincoln's re-election. Now Hood moved north to threaten Sherman's lines of communications in Tennessee, but Sherman persuaded Grant to allow him to pursue one of the most innovative operational concepts of the Civil War: while a part of his army under George Thomas fell back to cover central Tennessee, Sherman cut loose from his supply lines and marched into the heart of Georgia on the way to the sea. Grant eventually approved the move. Hood pursued Thomas's forces first to Franklin where, after accusing his general officers of cowardice, he launched his troops against well-entrenched Federals. The result was a slaughter in which many of his generals died. Unrepentant to the end, Hood advanced to Nashville, where Thomas destroyed the remnants of an army the Confederate commander had begun wrecking at Atlanta.

General William T. Sherman (1820–91), pictured here at the battle of Atlanta, directed much of the savage destruction of the South in what was called the 'hard war'.

Meanwhile, Sherman marched through Georgia. The war had taken a vicious turn, as troops carried the war to the South's heartland. While Sherman did not aim his campaign directly at civilians, its 'collateral' effects – wrecking habitations, destroying the crops, stealing the farm animals – underlined how far the Federal government was willing to go to destroy the Confederacy. Sherman's troops took great delight in the 'Chimneyvilles' that remained in the wake of their march. As Sherman warned the citizens of northern Alabama:

> The government of the United States has in North Alabama any and all rights which [it chooses] to enforce in war, to take [Confederate] lives, their houses, their lands, their everything, because they cannot deny that war exists there, and war is simply power unconstrained by constitution or compact. If they want eternal warfare, well and good. We will accept the issue and dispossess them and put our friends in possession…[T]o the petulant and persistent secessionists, why, death is mercy and the quicker he or she is disposed of the better. Satan and the rebellious saint[s] of heaven were allowed a continuance of existence in hell merely to swell their just punishment.

The destruction wrought in Georgia and in South Carolina represented a portion of a larger policy aimed at breaking the southern will to continue the war. It served a clear warning to Confederate soldiers that they could no longer protect even their homes from the war.

As Sherman was driving to the sea, Grant unleashed General Philip Sheridan on the Shenandoah valley. Sheridan was one of the most competent battlefield

Robert E. Lee (1807–70).
Lee was the best operational
commander of the war. His
dominance over the Army of
the Potomac, at least until
Grant arrived in the east, was
almost complete. A notably
aggressive commander, Lee
was to demonstrate in his last
campaigns the immense
advantage that modern
firepower provided
the defence.

commanders of the war; he was also, like Jackson, one of the most ferocious. Grant's instructions underline that what Sheridan did to the Shenandoah was the general policy of the Union high command; he ordered Sheridan to turn the Shenandoah into 'a barren waste... so that crows flying over it for the balance of this season will have to carry their provender with them.'

Sheridan enthusiastically executed his orders. A remark to his Prussian hosts in 1870 when he toured the battles of the Franco-Prussian War suggests how far the Union's strategy had become a relentless war against the South's popular resistance: Sheridan noted that the Prussians were being far too 'humanitarian' in their treatment of the French and added for the benefit of his avid German listeners that 'The people should be left nothing but their eyes to weep with over the war!' Admittedly, neither Sherman nor Sheridan achieved the level of Bomber Command's 'dehousing' campaign in World War II, but northern military forces fought only on the ground: they could thus spare the wretched inhabitants their lives while destroying the South's economic infrastructure, homes, foodstuffs, and farm animals. And everywhere that they moved they destroyed the institution of slavery, the heart of the South's cultural and political identity.

By early 1865 the Confederacy's position was hopeless. Re-election of Lincoln in autumn 1864 had removed its last hope; the great emancipator would see the war through to its conclusion. Through every Confederate state Union armies moved at will. Lee's army was gradually disappearing through desertion; Sherman was destroying South Carolina. His troops revelled in wrecking the state that had led the move towards secession and which had begun the conflict four years earlier by firing on Fort Sumter. North Carolina soon felt the weight of Union armies and the Confederates' last port, Fort Fisher, fell to a combined navy-army operation.

THE COSTS OF 'THE LATE UNPLEASANTNESS'

In April Lee's position at Petersburg collapsed as the Army of the Potomac won its first offensive victory at Five Forks. A rapid pursuit with Sheridan in the lead eventually caught Lee at Appomattox. Recognizing the inevitable, Lee surrendered. He then took on the mantle of one of the great statesmen in American history by spending his last years urging his countrymen to accept the results. Unfortunately, the destructive war waged by Union armies in the conflict's last year, the problems of race relations in a defeated country, and the bitterness of the lost cause perpetuated the division between North and South for well over a hundred years. But a simple grammatical change underlined the transformation wrought by the Civil War. Before 1861 Americans said 'the United States are'; after 1865 they said 'the United States is.' The North's victory had important consequences for the twentieth century. The maintenance of a united nation in North America with its immense industrial and agricultural power was to play a crucial role in winning both world wars against Germany; a fragmented sub-continent would have played little role in such a conflict.

The Civil War was the first modern war: one in which military power, built on popular support and industrialization, and projected by the railroad and steamship over hundreds of miles, approached the boundaries of total war. Neither strategic vision nor military capabilities to wage a great war existed at the beginning: the mere creation of military force and its requisite support created problems that were not readily apparent nor easily solved. Nevertheless the Union's political and military leadership eventually evolved a strategy that brought victory, a strategy of attrition rather than decisive battle. Along with the general assault on the South in 1864 went a war to break the popular will of the southern population. But the cost of such a war was appalling: around 625,000 soldiers died in the war on both sides, a figure equal to the total of all other American wars up to and including most of the Vietnam conflict. A comparable level of losses for the United States in World War I would have been about 2.1 million lives (instead of 115,000). The Civil War indicated that the new technological battlefield would take a heavy toll in lives, and that the capacity of the modern state to mobilize its human and industrial resources could feed that technological battlefield almost indefinitely. And those resources, both human and industrial, were growing by leaps and bounds as western civilization entered the twentieth century.

BISMARCK'S WARS

However, at approximately the same time, the Europeans learned different lessons about modern war. Almost concurrently with the American Civil War a series of wars achieved the unification of Germany under Prussian leadership. These successes involved a series of short, triumphant wars, but they did not rest on the tactical or technological superiority of Prussia's armies; rather they reflected the brilliance of its statesmanship and the professionalization of its officer corps. The latter arose in part from the reaction to the devastating defeat of Jena-Auerstadt in 1806. The creation of a *Kriegsakademie* (war college) to produce trained staff officers allowed the Prussians to establish the nucleus of an effective staff system in time for the War of Liberation against the French in 1813 and its success in managing the myriad details involved in fighting Napoleon prevented the retrenchments of the post-war period from dismantling the *Kriegsakademie* and a nascent general staff.

In the period leading up to the 1860s a small, elite general staff pushed the Prussian army towards a recognition of the advantages that railways and changing weapons technology would provide in the next war. The appointment of Helmut von Moltke as the chief of the general staff in 1858 accelerated the process, for Moltke encouraged the construction of strategic railways throughout Germany, arguing that they would prove more valuable in future wars than fortresses. The rate of railway expansion in Germany was over twice the rate in France during the 1840s, and by 1854 the German Confederation possessed nearly 7,500 miles of railways. By 1860 Prussia itself possessed 3,500 miles of railways (and Moltke had

Prince Otto von Bismarck (1815–98). Bismarck was one of the few statesmen in European history who truly understood that war was an extension of policy by other means. Consequently, he always aimed for what was achievable and instinctively understood when it was time to end the game. But Bismarck never explained his policies or educated the next generation of German leaders: the consequences eventually proved fatal for the Second Reich and almost destroyed Europe.

grown rich from his investment in railway stock). The crucial point was that the Prussian general staff, unlike other military organizations in Europe, systematically thought through how best to exploit this expanding potential for mobilization and deployment of military forces. However, Prussia's advantage lay not only in its capacity to mobilize, deploy, and support its forces. The Prussian army was also first in Europe to adopt a breech-loading rifle, the needlegun, which allowed its soldiers to reload three to four times faster than their opponents – and to do so while lying down, an obvious advantage in any firefight.

But such changes represented only potential; it took skilful strategic and political moves to turn this military potential into strategic reality. In the early 1860s the Prussian state had come to a constitutional impasse between the king's demand that the legislature support a three-year term of military service and the legislature's refusal to provide the funding. In desperation Wilhelm I turned to an aristocrat of the old school, Otto von Bismarck, to break the deadlock.

Bismarck was an extraordinary character. He had enjoyed little success in a short army career, while he had spent his days in university drinking and wenching. His diplomatic service won him few friends. But he did have qualities that few recognized at the time. He possessed an extraordinary capacity to size up his opponents; and he was a first-class politician with a gambler's instinct of when to play and when to leave the table. Unlike most Prussian conservatives, he understood the strength of German nationalism and saw that Prussia must either swim with the tide or be swamped by it.

Bismarck's greatest advantage lay in the weaknesses in the European system. Few in Europe recognized Prussia's latent strengths with its ongoing industrial revolution; equally important, most Europeans regarded the Prussian army as one of the least effective on the continent. Moreover, after the Crimean War Britain had largely removed itself from continental affairs; France had no effective focus to its strategic policy; and Austria and Russia were at odds due to Austria's behaviour during the Crimean War. In this vacuum the new Prussian chancellor moved to make his mark. As he had warned the Prussian assembly: 'The great questions of our day are not decided through speeches and majority votes – that was the great error of 1848 and 1849 – but through iron and blood.' The first opportunity came with Denmark.

When the Danish king died without a male heir it made no difference for the throne of Denmark, but for the German duchies of Schleswig-Holstein, it did. In 1864, the German Confederation, led by Prussia and Austria, refused to recognize Danish claims to the duchies. The allied armies of the German states then made short work of the Danes, but the question of what to do with the liberated provinces remained. Bismarck welcomed the confusion, since the Austrians received territories to administer but the lines of communications to them ran entirely through Prussian territory. The chances for misunderstanding were numerous and Bismarck was only too glad to maximize them.

It appears that Bismarck hoped to negotiate a deal with the Austrians whereby Prussia would control northern Germany, while Austria controlled the south. But the Austrians displayed no appreciation of the altered balance in Germany. Not only did they refuse to recognize Prussia as an equal, they actively courted war. The other European states, except for France, displayed scant interest in the brewing conflict in central Europe; the French for their part believed that the war between Austria and Prussia would be a prolonged affair in which they could intervene to advantage.

Prussia did suffer from some significant disadvantages: the other German states rallied to Austria; Prussia's territory was divided in two; and Bohemia offered an easy launching pad for an Austrian attack on Berlin. But Moltke and the general staff capitalized upon these challenges. A Prussian army swiftly disposed of Hanover, and thereby united Prussian territory. Meanwhile in June 1866, utilizing the north German railroad system, Moltke rapidly deployed three armies on the Austrian frontier with the intention of uniting them in Bohemia. Austrian staff work was abominable, reflecting the casual approach to the profession of arms that the Austrians had displayed throughout the preceding decades. Consequently, the Austrian armies gathered slowly in central Bohemia, while the westernmost Prussian army overran Saxony, and three other Prussian armies moved swiftly into Bohemia. The needle gun gave the Prussians an overwhelming tactical advantage, which the initial skirmishes confirmed – casualty exchange ratios were on the order of one Prussian for four or five Austrians. Even more important, the early defeats sapped Austrian morale.

Surprised by the speed of the enemy's advance, the Austrian commander, Prince Benedek, fell back on a series of low hills just north of the town of Königgrätz. The Austrian army numbered 190,000 men with 25,000 Saxons in support. The Prussian forces exceeded 200,000 men, but only two of their armies were on the

German unification and expansion, 1864–71. Prussia waged and won three great wars against her neighbours: against Denmark in 1864, against Austria in 1866, and against France in 1870–71. While her victories extended German territory to the north and west, Prussia's major gains came with the amalgamation of the German states into one, less than perfect, union. The results fundamentally altered Europe's balance of power.

General Helmut von Moltke (1800–91) combined an extraordinary operational mind with a far-reaching recognition of where technology was driving war. Consequently, he pushed the Prussian army to utilize the full potential of both the breach-loading 'needlegun' and the railway. However, Moltke proved less able to discern the political constraints that must bind all operations, and his quarrel with Bismarck was to mislead Germany's generals in two world wars in the next century.

field (and Moltke's telegraph system had broken down) when the battle of Königgrätz began on 3 July. By this point Benedek had a keen appreciation of the danger that needle guns posed to his troops; he ordered his subordinates to hold their troops back and rely on their artillery, which was generally superior to that of the Prussians. But Austrian senior officers displayed a cavalier disregard for their orders. As a result, when the 7th Prussian Division gained a local success in a small wooded area, the Swiewald, on the Austrian right, Austrian commanders threw in counter-attack after counter-attack. All withered before Prussian firepower. Out of fifty-nine battalions in the area, the Austrians committed forty-nine in the firefight in the Swiewald, twenty-eight of which simply disappeared. In effect this wrecked the entire Austrian right wing. The difficulties on the right turned into a catastrophe when the third Prussian army, commanded by the Prussian Crown Prince, arrived on the battlefield.

Meanwhile the Prussians managed to work the Elbe army around the enemy's left flank. Only the most desperate efforts by Austrian artillery and cavalry prevented the Prussians from surrounding Benedek's entire force. What survived was a wreck; in one day's fighting the Austrians had lost 40,000 men killed or wounded, with a further 20,000 prisoners of war. The road to Vienna lay open, and the complete destruction of the Habsburg state seemed imminent. The Prussian generals, Moltke included, were champing at the bit to acquire the laurels of their great victory.

But Bismarck would have none of it. He persuaded his king to halt the Prussian advance and open negotiations with the Austrians, for he saw that only France and Russia would benefit from the war's continuation. If, however, Prussia offered generous terms, it would persuade Austria to accept a long-term settlement. Prussia should limit its territorial gains to northern Germany; the south German states would merely come under its sphere of interest. Such a peace would be most attractive to the Austrians, since they would lose no territory themselves. Bismarck's settlement represented inspired statesmanship. Prussia absorbed the north German states; it controlled the military and foreign policies of the south Germans; the peace placated Austria; and Bismarck had entirely excluded the French. The Austrians accepted with alacrity. But such strategic wisdom did not find favour with Prussia's soldiers; to them, Bismarck's manoeuvres had robbed them of their chance to pursue a beaten foe to his capital.

THE FRANCO-PRUSSIAN WAR

For the immediate future Bismarck wanted to consolidate his gains. He felt no great desire to create a united Germany; after all, southern Germany was the bastion of two of his great hates: liberalism and catholicism. But the French refused to accept the results of 1866. The following year they attempted to buy the duchy of Luxembourg, but backed down before a storm of British and German protests. That diplomatic setback did not end French interference in southern Germany and, in the end, French intransigence persuaded Bismarck that he must risk another war in order to stabilize his gains. The French accommodated him. The empire of Napoleon III had come under increasing political pressure at home to liberalize the constitution, while setbacks in foreign policy had steadily eroded the regime's popularity. Therefore, the emperor sought relief in foreign policy or military success.

The military balance favoured Prussia even more than it had in 1866. The Prussian general staff had honed its administrative and organizational skills to a new pitch. Staff work allowed the Prussians to utilize further the enormous potential of railroads, while the general staff system provided a means to convey orders and ensure their obedience; the Prussians would find it relatively easy to manage the deployment and operations of the great armies they mobilized in 1870. Without such a system, the French did not.

Ironically, the Prussians lacked the technological edge they had enjoyed in 1866 – the French *chassepot* rifle was superior to the needlegun – but the Prussians had rectified their weakness in artillery: their new steel breach-loading cannon gave them an advantage over the French in both rapidity and accuracy of artillery fire. Nevertheless the French possessed another weapon that might have provided them a great advantage – the *mitrailleuse*, the first machine gun – but the Ministry of War had kept the weapon so secret that few French commanders even knew of its existence. Beyond their staff system, the Prussians enjoyed other advantages. They possessed an effective reserve system; two wars had blooded their senior officers; and Moltke was an outstanding operational commander. Most importantly, in Bismarck they possessed a brilliant strategist whose policies ensured that the other European powers remained outside the conflict. The French had no reserve system, a weak staff, and no general of particular competence.

Seriously miscalculating the balance, Napoleon III challenged the Prussians. The all-too-clever Bismarck edited the account of a minor confrontation between his king and the French resident ambassador into a dispatch where Prussians believed their king insulted and Frenchmen their honour impugned. France declared war and both sides mobilized and deployed, the French believing that war would begin with their invasion of the Rhineland – to what purpose was unclear – and with their army in firm control of the initiative as at Jena-Auerstadt in 1806. Despite the fact that the Prussians deployed over greater distances, their effective staff work and reserve system allowed them to put 380,000 men on the French frontier while, at the same time, they deployed 95,000 men to watch Austria. By 31 July 1870, by contrast, the French had only 224,000 soldiers on the frontier. Napoleon III established two provisional armies under marshals who had never held such responsibilities before, and neither French army possessed a staff to control the operational and logistical movements of its component corps. The three Prussian armies, on the other hand, had effective staffs to co-ordinate their operational and logistic movements; and they were led by commanders who had won their spurs in the wars of 1864 and 1866.

The opening skirmishes displayed a pattern that would hold throughout the fighting between the Prussian and French imperial field armies. The French displayed considerable competence on the tactical battlefield, while the *chassepot* proved its worth again and again. But French ineptitude at the operational level more than counter-balanced successes on the tactical battlefield. On 6 August the Crown Prince of Prussia's army bested its French opponents at Weissenburg; both sides suffered approximately 6,000 casualties, but the Prussians also captured 6,000 Frenchmen. Even more important than the local success was the fact that the Crown Prince succeeded in getting around Marshal MacMahon's army and forced a general retreat of French forces from Alsace. Meanwhile, the main French army under Marshal Bazaine also came under attack. On the heights of Spickern, vastly superior Prussian forces attacked the French II Corps. The French inflicted over 5,000 casualties on the attackers, while suffering barely 3,000 casualties themselves, but Bazaine failed to support his corps commander (not the last occasion in which he remained mired in inaction while subordinates fought for their lives). However, the significance of Spickern lay in the fact that Moltke interposed his First and Second Armies between the two French armies, while the Crown Prince's Third Army was outflanking MacMahon's forces on the Prussian left.

On 16 August Moltke, controlling the movements of First and Second Armies, brought Bazaine to battle. By this point the Prussians were close to enveloping their opponent. That day a massive encounter battle took place at Mars-la-Tour. The French suffered 16,000 casualties, the Prussians 17,000. Significantly, Bazaine retreated northwards instead of to the west, further increasing the chances that the Prussians would encircle his forces.

Two days later the armies tangled again and the French came close to scoring a major victory that might have reversed the course of the Franco-Prussian War. At St Privat, Bazaine's VI Corps of 23,000 men held off nearly 100,000 Prussians for an entire day; reinforced, the VI Corps might have turned a local tactical success into something of operational significance. Meanwhile, at Gravelotte, two Prussian corps achieved initial success, but as they advanced they became entangled. They then launched a series of confused attacks that only added to their losses. French defenders smashed the last German attack so decisively that the attacking units entirely collapsed: any French counter-attack at this point would have resulted in a serious operational reverse for the Prussians. But the French commander on the scene refused to take independent action, while Bazaine, like McClellan at Antietam, again refused to intervene in the battle. Casualties were heavy on both

Prussian infantry advancing towards French positions near Sedan in 1870. Throughout the Franco-Prussian War, the French normally possessed superior firepower in infantry weapons, and so the Prussians generally took heavier casualties, even though they were usually able to dominate the battlefield. However, at Sedan the Prussians were able to bring the superiority of their artillery to bear, and in short order the out-gunned French were forced to surrender.

sides, but the balance in favour of the French suggest how close they were to success: the Germans lost 20,163 men, the French only 12,273. In the end, Bazaine pulled back into Metz and thereby allowed the Prussians to entrap his entire force.

The encirclement of one French army at Metz constituted a political disaster for Napoleon III – one that threatened his political survival. The French therefore gathered together all the remaining forces of their professional army: Marshal MacMahon led the expedition and the emperor himself accompanied the troops in a desperate bid to win back his waning prestige. However, the French approached Metz by manoeuvring along the Belgian frontier; they could have chosen no more unfortunate route of approach. The result was predictable: Moltke manoeuvred around MacMahon's flank, in order to trap and then destroy a second French army at Sedan. The Prussians had learned from their bloody experiences at St Privat and Gravelotte and battered the surrounded French into surrender with their artillery. This marked the end of the Second Empire.

GERMANY TRIUMPHANT

In Paris the French declared a republic and its new leaders proclaimed a *levée en masse*. The war had unleashed the full flood of nationalist feeling on both sides. The problem for the French was that as thousands flocked to the colours, the trained professionals were all in Prussian prisoner-of-war camps. Thus, the new republic was in the same situation as the contending sides in the American Civil War in 1861; it had to create military organizations out of the fabric of civilian society with little professional expertise available. The Prussians of course did not face that problem. In October, with the destruction of the Metz pocket completed, Moltke moved on Paris. The French desperately prepared to withstand a siege; at the same time they attempted to put their army back together. As soon as the siege of Paris began, Bismarck demanded that the Prussian generals open a bombardment to force the republic to the peace table. While siege and bombardment proceeded, the French launched a series of efforts to relieve the capital and a guerrilla war against Prussian lines of communication through northern France. The relief efforts failed with heavy casualties, while attacks on supply lines angered the Prussians and further embittered the war, but failed to achieve their objective. The French Republic eventually surrendered to the logic of its situation, undoubtedly assisted by the growing threat of revolution in Paris.

The peace that resulted had a number of unfortunate repercussions on the history of the twentieth century. First, acquisition of Alsace and Lorraine by the Germans created a permanent rift between the two powers. Secondly, the short, swift nature of Prussia's victories in 1866 and 1870 convinced most of Europe's statesmen and generals that wars in the modern age would be brief and relatively painless. By and large, analysts of these conflicts missed the extraordinary nature of Bismarck's statesmanship as well as the gross incompetence of Prussia's opponents on both the strategic and operational levels.

The most dangerous result of these wars was their impact on the Germans, who believed that they had won because of their prowess on the battlefield. Their military performance had of course played a role, but the crucial component had been Bismarck's political and strategic realism and restraint. The victories of 1866 and 1870, however, seduced German statesmen, soldiers, and intellectuals into believing that military and operational concerns should always outweigh strategic and political factors. The new German Empire, proclaimed in the Hall of Mirrors in Versailles, carried the military glory of that founding to its death in 1918. And the new state enshrined the principle on which Bismarck had come to power: namely that the Prussian military would remain independent of constitutional constraints. That had not mattered in a state where a statesman such as Bismarck, with direct access to and great influence with the emperor, remained in control; but in post-Bismarckian Germany, the political sphere would lose all control over the state's military institutions.

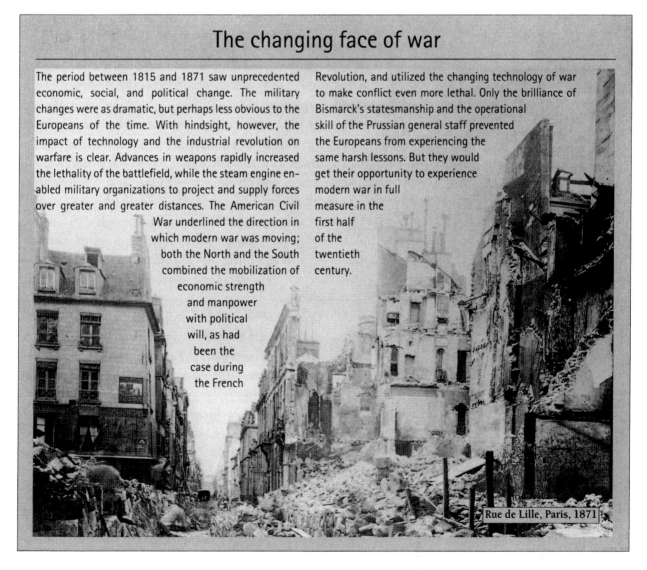

The changing face of war

The period between 1815 and 1871 saw unprecedented economic, social, and political change. The military changes were as dramatic, but perhaps less obvious to the Europeans of the time. With hindsight, however, the impact of technology and the industrial revolution on warfare is clear. Advances in weapons rapidly increased the lethality of the battlefield, while the steam engine enabled military organizations to project and supply forces over greater and greater distances. The American Civil War underlined the direction in which modern war was moving; both the North and the South combined the mobilization of economic strength and manpower with political will, as had been the case during the French Revolution, and utilized the changing technology of war to make conflict even more lethal. Only the brilliance of Bismarck's statesmanship and the operational skill of the Prussian general staff prevented the Europeans from experiencing the same harsh lessons. But they would get their opportunity to experience modern war in full measure in the first half of the twentieth century.

Rue de Lille, Paris, 1871

CHAPTER 13   *Towards World War*

The forty-three years between the Franco-Prussian War and World War I (1871–1914) constituted an unprecedented period of peace in Europe. This partially resulted from a common interest among the European powers in seizing those areas of the world still independent from western control. Expansion of western influence in Africa, Asia, and the Pacific did cause considerable tension, but pursuit of empire remained sufficiently distant to prevent a major European war over imperialistic competition.

The late nineteenth century saw an acceleration of industrialization in the United States and Germany, while France, Austria-Hungary, and even Tsarist Russia participated in the expansion of the western world's economic power. This growth in turn fuelled a world economy that showed every prospect of spreading wealth beyond the narrow band of upper classes. In the end, the West's economic power provided the resources for the catastrophic wars of the twentieth century; but for the time being Europeans drew the comforting illusion from their prosperity that they alone possessed the key to the future.

There was a darker side to progress. The western system rested on competition between distinct national states (with the exception of Austria-Hungary): as long as that competition remained confined to seeking economic and diplomatic advantage, it did not threaten the structure's basic stability. But economic expansion placed enormous military power in the hands of these states and in the long run made war both inevitable and disastrous. Western political sophistication failed to keep pace with its burgeoning military and economic power. Above all, nationalism drove statesmen and generals to pursue policies that raised the stakes and made war seem an increasingly acceptable alternative, while public opinion accepted careless notions of national rights and aspirations, regardless of their political or strategic consequences. The result was a mix of unprecedented power with general irresponsibility.

THE MARCH OF TECHNOLOGY

The decades of imperialism also saw a revolution in military and naval technology, as well as an increasing professionalism in the officer corps. But that process of professionalism provided Europe's military leaders with a narrowing view of the world. The contrast between the broad sophistication of Prussian officers in 1813 – men like August von Gneisenau, Gerhard von Scharnhorst, and Carl von Clausewitz – with the narrow, parochial pedants of 1900 – Alfred von Schlieffen, Theodor von Bernhardi, and Erich Ludendorff – could not be more graphic; and the same process was at work in other nations.

There were two causes: the increasing complexity of societies and military organizations during the nineteenth century, and a technological revolution that

Opposite: A gun-finishing shop at the Krupp armaments factory in Essen, Germany. The massive industrialization of the European economy between 1840 and 1900 spread wealth widely, albeit unevenly. The rapid advance of technology also provided increasingly sophisticated weapons to Europe's military forces. By 1900 Krupp manufactured weapons not only for the German army but for foreign buyers as well, and its capacity to manufacture weapons in increasing numbers would lie at the heart of Germany's ability to fight two great wars against the whole world. However, it was but one of several massive arms manufacturers in the industrialized world – which now included Japan – capable of rapidly expanding production to meet demand.

altered and extended the nature of war as well as society's capacity to support conflict. In response, European armies increasingly turned to the German general staff and its emphasis on serious study as a model for professionalizing the careers of their officers. But even the German officer corps proved resistant to the general staff's ideal, while the creation of staff colleges at Camberley (Britain) and Leavenworth (United States) was fraught with difficulty. Navies resisted profess-ionalization even more: the Royal Navy lacked a staff college and a proper naval staff until 1911.

One must not underestimate the complexity of the problems confronting generals before World War I. To do so is to miss the real reasons for the blood bath. The fact that there had been no major wars between the great powers since 1871 added to the uncertainties. Moreover, the military had to rely on civilian estimates of the economic and political stability of European society, and that advice proved wildly inaccurate.

In the military sphere, technology moved at a dizzying rate and the adjustment to technological changes sufficed to occupy the time of most officers. The admirals who led the fleets into battle in 1914 had entered navies in the 1880s whose traditions and technology were closer to Nelson's day than to the twentieth century. From primitive steam-driven and partially metalled ships of 1880, many still possessing sails, navies had progressed to great oil-powered dreadnoughts with weapons that could throw projectiles over twenty miles and could move at speeds of over twenty knots (cruisers and destroyers could reach speeds of thirty knots). With radio, navies could control and deploy ships around the world. By the end of World War I the introduction of submarines, aircraft, and aircraft carriers underlined the extraordinary technological changes that affected the conduct of naval war.

The impact of technology on armies was somewhat less dramatic, but World War I still represented a watershed. The armies of 1914 retained the tactical and operational concepts of those of the nineteenth century. But the harsh realities of combat in an era of bolt action rifles, machine guns, and howitzers rendered obsolete virtually every tactical conception with which the armies went to war. Smokeless powder allowed riflemen to remain concealed from their opponents, and – because it also provided higher velocity – to hit targets at great distances, while the creation of nitrate explosives made possible shells with great destructive potential. Finally, recoil-absorbing gun carriages allowed artillerymen to fire shells over great distances and to do so at greater rates because they did not have to resight their weapons after each firing.

Yet, if such changes seem obvious to us at the end of the twentieth century, they were not so obvious in July 1914. Military organizations rarely have the opportun-ity to conduct the dirty business of war. In times of peace they cannot replicate wartime conditions; thus they find it difficult to evaluate the implications of technological and doctrinal changes. It is as if surgeons did not perform surgery for decades and then had to execute thousands of operations in cold, damp operating rooms, without food or sleep, and with rivals shooting at them from the balconies of operating theatres. The generation of peace before 1914 prevented European generals from fully understanding the implications of the murderous combination of technology and conscription.

Moreover, the wars waged on the periphery, mostly against the hapless natives of Africa, Asia, the American west, and central Asia, provided the illusion for many that war still remained a simple, easy matter. Such wars involved a relatively small commitment from the European powers, because they were mostly waged against indigenous frontier peoples who had minimal capacity to mobilize economic or technological support in their own defence. These small wars consequently pitted well-trained, disciplined, and organized military forces against tribesmen who, whatever their bravery, had no capacity for sustained resistance.

THE MAHDI AND THE ZULUS

As the greatest colonial power in the world, Britain was involved in the largest number of conflicts with non-Europeans. The construction of the Suez Canal gave Egypt a central position in the British Empire because of the importance of the lines of communication to India. In 1882 severe anti-western rioting in Alexandria resulted in British intervention. In September a British army under Sir Garnet Wolseley launched a surprise night attack that crushed the Egyptian army at Tel-el-Kebir; an immediate pursuit finished off the war and placed Egypt under British domination for the next seventy-four years.

Troubles in Sudan then pulled the British into involvement at the headwaters of the Nile. In 1883 followers of the Islamic fundamentalist ruler, the Mahdi, wiped out an Egyptian army of 10,000 men and preserved the independence of the Sudan for another decade. In 1896, however, the British under General Horatio Kitchener began a systematic conquest of the region. Supported by a railroad constructed as his advance proceeded, Kitchener brought modern military power to bear on his opponents. At Omdurman, an army of 40,000 Dervishes struck Kitchener's Anglo-Egyptian army of 26,000 troops, but commitment was not proof against rapid-fire weapons and artillery. The high point of the battle saw the 21st Lancers launch one of the last cavalry charges in history to crush a final Dervish attack. When it was over the British had suffered fewer than 500 casualties (only fifty dead), while 30,000 Sudanese lay dead and wounded.

Further south on the continent, the British regarded South Africa as of great importance for its links to India until construction of the Suez Canal. Here they encountered hostility not only from the original Dutch settlers, the Boers, but also from native Blacks, in particular the Zulus. With construction of the Canal the British might have let South Africa slide into oblivion, but for the fact that the world's greatest lode of diamonds was discovered along the Orange River; further discoveries of South Africa's mineral worth only fuelled British ambitions.

Scottish troops pose before the Sphinx in 1882 after helping to defeat Egyptian nationalist forces at the battle of Tel-el-Kebir. By the late nineteenth century European military and technological superiority had reached the point where other civilizations had no hope of resisting western intervention.

In April 1877, the British annexed the Transvaal, a Boer stronghold, and thereby acquired the locals' problem with their Zulu neighbours. The Zulu king in the early nineteenth century, Shaka, had created an extraordinary military system that could deploy 40,000 well-trained, highly disciplined warriors; yet one that possessed the arms and tactical capabilities of the primitive Romans. Fighting with shields and short spears, Zulu formations (impis) displayed extraordinary fortitude, as well as an amazing capacity to move great distances on foot and camouflage themselves when need arose. Nevertheless, the British underestimated their opponents. The leader of the expedition to punish the Zulus in 1879, Lord Chelmsford, split his forces, and the Zulus moved around his advance troops unseen. On 22 January they smashed into the British base camp at Isandhlwana; there, because of serious tactical errors by British officers on the spot and the imbecility of a supply system that required written receipts from the defenders for ammunition as it was being used, the Zulus slaughtered almost everyone.

Later that day and night, victorious Zulus struck the small outpost of Rorke's Drift, defended by barely 100 soldiers – including the sick. In an epic defence, the British fought off waves of Zulus; the killing power of rifles devastated the attackers. A series of desperate engagements then occurred that allowed substantial reinforcements to arrive. On July 4, 1879, Chelmsford, leading 4,200 European and 1,000 native troops, reached the Zulu capital; despite coming under attack from Zulu impis of over 10,000 soldiers, the Europeans slaughtered the attackers and broke the back of Zulu power.

Isandhlwana 1879

Early in 1879 British forces in South Africa invaded Zulu territory after the Zulu king had rejected British demands for a protectorate. The British deployed approximately 5,000 white troops and 8,000 native levies; the Zulus 40,000. The Zulus, unlike many of those who were to go down before western imperialism in the late nineteenth century, possessed a highly disciplined and effective army capable of great flexibility on the battlefield; but they were equipped with spears, not rifles.

Lord Chelmsford, the British commander, launched his forces into Zululand in three widely dispersed columns. The Zulus caught the main camp at Isandhlwana by surprise and launched a series of savage attacks which inflicted terrible losses; then the British supply system broke down at a critical point when those in charge of handing out ammunition demanded receipts. Finally, as ammunition ran out, the Zulus' numerical superiority told. Only a few survivors escaped from the camp and got away. Nevertheless, the Zulus lost the war.

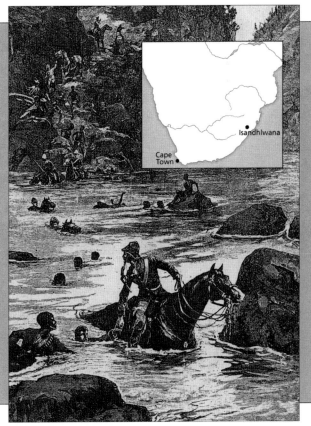

But Britain's troubles in South Africa were far from over. In late 1880 the Boers rose in the Transvaal. Within a month they had invaded Natal and defeated British forces that – as with the Zulus – thoroughly underestimated their opponents. In February 1881 the Boers again caught the British in the open and with superior use of cover and rifle fire inflicted a second defeat, this time killing the general officer commanding. The British government, deciding that the Boers were not worth the effort, recognized their independent republic; but the two battles should have underlined the fact that the Boers were formidable opponents.

HOW THE WEST WAS WON

While the British waged wars against Blacks and Boers in Africa, the Americans, fresh from the Civil War, completed the solution of their own 'native problem', in effect ending the frontier in the west and bringing 'civilization' to the entire area ruled by the United States. General Philip Sheridan's memorable comment, that 'the only good Indians I ever saw were dead' sums up the attitudes of all too many of those charged with the 'police actions' in the west. The Indians proved to be skilled fighters and tenacious opponents, but they lacked the organizational skills and the capacity to sustain a conflict. Once they became isolated from their hunting grounds and access to weapons and ammunition, their defeat was a foregone conclusion.

The largest Indian war occurred in the mid-1870s against the Sioux. In June 1876 one column of US troops fought a pitched battle with Sioux warriors led by Crazy Horse. Both sides pulled away, but a second column continued its advance, and sent the 7th Cavalry under George Armstrong Custer ahead to cut off the Sioux. Custer, however, disobeyed his orders. With golden curls and buckskin jacket, the colourful Custer led a portion of his regiment directly against the main Indian camp, while the remainder, led by men less hungry for glory, followed the precept that discretion is the better part of valour. Custer and his troops went down to complete destruction, a defeat immortalized in paintings on the walls of every saloon west of the Missouri.

For the next several months, the victorious Sioux eluded US troops, but those charged with the campaign continued their pursuit into the winter. In November 1876 the regulars discovered one of the main Indian encampments and, in a surprise night attack, destroyed most of its inhabitants. In early January 1877 US troops caught up with Crazy Horse; by shelling his camp they stampeded the Indians, and Sioux resistance collapsed.

Even more impressive than Sioux resistance was that of the Nez Percé. The tribe had defied orders to abandon tribal lands in Oregon; fighting then broke out; and the Nez Percé leader, Chief Joseph, led 300 warriors and 700 tribesmen eastwards. In summer 1877 Joseph fought his way through superior numbers of white soldiers in Idaho and reached Montana. His warriors displayed extraordinary discipline on the battlefield, besides the natural skills of their warrior-hunting society. The Nez Percé continued their march through Montana and had almost reached sanctuary

Chief Joseph (Heinmot Tooyalaket) of the Nez Percé provided the skilled military leadership which allowed his people to fight their way from Oregon almost to Canada when the US army tried to move them to Indian territory. But the white man's numbers eventually ran the Nez Percé to ground in Montana in 1877. Joseph died in 1904.

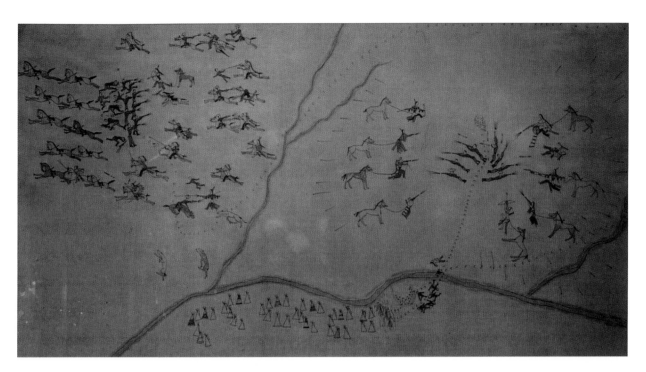

in Canada when US forces, outnumbering them by ten to one, finally brought them to bay at Eagle Creek and forced their surrender.

Ten years later US troops found themselves waging a guerrilla war against the Apaches in Arizona and New Mexico who, led by Geronimo, waged an effective hit-and-run war. What made the war particularly frustrating was the Apaches' ability to cover great distances on foot. Only by massing enormous forces in the region's arid deserts was the regular army able to bring them to heel.

While Americans and British waged particular colonial wars, a number of similar conflicts occurred elsewhere. The Russians waged campaigns in central Asia; the French, having brought Algeria under their control by 1847, expanded their empire to include Indo-China and substantial territories in central Africa. Everywhere the West was on the advance while other centres of civilization, if they survived, stood on the defensive.

For the Ottoman empire the long decline towards extinction in World War I continued. In 1876, with the enthusiastic help of local Muslims, the Turks put down a rebellion by Christians in Bosnia. The Serbs came to the help of their brothers and themselves suffered another thrashing at Turkish hands. At this point, in early 1877, the Russians intervened. A Russian army, with naval support, seized the mouth of the Danube. The Russians then won a series of victories over the Turks, and their rapid advance threatened to destroy Turkish control in the southern Balkans. But the Russians halted to attack the fortress at Plevna which, five months later, they gained; then, in December they carried their campaign to the gates of Constantinople. However, by this point the other major powers intervened to prevent Russia from gaining the fruits of its victory. The Treaty of San Stefano

Battle of the Little Big Horn, painted by White Bird, a Northern Cheyenne Indian who was there. George Custer had over-confidently launched his troops against Sioux warriors armed with repeating rifles, who destroyed his cavalry column to the last man.

(1878) recognized the independence of Serbia, Montenegro, and Rumania, while Bulgaria became autonomous. The Turks still maintained a presence in Europe as well as control over the Middle East: the Europeans, although highly successful, remained too fragmented to complete the destruction of the Ottoman state.

THE BOER WAR

The discovery of gold in the Witwatersrand (Transvaal) in 1886 added to the known mineral worth of the Boer republics. By now, through annexation of Zulu territory in 1887, the British were cutting the Boers' access to the ocean. Ambitions in both the Cape Colony and London exacerbated tensions in South Africa. Thousands of adventurers flocked to the Transvaal to seek their fortune; not surprisingly, tensions between outsiders and Boers rapidly rose.

The Boer republics lacked a military force in the conventional sense; rather they possessed a militia loosely grouped in commandos. Their leaders possessed a coherent grasp of neither strategy nor tactics, while the commandos at the best of times held to the loosest of discipline. But the Boers did have modern rifles, and their men were marvellous marksmen. They knew the veld and had the toughness born of struggling to farm a harsh and forbidding land. The British army that fought against them was well-disciplined and organized, but few of its generals understood South African conditions, and officers as well as men were generally contemptuous of the farmers against whom they would fight.

The Boers, recognizing that the British were assembling superior military forces, initiated hostilities with an invasion of Natal in October 1899. By so doing, they forfeited the possibility of manipulating British public opinion in their favour. Nevertheless, most Europeans saw British preparations as indicating hostile intent and, throughout the war, European sympathies consequently lay with the Boers, although the Royal Navy made it impossible to translate that sympathy into meaningful support. Nevertheless, fast-moving Boer columns soon isolated both Mafeking and Kimberley, and within a month had trapped a third force at Ladysmith. The British hastened to relieve the besieged towns. At the end of November a column of 10,000 troops under General Paul Methuen fought their way to the Modder River in an effort to reach Kimberley, but suffered nearly 500 casualties while the Boers scarcely lost a man. With smokeless powder and bolt action rifles, the Boers put down a murderous fire. Neither British troops nor their artillery could see the enemy; yet any movement across the killing zone covered by unseen Boers resulted in unacceptable casualties.

Worse was to come. In the second week of December 1899, the British suffered a series of defeats that became known collectively as 'Black Week'. On 10 December, a column under Sir William Gatacre got lost; the Boers ambushed the muddled advance near Stormberg and inflicted heavy casualties. On the same day, at Magersfontein, Methuen launched heavy attacks on firmly entrenched Boer positions: his troops achieved nothing, but again suffered heavy losses (210 dead

Opposite: Boer commandos looked like an ill-dressed rabble by British army standards, which evaluated military effectiveness almost entirely on the basis of appearance. But the Boers carried the most modern rifles, had spent their lives from childhood in the saddle on the veld, and had inherited an innate stubbornness and courage from their Dutch ancestors. In the right circumstances they made extraordinarily good soldiers. In the first battles of the Boer War these qualities showed to full effect, assisted by the tactical obtuseness and incompetence of British commanders.

and 675 wounded). Since the British soldiers and gunners hardly ever saw the defenders, the Boers again suffered few casualties. Five days later the commander-in-chief in South Africa, General Redvers Buller, attempted to turn the flank of Boer forces after crossing the Tugela River. But the British got entangled in difficult country, while Boer riflemen devastated their columns. British artillery once more failed to make out the defensive positions, and the Boers killed most of the gun crews. The attackers lost 143 dead, 756 wounded, and 220 missing. The Boers gained eleven guns, while losing barely fifty men.

If the Boers had been a well-disciplined force, they could have turned their victories into a genuine success. But they were not, and the British withdrew. The Boer commanders now found it difficult to keep their men in the field since most viewed the war as already won: their lack of discipline caused the commandos to melt away and then reform as the individual soldiers addressed their own needs. On the other hand, the British refused to allow themselves to be humiliated. The four corners of the empire rallied to the Union Jack, as substantial forces moved from Britain, Canada, Australia, and New Zealand to South Africa. The resources of the Empire made the final result inevitable, no matter how poor the preparation of generals and soldiers for the first clash. But things did not turn around quickly. Buller made two more – and larger – attempts to break through the Boer positions, but at Spion Kop and Vaal Kranz his troops suffered even heavier casualties and achieved nothing. Total losses for the two battles were 408 killed, 1,390 wounded, and 311 captured, against under a hundred Boer casualties.

A new commander assumed control of the campaign, General Lord Roberts, with Kitchener as his chief of staff. Roberts introduced movement into the campaign by using cavalry to outflank Boer positions, and in February 1900, the British relieved Kimberley and broke the major Boer force in front of Magersfontein. With Roberts temporarily sick, however, Kitchener launched a direct attack on the enemy laager at Paardeberg with the usual results: 320 British soldiers killed and nearly 1,000 wounded. The Boers might have made good their escape, but their commander, Piet Cronje, refused to abandon his wounded. By the end of the month Roberts had captured Cronje's Boers, and the British enjoyed their first major victory. More victories followed as the empire's military forces placed overwhelming pressure on the enemy. As Cronje's force surrendered, Buller broke across the Tugela River and drove on to relieve Ladysmith. The British soon finished off the Boer republics, and annexed the Orange Free State in May and the Transvaal in September 1900.

In conventional terms the war was over, but in reality it had only just begun. The Boers returned to their homes as conventional resistance collapsed, but refused to accept the result that brought their country under British colonial administration. They turned to guerrilla warfare, in which raiding parties wrecked British communications and supply lines, while the local population provided hiding places, food, and intelligence on British movements. Well-informed about the

'Breaker' Morant (seen here in a studio photograph taken before he sailed from home) and other Australian soldiers were executed for murdering Boer civilians. Although their punishment was justified by military law, much of what the British did lay outside 'military law'. To many Australians it seemed that their soldiers had been singled out for activities in which many others were equally guilty. As a result of the eventual outcry, the Australian government did away with capital punishment for its soldiers – and many Australians during World War I felt free to express their opinions about staff officers and military policemen with an independence and virulence that set them apart from British soldiers and those of the other Dominions.

enemy, the Boers were able to hit and run without suffering significant casualties. On the other hand, the British operated almost totally in the dark.

To meet a deteriorating situation, the British erected a series of blockhouses and fences to protect their supply and communication lines. When this failed to break Boer resistance, they attacked the civilian support on which Boer guerrillas depended, rounding up the civilian population and placing some 120,000 Boer women and children in camps. Indifferent care led to the death of perhaps 20,000 from disease and hunger. The British also used large numbers of irregulars to track Boer guerrillas and carry the war into the countryside. Consequently, a number of unsavoury incidents occurred in which civilians were mistreated and in some cases murdered. 'Beastliness' eventually broke the guerrillas: in May 1902 the Boers accepted British sovereignty and the British 'won' the war. But the sad history of South Africa since 1902 suggests that no one won: not the British, not the Boers, and certainly not the Blacks, who at best were observers of the contest for their lands between the whites.

The British had won because of their superiority in resources and manpower – by war's end they had assembled 300,000 troops there – and their willingness to

The battle of Spion Kop, like the other early battles in the war, mostly took place at ranges well beyond that of hand-to-hand combat. Boer rifles imposed heavy casualties on advancing British troops well before the attackers could even make out where the Boer positions lay. And, as later occurred in the first years of World War I, artillery could not hit targets it could not see.

concentrate their power in South Africa. The Boer War had considerable impact on the British army: above all it resulted in an emphasis on infantry training which created the best soldiers, man for man, in 1914. But it did little to change basic attitudes in the officer corps. Historians have harped on the inability of British generals to learn the lessons of the Boer War. In fact, they did recognize the killing power of modern weapons, but against a better-armed foe in Europe British generals would not find it so easy to adapt to the conditions of war, or to innovate.

THE RUSSO-JAPANESE WAR

Of the non-western civilizations, only the Japanese displayed the ability to adopt the weapons of the West and turn them against their developers. Few would have predicted it. From the early seventeenth century the Tokugawa shoguns, having destroyed their rivals, sought to demilitarize Japanese society by restricting possession of firearms (indeed, of any arms) and destroying all but one castle on each noble estate. They also discouraged contact with the outside world, censored all foreign books (especially those concerning military affairs), and concentrated foreign trade in the remote port of Nagasaki. On the other hand, thanks in part to an unprecedented two centuries of peace, Japan prospered: agricultural production, internal trade, manufacture, and credit all developed rapidly; by 1800 as much

Japanese artillerymen load one of the eighteen 'Osaka babies' – artillery pieces brought from mainland Japan to fire 500-lb shells against the Russian forts and garrison as the siege of Port Arthur began in 1904. Japan had already joined the camp of the modern industrialized nations in terms of the capacity of its industry to manufacture modern weapons, as the Russians found out to their cost.

as 20 per cent of the population lived in towns; and by 1850 perhaps 40 per cent of all Japanese males could read. The country may have lacked the power-driven machines and the scientific knowledge of the West, but it possessed superbly skilled craftsmen, an efficient commercial and financial network, and a sufficient degree of prosperity in both town and country to respond successfully to the pressure, first exerted by the United States in 1853, to 'open' Japan to western trade. The Tokugawa regime fell in 1868, delivering power to leaders who recognized that Japan must either adapt or succumb. Within a quarter of a century, the country had modernized so effectively that it was able to deploy its new-style armed forces on the Asian mainland – the navy trained by the British, the army by the Germans – and rout the Chinese (1894–95). The Japanese acquired Formosa, and lost direct control over Korea only because of Russian interference.

Over the next decade, Japan and Tsarist Russia moved towards conflict. Most Europeans believed that the Russians would easily defeat the Japanese in war (racial prejudice would lead the West to underestimate Japan's military capabilities right down to Pearl Harbor in 1941); and, indeed, in terms of military and economic power, the Russo-Japanese War was a conflict Russia should have won. But two problems confronted the Tsarist regime. On the one hand, it could only deploy a limited portion of its military power across Siberia. The Trans-Siberian railroad was a single track line which stopped on each side of Lake Baikal, where everything had to be unloaded, transported across the lake, and then loaded up again. On the other hand, and far more serious, Tsar Nicholas II brought a facile naiveté to the problems of government and tended to pick irresponsible and corrupt councillors who precipitated Russia into revolution.

Both sides courted confrontation because each aimed to control Korea and Manchuria. The Russians, however, possessed barely 100,000 troops east of Baikal and could only laboriously build up and supply that force. The Japanese, by contrast, could immediately throw a standing army of 250,000 men onto the Asian mainland, while their reserves would double those forces. On the naval side, the Japanese fleet was superior in Asian waters, while the Russian Baltic fleet faced an extraordinarily difficult journey across thousands of miles to reach the Pacific. Moreover, the conclusion of a defensive alliance with Britain provided security for Japan: Russia could not receive direct help from its French allies without bringing Britain into the war.

In February 1904, Japanese torpedo boats attacked the Russian fleet in Port Arthur before the declaration of war. The attackers sank a few vessels and bottled the Russians up. Ironically, the British and American press, largely pro-Japanese, saluted the attackers for their daring (an interesting contrast to their response to Pearl Harbor thirty-seven years later). The Japanese also attacked Russian ships at Inchon; a week later their First Army landed and seized Seoul. With a secure base in Korea, the Japanese moved north to the Yalu and towards direct military action against Russian forces in Manchuria.

The Russian commander, General Alexei Kuropatkin, planned to withdraw into the depths of Manchuria and allow Port Arthur to withstand a siege, while he awaited reinforcements across Siberia. Such an approach made considerable sense, but the Tsar's viceroy ordered an immediate offensive and, as a result, the Japanese First Army inflicted a major defeat on the Russians defending the Yalu. Meanwhile, the Japanese navy landed a second army northeast of Port Arthur on the Liaotung Peninsula. A third army landed west of the Yalu, and Japanese troops moved to lay siege to Port Arthur, while other units screened the siege from the Russians in central Manchuria. In operational terms the situation resembled the siege of Sebastopol in 1854–55 (see pages 219–20), where those conducting the siege also had to prevent Russian armies from breaking through to the besieged port.

In late May, the Japanese launched their first attack on the outposts surrounding Port Arthur: they drove Russian troops off the heights at Nanshan, but suffered over three times the casualties of their opponent. With sufficient stocks to last over the summer the Russians possessed a strong position, and inconclusive skirmishing both by land and sea characterized the fighting in early summer. In mid-August, however, the Japanese launched a massive assault that eventually captured crucial Russian positions, although machine guns and artillery inflicted 15,000 casualties on closely packed Japanese assault columns. Russian losses were only 3,000.

At the end of September the Japanese resumed the offensive. This time they suffered even heavier casualties and made no important gains. A fourth offensive at the end of October and a fifth at the end of November only added to their losses without significant results. The Japanese then concentrated their whole effort at capturing 203 Metre Hill, the lynch pin of Russian defences. By 5 December they finally pushed the defenders out of the position, but suffered 11,000 casualties in the process. Possession of Hill 203 allowed Japanese artillery to destroy the remnants of Russia's Far Eastern Fleet, but not until January 1905 could they force the Russians to surrender. Ironically, the Japanese discovered that, despite the garrison's state of starvation, substantial food dumps still existed within the fortress.

While the Japanese attacked Port Arthur, major fighting also took place in central Manchuria. Beginning in June 1904, the two sides moved towards a major military confrontation. In late August the two armies clashed in the battle of Liaoyang, where the Japanese numbered 125,000 and the Russians, with the first reinforcements from Europe, 158,000. The Russians attacked first, but aggressive Japanese counter-attacks persuaded the Russian generals that their enemy possessed greater strength. Losses were approximately equal, with 23,000 Japanese casualties against nearly 20,000 Russians, but the Russians conceded defeat and pulled back.

Reinforced by a steady flow of troops from Europe, Kuropatkin's forces increased to 200,000 while Japanese reinforcements raised their totals to 170,000. In early October at Sha-Ho the Russians attacked the Japanese right wing to cut their lines of communications; however, the Japanese counter-attacked the Russian centre and almost broke through. Kuropatkin stopped his attack and desperately shored up his centre. This time, the Russians lost more heavily: 40,000 against 20,000.

The strength of both armies continued to accelerate despite the rigours of the Manchurian winter. By mid-January the Russians had 300,000 men, while Japanese strength reached 220,000. On 26 and 27 January 1905, the Russians again attacked and came close to breaking their opponents; had they pushed their advantage, they might have broken through Japanese lines. But the fighting occurred during a snowstorm and the resulting confusion and uncertainty led the Russian generals to miss their opportunity. The front again returned to stability.

By the end of February the Japanese, reinforced by troops from Port Arthur, finally gained parity with their opponents: both sides now possessed approximately 310,000 men. On 21 February the battle of Mukden began. Field Marshal Iwao Oyama launched his Third Army to outflank the Russian right wing. While both sides focused on outflanking their opponents throughout the campaign, the speed of advancing troops and the lethality of weapons made it inevitable that such attempts would fail. The Japanese put the Russians in desperate straits – only the movement of reserves from the rest of the front prevented a collapse – and, although their advance did not envelop the Russians, after two weeks of fighting the Japanese entered Mukden. Three more days of heavy fighting forced the Russians into a general retreat. They had been thoroughly defeated and suffered over 100,000 casualties. The Japanese lost 70,000 men.

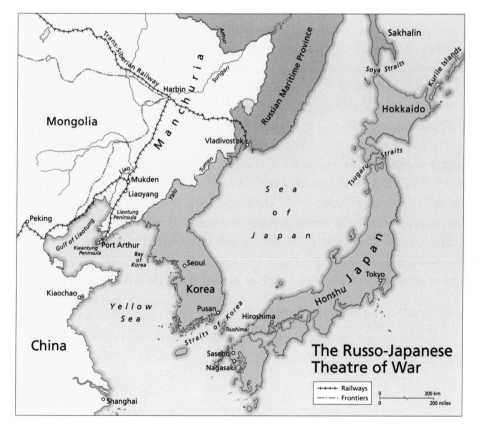

The Russo-Japanese War was fought close to Japan's power-base, whereas Russia had to transport its forces and their supplies either 6,000 miles across Siberia or 20,000 miles by sea around Africa and Asia. Twenty years earlier, this might not have mattered, because of the superiority in technology that the Russians would have enjoyed; by the beginning of the twentieth century, it did, since the Japanese by then disposed of equally modern arms.

While the fighting was occurring in Manchuria, the Russian Baltic fleet embarked on a round-the-world expedition to relieve pressure on Port Arthur. This fleet, an odd conglomeration of obsolete vessels, lacked both the training and the material preparations for such a journey, much less for a major fleet action, and it received little help along the way. After an epic 20,000-mile journey the thirty-two Russian vessels eventually reached East Asian waters, only to find themselves outranged and outmanoeuvred by their opponents in the Tsushima Straits, on 27 May 1905. The fleet action lasted through the night when Japanese superiority was even more pronounced. Although a few Russian vessels escaped, the Baltic fleet had ceased to exist.

Tsushima represented Russia's last gasp. Revolution had already broken out in most urban centres in Tsarist Russia, for the humiliation of their military forces represented the last straw to many Russians who had watched Nicholas and his advisers botch every major internal and external decision. For a time, it appeared the regime might fall, but it did not. But while Russia seethed with discontent, the Japanese had also suffered heavy casualties in the war and stood on the brink of financial collapse. In September 1905, both sides consequently accepted a compromise peace brokered by the American president, Theodore Roosevelt. The Russians abandoned Port Arthur, Korea, and Manchuria; the Japanese gained a decisive interest in the first two but would not gain complete control of Manchuria until 1931. Ironically, defeat in Asia focused Russian attention on European aspirations once more, particularly in the Balkans.

In retrospect, the war in Manchuria anticipated much of what became all too familiar on World War I battlefields. Everywhere, firepower dominated and killed soldiers in huge quantities, a fact recognized by most of Europe's military establishments, some of whose most sophisticated soldiers were on the scene – for the British, Sir Ian Hamilton and, for the Germans, the brilliant and acerbic Max von Hoffman (among others). But the war also confirmed the belief of economists and politicians that nations could not long withstand the economic and political pressures that would come in a major conflict. After all, had not Russia collapsed into anarchy and revolution after less than eighteen months of war? And was not Japan on the brink of bankruptcy? The lesson, then, seemed obvious: nations must win a major war at the outset, using every ounce of military power they could muster. Some analysts believed victory would require the sacrifice of the last battalions in their armies, fighting with the same desperate, suicidal spirit the Japanese had displayed in attacking Port Arthur. It was the wrong lesson.

THE ROAD TO ARMAGEDDON

Few have portrayed the outbreak of World War I better than Winston Churchill. In his account of the war he comments that:

> One rises from the study of the causes of the Great War with a prevailing sense of

the defective control of individuals upon world fortunes. It has been well said, 'there is always more error than design in human affairs.' The limited minds even of the ablest men, their disputed authority, the climate of opinion in which they dwell, their transient and partial contributions to the mighty problem, that problem itself so far beyond their compass, so vast in scale and detail, so changing in its aspect...Events...got on to certain lines, and no one could get them off again. Germany clanked obstinately, recklessly, awkwardly towards the crater and dragged us all in with her.

Bismarck's strategic triumphs in the wars of unification, and his skilful diplomatic policies afterwards, had guided the new Reich to a unique position in Europe (see page 241). But his successors failed to see the advantage of Germany's position or that any attempt to make Germany the hegemon of Europe would lead the other powers to band together against the threat. Some of this was Bismarck's fault: he never clarified his policies, and he created a state with no constitutional controls over its military instruments. Bismarck's dismissal by the young Kaiser Wilhelm II in 1890 brought a new generation of Germans to power, a generation that felt few of Bismarck's inhibitions about the use of force. They worshipped the military, whereas Bismarck had merely regarded it as a tool. Above all, they believed that Germany possessed infinite potential and the *right* (because of Germany's culture and civilization) to translate that potential into a 'place in the sun'. Making the situation more dangerous was the fact that Germany's senior military leaders had dispensed with Clausewitz's belief in the primacy of strategy; to German generals of the new century what mattered was military and operational necessity alone.

Almost immediately after Bismarck's removal, the experts in the German Foreign Office, relieved of the chancellor's interference, persuaded Wilhelm to dispense with the 'Reinsurance Treaty' with Russia, signed in 1887 and promising neutrality should either power become engaged in war with a third party. They believed that republican France and Tsarist Russia could never ally; yet in 1891 the Tsar was standing bareheaded at the playing of France's revolutionary anthem the *Marseillaise*, and one year later the two powers had become allies. Germany now confronted the likelihood of a two-front war, should conflict break out among the major powers.

It is hard to see much purpose in the policies pursued by Germany over the next two decades. In 1894 the Kaiser read the work of the American prophet of naval power, Alfred Thayer Mahan, and immediately concluded that Germany's rise to the status of a world power could only occur through creation of a great fleet. The Kaiser's enthusiasm was undoubtedly fuelled by his love–hate relationship with his British cousins. Not until 1897 did he find an admiral, Alfred von Tirpitz, who possessed both the ambition and political acumen to carry out his dreams.

Tirpitz created an effective political coalition of landed aristocracy and industrialists to secure resources for the naval build-up. He argued both that construction

Kaiser Wilhelm II (1888–1918) loved his navy and the naval uniforms that his position allowed him to wear. His empire, however, paid a heavy price for the Kaiser's dilettantish dreams of a 'world empire': Britain, alienated and alarmed by Germany's naval programme, joined France and Russia to block her drive towards European hegemony.

of a great fleet would force Britain to respect the Reich's worldwide interests and that, because Britain and the Franco-Russian alliance held mutually hostile interests, Germany could create such a fleet without fear of British interference. Moreover, Tirpitz held to a number of other assumptions: that the cost of battleships would remain stable; that Britain as a liberal state could not stay the course in a major arms race; and that the British would never make agreements with their ancient rivals, the Russians and French. Finally, at the heart of Tirpitz's strategy lay the assumption that the German fleet would eventually reach sufficient strength to defeat the Royal Navy in battle and that in a single afternoon his fleet would wrest control of the world's oceans and empires away from the British. Ironically, however, right down to the outbreak of war in 1914 the Germans never devised a plan for how they would use their navy if the British did not launch a close blockade of Germany's ports. Tirpitz's greatest mistake lay in his failure to recognize that geography had given Britain an almost unassailable naval position: the British Isles lay astride Germany's path to the Atlantic, and it would be an easy matter for the Royal Navy to block Germany in the English Channel and across the exits from the North Sea, whilst Britain's position also shielded its own trade routes. But nothing deterred the Germans from their course.

THE ARMS RACE BEGINS

In 1906 Admiral Sir John Fisher, the reforming head of the British Admiralty, introduced a revolutionary class of battleship, the *Dreadnought,* an all-big-gun, heavily armoured vessel that rendered all previous battleships obsolete. With that technological lead the British laid down battleships as fast as they could. Although the change in ship design doubled costs for the short run and raised them even higher over the long run, the threat to British naval mastery posed by the German build-up spurred Parliament to match – and in fact exceed – every step in Tirpitz's programme. As Churchill characterized the situation in one year: 'the Admiralty asked for six [battleships], the Cabinet proposed four, and we compromised on eight.' Moreover a series of diplomatic agreements (starting with an alliance with Japan in 1902) allowed the British to concentrate their fleet in the North Sea against the German menace.

The continuing German naval build-up prompted Britain to form an entente with France in 1904 that resolved outstanding disagreements between the two countries. The Germans replied by causing a major diplomatic crisis over Morocco, intended to break up the growing Anglo-French friendship; instead, they only drove the two powers more closely together. In 1907, the British and Russians responded to German policy with a similar entente that also resolved outstanding differences. While these agreements did not create formal alliances between Britain and the continental powers, they created a community of interests that the Germans correctly perceived as hostile. In succeeding years Britain strengthened its ties to France with military agreements and in 1912 even pulled its Mediterranean

Opposite: A British battle squadron steaming down the English Channel in 1911. HMS *Dreadnought,* launched on 10 February 1906 represented a significant change in the balance of navel power. With its emphasis on big guns (ten 12-inch guns) and its heavy armour, the *Dreadnought* set a standard for battleship construction that would last through to World War II. All the major powers (and most of the smaller imitators) now hastened to pour massive resources into the construction of 'dreadnoughts'; Britain, however, thanks to its superior industrial strength and its head-start, always retained the lead.

fleet into the North Sea: in return for Britain's promise to protect French interests in the Atlantic, France agreed to protect British interests in the Mediterranean. But the largest commitment – not reported to the whole cabinet – was that a British Expeditionary Force should be sent to the continent in defence of France, if the need arose.

None of this caused the Germans to desist from an armaments programme that endangered the Reich's long-range strategic interests, but the increasingly tense European situation did lead in 1912 to a change in emphasis. Up to that point, the German army had undergone no major expansion of active or reserve components since 1900. Such a state of affairs is extraordinary when one considers that German strategy in case of war rested almost entirely on the Schlieffen plan (see page 262) and that until 1913 the army lacked the necessary troops to execute that operational plan on which Germany's fate would rest. This shortage of troops resulted from two facts: first, until 1912, the general staff failed to give the war ministry a complete picture of its grand strategy; second, the war ministry, a haven for conservatives, consistently opposed expansion of troop strengths because such a step would increase the number of middle-class officers and thereby dilute aristocratic control over the officer corps. Since the Kaiser lacked a central authority to run the army – over forty general officers possessed the right of direct

access to him – a variety of powers squabbled and argued, but essential questions remained unanswered.

In 1912 the general staff, led by Colonel Erich Ludendorff, among others, finally broke war-ministry opposition to a major increase in army authorizations. As a result the Reichstag increased spending levels for the army to support 165,000 more men in 1912 and 1913, as part of a programme to increase peacetime strength from 544,000 to 877,000 men. Thus, the army would just have sufficient troops in 1914 to execute the Schlieffen plan. In revenge the conservatives had Ludendorff removed from the general staff and sent to an obscure troop command; but he would be back.

THE GATHERING STORM

A series of crises in the Balkans provided tinder for the impending European conflagration. The weakness of the Ottoman empire combined with Austrian and Russian ambitions to exacerbate the situation. Moreover, each of the eastern empires felt threatened by internal political developments and therefore sought to escape their domestic dilemmas through foreign policy successes – starting in the Balkans. In 1903 a group of radical nationalist officers seized power in Serbia and pursued a fiercely anti-Austrian policy. The Austrians increasingly regarded Serbia, which France and Russia supported, as a direct threat to their existence. In 1908, motivated by a desire to separate Serbia and Russia, they made a deal with the Russians by which Austria would acquire title to Bosnia-Herzegovina in return for helping Russia open the Bosporus to its warships. In the event, the Austrians annexed Bosnia, but the Russians got nothing (because the other powers objected). The Germans played an active role in humiliating the Russians, the Kaiser portraying himself as a knight riding to Austria's rescue.

The next round of Balkan troubles began in September 1911 when the Italians attacked the Turkish province of Libya in North Africa and followed up by seizing the Dodecanese islands. These Italian moves led the Balkan states to jump on the prostrate Turks; Serbia, Bulgaria, Greece, and Montenegro all participated. But the thieves immediately fell out over the spoils. Serbia, Greece, Montenegro, and then Rumania banded together to pummel Bulgaria. Even the Turks joined in. While the Serbs gained much from the war, doubling the size of their state, the Austrians prevented them from gaining access to the Adriatic and the world's oceans: once again the Germans deterred the Russians from supporting the Serbs, and before the united might of Austria and Germany, Serbia conceded.

In the nineteenth century Bismarck had stated that the Balkans were not worth the bones of a single Pomeranian grenadier. What had changed to alter German policy? Most notably the Germans, for all their bluster, believed they stood in terrible danger. Internally, the Social Democrats, a party which had only recently abandoned its revolutionary Marxist platform, had steadily enlarged its share of the votes in recent elections. By this point it was the largest party in the Reich. In external terms, the naval race with Britain, despite expenditure of huge sums, was no closer to resolution; and the British seemed to have allied themselves with Germany's continental enemies. Moreover, those enemies, Russia and France, were steadily improving the strength of their ground forces on the continent. Russia had already cast a defence programme for completion in 1917 that would radically improve its ability to project military power into central Europe. Consequently, Austria was Germany's last significant ally; and if the Reich did not support Vienna, was it not possible that Austria might also turn away, leaving Germany alone on a continent of enemies?

While Germany's leaders viewed the international environment with gloom, Austria was desperate. The Habsburg monarchy was the only power in Europe that did not base its legitimacy on nationalism. Internally, Czechs, Poles, and Slovaks all clamoured for autonomy; even the Hungarians were not entirely reliable; and on the frontiers, Italians, Serbs, and Rumanians demanded freedom for their brothers living under 'the Habsburg yoke'. With enemies everywhere, was not war the only option? As the chilling German phrase went: 'Better a terrible end than endless terror.' Eventually, it was Germany that grasped most eagerly at war. In a 1912 conference between the Kaiser and his military leaders, the chief of the general staff, Count Helmuth von Moltke, urged a preventative war, 'the sooner the better'. The others enthusiastically agreed. Significantly, the German leadership failed to make coherent preparations for war over the next two years, but its mood was clear: at the first opportunity it would push Europe over the precipice.

On 28 June 1914 the chance occurred. A group of young terrorists, trained, supported, and organized by the Serbian government, assassinated the heir to the Austro-Hungarian throne as he visited the newly annexed Bosnia. The event outraged Europe. But Austria hesitated, while its police investigated the affair in the best traditions of Austrian incompetence. For most of July the Austrians dithered and lost much of Europe's support; when they acted, the assassination was on the back pages of European newspapers. Meanwhile, the British made desperate efforts to defuse the crisis, in the belief that they were acting in concert with the Germans; but the Kaiser and his government were playing a double game. Germany gave overt support to British initiatives, but privately urged the Austrians to act as decisively against Serbia as possible.

In fact, the Germans issued the Austrians a 'blank cheque' which they expected and *wanted* their allies to use. On 23 July the Austrians therefore issued an ultimatum to Serbia that allowed no room for negotiations. Despite a conciliatory answer from the Serbs, Austria declared war on 28 July. Ironically, Austrian incompetence prevented substantial military action for the next two weeks; but to ensure that the Rubicon remained crossed, the Austrians immediately shelled Belgrade. Consequently, the Russians confronted a situation where surrender to German and Austrian pressure again would do irremediable harm to their interests in the Balkans.

Austrian police and army officers lead away a suspected terrorist in Sarajevo, Bosnia, on 28 June 1914, the day Archduke Franz Ferdinand, heir apparent to the Austro-Hungarian empire, and his wife were assassinated in the city. Because the plotters were all under age, they did not suffer the death penalty: Gavrilo Princip, who fired the fatal shots, received a twenty-year prison term (but died of tuberculosis in 1918). However, Austria took a strong line against Serbia, which it held ultimately responsible for the outrage, and determined to exploit the incident in order to end Serb opposition to Austrian expansion in the Balkans.

THE WARPLANS OF THE GREAT POWERS

By this point, military planning had made war almost inevitable. Of all the plans for war that European armies cast before 1914, only Britain did not expect their army to achieve decisive results – although that merely reflected the size and strength of a British army prepared to play an ancillary role on the continent. Yet even the British army possessed a mission that foresaw it supporting a decisive French offensive to defeat the German army in the Rhineland.

In understanding these plans, the historian must bear in mind that military planning reflected the best estimates of economists and politicians as well as soldiers. European general staffs fully understood that modern battlefields would be terrible killing grounds. But civilian experts believed the modern state to be a fragile edifice with neither staying power in economic terms nor stability in political terms. Few believed that a major war could last more than a year before political and financial collapse occurred. Even fewer believed that a great struggle could last a second year. There had been a few prophets in the wilderness: the elder Moltke had warned that the next European war might last thirty years. (He was closer than one might think. If one considers World War I and World War II as a single great struggle – as Thucydides thought about the Peloponnesian War – then Moltke was exactly on target.) The Polish entrepreneur, Ivan Bloch, issued a similar warning in his book *Is War Impossible?* (1899), which predicted that 'Everybody will be entrenched in the next war'; but such estimates were very much the exception. All the recent wars involving European powers had been relatively short, and in the case of Russia, revolution had broken out and political and economic stability had collapsed. Thus, the principal strategic requirement seemingly confronting Europe's militaries was to win the next war quickly before financial and political collapse ensued.

The foremost example of how political assumptions combined with military perceptions to produce strategic disaster is Germany's Schlieffen plan. The German mistakes were similar to those of their military opponents, except on a grander scale and with greater impact on the course of the war. The Schlieffen plan reflected the strengths and weaknesses of the German 'way of war'. Since that 'way of war' would dominate the first half of the twentieth century, it is particularly useful to examine the plan in detail.

Count Alfred von Schlieffen had become chief of the general staff in 1891; as such his primary responsibility lay in establishing plans to deal with potential conflicts. By 1891 the German nightmare of facing a two-front war with France and Russia in case of hostilities had turned into reality. In such a situation Schlieffen's predecessors had thought in terms of defending Alsace-Lorraine in the west, and assuming the offensive against Russia; but Schlieffen believed that Russia's vast expanses would prevent the achievement of a decisive victory. France, however, confronted Germany with a solid barrier of fortresses along its frontier so that a quick victory in the west seemed equally problematic. But Schlieffen was a student

Count Alfred von Schlieffen (1833–1913) represented the archetype for the general staff officer. He allowed himself no diversions from his ruthless pursuit of military excellence: he would even set his subordinates tactical problems on Christmas Eve and expect to receive their answers on Boxing Day. But for all his brilliance and studious attention to war, he was peculiarly blind to its political dimensions. Like most of his contemporaries in the German army he dismissed Clausewitz's *On War* as a 'book to be read by professors'.

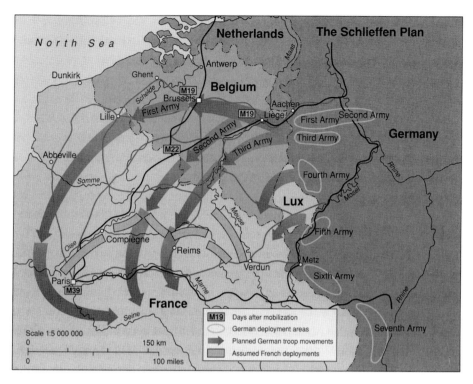

The Schlieffen plan was an audacious attempt to surmount the operational and tactical problems raised by the spiralling size of armies, as well as the increasing effectiveness of infantry and artillery weapons. It involved moving 1.5 million men in seven armies according to a day-by-day, railway-car-by-railway-car schedule which required Liège (where the three main armies began to fan out) to be taken by M-12 (the twelfth day after mobilization), Brussels subdued by M-19, the French frontier crossed by M-22, and Paris captured by M-39. This would knock France out of the war within six weeks – the precise time which Schlieffen estimated Russia would need to complete full mobilization – and so allow Germany to transfer its victorious forces eastwards in time to meet and beat the Russians in East Prussia.

of military history; as such he had drawn the conclusion from his studies, particularly Hannibal's victory at Cannae (see pages 48–9), that envelopment was the only route to decisive victory. He now proposed to sweep around the French fortifications by invading Belgium. Once deployed in the Low Countries, German armies could outflank French defences and destroy the French army in a gigantic envelopment east of Paris. With France eliminated, Germany could deal with Russia in a more leisurely campaign.

In every respect, the Schlieffen plan seemed to represent a brilliant operational solution to Germany's strategic problems. But on the political level it had extraordinary weaknesses that resulted from both its narrow definition of the problem and its faulty operational assumptions. Its most obvious weakness lay in the strategic realm: by violating Belgian neutrality, the Germans guaranteed that Britain would enter the war at France's side. If Germany won quickly, such interference would count for little; in Schlieffen's words, it would allow the Germans to sweep the British army up along with the French. But if the war were long, Britain represented a serious threat to Germany's conduct of the conflict, while German violation of Belgian neutrality would also have considerable impact on American attitudes. However, because of the 'short-war scenario' (see pages 256 and 262), such considerations did not overly concern Schlieffen or his successors.

In fact the Schlieffen plan held the seeds of its own operational failure. It depended on the French doing everything expected of them – namely committing their forces to an invasion of Alsace and Lorraine – and on Belgium acceding to a

German invasion of its territory. Any serious Belgian resistance would confront German forces with enormous logistic difficulties, particularly if the Belgians sabotaged the railroad tunnels and bridges.

Moreover, Schlieffen and his planners never came to terms with the problem represented by Paris. Where would the troops to blockade the city come from, if the German right wing proceeded on its march to envelop French forces deep within France? And if Germany's forces stopped to eliminate the French troops in Paris, would not the French army have sufficient time to redeploy? In effect, like other grand strategies in Europe, the Schlieffen plan existed in a realm of pure, intellectual war, in which each opponent followed the moves choreographed for him and in which no mistakes or faulty assumptions delayed the onward sweep to military victory.

The new chief of the general staff, the younger Moltke, modified the Schlieffen plan by adding troops to the centre and left wing, but he left the right wing as strong as Schlieffen had intended. (Logistically, it is doubtful whether the Germans could have pushed more troops out on the right and supplied them.) Ironically, the most disastrous tinkering that occurred in the last years of peace had to do with military options, for in 1913 Moltke and Ludendorff discarded the alternate plan for an offensive deployment against Russia. Thus, however the war might begin, Germany's opening move would have to be made in the west. In addition, Moltke and Ludendorff decided that military operations would begin, immediately upon notification of mobilization, with movement into neutral Luxembourg and Belgium to prevent last minute second thoughts by the Emperor or his diplomats.

Military plans of other states reflected the same 'short-war scenario' that Germany's military and civilian leaders had cast. They also reflected the fact that few planners had experienced war, and none had experienced war on the scale of what was to come in 1914. As a result, their efforts appear generally unrealistic, but in the circumstances they reflected attempts to analyse realistically the military, political, and economic realities. They were, however, wrong in almost all of their assumptions.

COUNT-DOWN TO WAR

Austria's declaration of war on Serbia on 28 July started the clock ticking on the time bomb; there was no way now to stop the bomb from going off. Twice in the previous decade Russia had backed down before Austro-German challenges. They would not do so again. The Tsar made a half-hearted effort to mobilize only the Russian forces facing Austria, but not those facing East Prussia. However, his generals persuaded him that such a deployment could not work and would give the advantage to the Germans.

Once the Russians decreed full mobilization on 30 July, the Germans acted. The Kaiser, after assuring his advisers throughout July that he would not 'chicken out', got cold feet at the last moment. He asked an appalled Moltke whether the army could mobilize against Russia, while remaining on the defensive in the west. A shattered chief of staff, almost reduced to tears, replied that there was only one option, the Schlieffen plan. The Kaiser's devastating rejoinder was that Moltke's uncle – the great Moltke – would have given a different answer. Nevertheless, on 1 August the Kaiser authorized mobilization and therefore – given the exigencies of the Schlieffen plan – war. The same day the French also mobilized, but announced to the German ambassador that their troops would remain well behind the frontier. It did not matter: when Germany declared war on France on 3 August, her troops were already in Luxembourg and Belgium. Germany, in support of Austria's claims against Serbia, was now invading Luxembourg, Belgium, and France. When the British ambassador suggested to the German chancellor that Germany had treaty obligations to respect the neutrality of the Low Countries, Bethmann-Hollweg replied that the treaty was only a 'scrap of paper'.

It did not take much more to persuade the British cabinet that their country must side with France and Russia. It had taken only a week from Austria's declaration of war on Serbia to bring the major European powers into a disastrous conflict. As Viscount Grey, the British foreign minister suggested: 'the lamps are going out all over Europe and we shall not see them lit again in our lifetime.' He was right: they would not be relit across the whole continent until 1989.

The telegraph, invented in 1832, played an essential role in the coming of war in 1914. Statesmen used it to communicate. Austria declared war on Serbia by telegraph on 28 July; the next day Kaiser Wilhelm and Tsar Nicholas (just 45 minutes apart by wire) exchanged several personal messages in a final attempt to avoid hostilities. War offices used it to mobilize. Just after 6 p.m. on 30 July, in St Petersburg, telegraph operators began to send out orders for an unprecedented simultaneous movement of troops: 744 infantry battalions and 621 cavalry squadrons – some 2 million men in all – were called to arms.

CHAPTER 14   *The West at War*

British cavalry charge near Mons in Belgium on 21 August. When the European armies went to war in August 1914, they had not engaged in a major continental war since 1870. As a result they retained many concepts that were more applicable to the conflicts of the early nineteenth century than to war with machine guns, rapid fire rifles, and long-range artillery. For the first few months, cavalry floundered around the battlefield with neither a clear mission nor the ability to survive for long – despite a few successes, like this one. By October 1914, however, with the creation of the great trench line from the Channel to Switzerland, they had no role on the battlefield and were soon relegated to rear-area security duties.

The failure of diplomacy in July 1914 brought on the great conflict feared by some and welcomed by many. Throughout Europe, while reservists flocked to the colours, crowds acclaimed the declarations of war. The hostilities, however, failed to live up to expectations of a short, decisive, conflict; rather, a terrible, seemingly endless struggle ensued. From our vantage point it is difficult to see how the Germans lasted as long as they did: after all, they went to war with three of the greatest powers in the world, Britain, France, and Russia, a coalition backed by the United States, a power that German efforts would eventually enlist in the roll of their enemies. But last they did, and in 1918 they finally achieved total victory in the east, and at one point seemed close to it in the west as well. Nevertheless, in the end, despite their tactical and operational skills, they could not overcome their fundamentally flawed strategy and the weight of the coalition ranged against them.

In 1914 European armies confronted a technological revolution on the battlefield. The weapons developed over the previous decades – bolt-action rifles, machine guns, modern howitzers – provided firepower in unprecedented measure and presented insoluble problems to western military organizations. Modern weapons allowed armies to set up impregnable defensive positions, and neither the officer corps nor the general staffs worked out how to use modern technology, or evolved tactical concepts to break through such defences, until 1918. Moreover, during the course of the war, gas, tanks, aircraft, and a panoply of new infantry weapons made tactical problems daunting and solutions elusive, while battlefield doctrines grew ever more complex. The front lines – at least in the west – remained relatively stable, but conditions within the battle zone underwent enormous changes, while military forces had to adapt and innovate in accordance with developments on the other side of the hill.

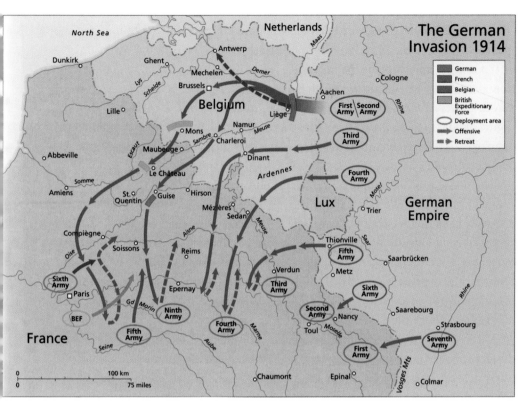

The German
Invasion 1914

The Schlieffen plan (see page 263) almost worked: Germany mobilized her forces on 1 August and, although Liège did not fall until 16 August, the Germans took Brussels on 20 August and entered France on the 24th – only two days behind schedule. However, Schlieffen ignored the problem of how to neutralize the strong garrison of Paris, and the logistical nightmare of supplying and sustaining the men in the powerful First Army, on the right flank, who were required to march between 20 and 25 miles a day. His plan also guaranteed, by violating Belgian neutrality, that Britain would enter the war at its outset.

The armies moved forward towards the first clash in 1914 on the basis of carefully laid plans. Most senior officers recognized the lethality of modern weapons, but generals, as well as politicians and economists, believed that modern societies could not support the cost of a prolonged struggle. Consequently, they planned to launch a knock-out blow that would win quickly, whatever the cost. The Russians aimed to grab East Prussia as well as deal Austria a crushing blow. The French hoped to slice behind German forces with a drive through Alsace-Lorraine to the Rhineland. However, as in 1870, they miscalculated by estimating that Germany would not use reserve forces; therefore, while the French recognized that the Germans might launch their main attack through Belgium, they mistook its size and power.

THE OPENING MOVES

The German plan, named after its designer Count Schlieffen, assumed that the Reich could only win a two-front war by crushing France before Russia could mobilize (see pages 262–4). Since French frontier fortifications presented a major problem, Schlieffen called for the invasion of Belgium, thus outflanking France's defences and allowing German forces to sweep south, mask Paris, and envelop French armies from the west. Germany would not attempt a minor violation of Belgian territory; rather, it would use the country as a launching pad to hurl three armies of thirty-two divisions at the French left. Accordingly, on 4 August 1914 one million German troops began the invasion of Belgium, a move that sufficed to end the political debate in Britain on whether to honour informal military commitments made in the previous decade to France: the British immediately declared war.

First of all, the Germans had to gain Liège and its gap in order to deploy the forces necessary to execute their plan. Great mortars, manufactured by Krupp and Skoda, wrecked the Belgian fortresses, while Colonel Erich Ludendorff, already a figure of note in the German army (see pages 258, 264), drove into Liège and then demanded and received the citadel's surrender. His success led to his appointment as chief of staff to German forces in East Prussia. Belgian resistance at Liège did little to detain the Germans, although it caused annoyance, while the withdrawal of the Belgian army to Antwerp threatened the German flank. To cover that threat, the Germans had to detach two corps. Elsewhere the Belgians sabotaged roads, wrecked communications, blew up railway tunnels and bridges, and sniped at the enemy. In fury, the Germans retaliated. They bombarded the university town of Louvain and in places that resisted shot civilian hostages: 664 hostages executed at Dinant and 150 at Aerschot set the tone – small change to later generations, but enough to outrage the world of 1914.

While the Germans moved into Belgium according to the Schlieffen Plan, the French followed their own strategy – 'Plan XVII', prepared by Joseph Joffre, chief of their general staff. Just as Schlieffen had anticipated, in massed brigades, with officers wearing white gloves, the French First and Second Armies moved into Alsace-Lorraine in mid-August, where German defenders under Crown Prince Rupprecht of Bavaria slaughtered them. Shaken, the French reeled back; Rupprecht requested permission to pursue and Helmuth von Moltke, the chief of staff, acquiesced in the hope that his armies could execute a double envelopment – even though by so doing he violated Schlieffen's basic conception, which was to roll the French up from the west.

French attacks now shifted to the Ardennes but once again they ran into numerous German forces which drove them back. Here too German troops pressed forward, although their action again pushed the French out of the trap that Schlieffen had hoped to set. By now the German right wing had completed its deployment in Belgium and was moving forward. Initially, the French high command failed to recognize the growing threat to its position, but the Fifth Army commander, Charles Lanrezac, acted on his own: with his troops battered in the Ardennes he ordered a timely withdrawal. On the far left of the Allied line the newly arrived British Expeditionary Force, badly mauled at Mons on 23 August, also retreated. At this point, the German right wing was positioned to envelop the entire Allied left, but Karl von Bülow, commander of the right, refused Alexander von Kluck, First Army commander, permission to swing west to envelop the British Expeditionary Force.

The French high command finally recognized the danger. 'Papa' Joffre did not panic: instead he desperately reshuffled French forces to his left wing. The German

Opposite: Christmas Day, 1914. After the terrible killing of late summer and autumn 1914, the exhausted armies collapsed into stalemate on the Western Front. In appalling conditions, exacerbated by bad weather, the troops shivered with only the minimum of protection. On Christmas Day, soldiers in the forward lines simply stopped firing; some more adventurous souls then clambered out of the trenches. By late morning large groups of soldiers were exchanging Christmas greetings in no man's land between the trenches, and by afternoon they had begun to play football. At midnight, however, the undeclared truce ended and the armies went back to the business of killing. There would not be another truce until November 1918.

advance and Allied retreat, both moving at approximately 20 miles a day, set in motion a race towards Paris, but the Allies held the advantage in that they were falling back on their supply dumps. The Germans, short of resources, were soon exhausted. Moreover, the German high command chose this moment to pull two more corps off the right wing because of the Russian threat to East Prussia (see page 270).

At this point, mounting losses combined with Schlieffen's miscalculations to confront German commanders with a difficult choice: what to do about Paris. With insufficient troops either to attack or screen the capital, the Germans swung east on 1 September intending to by-pass Paris and finish off the French army. But Joffre had rushed reinforcements into the capital and, when aerial reconnaissance revealed the German move to the east of Paris, he struck. The battle of the Marne, between 5 and 10 September, involved over two million soldiers – perhaps the largest encounter ever fought to that date – and began with a French attack which forced Kluck's First Army to face west, in the opposite direction from Bülow's Second Army, which was facing almost due east. A gap opened between the two forces which the British Expeditionary Force stood poised to exploit; had it moved with dispatch the Allies might have destroyed the German right wing.

In fact, the British moved too slowly, but the Germans remained in serious straits: their right wing had fragmented and possessed no clear focus, while their logistical system was near collapse – its railheads lay deep in Belgium – and their troops were exhausted. As one officer noted: 'We can do no more. The men fall in the ditches and lie there just to breathe…The order comes to mount. I ride bent over with my head on the horse's mane. We are thirsty and hungry. Indifference overcomes us.' The general staff's representative, Colonel Richard Hentsch, sent to assess the situation, recognized the makings of a disaster; in Moltke's name, he ordered a retreat to the Aisne. The Schlieffen plan had failed; France had survived.

After the initial movements dictated by the Schlieffen plan and the race to the sea, the Western Front solidified into a prolonged stalemate, with minimal movement in the positions of the opposing sides despite massive battles in which millions of young men were killed or wounded.

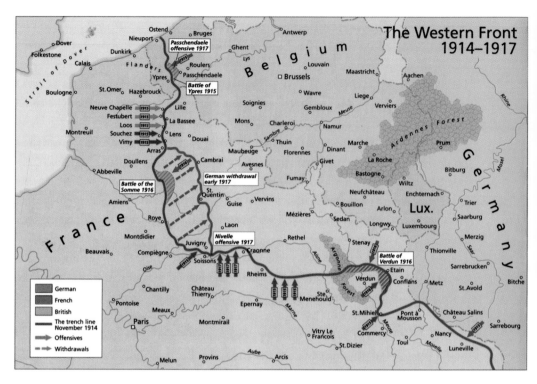

The pursuit by Allied forces, however, was hesitant. Once on the Aisne, the front stabilized and the opposing armies attempted to regain freedom of manoeuvre by outflanking their opponents. But the ensuing 'race to the sea' only extended a ragged line of trenches to the Channel. In October, the new chief of the German general staff, Erich von Falkenhayn, ordered an offensive in Flanders to drive the Allies from Antwerp and the Channel ports. The German cupboard, however, was so bare that he threw in a corps of inexperienced university students who had begun training only in August. The Germans took Antwerp, but of 36,000 in the university reserve corps, only 6,000 survived unscathed. One of them was Adolf Hitler. By November the opposing armies had become locked in a tight embrace on a 500-mile front running from Switzerland to the Channel. The four months of fighting had resulted in a general stalemate, while nearly half a million French, British, and German soldiers lay dead. The battle lines would change but minimally over the next three years despite horrendous casualties.

GERMAN VICTORY IN THE EAST

In the east equally significant battles occurred, also involving terrible casualties, stalemate, and the collapse of pre-war plans. Schlieffen had accepted the possibility of the temporary loss of East Prussia while Germany committed her main forces in the west; but by 1914 Russia's military organization had improved significantly and it managed to mobilize and deploy its forces far more quickly than expected. Two armies, under Paul Rennenkampf and Alexander Samsonov, struck East Prussia. Rennenkampf's forces moved from Russian territory to attack Königsberg from the east, while Samsonov's army attacked from Poland and struck north. Had the Russians co-ordinated these movements, they had some prospect of capturing East Prussia and destroying the German Eighth Army. But little co-ordination occurred: the two commanders hated each other, and the Russians' uncoded messages gave the Germans an accurate picture of their intentions.

Rennenkampf moved first. At Gumbinnen, a small town in East Prussia, his forces defeated the Germans on 19–20 August; had he followed up his initial victory, he could have placed the Germans in desperate straits: as it was, the German commander in East Prussia panicked and urged abandonment of the whole province. Moltke and the Kaiser demurred, sacked the commander, and replaced him with a retired general, Paul von Hindenburg, together with Ludendorff as his chief of staff. Even before the new team arrived in East Prussia, the general staff officer on the scene, Max von Hoffman, had laid the basis for victory. Signals intelligence had made it clear that Rennenkampf planned to remain stationary, so that the Germans possessed a brief window of opportunity to isolate and destroy Samsonov, whose army was advancing north from Poland. Hoffman withdrew most of the forces facing Rennenkampf by rail and concentrated them instead at Tannenberg against Samsonov. By 26 August, Samsonov recognized that his army was in serious trouble, but he determined to stay and fight in the belief that Rennenkampf would move rapidly to his rescue. Rennenkampf, however, failed to advance and on that day German attacks overwhelmed both of Samsonov's flanks; a moderately successful Russian attack in the centre only moved their forces deeper into the net. By 30 August the Germans had destroyed Samsonov's army and captured 92,000 Russians and 400 guns. They now moved east and by mid-September the Eighth Army had chased Rennenkampf out of East Prussia and inflicted heavy casualties on his army as well. The victories established Ludendorff and Hindenburg as national heroes.

Since the Germans wrote the history of the Eastern Front, Russia's defeat in East Prussia has largely obscured its successes elsewhere. In fact, the major Russian effort of 1914 was not directed against East Prussia, but rather against the Austro-Hungarian empire in Galicia. In the south, the Austrians had struck first. Conrad von Hötzendorf, their chief of staff, launched three armies on divergent lines of advance into Poland, where they quickly ran into trouble. The Third Army fell back to its starting point, while the Russians almost cut off the Fourth Army by severing its lines of communication for a time; and although the Austrians eventually fought their way out, they retired in complete shambles to their territory – a retreat that continued across Galicia. In late September, the Russians almost broke onto the Hungarian plain, which might have led to Austria's collapse in 1914, but their advance eventually faltered from logistical difficulties and heavy losses.

Fighting continued on the Eastern Front – which extended for twice the length of the Western Front – through the autumn, as the opposing sides attempted to pick up the wreckage of their failed war plans. By pushing their reserves of equipment and ammunition forward, the Russians posed a significant threat to Austria-Hungary; but in so doing they mortgaged their future, because Russian industry, incompetently mobilized by Nicholas II's bizarre autocracy, proved incapable of restocking what the army expended in its operations. Nevertheless, the autumn campaign was a close-run thing for the Central Powers. Germany had to bolster the Austrians with eighteen divisions and only after desperate efforts were the combined forces of the Central Powers able to fight their adversaries to a standstill in the early winter. Even then, the stinging defeat suffered by Austria-Hungary in autumn 1914 removed its army as a major player on the Eastern Front for the remainder of the war. But the Russians themselves were thoroughly weakened too: they had exhausted their armies and, even more dangerously, their logistical structure. The Ottoman decision to attack Russia in October 1914, with offensives in the Caucasus and raids in the Black Sea, increased the strains even further.

Mobilizing industry for World War I

The failure of the offensives in 1914 resulted in a military stalemate that only sustained attrition could break. Thus the war came to turn, as had the American Civil War, on industrial power and on access to raw materials and the world economy. The Germans possessed an advantage at the beginning in the military potential of their industry, but the Allied blockade denied them access to world markets.

As the fighting increased in intensity, the battlefields required ever greater amounts of weapons and the ammunition to supply the guns, not to mention food, clothing, barbed wire, and soldiers. But the battle fronts caused a steady drain on national manpower at a time when requirements for agricultural and military production demanded increasing numbers of workers. As a result, both sides resorted to the widespread use of women in factories and in professions which would never have considered such employment before the war. By 1918 60 per cent of the workers in British munitions factories consisted of women and virtually every sector in the economies of the democracies as well as the autocracies had come under some form of government control.

In the long run the Allied blockade exercised its greatest influence by putting the American economy at the disposal of the Allies and limiting the Germans to the resources of Central Europe alone. American loans and then entrance into the war furthered that access; German efforts under Ludendorff at the end of 1916 to increase German war production drastically, by contrast, eventually wrecked the economy and contributed to the collapse in 1918. In the end, to paraphrase Napoleon, God was on the side of the bigger industry.

Even heavy work, such as that in the coke and steel industries of the opposing economies, saw the widespread introduction of women into the work force. Here British women coke workers underline that they could do any job that men did.

1915: YEAR OF ALLIED FAILURE

At the end of 1914 Winston Churchill, First Lord of the British Admiralty, wrote a sharply perceptive memorandum for the British cabinet. He warned that the war had settled into a stalemate with little prospect of a breakthrough by either side: the generals would of course try, but would only add to the huge casualties suffered thus far. Churchill suggested that only mechanical means held the prospect for breaking the tactical deadlock, but development of such means would take months if not years. The fighting in 1915 mirrored Churchill's expectations. For the British, the Western Front involved several attacks that extended the heavy casualties suffered by their regular army in 1914; but the volunteers who flocked to the colours at the war's onset were not yet ready, so the French had to shoulder the bulk of fighting in the west in 1915.

Russian prisoners move into German captivity after their defeat around the Masurian lakes in East Prussia in 1914. The traditional view of the opening fighting on the Eastern Front emphasizes Germany's victories in East Prussia. However, at the same time, Russian armies scored great successes against the Austrians in southern Poland and Galicia.

French doctrine still emphasized morale as the most important factor in battle. In the larger sense they were right, but their troops lacked the technology, artillery support, and tactical conceptions necessary to break into and through German defences. In both March and May, the French launched major attacks on the Champagne front, while the British attacked further north. Both offensives caused excruciatingly heavy losses and, in any case, the Germans had constructed second-line defences behind the most important segments of their front. Allied commanders believed that the only path to mobile warfare lay in massive artillery bombardments that would saturate enemy defences and allow attackers to cross the killing zone. What they missed was that lengthy bombardments served to alert the Germans, who then had time to move reserves to threatened sectors. At Loos, in September, the British actually broke through German defences but Sir John French, commander of the British Expeditionary Force, had placed his reserves too far in the rear and the Germans closed the gap before reinforcements could arrive. Further French attacks only added to the casualties: in the course of 1915 over a million Frenchmen were killed or wounded, in return for no significant success.

In the east the situation proved even gloomier for the Allies. In view of Austrian weakness, Falkenhayn decided early in 1915 that Germany must assume the offensive. His aim was not a massive invasion of Russia, as Hindenburg and Ludendorff urged, but rather a limited campaign to damage the Russian army and push the Russians back, so that they would no longer pose a strategic threat to Austria. Along with this limited campaign, the Germans embarked on a sophisticated effort to undermine popular Russian political and military morale (an effort that culminated in revolution in 1917). By making minimal incursions into Russian territory, the Germans did not threaten 'Mother Russia' directly; rather, they exacerbated their opponents' difficulties by forcing the Russian High Command to fight at the end of long and inadequate lines of communication.

The initial German offensive came in Galicia. On 2 May 1915, General August von Mackensen attacked Russian positions between Gorlice and Tarnow, catching them by surprise. Within two weeks the advancing Germans had driven their opponents from Galicia. Russian forces were desperately short of everything; as a Tsarist officer despairingly noted: 'At the beginning of the war, when we had guns, ammunition, and rifles, we were victorious. When the supply of munitions and arms began to give out, we still fought brilliantly. Today, with its artillery and infantry dumb, our army is drowning in its own blood.' In one month, the Germans had advanced almost 100 miles and captured 400,000 Russians.

In July, Falkenhayn ordered Hindenburg from the north and Mackensen from the south to drive Russian forces out of Poland. Ludendorff argued that greater reinforcements would enable him to destroy more Russians, but Falkenhayn refused because of the situation in other theatres. In particular, he wanted to eliminate Serbia – where repeated Austrian efforts to take Belgrade had failed – while the British assault on the Dardanelles posed a considerable threat to the position of the Central Powers in the Balkans and made it advisable to hold back substantial reserves in case of an Ottoman collapse.

The attack on the Dardanelles represented the one strategic masterstroke of the war. It was Churchill's brain-child: the First Lord argued that a successful attack there would force Turkey from the war, open up crucial supply lines to Russia, bring

The Eastern Front saw far greater movement than was the case with military operations in the west. First of all, the force to space ratio was far lower – mainly because the front extended twice as far – which allowed a greater potential for breakthroughs and subsequent exploitation. But of far greater importance was the incompetence of the Tsarist government, which failed to mobilize Russia's industrial potential for the 1915 battles, and the strategy adopted by the Germans – who never directly advanced into the depths of Russia, but rather waged a highly successful campaign to destabilize the Tsarist regime from within, while carrying out limited attacks on the periphery.

Romania and Bulgaria into the war on the Allied side, provide direct support to Serbia, and create a third front against Austria-Hungary. None of these possibilities came to pass because, whatever the campaign's strategic merits, the operational and tactical execution of the venture was abysmal. First, at Churchill's urging, and over the admirals' objection, the Royal Navy tried to force its way through the forts protecting the Dardanelles into the Sea of Marmara in the hope that, once the obsolete Allied battleships had got through, they could attack Constantinople and cause Turkey's collapse. But stiff resistance from Turkish shore batteries combined with mines to thwart the attempt. Now the war office agreed to support the attack with ground forces – the 29th Regular Division and Imperial troops in Egypt – under Sir Ian Hamilton; but planning remained haphazard and the landing forces detailed for Gallipoli received no training in amphibious warfare. Moreover the simplest of questions remained unanswered: was there water ashore? were there roads? what sort of fighting would occur? what were the strengths and weaknesses of Turkish defences?

The campaign began on 25 April 1915, when Allied forces struggled ashore on the Gallipoli peninsula. At the tip, Turkish machine gunners slaughtered British troops attacking from the steamer *River Clyde*. Just up the coast British troops made successful landings against no enemy resistance, but the commanders on the spot had no idea of what to do and displayed no initiative. Their troops gained a foothold but not the heights. Further along the coast, Anzac (Australian and New Zealand) troops mistakenly landed in an area later called Anzac Cove. No Turks confronted them, but the Anzacs advanced too slowly towards the heights looming above. Before they reached the ridge, an obscure Turkish colonel, Mustafa Kemal, arrived; he immediately recognized the position's critical importance and rushed

Anzac (Australian and New Zealand army corps) troops landing on the beaches of what became known as Anzac Cove in the Dardanelles in April 1915. By a stroke of luck, this amphibious assault occurred in an area that the Turks regarded as of little tactical importance, and so they failed to defend the area with significant forces. However, the bluffs overlooking the beaches explain the Turkish confidence – the Anzac troops would fail to scale the heights before the Turks arrived to defend them.

Massive bombardment around the Verdun battlefield had blown the vegetation and topsoil off the countryside by summer 1916. The landscape, looked much like that of the moon. By summer 1915 artillery was master of the battlefield in the west, a role that it never fully surrendered during the war. But in no other battle was it as dominant as at Verdun, where infantry units could spend their entire spell in the trenches and never see an opposing soldier, yet lose 75 per cent of their strength though the endless bombardment.

reinforcements to hold the heights. As Churchill noted in his history of the war: 'The terrible "ifs" accumulate.'

The landing settled into a murderous stalemate in which the killing power of modern weapons made it impossible for either side to break the deadlock. The Turks held the heights, Imperial troops the shore, and neither could shake the other from their defensive positions. In August, the British raised the stakes. After receiving reinforcements, Hamilton's staff planned an impossible night attack from Anzac Cove against the heights, in which Australian and New Zealand troops suffered severe losses, while at Suvla Bay new divisions commanded by General Stopford, who had not led troops since 1882, successfully landed but then sat down in general disorganization to await the Turks. Stopford had not been informed that the heights 4 miles east of Suvla were his objective and by the time he moved, three days later, the Turks were ready. These failures sealed the fate of the Gallipoli campaign and, in the winter, the British withdrew. Nearly half a million Allied troops had fought in the area; approximately half became casualties. As a result of the failure, Bulgaria joined the Central Powers and, in conjunction with German and Austrian troops, eliminated Serbia by the end of the year. The Central Powers thus established a stranglehold over the Balkans.

However, another significant front opened in 1915. The Gallipoli expedition, as well as their own miscalculations, led Italian leaders to believe that the war was almost over and that the Allies would win. In May 1915 they therefore joined the war against Austria. The Italians confronted the problem of breaking Austrian positions in the Alps – one that no army in World War I could have solved – but proved successful only in dragooning large numbers of peasants and throwing the poorest of Italian society into endless unsuccessful offensives against Austrian positions along the Isonzo river. These offences, as much as any in the war, underlined the inadequacies of Europe's military organizations. By November 1918, the Italians had lost over 500,000 dead merely to pin down for three years considerable Austro-Hungarian forces that might otherwise have served on the Eastern Front.

1916: THE KILLING WAR

At the end of 1915 Falkenhayn presented the Kaiser with a strategic memorandum. He indicated that the Reich confronted a massive struggle of attrition against opponents with greater resources and manpower; after surveying the various war zones, he argued that no possibility for a decisive victory existed anywhere. Britain clearly remained the Reich's greatest opponent, but Germany lacked the means to strike at it directly; the French, however, represented Britain's continental sword. Therefore, Falkenhayn proposed a battle of attrition to break French morale, with the fortress city of Verdun as his target. The general staff set in motion plans for the battle, but Falkenhayn did not inform the local commander, Germany's crown prince, that the assault on Verdun was only to lead to attrition. Moreover, Falkenhayn as chief of staff controlled the reserves, and by having the attack move down the right bank of the Meuse, he ensured that the crown prince's forces would not capture Verdun by surprise.

Falkenhayn believed that an unprecedented heavy use of artillery would allow the Germans first to make substantial initial gains at minimal cost and then slaughter all French counter-attacks; he also mistakenly assumed that his forces would be able to maintain their superiority in artillery. Even so, the initial attack came close to success. French commanders had long neglected the sector; only at the last moment did they react to intelligence warnings of a major German offensive. Four days after the opening hurricane bombardment, on 21 February 1916 the Germans captured Douaumont, one of the outer ring of defences, with few losses and for a moment it appeared they might force the French out of Verdun. But the Germans suffered heavier casualties than expected; reserves failed to arrive in timely fashion due to Falkenhayn's cautious policies; and French defenders on the left bank of the Meuse imposed increasingly heavy losses on advancing German troops. Nevertheless, as in August 1914, the French did exactly what the Germans wanted: they decided to defend Verdun at all costs. The day after Douaumont fell, they also brought in their best general, Philippe Pétain.

At the beginning of the war Pétain had been a colonel with little prospect of promotion, for he had espoused the power of defensive war in the modern age, becoming an expert in what most French officers regarded as an arcane art. But after August 1914, Pétain's rise had been meteoric. He arrived at Verdun to find everything in shambles, but commented acidly, on seeing that the Germans had attacked only on the right bank, '[Those gentlemen] don't know their business.' He reinforced French artillery on the left bank, restored shattered morale, and conducted an effective defence of Verdun from his bed as he recovered from pneumonia.

A German 210-mm howitzer prepares for action. The Germans possessed superiority in artillery at the start of the Verdun battle, but their refusal to attack on the left bank of the Meuse negated their advantage.

The battle resulted in a gigantic slaughter, with artillery the butcher and infantry the cattle. A French captain reported after service on Le Mort Homme (high ground west of Verdun) in April 1916:

> I have returned from the toughest trial that I have ever seen…four days and four nights – ninety-six hours – the last two days soaked in icy mud – under terrible bombardment, without any shelter other than the narrowness of the trench, which even seemed to be too wide. The Boche did not attack, naturally: it would have been too stupid. It was much more convenient to carry out a fine firing exercise on our backs…result: I arrived there with 175 men, I returned with thirty-four, several half mad. And a platoon of little chasseurs is in our place. It's the next course; there will be another to serve before long, for the appetite of the ogre is insatiable.

A lieutenant wrote:

> First came the skeletons of companies occasionally led by a wounded officer, leaning on a stick. All marched or rather advanced in small steps, zigzagging as if

intoxicated…It seemed as if these mute faces were crying something terrible, the unbelievable horror of their martyrdom. Two territorials who watched us return wept in silence.

By 1 April German losses reached the point where the Crown Prince recommended that Falkenhayn shut the battle down; misled by optimistic intelligence reports of heavy French casualties, however, the chief of staff declined and instead ordered a last attempt to capture the city. On 7 June the Germans took Fort Vaux, after desperate resistance by its garrison of 100 had inflicted nearly 3,000 casualties on the attackers, and seemed on the brink of breaking through to Verdun. At this point Russian success against the Austrians (see page 282) and the British offensive on the Somme forced Falkenhayn to disengage and rush reinforcements to other fronts, but the battle did not end. With the Germans only 6 miles from Verdun, the French counter-attacked. Using tactics developed by Captain André Laffargue that emphasized small units and decentralized leadership, French forces under General Robert Nivelle recaptured Douaumont and Vaux and almost drove the Germans back to their original starting positions. Verdun had cost the two sides over 400,000 killed and 800,000 wounded – split almost evenly between the opponents.

THE SOMME

As the German attack on Verdun ended, the British army made its debut as a major player on the Western Front. At a conference in December 1915, Allied leaders had selected the Somme for their major effort in 1916, but Verdun limited French involvement. Now, Sir Douglas Haig, the British Expeditionary Force's new commander, confronted two major problems: on the one hand, the German

The first day on the Somme: troops of the 29th Division advance into no man's land on 1 July 1916, the worst day in the history of the British army. During the rest of the battle, however, the British inflicted heavy casualties, because the Germans defended every position and placed most of their infantry in the front line trenches, where artillery decimated them.

defences with deep dugouts and barbed-wire entanglements represented a serious impediment to any attack; on the other hand, the British troops who had volunteered in 1914 and 1915, while filled with enthusiasm, were still amateurs in the business of war. One of Haig's chief subordinates, Sir Henry Rawlinson, argued that, in view of British tactical weaknesses, the British Expeditionary Force should treat its operations on the Western Front as a gigantic siege: by launching a series of distinct, small attacks, British troops would gain experience while using their nation's industrial strength, now fully mobilized, to hammer the Germans. But Haig would have none of it: instead he settled on a great artillery bombardment followed by a massive, tightly controlled infantry attack, advancing at a walk against the wrecked German positions.

British artillery preparations lasted a week; 1,437 artillery pieces fired a million and a half shells on German positions. Then, on 1 July, after reaching its climax, the bombardment halted; along an 18-mile front fourteen British divisions came on in waves. However, the bombardment failed to do what Haig expected: much of the barbed wire remained intact and the German infantry moved smartly out of their dugouts and on a bright, clear day slaughtered the attackers. A German observer reported:

> As soon as the men were in position, a series of extended lines of infantry were seen moving forward from the British trenches…[W]hen the leading British line was within a hundred yards, the rattle of machine gun and rifle broke out along the whole line…Some fired kneeling so as to get a better target over the broken ground, whilst others, in the excitement of the moment stood up regardless of their own safety, to fire into the crowd of men in front of them. Red rockets went up into the blue sky as a signal to the artillery, and immediately afterwards a mass of shells

from the German batteries in the rear tore through the air and burst among the advancing lines. Whole sections seemed to fall, and the rear formations…crumbled under this hail of shells…With all this were mingled the moans and groans of the wounded, the cries of help and the last screams of death…[T]he extended lines of British infantry broke…like waves against a cliff, only to be beaten back.

On 1 July 1916, some 120,000 British infantry went over the top; of those 19,240 were killed, 35,493 wounded, 2,152 missing, and 585 prisoners. Close to 50 per cent of the attackers were casualties – yet in only a few spots did the British gain the first-line enemy trenches.

Quite understandably, but mistakenly, British historiography has focused on the first day's tragedy and ignored the remainder of the battle. The British did not repeat their mistakes, but rather concentrated on more limited attacks that emphasized their artillery superiority. On the other hand, the Germans fought according to Falkenhayn's demands that they hold on to every foot of French territory, counter-attack all British gains, and dominate the forward edge of the battlefield. As a result, German infantry were consistently exposed to the full weight of British bombardments, while their counter-attacks added to a spiralling level of casualties. From 2 July the British inflicted a ratio of casualties close to what they suffered and in some cases they even achieved major successes. On 14 July, a dawn assault by 22,000 men of Rawlinson's First Army punched a hole 6,000 yards wide in German defences; only the failure of their reserves to move quickly prevented a breakthrough.

Given Allied superiority in men and material, such levels of attrition represented a serious drain on Germany's overall position. The *Materialschlacht* – battle of resources – which typified both the Somme and Verdun slowly but steadily drove the German army towards defeat. At the end of August, under intense political pressure caused by military failures, the Kaiser dismissed Falkenhayn and replaced him with Hindenburg and Ludendorff, the latter clearly in the dominant position. Historians have correctly emphasized the misshapen industrial and political policies that Ludendorff would impose on the Reich as contributing significantly to the final collapse, but they have overlooked Ludendorff's recasting of German battle doctrine. In effect the Germans invented the modern battlefield and that invention prolonged the war into 1918. Upon assuming control, Ludendorff recognized that German troops were receiving a terrible beating on the Somme. Unlike most other World War I commanders, he went out to the front to discover at first hand what was actually happening. His memoirs noted that 'it was my duty to adapt myself to [actual conditions]' and, in his fact-finding tour, he demanded that soldiers and staff officers speak their minds and not pass along something 'made to order'. What he learned confirmed his worst fears; the army's tactical approach was maximizing German casualties.

Ludendorff turned the problem over to a group of expert general staff officers with recent battle experience. That group evolved a new doctrine encapsulated in

Wounded Australian soldiers in a trench awaiting evacuation to a hospital during the battle of the Somme. By 1916 medicine had advanced to the point where the wounded had some prospect of survival if they could be brought to casualty treatment stations; but blood transfusions and antibiotics still lay in the future, and death rates remained high.

the manual, *Conduct of the Defensive Battle*, completed in autumn 1916. The changes came too late to affect the Somme, but the new doctrine transformed how the Germans fought in 1917 and 1918. Instead of packing masses of infantry into the front lines, only a thin screen of machine gunners would man forward positions. Then, a series of strong points, increasingly dense the deeper one advanced into the system, would inflict heavier losses on the attacker. Meanwhile, the bulk of the infantry remained out of enemy artillery range to launch local and general counter-attacks on any penetrations. Above all, the new doctrine devolved authority for tactical decisions down the chain of command. Lieutenants and captains on the scene would now make the critical decisions as to whether to retreat, hold, or counter-attack.

Meanwhile, in the east, things had gone relatively well for the Central Powers. After the successes of 1915, Falkenhayn saw no reason to pursue the beaten Russians into the depths of their country. However, his contempt for the Austrians created a dangerous situation. In early 1916 Conrad suggested that the Central Powers knock the Italians out of the war; Falkenhayn turned the proposal down but, without telling the Germans, the Austrians went ahead anyway and siphoned their best troops off from the Eastern Front to attack the Italians just before, in response to desperate French appeals, the Russians launched a major offensive.

Under new leadership, the Tsar's war ministry had finally mobilized Russia's industry, and equipment and supplies began to flow to the front. Now, after successful operations against the Turks in the Caucasus, the STAVKA – the Russian high command – determined on a series of limited offensives, beginning with General Alexei Brussilov's army in the south which would set the stage for larger offensives in the north against the Germans. Brussilov himself was a cut above other Tsarist generals. He planned the attack in great detail and emphasized thorough preparations to his subordinates. They in turn were thoroughly familiar with the Austrian defences, weakened by Conrad's decision to withdraw troops for the attack on Italy.

On 4 June 1916 Brussilov's offensive began, and the Austrians collapsed. Within two weeks the Russians had captured 200,000 prisoners and advanced over 40 miles; Austria again appeared on the brink of defeat. Only by shutting down Verdun could Falkenhayn assemble sufficient reinforcements to bolster his ailing ally, although in fact subsequent attacks by the Tsar's commanders displayed the same lack of preparation that had characterized previous Russian operations. Nevertheless, Brussilov's success convinced the Romanians that Austria-Hungary was collapsing and in August they rashly declared war on the Central Powers. By then, Germany and Austria possessed sufficient forces to smash Romania and gain control of its valuable resources – wheat and oil. Thus, the only strategic result of Romania's entrance into the war was to extend the length of front that the exhausted Russian army had to defend.

1916 had brought success to none of the participants. Verdun had hurt the French severely; the British had failed to make significant gains on the Somme; the Russians were on the brink of a revolution. On the other side, Austria had suffered new defeats and the Germans had experienced a rate of attrition they could not afford. Like punch-drunk fighters, the opponents entered 1917 in a state of exhaustion; but no one could discern an end to the interminable slaughter.

The war at sea, 1914–1918

The opposing navies entered the war with the belief that a massive naval battle would determine the command of the seas. The German High Seas Fleet expected the Royal Navy to establish a close blockade in the Heligoland Bight, where mines, submarines, and torpedo boats could inflict heavy casualties; then the German battle fleet would sortie and destroy the remnants. But the British failed to establish a close blockade. Instead, the Grand Fleet moved to Scapa Flow in the Orkneys and from that base maintained a distant blockade. Smaller units of the Allied navies closed the Channel. In effect, this excluded Germany from world commerce and, as the war continued, the British imposed more stringent limitations on neutral trade. Meanwhile, in the war's first months the Royal Navy cleaned up the fragments of the German navy on foreign station and swept the seas of enemy commerce.

This depressing situation led the Germans to undertake a series of naval raids on the east coast of England. However, by late 1914 the Royal Navy was able to read much of their opponents' ciphered signal traffic and in January 1915 the British battlecruisers caught German raiders at the battle of Dogger Bank. Through a series of mistakes the British allowed the enemy's main force to escape, but they did sink the battlecruiser *Blücher*.

In May 1916, the Germans again put to sea, this time in full force. Admiral Reinhard Scheer brought out the High Seas Fleet, including a squadron of pre-dreadnought battleships which slowed the rest. He hoped to catch a portion of the Royal Navy, destroy what he found, and return to safety before the main British forces came up. However, since the British were still reading German signals, they sortied while the High Seas Fleet was making steam. The German scouting force consisted of five battlecruisers under Admiral Hipper; Scheer had sixteen dreadnoughts and six pre-dreadnoughts. The British had overwhelming superiority: Sir David Beatty, commander of the scouting forces, had six battlecruisers and four super-dreadnoughts, while the main fleet under Sir John Jellicoe consisted of twenty-four battleships and three battlecruisers.

The screening forces encountered each other first on 31 May. Hipper turned south towards the High Seas Fleet, and Beatty pursued. A running fight ensued in which the British battlecruiser *Indefatigable* blew up, followed by the *Queen Mary*. Shortly thereafter, the High Seas Fleet appeared on the horizon. Beatty turned back north on a course straight toward Norway. Instead of recognizing that the British battlecruisers were moving towards a rendezvous with another force – the only explanation for Beatty's course – the Germans pursued. At approximately 6 pm, the Germans sighted the Grand Fleet and, at precisely the right moment, Jellicoe deployed his battle squadrons from column into line. A terrifying weight of shells fell on the High Seas Fleet and only the desperate expedient of turning his entire battle line at the same time saved Scheer from destruction. The Germans misread the situation and turned back in an attempt to reach their bases, and an hour later once more ran into the massed firepower of the British fleet. Scheer again ordered his ships to flee west, this time in greater confusion.

As evening fell, the British had the prospect of repeating the 'Glorious First of June' (see page 208): they lay between the Germans and their bases, had battered the enemy

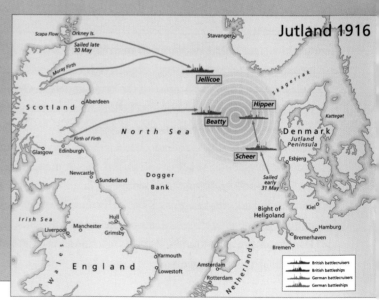

Left: HMS *Royal Oak* in action at the battle of Jutland. Geography blocked the German High Seas Fleet from access to the Atlantic, and within the North Sea superior intelligence allowed the British to follow the moves of their naval opponent, as the approach to contact at Jutland – depicted on the map below opposite – suggests.

severely, and had excellent intelligence. But the British failed to utilize their advantages. The Admiralty did not pass its information to Jellicoe and the captains of the Grand Fleet displayed little initiative – in some cases British battleships allowed German vessels to sail right past them. On the next morning the Grand Fleet rode alone in the North Sea. In percentage terms, the tonnages lost by both fleets were roughly equal, while two German battlecruisers crept back into Kiel with their forward decks awash; what mattered was that the British maintained control over the North Sea.

But if the German High Seas Fleet achieved little, German submarines posed a lethal threat. In November 1914, in response to the British blockade of the Central Powers, Tirpitz announced a submarine blockade of Britain even though the navy had only twenty-nine U-boats in service. A year later that number had reached fifty-four, but due to engineering difficulties the Germans averaged only 1.3 U-boats on station for every one in dock.

Even more astonishingly, Germany undertook its submarine campaign as if the military and economic potential of the United States counted for nothing. In spring 1915 the German consul announced on the front page of the *New York Times* that his country was going to attack and sink the Cunard liner *Lusitania* as it sailed to Britain; it did, killing 1,198 passengers. That action almost brought the United States into the war despite the isolationism of much of the country. Only President Woodrow Wilson's perseverance cooled the crisis until the Kaiser, at least, had the sense to recognize that it

was not in the Reich's interest to add the United States to Germany's enemies and announced an end to unrestricted submarine warfare. Nevertheless, for the remainder of 1915 and 1916 the German naval leadership waged an intense campaign to resume such attacks and, with no thought to US potential, the army's leaders lent their support. At the beginning of 1917 Hindenburg and Ludendorff forced the issue, and the Kaiser caved in. As Ludendorff remarked: 'The United States does not bother me...in the least; I look upon a declaration of war by the United States with indifference!' Germany resumed unrestricted submarine attacks in February 1917 and the United States declared war in April.

Ironically, the Germans had done little to prepare their navy for the campaign; its construction programme continued to favour capital ships. Nevertheless, U-boats represented a greater threat in 1917 than two years earlier. The British Admiralty remained adamantly opposed to convoys to protect Allied commerce until, in spring 1917, losses of merchant vessels began to threaten Britain's economic survival and the prime minister, David Lloyd George, demanded that the Royal Navy introduce convoys. In April 1917 U-boats sank 841,118 tons of Allied merchant shipping; with the introduction of convoys that total fell to 365,000 tons in July and to 200,000 tons in September. By now the threat had returned to manageable levels. Of the great troop convoys that carried a quarter of a million American soldiers to Europe each and every month in the summer of 1918, the Germans hardly damaged a ship.

1917: THE DARKEST YEAR

At the end of 1916 the French replaced Joffre, whose lack of success had destroyed his prestige, with Robert Nivelle. Nivelle had achieved a reputation as an innovator, especially at Verdun, where his success in regaining the territory lost in the first stages of that battle had given him great prestige. Now in charge of the army, Nivelle set about changing its battle doctrine in early 1917, based upon a tactical pamphlet written by André Laffarge (which had also profoundly influenced the Germans). Laffarge's approach aimed at developing decentralized manoeuvre tactics that would allow troops to break into and through the heavy defences of the opposing front line trenches, and the successes at Verdun suggested that he was on the right track. Nivelle proposed a great offensive thrust in spring 1917, using this new tactical doctrine to break through German lines at the base of the great bulge formed by the enemy's positions in France.

However, all these assumptions proved faulty because in mid-winter Ludendorff ordered a withdrawal from much of the bulge. Several reasons explain this decision. Although some saw the abandonment of French territory as a sign of weakness, the shortened front provided the Germans with a substantial bonus of troops, and enabled them to site their new defences with great care, utilizing terrain to support new doctrinal concepts. Finally, the Germans created a desert in the abandoned areas, quite accurately giving their retreat the code name 'Alberich' after the vicious dwarf of the Niebelungen sagas. Ludendorff's retreat removed the operational rationale for Nivelle's offensive. Moreover, the new German system of defence in depth (see page 281) undercut the offensive tactical innovations that the French had made.

In any case, the French army of 1917 was a brittle instrument. Interminable attacks and bloodletting had exhausted French troops as well as the nation. Moreover, the French army had taken execrable care of its soldiers throughout the war: its medical services were an outrage; French generals had been profligate with their soldiers' lives; food was a travesty; and leaves for soldiers were entirely inadequate. Nivelle, perhaps sensing these weaknesses, promised that the coming offensive would break the German army. It did not. Admittedly, the French experienced little difficulty in getting through first line positions but, just as Ludendorff had intended, the deeper they drove, the higher their casualties became. By the end of the second day, 120,000 French soldiers lay dead or wounded and there was little evidence that the survivors had any prospect of breaking through German defences. To complete the disaster, Nivelle refused to halt the offensive once it had failed; like his predecessor, he continued the slaughter.

In response the troops mutinied. At first, a few regiments refused to attack; but soon disorder spread throughout the army and, within a week, large numbers of regiments were displaying the red flag. For the most part the mutineers simply wanted decent treatment – in some cases mutinous troops even continued to man front line trenches – but disorders also occurred in rear areas and, in several cases,

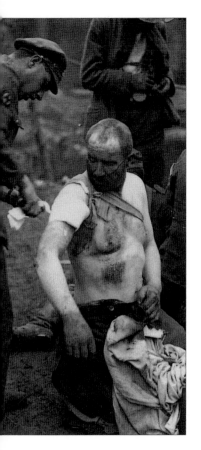

Wounded German prisoners of war being treated at a forward aid station of the New Zealand division during the third battle of Ypres. In this conflict, unlike World War II, all sides showed humanity towards those captured in battle and generally adhered to international law.

drunken soldiers attacked staff officers while others beat up members of the medical service. In Paris defeatists became vocal in their demands for peace.

France trembled on the brink of collapse. Desperate, French politicians turned to Georges Clemenceau, the one politician with the ruthlessness to see the crisis through. In turn, he appointed Pétain to rebuild the army. Clemenceau brought order to Paris and Pétain brought discipline to the army. At least twenty-three mutineers were shot and a further 250 were marched out into no-man's land and annihilated by artillery. But, besides such measures, Pétain visited virtually every division to hear complaints and implemented a thorough-going reform of medical treatment, leave policies, and other causes of grievance. Above all, he made clear that he would husband the lives of his soldiers. Nevertheless, the French army remained incapable of major military operations for the remainder of 1917. With revolution in Russia, and America only beginning its mobilization, the burden of the fighting therefore fell on the British Expeditionary Force.

Little in the historical record suggests that Haig had come to grips with the failures of 1916. The British High Command had left the development of tactics to the various armies that served under it on the Western Front. Consequently, no coherent effort to introduce new approaches, as in the German army, had evolved. Instead, each British army attacked the problem of tactical innovation in its own idiosyncratic fashion; in some cases, in particular Rawlinson's and Plumer's armies, the measures adopted were both realistic and innovative, emphasizing careful preparation, surprise, and deception as well as the considerable artillery strengths of the British army. An attack by Plumer's troops took Messines Ridge in June 1917 through careful operational planning that effectively co-ordinated artillery with the infantry attack and destroyed the German positions in exchange for only light casualties. This success suggests how much the British might have achieved in 1917. However, such an approach would not have resulted in a brilliant break-through on the Western Front, which was what Haig desired. Hence he preferred the bold and unrealistic proposals of his fellow cavalryman Hubert Gough.

Since his first days in command, Flanders had interested Haig as a site for a possible offensive but in 1916 the French pushed the British into the Somme offensive; in 1917 Haig could pick his own ground, however, and he chose Flanders. A sound strategic rationale lay behind the choice, for the U-boat bases in occupied Belgium represented a significant threat to Allied shipping; nevertheless, Haig's plans, like those of 1916, rested in a dream world of Napoleonic war – he expected artillery to pound German front-line forces into submission, then the infantry would create a breakthrough for the cavalry, which would execute a vigorous pursuit of the beaten enemy.

Flanders had been a great primeval swamp until, in the middle ages, its inhabitants had dug a complex maze of canals for draining. August brings considerable rain to the region every year; yet it was precisely this time, and this area, that Haig selected for his great offensive. On 15 July 1917 the British bombardment began and continued for the next sixteen days, wrecking the drainage system completely. On 31 July the infantry went over the top at Passchendaele, near Ypres, and on the next day the rains began. Bombardment and rain soon turned the countryside into a morass of glutinous mud. Moreover, the bombardment fell most heavily on German outposts and left the major defensive positions in the rear largely untouched, so that the initial British attacks gained minimal ground. Nevertheless, Haig, bolstered by his optimistic staff, reported to London that all was well. His chief of intelligence, General Charteris, and chief of staff, Launcelot Kiggell, were particularly willful tools of such deceptions; when the battle had ended and Kiggell was returning to London, he visited the front line for the first time. His mournful comment – 'Good God, did we really send men to fight in that?' – speaks volumes on the leadership of the British Expeditionary Force.

As with the Somme, Passchendaele turned into another grim battle of attrition. On 13 September Sir Herbert Plumer's army attacked on a front of 4,000 yards with a pre-attack bombardment of 3,500,000 shells. But much of the German infantry waited out of artillery range, and their losses dropped significantly compared with the Somme. Nevertheless, Passchendaele was a terrible experience for all concerned. An Australian officer noted after a reconnaissance patrol:

> The slope was littered with dead, both theirs and ours. I got to one pill box to find it just a mass of dead so I passed on carefully to the one ahead. Here I found about fifty men alive, of the Manchesters. Never have I seen men so broken or so demor-

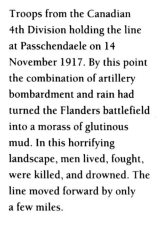

Troops from the Canadian 4th Division holding the line at Passchendaele on 14 November 1917. By this point the combination of artillery bombardment and rain had turned the Flanders battlefield into a morass of glutinous mud. In this horrifying landscape, men lived, fought, were killed, and drowned. The line moved forward by only a few miles.

alized. They were huddled up close behind the box in the last stages of exhaustion and fear. Fritz had been sniping them off all day and had accounted for fifty-seven that day – the dead and dying lay in piles. The wounded were numerous, unattended and so weak they groaned, some had been there four days already.

When Haig finally called off the Passchendaele offensive at the end of October, British casualties had reached nearly 300,000; with French and Imperial casualties included, the allies had lost over 400,000 men, the Germans 270,000. One might argue that the Germans could afford their casualties even less; but such reasoning hardly excuses the unimaginative leadership that sent so many soldiers to their deaths in such conditions.

In November 1917, the British showed that an alternative existed to Haig's leaden approach. Tanks had first appeared on the Somme but, like all new weapons, they had teething troubles. As the battle in Flanders ground to a halt, however, the tank corps commander, General Hugh Ellis, suggested that a tank raid on German positions away from Flanders might achieve a success. Under political pressure from Lloyd George because of the heavy casualties in Flanders, Haig agreed. On 20 November, after a brief preliminary bombardment, British tanks attacked German positions in front of Cambrai. The defenders had no reserves available and the defending divisions were 'Class B', the weakest in the German army. The position collapsed; in one day, at a cost of less than 5,000 casualties, British tanks and supporting infantry gained more territory than the Passchendaele offensive had gained in three months. But there were no reserves available, and efforts to prepare defences were inadequate. Within the week a murderous German counter-attack hit the British positions around Cambrai, for the first time using a new offensive doctrine prepared by Ludendorff and his planners (see page 288), and drove the British back beyond their start line. Haig as well as Ludendorff concluded that the tank was a flash in the pan.

While grinding battles continued in the west, momentous events occurred in Russia. In February 1917, the Tsarist government collapsed; in a matter of days all vestiges of the regime disappeared and, in its place, a hodgepodge of ill-prepared political parties established a provisional republic. To add to the confusion, the Germans allowed the outlawed revolutionary leader, Vlamidir Ilyich Lenin, to cross their territory in a sealed train from Switzerland so that he could return to Russia. Over 1917 and 1918 they kept him and his Bolshevik party well supplied with gold to run a campaign of subversion against what remained of the Russian war effort, for alone among Russian politicians Lenin urged an immediate end to war; he propagated the Bolsheviks' slogan of 'peace and bread', a stance that reflected the needs of his German paymasters as well as his own instincts. With their well-financed propaganda the Bolsheviks undermined the provisional republic and significantly affected the army's morale, while a badly prepared offensive in July fuelled the collapse of discipline among Russian units. That month saw a Bolshevik

Conditions in the front line trenches, particularly during the wet winter months, constituted almost as harsh a burden for the front-line troops as enemy attacks. While medicine had improved considerably over earlier decades, it could not handle the lung and infectious diseases that such conditions encouraged. The state of this Australian communication trench near Messines in Belgium in January 1918 suggests the kinds of hazards that confronted troops in the fourth winter of the war.

coup in St Petersburg fail, but four months later a general collapse of the army and civil government allowed Lenin to seize power.

With the discipline and stamina of the Russian army destroyed, and faced now with German and Austrian demands, the new regime could only follow a path of craven submission. Initial negotiations failed, but a rapid German advance quickly persuaded Lenin that revolutionary rhetoric could not halt military power. In March 1918, with the Germans only 100 miles from their capital, the Bolsheviks made peace at Brest-Litovsk and surrendered the Baltic states, Poland, Finland, and much of the Ukraine. But German ambitions were almost limitless; instead of transferring troops to the west, Ludendorff left substantial forces in the east to grab further territory. By early May the Germans had occupied the rest of the Ukraine, the Crimea, and Finland, and Ludendorff dreamed of a Teutonic empire running all the way to the Urals. The treaty of Brest, and its aftermath, underlined the extent of Germany's territorial ambitions and gave a hollow ring to her subsequent protests about the injustice of the Versailles settlement.

As Russia collapsed, the Germans provided a small group of elite divisions to the Austrians for a new attack on Italy. On 24 October 1917 an Austro-German offensive struck an Italian army already in desperate shape: sustained military failure, the dismal treatment of the troops, and a collapse of national morale had created a situation ripe for disaster. Within a day the front line collapsed in the Isonzo valley at Caporetto, and in some areas the Austro-German advance carried the unheard-of distance – at least in the west – of 10 miles. One German officer (Erwin Rommel) with a reinforced company captured nearly 10,000 Italians over the course of the day. For a while it appeared that Italy would have to sue for peace, but the Germans were incapable of a sustained effort in the theatre, while Austria alone did not possess the strength to knock Italy out of the war. With considerable help from Anglo-French forces, the Italians halted the enemy's advance on the Piave. But the Caporetto débâcle provided one more sign of the desperate straits the Allied cause was now in.

1918: THE YEAR OF DECISION

By autumn 1917 Ludendorff's tactical experts had created a new offensive doctrine – an 'attack in depth' to parallel its successful 'defence in depth' – and over the following winter the Germans intensively reorganized and retrained a small group of elite divisions in these new tactics. Approximately forty 'storm troop' divisions received new equipment, the best NCOs and officers, and a solid dose of training in new concepts. Significantly, all officers, including division commanders, went through the training schools to provide a thorough understanding of the doctrine at all levels. The new approach emphasized delegation of authority all the way down to NCOs and reintroduced manoeuvre on the battlefield, but manoeuvre that remained closely tied and co-ordinated with firepower. Moreover, the new doctrine demanded that German troops gain and maintain the initiative by exploiting breaks in the enemy's line; they must drive as quickly and ruthlessly as possible into rear areas. Tempo was key.

Nevertheless, considerable weaknesses undermined the German position. Outside elite storm troop units, the remainder of the army lacked the equipment, human material, and training to conduct the new form of war. Moreover, the concentration of better NCOs and officers in the storm troops ensured that other units declined precipitously in combat potential. Ludendorff would have to win the war with his few elite divisions before the Americans arrived; if not, the rest of the army could not hold out for long. Finally, while the Germans had admirably thought through the tactical problems of the battlefield, they had little conception of how tactical successes might translate into victory. As Ludendorff replied to Crown Prince Rupprecht, when the latter asked about the operational goals for the spring offensive: 'I object to the word "operation". We will punch a hole into [their line]. For the rest we shall see.' Ludendorff decided to aim the first great blow against Gough's Fifth Army and Plumer's Third Army.

Over the winter of 1917–18 Haig also announced a policy of defence in depth but his headquarters proved incapable of promulgating a consistent doctrine throughout the British Expeditionary Force. In most British defensive positions, infantry still lay in forward positions within range of enemy artillery fire; co-ordination between artillery and infantry remained lackadaisical; and few officers had the training to operate independently once the command structure broke down. Haig

A British Firespit II tank crushes its way through wire obstacles in 1917. The picture underlines one of the major roles of the tank on the First World War battlefield: to destroy the enemy's wire without a prolonged artillery bombardment so that the infantry could come to grips with their opponents. By 1918, tanks were capable of influencing battles in a decisive fashion.

and his staff, however, were oblivious to such weaknesses. On 2 March, the commander of the British Expeditionary Force recorded in his diary:

> I…told the army commanders that I was very pleased at all I had seen in the fronts of the three armies. Plans were sound and much work had already been done. I was only afraid that the enemy would find our front so very strong that he will hesitate to commit his army to the attack with the almost certainty of losing very heavily.

At 5 am on 21 March 1918 the German offensive began; 6,473 howitzers opened up on a 40-mile front with a bombardment that saturated every trench, battery position, and supply dump. At 9.35 am, 3,500 trench mortars added their voice to the bombardment; 5 minutes later, thirty-two divisions advanced; thirty-nine divisions stood in reserve. The Germans launched over a million men in the 'Michael' offensive. Almost immediately the British defences unraveled. By the second day, German attacks had shattered Gough's Fifth Army, although in the

Battlefield tactics in World War I

The World War I battlefield required that the opposing sides develop a number of complex, interwoven tactical schemes before their troops could successfully break through the enemy's defensive positions. The foremost requirement was to develop artillery tactics that could hit targets precisely without 'pre-registration', since any registration fire would only serve to alert the enemy that a major offensive was imminent.

Such capabilities needed detailed aerial photography, a thorough knowledge of artillery ballistics, an ability to forecast reliably the impact of weather conditions on the flight of shells, and an accurate estimate of the nature of the enemy's defensive system. At the same time that the armies were experimenting with artillery tactics they also had to develop decentralized infantry tactics that would allow junior officers and non-commissioned officers to make decisions on the battlefield on their own authority. This was not an easy process, particularly given the strongly hierarchical nature of military organizations. Moreover, the opponents developed increasingly sophisticated weapons that often increased the firepower of the infantry and the artillery and hence made the defence even stronger.

Thus tactics underwent radical changes throughout the war as the opposing sides attempted to gain an advantage over their opponents. The development of new offensive tactics could be negated by a defence in depth (diagrammed below), increasingly dense the deeper one advanced into the system, which inflicted heavy losses on the attacker. This happened to the French during their ill-fated offensive in April 1917. By 1918 the Germans had developed offensive tactics that finally allowed them to break the deadlock on the Western Front – but at such catastrophic costs in casualties that military collapse soon followed.

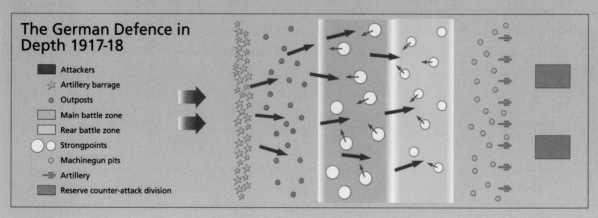

The German Defence in Depth 1917-18

- Attackers
- Artillery barrage
- Outposts
- Main battle zone
- Rear battle zone
- Strongpoints
- Machinegun pits
- Artillery
- Reserve counter-attack division

north Plumer's forces held more effectively in an area where the Germans aimed to achieve major gains. At this point, Ludendorff threw away his last chance to win the war. Despite the fact that the advance in the south was threatening to split the British and French apart, he decided to reinforce the northern drive that had achieved little. There were also upsetting incidents during the German advance: even the highly disciplined storm troops displayed a propensity to loot Allied supply dumps in their path. Even among the best, the bonds of discipline were loosening.

For a time Haig prepared to fall back on the Channel and cut his links with the French, but two crucial things happened. First, Pétain intervened admirably to rush reinforcements from the south; second, the Allied governments, confronting defeat, established a supreme command to control and co-ordinate the overall effort. Ferdinand Foch, a brilliant military teacher and leader, became commander-in-chief of all Allied forces. Within a week his troops had halted the offensive. However impressive their advance, the Germans were the real losers from 'Michael': the new tactics were not cheap, for the attackers suffered heavy casualties; moreover, the Germans gained nothing of strategic or operational significance. Finally, the new lines established after the offensive ended proved harder to defend and required more troops.

Nevertheless, Ludendorff next turned his attention to the northern portion of the British line. He had intended to attack there all along, but because of heavy losses had only eleven divisions available. Again the Germans achieved an impressive tactical success that led nowhere. Helped by the collapse of some Portuguese

The offensives of 1918: the German attacks in the spring (left) and the Allied advances the last half year of the war (right). The German attacks brought unheard-of advances, but no decisive results. These drives captured only territory, but no strategic objectives, and the resulting gains proved harder to defend than the start lines for the attacks. Actually, the crucial result was the fact that the German army destroyed itself in the process of its attacks. The Allied troops advanced against a defeated and collapsing opponent. The bulk of that effort would be carried by the British army – in one of the most successful but least examined campaigns in its history.

units, the storm troopers surged forward; but they lacked the ability to exploit breakthroughs on the operational level, while Haig had sufficient reserves in the area, and after heavy losses the advance stopped short of significant gains. With Allied reserves concentrated in the north, Ludendorff now decided to attack the French on the Aisne. By the end of May, he had concentrated forty-four divisions along the Chemin des Dames. Ironically, three of the British divisions badly mauled in March had arrived in the area for rest and refit. Pétain ordered French commanders to prepare defences in depth, but General Duchesne, First Army commander, disobeyed and so even the British, who knew better, had to pack the front line trenches with infantry.

On 27 May a massive bombardment by 4,000 guns began, with liberal dosages of gas shells intermingled with high explosive. Three hours later German infantry went over the top. The Allied line collapsed and in one day the German Seventh Army crossed two – in some places three – rivers and created a salient with a base of 25 miles and extending 12 miles into Allied lines. The attackers destroyed four divisions holding the line and another four moving up, and their advance continued unabated the next day. Ludendorff had only intended the attack on the Chemin des Dames to pull Allied reserves from the north before a final assault in Flanders. However, success went to his head and he gave the commanders carte blanche, and rushed in reserves to continue the advance despite the lack of a discernible goal. Nevertheless, on the afternoon of 30 May 1918, the Germans reached the Marne, less than 40 miles from Paris. National panic occurred in France as the government again prepared to decamp to Bordeaux.

Pétain, however, refused to panic. Within a day of the start of the battle, he had sixteen divisions moving towards the Marne. He made clear to subordinates and politicians that Anglo-French forces had only to hold for a few more months before the flood of Americans arrived and, indeed, the United States now began to provide substantial aid to their hard-pressed allies. At Château-Thierry on 4 June, US troops gave a good account of themselves and managed, with French support, to halt the German advance. While the Americans proved tactically inept, their enthusiasm and vigour provided a crucial uplift to French morale. Meanwhile, the Germans prepared to launch their fourth offensive. This time they targeted the French to iron out the gap between the salients formed by the spring offensives, but preparations were so badly managed that their opponents had plenty of warning. French commanders in this sector still packed their front line trenches with infantry, where the artillery bombardment could butcher many of them; but at least they were prepared. German casualties were again high with few gains.

It was a battered and weary German army that now prepared for its last great offensive of the war. Out of ideas and almost out of manpower, Ludendorff aimed his last blow at Rheims. He still believed that he could launch a great blow to break the British; nevertheless, for purposes of morale, he code-named his coming strike *Friedensturm* – peace offensive. Forewarned again, the Allies finally prepared a defence in depth and Foch provided eleven divisions as reinforcement. The last German assault proved even more disastrous to the attackers than the Nivelle spring offensive of 1917 had been to the French. The Germans barely got a foothold in the front line trenches, although suffering extraordinarily high casualties, and German morale hit rock bottom. Since launching 'Michael' one million German soldiers had been killed or wounded, the storm troop divisions suffering particularly heavily; and, after four years of slaughter, these losses proved irreplaceable. Morale fell so low that more than half a million German troops deserted. Ludendorff's incessant attacks had ruined the army and brought it to the breaking point, while Allied strength was on a rapid upswing with the arrival of hundreds of thousands of Americans.

The French attacked first. On 18 July their Tenth Army struck the western side of the Marne salient. Within the first hours the attack threatened Soissons, on which German forces in the salient depended for their supplies. In the end, the Germans escaped, but they had suffered their first significant defeat of 1918. Foch now ordered his subordinates to launch a series of attacks to keep constant pressure on the exhausted Germans. The next blow fell in the north. On 8 August 1918 Imperial troops, Australians and Canadians, supported by large numbers of British tanks, struck an unprepared opponent near Amiens. British artillery suppressed enemy artillery, while tanks covered the infantry crossing the killing zone. Six German divisions collapsed – in fact, their collapse was so complete that retreating troops attempted to prevent reserves from restoring the front. British armoured cars got into German rear areas and wrecked reserves' preparations to counter-attack. More than two-thirds of German losses were POWs – a dangerous sign. Ludendorff admitted after the war that 8 August was the 'black day of the war for the German army'.

This stunning British success came with minimal casualties. The tanks were a war winner and, although there were still relatively few, the British could never-theless have launched at least one and probably two more attacks utilizing the tank force as the linchpin; but the senior leadership of the British Expeditionary Force failed to recognize the potential of the weapon. Instead, Haig used tanks in small packets and relied as usual on a combination of artillery and infantry for succeeding offensive operations. Nevertheless, by September the British Expeditionary Force had broken the main German defences in the west, the Siegfried Line, pushed the enemy away from the Belgian coast and almost recaptured Brussels. But they achieved these successes at great cost: ironically, British casualties from August to November 1918 exceeded those suffered at Passchendaele the year before, although the gains were of course on an entirely different level.

As the British drove the Germans back, the French launched carefully controlled assaults in the centre that battered their adversaries, but caused relatively few casualties to the attackers. The first major American offensive came against the Saint-Mihiel salient, southeast of Verdun. US preparations were so inept that the

Opposite: The arrival of American troops in the summer of 1918 at the rate of a quarter of a million every month threatened completely to undermine the precarious balance that existed on the Western Front. But America's lack of preparations, either military or economic, before her entrance into the war made it difficult for US forces to make their presence fully felt on the battlefield. However, Franklin Roosevelt, then Assistant Secretary of the Navy, observed and learned from these mistakes. In the next war, fought while he was President, America's armed forces would be substantially better prepared to handle the crisis occasioned by foreign aggression.

Paul von Hindenberg (1847–1934, left) and Erich von Ludendorff (1865–1937, right) led Germany in the last half of World War I. Propelled to popularity by their 'victory' at Tannenberg (in fact, the work of others), they assumed command of the country's fate in the summer of 1916. Ludendorff would soon develop the concepts from which modern war would evolve, but his strategic and political obtuseness – particularly in provoking the United States to enter the war – ensured that Germany would eventually lose.

Germans believed that it was all a deception effort; nevertheless they were withdrawing in order to shorten their lines at the moment the Americans struck, supported by a force of over 1,000 planes. The salient was recaptured. After Saint-Mihiel, the growing US forces moved against more forbidding enemy positions in the Meuse-Argonne sector, where they ran into formidable opposition: the blood-letting, exacerbated by inadequacies in training, was terrible – albeit no worse than the experience of their Allies earlier in the war.

On the Western Front, defeat stalked the Germans. Virtually nothing remained of the storm troops; defensive divisions fell to 20 per cent of their table of organization; only the machine gunners put up sustained resistance. But the situation in the west was by now the least of German worries. Famine stalked the homeland, while strikes and worker unrest seriously jeopardized industrial production. In September and October Germany's allies, Bulgaria and Turkey, exhausted by four years of war, made peace; by November Allied troops from Salonika had reached the Hungarian plain; while Italian and British troops crossed the Piave and moved on Austria, which signed an armistice on 3 November. A desperate Ludendorff asked the politicians to secure a cease-fire in order to stabilize the deteriorating military situation, but it was too late; Germany had no cards left to play. The appointment of a liberal chancellor, Prince Max of Baden, could not soften Allied demands that Germany abandon the struggle, and the high command's confession that the war was lost unleashed revolution at home. The navy added to the Reich's troubles by deciding to take the High Seas Fleet into the North Sea for a 'death ride' to maintain its honour. The enlisted men, however, brutalized by four years of bad treatment and wretched food, had no intention of dying for the navy's honour. They raised the red flag, and revolution, with the collapse of Bismarck's empire, followed. The emperor abdicated and, choosing dishonour over death, fled to Holland; Ludendorff, disguised by a fake beard, fled to Sweden. Hostilities ceased on the Western Front on 11 November 1918.

THE WAR AT HOME

The war's conduct at political and strategic levels left much to be desired. If Europe's generals had difficulty in adapting to the challenges of war, politicians proved little better. The French government fled Paris for Bordeaux at the German approach in 1914, and remained there for much of the next year. Their pusillanimity hardly placed them in a position to challenge Joffre's strategy. In Britain, Prime Minister Asquith confronted crisis in 1915 due to the difficulties at Gallipoli – Churchill fell from power, while the Conservatives joined the government to form a coalition – but national government did not alter the laissez-faire approach. Only severe national dissatisfaction combined with the escalation of the war brought change in Britain: in December 1916 David Lloyd George executed a palace coup and replaced Asquith, but in the process destroyed his own party and undermined the government's ability to control Haig. In France the army's collapse in 1917 and a weak government finally brought the ferocious Clemenceau to power. In part these political difficulties reflected the pressures placed on societies by the war as well as the tension between generals and civilian leaders.

The Germans selected a different path. Instead of placing direction of the war under a strong political leader, they turned it over to the generals. The rise of Hindenburg and Ludendorff to virtual dictatorship elevated military expediency in every case above political wisdom. The declaration of war on the United States offered the most egregious example of the deficiencies of military rule. But the so-called Hindenburg plan, with its crippling demands on German industry, wrecked a tenuous national unity and eventually the economy. From beginning to end, the German military doubled its bets with no sense of the relationship between means and ends. They aimed at *Weltmacht oder Niedergang* – world power or defeat – and eventually got the latter.

In the east, the two great autocratic empires, Austria-Hungary and Russia, adapted least successfully. Tsarist Russia extended its people to the breaking point by the amateur decisions of its rulers, until military collapse brought down the edifice of civil government and turned the nation over to radical revolutionaries who soon made many Russians long for the ineptitudes of the former regime. The Austrians muddled through the war to the end, undoubtedly surprising themselves as well as their opponents, but their multi-national state then splintered and the fragments still plague the world in places like Bosnia.

The human cost of the war is almost unimaginable to those living at the end of the twentieth century. Over 70 million men were mobilized, over nine million of whom died in service, the great majority of them still in their teens and twenties. Perhaps 700,000 British soldiers perished; the Dominions lost another 250,000. The Italians lost over 500,000 men, Austria 1.1 million, France 1.3 million, and Germany 2 million. The impact of these losses was unequal. Almost half of Australia's eligible men between the ages of eighteen and forty-five volunteered to fight in the war, of whom over one-third were wounded or maimed and almost one-sixth were killed. Almost 40 per cent of all Serbs who served were killed, as were about 30 per cent of all Turks and 25 per cent of all Romanians and Bulgarians. France, Russia, Britain and her Dominions, Austria-Hungary and Germany all lost between 11 and 17 per cent of their soldiers, sailors and airmen. Only United States forces could boast a death rate of under 5 per cent.

In order to fight a war of such duration and intensity, the combatants had to mobilize not only manpower, but also economic resources and financial strength to an extent unprecedented in the history of war. With so many men at the front, nations brought women into the factories and the workplace to an extent previously unseen, and that in turn produced massive social changes throughout Europe in everything from morals to the position of women in society. The granting of women's suffrage in Britain and the United States was but one small indication of the social changes occasioned by the conflict.

Two war loan posters from 1917. The bottom one (from Austria-Hungary) looks to the past for its support, while the German poster (above) couches its appeal with the modern battlefield soldier, obviously a storm trooper, equipped with the accoutrements and weapons of the new age, and with the barbed wire of the trenches very much in evidence.

But the war's greatest impact concerned the death of the belief in progress that had marked western civilization before June 1914. Nothing indicated this collapse in Europe's morale more clearly than the triumph of radical ideologies – poisons of both left and right – in the post-war world. Quite literally, the war led Europe's intellectual elites into a desperate search for simple, clear answers in the grim shadows left by war. Perhaps poetry best suggests the journey that Europe travelled. In 1915, Rupert Brooke, a young British poet, soon to die, penned the following lines:

> If I should die, think only this of me:
> That there's some corner of a foreign field
> That is for ever England. There shall be
> In that rich earth a richer dust conceal'd
> A dust whom England bore, shaped, made aware,
> Gave, once, her flowers to love, her ways to roam,
> A body of England's, breathing English air.
> Wash'd by the rivers, blest by suns of home.
> And think, this heart, all evil shed away,
> A pulse in the eternal mind, no less
> Gives somewhere back the thoughts by England given;
> Her sights and sounds; dreams happy as her day;
> And laughter, learnt of friends; and gentleness,
> In hearts at peace, under an English heaven.

Three years later Siegfried Sassoon, another British officer, penned a very different poem about the Western Front:

> At dawn the ridge emerges massed and dun
> In the wild purple of the glowering sun
> Smouldering through pouts of drifting smoke that shroud
> The menacing scarred slope; and, one by one,
> Tanks creep and topple forward to the wire.
> The barrage roars and lifts. Then, clumsily bowed
> With bombs and guns and shovels and battle-gear,
> Men jostle and climb to meet the bristling fire.
> Lines of grey, muttering faces, masked with fear,
> They leave their trenches, going over the top,
> While time ticks blank and busy on their wrists,
> And hope, with furtive eyes and grappling fists,
> Flounders in the mud.
> O Jesu, make it stop!

The journey that western civilization had travelled over those three years was indeed terrifying. It is not yet over.

CHAPTER 15 *The World in Conflict*

In early 1919 the victorious leaders met at Versailles to settle the enormous issues raised by Germany's defeat, the collapse of Austria-Hungary, Russia, and Turkey, and the spectre of left-wing revolution. In retrospect, they had little chance of constructing a lasting peace, for the fashion in which the conflict had ended ensured the inevitability of another great struggle. Allied troops remained outside German territory at the signing of the armistice, while Germany still ranked as the most powerful European nation in terms of both economic and political potential. Messianic Marxists had seized power in Russia; their ideology removed that nation from European discourse for the next seventy years. Finally, in eastern Europe, a plethora of weak states emerged to replace the great empires. The success of the settlement therefore depended on the willingness of the western democracies to defend its provisions. But the United States withdrew from world affairs after 1920, and Britain displayed a decreasing willingness to involve itself in Europe. This left France to contain a Germany furious at having to abide by the treaty's humiliating provisions; France responded by constructing a massive fortified barrier along its eastern frontier, the Maginot Line.

By the early 1920s many Germans believed that their defeat in 1918 had resulted from political sabotage by Jews and communists within the Reich, while the surrender of territory to Poland, Denmark, and Belgium, the requirement to pay huge reparations, as well as the confiscation of both the overseas empire and the navy, exacerbated a national mood of outrage. The military and political elite responsible for defeat therefore settled the blame for their own errors on the shoulders of the new Weimar Republic, which had accepted the peace terms imposed by the victors. Meanwhile, French pressure increased the weakness of the new democracy: in 1923, with Germany lagging behind in its reparation payments, French troops occupied the Ruhr. The German leaders replied by committing economic suicide; deliberate inflationary policies destroyed the savings of the middle class as well as the trust on which the republic depended for its stability.

PREPARING FOR THE NEXT WAR

After 1923, however, Europe enjoyed an illusory stability dependent on loans from an unreliable United States, and the major powers reduced their armaments. But everything depended on mutual good will and the collapse of the Wall Street stock market in October 1929 heralded grimmer times. American banks called in their loans, causing the collapse of the Central European economy and, as unemployment reached tens of millions, the Weimar Republic dissolved. In January 1933, Adolf Hitler became Chancellor of Germany; he joined Benito Mussolini in Italy, Joseph Stalin in the Soviet Union, and militarists in Tokyo in a common desire to overturn the world order.

Meanwhile Europe's military grappled with the lessons of the Great War. They confronted rapidly changing technology in an era of reduced budgets, as well as the fact that the skies now represented as distinct an arena for operations as the land and sea. The key decisions that determined the course of ground conflict in World War II occurred in the 1920s. The crucial element in German innovation was the appointment of General Hans von Seeckt as commander-in-chief of the army. Confronted with the Allied demand for a reduction of the German army to 100,000 men and 4,000 officers, Seeckt placed the general staff in control of the army and its officer corps. Largely as a result of this, the *Reichswehr* (as the new German army was known) became the only European force to undertake a ruthless, clear-headed analysis of recent military experience. Historians like to argue that generals always prepare to refight the last war. In fact, they rarely do; but Germany between the wars offers the exception. Seeckt established no less than fifty-seven committees to re-examine World War I, with general staff officers chairing committees composed largely of the men who had developed the offensive and defensive doctrines that proved so effective in 1917 and 1918. Consequently, the German army developed a coherent picture of the 1918 battlefield and by 1924 had published a doctrinal manual – *Die Truppenführung* (Troop Leadership) – based upon a thorough and complete assessment of the last war.

On this solid foundation, the Germans innovated during the interwar period: their doctrine emphasized flexibility, initiative at all levels, exploitation, and leadership from the front. This approach was common to German combat officers whatever their branch. As a result, those who developed the armoured force in the 1930s built on a coherent operational and tactical framework and created a conception of armoured warfare that represented a crucial evolutionary development in military capabilities.

In 1933 Hitler initiated a massive rearmament programme. At this stage, however, he did not interfere with the tactical or operational decisions of his army commanders: the crucial players in rearming Germany remained the army's commander-in-chief, Werner von Fritsch, and the chief of the general staff, Ludwig Beck. Looking at Germany's strategic situation in 1933 both came to the conclusion that the Reich required an army consisting largely of infantry divisions, for it lacked the resources, technology, and expertise to gamble on the creation of an all mechanized or motorized force.

Nevertheless, the Germans did conduct armoured experiments with enthusiasm. They already possessed two solid assets – a coherent doctrine and knowledge of British experiments in the late 1920s and early 1930s – and as early as 1934 Beck conducted general staff exercises to examine the potential of panzer corps and armies, well before authorization of such formations. The German army boasted three panzer divisions in 1935, six by 1939, and ten by 1940. These developments took place within a framework in which the Germans thoroughly examined the lessons of peacetime exercises as well as combat experience. For the proposed invasion of Czechoslovakia in 1938, panzer forces were to operate only as divisions; but in Poland and France they functioned as corps and finally in 1941 as panzer groups, armies in everything but name.

Development of army doctrine in the rest of Europe was not so smooth. The British failed to examine the lessons of World War I until 1932 and then, when presented with a highly critical document, the chief of the imperial general staff, Montgomery-Massingberd, buried the findings. Nevertheless, there was considerable intellectual ferment in the British officer corps, with a group of innovative commanders pushing for development of armoured warfare. Two pundits, J. F. C. Fuller and B. H. Liddell Hart, provided intellectual justification for new approaches as well as pressure for reform, and they received a sympathetic hearing from many officers. Even more important, one chief of the imperial general staff, Lord Milne, supported experimentation in mechanized warfare: at a time of financial constraints, he expended scarce resources that made extensive experiments possible.

But in 1934 British advances ran into a dead end. Two things militated against a coherent programme of innovation. First, politicians as well as public opinion resolutely opposed the commitment of British forces to the continent: as a result, up to 1939, British governments provided minimal funding to the army. Second, most officers remained enamoured of traditional regimental soldiering; they regarded officership as a comfortable position rather than as a profession demanding serious study, and regimental tradition combined with the narrow perspectives of the various combat branches to prevent the development of coherent doctrine. Consequently, sports, pig sticking, and fox hunting remained more important to most regimental officers than serious study in preparing for war.

The French devoted some study to the last war, but over their efforts hung the grim experiences of 1914–17, which pushed their planners towards a carefully controlled approach to battle. Termed the 'methodical battle', the doctrine evolved by a small group in the *École supérieur de guerre* (the French war college) seemed to offer an escape from the terrifying casualties of the last war; but it drew upon the experience of only a few carefully selected battles in 1918. Worse still, the army's senior commanders, led by Maurice Gamelin, refused to countenance dissent or new ideas. In the end the French high command proved incapable of imagining or preparing for possibilities beyond its own narrow conceptions.

The case of the Soviet army was perhaps the most tragic. In the 1920s and 1930s – well before any significant threat existed – the regime lavished production from its ruthless programme of industrialization on Soviet military forces. By the mid-1930s the Red Army had evolved into two distinct forces: a mass army of peasants, the traditional form of Russian military power; and an emerging mechanized force, well-equipped and partially trained to execute wide-ranging movement. But in May 1937 Stalin began to purge the Soviet military. Those who supported innovation and change went before NKVD (Stalin's secret police) firing squads, and tens of thousands of officers were, in the euphemism of the time, 'liquidated'.

AIR AND SEA POWER

By the end of World War I, aircraft had appeared in every role that delineates air war today: close air support, reconnaissance, interdiction, air defence, air superiority, and strategic bombing. Ironically, postwar air power prophets displayed little interest in the experiences of the past; rather, they centred their arguments on its future potential. Two schools emerged. In Europe, Italian general Giulio Douhet, and the first postwar commander of the RAF, Lord Trenchard, argued that the strategic bombing of population centres would win the next war. Civilian centres, they believed, were particularly vulnerable: aerial bombardment would soon result in mass rioting, collapse of civil authority, and revolution. Both argued that other forms of air power represented a misuse of its potential. They also believed that armies and navies would prove irrelevant to the conduct of war in the future. Before World War II, Douhet exercised little influence outside Italy; Trenchard, however, played a crucial role in forming the RAF and provided that service with a doctrinal justification that does much to explain Arthur Harris's intransigent leadership of Bomber Command during World War II – although in fairness, Trenchard also cultivated a number of officers who were not fanatical exponents of his views (such as Hugh Dowding and Arthur Tedder).

Another approach, however, evolved in the United States, where Congress would not have permitted the development of a bomber force whose primary target was civilian population centres. The Air Corps Tactical School evolved a concept of air power that aimed at disabling the enemy's economic system. By targeting and destroying crucial industries such as electric power or ball bearings, it was argued, aerial bombardment could bring its enemy's industrial effort to a halt. The theory depended on bombers flying great distances through enemy air defences without suffering serious losses, as well as the ability to hit targets with pinpoint accuracy.

All exponents of air power assumed that the bomber would always get through, so that air defence did not represent a viable alternative. However, the Chamberlain government in the late 1930s forced the RAF to devote significant resources to creating a defensive system based on radar and fighter aircraft. The officer in charge of developing Fighter Command was Hugh Dowding, who possessed a clear understanding of the technology and the organizational requirements to make an air defence system work.

In Germany the Luftwaffe recognized early on that, however well it might perform, the fate of the army would prove decisive for national survival. Consequently, it developed a broadly based doctrine that emphasized co-operation with other services. But the Germans were also interested in strategic bombing. There was nothing inimical in Nazi ideology to attacks on an enemy's population or economy – indeed, the Nazis believed that their values would provide a substantial edge in a conflict involving strategic bombing by assisting the German population to withstand the pressures of such attacks better than any other nation. Significantly, they developed sophisticated navigation and blind bombing devices to

The modern aircraft carrier had emerged in the United States navy by the mid-1930s. A naval arms-control agreement in 1922 between the Great Powers required the US to scrap two battle-cruisers under construction, but their hulls became fleet carriers instead: the *Saratoga* (above) and the *Lexington*. Both provided unprecedented deck space, carrying capacity, and speed (33 knots). Their 'island' structure allowed for maximum freedom to land and launch aircraft.

identify targets under night-time or bad weather conditions – capabilities the RAF did not possess until 1942 – and only technological difficulties in engine development and mistakes in the He 177 programme prevented the Nazis from producing an effective strategic bomber.

Navies paid the least attention to the lessons of World War I. The Royal Navy spent the interwar years preparing for a replay of Jutland. Despite the fact that U-boats had come perilously close to winning the last war, the British devoted little time and fewer resources to countering the submarine menace: the appearance of Sonar ('Asdic' in the Royal Navy), which used sound waves to identify and track submarines, misled British admirals into believing that U-Boats no longer represented a significant threat. The German navy differed little from its rival. German admirals believed British claims to have mastered the submarine, and when rearmament began they set out to create a great battle fleet and undertook minimal steps to build up their submarine force for an assault on North Atlantic trade.

The Japanese and the Americans were more innovative. Both centred their preparations on the Pacific and both thought in terms of a climactic battle between their fleets. While the emphasis in both navies centred on battleships, they also developed fleet carriers and naval aircraft to extend the fleet's hitting range. While battleship admirals still ruled in the Pacific, a new generation of naval airmen, some promoted to admiral, had already gained positions of influence by 1941. They would take naval operations in radical new directions on the outbreak of the Pacific war.

THE ROAD TO WAR

Hitler's appointment as German chancellor on 30 January 1933 set in motion forces that resulted in a new world war. Hitler had a coherent and terrifying ideology that identified the enemies of civilization in terms of race (unlike Marxists who identified their enemies in terms of class) and believed that Germans formed the foremost Aryan race, the creator of the world's greatest civilizations. Germany, Hitler argued, must either seize the territory and resources required for its world-historical mission or sink into insignificance. To the east the spaces of Russia and the Ukraine beckoned; there Germany would realize its destiny by dispossessing the Slavic 'sub-humans'. But above all, Germans, according to Hitler, must beware the insidious danger of Jews and their twin creations: capitalism and communism. Germany must eliminate Jews and their influence from Europe, if the Aryan race were to realize its full potential. Hitler had no intention of restoring the 1914 frontier of Germany, but rather intended a fundamental restructuring of the entire continent. He immediately proceeded to dismantle the Versailles settlement and not surprisingly, given his goals, began a massive programme of rearmament in 1933. In 1935 he concluded a naval agreement with Britain that legitimized his efforts at rearmament and in 1936, despite army fears that France might act, ordered remilitarization of the Rhineland. Europe, however, shifted its attention away from this provocative move. In 1935 Mussolini attacked Ethiopia; under doses of

Terror bombing and the Spanish Civil War

When the Germans intervened in the Spanish Civil War they determined to keep their commitment small and not deploy regular units of the Luftwaffe or the army. Nevertheless they set out to learn from their experiences in the Spanish fighting and consequently were most interested in testing such things as the impact of terror bombing on civilian morale: hence the attack on Guernica – a small town in the Basque country – in April 1937. The attack levelled much of the town, but the international outcry, enthusiastically taken up and fanned by Soviet propagandists, was disproportionate – especially in comparison with what would come in World War II – and the strategic benefits minimal.

Nevertheless, the Germans learned a great deal from the air war in Spain beyond the fact that terror bombing would not necessarily change the military equation to any great extent. They discovered that finding and then hitting targets accurately

would be no easy task. They also learned a great deal about how to provide close air support for the army – a very important lesson that they would take into World War II. Most importantly they mastered the 'finger four' tactics of air-to-air combat. The result was that the Luftwaffe was able to take a broad range of capabilities into the coming war, capabilities that allowed them to influence the course of the ground battle as well as the war in the air.

The Spanish Civil War lasted nearly three years. Its length reflected the fact that neither side possessed the skill to win quickly, but in addition, General Franco, the rebel leader, may have deliberately prolonged the war so that he could kill the maximum number of his enemies.

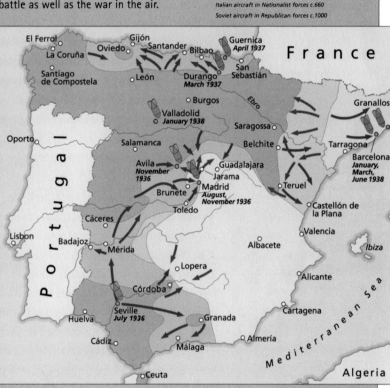

German aircraft in Nationalist forces c.600
Italian aircraft in Nationalist forces c.660
Soviet aircraft in Republican forces c.1000

mustard gas Ethiopian resistance collapsed and the country was annexed by Italy. In 1936 a revolt by Spanish generals under Francisco Franco began a vicious three-year civil war and added another distraction. The European Left feared Fascism as an internal political threat, a belief which the insurrection in Spain only exacerbated; but although British and French socialists vigorously supported the Spanish Republic, they consistently attacked defence spending by their own governments.

Meanwhile, in Germany, the heavy rearmament programmes strained the economy and occasioned tensions between Hitler and his advisers. As a result, Hitler replaced his senior generals and ministers early in 1938 with individuals

German troops enter Warsaw in September 1939. Two great German army groups began their invasion of Poland on 1 September 1939. The combined drive cut Poland in half within a week, aided by the fact that the Poles attempted to defend everything and consequently safeguarded nothing. On 17 September Soviet armies invaded from the east and Poland was partitioned by the victors twelve days later.

more amenable to risks, and within a month he invaded Austria. The British looked on; the French government resigned in protest.

The lack of international pressure convinced Hitler that he could also destroy Czechoslovakia, now surrounded on three sides by the Reich, and over the summer of 1938 he manufactured a crisis to destabilize the Czech Republic and indicated his intention to destroy it. To the British Prime Minister, Neville Chamberlain, it was inconceivable that anyone would court another European conflict after the slaughter of World War I. He therefore set out to appease Hitler – a policy which, ironically, involved Britain more and more deeply in European affairs – and made three personal trips to Germany in September 1938. On Chamberlain's last visit, he, Hitler, Mussolini, and the French premier, Edouard Daladier, dismembered Czechoslovakia to Germany's advantage: despite a generally favourable military situation, Britain surrendered France's most important eastern ally in return for promises of good behaviour from Hitler. Chamberlain defended his policy towards Czechoslovakia on the basis that appeasement of Germany would work and that Britain's deficient defences – for which he held considerable responsibility – demanded a peaceful settlement.

But Czechoslovakia's surrender opened up the flood gates. Over the next six months, the British and French did little to repair their perilous position; the Germans, on the other hand, made major advances in their rearmament efforts while the economic and financial gains from Austria and Czechoslovakia aided their strategic position. In March 1939 Hitler annexed the remains of Czechoslovakia. The lightning German occupation of Prague finally awoke British leaders to the extent of the German threat, and under intense political pressure, Chamberlain attempted to isolate Germany by creating a diplomatic bloc based on the surviving smaller nations of eastern Europe. Because he refused to recognize the inevitability of war, however, he failed to approach the Soviets. It was probably too late in any case; for by inclination Stalin favoured a deal with Hitler, and he now stood to gain far more from the Nazis than from the western Allies.

When Britain guaranteed Poland's independence in March 1939, Hitler was furious. As a result, he underestimated both the political pressures under which the British government now operated and Chamberlain's moral strength; he declared to his entourage: 'I saw my enemies at Munich and they are worms!'. So German political and diplomatic pressure accompanied a massive military build-up on the Polish frontier until on 23 August Hitler and Stalin agreed to a non-aggression pact that made their nations partners in crime. Germany would have its war against Poland, and possibly against the western powers, undisturbed by the threat or reality of Soviet intervention; in return, Stalin would gain eastern Poland, the Baltic states, Finland, and the Romanian province of Bessarabia. Assured of Soviet neutrality, Hitler took the plunge: on 1 September 1939 German troops invaded Poland. Two days later the unwilling British and French governments declared war on Germany.

GERMANY'S EASY WAR

German planning for the attack on Poland had begun in April 1939. The high command designated two army groups with a total of 1.5 million men to annihilate the Poles. Army Group North, under Fedor von Bock, would destroy enemy forces in the 'Polish Corridor' that separated the two parts of Germany; its armoured forces would then drive deep behind the Polish front while the main attack would come from Army Group South under Gerd von Rundstedt. Containing three armies, it would strike into the heart of Poland to reach Warsaw as quickly as possible. The Poles had no clear idea where the main German blow would fall, so instead of defending their heartland they attempted to defend everything and deployed their army in loose formations all along their extensive frontiers.

In a matter of days, German panzer units had broken loose and were approaching Warsaw while, with a combination of interdiction strikes and attacks on the Polish capital, the Luftwaffe made the difficult Polish situation impossible. Within a week the Germans had broken Polish resistance except in Warsaw and chopped the Polish army up into encircled pockets that had little choice but surrender. On 29 September, Stalin (whose forces had invaded just before the Polish collapse) and Hitler partitioned the country. During the whirlwind campaign the Poles had lost 70,000 killed, 133,000 wounded, and 700,000 captured; the Germans only 11,000 dead, 30,000 wounded, and 3,400 missing.

On the surface, the victory over Poland appeared a stunning success. In less than a month, the Wehrmacht had crushed enemy resistance, and by every measurable factor the army had excelled. However, the German army's higher leadership did not estimate the performance of its units as being equal to its standards. For the next several months the high command waged a furious row with Hitler, its leaders arguing that German troops were not ready for major offensive action against the West and that only a massive training programme could correct the deficiencies that had appeared in Poland. Hitler, on the other hand, confronted an economic situation that placed the Reich in a dangerous position. Not only did the Anglo-French blockade, imposed immediately after the declaration of war, drastically reduce imports, but Germany's oil position showed serious strain. In fact, throughout the war Germany's synthetic oil factories, in combination with Romanian oil imports, barely kept up with the wartime demands of the economy and the military: the loss of either would threaten the Reich's strategic stability. In 1939 imports from Romania dried up and, as a result, Germany's oil reserves dropped dangerously low. Consequently, Hitler pushed his generals to launch an immediate offensive in the west before economic difficulties compromised Germany's ability to conduct the war, although in the end bad weather and Allied inaction allowed the Germans to delay their attack until spring.

Meanwhile the Soviets, having occupied eastern Poland and the Baltic states according to plan, attacked Finland in November 1939; but their preparations were poor. Finnish workers did not rally to join the workers' and peasants' paradise, as

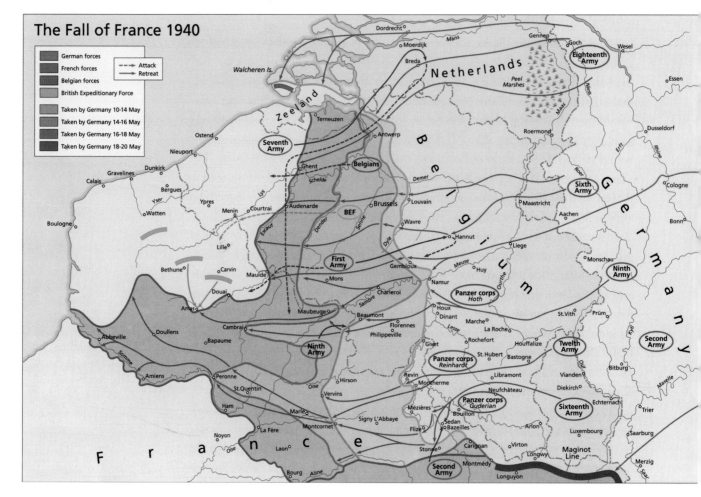

The Fall of France 1940

German forces
French forces
Belgian forces
British Expeditionary Force
Taken by Germany 10-14 May
Taken by Germany 14-16 May
Taken by Germany 16-18 May
Taken by Germany 18-20 May
--- Attack
→ Retreat

The German attack, expected through northern Belgium in a replay of the Schlieffen Plan of 1914, came instead through the Ardennes, with German armour advancing in a powerful fist to the banks of the Meuse by the evening of 12 May. The panzer divisions, each a powerful combined-arms team of infantry, artillery, engineers, and tanks, broke through and crossed the Meuse. French responses always came too late or in insufficient strength, and by 16 May the Germans were in the open, rolling down the defenceless roads of northern France towards the Channel coast.

Stalin expected, but fought furiously at the side of their middle-class brethren. Eventually, although the Finns inflicted heavy casualties on the attackers, the Soviets brought sufficient power to break Finnish defences and force an armistice in March 1940; but the Winter War did serious damage to the reputation of the Red Army, which lost some 200,000 men against only 24,000 Finns – a factor that would figure in Hitler's calculations later on.

Worried by indications of an Allied move to aid the Finns and thereby block export of Swedish iron ore, essential to the German war economy, Hitler decided on a pre-emptive strike against Scandinavia. In April his forces attacked Denmark and Norway. The former fell with hardly a shot. Further north, screened by their battle fleet and aided by treason and incompetence in the Norwegian government, the Germans seized the key Norwegian harbours; at the same time, paratroopers grabbed the major airfields. Only in Oslo fjord did the Norwegians mount a successful defence, where their reservists sank the new heavy cruiser, *Blücher*, and stalled the Germans long enough for the government to escape.

The Royal Navy's response was hesitant except at Narvik, where British warships surprised the Germans, sinking ten destroyers and isolating the mountain troops from reinforcement. Elsewhere the Allies moved too slowly. In the short run, the Scandinavian campaign was a disaster, but it had two results that benefited the Allied cause. First, the political crisis occasioned by Allied reverses in Norway resulted in Chamberlain's fall from power. On 10 May 1940 Winston Churchill became Britain's prime minister. Second, the campaign in Norway crippled the German navy. On 1 July 1940 the German navy had only one heavy cruiser and four destroyers – a force entirely insufficient to cover a cross-channel invasion.

THE FALL OF FRANCE

In early October 1939 Hitler ordered the army high command to draw up plans to seize the Netherlands, Belgium, Luxembourg, and northern France to the Somme. While the Führer and the army high command quarrelled about when and whether to launch 'Yellow' (the plan for a western offensive), Hitler, urged on by Army Group A's chief of staff, Erich von Manstein, pushed for redeployment of several panzer divisions to the Ardennes whence they could bypass the Maginot line and make a lightning attack upon Allied defences along the river Meuse. In February 1940 the chief of the general staff, Franz Halder, though still sceptical about an Ardennes drive, duly placed virtually all the German armour in this area. He and most senior officers also doubted whether mechanized forces alone could achieve a breakthrough on the Meuse. As a result, infantry divisions were ordered to follow up the armoured units. But the panzer commanders retained the authority to act on their own: if they did reach the Meuse and cross it, they could then exploit their success. The new plan envisaged the panzers driving to the Channel coast at Abbeville and trapping the French, British, and Belgian forces with their backs to the sea, while airborne and ground forces overwhelmed the Netherlands, the main

German infantry advances westward in May 1940. After a whole winter of extensive and ruthless retraining based on an accurate examination of the 'lessons learned' during the Polish campaign, the German infantry had become the finest fighting soldiers in the world by the spring of 1940.

army fell on Belgium, and a smaller force (with no armour) engaged the garrison of the Maginot Line.

The Allied conception for the campaign played directly into German hands. Gamelin, the French commander-in-chief, magnified Allied tactical weaknesses by relying on the Maginot line to hold the right and centre, and by shifting Seventh Army, his only reserves, to the far left of the Allied line to link up with the Dutch. He thus removed France's entire operational reserves from the board.

On 10 May 1940 the Germans moved. In the north paratroopers took the key bridges reaching into Holland, so that 9th Panzer Division could break into the heart of the country; airborne troops also attempted to seize the main airfield at the Hague and capture the Dutch government. Although this *coup de main* failed, the rest of the German plan succeeded. With Dutch defences crumbling, the Germans blasted Rotterdam, causing 3,000 civilian casualties, and threatened the Dutch with more such attacks. The Dutch army, which had not fought since 1830, capitulated on 14 May. Meanwhile Bock's Army Group B, consisting of infantry formations, kept up a hammering advance against the Belgians. The seizure of the 'impregnable' Fort Eben Emael by glider-borne infantry added to the sense of bewilderment on the Allied side. Nevertheless, the best units in the French army and the British Expeditionary Force rushed to the rescue: Bock's advance confirmed their assumption that the Germans would replay the Schlieffen plan (see pages 262–4).

They did not. Unhindered by Allied aircraft, nine panzer divisions in three corps advanced through the Ardennes. French and Belgian troops put up minimal resistance and by the evening of 12 May all three corps had reached the Meuse. On the next morning, the northernmost attempted a crossing at Dinant. Seventh Panzer's rifle regiment, led by its commander, Erwin Rommel, established a foothold and, as division engineers bridged the river to get the tanks across, Rommel led his infantry with machine guns to fend off French tanks. By evening, 7th Panzer's infantry regiment had suffered nearly 70 per cent casualties, but the tanks were over, and French defences crumbled. Rommel's success allowed the rest of the panzer corps to cross and exploit a collapsing enemy situation.

In the centre, the panzers failed to achieve a breakthrough and in the south, at Sedan, the force commanded by Heinz Guderian also ran into tenacious resistance. Tenth Panzer Division only got a company across the Meuse with the loss of forty-eight out of fifty assault boats; 2nd Panzer Division failed to get across at all. But 1st Panzer Division's rifle regiment, aided by an infantry regiment, broke French defences and by early evening had gained the western heights overlooking the Meuse. Over the next three days, Guderian expanded his bridgehead and rapidly thrust a knife into the Allied defensive positions. The race to the Channel was soon on. As the panzers reached deeper into French territory the German high command (*Oberkommando der Wehrmacht*) and the army high command (*Oberkommando des Heeres*) became deeply nervous. Nevertheless, on the 17th Guderian subverted an order for only a 'reconnaissance in force' by turning off his radio as the tanks raced westward down the Somme valley and, on 20 May, reached Abbeville on the coast just as Bock's army took Brussels – all exactly according to plan.

The initial Allied response was at first lethargic but soon turned into panic and collapse. The French government sacked Gamelin, but his replacement, Maxime Weygand, arrived with the battle all but over. For the Germans the success seemed too good to be true; as Guderian commented, the battle was 'almost a miracle'. As its troops captured the French ports, nagging doubts tugged at Hitler, the German high command, and the army high command: might not the panzers lose heavily among the numerous water obstacles of Flanders; might not the French recover when the battle turned to France?

Consequently, the German army high command halted the panzers after the capture of Boulogne on the 26th and the capitulation of Belgium on the 28th; senior generals deemed infantry and Luftwaffe sufficient to finish off the broken allied forces in the north. At this point, however, with the German command structure in a jumble, the Royal Navy brought its skill into play to withdraw the British Expeditionary Force, and in skies obscured by smoke over Dunkirk, the Luftwaffe ran into tenacious resistance from Spitfires flying from Britain. By the end of

A French tanker surrenders to German infantry. The French high command had finally established three armoured divisions in 1939, but by then it was too late. In the coming battle, French armoured divisions lacked the doctrine, training, communications, and above all the conception of combined arms to handle the complex and fluid environment within which the Germans fought. As a result the French fought as individuals rather than as units and the resulting discrepancy between the opposing forces was all too obvious.

operation 'Dynamo' on 3 June, Allied ships had brought out nearly 350,000 Allied troops – not enough to save France, but enough to allow Britain to fight on.

The rest of the campaign was a smooth ride for the Germans. After initial tenacious resistance, the French collapsed and the Germans flooded south. A few French wished to continue the struggle, but most were eager for peace. Verdun's aged defender, Marshal Pétain, emerged to sign an armistice with the victors on 22 June. Thus began the long, dark chapter of French collaboration with the Nazi conquerors.

THE BATTLE OF BRITAIN

For most Germans, including Hitler, victory over France spelled the end of the war in the west. In euphoria, they eagerly awaited peace overtures from Britain, but the placatory days of appeasement had ended. Despite opposition from some Chamberlain supporters, Churchill steeled the nation to stand; he calculated that the United States could not indefinitely remain aloof and that Germany and the Soviet Union would not long remain allies. He received confirmation from President Franklin D. Roosevelt in June that the United States would provide weapons and economic support – for a price – and refused to countenance any negotiations with Hitler.

Not until the end of July did the Germans awake to the fact that Britain was still in the war. They then cobbled together an air offensive against the British Isles. If that did not break British will-power they proposed, as a last resort, a cross-channel invasion, operation 'Sealion'. The latter never had the slightest chance of success: the German navy had virtually nothing left after Norway, and neither army nor navy had examined the problems involved in a major amphibious operation. The plans for 'Sealion' called for Rhine River barges to transport the army across the Channel; one can imagine their chances in such waters against British destroyers.

The Luftwaffe faced daunting problems in attacking the centres of British power. No one had ever undertaken a major air campaign and, to add to uncertainties, Luftwaffe intelligence proved wrong in almost every respect about Royal Air Force strengths and weaknesses. Moreover, the Luftwaffe had suffered heavy casualties in France, while the surviving aircraft and pilots had undergone great strain. By contrast, the British possessed an effective force of fighters, the first early warning system, based on radar, and a first-class leader in Sir Hugh Dowding. Dowding deployed his forces to protect all of Britain, while also providing locations in the north where squadrons could refit. He aimed to fight a battle of attrition until autumn's bad weather brought relief. For the first time, the British also enjoyed an advantage they would possess for the rest of the war: the ability to decipher many of the top secret transmissions of the German high command. Based on extensive radio interception

The Spitfire was the crucial fighter aircraft in Britain's battle against the Luftwaffe in summer 1940. It was the equal of the Bf 109, unlike the Hurricane which was inferior, and hence it could contest with German fighters for control of Britain's skies. With the help of radar, British fighters were able to locate the incoming German raids and in a sustained battle of attrition make the Luftwaffe pay an unacceptable price for its efforts.

capabilities, an intimate knowledge of how the
main German encryption devices worked (provided by the Polish secret service), and a
careful study of German radio procedures,
the British built up an increasing ability
to look into the enemy's conduct of the
war. They also proved capable of getting
'Ultra' messages (the intelligence based on this
deciphering) out to commanders in the field without compromise.

The initial German air offensive drove the RAF back from the
Channel, but provided the British with useful experience of Luftwaffe tactics
and operations. On 13 August, the Germans began their duel with the RAF:
attacks in the north failed with heavy losses, but in the south savage assaults rocked
Fighter Command's bases and squadrons. German losses proved devastating,
however, and British resistance remained tenacious. In September, under great
pressure to knock the British out before the weather broke, the Germans switched
their attention to London, a decision that allowed Fighter Command time to
recover. British fighters decimated a massive raid on 15 September so effectively
that the Luftwaffe's daytime offensive ended. The Germans continued bombing at
night, however, and, with their blind bombing system, might have brought Britain
to defeat during the Blitz had British scientific intelligence not discovered the
system and devised countermeasures. Thus ended the war's first strategic bombing
offensive; Anglo-American air forces absorbed few of its lessons.

The Bf-109 was the
finest fighter in the
world when it first went
into production in 1937
and it remained the
Luftwaffe's mainstay
fighter through-
out World War
II as German
industry
steadily improved its
engines and its capabilities.
Although Britain began to
manufacture two comparable
fighters – the Hurricane and
the Spitfire – in 1938, in the
hands of a capable fighter pilot
the Bf-109 remained a deadly
opponent right up to the end
of the war.

WAR IN THE BALKANS

On 10 June 1940 Benito Mussolini declared war on Britain and France. He entered
the conflict with no clear strategic or operational conceptions, except that Italy
must regain Rome's ancient patrimony in the Mediterranean, and with a military
establishment unprepared both intellectually and professionally for modern war.
Throughout the summer the Italians dithered, thwarted both by their own in-
decision and by prohibitions imposed by the Germans, until in September
Mussolini forced Marshall Graziani in Libya to move against Egypt. His forces
reached Sidi Barrani where they entrenched themselves in a series of isolated defensive positions.

In the Balkans, also in September, Hitler moved to secure Romania and its oil by
sending as military 'advisers' a panzer and a motorized infantry division, two flak
regiments, and two fighter squadrons, without informing his Italian allies. In
retaliation, in October, Mussolini attacked Greece without informing Hitler. But the
Italian army had just demobilized its reserves and there were only enough Italians
in Albania – the launching pad for the attack on Greece – to achieve a one-to-one
ratio even before Greek mobilization. Moreover, the ports of Albania proved
insufficient to support major military operations as well as the build-up of Italian

forces. Within a week, the Greeks had driven the Italians back in disorderly retreat into Albania, and British forces began to arrive in both Crete and Greece. Mussolini had thoroughly upset the stability of the Balkans.

Further Italian disasters followed. In November 1940 a handful of British torpedo aircraft struck the Italian battle fleet at Taranto, sinking three Italian battleships and permanently altering the naval balance in the Mediterranean. In December British forces from Egypt raided Italian positions in front of Sidi Barrani. They achieved total success and almost drove the Italians out of Libya. Meanwhile other Commonwealth troops invaded Italian Somaliland, Eritrea and finally Ethiopia: all had fallen by May 1941. At first, the Germans displayed considerable glee at Italy's difficulties. But as Italian disasters threatened to unravel the Axis position in the Mediterranean and Balkans, and perhaps even drive Italy from the war, Germany acted. In February 1941 Rommel led the advance guard of the Afrika Corps to Tripoli. Contrary to his orders, he attacked immediately and soon began to drive the British – weakened by the departure of 60,000 men to Greece – back to Egypt.

To restore the Balkan situation, however, required more considerable effort. To get at the Greeks and relieve pressure on the Italians in Albania, the Germans negotiated deals with the Hungarians, Romanians, and Bulgarians. In March 1941, Yugoslav envoys also signed a treaty of alliance with the Axis, but then a coup by Serb officers overthrew their government. Hitler was furious, and in response ordered the Wehrmacht to beat the Yugoslavs 'down as quickly as possible'. He also ordered the Luftwaffe to wipe Belgrade off the face of the earth. Two weeks later the Luftwaffe complied: round the clock bombing wrecked the Yugoslav capital and killed 17,000 of its citizens. Meanwhile the panzers destroyed Yugoslav defences and overwhelmed the country within twelve days. So swift and stunning was their success that almost immediately the Germans began withdrawing troops for the coming invasion of the Soviet Union. This left thousands of Yugoslav soldiers in mountain areas. Within a matter of months a ferocious guerrilla war flared up that would eventually cost the Germans dearly.

The campaign against Greece also proceeded smoothly. The Greek high command had placed its forces on the Bulgarian border, so the Germans easily outflanked Greek defences through Yugoslavia while the British scurried to escape before the Germans cut their lines of retreat. Most Commonwealth troops got away, albeit without their equipment, but the Greeks facing Bulgaria and those in Albania fighting the Italians went into Axis prisoner-of-war camps.

The fall of mainland Greece still left the British in control of Crete, from which the RAF could threaten Romania's oil wells, as Hitler recognized. Since the British had blown three Italian heavy cruisers out of the water at Cape Matapan, thus eroding what little self-confidence remained in the Italian navy, any assault on Crete would have to come by air. The Luftwaffe's 7th Airborne, the world's first paratroop division, backed by 5th Mountain, executed the attack. The Germans faced considerable odds: not only did the British have nearly twice as many troops on Crete as German intelligence estimated, but the intercepted information from 'Ultra' gave advance warning of a major airborne attack against Crete's three airfields. But British commanders on the scene disregarded this intelligence and deployed their troops to meet an amphibious attack. Nevertheless, it proved a close call for the Germans. The defenders butchered most of the first day's airborne drop on 20 May 1941; only at Maleme did the Germans establish a precarious toehold. However, once the paratroopers won control of that field and the Luftwaffe was able to fly in reinforcements, the balance slowly shifted. The Royal Navy again executed a successful withdrawal, but the Germans gained Crete and the Allies would not be able to attack the vital Romanian oil fields until early 1944 (from bases in Italy).

In achieving their victory the Germans had suffered grievously, losing nearly 60 per cent of their transport aircraft, while their paratroopers had taken such heavy casualties that Hitler refused to authorize further airborne attacks. The British and Americans, however, impressed by the German attack, created airborne units that would play a major role in their later assaults on the continent.

German troops advance over a dynamited road-bed in northern Greece in April 1941. As in France the previous year, German skill at combined arms – as well as the outstanding leadership and training of officers and non-commissioned officers – once again provided the Nazis with a significant advantage over their opponents. The only option for the outnumbered and outfought British and Greek forces was to flee to the south – the British to escape by sea, the Greeks to surrender and endure occupation.

The German invasion of the Soviet Union involved operations over far larger distances than in previous campaigns. Consequently, while the Germans could wish away the logistical difficulties in the first stages of the campaign, by the end of July they confronted almost insoluble problems. Their advance thereafter, particularly in the autumn, drew the Wehrmacht well beyond the point of prudent logistical calculation and confronted its troops with the collapse of their supply system under the ferocious conditions of the Russian winter.

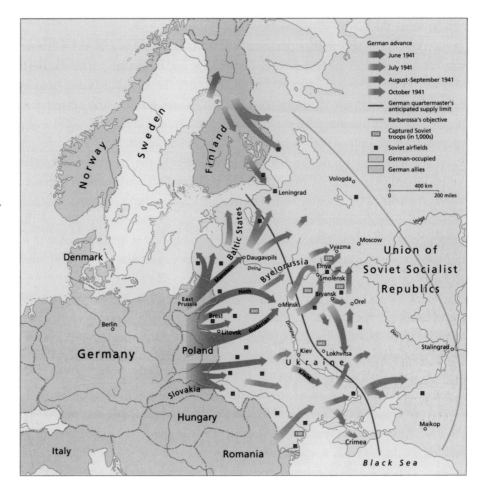

BARBAROSSA

At the end of July 1940, immediately after the fall of France, Hitler determined to invade the Soviet Union. Strategic as well as ideological reasons pushed him east, but the latter dominated his approach to the coming campaign and coloured his assessment of the Soviet Union. The Germans came as conquerors, not as liberators. Hitler aimed to destroy eastern Europe's Jewry as the advance progressed, and to enslave the Slavic peoples; 'special action' commandos (*Einsatzgruppen*) therefore accompanied each invading army group specifically charged to liquidate Jews, communist officials, and other undesirables. Hitler made all of this crystal clear to the senior army leaders, and most of them willingly complied. 'Barbarossa' – as the invasion was known, after a famous medieval German emperor – unleashed an ideological conflict, the ferocity of which Europe had not seen since the religious wars of the seventeenth century.

German military planning for Barbarossa was a mixture of tactical and operational genius with woolly-headed political optimism and logistical imbecility. It was clear that a major factor in the campaign would be Russia's sheer size and that it would be difficult to support advances beyond Riga, Smolensk, and Kiev. Since the Germans had become intimately acquainted with conditions in Russia during World War I, they should also have had few illusions about the weather. Nevertheless Hitler leaned towards attacking the Ukraine and Leningrad while the army high command targeted Moscow in the belief that its fall would automatically result in the Soviet Union's collapse. The high command planners aimed to destroy the Red Army in the border areas, to prevent them withdrawing to the interior, and then (like Hitler) expected the enemy to fold 'like a house of cards'.

The German army was by now a formidable instrument. Two years of unbroken success had honed its generals, unit commanders, officers, and non-commissioned officers. But there were also weaknesses. Only by scraping together military equipment from all over Europe, including Czech tanks, Norwegian mountain artillery, and Belgian, French and British trucks, could the Germans launch an invasion. Moreover, the armoured forces moved almost twice as fast as the infantry, and so repeatedly had to wait – both for fuel and for reinforcements. Finally the Germans embarked on Barbarossa with virtually no reserves. On the other hand, Stalin's actions magnified the German advantages. Purges had decimated his officer corps; pervasive fear hampered initiative at every level; and a cloying belief in 'Comrade Stalin' magnified the unreality of preparations. To the end Stalin believed that Hitler would stick to their 1939 non-aggression pact (see page 304) and, fearful of his political vulnerability, packed frontier districts with Red Army regular divisions and demanded that his commanders never retreat.

Not all Soviet difficulties in 1941 resulted from the superiority of German forces; some were entirely self-inflicted. In the first week of the campaign, tank units were directed to advance on the Germans through a swamp and launch a counter-attack. Their officers obeyed and drove their T-34s, weighing 42 tons each and the finest armoured vehicle in the world at that time, into a swamp.

German assault boats attack across the Dniester. The speed and depth of the Nazi advance provided Soviet forces scant time for recovery. The Red Army's commanders proved incapable of handling the flexibility and swiftness of German operations, while Stalin and the high command refused to prepare the nation for a defence in depth (perhaps through a realization of the Soviet regime's vulnerability in political terms). As a result, the Soviets failed to hold any of the major river lines against the onrush of the invaders.

At 1.30 a.m. on 22 June 1941 the last goods train, one of literally thousands that spring, all filled with raw materials from neutral Russia to feed the Nazi war machine, crossed into German territory at Brest Litovsk. Two hours later German artillery on a 2,000-mile front from the North Cape to the Black Sea opened fire, a shattering series of air attacks began, and over three million Axis troops rolled east. Everywhere they caught the Soviets by surprise. One front line Soviet unit plaintively inquired from its superiors: 'What should we do? We are being attacked.' The reply was: 'You must be insane, and why is your signal not in code?' Later that morning, when the German ambassador presented the Reich's declaration of war, the Soviet Foreign Minister equally plaintively asked: 'What have we done to deserve this?'

Within four days, the Soviets had lost over 3,000 aircraft. On every front, German armour drove deep into Soviet rear areas: Manstein's panzer corps in the north covered 200 miles and reached the Dvina River at Dvinsk in four days. In Army Group Centre's sector, panzer groups under Hoth and Guderian encircled a significant body of Soviet troops at Minsk in the first week (324,000 prisoners with 3,300 tanks destroyed or knocked out); they then swept out to entrap an equally large body of troops near Smolensk by mid-July (another 300,000 prisoners and 3,000 tanks). German successes led Halder to exclaim in his diary in early July: 'It is, therefore, truly not claiming too much when I assert that the campaign against Russia has been won in fourteen days'. Only in the south did the Germans encounter effective resistance; nevertheless, even there, they had neared the gates of Kiev by mid-July.

But by the end of July the advance ground to a halt. The Nazi logistical system could barely provide panzer and motorized infantry divisions with enough supplies to defend themselves, since the lead formations had used up most of their reserves of ammunition and fuel and nothing remained for a push further east. Infantry divisions, slogging forward on foot, lagged well to the rear. Moreover, while the advance had destroyed many of the regular units of the Red Army, waves of Soviet reserve formations hit the spearhead troops. Halder commented despairingly in his diary at the beginning of August:

> The whole situation shows more and more clearly that we have underestimated the colossus of Russia…This conclusion is shown above all in infantry divisions. We have already identified 360. These divisions are admittedly not armed and equipped in our sense, and tactically they are badly led. But there they are; and when we destroy a dozen the Russians simply add another dozen.

During August the forward units of the German army fought to survive; logisticians struggled to control the desperate supply situation; and the infantry marched to catch up. Although they had worked wonders, the field armies had suffered substantial casualties: almost 400,000 by mid-August, over 10 per cent of its total strength. The army high command, the German high command, and Hitler again quarrelled, with the generals urging a drive on Moscow while Hitler wanted to capture the Ukraine, with its grain, and Leningrad, where revolution had originated. As usual, Hitler won the argument and when in late August the Germans finally amassed sufficient supplies to resume their advance, Army Group North surrounded Leningrad, where Stalin's henchman refused either to move civilians to safety or to provision the city for a siege – for to do either would suggest defeatism. Deaths in Leningrad as a result of starvation and disease would eventually exceed one million. Meanwhile in the centre, Guderian's panzer group drove south into the Ukraine. Stalin again refused to countenance any withdrawal; 600,000 Soviet soldiers in the Kiev pocket went into German prisoner-of-war cages. Few survived.

Despite the lateness of the year, these successes at Kiev and Leningrad led Hitler and his senior commanders to throw everything into a massive assault on Moscow. The logistical alternatives were clear: either remain in position on an arbitrary line stretching from Leningrad to the Crimea and prepare for winter, or drive to Moscow and arrive at the Soviet capital with no thermal clothing and no supply dumps. The generals enthusiastically signed on for Moscow.

'Operation Typhoon' began in late September with Guderian's panzer group moving first. The two other panzer groups followed with attacks on 1 October. Within one week, the Germans had completed two more massive encirclements at Bryansk and Vyazma; within two, they had another 600,000 prisoners of war, and a yawning gap existed in front of the Soviet capital. But autumn rains slowed the advance to a crawl and allowed the Soviets to scrape together a last ditch stand. In November, cold weather froze the mud and returned movement to the battlefield,

Soviet prisoners captured by the Germans. By March 1942, 2 million of the 3.6 million Soviet prisoners of war were already dead – 600,000 shot out-of-hand (about 6,000 a day) because they were commissars, communists, or Jews. Of the prisoners captured in 1941 barely 100,000 would return to the Soviet Union alive.

allowing the Germans to make a final attempt to encircle Moscow. Some units came within sight of the Kremlin spires in early December, but the Germans had shot their bolt. Their tanks and other equipment ceased to operate in the extreme cold; front line units were exhausted, fought out, and completely unprepared for winter

The Battle of Moscow

The German victory over the Soviet armies in the Kiev pocket – with well over 600,000 prisoners along with immense amounts of material – brought a feeling of euphoria to the German high command. But even as the Kiev battle burned to its conclusion, Hitler set in motion the next major operation: an offensive against the forces defending Moscow in an all-out attempt to capture the Soviet capital and destroy Stalin's regime before winter closed in.

Hitler's decision received the enthusiastic support of the senior German commanders on the Eastern Front. Field Marshal Bock of Army Group Centre and the army high command were particularly supportive, for they had been arguing since before the campaign began that Moscow was the decisive objective, the capture of which would bring victory. Only the logisticians had some doubts: they were barely able by this point in the campaign to begin building up supply dumps for the winter. Another major drive forward would not only prevent the establishment of stockpiles for winter but also prevent them from bringing up winter fuels and especially winter clothes.

Given German disdain for logistics the choice was simple: advance. At the end of September Guderian, hurrying back from the Ukraine, launched his panzer group against the southern flank of the Soviet armies defending Moscow. On 1 October two other panzer groups jumped off in what the Germans code-named 'Typhoon'. Within the first days German armour had gained operational freedom. So successful was the German offensive that the Soviets only realized that their forces lying to the east of Smolensk had come under attack through British queries (on the basis of 'Ultra' intelligence) and Hitler's announcement in Berlin that the Wehrmacht had launched a great offensive on the Eastern Front. Soviet reconnaissance aircraft soon confirmed that German columns were deep behind the front lines at the same time that communication lines went dead with all of the troops lying in front of Moscow. The Germans were on the way to a devastating double victory at Bryansk and Vyazma that would see over 600,000 more Soviet troops captured, hundreds of thousands killed, and masses of military equipment captured.

But as the Germans were finishing off the twin pockets in mid-October, the weather broke and the annual torrential rains of autumn began. Despite the fact little lay between the Germans and Moscow, the glutinous mud stuck the German armour and motorized infantry in a quagmire. That respite gave the Soviets sufficient time to bring up reinforcements and to appoint one of the few competent general officers to survive the purges, Georgi Zhukov, to command the defences of Moscow. Zhukov hustled forward enough troops to hold off the attackers in the mud and began to assemble a substantial reserve for the climactic point in the battle.

In November the weather began to turn again; cold weather began to freeze the mud and snow replaced the rain. Once again the German high command confronted the problem of whether it should resume the advance on Moscow. The logistical situation carried even more dangerous consequences for the German advance: winter was on the doorstep yet no winter clothes and few supply dumps were

Eastern Front 1 October–5 December 1941

German advance by 16 September
German advance by 1 October
German advance by 3 October
German advance by 7 October
German advance by 5 December
Surrounded Soviet armies

conditions; and the Germans had no stockpiles. On 6 December, the day before Japan attacked the US Pacific fleet at Pearl Harbor, the Red Army counter-attacked and relieved the pressure on Moscow. Hitler's gamble to conquer the Soviet Union in a single campaign had failed.

German troops disappear into a snowstorm just ahead of a tank carrying Nazi insignia (to identify it to German aircraft). However, the German troops lacked the winter gear and their tanks lacked the lubricants essential for winter operations, and in early December their efforts stalled before Moscow (see map, right).

Moscow 5 December 1941

Kalinin · Ninth Army *Strauss* · Third Panzer Army *Hoth (Reinhardt)* · Thirtieth Army *Lelyushenko* · Sixteenth Army *Rokossovski* · Twentieth Army *Rokossovski* · Fifth Army *Govorov* · Rzhev · Volga · Klin · Thirtythird Army *Efremov* · Moscow · Zhukov · Gzhatsk · Mozhaisk · Borodino · Fortythird Army *Sobennikov* · Dnieper · Jarzewo · Vyazma · Bock · Fourth Panzer Army *Hoepner* · Kolomna · Fortyninth Army *Zakharkin* · Tenth Army *Golikov* · Maloyaro slavets · Oka · Saraisk · Fourth Army *Kluge* · Ugra · Juchnoff · Kaluga · Fiftieth Army *Boldin* · Desna · Rosiavl · Tula · Ura · Second Panzer Army *Guderian* · Belev · Second Army *Schmidt* · Oka · Misensk · Orel

0   150 km
0   100 miles

General Franz Halder, the chief of the general staff, suggested, perhaps the freeze would allow renewed mobility and just possibly it would not snow until mid-January.

The senior commanders, and particularly the high command, had clearly lost touch with how rapidly conditions on the front were deteriorating. By mid-November the really cold weather had arrived. German tank crews discovered that the oil in the crank cases of their vehicles had solidified; the only way they could warm their vehicles sufficiently to start the engines was to light tank-fuel fires under the engines, often with spectacular, though unwished for, results. Exhausted by five months of heavy fighting, with their logistic system collapsing, and with precipitous drops in the temperatures, the German troops struggled towards Moscow.

Zhukov refused to commit his reserves until the attackers had shot their bolt. As the German advance ground to a halt within sight of the Russian capital in early December, in heavy snow and temperatures below zero Fahrenheit, the Soviets finally counter-attacked. Everywhere on the Eastern Front Hitler's forces lay in desperate straits — straits that threatened to destroy the entire invading army.

available for the troops. Senior German commanders, however, locked in their belief that the failure to continue the battle on the Marne in 1914 had cost them the war, believed that one final push would gain them Moscow and topple the Soviet regime. They once again discounted the logistical situation and ordered the advance on Moscow to continue. As

CHAPTER 16 | *The World at War*

In December 1941 and January 1942 the German army in the east lay marooned in a series of fortified areas, nicknamed 'hedgehogs', around the main centres of communication and teetered on the brink of collapse. Nevertheless, upon hearing of Japan's entry into the war (see page 333) Hitler rashly declared war on the United States on 11 December, a decision that sealed Germany's fate. The navy actively encouraged the move while the army and air force displayed little interest in the issue, since their attention remained absorbed on the Eastern Front, where Soviet armies had just begun a powerful counter-attack against Army Group Centre. The Soviets eventually fell short of a major success, because Stalin refused the advice of his most successful general, Georgi Zhukov, to concentrate on a single front. Consequently the Red Army sought victory in all sectors, and failed.

When the fighting died down in mid-March the two sides were completely fought out, but Hitler believed that Germany must finish off the Soviet Union before America's potential told. By this point, he had assumed direct command of the German armies and most of the senior officers who had won the victories of 1939–41 had retired. In April 1942 Hitler decided that his forces would stand on the defensive in the north and centre while in the south they would launch an offensive to gain the oil of the Caucasus. However, he remained unclear about whether the troops should drive into the Caucasus to capture the oil or whether they should capture Stalingrad on the Volga to block the northward movement of that oil. Throughout the campaign he was to vacillate between these two approaches.

The Soviets moved first, but their attack on Kharkov in May turned into a disaster, destroying all reserves on the southern front. The Germans then attacked in the Crimea, where Manstein's Eleventh Army broke all remaining Soviet positions. The main offensive began on 27 June: striking west at Voronezh, the Germans established a blocking position and swung down the Don. This time Soviet forces gave way – there would be no more encirclement battles – and behind the panzers, Romanian, Hungarian, and Italian troops moved forward to guard Army Group South's lengthening flank, since the Germans lacked sufficient troops of their own for the task.

By late July, German forces had swept forward to the Don and a month later had reached the Volga. On 13 September a ferocious assault hit Stalingrad, which sprawled for 12 miles along the west bank of the river, and for the next two months the city became the Verdun of World War II. Block by block German troops of Sixth Army drove the Soviets back towards the Volga and by mid-November had taken most of the city, albeit with huge losses in men and material. Meanwhile the Red Army fed enough fresh troops into Stalingrad to keep the fighting going, but kept most of the reinforcements flowing into the theatre in reserve for a great

German infantry with mortars move out across the moon-like landscape of Stalingrad. Beginning in late August 1942, the Germans attacked Stalingrad block by block, but casualties mounted and the battle sucked in troops from both flanks, leaving the overall German position along the Volga increasingly vulnerable. By early November, even though they had captured 90 per cent of the city, the German forces were exhausted.

counter-attack. Unlike Soviet offensives the previous year, Stalin aimed for a limited goal: the destruction of Sixth Army.

Hitler was trying to deal with the Axis collapse in the Mediterranean (see pages 322–4) when the massive Soviet counter-attack, 'Operation Uranus' with 1 million soldiers, 13,000 guns and almost 900 tanks, caught the Sixth Army by surprise. Launched on 19 November 1942, the spearheads met behind Stalingrad four days later, trapping over 200,000 men in a classic 'Cannae' manoeuvre (see pages 48–9) that (in other circumstances) would have appealed to the Prussian general staff. Reassured by Göring that the Luftwaffe could supply Sixth Army, Hitler ordered General Friedrich Paulus to hold and await relief while Erich von Manstein, promoted to field marshal for his victories in the Crimea, assumed control of relief efforts. The German counter-attack came close to Stalingrad, but Paulus declined Manstein's order to break out without Hitler's concurrence, and the Führer refused.

In December the Soviets launched another attack, underlining how much the balance in the east had shifted. A massive offensive against Italian and Hungarian armies along the Upper Don caused their complete collapse. This Soviet success shut down the airlift to Stalingrad and Paulus surrendered on 31 January 1943. In all, the battle of Stalingrad may have cost the Germans more than a million men killed, wounded, missing, and captured – nearly one-quarter of their strength on the eastern front. It also threatened all of Army Group South. Throughout January and February Manstein confronted catastrophe: he barely got First Panzer Army out of the Caucasus, while Seventeenth Army remained on the Kuban Peninsula because Hitler demanded a launching pad for the 1943 summer offensive. The Soviets continued their advance and threatened to cut Army Group South off by reaching the Black Sea west of the Crimea but, lacking a coherent focus to their advance, they overextended themselves. Manstein quickly perceived the Soviets' vulnerability and in late February and early March dealt them a devastating counter-thrust, inflicting heavy casualties on their forces and even regaining Kharkov before the spring rains caused a temporary halt.

THE MEDITERRANEAN AND ALLIED STRATEGY

While millions of Nazi and Soviet troops fought on the Eastern Front, in North Africa the British faced only a few demoralized Italian units (see page 311) reinforced by a German corps commanded by Erwin Rommel. Although consistently outnumbering their adversaries, the British suffered a series of humiliating defeats that reflected an army that learned too little and too late from its battlefield experiences. Rommel by contrast displayed a coherent and effective approach that emphasized initiative, speed, and exploitation until in July 1942 his troops reached El Alamein, only 70 miles from Alexandria.

Anglo-American strategic planners, like their Soviet counterparts, had come to recognize the crucial importance of industrial production. From summer 1940 the British and Americans emphasized the mobilization of industry, manpower, and

Soviet infantry counter-attacks at Stalingrad in November 1942. The Soviets held on to enough of the city to pin the Germans down. Their attack on the flanks positioned them to win one of the great victories of World War II.

resources to prosecute the war; the Germans, on the other hand, maintained a 'guns and butter' economy until 1942. By then, they were well behind in harnessing all available resources for war, as well as being vastly outranked by the industrial capability of the Allies. Hitler's armaments minister, Albert Speer, performed miracles in the second half of the war, but by 1942 the Germans had lost the race: the American economy was coming on line and undreamed of production levels would soon flow from US factories. As a British historian of the Combined Bomber Offensive has noted, by 1944 American factories were turning out four-engine bombers 'like candy bars', while by 1944 the main US battle fleet in the Pacific was larger than all the other navies of the world combined.

Faced with declarations of war by both Japan and Germany in December 1941, President Roosevelt and his advisors chose a 'Germany first' strategy and called for a cross-channel invasion in 1943 to attack Hitler's empire directly. The British chiefs of staff argued that sufficient forces were not yet available and that the western powers should allow another year of war in the Mediterranean and in Russia to grind German power down. Such differences threatened to unravel Anglo-American strategy, but Roosevelt stepped in and ordered his commanders to co-operate with the British in a major operation in the western Mediterranean.

The ensuing operation, code-named 'Torch', targeted Morocco and Algeria to squeeze Axis forces from the west; but just before 'Torch' began the British attacked Rommel at El Alamein. Churchill had responded to earlier defeats in North Africa by replacing most of the senior commanders in the Mediterranean, and entrusting Eighth Army to Bernard Law Montgomery. Whatever his faults, Montgomery was a great motivator, trainer, and realist. However, unlike William Slim in Burma (see page 337), he never possessed the time to correct the tactical deficiencies of the troops he commanded, and he therefore determined to make the Germans fight a battle that played to Eighth Army's strengths: as a result, El Alamein was a battle of attrition rather than movement. Moreover, he displayed a considerable ability to adapt to actual battle conditions until his superiority in men and equipment told. On 23 October, with some 230,000 men and 1,030 tanks, Montgomery attacked the 100,000 men and 500 tanks commanded by Rommel. On 3 November the Afrika Corps began its retreat and did not stop until it reached Tunisia.

As Montgomery pursued the Germans, on 8 November American and British forces landed simultaneously at several points in French Morocco and Algeria. The French put up considerable resistance but eventually surrendered, and the Germans decided to create a fortified redoubt in Tunisia. The decision to reinforce North Africa was one of the worst of Hitler's blunders: admittedly, it kept the Mediterranean closed for six more months, with a negative impact on the Allied shipping situation, but it placed some of Germany's best troops in an indefensible position from which, like Stalingrad, there would be no escape. Moreover Hitler committed the Luftwaffe to fight a battle of attrition under unfavourable conditions, and it suffered losses that it could not afford.

German observers watch for approaching British tanks. The Germans in North Africa in 1941 and 1942 repeatedly selected strong defensive positions and then allowed the British to destroy themselves with futile attacks upon their well-entrenched adversaries.

The North African campaign, which lasted to May 1943, had important consequences for the Allies too. On the one hand a tactical defeat at Kasserine Pass provided the US army with a grim warning about its deficiencies; on the other, as the US military had feared, it prevented a cross-channel invasion in 1943. Instead a conference of senior Anglo-American political and military leaders at Casablanca in January 1943 determined that Sicily should be the next objective. Allied forces landed successfully there on 10 July and by 17 August had overrun the entire island, although the German forces opposing them managed to escape. The invasion of Sicily finally energized the Italian king to remove Mussolini. Marshal Badoglio, a man notable for his military incompetence, attempted to negotiate Italy's way out of the war, but his lack of resolve allowed the Germans to strengthen their forces in the peninsula. The Allies failed to cross over to the mainland until early September. After a few nasty moments at Salerno, they drove north to Naples where their advance came to a glutinous stop in the mud of the Apennines, but most of Italy remained in German hands.

The inability of Allied forces to dislodge German forces south of Rome caused severe disappointment. In February 1944 the Allies got amphibious forces ashore at Anzio, catching the Germans by surprise, but failed to take advantage of the situation. As Churchill put it, the Allies had expected to throw a wildcat ashore but instead had come up with a beached whale. Only in May did the Allies break the stalemate in Italy: spearheaded by Free French infantry who crossed terrain that the Germans regarded as impassable, they closed on Rome and threatened the German

Erwin Rommel (1891–1944) was a commander who led from the front, and on innumerable occasions his presence both inspired his troops and provided him with a sixth sense of what was occurring on the battlefield.

Tenth Army. But the US commander, General Mark Clark, decided that the glory of Rome's capture should go to American troops, and the Germans escaped. The Allies next drove the Germans north of Florence over the summer, but Italy had by then become a backwater theatre.

THE BATTLE OF THE ATLANTIC

The successful defence of the sea lines of communications on which Britain and the United States depended for the projection of military power as well as for economic production constituted the most important victory of World War II in the west. In 1939 neither the Royal Navy nor the *Kriegsmarine* had expected a great U-boat war against commerce: a minuscule U-boat fleet – never more than fifty – inflicted heavy, but not significant losses on British convoys in the war's first year. Control of French and Norwegian naval bases after 1940 greatly aided the Germans, but still the U-boat fleet grew only gradually, partially due to the *Kriegsmarine's* continuing emphasis on battleship construction. Moreover, during this period the Royal Navy gained the cypher keys that enabled British signal intelligence to break German naval codes on a continuing basis. Consequently, the rising tide of merchant losses to U-boats in the first half of 1941 dropped dramatically in the second half.

At the end of 1941, the Germans introduced a new complexity into the encoding system, depriving their intended prey of vital intelligence, while Hitler's declaration of war on the US led U-boats to strike at commerce along the east coast of the United States. Inexcusably, the Americans refused British advice and repeated every mistake their Allies had made – no convoys, no black-outs, no radio silence. The result was a slaughter. In spring 1942, after the Americans introduced proper procedures on the east coast, Admiral Karl Dönitz, commander of the U-boats, switched his attacks to the Caribbean where defences were just as lax. The Germans, however, made crucial errors. Hitler kept many boats in a defensive role to protect Norway and North Africa and to operate against Allied shipping in the Mediterranean; Dönitz overcontrolled the boats on station, thereby robbing his

The routes of convoys SC-122 and HX-229 between 6 and 22 March 1943, and their plight on 15 March. By 1943, better-trained and more numerous Allied naval forces in the North Atlantic, supported by long-range land-based air power and improved technology, had reached rough equality with their tormentors. In April and May 1943, the balance shifted drastically in the Allies' favour and the U-boats began to suffer catastrophic losses in their attacks on convoys. Victory in the battle of the North Atlantic constituted the most important strategic achievement of the western Allies during World War II.

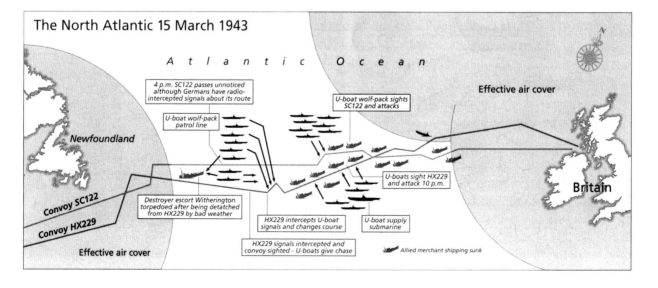

The North Atlantic 15 March 1943

Atlantic Ocean

4 p.m. SC122 passes unnoticed although Germans have radio-intercepted signals about its route

U-boat wolf-pack patrol line

U-boat wolf-pack sights SC122 and attacks

Effective air cover

Newfoundland

Destroyer escort Witherington torpedoed after being detatched from HX229 by bad weather

U-boats sight HX229 and attack 10 p.m.

Britain

Convoy SC122

Convoy HX229

HX229 intercepts U-boat signals and changes course

U-boat supply submarine

HX229 signals intercepted and convoy sighted – U-boats give chase

Allied merchant shipping sunk

Effective air cover

subordinates of flexibility and increasing the risk that plans would be intercepted; and the German staff was so small that it eventually lost contact with the larger picture. As one opponent remarked, Dönitz pursued 'an eighteenth century way of war in a twentieth century age of technology'.

Despite the fact that hundreds of U-boats now operated in the Atlantic, the situation in 1943 swung to the Allies' advantage. Production of merchant vessels and escort ships in American dockyards surpassed losses, while Allied defences improved. Long-range aircraft reached out deep into the Atlantic, leaving few areas untouched by aerial surveillance, while the tactics and technology available to defenders advanced significantly. Finally, at the beginning of 1943, the British regained the ability to penetrate the U-boat message traffic. The battle of the Atlantic culminated in spring 1943. In March U-boats sank 627,000 tons of merchant shipping; in attacks on convoys SC122 and HX229 by forty submarines, the Germans sank twenty-one vessels for the loss of one U-boat. But in the last week of April, when forty-one U-boats assaulted convoy ONS5, the attackers sank twelve merchant ships but lost seven submarines with another five severely damaged. In May the Germans lost forty-one U-boats with hardly any successes, leading Dönitz to pull his boats from the Atlantic. The Allies had won the battle.

A damaged German U-boat, hit by depth charges and strafed by a United States navy plane, sinks as members of the crew prepare to abandon ship. By late 1943 the U-boats had become the hunted rather than the hunters.

THE AIR WAR

No other aspect of the Allied war effort has occasioned more controversy than the Combined Bomber Offensive. Until February 1942, when Arthur Harris took over Bomber Command, British efforts to attack the Reich's economy and cities proved a dismal failure. His aircraft devastated Cologne in a thousand-bomber raid in May, but enjoyed few successes over the remainder of the year. Nevertheless, Harris provided strong leadership and a steadfast belief that area bombing would eventually break enemy morale. In 1943 Bomber Command nearly lived up to Harris's expectations: in the spring it blasted the Ruhr and at the end of July it destroyed Hamburg, killing 40,000 of the city's population. Speer warned Hitler that if Bomber Command achieved similar effects on five or six other cities, German morale would entirely collapse.

However, Harris's forces failed to achieve another Hamburg for the rest of 1943 and in late autumn they turned on Berlin. That campaign came close to wrecking Bomber Command because German defences, particularly night fighters, proved increasingly effective and the length of the flight to targets deep inside Germany magnified the vulnerability of British bombers. The disastrous raid against Nuremberg in late March 1944, where the attackers lost 105 aircraft, mostly to enemy fighters, forced Harris to abandon attacks against remote targets.

While the British bombarded the Reich at night, in June 1943 the Americans began daylight attacks on German industrial targets. American air strategists believed that large formations of well-armed B-17s could fight their way through German defences without heavy casualties. But the German fighter force represented

1944: a B-24 from the United States Fifteenth Air Force takes a direct hit from German anti-aircraft fire. The fuel explodes, no one survives, but the formation continues on its course.

a far more formidable opponent than the Americans had calculated: in August sixty bombers were lost in attacks on Schweinfurt and Regensburg, and sixty more two months later in another raid against the ball-bearing factories of Schweinfurt. Throughout the summer and autumn the Americans lost 30 per cent of their crews every month and, although they also imposed heavy losses on the Luftwaffe's fighters, the second Schweinfurt catastrophe forced the Americans to abandon unescorted raids deep into the Reich. However, early in 1944 a true long-range escort fighter, the P-51 'Mustang', became available and the US Eighth Air Force again struck targets in the heart of Germany and began a terrifying war of attrition against the Luftwaffe until, in May, the German fighter force finally broke.

By themselves, the 2.6 million tons of bombs dropped on 'Fortress Europe' did not win the war. Nevertheless, they had a significant impact on German morale, and that impact in turn explains why the Germans expended so many resources on the V-1 and V-2 programmes – resources that the Strategic Bombing Survey estimated would have allowed production of 24,000 more fighter aircraft in 1944 alone. Furthermore, approximately 12,000 heavy anti-aircraft guns and half a million soldiers participated in the task of throwing huge numbers of badly-aimed shells into the skies night after night, all to reassure the Reich's population. Most important of all, the daylight air offensive gained air superiority over Europe, a prerequisite for a successful cross-channel invasion. The attack on the French roads and railways proved crucial for the ground battle in Normandy, while destruction of the Reich's synthetic oil production further lamed both the Wehrmacht and the Luftwaffe. Finally, the systematic bombardment of the transportation network over the winter of 1944–45 (see page 332) broke the German war economy and explains why there was no last ditch defence of the Reich. Purchased with the lives of 158,000 flying personnel (and of perhaps 650,000 civilians), the Combined Bomber Offensive made an essential contribution to Allied victory.

THE EASTERN FRONT 1943–44

Soviet successes and German counter-attacks in early 1943 (see pages 321–2) had left a great bulge or salient around Kursk, between Orel and Kharkov, and Manstein convinced Hitler that destruction of Soviet units in the Kursk salient would stabilize the front. However, the Führer delayed the start of the offensive until German forces reached peak strength. North of Kursk Model's Ninth Army eventually possessed three panzer corps with 900 tanks; in the south Manstein held four panzer corps with over 1,000 tanks; and the Luftwaffe concentrated 2,500 aircraft for the offensive, code-named 'Zitadelle'. But when ready, the Germans ran into a fully prepared opponent. The Soviets intended to catch the German assault in a colossal web of defensive positions, stretching up to 200 miles, and only then launch their armour. Moreover, their intelligence sources picked up both the day and the hour of the intended German attack – dawn on 5 July 1943 – and so allowed Soviet artillery to fire the greatest pre-emptive barrage in the history of warfare: hundreds of guns and mortars pounded the German forces as they prepared to advance. Within two days the German efforts had stalled and the Soviets now

V-1 and V-2: The vengeance weapons

Although it was clear by the late 1930s that the project to develop long-range rockets would prove inordinately expensive – and produce weapons of no great accuracy – the German army funded the effort. By 1942, as British bombers began to inflict serious damage on German cities, the V-2 (for 'vengeance weapon') became a crash programme; at the same time the Luftwaffe came up with the V-1, a pilotless aircraft powered by a ramjet. However, neither system possessed any degree of accuracy: hitting an area the size of southern England was the best they could do. The cost of the 'vengeance weapon' programmes approached one quarter of the Manhattan Project that developed the atomic bomb – an enormous outlay considering that the payload was less than a fifth of that carried by a Lancaster bomber.

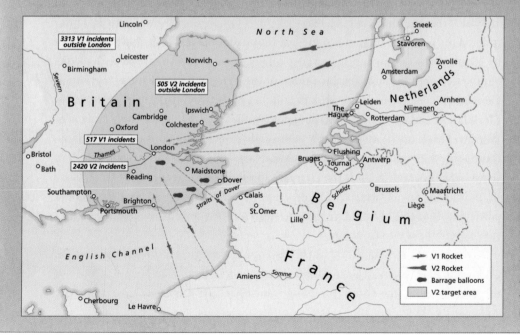

V-1 attacks on England were launched from northern France, while V-2 rockets were fired from sites – sometimes mobile platforms – in western Holland: in both cases, the target was London. Although neither weapon possessed much accuracy, the V-1s nevertheless possessed considerable psychological impact (the V-2s less so, although they were virtually indestructible). In the end they merely proved a nuisance and had little impact on the Allied conduct of the war, but they wasted a huge amount of Germany's resources.

committed their tank armies. At Prokhorovka, to the south, on 12 July over 1,000 tanks clashed and a massive Soviet counter-attack followed.

Kursk proved that the Red Army had acquired formidable skills at the operational level of war. They had also mastered deception – *maskirovka* – so that, from the end of 1942, every major Soviet offensive took the Germans by surprise. After the victory at Kursk, Stalin committed 2.6 million men, over 51,000 guns and mortars, 2,400 tanks and assault guns, and 2,850 combat aircraft on a 400-mile front between the Pripet Marshes and the Sea of Azov. They first retook Kharkov and then at the end of September, as Army Group South's left flank unravelled, entered a desperate race with the Germans for the Dneiper. The Soviets thus regained the critical agricultural and industrial portions of the Ukraine. To complete the catalogue of German disasters, the Red Army also reached the Black Sea and isolated Seventeenth Army in the Crimea.

The arrival of the October rains gave the Germans a respite, but winter allowed the Red Army to operate again, this time with 4 million troops and over 4,000 tanks, with US four-wheel and six-wheel trucks aiding the advance by providing logistical support. By May 1944 they had reached the Carpathians as well as the frontiers of Hungary and Romania, while attacks elsewhere pried the Germans from their positions around Leningrad and recaptured the Crimea (destroying the German Seventeenth Army).

In late spring the Soviets fed the Germans bogus intelligence indicating that the next major Soviet attack would come against Army Group South in preparation for a drive into the Balkans, while in fact the Red Army built up its forces opposite Army Group Centre. Stalin bided his time until after the Anglo-American landings in Normandy and then, on 22 June 1944, just three years after the launching of 'Barbarossa' (see page 315), Operation 'Bagration' (named after one of the heroes of 1812–13) began, aimed at the heart of the German line around Minsk. Hitler ordered his troops to hold out to the last round and the last man, and so they did: by 20 July Army Group Centre had been totally destroyed, with seventeen divisions annihilated and fifty losing half or more of their strength. On that day a group of German officers, dismayed by Hitler's conduct of the war, made an attempt on his life. It failed, and the Red Army kept on for another month to reach the Vistula near Warsaw. There, on 29 August 1944, Stalin called a halt. The Polish underground – thoroughly anti-Communist as well as anti-Nazi – had risen, and it made excellent sense in Stalin's eyes to allow the Germans to destroy his enemies in Poland before he moved in. Soviet armies had advanced far enough west so that they could participate in the kill, should Anglo-American forces win an overwhelming victory that carried them into Germany.

In the meantime, Stalin set about achieving his strategic aims in the Balkans. On 20 August 1944 Soviet artillery pounded German and Romanian positions north of the Danube delta, the latter crumbling immediately. It was more than a military collapse, for three days later the Romanians abandoned the German alliance and

The battle for the Razdelnaya Station near Odessa in April 1944. By then, the Soviets' combination of firepower, manoeuvre, and effective battlefield weapons with numerical superiority had altered the tactical balance on the Eastern Front entirely in their favour.

within a week most of Romania was under Soviet control with Romanian forces now attacking the Germans. Hard on the heels of Romania, Bulgaria quit. Nevertheless, German troops in Greece and Macedonia had time to escape and reknit a front in Hungary. But even the Hungarians were desperately trying to abandon the sinking ship; though the Nazis nipped an anti-German coup in the bud, by November the Germans and the remnants of the Hungarian army were fighting in the suburbs of Budapest. The Soviets had now gained territorial control over much of what became their empire during the Cold War.

VICTORY IN THE WEST

The most complex military operation of the war was the Allied landing in France in 1944. The failure of a seaborne raid on Dieppe in 1942 demonstrated that seizing a port at the start of the invasion would prove almost impossible; the invaders would need to bring all their landing gear with them. The venture would therefore require not only air superiority, but also the controlled movement of troops, equipment, and supplies ashore over beaches. Only in 1944 did the Allies possess enough landing craft and logistical support to make such an operation possible. By January 1944 the high command for Normandy was in place, with the American Dwight Eisenhower in overall charge and the British Bernard Montgomery commanding the ground forces during the initial phase. Upon arrival in England, Eisenhower and Montgomery recognized the inadequacy of the proposed landing force of one paratroop and three infantry divisions: those numbers were increased to three paratroop and five infantry divisions. The former would guard the invasion's flanks while the infantry seized the shoreline over which the great logistical build-up would proceed.

In France, Rommel put his restless energy to work in preparing the defences. Unlike other German commanders, he recognized that the invaders must be stopped on the beaches or the war was lost. But considerable confusion existed among the Germans: Gerd von Rundstedt, in overall command of western Europe, adopted a fundamentally different approach from Rommel, while Hitler retained personal control over the deployment of the armoured reserves.

At dawn on 6 June 1944 a force of some 6,500 naval and transport vessels, protected by 12,000 aircraft, brought the invaders to Normandy. Only at 'Omaha' beach did the defences seriously delay the attackers; elsewhere the Germans reacted slowly and hesitantly. For much of the battle, Hitler and the German high command remained convinced that further landings would occur around Pas de Calais – another victory for Allied deception efforts – and on the first day, the Allies got 177,000 men ashore. But now local German forces proved grimly tenacious and atrocities occurred: on 7 June, for example, troops of the Waffen SS division *Hitlerjügend* massacred nearly a hundred Canadian prisoners of war and drove their tanks over the bodies. On the eastern side of the battle the British and Canadians failed to break the outnumbered enemy or gain access to the plains beyond

Rommel's arrival in France as Inspector of Coastal Defences at the end of 1943 resulted in a massive programme to construct barriers between the low and high water lines on the French coast. Here, German soldiers working on the beach obstacles run for cover as an Allied reconnaissance aircraft sweeps over at low altitude. In June 1944 these obstacles would force the Allies to land their forces in Normandy at low tide.

By 1943 the combined production of the Allied war economies had reached the point of overwhelming superiority over that of Nazi Germany. Nevertheless, the campaigns to regain the territories lost to the Wehrmacht in 1940 and 1941 proved protracted and costly. With attacks from four directions – from the east, from the west, from the south, and from the air – German defeat was inevitable, but the very length of those campaigns allowed the Nazis to continue their crimes against humanity into the spring of 1945.

Normandy. In the west the Americans captured Cherbourg, but then bogged down in the bocage country. During June and July a massive battle of attrition, reminiscent of World War I, consumed vast quantities of men, equipment, and ammunition. But eventually, while Montgomery's persistent attacks pinned German armour in the east, the Americans levered the enemy away from the coast and on 31 July captured Avranches. From there, they could have enveloped the entire German line; instead they headed west into Brittany. Hitler, however, played into the Allies' hands by ordering a counter-attack at Mortain. 'Ultra' (see page 311) warned the Allies, and their air and ground forces stopped the Germans cold, while American armoured forces finally turned east to threaten the whole German position in Normandy. Meanwhile, on 15 August, Allied forces effected another successful landing on the Mediterranean coast of occupied France.

The campaign now turned into a wild pursuit to the German frontier. Montgomery argued for a narrow advance into the Reich – under his command, naturally – but Eisenhower pursued a broad front strategy, although he provided Montgomery with most of the necessary supplies. On 2 September the British liberated Brussels; two days later they captured Antwerp with its dockyards undamaged. But then Montgomery stopped the advance in preparation for operation 'Market Garden', designed to outflank the German defences by an attack through the Netherlands and capture of the bridges across the Rhine at Arnhem.

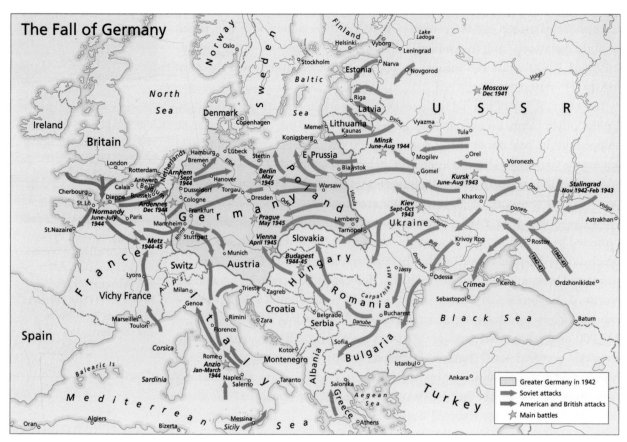

The Fall of Germany

As a result, the Germans recovered, their Fifteenth Army escaped into Holland and managed to close off access to Antwerp. Nearly two weeks later, 'Market-Garden' began. However, the British 1st Airborne failed to secure Arnhem; supporting armour advanced lethargically; and the plans fell into German hands in the first hours of the attack. This failure ensured that the Germans would be able to hold on to their western borders until the winter, and it confronted the American and Commonwealth forces with the unpleasant prospect of dislodging the Germans from difficult terrain and prepared positions at a time when their own formations had suffered heavy casualties and lacked the reserves to allow burnt-out divisions time for rest and refit. Moreover, the destructive power of the Allied air forces had wrecked France's logistical infrastructure and road network, making the supply of Allied forces on the German frontier difficult until access to Antwerp was restored in late November.

THE END IN EUROPE

Nevertheless, by autumn 1944 Germany stood on the defensive on all fronts. Its enemies menaced the gates of the Reich while air attacks pounded German industry and cities. Yet the Germans hung on in a mood somewhere between fanatic determination and desperate resignation. As many put it: 'Enjoy the war, for the peace will be hell.' The Germans had indeed much to fear: the extermination camps continued their grim work largely undisturbed until the autumn of 1944 and most Germans realized that their country had committed unspeakable crimes for which they would be called to account. For the time being, however, tenacious resistance combined with appalling weather to keep the Allies at bay.

Then on 16 December the Germans struck at weakly held US defences in the Ardennes; they aimed to separate the British and Canadian forces in the north from the Americans in the south, and to recapture and destroy Antwerp. The American line buckled and in some areas collapsed; moreover, the only reserves available were two airborne divisions. They were immediately rushed to shore up the flanks – the 82nd to the north side of the growing German bulge, the 101st to Bastogne. There, the 101st put up an epic resistance: for a time the Germans surrounded the town, but the 101st's control of the crucial road junction added to the attackers' problems because they had only enough fuel to get half way to Antwerp. They never came close. The Allied high command of 1944 was not that of 1940; its response was smooth and swift. Patton's Third Army was on the road north even before its commander received orders to support US forces in the Ardennes. Bad weather had played a major role in the initial German successes, but when it cleared, Allied tactical air forces inflicted heavy casualties and by the end of December the Germans had been stopped and began to fall back. The battle of the Bulge destroyed the Reich's last operational reserve.

Meanwhile, Allied air forces, strategic as well as tactical, registered notable successes against the German transportation network. By December railroad

Dresden after British and United States bombers attacked the city in mid-February 1945. The resulting fire-storm killed more than 30,000 civilians. An angel on the cathedral surveys the wreckage of what had been one of the most beautiful cities in Europe.

loadings had fallen to 60 per cent of normal and by February 1945 the capacity of marshalling yards was down to 20 per cent of normal. As a result, production of military equipment and ammunition almost completely ceased. There would be no 'Twilight of the Gods' death struggle for, without the tools of war, the Germans had no capacity to resist.

The end was not slow in coming. In mid-January 1945 Russian armies attacked in the east. East Prussia, Pomerania, and Silesia fell to a hurricane of violence and revenge; terrible killing and suffering occurred wherever Soviet soldiers trod. The Germans now reaped the whirlwind of the ideological war they had sown in 1941. The Red Army closed on the Oder and its commanders halted for the last push on Berlin. Meanwhile, the western Allies finally broke loose. In the north, British and Canadians moved to the Rhine and prepared a carefully planned blow across the river. In early March, the Americans reached the Rhine and German resistance collapsed: at Remagen they captured the Ludendorff bridge intact, rushed as many troops over the Rhine as possible, and joked about Montgomery's apparently superfluous preparations. By April, in the west, Allied armies could drive where they wanted: over the north German plain, the Ruhr, Bavaria, even into Austria. In the south, the German forces in Italy surrendered. In the east, the Soviets slammed across the Oder and into Berlin. In his wretched bunker, one of Europe's nightmares ended as Hitler blew out the roof of his mouth on 30 April. His commanders surrendered unconditionally a week later.

JAPAN'S EXPANSION

Perhaps the greatest indication of America's strength was that, besides its role in Africa and Europe, it also conducted a relentless struggle against Japan. Japan and the United States had been on a collision course from the early decades of the twentieth century, but American immigration and tariff policies combined with Japan's ruthless conquest of China to create tensions that worsened throughout the 1930s. By closing their markets during the depression, the western powers encouraged aggressive Japanese policies towards the Asian mainland and helped Japanese militarists to gain power. In 1931 Japanese army units seized Manchuria without Tokyo's authorization. Six years later that army initiated an undeclared war against China, and Japanese troops soon controlled China's coastal regions and most of the important Chinese cities, leaving a trail of atrocities in their wake.

Japanese ambitions, in spite of limited resources, proved almost boundless. Ever since her great victory in 1905 (see pages 252–6), Japan's Imperial Defence Plan had identified Russia as the major threat. Now, even as the war in China sucked in its forces ever more deeply, the Japanese army also initiated a series of incidents along the Manchurian frontier to test the Red Army, until in August 1939 Soviet forces commanded by Georgi Zhukov annihilated a reinforced Japanese division at Kalkhin Gol on the Mongolian border. This resounding defeat persuaded the Japanese that the Red Army was not an easy mark. But France's collapse the

Japan's attack on the warships anchored at Pearl Harbor (Hawaii) in December 1941 brought the United States into the war with a vengeance. However, the spectacular tactical success masked a major strategic disaster, for the Japanese entirely missed the targets that really mattered: Pearl Harbor's repair facilities and the great petroleum farms which would underpin the United States Navy's war in the Pacific for the next year.

following year offered new prospects, although US forces in the Philippines represented a great question mark. Could Japan risk moving against the European colonies in Southeast Asia, while leaving a major American base on the flank of the advance? In June 1940 the Japanese occupied the northern portion of French Indo-China and in September signed a ten-year treaty of military and economic co-operation with Germany and Italy. On 13 April 1941, however, to protect its northern flank during the anticipated war with the western powers, Japan also signed a non-aggression pact with Russia. The United States made no response, but when the Japanese extended their control to the southern provinces of Indo-China in July 1941, President Roosevelt acted. Moved by China's plight and fearful of Japanese designs, the US declared a general embargo on trade with Japan, which was immediately supported by the British and the Dutch. Dependent on the US for 80 per cent of its oil imports, Japan faced an intolerable choice: either war, or the surrender of all its mainland gains since 1931 (America's terms for the resumption of trade). So the Japanese leaders devised a plan to conquer Southeast Asia and thereafter establish a defensive perimeter around their gains which would bring any counter-attack to a standstill. Aware that inferior resources precluded any chance of outright victory against the US, they nevertheless hoped that a long and costly war would sap American will and facilitate a compromise peace.

The Americans, unaware of all this, confronted the possibility of war with equanimity. As *Time Magazine* suggested shortly before the outbreak of hostilities: 'A vast array of armies, of navies, of air fleets were stretched now in the position of track runners, in the tension of the moment before the starter's gun.' In the early morning hours of 7 December 1941 such comfortable assumptions came crashing down at Pearl Harbor, Hawaii, headquarters of the US Pacific fleet. A Japanese air attack, launched entirely from carriers, sank five US battleships, damaged a sixth, and destroyed three cruisers and nearly 200 aircraft. Nevertheless, the Japanese made a number of mistakes. The surprise attack on Pearl Harbor united Americans as no other action could have done. Moreover while loss of the battleships appeared devastating, these ships were of World War I vintage, while no carriers were in harbour. Finally and most seriously, the Japanese failed to drop a single bomb on the power stations and great oil storage tanks that surrounded the harbour. Had they also concentrated on these targets, they would have forced the US navy to base its ships in San Diego for the next year and a half.

Pearl Harbor was a harbinger of the disasters that soon befell the colonial powers in southeast Asia. America's defence of the Philippines was a disgrace; the British did no better in Malaya, where they lost two capital ships in December 1941 and 130,000 troops at Singapore in February 1942; and the Dutch had lost their empire in Indonesia by March. Burma was occupied between January and May, driving British-empire forces back to the borders of India. In the first sixth months of war, Japan achieved its goals even faster and at less cost than its most optimistic plans had estimated, with a minimum commitment of ground troops and minimal losses.

Sailors from HMS *Prince of Wales* wait to abandon ship off Malaya in December, 1941. By moving into the Gulf of Siam, beyond cover of land-based air support, Admiral Sir Thomas Phillips placed his ships in an impossible situation. The sinking of the *Prince of Wales* and *Repulse* by Japanese aircraft underlined that battleships could not survive in a hostile environment unless protected by air power. Phillips went down with his ship.

Japan's luck began to run out in May 1942. In the Coral Sea, the first battle in which opposing surface fleets never sighted each other, the Americans sank one carrier, damaged another, inflicted heavy casualties on the Japanese air groups and prevented the Japanese from landing on the southern shore of New Guinea. Meanwhile the Americans had managed to break the Japanese navy's codes, and their intelligence (known as 'Magic', and as useful as the 'Ultra' information intercepted from the Germans – see page 311) revealed that the Japanese were trying to create their strategic perimeter with dangerously dispersed forces. While one force sought to attack and occupy certain Aleutian islands off Alaska, another – with four aircraft carriers – aimed to take Kure and Midway islands in the central Pacific, while a third patrolled the waters between as a strategic reserve. The Japanese had devised an intricate plan to mislead the Americans, but 'Magic' revealed the truth. The climactic moment in the Pacific war saw American dive bombers arrive over the three Japanese carriers near Midway at the precise moment the latter turned into the wind to launch decks full of loaded and fuelled aircraft. Combat air patrols of 'Zero' fighters were at deck level and anti-aircraft guns depressed to handle a torpedo aircraft attack. In moments, the Japanese carriers were seas of flames, and all had to be abandoned. By the battle's end they had lost a fourth carrier. The balance in the Pacific irrevocably shifted to the Americans.

In August 1942, the United States made its first offensive move in the Pacific. The 1st Marine Division landed on Guadalcanal, an island in the Solomons. Despite a devastating setback at the battle of Savo Island, where the Japanese sank four heavy cruisers at night, the Americans hung on. For the next nine months fighting raged on Guadalcanal and in the waters of the Solomons; major hostilities also occurred in New Guinea as Australian and American troops slogged through the jungle to drive the Japanese back from Port Moresby. In both campaigns the Allies failed to win a decisive victory, but slowly and steadily ground the Japanese down.

In Europe the Americans had often minimized the political factors in Allied strategy. In the Pacific, however, US domestic politics resulted in a division of the offensive against the Japanese empire. General Douglas MacArthur's record in defending the Philippines had not been impressive; yet his political connections were such that Roosevelt dared not bring him back to Washington to conspire with the Hearst Press and Republican Party. Consequently, it seemed safer to leave him in the Pacific. As the senior American officer, he could claim command in a unified theatre, but the navy was not about to put MacArthur in charge of its forces. The result was a compromise: MacArthur would direct the southwest Pacific theatre, and Admiral Chester Nimitz, the senior naval commander, ran the central Pacific theatre.

While MacArthur drove the Japanese back in New Guinea in late summer and autumn 1943, the navy launched its drive across the central Pacific. By this point new Essex class carriers began arriving at Pearl Harbor; at 27,000 tons, with a top speed of 32 knots and 100 aircraft, they represented a major increase in hitting

American carriers in the Pacific, such as this Independence class, followed by an Essex class, possessed unmatched striking power by 1944. Launching aircraft equal or superior in performance to those flown by any air force in the world, with the aid of supplies received from bases over thousands of miles away, the carriers could attack and destroy any target they chose.

Kamikaze Attack, painted from memory by Richard Gibney, who served with the US marines. Japan's response to overwhelming American superiority at sea and in the air was to launch 'kamikaze' pilots. These volunteers flew their aircraft on suicide missions directly into their targets, maximizing the damage done by the bombs, the ammunition and the fuel remaining on board. Consequently, American naval casualties in late 1944 and early 1945 began to rise dramatically despite the fact that Japan had no navy left.

power. Moreover, US shipyards were producing them at the rate of nearly one a month, as well as turning out Independence class light carriers (11,000 tons) almost as fast. These vessels supported the F6F 'Hellcat' fighter, which finally proved superior to the 'Zero', ensuring that Japan could not defeat the Americans either at sea or in the air.

JAPAN'S DEFEAT

Nimitz's first move came against Tarawa in the Gilbert Islands. There, the navy and marines made a number of mistakes: the bombardment was too short, the marines misestimated the tides over the barrier reef so that assault troops had to cross 700 yards of open water under fire, and communications broke down. Tarawa was a bloody shambles, leaving 1,000 marines dead and 2,000 wounded; but the experience taught the Americans a great deal. In early 1944, when the next blow fell upon the Marshalls, Nimitz forced his fleet commanders to attack the centre of the island chain and to rely on the carriers to neutralize enemy air power. The Japanese were building formidable defences, but they were not yet ready. As a result, Kwajalein fell at a fraction of Tarawa's cost. One month later, the Americans jumped to the northern side of the Marshalls by seizing Eniwetok, while neutralizing the great naval base at Truk with air strikes. These 'island hopping' moves left considerable Japanese garrisons isolated on the other atolls; without air or sea power these positions became strategically useless.

Not to be outdone by navy and marines, MacArthur moved on the Admiralty Islands. Backed up by General George Keaney's highly effective tactical air units, MacArthur's forces attacked Biak, a small island 300 miles west of New Guinea. By

General Tomoyuki Yamashita (1885–1946). In 1946 the American occupation authorities hanged Yamashita for war crimes committed by Japanese marines (not under his command) in Manila. One suspects his sentence resulted mostly from pique at a superior performance in Malaya and the Philippines that stood in stark contrast to that of his eventual conquerors.

mid-May 1944 the Americans had captured it, putting the Philippines within reach of long-range air attacks. In reply the Japanese resolved to launch their fleet against the exposed forces on Biak. The situation underlines the high risks that the separate American drives involved, but just as the Japanese were about to move, Nimitz attacked Saipan in the Marianas, control of which would place American air power within range of the Home Islands.

The conquest of Saipan was no easy matter against stiff resistance: US soldiers and marines suffered no fewer than 14,000 casualties. As fighting continued on Saipan, the Japanese navy sortied against the Marianas, instead of Biak, and a huge air battle ensued, called by the Americans the 'great Marianas turkey shoot'. US aircraft managed to sink three enemy carriers – two by submarines – but the crucial result was the destruction of the Japanese naval air forces, with few American losses. The taking of Biak and Saipan positioned the Americans to invade the Philippines.

Ironically, by this point even if the Americans had done nothing for the remainder of the war, the Japanese had already lost. US submarines, hindered at first by defective torpedoes and weak leadership, had eventually swung into high gear. Their opponents had made no preparations to defend their sea lines of communications against attack, so that by the end of 1943 American submarines, aided by extensive 'Magic' intelligence, could savage Japanese commerce. By the end of the war they had sunk half of the Japanese merchant fleet and two-thirds of the tankers. Movement of oil from the Dutch East Indies stopped, while shipments of raw materials to the Home Islands slowed to a trickle.

In October MacArthur and Nimitz attacked the Philippines. As infantry landed on Leyte, the Japanese again sortied. Their fleet took three separate tracks: from the north came a force of carriers – with virtually no aircraft on board due to losses in the Marianas – in order to draw off the main US fleet. Meanwhile, two small task forces moved through the Surigao Straits, while the main battle fleet drove through the San Bernardino Straits to attack the invasion fleet off Leyte. The plan almost worked. While the older US battlewagons (several refloated and repaired after being damaged at Pearl Harbor) destroyed the Japanese vessels in the Surigao Straits, the Americans took the bait and went north after the enemy's carriers. The main Japanese force, after initial losses to American carrier aircraft and submarines, made it through the San Bernardino Straits and ran into a weak force of escort carriers and destroyers; but a heroic defence by these outnumbered and outclassed ships eventually persuaded the Japanese admiral to withdraw, despite explicit orders to use and lose his fleet. US victory at Leyte Gulf ended the ability of the Japanese navy to fight a major naval action.

Yet the Japanese fought on. They held Burma until May 1945, when Commonwealth forces under William Slim recaptured Rangoon. In the Philippines under the skilled leadership of General Yamashita, the conqueror of Malaya and Singapore, the Japanese did a better job of defending the islands than had MacArthur in 1942 and resistance there continued to the war's end. However, by early 1945 the strategic portions of the islands were in American hands. Meanwhile, in autumn 1944 B-29s based in the Marianas began operations against the Home Islands. To provide an emergency landing strip for damaged bombers and to capture Japanese radar installations, the marines attacked Iwo Jima in February 1945. A preparatory bombardment of only four days, instead of ten as requested by the marines, left most of the Japanese defences intact. Two marine divisions were bled white in wresting Iwo's volcanic ash and rubble from the Japanese, and when it was over 6,821 marines were dead and nearly 20,000 wounded. Few from the Japanese garrison of 21,000 survived.

Next came Okinawa where, for the first time, the Americans ran into Japanese forces in formations larger than a division: an army of over 70,000 troops waited on the southern portion of the island in well-prepared positions. On 1 April the invasion force began to discharge its soldiers and marines. On 6 April the Japanese replied with assaults of 'kamikaze' aircraft, loaded with explosives and flown in suicide missions against American targets. On that day alone 700 aircraft, over half of them suicide planes, struck the US fleet. Attacks continued throughout the invasion period; kamikazes sank thirty ships and damaged another 368; 5,000 American sailors died, with another 5,000 wounded. The conquest of Okinawa formed the bloodiest chapter in the Pacific war. As one weary marine exclaimed: 'They send you up to a place…and you get shot to hell…But then they send you right back up again and then you get murdered. God, you stay there until you get

Slim's Burma campaign

Field Marshal the Viscount William Slim (right, 1891–1970) is perhaps the only premier commander of World War II whose reputation has remained intact. Slim came from a lower middle class background and without World War I would have had little chance of becoming an officer. But he volunteered for service in 1914, soon gained his commission and served with distinction. He then moved to the Indian Army.

At the outbreak of World War II, Slim served with Indian units in East Africa and the Middle East before arriving in Burma in 1942, where he extricated his Commonwealth forces to India relatively intact. Because the Burma theatre was regarded as a backwater by Allied strategists, Slim's Fourteenth Army received few resources, but he used the opportunity to retrain his troops for jungle conditions before beginning operations to regain Burma. In 1944 the Japanese moved first, but in the brilliantly conducted defensive battle of Imphal, Slim's troops first broke the Japanese and then pursued them all the way to Rangoon – the most successful exploitation campaign conducted by a British general in World War II.

US marines advance across the battle-scarred and surreal landscape of Iwo Jima. Like the succeeding battles on Okinawa, the fighting on Iwo Jima saw no mercy and no quarter: the marines fought until there were no Japanese left alive and until most of them were either dead or maimed. Both Okinawa and Iwo Jima indicated the losses that would have occurred had Allied forces landed on Kyushu in November, 1945.

killed or you can't stand it any more.' In the end the Americans destroyed all 70,000 troops, while well over 100,000 civilians died as a direct or indirect result of combat.

DROPPING THE BOMB

The conquest of Okinawa had cost the Americans 65,631 casualties – a frightening foretaste of what an attack on the Home Islands might involve. Thus far, the Americans and Japanese had fought a vicious war on small atolls and islands, which limited the numbers of troops involved; but for the coming invasion of Japan the full weight of US ground forces would make contact with the massed Japanese army. The American high command had selected 1 November 1945 as the date for 'Operation Olympic', the invasion of Japan: it would involve a great attack on the island of Kyushu in an operation approximately twice the size of D-Day. Unlike the Germans in Normandy, however, the Japanese expected the American landing precisely where it was to have taken place. As a staff officer testified after the war:

> We expected an Allied invasion of southern Kyushu and a later invasion of the Tokyo plain. The entire army and naval air forces had volunteered for an all-out kamikaze defence, and each had from four to five thousand planes…We planned to send over waves from 3–400 at a rate of one wave per hour. On the basis of Leyte and Okinawa we expected about one out of four planes to hit a target.

'Olympic' would have involved a level of casualties that would have been devastating for both Japan and the United States.

'Olympic' never occurred, however, because of scientific developments. The American strategic bombing campaign against Japan achieved little before spring

1945, for precision bombing had not been able to reach the dispersed economy of the Home Islands. But then the B-29s began replicating the area bombing that had characterized Bomber Command's efforts in Europe. On the night of 8 March, the B-29s destroyed much of Tokyo in a firestorm: by morning 83,000 Japanese had died, with 41,000 more injured. The Americans then proceeded to destroy the other major Japanese cities one by one. By summer Japan was totally isolated; its fleet sunk; its air force helpless; its industry dead. But the Japanese high command showed little interest in ending the war, preferring to concentrate on achieving an honourable death for its officers and men.

On 6 August, however, three B-29s flew over Hiroshima; one dropped the first atomic bomb and 90,000 died in a flash brighter than the sun. Two days later the Red Army broke the 1941 non-aggression pact and rolled across the Manchurian frontier and through Japanese defences. Then on 9 August a second atomic bomb fell on Nagasaki and another 35,000 Japanese died. At this point, the emperor stepped into the political process to resolve a deadlock among his advisers. He ordered a general surrender, a decision of great moral and physical courage; for several weeks it was touch and go whether the military, particularly the junior officers, would obey his command. In the end they did, and on 2 September representatives of the Japanese government signed the terms of surrender on the deck of the battleship *Missouri*. The war was over. Japan, like Germany, came under Allied occupation.

World War II had ripped across the planet and involved by its end in one fashion or another virtually everyone. When it was over it had killed tens of millions, wrecked virtually every major city in Europe, ravaged China and Japan, and caused mass migrations, untold misery and limitless destruction. Was the victory worth the cost in treasure, lives, and destruction?

It is perhaps only by looking at the reverse scenario – the alternative to fighting the war through to unconditional surrender – that one can judge the measures taken to achieve total victory. And the consequences of either an Axis victory or a survival of the Axis powers explains why the Allies felt it necessary to fight the war to the end. The catalogue of crimes committed by the Italians (Somalia, Ethiopia, Libya) or the Japanese (China, Korea, Manchuria) suggests what these two powers would have been capable of in a world unrestrained by peacetime conventions or the pressures of war. As for the Germans, not only their list of crimes but their megalomaniac desire to remake the continents along the lines of biological-racial 'science' suggests an almost unimaginable world had they succeeded. As Churchill had warned in a speech calling upon Britain to resist to the last in June 1940: 'if we fail, then the whole world, including the United States, including all that we have known and cared for, will sink into the abyss of a new Dark Age made more sinister, and perhaps more protracted by the lights of perverted science.' Indeed it would. And that vision accounts for the insistence of the Allies on the unconditional surrender of their enemies, and their single-minded determination in securing it.

Beneath the great mushroom-shaped cloud above Nagasaki on 9 August 1945 25,000 people died. The horror caused by the use of the atomic bomb would cast a shadow over the rest of the twentieth century but helped to avert a terrible clash of extinction between the Soviet Union and the United States.

CHAPTER 17

The Post-War World

Foreign Minister Mamoru Shigemitsu signs Japan's surrender in a ceremony on board the American battleship, *Missouri*, watched by army chief of staff General Yoshijiro Umezu and other members of the Japanese delegation. Having learned the lesson of World War I (when only Germany's political leaders signed), the victors in 1945 ensured that both the military and diplomatic leaders of Japan and Germany signed the instruments of defeat.

The end of World War II ushered in forty-five years of uneasy peace known as the 'Cold War'. In the wreckage of the Axis collapse, two superpowers emerged to contest worldwide hegemony, their forms of government representing vastly different political and economic systems. In any other period, such differences and suspicions would have resulted in another great war; but over this contest hung the shadow of nuclear weapons whose destructive potential was such that in the end neither side dared resort to a direct military challenge to its opponent. After Hiroshima some predicted that nuclear deterrence would eliminate war and, in the sense that the United States and the Soviet Union never directly engaged each other in war, they were right. Hostilities still occurred, but for the most part they reflected the collapse of the colonial empires of the West in the aftermath of the world wars; and, while both the United States and the Soviet Union dabbled in these conflicts, they remained peripheral to the larger interests of the superpowers. In retrospect, one of the Cold War's great ironies was that it brought an unparalleled time of stability during which the contestants deterred each other from going over the brink.

World War II also heralded the arrival of science as the dominant theme in warfare. The extraordinary development of technologies to support strategic nuclear weapons represented a quantum change in the capabilities which the opposing sides in the post-war world deployed. Yet, as Vietnam underlined, technology alone could not compensate for defects in policy, strategy, or even tactics.

Finally, the post-World-War-II era encompassed the destruction of the colonial empires that had formed in the nineteenth century. The humiliation of European armed forces at the hands of the Japanese destroyed whatever legitimacy remained for western domination of Southeast Asia, although it took a number of costly wars to underline that point; and once the tide of liberation had spread through Asia, Africa soon followed. The last colonial empire, Russia's, would not dissolve until the early 1990s.

THE AFTERMATH OF WORLD WAR II

As the Japanese surrendered on the battleship *Missouri* in Tokyo Bay, the great imponderable was how long the United States would involve itself in affairs outside the western hemisphere. During the war Roosevelt had suggested to Stalin that American troops would stay in Europe no longer than three years after the war's end and, certainly, America's flight from responsibility in 1920 did little to suggest a long American commitment to Europe. However, even more than after World War I, in 1945 America bestrode the world with its economic power, since only the western hemisphere had remained untouched by the catastrophic destructiveness of modern weapons. The Combined Bomber Offensive had wrecked Germany from one end to the other, while the remainder of central Europe lay prostrate after Axis and Allied armies had finished fighting back and forth across the scarred landscape. France, torn by Vichy and occupation experiences, as well as by the fighting, was a shadow. Britain itself was hardly poised to resume its position as a world power, while India, the crown jewel of Britain's empire, stood on the brink of independence.

In the east, the Soviet Union had emerged victorious from its great ideological war against Nazi Germany, but that victory had come at almost unimaginable cost; somewhere over twenty-five million Soviet soldiers and civilians had perished. Even more serious from Stalin's point of view was the economic damage inflicted on the Soviet economy. While the Soviets had gained a great empire, the battles marking their advance (coming after four years of Nazi exploitation) hardly rendered eastern Europe an economic plum. Allied air attacks had also brought Japan to the edge of starvation: by summer 1945, the Americans had turned Japan's cities and industries into smoking ruins, sunk its merchant fleet, and reduced the Japanese economy to subsistence level. Moreover, the Japanese had destroyed China from north to south and, in the destruction, the nationalists and the communists began to fight over the bones of a broken nation.

As the new president, Harry S. Truman, and his advisers surveyed the world in 1945, they recognized the damage that US withdrawal had occasioned in 1920. While some understood the menace of Stalin's Soviet Union, most hoped to live harmoniously with Russia and so the initial steps of US foreign policy after World War II combined preparation for confrontation with efforts at accommodation. The Americans offered to extend the Marshall Plan, the aid package that assisted western Europe's recovery, to the Soviet Union and eastern Europe – an offer the Soviets considered but rejected for fear that prying American eyes would discern the weaknesses of their shattered economy. On the other hand, the Americans did send their armed forces to Greece and Turkey in 1947 when economic weakness forced Britain to withdraw. Even more important was American sponsorship in 1949 of the North Atlantic Treaty Organization (NATO), which signalled continuing US military and political commitment to western Europe.

Nevertheless, the Americans hoped that their possession of atomic weapons would allow them to maintain their responsibilities cheaply and, until summer 1950, they stripped their conventional military forces to minimal levels. Without the Korean War, these reductions in military strength would have probably forced an eventual withdrawal of America's commitments in much of Asia and Europe. Instead, that war stimulated a major US rearmament effort aimed at maintaining nuclear superiority and the defence of western Europe. In the first year of the Korean War (1950–51), the Truman administration drafted 585,000 men and recalled 806,000 reservists and national guardsmen. In retrospect, the Americans appear to have overestimated Soviet capabilities and intentions, but then the Soviets – certainly down to the death of Stalin in 1953 – gave every indication that they represented a direct challenge to western values.

General of the Army Douglas MacArthur, commander-in-chief of United Nations forces in Korea, accepts the UN flag presented to him by General Lawton Collins, US army chief of staff, on 14 July 1950. The flag symbolized that MacArthur was to lead a multi-national force to repel North Korean aggression in the Korean peninsula.

From the late 1940s, American foreign policy therefore aimed at deterring the Soviet Union and containing the communist world, including China, within the territories it then held. That policy led the United States to fight two wars in Asia and commit substantial forces to the defence of Europe. It also involved massive outlays on increasingly complex technologies to upgrade nuclear and conventional weapons and delivery systems. For much of the Cold War the United States relied on the United States Air Force (USAF) to deter the Soviets, although with the appearance of Polaris submarines in the mid-1960s the navy played an increasingly important role in deterrence.

As a result, until the late 1980s, the focus of the USAF remained on the nuclear mission. Admittedly that emphasis achieved its aim of deterring the Soviets; but it also ended serious thinking within the air force about how the changing technological capabilities of air power could affect the military balance in conventional conflicts. Most air force officers saw their mission as deterrence; if they failed in that, war would simply become a matter of laying down vast numbers of nuclear weapons. A saying in the 1960s summed up this state of mind: 'Nuke them till they glow in the dark.'

The technological revolution executed by the US in support of its military build-up had an enormous impact on the world. From miniaturization of nuclear weapons, to jet aircraft and ballistic missiles that could cross continental distances, to cruise missiles that could hit targets with incredible accuracy, the Americans drove technology to the limits. This effort did not always come at the expense of the civilian economy: the computer revolution of the 1980s stemmed entirely from the miniaturization efforts that the space and military programmes demanded. But, for the Soviets, the technological revolution proved a nightmare since none of its aspects played to the strengths of their centrally planned economy. Throughout the Cold War Soviet factories ground out tens of thousands of tanks, artillery pieces, armoured personnel carriers, and even jet aircraft. But problems existed here too, since technology increasingly affected the capabilities even of ground weapons, and rendered vast numbers of them obsolete. The Gulf War of 1991 would underline how far the Soviets had fallen behind in the race, and yet the competition to keep up with the US in complex areas such as nuclear submarines, guided missiles, and space-based capabilities eventually broke both the morale and the economy of the Soviet Union.

THE KOREAN WAR

As a result of casual decisions made by US and Soviet leaders in 1945 to disarm surrendering Japanese forces in Korea, two separate states appeared in the peninsula. In the North, a regime based on xenophobic nationalism and Stalinist communism established itself under Kim Il-Sung. In the South, Syngman Rhee created a dictatorship as xenophobic as that in the North, but without the communism. By early 1950 the South had run into trouble both economically and

Red Square 1951: Soviet armed forces celebrate the anniversary of the October Revolution. In the 1980s considerable argument took place over whether CIA estimates on Soviet military spending were accurate or overinflated; it is now clear that such estimates were accurate, but that the CIA enormously overestimated Soviet gross national product. In effect, the Soviets spent themselves into bankruptcy, with a level of defence expenditure that eventually caused the collapse of an unworkable economic system.

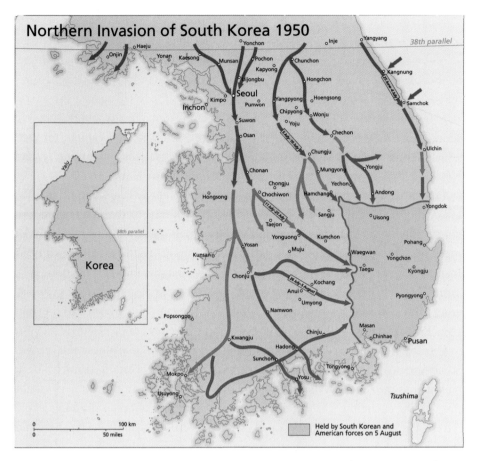

Northern Invasion of South Korea 1950

The invasion of South Korea, 1950: liberally supplied with Soviet equipment, including tanks, the North Korean Army possessed enormous superiority over its opponent in the South. Kim Il-Sung's forces rapidly destroyed both South Korean troops and the first Americans to arrive on the scene. But American firepower and South Korean tenacity allowed the creation of a defence perimeter around Pusan, where the North Korean invasion came to a halt.

politically; communist guerrillas enjoyed some success, while American military and economic aid remained at minimal levels. Misled by US pronouncements, Stalin allowed Kim Il-Sung to invade the South. It was one of the worst mistakes the Soviet dictator made.

In June 1950 North Korean armies swept aside ill-equipped South Koreans and, in their wake, began a murderous effort to cleanse South Korea of its incorrect class structure. However, communist savagery rallied South Koreans to their regime and undercut whatever chances existed for a peaceful reunification of Korea for generations. The invasion also brought an unexpected American reaction: President Truman committed the US military to the defence of South Korea. So unexpected was his action that the Soviets, boycotting meetings of the United Nations Security Council, were not present for the debate over Korea; consequently, the Americans were able to cloak their rescue efforts under the United Nations flag. From Japan, General Douglas MacArthur rushed his ill-trained and ill-prepared garrison troops to Korea. A series of humiliating defeats followed, and by August the North Koreans had driven the Americans and the remaining South Korean forces back to a small perimeter around the port of Pusan in the south-east. There the front stabilized, as US firepower and aircraft took a terrible toll on the attackers and interdicted supply routes running the entire length of the peninsula.

US marines try to rest along the icy trail in sub-zero temperatures as they retreat through mountainous terrain in North Korea. The massive intervention of Chinese ground forces in the Korean War in December 1950 placed the American spearheads advancing to the Yalu river in great danger. For a while, marine and army troops on the eastern side of North Korea were encircled, but they fought their way out, bringing their dead and wounded with them.

As savage battles enveloped Pusan, MacArthur launched one of the master-strokes of his career: husbanding his reinforcements, in September 1950 he threw a combined marine and army force ashore at Inchon, near Seoul. Tidal conditions at Inchon represented a nightmare for planning the landing, and MacArthur's military advisers along with the US joint chiefs of staff advised against the operation. But MacArthur was right; the North Koreans were not ready and Inchon fell, soon followed by Seoul. With the capture of the South Korean capital, through which North Korean supply lines ran, the enemy's position around Pusan collapsed. Those not taken prisoner fled in disorder to the North.

For the Americans the question was 'what next?' At the beginning of the war, MacArthur had argued for the rearmament of the Chinese Nationalists in order to launch them back against the mainland from which the communists had driven them in 1949. Truman answered with a resounding no. Now, with victory at Inchon, MacArthur urged pursuit across the 38th parallel into North Korea; here Truman agreed. But MacArthur's towering ego led him to discount warnings emanating from communist China that it would not tolerate a US advance to the Yalu river, Korea's frontier with China. The Americans therefore continued their advance in two separate pushes to the North and in late autumn the Chinese intervened. Some American units collapsed under their attacks: in the west, the army fell back pell-mell to the south; in the east, the marines and accompanying soldiers fought through the encircling Chinese armies and even brought out their dead in an epic retreat. The advancing Chinese, honed by years of struggle against the Japanese and the Chinese Nationalists, endured enormous hardships with minimal logistical support; they moved with speed over the mountainous terrain of North Korea, around and through blocking positions established by United Nations forces.

As Chinese forces drove south of Seoul, MacArthur suggested extreme options ranging from nuclear attacks to the abandonment of the peninsula. Not surprisingly, a growing estrangement marked relations between Truman and his general. As the chairman of the American joint chiefs of staff, Omar Bradley, noted about MacArthur's suggestion that the United States wage an all-out war on communist China: it would be 'the wrong war, at the wrong place, at the wrong time, and with the wrong enemy'.

In early January 1951 the situation stabilized south of Seoul as UN forces under the command of the best US combat general of World War II, Matthew B. Ridgway, solved serious morale problems and developed tactical solutions that emphasized firepower to deal with massed Chinese attacks. At this point the long supply lines supporting Chinese troops came under heavy air bombardment, while Ridgway's forces counter-attacked and shortly afterwards regained Seoul. In April the communists tried but failed to recapture what was left of the South Korean capital. This time, United Nations forces did not collapse but instead resumed their offensive after the Chinese had exhausted themselves. In the face of overwhelming American firepower, the communists took appalling casualties and appeared to be on the brink of collapse; certainly their desperate appeals for talks suggested the serious straits in which they found themselves. The US then made one of its most serious mistakes of the Cold War: it agreed to halt the advance and begin peace talks. There was of course nothing wrong with beginning talks, but halting the United Nations troops allowed the enemy to regroup and so ended their need for an armistice.

The American decision to move as quickly as possible to the peace table reflected a number of factors. First, Truman had found it necessary in April to dismiss MacArthur because of the general's insistence that the United States follow an 'Asia first' strategy – one that would have carried the war to Manchuria and perhaps even mainland China. By challenging the president, MacArthur left Truman no alternative. Truman and his advisers recognized that Korea represented only a pawn in a larger geopolitical match between the Soviet Union and United States: they wanted peace in Asia in order to concentrate on what they regarded as the Cold War's crucial theatre – western Europe.

Undoubtedly, in summer 1951 neither the US nor China desired to see the Korean War continue; but Stalin did, since he perceived that the war was placing considerable strain on the United States. Consequently, armistice talks dragged on for two more years, while the killing continued on a battlefront that resembled the trench lines of World War I. For strategic reasons, the Americans never increased their forces sufficiently to break the stalemate, while massive interdiction efforts by the US air force limited the extent to which the Chinese could support their ground forces. The stalemate pitted western firepower against the masses of China's revolutionary soldiery.

The length of the war and its lack of results – as MacArthur commented when he resigned: 'there is no substitute for victory' – made Truman highly unpopular to Americans, and in November 1952 they elected Dwight D. Eisenhower as president. His electoral success reflected not only his popularity, but also his promise to end an interminable struggle. He made it clear to the communists that unless they made real moves towards peace, he might consider using nuclear weapons. However, the armistice of summer 1953 resulted largely from Stalin's death the previous March, because the new Russian leaders did not look on escalation of the war with the same cynicism as the dictator – especially since a succession crisis was brewing in the Soviet Union.

In retrospect Korea was the crucial turning point in the Cold War. It brought the United States and its full potential back into the contest. It stabilized the situation in East Asia and, with the infusion of massive American resources to fight the war, began the process by which Japan ascended to the status of an economic superpower. It also created an atmosphere in the United States where the commitment of conventional forces to the defence of western Europe became possible. However, the Korean War also fanned the flames of an anti-communist witch hunt in America and ended whatever possibility might have existed for substantive accommodation with the Soviet Union in the post-Stalin period.

Throughout the Korean War, Allied forces enjoyed immense superiority in firepower, whether land-based artillery, air power or naval gunfire. Here, on 28 November, 1951, the 6-inch guns of HMS *Belfast* blast shore targets in North Korea.

THE THIRTY YEARS WAR: VIETNAM, PART I

In the nineteenth century the French expanded into an area that they misnamed Indo-China which included three distinct peoples: Laotians, Cambodians, and Vietnamese. The last had waged a tenacious and successful effort to avoid the snares, cultural as well as political, of Chinese civilization to the north, only to succumb to French technology and organization in the nineteenth century. But the Vietnamese only grudgingly accepted French overlordship.

By the early twentieth century French education in Vietnam was turning out voracious nationalists prepared to challenge France on its own terms. In particular, a Vietnamese who eventually settled on the *nom de plume* of Ho Chi Minh set in motion a revolution that defeated first the French and eventually the Americans. As a young man he journeyed to Europe and there became one of the founders of the French Communist party. In the 1920s and 1930s, he continued his education by working for the Comintern in Moscow and eventually for the Chinese communists. But whatever his politics or his location Ho remained a fervid Vietnamese nationalist.

The Battle of Dien Bien Phu

By late 1953, the French position in Indo-China showed serious signs of deterioration. The armistice in Korea allowed the Chinese and Soviets to increase significantly their aid to the Viet Minh; moreover, French efforts to inflict defeats on Vietnamese forces by launching raids into enemy territory had failed dismally.

At this point, the French decided to undertake a high risk strategy. They would launch their airborne forces in a deep raid to seize the town of Dien Bien Phu, which lay on the supply routes to Laos. The French high command gambled; first, that they could tempt the Vietnamese leaders to move significant forces into the area around the town and, second, that French superiority in firepower, discipline, and training would allow the defending force to decimate Viet Minh attackers (as had happened in fighting along the Red River in 1951.)

But the French assumptions were dangerously flawed. First, the North Vietnamese proved able to deploy far more forces and firepower than the French expected; second, they were able to supply those forces over the course of a prolonged engagement. The battle began in March 1954, as Viet Minh elite units stormed the outlying positions that protected Dien Bien Phu and particularly its airfield. With their artillery on the heights the Viet Minh possessed a bird's-eye view of the valley of Dien Bien Phu below: almost immediately, the airfield became unusable. The French air force proved incapable of suppressing either Viet Minh howitzers or supply lines, and the Viet Minh infantry, as the Americans would find out a decade later, were ruthless, well-trained, and disciplined.

Despite the hopeless situation, French paratroopers continued to drop into the beleaguered compound until the last days. The garrison, for the most part, fought with extraordinary courage but by May the Viet Minh had overrun the entire position. The French lost both the battle and the colony.

French troops within Dien Bien Phu run between positions under fire.

In March 1945, the Japanese destroyed the last vestiges of French military and colonial power in Vietnam. Ironically, the United States refused any support for the French as they went down to defeat. Six months later the Japanese surrendered: Nationalist Chinese troops occupied the North while the British moved into the South to disarm the defeated forces, since the French, recovering from occupation, were not yet prepared to return. In the vacuum the only disciplined local forces were those of Ho Chi Minh, the Viet Minh. At first the French recognized Ho's regime, but the new Fourth Republic could not enforce its political decision: French commanders on the scene committed their forces to re-establishing French rule and, given Ho's intransigence, war was the only outcome. The French quickly re-established control of the cities, but Vietnamese resistance did not collapse; rather Viet Minh guerrillas gained effective control over the countryside and waged a bloody hit-and-run war against French troops. In 1949, the victory of the communists in China altered the balance. Their leader, Mao Tse-tung, provided substantial weaponry and training to the Viet Minh and in October 1950 Ho's forces dealt the French a series of devastating blows along the frontier. The French position in northern Vietnam collapsed.

Hitherto, the Americans had taken a decidedly hostile position towards French attempts to re-establish their colony in Southeast Asia, but with the Korean War in progress, the US sent substantial military aid which allowed the French to make a stand in the Red River Valley. In early 1951 Vo Nguyen Giap, a former history teacher and now Ho's military commander, threw Viet Minh forces against the French in a savage offensive. Overwhelming French firepower and first-class leadership taught Giap and his commanders a grim lesson: they could not beat their enemy in the open.

The war therefore became a stalemate. The Vietnamese controlled the areas around the Red River Valley and the countryside throughout much of the rest of the country, especially at night. The French launched sweeps to catch and destroy guerrilla forces in the open, where French firepower and training would prevail, but their operations mostly fell on thin air: the Viet Minh fought only when it was to their advantage. Although mounting losses made the war increasingly unpopular in France, the stalemate held as long as the Korean War continued; but when that conflict ended in 1953, the Chinese were able to provide increasing aid. To forestall a worsening situation, the French baited a trap for Giap; they aimed to pull the Viet Minh into a battle where superior French firepower would tell. Late in 1953 an airborne attack captured Dien Bien Phu, a position that the French believed critical to Giap's logistics, hoping that the Viet Minh would appear in strength so that their elite troops could deal them a devastating blow. However, the French had greatly underestimated the sophistication, dedication, and capabilities of their opponents. In March 1954 Giap struck. Viet Minh attacks overwhelmed the outer defence redoubts at Dien Bien Phu while their artillery dominated the main French positions. Airborne re-supply proved extraordinarily difficult since the Viet Minh

D-Day at Dien Bien Phu: the French paratroop drop on Dien Bien Phu in December 1953. The French attack caught the Viet Minh by surprise and the few cadres in the valley ran away. But the surprise did not last long (see box opposite).

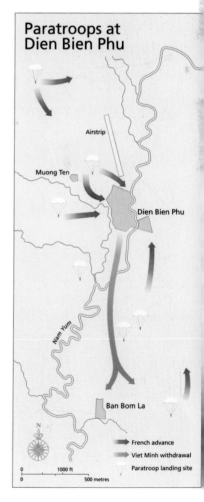

Paratroops at Dien Bien Phu

Airstrip

Muong Ten

Dien Bien Phu

Nam Yum

Ban Bom La

N

French advance
Viet Minh withdrawal
Paratroop landing site

0   1000 ft
0   500 metres

soon rendered the airfield unusable. By early April, only US intervention could have restored the situation.

Policy debates in the United States revolved around the issues of the strategic cost, significance, and burden that such a war might involve, and eventually concluded that the benefits of holding Vietnam for French colonialism were not worth the expense. And so the Americans watched while Dien Bien Phu and its garrison went down to defeat. The refusal of American aid thoroughly soured Franco-American relations, while Dien Bien Phu sealed the fate of French colonialism in Southeast Asia. The Americans did establish an anti-communist regime in South Vietnam as a result of the peace accords signed in Geneva (July 1954); but how they thought such a regime would survive when even its leaders recognized that they owed their independence to Ho's Viet Minh remains one of the tragic, unanswered questions of the 1950s.

THE ALGERIAN WAR

Few bands turned out to welcome the French troops returning from their Asian defeat. Instead, France plunged into another war. On 1 November 1954, Algerian rebels attacked French positions across North Africa and initiated a struggle for national liberation. Their opening assaults failed to win outright victory, but they achieved the larger aim of mobilizing Arab sentiment against the French. Complicating the situation was the fact that the large European population in Algeria adamantly refused to countenance any change in Algeria's status as an integral part of France. Escalating guerrilla activity confronted the French with problems similar to those they had faced in Vietnam, but in Algeria the FLN – *Front de Libération Nationale* – could also strike at the European population. This resulted in harsh responses that only exacerbated the war and turned it into a conflict between hostile nationalities and religions.

French officers had returned from Asia determined not to repeat the mistakes they had made in Vietnam. They exhibited a coherent understanding of revolutionary war and the nature of their opponents, but their desire to make the Algerians citizens of France flew in the face of French as well as Algerian political realities. The year 1956 marked the turning-point. The French introduced conscripts to the fighting, which they had never done in Vietnam, and almost immediately these inexperienced troops ran into difficulty. In September the FLN brought the war into the cities by directly attacking French civilians, increasing the war's rising cost as well as its savagery. Even more destructive to the French position was the failure of Anglo-French operations against the Suez Canal in early November (see page 357), because the collapse of that effort heavily reinforced the suspicions of many French officers concerning the competence of their political leaders.

By late 1956, the FLN controlled the Arab quarters of the major cities, while its terror attacks had brought European Algeria to a virtual halt. Up to this point, urban security had rested on the police; the army had been responsible for the war in the *bled* – the back country. Now, with control in the cities collapsing, French authorities sent in the army. In January 1957, General Jacques Massu's paratroopers took control of Algiers and immediately instituted a ruthless, no-holds-barred war against the FLN's cadres. Massu used preventive detention, ruthless searches, constant patrolling of the Casbah, a general disregard for civil rights, and even torture against the FLN. It was a war of the dirtiest kind – unflinchingly portrayed in the film *The Battle of Algiers* – and in the end it broke the FLN; but its methods did nothing to improve Algerian attitudes towards French rule. Even more important, the use of torture eroded support for the conflict in Metropolitan France. The French government proved incapable of handling the complex issues raised by Algeria and on 15 April 1958 it fell. No politician proved able to put together a replacement administration for the next thirty-seven days and in Algeria the army's fury mounted at the lack of political leadership in Paris. The officer corps refused to lose another war because of what it regarded as cowardly behaviour on the part of the politicians, so in mid-May a mob in Algiers, supported by the army, seized the government buildings and demanded that Charles de Gaulle, leader of the French government-in-exile in World War II, take over a bankrupt state. By 1 June 1958 de Gaulle was in power in Paris and, over the next four years, conducted a difficult and often contradictory policy towards Algeria. It is not clear when he made the decision to abandon the conflict, but by September 1959 he was offering 'self-determination'.

Meanwhile, he allowed the French military to continue its skilful campaign. By isolating the FLN from its bases in Tunisia and Morocco and by sophisticated use of helicopters and mobile formations, the French army destroyed their opponents in the field. Despite the military success, however, de Gaulle prepared to withdraw. He faced a significant challenge from many French officers, some of whom went so far as to join a terrorist organization, the OAS (*Organisation de l'Armée Secrète*), which plotted his assassination; but de Gaulle survived, and extricated France from Algeria without a civil war. The generals could boast that they had won the military conflict, but this ignored the crucial fact that they had lost the political war. In 1962 Algeria became independent.

UNCONVENTIONAL WAR: THE BRITISH EXPERIENCE

Where the French fought and lost two disastrous wars, the British came through the process of decolonization relatively unscathed. The great challenge was that of freeing India, which Britain overcame by a combination of statesmanship at home and stable and responsible military leadership on the scene. But the British also confronted serious military challenges elsewhere. Some they defeated; others they finessed. In February 1948, communist guerrillas in Malaya began a well-run campaign to terminate British rule and create a communist dictatorship. Over the next four years, they gained strength and improved their position. But in February 1952 the British began an effective drive against the insurgents with several factors

American helicopters fly over the Vietnamese rice paddies. The helicopter was the US army's answer to the problems associated with dealing with 'invisible' guerrillas. Admittedly, helicopters did provide greater mobility as well as the ability to bring reinforcements rapidly to troops in action on the ground; but they also proved vulnerable to enemy ground fire, and deluded American commanders into thinking that they could focus on operations and ignore the political and social issues associated with unconventional war.

favouring the effort. Malaya had two main ethnic communities, Malays and Chinese; the communists drew their support almost entirely from the latter. Moreover, Malaya had no frontier with a communist nation; consequently, the insurgents found it increasingly difficult to import arms and munitions.

The British recognized that the insurgency was a political problem and, as they embarked on their campaign to suppress the guerrillas, announced their intention to grant Malaya independence in the immediate future. Thus, they encouraged Malay nationalism while splitting the Chinese community from both the Malays and the guerrillas by careful police measures. Finally, the military effort rested on soldiers who knew the jungle better than the enemy. Conditions of guerrilla war in Malaya led the British to recreate several special units that had done so well in World War II – particularly the Special Air Services Regiment (SAS) – and this ability to fight unconventional war would pay the British armed forces big dividends in a number of future conflicts from Kenya and Aden to Ulster and the Falklands. By 1954 the communist high command in Malaya had withdrawn to Thailand and the war sputtered out. The British had won the political as well as the military struggle.

THE THIRTY YEARS WAR: VIETNAM, PART II

In 1954 President Eisenhower and his advisers had decided that Vietnam was not worth the blood and treasure that it would take to defeat the Viet Minh. However, the American bureaucracy failed to translate that decision into policy and the United States slipped slowly towards involvement through half-measures.

The Geneva Peace Accords of 1954 established an anti-communist regime in South Vietnam, led by the autocratic Ngo Dinh Diem, which combined the worst aspects of French colonialism with mandarin rule. It possessed little legitimacy in the countryside, while Diem and his family remained firmly wedded to the idea that only loyalty to the regime really mattered. Because Saigon remained low among American strategic priorities until 1961, military and civilian advisers from the bottom levels of American bureaucracy, most of whom knew neither French nor Vietnamese, influenced policy inordinately and, using Korea as a paradigm, laboured to establish a conventional army to defeat a conventional invasion.

Meanwhile, Ho and his cohorts laboured to establish their version of Stalin's socialist paradise in the North and eventually provoked rebellion among peasants in the Red River Valley, which they put down with enthusiastic ruthlessness. Then in 1959, recognizing Diem's weakness, they launched a campaign of infiltration, political action, and military and logistical support for an insurrection to overthrow the regime in South Vietnam. They began to construct a road through Laos and Cambodia that the Americans eventually named the 'Ho Chi Minh Trail'. Against an unpopular regime with little sense of what was happening in the countryside, the insurgency spread rapidly until, by the time John F. Kennedy became president in 1961 and announced that America would 'pay any price, bear any burden' to defeat communism, the situation in South Vietnam had disintegrated alarmingly.

The US military were hardly prepared to meet the challenge posed by the 'Viet Cong' (the derogatory name for the Viet Minh). Senior commanders and staffs took the conceptions within which the US army had trained – namely preparation for massive conventional or nuclear war against the Soviet Union – to the highly politicized guerrilla war in the difficult terrain of Southeast Asia and, throughout their involvement, proved incapable of absorbing the lessons of the conflict. A system of one-year tours of duty, combined with a general lack of knowledge of Vietnamese culture and language, only reinforced such weaknesses.

Kennedy selected the president of the Ford Motor Company as his secretary of defense. Robert Strange McNamara brought to the job a punctilious accountant's mind and a firm belief that there were few problems that systems analysis could not solve. McNamara did ensure that the Defense Department held the services to higher accountability in spending their funds; however, he possessed a totally unrealistic desire to eliminate all ambiguities and uncertainties from defence analysis as well as from the conduct of war. Under his tutelage the American military would fight the war in Vietnam entirely on the basis of statistical indices: numbers of enemy dead and wounded, numbers of battalion-days in combat, tons of bombs dropped, tons of cargo moved through the ports. The lists seemed endless, and all proved essentially meaningless in judging the progress of the war.

McNamara and Kennedy inherited their first test from Eisenhower: the invasion of Cuba by a brigade of exiles organized and trained by the US Central Intelligence Agency. Although some advisers protested, as Secretary of State Dean Rusk later remarked, since 'Kennedy had let us all know he didn't like having a bunch of memos shoved at him', critical memos seldom reached his desk. Even McNamara and the joint chiefs of staff raised no objection, while Rusk 'never expressed my doubts explicitly in our planning sessions...because [Kennedy] was under pressure from those who wanted to proceed'. Those 'who wanted to proceed' included some eloquent and wealthy Cuban exiles who pointed to the successful recent invasion by Fidel Castro and only a few associates. In April 1961, with Kennedy's blessing (but without support from America's armed forces), 1,500 exiles stormed ashore at the Bay of Pigs. Castro's troops swiftly overwhelmed them. Kennedy later analysed why he and his advisers had erred and found the answer in 'groupthink': a management style that fosters a premature sense of apparent unanimity among decision-makers (both actively, by discouraging the expression of dissenting views, and passively, by guiding discussions in ways that minimize disagreement). Eighteen months later, when US spy planes discovered Russian missiles deployed on Cuba, Kennedy abandoned groupthink and made his advisers meet separately in

US troops advance through the Vietnamese bush. The North Vietnamese managed to maintain enough pressure on the US military to keep the Americans' focus off the battle for the hearts and minds of the Vietnamese population. In the hills and the jungle, North Vietnamese regulars proved enormously effective in nullifying the advantages that the Americans enjoyed in technology and in firepower.

William Westmoreland. No general has so thoroughly condemned himself in his memoirs since George McClellan (see pages 222–6). General Westmoreland noted that he kept beside his bed during his service in Vietnam 'a Bible; a French grammar; Mao Tse-tung's little red book on theories of guerrilla warfare; a novel, *The Centurions*, about the French fight with the Viet Minh; and several works by Dr Bernard Fall, who wrote authoritatively on the French experience in Indo-China and provided insights into the enemy's thinking and methods. I was usually too tired in late evening to give the books more than occasional attention.' *The Centurions* is in fact a novel about Algeria; only the early chapters deal with the French defeat in Vietnam. But the General is obviously a man of his word; he never got beyond that point in the book. There is no reason to suspect that he got any further in the other books.

sub-groups, encouraged scepticism among them, and sometimes left the room to avoid dominating the debate. Although most initially favoured air strikes on Cuba, instead in October 1962 they merely blockaded the island while the protagonists worked out a face-saving retreat.

Although Kennedy changed his position towards Cuba in the light of experience, by contrast, from his first days in office up to his assassination in November 1963, he pursued an active, aggressive policy in Vietnam that steadily raised the stakes. Enthusiastic about meeting Ho's challenge, the president and his advisers underestimated their opponents and overestimated their Saigon allies. As American aid and advisers poured into the South, the political and military situation grew darker. Newspaper reporters noted the deterioration, but the commander of the advisory effort, General Paul Harkins, depicted the war in rosy terms to Washington while contemptuously dismissing the press. Only in autumn 1962 did the Americans finally recognize that Diem was a loser. Threats of US withdrawal eventually led to a coup by the Vietnamese military that overthrew the regime and assassinated the dictator and his brother.

But the coterie of generals who succeeded Diem proved even more inept than their predecessor, and by summer 1964 resistance in the South was collapsing. The new US president, Lyndon Johnson, refused to admit defeat at the hands of what he termed a 'piss-ant country'. In summer 1964 he therefore launched a series of air raids against the North Vietnamese navy, supposedly in response to attacks on American destroyers in the Gulf of Tonkin. Johnson and his advisers hoped that such strikes would persuade the North Vietnamese to desist. Ho and his colleagues, however, had no intention of desisting. As they told Bernard Fall, a noted western expert on Vietnam, they had no fear of American firepower; after all they had already beaten the French. Nevertheless, Johnson campaigned for re-election on a platform that portrayed his opponent, Senator Barry Goldwater, as a warmonger. Johnson won but, as one voter later commented, 'I was told that if I voted for Goldwater, I would get war, and I voted for Goldwater and got war.'

In early 1965 Johnson authorized a bombing campaign against the North, code-named 'Rolling Thunder', which severely limited targets that US aircraft could attack. Although even unrestricted bombing could not have stopped the North Vietnamese offensive against the South at this stage, 'Rolling Thunder' was a totally misconceived effort with no chance of success. Johnson therefore tipped American ground forces directly into the struggle for South Vietnam. The conduct of the war now fell to General William Westmoreland.

Westmoreland shared with most other American military leaders a contempt for past experience. For example, in 1964 the French, recognizing that it was increasingly probable that the United States would embroil itself in Vietnam, made available to the American government the after-action study of their defeat in Vietnam: it still sits in the classified library of the National Defense University, in the original French, and there is little evidence that senior military or political leaders in the Pentagon studied the volume. Not surprisingly, therefore, the American military repeated every mistake the French had made. They also refused to learn. Confronted in the Ia Drang Valley battles with serious tactical and operational problems, including the destruction of a battalion of the 1st Air Cavalry at 'Landing Zone Albany', Westmoreland denied the corps commander's request that Military Assistance Command Vietnam (MACV) set up a 'lessons learned board' to examine the tactical and operational weaknesses of US forces. Instead, throughout the war, firepower-heavy American military units blundered around the countryside wrecking everything.

Westmoreland also displayed little interest in reforming the South Vietnamese military, and at least until 1967 pacification remained at the bottom of his priorities. MACV emphasized search and destroy missions, in which American units sought to find, fix, and then liquidate main-force enemy units; it actively discouraged participation by its troops in the political war in the countryside. When marine commanders initiated a small-unit, civil action strategy to protect the population in their area, MACV placed severe limits on the effort. Statistical indices, beloved by McNamara, dominated the American approach. What counted were battalion days in action and the justly infamous body counts. One result of this score-card approach was the My Lai massacre in which American soldiers slaughtered Vietnamese peasants; MACV then covered up the incident until it exploded in the American press.

Besides search and destroy missions, the Americans cleared whole areas of the country to deny Viet Cong and North Vietnamese the support of the peasants and then dumped the transplanted civilian population into the hands of a government that lacked any facilities, resources, or interest in resettlement programmes. Elsewhere, free-fire zones allowed American artillery and aircraft to destroy the landscape and impose a terrible toll on civilians as well as the enemy. The approach was even less imaginative than the French effort had been, but the awesome firepower that the Americans deployed allowed them the illusion of 'military victory'.

The American people had greeted the introduction of US troops into Vietnam with enthusiasm, and in summer 1964 the Senate passed the 'Gulf of Tonkin Resolution', authorizing air raids on North Vietnamese targets, by a margin of eighty-eight to two. In October 1965 *Time* magazine enthusiastically crowed in its lead article about the American buildup:

> It was only three months ago that the lethal little men in black pajamas roamed the length and breadth of South Vietnam, marauding, maiming and killing with impunity...Today South Vietnam throbs with a pride and power, above all an esprit, scarcely credible against the summer's somber vista...The remarkable turnabout in the war is the result of one of the swiftest, biggest military buildups in the

Vietnam-War protestors at the Pentagon, October 1967. The *Harvard Crimson* commented in 1968, when President Johnson removed draft deferments for graduate school: 'The National Security Council's draft directive puts almost all college seniors and most graduate students at the head of the line for next year's draft calls. Three-fourths of the second-year law class will go off to war...Yesterday's directive is a bit of careless expediency, clearly unfair to the students who would have filled the nation's graduate schools next fall.'

history of warfare...Wave upon wave of combat-booted Americans – lean, laconic and looking for a fight – pour ashore from armadas of troopships. Day and night, screaming jets and prowling helicopters seek out the enemy from their swampy strongholds...The Viet Cong's once-cocky hunters have become the cowering hunted as the cutting edge of US firepower slashes into the thickets of communist strength.

Johnson laboured mightily to keep the war popular with the American people. He refused to call up either National Guard or reserves; the government provided bodies for the war through the draft, but a draft that allowed the 'best and the brightest' to escape military service entirely. The government issued exemptions to the male children of the upper and educated classes, who carefully ensured that their exemptions remained in place before joining demonstrations against the war. The burden of the conflict continued to fall on the shoulders of poor black and white Americans. In addition, Johnson and McNamara, in glaring contrast to Truman's actions during the Korean War, stripped the American military through-out the rest of the world to fight in Asia.

TET AND AFTER

Nevertheless, the American soldiers and marines staved off the South's defeat in 1965–66, imposing terrible casualties on their adversaries. In 1967 the North Vietnamese changed their strategy of direct military confrontation by targeting marine units in the northern part of the country, which possessed less firepower. In 1968 they changed the game again by launching a massive assault, the Tet Offensive, on South Vietnam's cities. As in his attacks on the Red River Valley in 1951, Giap calculated that such an operation would result in widespread popular uprisings and the collapse of his opponents; but he was wrong. In a military sense, the Tet offensive and its ancillary operations proved disasters for North Vietnamese and Viet Cong troops. The South Vietnamese military, to the surprise of even their American advisers, fought tenaciously; the country did not rise in rebellion; and American firepower devastated the attackers. Giap reinforced fail-ure by launching continued offensives throughout 1968 that failed even more decisively and at greater cost, while the Americans and their allies eliminated all the communist sympathizers in the South who, in responding to Ho's call, had shown their hand.

War, however, consists of far more than totalling up statistics. The savagery of Tet brought home to the American people the seriousness of the conflict, while their government offered no convincing strategic or political explanations for what it was doing. Johnson withdrew from the presidential race and ended the misbegotten and badly executed air campaign against the North. Westmoreland, like a broken record, could only ask for more of everything until his promotion to chief of staff of the army finally removed him from Saigon.

Last checks before an American fighter bomber carries aloft its load of bombs (marked 'for you Charlie') destined for Viet Cong positions.Overwhelming US firepower made extensive tracts of Vietnam's jungle landscape resemble the surface of a brown moon and killed large numbers of Viet Cong (nick-named 'Charlie').

Westmoreland's replacement, General Creighton Abrams, displayed more imagination and political sense in fighting the war. MACV now emphasized 'Vietnamization', and the Vietnamese forces received attention, arms, and comprehensive training. But it was too late, for domestic pressure had reached the point where the United States simply had to pull out of Vietnam. At least the savage blood-letting inflicted on the North Vietnamese and the Viet Cong in 1968 created some breathing space, and the new administration of Richard M. Nixon carried out both open and secret negotiations with the North Vietnamese. Nevertheless, while he removed American troops, Nixon continued to provide massive military and political aid to the South and carried out operations to improve the military situation. For example, in May 1970 the Americans launched a major invasion of Cambodia to destroy the logistical bases of the North Vietnamese. The action achieved its military objectives, but a storm of political protests at home underlined how little time remained for the Americans to escape from the war.

In 1972, as the last American combat troops made their exit, the North Vietnamese launched a massive conventional invasion to destroy South Vietnam. Their aim was to humiliate the United States and not just beat what the North Vietnamese termed its 'lackeys'. Again they made a terrible miscalculation: American air power inflicted horrendous casualties on the advancing North Vietnamese while Nixon was so angered that he ordered the air force and the navy to launch a great air campaign against the North itself. Equipped with precision-guided munitions, US fighter bombers destroyed all the important bridges in North Vietnam and much of the enemy's economic infrastructure in a matter of weeks.

The collapse of the ground offensive and the destruction of much of their homeland brought the North Vietnamese back to negotiations. By autumn the opposing sides had hammered out a peace agreement that allowed the United States to withdraw with some dignity. Once again, however, the North Vietnamese

Southeast Asia 1978-79

Southeast Asia, 1978–79. Buoyed by their success in reuniting Vietnam under their rule in 1975, the Vietnamese communists involved themselves in both Cambodia and Laos – in effect, taking over the lands of what they regarded as inferior peoples. Major Chinese attacks in the North, however, underlined to the Vietnamese that their megalomania would not remain unchallenged.

attempted to humiliate the Americans by pulling out of the deal at the last moment. Buoyed by his overwhelming victory in the 1972 presidential elections, Nixon again unleashed US air power. This time even B-52s participated and, surveying the wreck of their country, the North Vietnamese finally decided that humiliation of the United States by a third-rate power was not an achievable objective.

Nevertheless, the Paris Peace Accords in 1973 failed to end the war in Vietnam. The Watergate affair limited Nixon's ability to support South Vietnam, while Congress, in full cry of self-righteousness, did everything possible to undercut South Vietnam. In 1975 the North Vietnamese therefore launched yet another conventional offensive against the South and this time, without American supplies or air power, it collapsed – although the millions of South Vietnamese refugees who took flight from their 'liberators' suggested that communism hardly enjoyed unanimous support in the South. But the American performance in 1975 was a disgrace: the CIA failed even to destroy its intelligence files in Saigon and thereby compromised nearly all of the South Vietnamese who had co-operated with the United States.

The Vietnam War was a sobering experience for most Americans. For the first time since 1812 an opponent had defeated the United States. The US had floundered into the war with half measures. Never did its military or political leaders undertake a serious strategic assessment of their opponent or of the war's possible political or military costs. From the beginning, the American military underestimated the ideological commitment of their adversaries, while McNamara and those who thought like him contemptuously rejected such intangibles.

In the end, the United States managed to extricate itself; but the cost to American values and self-esteem was devastating. Conversely, the North Vietnamese achieved their objective of unifying Vietnam under their control, but in so doing they sacrificed whole generations of their people, as well as the economic potential of their nation. Indeed, their victory looks hollow today when one considers that Vietnam is one of the poorest nations in the world – in a region dominated by Taiwan, Japan, South Korea, Singapore, Malaya, and Hong Kong – thanks to its intransigent political system and the fanatical war of national liberation that it waged.

THE ARAB–ISRAELI WARS

During World War I the British promised both the Arab peoples of the Near East independence from Ottoman rule and the Zionist movement a national home in Palestine. Few decisions by great powers have resulted in more potential for conflict. By the 1930s Jewish immigration into Palestine – much of it due to events in Nazi Germany – created conflict between Arab and Jew. An obscure British captain, Orde Wingate, who achieved fame in World War II in special operations, played an important role in providing Jewish settlers with innovative approaches to war, while the participation of Jewish volunteers in the British armed forces during World War II further broadened military knowledge among Palestinian Jews.

In 1948, with communal fighting on the upswing and their resources and patience exhausted, the British withdrew from the area. The United Nations declared partition between the communities, but the local Arabs as well as the neighbouring Arab nations rejected a peaceful settlement and launched military operations against the new state of Israel. However, the Arabs failed to co-ordinate their offensives, while local Arab leaders possessed neither political wisdom nor military ability. The Israelis broke the back of both local resistance and invading armies and, as a result of the 1948–49 war, acquired considerable territory that the United Nations settlement had assigned to Palestinian Arabs.

The Arabs displayed no desire to come to terms with the new Israeli state. Instead most Arab nations expelled their Jewish minorities to Israel at the same time that they proclaimed their aim to destroy the new state and its population. After the Nazi experience, the Jews could not afford to take such threats lightly. In the early 1950s they faced a rising tide of terrorism on their frontiers while the Egyptians, by purchasing arms from the Soviet Union, appeared to represent a direct threat to Israel's survival.

Consequently, when in 1956 the British and French invited the Israelis to participate in military action against Egypt, which had just unilaterally seized the Suez Canal, they delightedly agreed. The efficiency of Israeli military operations in 1956 stood in stark contrast to that of the French and British. Using a combination of paratroopers and armour, the Israelis first blocked the Mitla Pass in the Sinai and then chopped the Egyptians to pieces. A high level of training, doctrinal cohesion, and moral determination provided the Israelis with a highly effective military system; Arab armies drawn from stratified class systems, with soldiers and officers who lacked solid grounding in the military profession, proved incapable of facing them on the modern battlefield.

Within a week, the Israelis were close enough to the Suez Canal to watch their European allies attack Egyptian forces in the Canal Zone. But as these operations unfolded, the Soviet Union and the United States stepped in and ended the war. Ironically, the Egyptian dictator, Gamal Abdel Nasser, who had lost the war in every military sense, won it in political terms: his prestige soared throughout the Middle East. The Israelis surrendered their conquests in the Sinai to a United Nations peacekeeping force in return for promises that the Egyptians would allow transit through the straits of Tiran. For the next eleven years Nasser basked in the glory of Suez Crisis and attempted to spread his influence throughout the Arab world. He found the Soviet Union a willing supporter of his designs and a provider of up-to-date military equipment, but for a decade Nasser also recognized the reality of the balance between his forces and those of Israel.

For reasons that remain obscure, peace in the Middle East collapsed in 1967. In May Nasser came to believe that the Israelis were about to attack; he then asked the UN to leave the Sinai, deployed Egyptian troops into the area, and declared a blockade of the straits of Tiran. Jordan and Syria made common cause with the

A smashed Syrian T-54 tank and an armoured car lie near the village of Bauias. Having finished with the Egyptians and the Jordanians, at the end of the Six Day War in June 1967 the Israelis turned on the Syrians. In perhaps the most graphic display of their military superiority, the Israelis drove their Syrian tormentors off the Golan heights in a single day and so thoroughly wrecked the Syrian armed forces that they could have driven right on to Damascus had they wished to do so.

Egyptians, and most military analysts believed the Jewish state stood little chance against Arab military might. Israel mobilized while the United States, thoroughly mired in Vietnam, abdicated its responsibilities to maintain the 1956 settlement.

On 5 June 1967 the Israelis struck. Flying out into the Mediterranean and then coming into Egypt at low level to avoid detection, Israeli fighter bombers wrecked the Egyptian air force in a series of morning raids. With enemy air power shattered, Israeli aircraft turned to supporting the ground forces. Against the Egyptians, Israeli armour cut off the Gaza strip, while other units crossed into Sinai where, consistently displaying an extraordinary willingness to take risks, the Israelis broke into, over, and then through Egyptian positions. The Egyptians, though often fighting bravely, proved incapable of adapting to the tempo of Israeli operations. Their collapse soon followed and, as Egyptian tanks and vehicles fled towards the canal through the Mitla Pass, Israeli aircraft completed the killing. Within four days, the Israelis had reached the Suez Canal, with all Sinai in their hands.

Shortly after Israel attacked Egypt, the Jordanians joined the conflict. Like the Soviets, they were misled by Egyptian claims that their aircraft had destroyed the Israeli air force. Not until the third day did the extent of Egypt's defeat become clear, and by then it was too late for the Jordanians, who had suffered their own defeat. Fighting began in Jerusalem where the Israelis had placed three brigades. The Jordanians fought well in small units, but were no match for the Israelis on the operational level. By 7 June the Israelis controlled the West Bank of the river Jordan.

With Egypt and Jordan defeated, the Israelis turned against Syria. Thus far, the Syrians had limited their military actions to shelling Israeli settlements lying below the Golan heights. On 9 June the Israelis, having redeployed, attacked the heights and in three days of furious fighting they seized Golan and the region behind. A wrecked Syrian army pulled back to Damascus and the Six Day War was over. In less than a week the Israelis had humiliated three Arab armies and air forces of much greater strength. Their success rested on the creation of a truly western army: one in which soldiers and officers worked as part of a closely integrated team with implicit trust between different levels of command. Above all the Israelis recognized that war requires serious professionals – individuals who not only train hard but who devote serious intellectual study to their career – as well as the latest technology.

However, the Six Day War led the Israelis to overestimate their strategic advantage as well as the significance of their operational and tactical victories. Unlike 1956, they held on to all the conquered territories in the belief that the Arabs would not dare unleash another war for the foreseeable future. Israeli intransigence also mirrored Arab intransigence. The Egyptians embarked on a war of attrition along the Canal, which hardly put Israelis in a mood to negotiate, while a series of terrorist outrages around the world angered the Israelis even more.

The Israelis therefore took a hard line toward the Arabs and, with little prospect of negotiations, the Egyptians had no choice but to think in terms of further military action. A new Egyptian leader, Anwar Sadat, possessed little of the self-indulgent mood that so characterized his predecessor and other Arab leaders. In 1973 Egypt and Syria agreed to launch a surprise attack on Israeli positions; this time they would provide as little advanced warning as possible. Ironically, US and Israeli intelligence services picked up many signals that indicated an Arab attack, but remained firmly convinced that such action was inconceivable.

On Yom Kippur, the Day of Atonement, 6 October 1973, the Israelis finally recognized what was about to occur, but they could only begin mobilization and hope that the troops in forward positions could hold for a few days. At 2.05 p.m. that same day a massive Egyptian air strike and artillery bombardment hit Israeli forward positions on the Suez Canal. The Egyptians then launched an all-out attack to regain the Canal and push the Israelis into the desert: their operation, rehearsed in minute detail, broke through the Bar Lev line and isolated the Israeli strong points. The reserve Israeli armoured brigade on the Canal counter-attacked without infantry or artillery support and suffered devastating casualties. Israeli aircraft attempted to intervene, but the Israelis had paid little attention to American experience with sophisticated Soviet-designed air defences in Vietnam and, lacking electronic equipment to counteract Soviet systems, their attacking aircraft also suffered heavy losses.

The Israelis had drawn the mistaken lesson from the Six Day War that armour could operate alone rather than as part of a combined arms team. The first days of

An Israeli Centurion tank advances during the Yom Kippur War of 1973. Over-reliance on tanks at the beginning of the war cost the Israelis heavily, except on the Golan heights. But by the end of the hostilities, the Israelis had recovered and had come close to destroying the armies of their opponents. The cost, however, had been very high and Arab successes provided the political basis upon which the two sides could negotiate.

the Yom Kippur War underlined the errors of such an approach. The Israelis quickly returned to a more coherent form of warfare in the midst of the conflict, but they paid a heavy penalty for misreading the lessons of the last war.

The one defensive measure the Israelis had taken before the war was to move another reserve armoured brigade onto the Golan heights. In the northern Golan, the Israelis lost their outpost on Mount Hermon, but the 7th Armoured Brigade shattered the attack of two Syrian divisions. In the south, the Syrians almost regained the heights but Israeli success in the north allowed them to concentrate reserves on the threatened southern sector and hold the Syrians. A general counter-attack then drove the Syrians beyond the start line and opened up the possibility of an advance to Damascus.

The Falklands War

Damaged by Argentinean air attacks, HMS *Antelope* explodes – one of several British ships that Argentinean aircraft (often using French-made 'Exocet' missiles) managed to sink or damage.

A series of miscalculations by the British Foreign Office persuaded the military leaders of Argentina that they could get away with an invasion and seizure of the Falkland Islands. Not only did they believe that Britain no longer possessed the military capabilities or will to regain the Falklands but they regarded Prime Minister Margaret Thatcher as merely a member of the 'weaker sex.' In both respects they made a costly mistake.

Despite considerable efforts at mediation by the United States, the Argentineans refused to take three-quarters of a loaf and the British therefore sent a 'Task Force' to the South Atlantic. The Argentinean fleet came out, but the British high command authorized a torpedo attack on the cruiser *Belgrano*, and its sinking removed the Argentinean Navy from the war. As British troops landed on the archipelago, the Argentineans launched a series of air raids on British ships sheltering in the waters around San Carlos. Argentinean air losses were heavy, as were British losses of ships; but Margaret Thatcher remained resolute.

Once ashore, the British paratroopers and marines, although outnumbered by their Argentinean opponents, overwhelmed the defenders, first at Goose Green and then in the advance on Port Stanley. British troops displayed once again the values of discipline, training, and preparation when pitted against opponents whose officer corps possessed more experience in torturing and murdering opponents of the regime in basements than in preparing for war, and enlisted ranks which consisted entirely of untrained conscripts. Not long after the surrender of the Argentinean forces on the Falklands, the government that sent them fell.

This forced the Egyptians to come out from behind their anti-aircraft and anti-tank defences and engage the Israelis in mobile warfare. In an open tank battle, the largest since Kursk thirty years before, the Israelis devastated the attackers. Taking enormous risks, they then counter-attacked. Driving across the canal they eventually gained a bridgehead on the western bank; from there they unleashed their armour. Driving south, Israeli tanks eliminated the Egyptian anti-aircraft missile sites and almost surrounded the Egyptian Third Army. At this point, the war ended; both sides could claim victory and on that basis, through American good offices, an Egyptian-Israeli peace treaty was eventually signed.

The Yom Kippur War had taken the Israelis, whose overconfidence and underestimation of their opponents had placed their nation in an extraordinarily dangerous position, by surprise; but once they regained equilibrium, they proved adept at adapting capabilities and doctrine to combat realities. The Arabs fought courageously; but since combat organizations reflect the societies that spawn them, their forces displayed considerable weaknesses on the modern, technological battlefield. The fault lines between classes, the lack of educational and technological skills, and weaknesses in professional military culture resulted in significant failures. The greatest impact of the Yom Kippur War of 1973, however, arose from the decision of the Organization of Petroleum Exporting Countries (OPEC) to support the Arab military effort by first halting oil production and then increasing its price by 250 per cent. The aim was to discourage western support for Israel; the effect was to trigger a major worldwide recession while at the same time increasing dramatically both the revenues and the political influence of the member states – especially the major oil producers around the shores of the Persian Gulf.

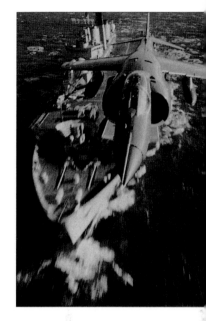

A Sea-Harrier rises from the deck of HMS *Invincible*. The Harriers, armed with American-built Sidewinder missiles, proved surprisingly effective against incoming air-raids. They also provided close air support for British ground forces as they overwhelmed Argentine defenders during the Falklands War.

THE GULF WARS

The reaction of the American military to defeat in Vietnam was sullen disbelief. A widespread use of drugs and near collapse into open racial conflict within the US services exacerbated the dark mood and it took the rest of the 1970s to restore the situation. But in the 1980s a number of factors contributed to a rebirth of American military power. After the bruises subsided, much of the American officer corps examined the lessons of the lost war, while publication of a superb translation of Clausewitz's *On War* fuelled a serious mood of self-examination. Moreover, a massive American military build-up unleashed by President Ronald Reagan after 1981 brought a revolution in technology to the battlefield. Finally, a small operation against a radical movement in the Caribbean island of Grenada pointed out major weaknesses in American military forces, particularly in the realm of inter-service co-operation.

The Reagan buildup aimed at preparing American forces to confront the Soviets on both conventional and nuclear battlefields. Such a war never occurred, and the collapse of the Soviet Union after 1989 initiated a policy of military reductions; but the new policy had hardly begun before those forces found employment in the

Persian Gulf. Even after the Soviet collapse, other states possessed immense ambitions and believed that the end of the Cold War brought with it auspicious opportunities.

Saddam Hussein began his rise to power in Iraq as an activist in the right-wing Ba'ath Party; he survived in the bloody world of Iraqi politics to become the ferocious dictator of a nation torn by insecurities. When Iran collapsed into seeming anarchy after religious ideologues seized power in 1979, Saddam invaded his neighbour in order to take advantage of the situation. Under ferocious Iranian counter-attacks, however, Iraq's military forces fell back to their own territory. A savage, seemingly unending war ensued in which two implacable tyrannies, one reinforced by Ba'athist ideology, the other by Islamic fundamentalism, aimed to break their opponents. The Iraqis bought great amounts of Soviet and western weapons and technology; the Iranians counted on religious enthusiasm and sent their youth in tens of thousands to clear minefields with their feet. In 1988 a series of carefully planned Iraqi attacks finally broke the Iranians, but while the Iraqis had bought technology from the Soviets and the West, their success reflected the weaknesses of their opponents rather than their own military competence.

To Saddam, 'victory' over Iran opened up the possibility of economic and political control of the Middle East. As leader of the Ba'ath Party he aimed to redress the ancient wrongs inflicted on the Arab and Islamic worlds by western interlopers over the previous five centuries. Burdened with debts from the war with Iran and believing it inconceivable that the US would use its military power, Saddam struck the small but oil-rich adjoining state of Kuwait in summer 1990. His invasion moved like clockwork and in less than a day Kuwaiti resistance collapsed. In response, the United States and its western allies deployed massive military forces into the Gulf. Little of this impressed the Iraqis. To the end they did not believe that the US would dare strike the victors of the Iran–Iraq War. As Saddam bluntly told the American ambassador in July 1990: 'Yours is a society which cannot accept 10,000 dead in one battle.' Above all, the Iraqis heaped scorn on the notion that technology might play any significant role in the war.

In fact, technology destroyed the Iraqis. In the first ten hours of the war in January 1991 a combination of Stealth aircraft, cruise missiles, electronic warfare, and precision-guided munitions took apart Iraq's complicated air defence system. Over succeeding weeks an aerial offensive battered Iraq's military infrastructure, wrecked Iraqi ground forces and inflicted minimal damage on civilian populations. Considerable squabbling between coalition commanders occurred over the level of damage that air attacks achieved, but in the end quantifiable measures proved meaningless: when Allied ground forces rolled into Iraq, the enemy surrendered with minimal resistance because the air attacks had shattered their morale.

Some air force planners argued that there was no need for a ground campaign, but they overlooked the political necessity for Allied ground forces to defeat the Iraqis and prevent the possibility that Saddam might claim that his army had remained unbeaten and unbroken in the field. Nevertheless, as a retired marine general noted after the war: 'This was the first time in history when the ground campaign supported the air campaign.' For many analysts the war simply demonstrated once again the technological superiority of western military power over that of third world nations. Yet technological superiority still only constitutes a portion of the equation; the course of hostilities since 1945 suggests that significant additional factors continue to affect the outcome of modern wars. Above all, training, discipline, and organization must undergird the efforts of military forces. That has been the essence of western way of war since the time of the Greeks. In Iraq the Coalition forces possessed those advantages. Their opponents did not.

The destruction of Iraq's air defences

Helped by French and Soviet technology, the Iraqis had by 1990 developed a highly sophisticated, integrated air defence system. But it possessed major weaknesses, particularly since the Iraqis underestimated the skills and technological sophistication of their opponents. The initial strikes by 'stealth' F-117 bombers and cruise missiles in January 1991 attacked the heart of the Iraqi air defence system, particularly the various command nodes, communication centers, and Iraq's main electrical system.

The next stage in the Allied plan sent two massive package of aircraft, combining jammers, drones, and aircraft carrying anti-radiation missiles, to strike any Iraqi radar installations that still functioned. By then, half an hour into the Allied assault, the Iraqi's realized that a major attack was in progress; but breakdowns caused by the initial strikes were already causing them considerable difficulties. At this point what appeared to be a massive two-pronged bombing strike aimed at Baghdad appeared on those radar screens still operating – but simply by 'tuning in' these installations attracted a large number of anti-radiation missiles. The Iraqi air defences failed to function in a coherent fashion for the rest of the war.

An RAF Tornado firing a rocket during the Gulf War of 1991. Allied air power, based not just a technological expertise but on extraordinarily well-trained and disciplined air crews, proved consistently superior to anything the Iraqis put in the air. After gaining air superiority, Allied air forces were able to pound Iraqi ground forces in Kuwait, as one air commander noted, like a tethered goat.

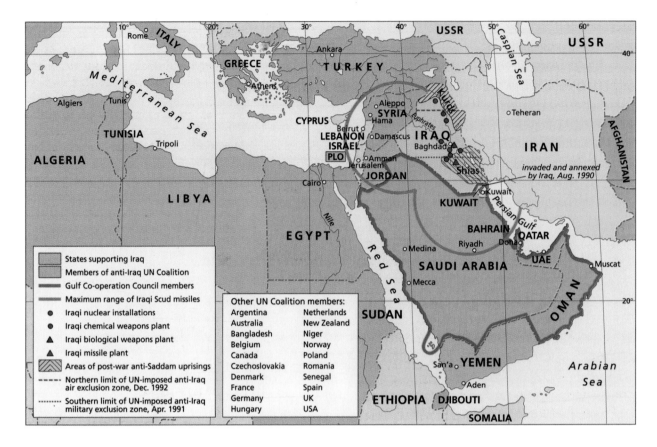

Legend:

States supporting Iraq
Members of anti-Iraq UN Coalition
Gulf Co-operation Council members
Maximum range of Iraqi Scud missiles
● Iraqi nuclear installations
● Iraqi chemical weapons plant
▲ Iraqi biological weapons plant
▲ Iraqi missile plant
▨ Areas of post-war anti-Saddam uprisings
- - - - Northern limit of UN-imposed anti-Iraq air exclusion zone, Dec. 1992
· · · · · Southern limit of UN-imposed anti-Iraq military exclusion zone, Apr. 1991

Other UN Coalition members:
Argentina	Netherlands
Australia	New Zealand
Bangladesh	Niger
Belgium	Norway
Canada	Poland
Czechoslovakia	Romania
Denmark	Senegal
France	Spain
Germany	UK
Hungary	USA

The Gulf War, 1990–1. In 1990, in an attempt to gain new resources with which to liquidate the debts incurred in his eight-year war against Iran, President Saddam Hussein of Iraq invaded and annexed another neighbour, Kuwait. The United Nations put pressure on Saddam to withdraw and, when he refused, United States President George Bush put together a broad coalition of states whose troops liberated Kuwait in 1991. The invasion stopped at the Iraqi frontier, however, and so Saddam Hussein survived in power, although the victors' economic sanctions, military 'no-fly zones' and 'weapons inspectors' prevented him from continuing his pre-war missile, nuclear, chemical and biological weapons programmes.

THE AFTERMATH OF VICTORY

The speed of the Coalition forces' victory in 'Operation Desert Storm' – less than four days of ground combat sufficed to drive the Iraqis into headlong retreat from Kuwait – seems to have taken the American administration by surprise: it had not yet decided when and how to terminate the war. On 27 February 1991 President Bush, apparently without directly consulting his theatre commanders, declared that a ceasefire would take effect at midnight – allegedly because the ground war would by then have lasted exactly one hundred hours. It proved a catastrophic decision for three reasons: first, contrary to early reports, Coalition forces had not yet sealed the border between Kuwait and Iraq, allowing many of Saddam Hussein's troops to escape; second, the elite 'Republican Guard' units had largely extricated themselves and remained ready and able to protect the regime against domestic opposition; third, although Kuwait was now free, the war had done nothing to improve 'the security and stability of the Persian Gulf' – one of the president's stated war aims. In the armistice arranged shortly afterwards, the Americans handed their vanquished adversaries another priceless asset: the continued use of their helicopters. So when the Kurds in the north and the Shi'ite population of southern Iraq, trusting in earlier American promises of support, rebelled against Saddam Hussein he easily crushed them, using chemical and biological as well as conventional weapons to massacre tens of thousands – some of them before the eyes of outraged American troops.

The American commanders had different priorities. Still obsessed by the stigma of defeat in Vietnam they resolutely opposed any protracted intervention in Iraq, whether by occupying its southern provinces or by supporting insurgents. Instead they wanted to declare victory as quickly and ostentatiously as possible (some wanted to hold the armistice talks on the USS *Missouri*, where the Japanese had surrendered in 1945!) and then hasten home for the victory parades. Saddam Hussein therefore remained in power, even though economic sanctions prevented post-war reconstruction (causing the death of tens of thousands of Iraqi civilians from dis-ease and deprivation) while UN arms inspections, and patrols of the southern and northern parts of Iraq (the so-called 'No-Fly Zones') by Coalition air-craft, prevented any military recovery. Although Saddam Hussein periodically refused to admit the inspectors and occasionally fired missiles at Coalition aircraft, he never regained the military capability he had possessed before the war. Nevertheless, the US left substantial armed forces deployed in the Arabian penin-sula, home of the holiest sites of Islam, as a 'rapid reaction force' in case of further trouble in the Gulf – despite the fact that their continued presence greatly offended many Muslims.

The impression created by Desert Storm that American arms might be invincible quickly faded. Late in 1992 some 33,000 troops (28,000 of them American) went to Somalia under a UN mandate to prevent a famine and halt a civil war between rival factions. Perhaps inevitably, they became sucked into the domestic conflict and, after a botched attempt to capture one of the local warlords in October 1993, his militiamen ambushed and murdered 18 American soldiers, wounded 78, and captured one. They also shot down two Blackhawk helicopters. At this point, Saddam Hussein's jibe that 'Yours is a society that cannot accept 10,000 dead in any one battle' (page 362 above) proved an exaggeration: public opinion in the United States found even eighteen deaths intolerable and demanded immediate disengage-ment. Early in 1994 the new US President, Bill Clinton, just like President Reagan following the murder of almost 200 American peacekeepers in Lebanon a decade before, recalled all remaining US forces. Although the 'Blackhawk Down' incident became the centrepiece of a popular book, film, and computer game, all Americans would live to regret the consequent display of weakness.

So would many others. Fearful that public opinion would no longer tolerate American casualties in humanitarian operations, President Clinton refused to inter-vene in 1994 when militia bands, soldiers, and policemen from the majority Hutu people of Rwanda massacred between 500,000 and 800,000 of the minority Tutsi in a matter of weeks, and forced another two million to flee. That same year he also did everything possible to avoid sending troops to end the excesses of a murderous regime in Haiti (and afterwards withdrew US forces as soon as he possibly could), and he refused to send a peacekeeping force to halt the genocide first in Bosnia and then in Kosovo, largely to avoid placing American troops in harm's way (pages 367–70 below).

THE CHECHEN WARS

Humanitarian intervention in these savage conflicts could scarcely have jeopardized the security of the United States, because in 1991 the Soviet Union – previously America's only potential challenger on the world stage – disintegrated into a Commonwealth of Independent States of which only the largest (the Russian Federation) continued to take orders from Moscow. Several military struggles emerged in the wake of the Soviet meltdown, above all in the Caucasus and in the Balkans.

Almost immediately, disputes arose between Moscow and the 'Near Abroad' (as Moscow termed the circle of states formerly included in the Union). Most were resolved peacefully, including control of the Black Sea fleet and the nuclear sites on non-Russian soil (albeit Ukraine, Belarus, and Kazakhstan now became nuclear powers); but a few led to war, especially where separatists managed to harness ethnic and religious passions. The worst conflict occurred in Chechnya, a region of the Russian Federation in the Caucasus mountains. The million Chechens, most of them Muslims, organized into 'clans', boasted a long tradition of autonomy and rebellion since their incorporation into Russia in the nineteenth century, and they refused to recognize Moscow's authority. Instead, their leaders declared independence and began to persecute the Russian minority, most of them living in and around the capital Grozny (meaning 'The Terrible', a fortress built by the original Russian invaders). Many fled. Then in 1993 civil war broke out among the different Muslim groups in Chechnya, leading Moscow to send in troops to preserve order (and also to maintain control of the vital oil pipelines that ran through the region). Although Russian armour managed to capture the cities, however, it proved incapable of defeating the Chechens in the mountains.

The war in Chechnya involved widespread brutality and caused perhaps 70,000 casualties, including some massacres of opponents captured by Russian troops. This served to unite all Chechens against the invaders until in 1996, reinforced by foreign Muslim fighters, the rebels launched a counteroffensive and recaptured Grozny. Unwilling to destroy the city in order to retake it, in August 1996 the Russian commander in the area negotiated a ceasefire and withdrew his troops: Chechnya became independent again in all but name. During the brief peace that followed, Chechen extremists carried out terrorist acts in Moscow and supported the efforts of Muslim groups elsewhere in the Federation to break free of Moscow's control until in 1999 Russian President Boris Yeltsin sent in 100,000 troops to restore control. Another bloodbath followed, with Grozny and other cities virtually destroyed while Chechen control remained unshaken in the mountains. In addition, Chechen militants continued to carry out numerous terrorist acts, including in 2004 the assassination of the Russian-appointed president, the downing of two Russian commercial airplanes, numerous suicide bombings around the Federation, and the capture of a school full of pupils, parents, and teachers. There, incompetence by both the terrorists and the Russian forces surrounding the school resulted in the death of over 300 hostages (half of them children) and the wounding of over 500 more.

THE BALKAN WARS

The collapse of the USSR caused deep ethnic divisions to resurface in Yugoslavia, a federation of six republics (Serbia, Croatia, Macedonia, Bosnia-Herzegovina, Slovenia, and Montenegro) held together by an authoritarian communist regime. After the death of the federation's founder in 1980, internal divisions appeared and, burdened by international debts, inflation, and rising unemployment, the economy declined. In 1990 multi-party elections in the constituent republics brought nationalists to the fore in Slovenia and Croatia, paving the way for their simultaneous declaration of independence in June 1991. The central Yugoslav government, dominated by the Serb leader Slobodan Milosevic, attacked; but in January 1992, after much bloodshed and destruction, UN peace-keepers and American diplomats forced him to recognize the secession of the two states.

Next, civil war broke out in Bosnia-Herzegovina, the most ethnically diverse of the former Yugoslav republics. The Bosnian Serbs wanted to remain in a union with Belgrade, while the Bosnian Muslims and Croats pushed for independence. From April 1992 each of the three ethnic groups sought to 'cleanse' the areas under its control of all opponents, and the Serbs, with support from Belgrade, conducted a particularly savage campaign in which the non-Serb men encountered were routinely killed and the non-Serb women systematically raped. Within a year Serb forces controlled around 70 per cent of Bosnia. They also blockaded the capital, Sarajevo, held by the Muslim-led government, but despite famine and high losses the city held out for over three years – one of the longest sieges in Western history.

In March 1994 President Clinton persuaded the Bosnian Muslims and Croats to form a federation, but the Bosnian Serbs refused all compromise. United Nations troops maintained five 'safe areas' for Muslim refugees in southeastern Bosnia (see map), but they were under orders to act with neutrality: UN troops could use force to protect deliveries of aid, but not to defend the intended recipients of that aid. In 1995, Bosnian Serb militia and police units commanded by Ratko Mladic decided to exploit this situation and surrounded the UN safe areas, including Srebrenica, a town close to the Serbian border protected by only two hundred lightly armed Dutch troops. Mladic's forces began to shell the town on 6 July and three days later shot one Dutch peacekeeper and took fourteen more hostage. By then, the fenced UN compound contained some 5,000 refugees, with 20,000 more outside. On 11 July the Dutch commander, Ton Karremans, called in a NATO air strike on the Bosnian Serb positions, but Mladic threatened to kill the Dutch hostages as soon as bombs began to fall. Karremans crumbled, and Mladic led his men into Srebrenica later that

The Balkan Wars.

The Yugoslav federation began to disintegrate after 1987, following the choice of Slobodan Milosevic as leader of Serbia, since he set out to expand Serbia's influence throughout the federation. Slovenia and Croatia made a simultaneous declaration of independence in 1991, provoking a vicious seven-month war when Serb forces intervened, allegedly to protect the ethnic Serb minority in Croatia. Another savage civil war broke out in Bosnia-Herzegovina, where Bosnian Muslims (44% of the population) and Croats (17%) demanded independence despite bitter opposition from the Bosnian Serbs (31%). Each ethnic group sought to 'cleanse' the areas under its control of all opponents until by 1993 the Serbs controlled around 70 per cent of Bosnia and besieged the capital, Sarajevo, held by the Muslim-led government. The war caused the death of at least 100,000 and displaced half of the region's 4 million inhabitants. In 1995 a renewed Serb offensive provoked NATO intervention, leading to an uneasy peace (the Dayton Accords) which left Bosnia divided between the three ethnic groups and utterly devastated by four years of war.

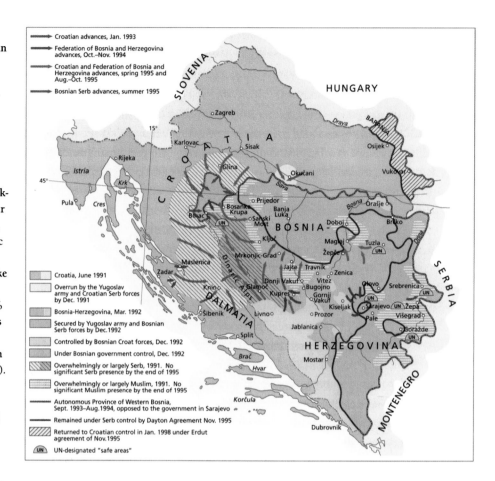

day, insisting that all Muslims surrender their arms if they wished to guarantee their safety.

Some Bosnian Muslims, foreseeing the outcome, fled to the mountains where the Serbs first shelled and then hunted them down; meanwhile Mladic oversaw the separation of the remaining men of military age, whom he detained, from the rest, whom he allowed to depart in safety. Next, Mladic offered to free the Dutch hostages and allow the peacekeepers to leave, provided they surrendered their weapons, food, and medical supplies. To save his soldiers, Karremans accepted these terms and abandoned all the Muslims still at his headquarters: Maldic's men promptly murdered them, along with any others they could find, burying their bodies in shallow graves before advancing on the other 'safe areas'. More than 8,000 Bosnian Muslims perished at Srebrenica – some with bullets and grenades, others through hunger, heat, or wounds as they fled. It was the worst military atrocity to occur in Europe since the end of World War II fifty years before.

The shallow graves showed up on satellite images released by the Clinton administration the following month and US journalists soon uncovered evidence of the massacres. NATO warplanes belatedly began a bombing campaign that forced the Serbs to pull back while Croatian ground forces seized the opportunity to invade

A survivor of the killings at Srebrenica grieves among the coffins of those murdered, whose bodies were about to be buried on 11 July 2005, the tenth anniversary of the massacres. Srebrenica was the first of the 'safe areas' established by the UN to protect Bosnian Muslim civilians from Bosnian Serb attempts to create an ethnically homogeneous and contiguous Bosnian Serb Republic bordering Serbia, whose border lay only ten miles away. More than 8,000 Bosnian Muslim men and boys over the age of twelve were executed, often hundreds at a time, in various locations, such as warehouses and playing fields selected in advance for this purpose.

and gain territory. In November, abandoned by Milosevic, the Bosnian Serbs bowed to American-backed pressure to accept a settlement, creating two fragile mini-states: a Serb Republic and a Muslim-Croat federation, each with a shattered economy. A UN 'High Representative' in Sarajevo monitored the peace process. The three-year Bosnian war had cost 250,000 lives (20,000 more remain missing, presumed dead), while by August 1995 over two million people from the former Yugoslavia had registered as refugees, about half of them from Bosnia.

In 2002, almost simultaneously, the United Nations unveiled a $12.5 million recovery package to improve the housing, the infrastructure, and the local economy of Srebrenica, and the Dutch Institute for War Documentation issued a detailed report that blamed both the UN and the Dutch government for failing to prevent the massacre. In an example of humility unprecedented among politicians, the entire Dutch cabinet resigned. Meanwhile the Dutch hosted an International Criminal Tribunal for the former Yugoslavia (ICTY), established by a 1993 resolution of the UN Security Council. By the end of 2007, the tribunal had indicted more than 160 persons for war crimes and tried more than 100 of them, including the Serb leader Slobodan Milosevic, the first former head of state to stand trial before an international court for his official acts. Milosevic, like most Serbs, vociferously denied that any atrocities had taken place in Bosnia (or indeed anywhere else in the Yugoslav wars he had unleashed), but the harrowing testimony of more than 5,000 witnesses, the exhumation of the bodies of many victims, and the publication of photos and films that showed their murder made this view untenable. In June 2004 Bosnian Serb officials finally admitted that their security forces had indeed carried out the massacre at Srebrenica, and the following year – a decade after the mass murders – they confirmed that police units from Serbia itself had also taken part.

Milosevic faced additional criminal charges arising from another war. In 1990 he had unilaterally ended the semi-autonomy enjoyed within Serbia by Kosovo, a province central to Serb national identity inhabited mostly by Muslims, and after six years of mainly passive resistance a group of militant Muslims formed the Kosovo Liberation Army (KLA), dedicated to gaining independence. In 1998, in response to KLA attacks on local Serbs, Milosevic sanctioned reprisals that forced hundreds of thousands of Muslims to flee, a process he proudly termed 'ethnic cleansing'. The threat of armed intervention by NATO led to peace discussions over the winter of 1998–9, but, although the Kosovar leaders declared themselves willing to accept autonomy within Serbia as a temporary compromise, with a later referendum on independence, Milosevic rejected the deal and ordered ethnic cleansing to resume.

NATO warplanes flew some 10,000 sorties in spring 1999, targeting both Serbia's main cities and Serb units in Kosovo in the hope of forcing Belgrade to accept the peace agreement. The mission failed. Even though their bombs caused enormous material damage, the fact that the NATO planes flew at or above 15,000 feet in order to avoid ground fire and the skilful use of camouflage enabled Serb forces to preserve most of their armament intact. Whenever night or bad weather kept NATO warplanes on the ground, Serb units in Kosovo continued to kill, rape, loot, and burn with impunity. By the time Milosevic eventually admitted defeat (more through Russian diplomatic pressure than through the eleven weeks of NATO bombing), approximately 600,000 Muslims had fled Kosovo and thousands of men had been murdered and thousands of women raped. Only when 40,000 NATO troops (KFOR) entered the province in June 1999 did Serb forces leave and the KLA lay down its arms. Milosevic's four wars, although allegedly waged to protect the Serb homeland, left much of Yugoslavia in ruins. Reconstruction began only after the Serbian opposition forced Milosevic from office in 2000 and sent him to stand trial for war crimes before the ICTY in The Hague.

OTHER CASUALTIES OF WAR

The war atrocities in the Balkans did not stand alone. The chilling events at Srebrenica, Kosovo, and elsewhere in the former Yugoslavia were paralleled in civil wars elsewhere in the late twentieth and early twenty-first centuries: in Sri Lanka and parts of Indonesia in Asia and in Algeria, Angola, Eritrea, Ethiopia, Liberia, Rwanda, Sierra Leone, Somalia, Sudan, and Zaire (also known as the Democratic Republic of Congo) in Africa. Each of these conflicts caused immense human and material destruction. The decade of war in Zaire (1996–2006), the most serious interstate conflict in modern African history, involved troops from nine states and directly affected the lives of 50 million Congolese: almost 4 million died (most of them from starvation and disease caused by the war rather than from the fighting itself); millions more fled their homes and became displaced either internally or in neighbouring countries. Even when the killing ceased, each country experienced economic dislocation, exacerbated by a very high birth rate that in time increased the number of young men for whom joining a militia group often offered the only chance of survival – at least in the short term.

In many Muslim countries in Central and West Asia, too, high birth rates produced far more young people than the local economies could absorb. In Afghanistan and Pakistan, in particular, many young males found material and spiritual sustenance in religious schools (*madrasas*), where they absorbed a radical ideology that demonized the West and its principal ally in the Middle East, the state of Israel. The continued Israeli occupation of areas conquered from its Arab neighbours in 1967 (see page 358), and the proliferation of Jewish settlements there, provoked passionate resentment among many Muslims and, from 1987, a campaign of civil disobedience (called the *Intifada,* from an Arabic word meaning 'shaking off') among Palestinian Arabs. Hundreds died in a cycle of killings and reprisals. For a time in the mid-1990s peace seemed possible when, under intense pressure from President Clinton, Palestinian and Israeli leaders agreed to interim self-government for the West Bank and the Gaza Strip, but the Palestinians rejected a further plan to create two independent states in the region.

A second *Intifada* began in 2000, and Palestinian suicide bombers and Israeli missile strikes caused significant losses of life and property, while Israeli ground forces invaded the territories controlled by the Palestinian authority in search of militants. The cycle of violence empowered the militants, and in 2006 democratic elections delivered a majority of seats in the Palestinian Legislative Council to Hamas (the acronym of *Harakat al-Muqawama al-Islamiyya,* Islamic Resistance Movement, but also an Arabic word meaning 'zeal'), an organization whose proclaimed political goals included the destruction of Israel and the raising of 'the banner of Allah over every inch of Palestine'. Israel and its Western allies now froze assets and revenues belonging to the Palestinian Authority, which produced political chaos, economic hardship, and mounting desperation. Armed clashes between Israelis and Palestinians increased.

Israel also faced a major security problem on its northern frontier. In 1982, in response to attacks launched on its territories by Palestinian exiles based in Lebanon, Israeli forces invaded and occupied the southern part of the country. The occupation encouraged the formation of new Muslim militant groups, including Hezbollah (Arabic for 'Party of God'), and in 2000, partly due to Hezbollah's successful guerrilla tactics, Israel withdrew its forces from southern Lebanon. This, too, failed to bring peace, and Hezbollah rocket attacks and raids continued until, in July 2006, Israel retaliated by land, sea, and air. A month-long campaign caused widespread disruption and devastation in Lebanon, but Hezbollah continued to hit targets deep inside Israel until a ceasefire imposed by the United Nations ended the fighting. Hezbollah's ability to acquire and deploy sophisticated Russian- and Iranian-made missiles, coupled with the failure of Israel's ground forces to prevail, suggested that the peace would not hold for long. Nevertheless, Israel's ability to penetrate and disable the entire defensive system of Syria (an outspoken supporter of Hezbollah) while its jets destroyed a suspected nuclear installation in September 2007 showed that it retained the edge in conventional warfare.

Although hostilities continued between Israel and some of its neighbours, several long-running conflicts in other parts of the world ended in the 1990s. In Latin America, negotiations terminated civil wars in Nicaragua, El Salvador, and Guatemala; while in Peru the capture of the leader of the Maoist 'Shining Path' movement ended a major insurrection. In Northern Ireland, where British troops had struggled in vain since 1969 to end the armed violence between Protestant and Catholic militants, US mediation helped to bring about the 'Good Friday Accord' in 1998 that largely ended the slaughter. When progress towards peace later stalled, the US decision to freeze the assets of all organizations suspected of aiding terrorism (see page 376) deprived the Catholics of Northern Ireland of vital support, and in May 2007 their leaders took office alongside their former rivals in a 'power-sharing' administration. Two months later they achieved one of their principal goals: the British Army withdrew from Ulster after the longest continuous deployment in its history: thirty-eight years.

LESSONS NOT LEARNED

These 'dirty wars' of the 1990s revealed significant weaknesses in the Western way of war. First, NATO's failure to halt 'ethnic cleansing' in Kosovo indicated important limits to the effectiveness of aerial bombardment. As early as 1922, a British report on the failure to end insurgency in Iraq concluded: 'Aeroplanes by themselves are unable to compel the surrender or defeat of hostile tribes'. The experience of first France and then the United States in Vietnam fully confirmed this verdict, and even in the Gulf War 'boots on the ground' proved essential in expelling Iraqi forces from Kuwait. Airstrikes alone, whatever the degree of 'surgical precision' achieved and whether delivered by fixed-wing aircraft or helicopters, could not entirely eliminate resourceful and determined opponents. The Kosovo campaign also confirmed a second legacy. Understandably, President Clinton showed extreme reluctance to put American troops in harm's way in the Balkans, since the Serbs posed no clear and present threat to US security. Less understandably, he advertised his reluctance by declaring publicly that he would commit no ground forces to Kosovo – thereby letting Milosevic know that he could carry out his murderous plans with impunity. So although Clinton's strategy ensured that not a single American perished in the Kosovo campaign, it also reinforced the impression created in Somalia that the US was no longer prepared to commit its troops to a ground war.

The second innovation in the conflicts of the 1990s occurred in war reporting. Saddam Hussein had allowed Western journalists to remain in Baghdad throughout the Gulf War and send live reports (albeit subject to censorship), so that astonished audiences could watch film shot by one camera crew of Coalition planes taking off from their bases followed by footage taken by their colleagues as the same planes avoided Iraqi anti-aircraft fire and dropped their bombs on the capital. Four years

Operation near Shatoi - 1996

Operation near Shatoi - 1996

Technology has allowed insurgents everywhere to spread their message quickly around the world: records and audiocassettes broadcast on radio have given way to videocassettes and digital images screened on television and on the Internet, in particular Internet sharing sites. YouTube, for example, although dominated by pop music videos and strange deeds recorded by strange people, also posts videos of armed conflicts (although YouTube regularly removes footage deemed to be offensive, so something viewed today may be gone tomorrow). The Chechen War of 1994–6 produced the first such videos and also the first 'video stars', like Amir al-Khattab, a Saudi mujahideen leader, who made his reputation (and raised money and support throughout the Muslim world) with film of his devastating ambush of a Russian armored column near Shatoi. The first of the two "frames" above, posted by the Turkish-based www.cihad.net and supplied with Turkish subtitles, shows the column take a direct hit; the second shows the Russian soldiers killed by the ambush.

later, although Boris Yeltsin forbade foreign journalists to enter the Chechen war zone he allowed Russian reporters to 'embed' with his troops and to broadcast film and commentary, even when the invasion bogged down. Furthermore, the spread of the Internet allowed the Chechens to broadcast to the world images that presented the cruelty of the invaders and the hollowness of Moscow's repeated claims of 'imminent victory'. They did the same again in 1999, when Russian forces launched their second invasion; so did supporters of Slobodan Milosevic, who staged rock concerts during NATO aerial bombardments to demonstrate both their contempt for the enemy and the inaccuracy of the bombing. Milosevic could not control foreign reporters, however. For example, two days after the satellite images revealed possible mass graves around Srebrenica in 1996, David Rohde of the *Christian Science Monitor* hired a translator and a driver and, almost single-handed, revealed the killing-fields to the world. Governments at war could no longer conceal from the wider world their atrocities – at least, not in areas about which the wider world cared.

Finally, operations in both Chechnya and Somalia demonstrated the extreme difficulty of crushing by conventional means highly motivated guerrillas fighting in areas – especially urban areas – which they knew far better than invading troops. Such asymmetrical warfare created two disadvantages for the invaders. On the one hand, the high degree of training and 'high tech' weaponry of modern war makes it relatively hard to convert human and economic resources from civilian to military use; but this is not so for militants able to use 'low tech' weaponry against the invaders' infrastructure or isolated positions. On the other hand, the longer the resistance lasts, the greater the opportunity for the resisters to receive reinforcements. Thus *mujahideen* (an Arabic word meaning 'those who struggle') flocked from all over the Muslim world into Afghanistan, Chechnya and Somalia. Prominent among these mujahideen were members of a small organization of Muslim fundamentalists known as al-Qaeda ('The Base') operating out of Sudan and led by a charismatic Saudi, Osama bin Laden. Early in 1992, Bin Laden issued a *fatwa* (religious edict) calling on all Muslims to undertake a holy war against the Western troops who had 'occupied' Islamic lands (especially Arabia). Somalia was his first proving ground, and he followed up the success of mujahideen there by supporting similar efforts in Chechnya, Bosnia, and elsewhere. From the first, however, he stressed that the battle could only be won by cutting off 'the head of the snake' – by which he meant the United States of America. He noted with interest the unsuccessful attempt in 1993 by an Islamic cell to bring down the twin towers of the World Trade Center in New York by detonating a truck filled with explosives. Its failure not only revealed America's casual, complacent, and confused attitude when under direct attack, but also prompted al-Qaeda leaders to devote close attention to the Center's structural weaknesses.

AMERICA UNDER ATTACK

At first Bin Laden sought 'soft targets', such as a joint Saudi–US military training facility in the Saudi capital, where al-Qaeda operatives detonated a car bomb in 1995, killing five Americans; but he also considered more ambitious strategies. Two years later, his agents bought a cylinder containing what they thought was weapons-grade uranium because, as one of them helpfully explained, 'it's easy to kill more people with uranium'. By then, international demands for Sudan to surrender Bin Laden had led him to flee to Afghanistan. When he arrived, control of the country was contested by the various warring groups, but in 1996 Kabul, the capital, fell to the Taliban (Sunni Muslim extremists, most of them Arabs rather than Afghans) and they made Bin Laden welcome, providing him and his associates with freedom of movement and allowing them to establish and run camps where between 10,000 and 20,000 devout Muslim recruits from around the world would learn how to attack Western interests.

Relatively few recruits would be deemed 'worthy' to become full members of al-Qaeda, however, for whereas in Sudan Bin Laden had merely provided training, weapons and funds to enable other groups to carry out the actual attacks, he now made plans to strike at 'the head of the snake' himself. In February 1998 he issued another *fatwa* claiming that the United States had declared war against God and his Prophet, and stating that the murder of Americans was now the 'individual duty for every Muslim who can do it in any country in which it is possible to do it'. Shortly afterwards, in an interview for American television, he re-emphasized that 'it is far better for anyone to kill a single American soldier than to squander his efforts on other activities', but immediately added that 'We do not differentiate between military or civilian. As far as we are concerned, they are all targets.' The following August, al-Qaeda suicide bombers simultaneously drove two trucks filled with explosives into the American embassies in Nairobi, Kenya, and Dar-es-Salaam, Tanzania, and detonated them, killing 12 Americans and over 200 others, and wounding thousands more (almost all of them Africans). Bin Laden immediately claimed responsibility and then, fearing American retaliation, took refuge in the Afghan countryside. Two weeks later, Tomahawk Cruise missiles fired from US warships struck a factory in Sudan allegedly manufacturing nerve gas for al-Qaeda and several of its training camps in Afghanistan. Although the missiles did extensive damage and killed between 20 and 30 people, Bin Laden was not among them.

In 1999, al-Qaeda planned a further operation designed to kill Americans and so persuade them to withdraw from the holy ground of Arabia. At first they thought of attacking an oil tanker with a boatload of explosives, but Bin Laden changed the objective to a US warship. In January 2000 a suicide team tried to sink one in the port of Aden, but their boat foundered en route; eight months later another team managed to damage – though not to sink – the USS *Cole* as it lay at anchor there, killing 17 American sailors and wounding 40 more. Once again, Bin Laden went into hiding to avoid the anticipated retaliatory strike, but this time none came.

Two factors explain the lack of any overt US response. First, three weeks after the attack on the *Cole*, America held a presidential election that produced a disputed result. For over a month, the nation focussed its attention on whether or not George W. Bush would succeed Bill Clinton as president, making it virtually impossible to coordinate another missile attack on Afghanistan. Second, even had a strike been considered, US intelligence and military officials feared that direct action – especially in the absence of direct evidence of Bin Laden's involvement – would provoke an Islamic backlash. Everyone in Washington remembered the verdict of *The Economist* of London after the 1998 strikes, that only time would tell whether the missiles 'had created 10,000 new fanatics where there would have been none'. They also recalled the outrage around the world the following year when a NATO bomb hit the Chinese embassy in Belgrade, apparently by mistake. Yet even without a provocative retaliation by America, the attack on the *Cole* served as a powerful recruitment tool for al-Qaeda. Bin Laden instructed the movement's Media Committee to prepare a propaganda video that included a re-enactment of the operation, footage of the training camps, and images of the sufferings of Muslims in Palestine, Indonesia, and Chechnya. Al-Qaeda's camps in Afghanistan soon received a fresh wave of zealous recruits.

Bin Laden already had fresh targets in mind. As George Bush focussed first on seizing the presidency and then on creating a 'missile shield' to protect America against the threat of a sudden catastrophic attack – for the number of countries with nuclear weapons continued to increase: Israel and North Korea; four states in the former Soviet Union; India and Pakistan – al-Qaeda prepared another daring and deadly operation. On 11 September 2001 members of the group hijacked three commercial airlines shortly after takeoff and crashed them into the twin towers of the World Trade Center in New York and the Pentagon in Washington. Passengers aboard a fourth hijacked airplane, which had taken off late, learned via their cell-phones of the intentions of the hijackers and forced them to crash in a field in Pennsylvania before reaching their designated target. Their extraordinary heroism saved either the US Capitol or the White House, and those in them that morning, from almost certain destruction. Even so, for an outlay of under $500,000, and their own lives, the nineteen hijackers selected by Bin Laden killed within the space of just under an hour approximately 3,000 Americans (and probably many others), caused billions of dollars of damage, and ended forever America's sense of invulnerability.

THE EMPIRE STRIKES BACK

With the exception of Palestine, Iraq, and a few other countries that felt little sympathy for the United States, the '9/11 attacks' (as they became known) outraged world opinion. In London, England, the guardsmen at Buckingham palace played the American national anthem; in Aberdeen, Scotland, all traffic lights turned to red for two minutes as a sign of solidarity. In addition, by 18 September 2001, 58 countries had pledged assistance (ranging from search-and-rescue equipment and personnel, through medical assistance teams, to troops) for a US-led invasion of Afghanistan. Two days later, President Bush issued an ultimatum: 'The Taliban must act, and act immediately', he announced in a televised address to Congress. 'They will hand over the terrorists or they will share their fate.' The following day he approved plans for air strikes and attacks on al-Qaeda and Taliban targets by Special Operations forces in association with the troops of sympathetic Afghan warlords, followed by a small-scale invasion by US ground forces stationed in neighbouring countries. Since the Taliban declined to surrender Bin Laden to President Bush, the aerial bombardment began on 7 October 2001, by coincidence the anniversary of the defeat of the Ottoman Turks at Lepanto in 1571 (page 122 above). The Taliban regime, which had become very unpopular after five years of brutal rule, collapsed within two months as the US and its allies launched 6,500 strike missions and Afghan forces opposed to the Taliban (aided by some US units) attacked surviving al-Qaeda fighters in the Tora Bora mountains along the eastern border. The whole operation cost the Coalition fewer than 20 dead. Shortly afterwards an exiled politician, Hamid Kharzai, 'returned to Kabul as interim head of state and in 2004, following Afghanistan's first democratic election in history, he became president. The new regime depended on support from two key allies: on the one hand, sympathetic Afghan warlords, now referred to as 'regional leaders', who continued to hold sway in most northern provinces, and, on the other hand, almost 40,000 troops maintained by NATO and the United States, tasked with maintaining order elsewhere. Although sustained military pressure, coupled with the deportation and imprisonment of suspected insurgents to Coalition prisons around the world (principally to a makeshift US facility at Guantánamo Bay, Cuba), temporarily crippled both the Taliban and al-Qaeda, their forces regrouped in remote areas on both sides of the Pakistan border and launched numerous attacks.

The initial success of the United States in Afghanistan restored the military prestige it had lost in Somalia and demonstrated that Western military technology could prevail even without the support of large ground forces. Yet it formed only the preliminary phase of President Bush's planned response to the 9/11 attacks. On 25 October 2001, he signed *National Security Presidential Directive 9*, entitled 'Defeating the Terrorist Threat to the United States'. It envisaged a global war of terrorism; it made no distinction between the terrorists and those who harboured them; and it declared that military force would be used if necessary. A series of annexes discussed each targeted terrorist group and how best to dry up its financial support and prevent it from acquiring weapons of mass destruction. The president's goal was the 'elimination of terrorism as a threat to our way of life'. At home, the US Treasury froze the assets and ended the financial activities in America of any organization suspected of terrorism or supporting terrorism: this included not only groups thought to have links with al-Qaeda but also networks operating elsewhere, including those suspected of funding the campaign of the Irish Republican Army to drive the British from Northern Ireland. Abroad, the president sought evidence that other regimes favoured al-Qaeda, and his suspicions immediately fell upon Iraq. Others in his administration agreed and some argued that US forces should strike Afghanistan and Iraq simultaneously because it seemed to them likely that Saddam Hussein had somehow sponsored the 9/11 attacks.

Although the president ruled out a simultaneous double strike, his senior military advisers began to plan for the invasion of Iraq in the near future. They were not alone. In February 2002, the British government commissioned a survey of the weapons of mass destruction capabilities of four countries, including Iraq, and shortly afterwards Prime Minister Tony Blair commissioned a similar enquiry, this time dealing only with Iraq. In September, Blair announced that his government would publish a full report presenting evidence that Iraq possessed both weapons of mass destruction and the capacity to use them and, with minimal direction from the Prime Minister's office, his intelligence experts obligingly declared that 'the Iraqi military were able to deploy weapons of mass destruction within 45 minutes of a decision to do so'.

President Bush cited this statement – and other claims provided by American and foreign intelligence sources – to justify designating Iraq (together with Iran and North Korea) as part of an 'axis of evil' that threatened world security. He now began to shift American resources (both military and intelligence) from Afghanistan and he sought a mandate both from the United Nations and from NATO to invade Iraq. The mandate was not forthcoming and, when Bush nevertheless pressed ahead, the solid sympathy for America in the wake of 9/11 began to fade. Instead, massive demonstrations against the impending war took place worldwide – one in February 2003, coordinated for the first time by Internet, brought millions of people out onto the streets. Spain, whose Prime Minister José Maria Aznar had declared unequivocal support for the invasion and promised to send troops, saw the largest mass demonstrations in its history: in Madrid, one million people – one-third of the capital's total population – marched against the war.

To no avail: in March 2003, President Bush issued an ultimatum that, unless Saddam left Iraq, he would order US forces to invade and, as soon as the ultimatum expired, US warplanes began a spectacular bombardment of Iraqi government buildings and other targets (including a 'decapitation strike' against Saddam himself). Coalition forces then invaded Iraq from Kuwait (Turkey refused to become involved) and, to the surprise of many observers (especially in the Arab world), captured Baghdad in less than three weeks. Organized resistance in most areas temporarily ceased, and although Saddam Hussein and many of his top advisers disappeared, by the end of 2003 Coalition forces had captured most of them (including Saddam Hussein).

In purely operational terms, the campaign had proved a resounding success. The Iraqi forces, which had never recovered their previous combat effectiveness after the last Gulf War, proved unable to resist either the enhanced firepower deployed by Coalition forces on the ground, by night as well as by day, or the 'smart' bombs and unmanned warplanes that could attack in all weather. Thus when a sandstorm halted the advance of American ground troops, Iraqi armoured forces decided to counterattack – unaware until too late that (unlike their colleagues over Kosovo) technology now allowed American pilots to 'see' the tanks through the dust and so destroy them. The rest of Iraq's armed forces, including the elite Republican Guard units, either fled or surrendered. The victors won the campaign with remarkably few losses: under 150 battle deaths.

Before long, some of the 'lessons not learned' in the wars of the 1990s changed this rosy picture. Above all, President Bush and his closest advisers overlooked the fact that America's successful wars in the past – World War II and Korea as well as the Balkans – had often led to open-ended commitments that lasted for decades and cost billions of dollars. They therefore did not plan for this possibility. Such an egregious failure to learn from history merits closer examination. The president offered three justifications for invading Iraq: first, Saddam Hussein possessed 'weapons of mass destruction' that threatened world peace; second, Saddam supported Al-Qaeda and other international terrorist groups and so threatened American security; finally, replacing a dictator who had already started two wars of aggression would bring stability both to Iraq and to the Middle East as a whole, reducing the deprivation, ignorance, and corruption that fuelled violent Islamist

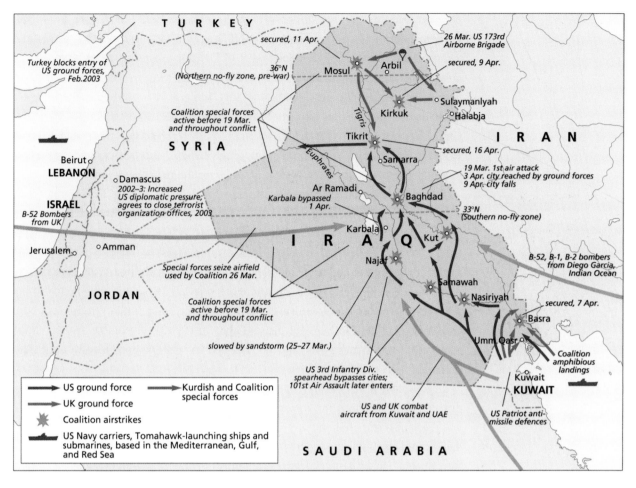

The invasion of Iraq 2003. The original US strategy to overthrow Saddam Hussein and his regime called for a devastating aerial bombardment (immodestly called 'Shock and Awe') followed by the simultaneous invasion of Iraq by US-led ground forces from Turkey and US and British forces from Kuwait in March 2003. The month before, the Turkish government announced that it would not allow US forces to pass through its territory but 'Shock and Awe' began anyway on 19 March (including an unsuccessful 'decapitation strike' intended to kill Saddam Hussein). Shortly afterwards, US airborne troops joined Kurdish supporters to take several northern cities, while British forces occupied Basra, Iraq's second-largest city, and surrounding areas. Meanwhile US infantry made a daring northward advance from Kuwait toward Baghdad, relying on close air support to weaken their opponents. They reached the Iraqi capital on 3 April and the city fell six days later. Within three weeks, a mere 125,000 Western troops had taken control of a country the size of California with 25 million inhabitants.

extremists. Bush believed that American forces could achieve all three goals within six months.

How could the president have been so wrong? To begin with, just like his predecessor John F. Kennedy when considering support for the Bay of Pigs operation forty years before (see page 350), George W. Bush received euphoric predictions of massive popular support for the invasion not only from the CIA but also from some eloquent and wealthy exiles (most of them long absent from their native land). One of them, Ahmed Chalabi (a Shi'ite who left Iraq in 1956, aged twelve), gained the ear of senior officials in the Department of Defense. Together, these advocates of armed intervention persuaded the president that, as soon as Coalition troops had eliminated Saddam Hussein, Sunni and Shi'a Iraqis alike would greet the invaders as liberators, just as had happened in Kuwait in 1991 and in Kosovo in 1999. Unlike Kennedy forty years before, President Bush resolved that this time US forces would invade alongside the exiles (including Chalabi), and he instructed his secretary of defense, Donald H. Rumsfeld, to draw up the necessary plans.

Rumsfeld resembled Kennedy's secretary of defense, Robert McNamara: both were veterans-turned–business executives who sought to streamline the US military by imposing commercial management techniques. Where McNamara favoured 'systems analysis', Rumsfeld embraced 'just-in-time logistics', which (he predicted) would enable lighter and more mobile forces equipped with 'smart' weapons to outperform larger, slower armies. He therefore rejected the plans drawn up by his generals to overthrow Saddam Hussein by deploying half a million troops, as in the Gulf War of 1991. Instead he insisted that just 130,000 combat troops could achieve the president's goals, and he harassed his generals relentlessly until they prepared plans to do this.

The success of 'Operation Iraqi Freedom', in which 130,000 Coalition troops defeated Saddam Hussein's forces in three weeks, not only vindicated Rumsfeld's vision but also lent credibility to his further contention that the same number of soldiers would also suffice to secure Iraq until a democratic government could take over. Nevertheless, some generals expressed doubts. Thus, at a congressional hearing a month before the invasion, a member of the Senate Armed Services Committee asked General Eric Shinseki, the US Army chief of staff, to 'give us some idea as to the magnitude of the army's force requirement for an occupation of Iraq following a successful completion of the war'. After some hesitation, the general responded: 'Something on the order of several hundred thousand soldiers'. He justified his figure, so different from that of Rumsfeld, his political superior, with some blindingly obvious facts:

> We're talking about post-hostilities control over a piece of geography that's fairly significant, with the kinds of ethnic tensions that could lead to other problems. And so it takes a significant ground-force presence to maintain a safe and secure environment, to ensure that people are fed, that water is distributed, all the normal responsibilities that go along with administering a situation like this.

Rumsfeld and his staff hastened to pour scorn on the caution of the Army's senior general. Two days later, in testimony to the House Budget Committee, Deputy Secretary of Defense Paul Wolfowitz observed that

> there has been a good deal of comment – some of it quite outlandish – about what our postwar requirements might be in Iraq. Some of the higher-end predictions

we have been hearing recently, such as the notion that it will take several hundred thousand US troops to provide stability in post-Saddam Iraq, are wildly off the mark. It is hard to conceive that it would take more forces to provide stability in post-Saddam Iraq than it would take to conduct the war itself and to secure the surrender of Saddam's security forces and his army – hard to imagine.

After this outburst, it was also 'hard to imagine' that other generals would risk public humiliation at the hands of their political superiors; criticism from the military establishment therefore temporarily ceased. The US government had returned to groupthink.

Nevertheless, Paul Wolfowitz was entirely correct that the idea of sending 'several hundred thousand US troops to provide stability in post-Saddam Iraq' was 'wildly off the mark'. The steady reduction in the size of the armed forces after 1991 meant that 'several hundred thousand US troops' could serve in Iraq (or anywhere else) on a prolonged basis only if the president kept every regular, reserve, and National Guard unit permanently mobilized. As it was, the 130,000 US soldiers already in Iraq included a significant number of reserve troops, because their skills and backgrounds were in short supply in the regular army, but even they had received no training in how to administer a country the size of California with a diverse population of 25 million (or, as General Shinseki had presciently put it: 'a piece of geography that's fairly significant, with the kinds of ethnic tensions that could lead to other problems').

Once they had toppled the huge statue of Saddam Hussein in Baghdad's Firdos Square on 9 April 2003, signalling the end of his rule, lacking specific orders Coalition forces stood aside while mobs looted and wrecked almost every unguarded installation of the fallen regime. As the journalist George Packer astutely noted, 'the gutted buildings, the lost equipment, the destroyed records, the damaged infrastructure, would continue to haunt almost every aspect of the reconstruction'; but even such extensive physical damage 'was less catastrophic than those effects that couldn't be quantified. Iraqis' first experience of freedom was chaos and violence.'

This catastrophe stemmed from the president's failure to prepare adequate plans for reconstruction and state-building. On 20 January 2003, less than sixty days before the planned invasion began, Bush entrusted the post-war administration of Iraq after its 'liberation' to the Department of Defense rather than to the State Department (which boasted extensive recent experience of state-building efforts in Haiti, the Balkans, and elsewhere). Rumsfeld, in turn, created a very small Office of Reconstruction and Humanitarian Assistance (ORHA) in the Pentagon and chose as its head a retired general, Jay Garner, who had handled humanitarian relief to Iraq's Kurdish population in the wake of the First Gulf War. With so little time to prepare, Garner decided (no doubt on the basis of his earlier exposure to Saddam Hussein's brutal way of war) that ORHA's overriding priority was to plan 'humanitarian assistance': how to cope with the mass starvation and epidemics, with the huge numbers of refugees and prisoners and, above all, with the aftermath of chemical weapons attacks that the general expected to follow Saddam's defeat. Garner expected that he would only deal with reconstruction and state-building later; because (happily) none of these anticipated disasters materialized, he lacked plans for the very different scenario that faced him in April 2003. Garner therefore decided to remove only the leading echelons of Saddam Hussein's ruling Ba'ath party, leaving the rest to work for an interim government of returned Iraqi exiles headed by Ahmad Chalabi. The looting and chaos that followed the fall of Saddam delayed implementation of even this minimalist plan: the military authorities did not deem the capital safe enough for the ORHA teams to enter until 23 April, and by then Washington had changed its mind about how to run post-war Iraq. The following day Rumsfeld informed Garner that he would be replaced and, two weeks later, President Bush announced the appointment of Paul Bremer, a former State Department diplomat who had studied counter-terrorism, as his representative in Iraq.

Like Garner, Bremer received his orders directly from Rumsfeld; unlike Garner, Bremer flew straight from Washington to Baghdad, where he created the Coalition Provisional Authority (CPA), eventually staffed by 1,200 officials (almost all Americans), to govern the country. All plans to form an interim Iraqi government were frozen; instead on 16 May 2003 Bremer issued a proclamation announcing the far-reaching powers assumed by the CPA, with himself as 'administrator', by virtue of 'the relevant UN security council resolutions, and the laws and usages of war'. In other words, Iraq was now an occupied country. If any entertained doubts on this point, the CPA's first order expelled all 'active members' of Saddam's Ba'ath party from government (including the hospitals, universities, schools, and social services). At least 35,000 civil servants, most of them Sunni, lost their jobs, salaries, and pensions overnight. The CPA's second order dissolved all of Iraq's armed forces. Jay Garner later recalled that he woke up the next day to find 'three or four hundred thousand enemies and no Iraqi face on the government'; his planning chief, Paul Hughes, believed that 'from the Iraqi viewpoint, that simple action took away the one symbol of sovereignty the Iraqi people still had'. Although later proclamations by the CPA claimed that it acted 'on behalf, and for the benefit, of the Iraqi people', Hughes believed that the dissolution of Iraqi's armed forces was 'when we crossed the line. We stopped being liberators and became occupiers'.

The CPA's opponents drew on two sources of strength: weapons and faith. Although Saddam Hussein had failed to stockpile 'weapons of mass destruction', he still possessed a formidable arsenal of conventional weapons. Fearing further domestic uprisings, like those that followed the end of the Gulf War in 1991, he had distributed caches of weapons and equipment all over Iraq, ready for his security forces to use in case of another insurrection. Instead, guerrilla groups seized these weapons as soon as it became clear that the CPA lacked the forces to control the country. Insurgents attacked with small arms, rocket-propelled grenades, and, most lethal of all, improvised explosive devices (IEDs: military or home-made munitions placed under or on the side of a road and exploded either by a command wire or by a remote controller such as a pager, garage door opener, or mobile phone). The insurgents, often former members of Saddam Hussein's security forces, killed or maimed hundreds of Coalition troops, who lacked sufficient armour for both themselves and their vehicles, thanks to Rumsfeld's 'just-in-time' logistics. The troops also had no mechanism to stockpile vital equipment in case of emergency. Meanwhile Shi'a militias took advantage of the power vacuum created by the CPA's purge of Ba'ath Party members to take over schools, hospitals and charitable institutions, imposing strict Islamic practices as they did so. They thus built up a valuable power base for future operations against the Coalition.

Media coverage, too, soon inflamed opposition to the CPA. The US military, just like the Russians in Chechnya, allowed journalists to travel 'embedded' in individual units, and so their reports reflected the viewpoint of the troops whom they accompanied; they provided little or no information about their Iraqi opponents. Soon, however, some French and Arab journalists began to report on resistance activity and placed their film footage on sympathetic television networks, which also carried material provided by 'media cells' created by the various insurgent groups. These media cells also publicized every success against the Coalition through posters, handbills, videos, DVDs, and, above all, the Internet (thanks to the CPA's efforts to promote increased access to the World Wide Web). Al-Qaeda, in particular, planned its operations according to their potential media impact rather than their direct military or economic impact. Yet it was the Americans themselves who provided the insurgents with their greatest propaganda coups. The US government held numerous Muslim suspects for years without trial in the makeshift prison at Guantánamo Bay; also, in spring 2004 images taken with digital cameras and camcorders of American military personnel (both male and female) torturing and humiliating Iraqi prisoners in Abu Ghraib prison near Baghdad appeared first on the Internet and then on television. A more powerful recruiting tool for the insurgents would be hard to imagine.

Three changes in insurgent strategy also compromised the ability of the CPA to govern Iraq. First, again like the Russians in Chechnya, Coalition troops became tied down in vicious urban warfare in which their enemies' superior knowledge of the terrain, and widespread popular support or acquiescence, neutralized many of the advantages conferred by superior weaponry. Second, the insurgents inside Iraq systematically chose 'soft targets': America's allies and the country's infrastructure. They launched suicide bombers against Italian troops; kidnapped and murdered Japanese and British contract workers; tortured and beheaded Iraqis who worked for the CPA; destroyed the offices and personnel of humanitarian organizations (including the UN and the Red Cross); and sabotaged the installations on which economic recovery depended. Images of each operation soon appeared on the Internet and on sympathetic television stations. Third, with so many of America's resources concentrated in Iraq, and now without a territorial base, al-Qaeda worked

US soldiers, together with members of the Iraqi Civil Defense Corps, patrol the Sunni neighborhood of Adhamiya, Baghdad, in January 2004 (on the left: one Iraqi wears a mask to avoid being recognized). Although the streets appear empty, all the cars have people in them; they have pulled to the sides of the road to allow the patrol to pass. Moreover, although Baghdad streets are normally filthy, Coalition forces paid local workers to keep them clean because insurgents would often hide bombs in the roadside trash.

through other Islamic groups to attack Western targets abroad: in Indonesia, in Morocco, in Turkey. Then, late in 2003, al-Qaeda strategists decided to launch direct attacks on America's principal allies, especially Britain, Poland, and Spain. They started with Spain for several reasons. The country had seen unprecedented popular demonstrations against Prime Minister Aznar's decision to invade Iraq (see page 377) and anti-war slogans still festooned every street. Also, Spain had scheduled general elections for 14 March 2004, and al-Qaeda calculated that exploding bombs that killed innocent civilians just before that date would intensify domestic pressure to withdraw all Spanish troops from Muslim lands.

The Spanish Constitution required all official campaigning to cease three days before elections 'to allow time for contemplation', and on the evening of 10 March 2004, despite widespread anti-war feeling and a promise by the Socialist opposition leader José Luis Rodríguez Zapatero that if elected he would immediately bring Spain's troops home from Iraq, every political indicator suggested that Aznar's Partido Popular would win the election. The following morning, exactly 911 days after the attacks on the World Trade Center and the Pentagon, Muslims linked to al-Qaeda exploded several bombs on commuter trains approaching Madrid, killing two hundred and maiming hundreds more. Aznar immediately blamed the Basque separatist group ETA and sought to suppress the mounting evidence of al-Qaeda involvement for fear that it would reveal to voters that his decision to invade Iraq had made their world less, not more, safe. On 14 March, although the Partido Popular received almost as many votes as in the previous election, the Socialists received three million more votes, and Zapatero kept his election promise: within one month he brought home all Spanish troops from Iraq (though not from Afghanistan).

The following month, April 2004, the CPA faced a new threat. The charismatic Shi'a cleric Muqtada al-Sadr, whose ancestor had helped drive out the last Western 'liberators' of Iraq (the British in the 1920s) and whose father had been murdered by Saddam Hussein, had built up a formidable militia (the Jaish al-Mahdi, or 'Army of the Messiah'). Now, with support from his co-religionists in Iran, whose own national security clearly benefited from keeping America tied down in Iraq, al-Sadr launched an offensive to gain control over the Baghdad suburbs and much of southern Iraq. When Coalition forces counter-attacked, Shi'a and Sunni joined forces for the first time to resist them and, although American troops eventually regained control of at least the cities, as soon as they left the insurgents returned.

In June 2004, the CPA dissolved itself and, with its last order, transferred limited sovereignty to an Iraqi interim government, which laid plans for elections to a new national assembly in January 2005. Because the Sunni population (still resenting their loss of power since the fall of Saddam) refused to vote, Shi'a and Kurdish parties won the election overwhelmingly and devised a new constitution for Iraq that largely favoured their interests. The competing sectarian agendas prevented the formation of an effective government, and, although security gradually improved in much of the north (where Kurdish leaders worked with the Coalition) and parts of the south (where British forces allowed the Shi'a militias an almost free hand), the rest of Iraq descended deeper into chaos. On 9 April 2005, the second anniversary of the fall of Saddam Hussein, tens of thousands of Iraqis again gathered in Firdos Square – this time begging the Americans to go home.

One success occurred in September 2005, when some 8,000 American and Iraqi troops captured the insurgent stronghold of Tal Afar, a city near the Turkish border,

US M1A1 tanks dominate the center of Karbala during heavy fighting to dislodge the Shi'a militia loyal to Moqtada al-Sadr in May 2004. Karbala, the site of one of the holiest Shi'a shrines, was once a wealthy city with a population of 500,000, more than 100 mosques, and more than 20 religious schools. After the US forces withdrew, Polish forces and Iraqi police continued to secure the city to prevent the return of the militias. The area in the photo had been completely restored by 2006, when the Coalition turned the city over to Iraqi control. Then militia forces attacked again.

and stayed on while they supervised both the rapid reconstruction of damaged infrastructure and the training of additional Iraqi security forces to hold the city. President Bush hailed this strategy, termed 'Clear, Hold, Build', as the key to military success in Iraq, but it was easier said than done, given the lack of adequate Iraqi security forces to hold ground once cleared of insurgents.

After the bombing of the Al-Askari Mosque in Samarra, one of the holiest Shi'ite shrines, by al-Qaeda operatives in February 2006, the Shi'ite Jaish al-Mahdi battled Sunni insurgents and al-Qaeda for control of Baghdad: every morning sixty or more bodies were found dead in the streets, usually with hands bound, a gunshot wound in the head, and (often) signs of torture. Meanwhile the insurgents, now reinforced by thousands of *mujahideen* from other Muslim countries, escalated their attacks on Coalition forces, detonating some 2,000 roadside bombs and more than 100 vehicle-borne IEDs each month. Hundreds of thousands of Sunni and Shi'a Iraqis fled their homes to avoid the sectarian bloodbath: some joined the two million displaced Iraqis living elsewhere in their own country, while others joined the two million refugees in Jordan and Syria. This exodus removed most of Iraq's middle-class citizens, who took with them much of the expertise needed to administer and reconstruct the country.

Finally President Bush realized that more American troops were needed to restore order in Iraq, even if it meant extending the tours of active duty for both regular and reserve units. In November 2006 he dismissed Donald Rumsfeld, and two months later he announced 'the surge': the transfer to Iraq of five brigade combat teams and two marine battalions – some 28,000 men and women in all – to secure Baghdad and its surrounding areas. General David Petraeus, the newly appointed theatre commander, implemented a counterinsurgency strategy in which the primary objective was to secure the base areas in which Iraqi insurgents and al-Qaeda terrorists operated. US forces now moved out of their large fortified bases and, coordinating their efforts with newly trained Iraqi army and police forces, began to live among the Iraqi people in smaller joint security stations and combat outposts and patrolled neighbourhoods on foot instead of in armoured vehicles. At much the same time, some Sunni tribal leaders in al-Anbar province began to ally with the Americans in order to battle al-Qaeda forces that had imposed a brutal and unwelcome ideology in the areas they controlled. These changes notably improved security: violent civilian deaths fell from 2,000 to 800 per month between May and October 2007, while the total US military personnel killed in action each month fell from 126 to 26.

Operation Iraqi Freedom, which by 2007 had lasted longer than US involvement in World War II, exacted an extremely high price. Estimates of violent Iraqi deaths since the American invasion in March 2003 varied wildly (the US government declined to collect these statistics, the Iraqi government figures were unreliable, and estimates by other groups often reflected an agenda that skewed the totals in one direction or another). At the lower end, the daily death totals reported by morgues

In autumn 2006, the Sunni sheikh Abdul Sattar Abu Reesha of al-Anbar province, tired of terrorist depredations against his tribe, aligned himself with US Army forces in Ramadi, the provincial capital. In March 2007 he met with General David Petraeus, commander of Coalition forces in Iraq, at a 'Ramadi Reconstruction Conference' to coordinate strategy. Six months later, al-Qaeda agents murdered the sheikh with a roadside bomb, but the new alignment of forces continued to spread across al-Anbar.

and newspapers across Iraq suggested a total of 100,000 violent deaths. At the higher end, a survey based on extensive (though, because of security concerns, not exhaustive) door-to-door sampling in July 2006 suggested a total death toll by then of 600,000. A poll by the British firm ORB in August 2007, also based on face-to-face interviews, asked Iraqi families that had lost loved ones in the violence how they died. The responses showed almost one-half killed by gunshot wounds and a further quarter by the impact of a car bomb or some other blast, with less than one-tenth killed by aerial bombardment. Most violent deaths in Iraq resulted from Muslims killing other Muslims. In addition, the invasion and the civil war that ensued led to extensive material damage, while the high unemployment, general austerity, and widespread insecurity in the contested parts of Iraq made life for the survivors both difficult and dangerous.

The United States also paid a high price for President Bush's decision to invade Iraq. By March 2008, 4,000 American troops had died (more than 3,000 of them in combat) and at least 30,000 had sustained physical injury (whereas most made a full recovery, many lost limbs and organs). In addition, perhaps one in twelve soldiers suffered mental problems such as post-traumatic stress disorder. Furthermore, more than 8,000 Iraqi soldiers and police officers working with the Coalition perished at the hands of the insurgents, as did more than 200 American civilian personnel (most of them voluntary contract workers). In material terms, total federal spending on defence doubled from a projected $350 billion for 2001 – before the 9/11 attacks – to a projected $700 billion for 2008, which included funds for

Afghanistan, Iraq, and Homeland Security. By 2007, American expenditure on Iraq alone exceeded $12 billion a month – with no end to the war in sight.

Some states exploited the weakening in America's international position caused by the commitment of so many troops and so much equipment in Iraq and Afghanistan. Admittedly a few formerly hostile regimes (notably Libya) made conciliatory gestures, but two other governments seized the chance to pursue their own nuclear ambitions. In July 2006, North Korea test-launched seven missiles and a few months later claimed it had successfully carried out its first nuclear test; meanwhile, Iran developed not only a nuclear programme but also missiles capable of delivering nuclear warheads. As in so many conflicts of the twentieth century, although Western governments displayed an enviable ability to win battles, they proved unwilling or unable to turn their military victories into a lasting peace.

The Future of Western Warfare

From the Greek hoplites to the Harrier jet, war has served as the driving force behind the West's rise to world domination. The history of the West, both at home and overseas, has centred around a ferocious competition for mastery among uncompromisingly ambitious powers, in which the ruthless, the innovative, and the decisive displaced the complacent, the imitative, and the irresolute.

WARS PAST

The western way of war has always involved high costs, however. On the one hand, the death and suffering caused in acquiring global dominion defy description: the invasion and conquest of the New World after 1492, in particular, exacted a terrible toll, causing not only the destruction of entire native American cultures and peoples, but also the forced displacement of millions of Africans to serve the needs of the victors in the New World. On the other hand, the endemic struggles between the western states seemed at times to banish peace entirely: the Thirty Years War (1618–48) devastated most of Germany and many of its neighbours; the Revolutionary and Napoleonic Wars (1792–1815) ravaged Europe from Lisbon to Moscow; the two world wars of the twentieth century all but destroyed the civilizations that spawned them.

This dark side has attracted trenchant condemnation. Homer's *Iliad,* first written down in the eighth century BC but composed long before, already shows a commander (Achilles) agonizing over the costs of the military action he is about to take; the Athenian assembly in the fifth century BC, according to Thucydides' account of the Peloponnesian War, likewise weighed the possible gains of their proposed Sicilian expedition against the probable losses. The history of Rome written by Tacitus bristles with vainglorious and ineffective leaders who squandered men and material for the wrong cause, in the wrong place, at the wrong time, and exudes a dry cynicism in describing the pitiless brutality which accompanied victory. Western poets, playwrights, and novelists have also regularly subjected the deeds of warriors to scrutiny and (on occasion) ridicule, from Euripides' *Trojan Women* and Aristophanes' *Lysistrata,* through the searing poems of Wilfred Owen and Siegfried Sassoon, or war-novels such as *Simplicissimus, War and Peace, Fields of Fire,* or *Catch-22,* down to films like *La Grande Illusion, Apocalypse Now* and *Saving Private Ryan,* or personal memoirs like *Storm of Steel* and *Born on the Fourth of July.* In addition, from AD 390, when Archbishop Ambrose of Milan forced Emperor Theodosius to do penance for slaughtering 7,000 people in reprisals, the Christian church has also called for responsible conduct both in declaring and in waging war – at least between Christians.

Making western war-makers the target of artistic, literary, and religious criticism has constantly provoked discussions of both the aims and the procedures of belligerents. Ironically, however, the ongoing debate often refined and ratified – rather than hindered – western aggression, for the need to justify each offensive act led to careful campaigns of propaganda that inflamed public opinion and increased support for hostilities, thus rendering wars more rather than less widespread and destructive.

The western way of war has exhibited some other remarkable consistencies over time. In most of the periods covered by this *History*, from the hoplites of Ancient Greece to the 'grunts' of Vietnam, the primacy of soldiers fighting on foot stands out: admittedly artillery, tanks, and aircraft have now somewhat eclipsed the foot soldier, but even during the invasion of Iraq in 2003 infantry remained essential. Furthermore, in most periods since the Greeks, the infantry's most common activity has been the siege. The West has shown an extraordinary predilection for complex defensive fortifications, from Jericho (the first walled city in the world) in 8500 BC to the trenches of the Western Front during World War I; and the requirement that armies capture fortified centres, whether castles or cities, before they advance has normally dominated military operations. Moreover, not only have sieges been numerous, they have also been prolonged: Paris in the fifth century resisted the Franks commanded by Clovis for five years, while Ostend in the seventeenth century, like Leningrad and Sarajevo and in the twentieth, held out for three years, and countless other places resisted for an entire campaign.

The logistical ability to maintain armed forces in action for protracted periods forms another constant feature of western warfare. Other military traditions also included sieges. Chinese armies, for example, regularly attempted to take fortified towns; but their enormous size (often exceeding 100,000) made it imperative to reach a decision swiftly for, with so many mouths to feed, no time could be spent on the arduous preparatory bombardment, trench-work, and mining favoured by European commanders. Most Chinese sieges therefore ended with a massed assault. In the West, by contrast, field armies above 100,000 remained rare until the eighteenth century; instead, the various states concentrated on military programmes that were capital- rather than labour-intensive. To this end, as noted in the Introduction, more resources normally went into the development of technology, discipline, and staying-power than into augmenting numbers. Once the West began to harness industrial power to its military endeavours in the eighteenth century, this strategy proved overwhelming. Thus, involvement in World War II caused the economy of the United States to undergo the largest, fastest, and most sustained expansion ever recorded: between 1941 and 1945 its gross national product increased by 50 per cent, steel output doubled, ship-building grew tenfold and aircraft production elevenfold. In concrete terms, the United States launched 51 million tons of merchant shipping during these years at the rate of three ships a day, with some vessels (at least for demonstration purposes) moving from start to launch in four and a half days; at the same time, it also produced a total of 300,000 aircraft, at a peak rate in 1944 of 250 per day.

The strategic decision taken by America's leaders – and by others in different times and places – to mobilize prodigious resources for war played an essential role in matching the successful innovations, both tactical and technological, made by their adversaries. Examples of rapid invention followed by equally rapid imitation abound throughout the twentieth century, perhaps most spectacularly in the field of atomic technology (where the nuclear monopoly of the United States lasted just four years, 1945–49); but the same process of replication also occurred in earlier periods. Thus in 1314 at the battle of Bannockburn in Scotland, the troops of Robert Bruce deliberately adopted the same technique of infantry combat against English knights that infantry at Courtrai in Flanders had successful deployed against French forces twelve years before (see page 93). Likewise, in the fifteenth and sixteenth centuries each development in gunpowder weaponry and in fortifications passed rapidly from one state to another (see chapter 6).

Although most if not all societies have displayed some ability to learn from defeat and imitate the military methods of successful adversaries, the West remained unusual in four respects. First, the almost permanent political fragmentation of Europe, coupled with the aggressiveness inculcated by its warrior values, produced prolonged and intense competition which placed a high premium on rapid adaptation and innovation within enduring institutional structures. Second, thanks in part to the high cost of military changes, the West developed not only a broad tax base but also an extensive network of credit which made possible both a host of expensive inventions and also the distribution of their costs over a far longer period. For these reasons a series of expensive technological and tactical revolutions have punctuated the military history of the West, especially since 1400: gunpowder weapons, the artillery fortress, the 'ironclad' battleship, the panzer division, nuclear weapons, 'smart' bombs. And each revolution has called forth rapid responses from those adversaries capable of mobilizing the necessary financial resources and of restructuring their economy so that military technology could receive sufficient support.

Third, the West normally judged military innovations on simple criteria of effectiveness. Some civilizations elsewhere rejected on cultural or religious grounds tactics or technology that were demonstrably superior: thus the military aristocracy of Mamluk Egypt refused to use firearms in battle, on the grounds that they did not fit their traditional way of war, leading directly to the Mamluks' overthrow by the Ottoman Turks in 1517. European warriors, by contrast, were always prepared to embrace any weapon or tactic that seemed to offer an advantage.

Fourth and finally, although China also developed close-order drill for infantry, both in classical times and again in the sixteenth century, western soldiers proved uniquely sensitive to the advantages of 'keeping together in time' (in the felicitous phrase of William McNeill) through drill. Thucydides described the Spartans marching into combat at the battle of Mantineia in 418 BC 'slowly and to the music of many fluteplayers in their ranks...to make them keep in step and move forward steadily without breaking their ranks'. The drill of the Macedonian army, recorded somewhat later by Aelian, became the basis of that adopted by the Dutch – and later by all other western armies – in the seventeenth century. The manoeuvres in formation of the Roman army, as described by Vegetius, likewise inspired subsequent imitations (see pages 4 and 66–7). The long-standing western tradition of popular participation in war may well explain this sustained importance of drill. The citizen armies of Ancient Greece and Republican Rome, the militias of the middle ages, the conscript armies of Europe and the United States since the nineteenth century: all needed to be rapidly 'broken in' to the military life – as professional soldiers did not – and, for this, precision manoeuvres in unison proved an ideal mechanism. But during the seventeenth century another benefit accrued: the combination of drill with the use of firearms to produce volley fire, perfected through constant practice, proved the mainstay of western warfare – and the key to western expansion – for the next three centuries.

This emphasis on finance, technology, eclecticism, and discipline has conferred a unique resilience and lethality upon western warfare. On the one hand, wars among western states have tended toward costly stalemate: the Peloponnesian War of classical Greece, the Hundred Years War of the middle ages, the Thirty Years War of the seventeenth century, the American Civil War, and the two world wars, all saw states fighting on for far longer than most observers (and participants) had believed possible. On the other hand, wars fought by the West against other societies have generally proved short and relatively cheap, because the western formula provided a decisive advantage. Far more Greeks perished in the Peloponnesian War than in halting the Persian invasions (almost 40,000 Athenians died on the single expedition against Sicily in 415–413 BC, against only 192 at Marathon in 490 BC); far more Roman legionaries met their deaths in the civil wars between 43 and 31 BC than in all the celebrated disasters in Germany and Parthia. And, on the other hand, small bands of western warriors achieved remarkable results abroad. Alexander the Great's army of fewer than 50,000 marched from Greece to the Indus and destroyed an empire of millions between 334 and 323 BC. western forces had by AD 1650 gained control over Siberia, most of the Americas, parts of the Philippines, and several other islands and archipelagoes off south and southeast Asia, as well as a necklace of fortified trading posts and cities around the coasts of Asia and Africa. By 1850, almost all of India and Australasia had been added; and by 1914 so had Africa and much of southeast and central Asia. Almost all of these additions came through the exercise of military power in a series of short, decisive wars.

WARS PRESENT

Will this pattern endure? The striking initial success of British forces in the Falklands (1982) and of Coalition forces in both Gulf Wars (1991 and 2003) might suggest continuance; but all three conflicts were fought in the precise way for which western forces had trained – to capture or recapture territory against a conventionally armed aggressor. They merely needed to relocate themselves to the South Atlantic or the Near East, and fight there rather than in Europe. Moreover the West has always excelled in its ability to project military force to distant theatres: the campaigns of Alexander and Caesar; the Crusades and the conquest of the western hemisphere; the suppression of the Indian Mutiny and the Boers; the Pacific War; the Gulf Wars.

In the 1990s the armed forces of the leading Western states underwent a series of linked changes that further enhanced this ability to project military force to distant theatres. These are normally referred to by the acronym 'RMA', standing for 'Revolution in Military Affairs', a phrase coined by the Office of Net Assessment within the Pentagon to refer to 'the interaction between systems that collect, process, fuse, and communicate information and those that apply military force' in order to make possible 'precision violence'. The RMA consists of a synergy between three elements: first, state-of-the-art intelligence, surveillance, and reconnaissance; second, advanced command, control, communication, computer, and intelligence assets; and, third, precision-guided munitions. Significantly, all its principal components had been present for decades. In 1943, both the United States and Germany began to use 'smart weapons' that were steered to their targets (some fixed, some moving) by radio signals sent from the launching platform; in 1958 the United States began to use precision-guided missiles against moving targets; and a decade later the first 'fire and forget' missiles, which required no human guidance after launch, came into use. Satellites were first used for reconnaissance in 1961 and for communications in 1965; the first tactical computers came into use in 1966; the first e-mail was sent in 1972. The operational use of each element remained isolated, however, until the collapse of the Soviet Union ended the nuclear threat (at least temporarily); only then, just in time for the Gulf War in 1991, did the military begin to integrate these innovations into a 'system of systems'.

The current RMA depends upon one of the distinctive characteristics of the Western way of war: a heavy investment in research and technology to offset marked numerical inferiority and, more recently, casualty aversion. At least since the days of Maurice of Nassau (see page 155), Western research and technology have been remarkably broad-based. They depend upon understanding, controlling, and exploiting the perceived regularities and irregularities *throughout* nature in order to create a broad background knowledge that expands in a path-dependent, sequential way. This enables individuals to formulate questions, and eventually to come up with answers, in many different fields of inquiry at the same time. As Francis Bacon wrote in 1620, 'the path to science is not, like that of philosophy, such that only one man can tread it at a time'. Six years earlier, his *New Atlantis* had suggested that experimental science should take place in research institutes like his fictional 'Solomon's House', with a staff of thirty-three (not counting research assistants) divided into observers, experimenters, compilers, interpreters, and 'merchants of light' – those who travelled in order to bring back knowledge. Before long, natural philosophers had formed societies in England along the lines suggested by Bacon, such as the 'Invisible College' which would later become the Royal Society. Other Western states soon followed suit.

The shared background among Western researchers in many different fields had an important consequence: discoveries tended to occur in clusters, and therefore became self-reinforcing. Sometimes the clusters occurred through competition, when several warring states all sought a technological edge; at other times practitioners in different places reached the same conclusion almost simultaneously simply because they started from similar premises. Often the advances could not be predicted, because (much to the irritation of governments through the ages) discoveries are seldom made to order; nevertheless, as Bacon predicted, the patient research and the soulless experiments that support them have steadily increased the sum of Western scientific knowledge.

Cultures that lack this broad base – for example, those endorsing 'Fundamentalist' beliefs that seek truth in revelation or instinct rather than in experiment; or those where the state micromanages all research – can still make scientific advances; but these advances will tend to be (in the phrase of Robert Merton) 'singleton techniques'. 'Singletons' are normally discovered by chance and, 'while their impact can at times be significant, further refinements and adaptations tend to be limited and soon run into diminishing returns'. That partly explains why although a Japanese warlord invented both the countermarch and the musketry volley in the 1560s – three decades before Maurice of Nassau and his cousin – it remained a 'singleton technique', abandoned when Japan 'gave up the gun' in the mid-seventeenth century.

The dependence of the Western way of war on simultaneous research by practitioners in many fields involved two important consequences (or, in current parlance, 'trade-offs'). First, each major innovation takes a long time to complete. It required six years to perfect volley fire (from a first sketch of the manoeuvre by William Louis of Nassau in 1594 to its first deployment in action at the battle of Nieuwpoort in 1600) and eleven years to develop the atomic bomb (from July 4, 1934, when Leo Szilard patented the idea of an atomic chain reaction in London – specifying that one of its consequences would be an 'explosion' – until August 6, 1945 when 'Little Boy' exploded over Hiroshima). The second 'trade-off' of the heavy dependence of the military on research and technology is the need to involve civilian expertise. As a prominent strategic analyst, Andrew Krepinevich, put it: 'Technologies that underwrite a military revolution are often developed outside the military sector, and then "imported" and exploited for their military applications'. On the one hand, some components are developed, or receive their first use, abroad: thus, among components of the current RMA, Egyptian forces first used both tactical missiles and smart weapons against a moving target. On the other hand, no single country can entirely supply the legion of components required by the various weapons systems: the United States currently depends on Germany, Japan, and South Korea to provide 'spare parts' for its principal armaments.

The involvement of experts from so many backgrounds and specialties naturally imperils security. So does the fact that many other countries have already acquired many of the components of the RMA, especially software. Enemies do not need to reproduce all elements of the 'system of systems' to challenge a Western adversary: they may only need enough to target one or more crucial component, or even to create so much 'friction' (above and beyond the normal hitches that can compromise a campaign) that the West loses its decisive advantage. In future, such threats are less likely to come from a sovereign power, but rather from a challenger based in cyberspace.

In fact few recent hostilities have been waged by sovereign powers using high technology arsenals: on the contrary, 90 per cent of all conflicts since 1945 have been civil wars fought with relatively simple weapons – a pattern likely to continue in the twenty-first century because high-technology wars, with their emphasis on arduous training, massive logistical backup, and copious state-of-the-art weaponry, make demands that few societies can meet. Regrettably, wars fought with less advanced weaponry, and especially civil wars, tend to be more brutal and to involve far higher civilian casualties. In the wars fought in Europe during the nineteenth and earlier twentieth centuries between 70 and 80 per cent of the casualties were military. By contrast, since 1945, the majority of the approximately fifty million people killed in war have been civilians – rising to 70 per cent or more in Vietnam. Moreover, almost all of them died from wounds inflicted by cheap, mass-produced weapons and small-calibre ammunition. Sometimes traditional weapons sufficed: most of the 500,000–800,000 Tutsis who perished in Rwanda over a three-month period in 1994 seem to have been hacked to death with machetes.

Nor did the slaughter of recent civil wars normally stem from mass violence, from a 'war of all against all' in a society intractably divided itself, as some suggested at the time (often to justify nonintervention). Subsequent studies have revealed that in Rwanda, as in Bosnia, Kosovo, Liberia, Sierra Leone, Somalia, and elsewhere, the massacres were the work of small groups, many of them professional criminals. In Rwanda, for example, the maximum number of 'hardcore' Hutu killers was 50,000, while perhaps another 150,000 played a supportive role – but even the combined total represented only 10 per cent of the total male Hutu population aged over thirteen. The vast majority of Hutu men took no part in the massacre; it follows that those who did could have been stopped relatively easily. Likewise in Bosnia and Croatia in the 1990s, although over eighty groups of irregulars held the country to ransom, most were small. Thus the 'Tigers', a much-feared Bosnian Serb group led by Zeljko Raznjatovic ('Arkan'), had a core of at most 200 men, most of them former members of the Official Fan Club of Belgrade's Red Star soccer team, of which Arkan had been president. The group numbered fewer than 1,000 overall, and yet they murdered hundreds if not thousands and robbed and plundered on a grand scale. An analyst of the Yugoslav wars has suggested that only 'one-to-five percent of any population, any nation' actively liked violence and 'wanted to hurt people'. For that small minority, whether in the Balkans or elsewhere, 'War was their dream come true' because the absence of government restraint allowed them to live their dream. And, all around the world in the 1990s, they did.

The link between civil war, low technology, and brutality is not unbreakable. George Grivas's justification of the guerrilla tactics he employed against the British in Cyprus in the 1950s makes a valid point:

> Our form of war, in which a few hundred fell in four years, was far more selective than most, and I speak as one who has seen battlefields covered with dead. We did not strike, like the bomber, at random. We shot only British servicemen who would have killed us if they could have fired first, and civilians who were traitors or intelligence agents.

But in most civil wars little attempt has been made to distinguish between qualitative and quantitative warfare, for political objectives may lead the forces of one side to attempt the extermination, rather than merely the defeat, of the other. Scholars have marshalled considerable evidence to suggest that Francisco Franco, leader of the Nationalist insurrection in Spain after 1936, deliberately rejected any option that might have brought a swift end to the Civil War in the interests of killing as many of his Republican adversaries as possible. Much the same pattern has characterized civil wars in southeast Asia, Africa, Central America, and Yugoslavia – as well as to a lesser extent in Northern Ireland and Lebanon – for savagery provokes reprisals and so becomes institutionalized, leading to a downward spiral of atrocity that rules out political compromise. Nor are these conflicts normally capable of resolution by the use of sophisticated weaponry, since such weaponry requires delivery from the air. Russia's experience in Afghanistan during the 1980s, the NATO bombing campaign in Kosovo in 1999, and the air campaign against Taliban fighters in the Tora Bora mountains of Afghanistan in 2001–2 confirmed the verdict of the Vietnam war (1965–73): it is almost impossible to eradicate guerrilla forces from 15,000 feet with conventional weapons.

Indeed it is hard to resolve civil wars at all, except by the total defeat of one side. The problem lies in the need for the warring parties to reach an agreement that will allow them to live together again in a single community. Since political power is hard to divide, and power-sharing arrangements normally remain brief, the weaker faction often does not dare to lay down its arms for fear of subsequent reprisals. Only the intervention of an outside power, capable of brokering a settlement and then of enforcing its provisions, tends to produce a compromise peace; but, as in the case of Sri Lanka or Lebanon, the cease-fire often lasts only as long as the broker's forces remain on the scene in strength.

Conventional wars between sovereign states have not ceased, however – witness the Indo-Pakistan wars, the Arab-Israeli wars, Iraq's attacks on Iran and then

Kuwait, the Falklands conflict and the invasion of Iraq by coalition forces in 2003. Moreover, the heavy military investment of so many governments in conventional weaponry continues: the Middle East and North Africa probably contain more soldiers, aircraft, missiles, and other weaponry than any other part of the globe, while the developing countries as a whole spent almost $150 billion on weapons and armies in 1988 alone, suggesting that more conflicts lie in the future. Conventional wars, too, prove hard to end, short of the unconditional surrender of one side. Few governments conduct serious negotiations while fighting, because to do so might imply weakness, provoke internal pressures to settle, or cause dissension with allies. Instead they escalate the conflict – either through the use of new weapons and new resources, or through attacks on new targets or new fronts – and thus prolong it. The Iran–Iraq war, which lasted eight years and caused hundreds of thousands of casualties, offers a terrible warning of the potential cost of inter-state wars to come.

WARS FUTURE

Since 1945 no one has been deliberately killed by a nuclear bomb. Although from the 1940s to the 1980s the superpowers built up massive arsenals, and although the initial response of NATO forces in the 1970s and 1980s to a Soviet attack on Europe called for the release of tactical nuclear weapons, both sides regarded nuclear war a 'worst case' catastrophe. The two or three other states possessing an atomic capacity felt the same.

In the wake of the collapse of the Soviet Union, however, the world entered an age of greater nuclear proliferation. Three other members of the Commonwealth of Independent States apart from the Russian Federation became nuclear powers in 1991 (Ukraine, Belarus, and Kazakhstan); so did India and Pakistan, both of which successfully tested nuclear weapons in 1998, as (apparently) did North Korea in 2007. Perhaps, in time, two, three, or four states in each major region of the world will acquire nuclear weapons. Most of them, especially those in densely populated regions and with closely regulated armed-forces, will probably regard nuclear bombs as the ultimate deterrent and use them only in desperation (in the bitter Kashmir dispute of 2002 both India and Pakistan backed away from nuclear threats.) But other states, some perhaps with a widely dispersed population, others with armed forces under looser control, may see matters in a different light. Moreover, nuclear weapons will not remain the only agents of mass destruction. Several aggressive states have shown interest in developing chemical and biological weapons, which are less expensive and easier to deliver.

In military terms, the world after the Cold War resembles the situation following other major conflicts that resulted in resounding victory: with the demise of the 'evil empire', a sense of euphoria creates pressure for a 'peace dividend'. After World War I, the British government declared that 'It should be assumed for the purpose of framing the estimates of the fighting services, that at any given date there will be no major war for ten years'; and this 'ten-year rule' was not rescinded until 1932 and not superseded until 1937. It would be rash for Western leaders to assume that, in the wake of the Cold War, another major challenge will not arise, just as both Nazi Germany and imperial Japan arose in the 1930s. The possibility that the West may face another major military threat may not be imminent, but it cannot be ruled out permanently.

Furthermore, the number and the nature of threats to international security facing the West are growing. On the one hand, the traditional causes of war – such as disputed boundaries and struggles for independence – remain. In sub-Saharan Africa, for example, where colonial boundaries were drawn with insufficient regard for the enduring hostility of different tribes, governments rarely serve as the focus of loyalty and ethnic tensions have produced innumerable civil wars in most of the forty-five states of the region, both large (like Nigeria, with its Biafran war in 1967–70) and relatively small (like Liberia and Sierra Leone, in a state of anarchy for most of the 1990s). On the other hand, new threats have emerged such as a growing pressure for land and sea resources caused by uncontrolled demographic growth combined with shrinking crop yields in many areas of the world. Anything that challenges a country's health, prosperity, social stability, and political peace may soon come to be seen as a threat to national security, and therefore as a potential cause of war.

Above all, global terrorists now challenge Western military dominance. They lack neither money nor recruits: the former comes from the deep pockets of those who disapprove of Western values, and the latter from the ranks of those who hate them. Terrorism is of course not new. In the West, the ruthless campaigns of murder and destruction carried out in the late twentieth century by the Irish Republican Army in the United Kingdom and ETA (a Basque separatist organization) in Spain followed a well-worn path: many others, from Protestant and Catholic extremists in the sixteenth and seventeenth centuries to the anarchists of the late nineteenth and early twentieth centuries, had done much the same. Western terrorists, however, rarely adopted the strategy adopted by a group of Muslims in Lebanon in the twelfth century: murdering their political enemies in suicide missions. Their name has passed into all Western languages: the Assassins. In 1983, America received a brutal reminder that this tradition lived on when Muslim suicide bombers destroyed the US marine base in Beirut. Fifteen years later, a team of Muslim suicide bombers blew up two US embassies in Africa, killing over 200 and maiming thousands; in 2000, another Muslim group sacrificed their lives in order to detonate a boatful of explosives next to the USS *Cole*, killing seventeen and wounding forty-nine more. Most spectacular of all, the following year fifteen Muslims hijacked three planes and deliberately flew them into the twin towers of the World Trade Center and the Pentagon, killing at least 3,000.

Americans were already familiar with terrorism: US newspapers and television stations regularly reported how IRA bombs had killed and maimed several thousand civilians in England and North Ireland. They were also used to asymmetrical casualties. In the Gulf War (1991) the coalition lost scarcely 200 combatants yet killed over 100,000 Iraqis; and they suffered no losses at all in the 'surgical strikes' of 1998–9 against Sudan, Afghanistan, and Yugoslavia, while again inflicting substantial casualties. But in all these scenarios, the disasters happened to someone else. On 11 September 2001, hijackers who lacked 'stealth' technology expertly steered three of the four aircraft they had acquired, free of charge, into their targets with a precision and destructive effect equal to that of a Tomahawk Cruise missile that cost $2 million. Although the hijackers suffered 100 per cent casualties, their 'kill ratio' exceeded 200:1 and they caused billions of dollars of immediate damage – to say nothing of the economic costs of heightened security thereafter and the psychological trauma arising from the shattered assumptions of invulnerability.

Admittedly, even in this complex scenario, certain considerations favour Western planners (apart from their possession of a huge nuclear arsenal). First, as John Keegan has pointed out, past encounters have tended to occur within a relatively limited compass, and may well continue to do so. For example, water, most of it ocean, covers approximately 70 per cent of the world's surface; yet almost all important naval engagements have taken place in a small fraction of that area, and usually within a few miles of land. Certain locations have been fought over repeatedly – such as the North Sea (site of the battles of Sluis in 1340, the defeat of the Spanish Armada in 1588, around twenty engagements in the Anglo-Dutch wars of the seventeenth century, Camperdown in 1797, and Jutland in 1916) or the narrows of the Central Mediterranean (Actium in 31 BC was fought remarkably close to the site of Lepanto in 1571 – itself the exact site of the battle of Naupactus, the first real seafight of the Peloponnesian War). Similarly, of the world's dry land, some 70 per cent is normally either too high, too cold, or too arid for the conduct of military operations; these areas therefore boast little or no military history. Instead, as with naval engagements, a disproportionate amount of military activity has occurred in a small fraction of the globe. Armies have fought over some places again and again: the vale of Boetia near Thebes in Greece, site of nine battles between Plataea in 479 BC and Chaeroneia in 338 BC; the Low Countries; the Lombard plain; Saxony. Edirne, formerly Adrianople in European Turkey, which saw fifteen battles or sieges between 323 and 1913, apparently holds the record. The explanation for such frequency is often geographical: Edirne lies in the last plain of Europe, so that invaders from both directions needed to secure it, and its resources, before resuming their advance. Other sites frequently visited by armies include other fertile plains surrounded by mountains, forests or desert, and the narrow avenues leading to them. Nature has also exerted a heavy influence on military activity through climate. Until recently, successful operations seldom occurred in the winter months; and even in World War II, the annual rains in March and October, accurately referred to by the Russians as the *rasputitsa* or 'roadless period', regularly caused all military movement to cease on the Eastern Front and proved an even greater hindrance than the more famous Russian winter.

Despite continuing improvements in military technology, conventional forces seem likely to operate at much the same times and in many of the same places as before (although the Falklands, Afghanistan and the Gulf Wars demonstrate that, when necessary, even inhospitable climes can become theatres of operations); and such geographical concentration dramatically simplifies the task of planning for war. Moreover, the surveillance systems currently available to support western forces present an unprecedented insurance against such threats materializing unexpectedly. During the Gulf Wars, reconnaissance satellites monitored the movement of enemy forces, pinpointed the location of military installations, and indicated the scale of the damage inflicted; early warning satellites gave advance notice of incoming attacks; communications satellites allowed continuous communications between headquarters and units in action; and weather satellites predicted the optimum conditions for every initiative. Although the 'friction', 'fog', and ambiguities of war can always jeopardize the proper use of this mass of data, the panoply of surveillance has substantially reduced the chances of strategic surprise against those who possess it – although Israel's success in taking over and disabling Syria's Russian-built early warning system while its planes destroyed a suspected nuclear reactor in 2007, using an electronic device known as 'Suter', shows that surprise is still possible.

But these sophisticated systems, like the weaponry they complement, require enormous expenditure. The future of the western way of war, and so of the western way of life and the advantageous economic system that sustains it, ultimately depends on three things: a sustained ability to manage international crises and prevent them from turning into armed conflicts, the outcome of which is always unpredictable; the continued willingness to pay (in both human and material terms) for defence against perils that are not immediately apparent; and the maintenance of each state's political control over its armed forces because, in the memorable epigram attributed to Georges Clemenceau, the architect of French victory in World War I, 'War is too important to be left to the generals'.

Concerning the first, there is always a risk that Western (or Westernized) states will repeat the mistake made so often in the past – twice in the twentieth century – and engage in mutual hostilities that inflict their awesome capacity for destruction upon each other. It may be true that, as John Mueller (a noted political scientist) has asserted in a recent study:

> In some very important respects, the institution of war is clearly in decline. Certain standard, indeed classic, varieties of war – particularly major war, or wars among developed countries – have become so rare and unlikely that they could well be considered obsolescent, if not obsolete. Also in notable decline, it appears, are international war more generally, conventional civil war, colonial war, and ideological civil war.

Nevertheless, as Mueller points out elsewhere in *The Remnants of War,* just a single charismatic individual can change this. In the 1930s, only one European leader really wanted war: Adolf Hitler; in the first years of the twenty-first century, only one world leader really wanted war with Iraq: George W. Bush. In both cases, the war that most of the world desperately opposed broke out.

The second condition for the continuation of Western military superiority has two aspects. On the one hand, there must be an unflinching determination to use force in extreme circumstances, even though it inevitably involves losses. United States intervention in Vietnam (1965–73) and in Somalia (1992–4) became seriously compromised by public reluctance to accept casualties: civilian revulsion at the sight of 'body bags' repatriating dead servicemen to their grieving families helped to precipitate ignominious withdrawal. Under these constraints even the most powerful and well-equipped military apparatus represents no more than empty bluff. In the lapidary phrase of Eliot A. Cohen, a prominent defence analyst:

> An unthinking requirement for 'force protection' as the first mission for American soldiers, ahead of any objective for which they might be put in harm's way, reflects an unwillingness to come to terms with what the use of force means; today, rather than the reckless dissipation of strength, it means an only slightly less reckless conservation of it.

On the other hand, continued Western military success also demands a high and continuing financial outlay. For example, the war in Iraq between 2003 and 2006 cost American taxpayers $526 billion, and by 2007 the war cost $12 billion a month. Will they be prepared to shoulder this burden – even if military casualties stay low – indefinitely, in the absence of clear evidence that the venture makes both the world and their own country safer? In 1692 John Hampden, an English political writer, asked (and answered) the same question during Britain's great war against Louis XIV of France. 'Great sums of money', he wrote, 'are the sinews of war'.

> Our dear-bought experience has taught us what vast taxes are absolutely necessary to maintain the armies and fleets, which are requisite for our security; and for the defence of our religious and civil rights; [but] provided we attain those ends, it will not be thought, at [the] long run, we have bought them too dear.

In the twenty-first century, as in the seventeenth, 'who pays and why' is almost as essential to the Western way of war as 'who fights and why'; and a congruence of outlook between the two is perhaps the most important of all.

The third condition on which the triumphant current military culture of the West depends is effective political control over the armed forces in each state. As Eliot Cohen has pointed out, leaving the conduct of modern war to professional soldiers has rarely produced lasting victories. In particular, successive US administrations between 1965 and 2001 largely abandoned the conduct of war to their senior military advisers. They failed to pick the right generals; they failed to conduct a meaningful strategic and operational dialogue with them; and they failed to set priorities and maintain proportion in what were, after all, only secondary conflicts. In short, the politicians lost sight of what they needed to do to run a war – whether in Vietnam, which saw a 'deadly combination of inept strategy and excessively weak civilian control', or in the first Gulf War, where the politicians disastrously accepted the military's narrow definition of 'victory' as 'success on the battlefield' rather than as 'ensuring the stability of the Persian Gulf'. George W. Bush and his defense secretary Donald Rumsfeld, by contrast, seldom listened to contrary advice: they marginalized Secretary of State Colin Powell, who had been chairman of the Joint Chiefs of Staff during the first Gulf War and therefore boasted a wealth of detailed experience, and they silenced any military personnel who challenged them. When General Eric Shinseki, army chief of staff, told the Senate Armed Services Committee just before the invasion of Iraq that 'several hundred thousand soldiers' would be needed for the effective occupation of the country after victory, he was publicly ridiculed by Rumsfeld's deputy, Paul Wolfowitz (see page 380).

According to Cohen, military success for the West depends on an 'unequal dialogue' between the military and their civilian masters. It is 'a dialogue, in that both sides expressed their views bluntly, indeed, sometimes offensively, and not once but repeatedly – and unequal, in that the final authority of the civilian leader was unambiguous and unquestioned'. Moreover, in preparing for this dialogue, successful Western wartime leaders have normally listened not only to their military advisers but also to linguists; not only to defence analysts but also to philosophers; not only to rocket scientists but also to historians. Thus the invention of the musketry volley in Europe during the 1590s only occurred because the cousins Maurice and William Louis of Nassau first studied at university under Justus Lipsius, who called for the re-introduction of the discipline and practices of the Roman legions described by Classical writers, and then read the works of some of them, above all Aelian (see page 154). Likewise Count Alfred von Schlieffen derived his celebrated 'double envelopment' strategy, which almost defeated France in 1914, from reading Hans Delbrück's vivid account of Hannibal's victory at the battle of Cannae (216 BC) in volume 1 of his *History of the Art of War*. Finally, the tragedy of 1914 presented in Barbara Tuchman's *Guns of August* played an important role in defusing the Cuban Missile Crisis. On 13 October 1962, President Kennedy's special envoy Chester Bowles asked the Russian ambassador in Washington if he had read it (and when Dobrynin said 'No', Bowles proceeded to summarize the first few chapters.) Two weeks later, Kennedy told his brother Bobby, 'I am not going to follow a course which will allow anyone to write a comparable book about this time, *The Missiles of October*'. ('If,' he added wistfully, 'anybody is around to write after this.')

But the 'unequal dialogue' requires not only gathering and digesting pertinent information from all available sources, including civilian experts, even those of one's allies, but also fashioning from it a stream of inquiries, probes, and suggestions to the military. Although they rarely overruled their generals and admirals, the great wartime leaders – Lincoln, Clemenceau, Churchill – all became world-class nags.

Each of them also won their war. Naturally, the unequal dialogue did not endear the leaders to their generals and admirals. Sir Alan Brooke, chairman of the Chiefs of Staff, wrote of Churchill in his diary, two months after D-Day: 'Never have I admired and despised a man simultaneously to the same extent'. Churchill never saw this entry, but had he done so he would probably not have cared. In an exchange with another senior officer who apologized after disagreeing 'very forcibly' with one of the Prime Minister's proposals, Churchill just smiled and said: 'You know, in war you don't have to be nice, you only have to be right'. His advice is as pertinent today as it was half a century ago: to maintain its military edge, the West must continue 'to be right'.

Reference Guide to The Cambridge Illustrated History of *Warfare*

Chronology

Glossary

Bibliography

Chronology

c.4000 BC Metallurgy developed: beginning of the Bronze age.

c.3000 BC Writing invented.

c.2500 BC Bow and arrow used in warfare.

c.2000 BC War chariot invented.

1600 BC Mycenaean period in Greece (to 1200 BC).

910 BC Assyrian empire (to 606 BC).

c.650 BC Development of the trireme in Greece.

600 BC Persian empire (to 330 BC).

c.600 BC Coinage invented.

490 BC First Persian expedition to Greece: battle of Marathon. Beginning of Roman expansion in Italy.

480 BC Second Persian expedition: battles of Salamis and Plataea (to 479 BC).

431 BC Peloponnesian War (to 404 BC).

415 BC Athenian expedition to Sicily (to 413 BC).

404 BC Spartan hegemony in Greece (to 371 BC).

401 BC Expedition of Xenophon and the '10,000' in Asia Minor (to 399 BC).

c.400 BC First use of catapults and onagers.

371 BC Thebans defeat Spartans at Leuctra.

371 BC Theban hegemony in Greece (to 362 BC).

359 BC Development of Macedonian phalanx (to 338 BC).

338 BC Philip II of Macedon defeats the Greeks at Chaeronea.

336 BC Alexander the Great becomes king of Macedon.

334 BC Alexander the Great invades Asia.

333 BC Alexander destroys Persian empire (to 330 BC).

330 BC Alexander king of Persia.

327 BC Indian campaign of Alexander (to 325 BC).

323 BC Death of Alexander.

c.320 BC Euclid writes *Elements of Geometry*.

c.300 BC Development of Roman legion begins (to 200 BC).

264 BC First Punic War (to 241 BC).

c.250 BC Archimedes makes advances in physics and siegecraft.

218 BC Second Punic War (to 201 BC).

216 BC Hannibal defeats Romans at Cannae.

190 BC Romans conquer Syria.

149 BC Third Punic War (to 146 BC).

107 BC Marius reforms Roman army (to 105 BC).

88 BC Sulla dictator in Rome (to 78 BC).

66 BC Pompey conquers Asia (to 61 BC).

58 BC Caesar conquers Gaul (to 51 BC).

53 BC Parthians defeat Romans at Carrhae.

46 BC Dictatorship of Julius Caesar (to 44 BC).

31 BC Octavian (Augustus) wins battle of Actium.

27 BC Augustus assumes proconsular power in Rome.

AD43 Roman conquest of Britain begins.

c.110 Aelian composes *Tactics*.

122 Hadrian's Wall built in Britain; Roman empire at greatest extent (to 136).

c.270 Use of the compass in China.

293 Diocletian divides Roman empire into four administrative parts.

324 Constantine reunites the Roman empire.

390 Vegetius composes *Concerning Military Matters* (revised c.440).

395 Final split of the east and west Roman empires.

407 Germanic tribes break through the Rhine frontier and overrun much of the West Roman empire.

410 Sack of Rome by the Visigoths.

451 Attila invades the West.

455 Sack of Rome by the Vandals.

476 Last Roman emperor in the West deposed by Lombards.

527 Reign of Justinian in Byzantium (to 565).

533 Reconquest of North Africa by Byzantine troops under Belisarius (to 534).

535 Reconquest of Italy by Belisarius (to 554).

570 Birth of Mohammed.

634 Muslim conquests begin.

673 Muslims attack Constantinople (to 677).

c.675 'Greek fire' invented.

c.700 Stirrups reach the West.

711 Visigothic Spain overrun by Muslims (to 715).

737 Danevirke built.

768 Reign of Charlemagne (to 814).

773 Charlemagne conquers Italy (to 774).

793 Charlemagne attempts to build Rhine–Danube canal.

c.800 Viking raids begin.

800 Charlemagne crowned emperor in the West.

c.850 Crossbow in use in France gunpowder invented in China.

955 Otto I defeats Magyars at the Lechfeld.

962 Otto I crowned emperor in the West.

1060 Normans conquer Sicily (to 1091).

1066 Battle of Hastings: Normans seize England.

1096 First Crusade (to 1099).

c.1200 Compass introduced in the West.

1204 Latin conquest of Constantinople (to 1261).

1237 Mongol conquest of Russia (to 1240).

c.1250 Introduction of plate armour.

1302 Flemish infantry defeat French army at Courtrai.

1314 Robert Bruce confirms Scottish independence by defeating the English at Bannockburn.

c.1320 First use of gunpowder artillery in Europe.

1337 Hundred Years War (to 1453).

1346 English longbows defeat the French at Crecy.

c.1350 Development of shipborne artillery.

c.1350 Development of hand-held gunpowder weapons.

1356 English defeat the French at Poitiers.

1385 Portuguese win independence from Castile at battle of Aljubarrota.

1415 English defeat the French at Agincourt.

1419 Hussite wars in Bohemia (to 1436).

c.1430 Development of 'full-rigged ship'.

c.1430 Development of 'corned gunpowder'.

c.1440 Leon Battista Alberti suggests the 'trace italienne'.

c.1450 Development of the matchlock musket.

1453 End of the Hundred Years War: England retains only Calais in France. Byzantine empire falls when Turks capture Constantinople.

1455 Wars of the Roses in England (to 1485).

1462 Ivan III crowned tsar of Muscovy.

1467 Charles the Bold, duke of Burgundy (to 1477).

c.1490 Rifled barrel invented.

1492 Columbus reaches the West Indies.

1494 Charles VIII of France invades Italy.

1497 Vasco de Gama circumnavigates Africa.

1511 First sailing warship launched in Scotland.

1515 First full artillery fortress (at Civitavecchia).

1519 Spaniards and Mexican allies under Cortés conquer Aztecs (to 1521).

1519 Magellan's ships circumnavigate the globe (to 1522).Charles V unites Spain, the Netherlands, the Habsburg lands and the Holy Roman Empire.

1531 Spaniards under Pizarro conquer Inca empire (to 1537).

1537 Niccolo Tartaglia develops science of ballistics.

1556 Reign of Philip II of Spain (to 1598).

1571 Christian galley fleet defeats the Turks at Lepanto.

1572 Dutch Revolt against Spain (to 1648).

1588 Spanish Armada fails to invade England.

1595 Dutch army develops volley fire and drill.

1600 Formation of the English East India Company.

1602 Formation of the Dutch East India Company.

1607 Jacques de Gheyn publishes first illustrated drill book.

1616 Count John of Nassau opens first military academy at Siegen in western Germany.

1618 Thirty Years War (to 1648).

c.1620 Flintlock musket invented.

1635 Franco-Spanish War (to 1659).

1642 Civil War in the British Isles (to 1651).

1648 Peace of Munster ends the Dutch Revolt; peace of Westphalia ends the Thirty Years War.

1649 English Republic (to 1660).

1659 Peace of the Pyrenees ends Franco-Spanish war.

1667 Louis XIV's War of Devolution (to 1668).

1672 Franco-Dutch War (to 1678).

1678 Ottoman wars against Russia and Austrian Habsburgs (to 1699).

1683 Ottoman siege of Vienna.

1688 William of Orange leads Dutch invasion of England and becomes William III, king of England, Scotland and Ireland. War of the League of Augsburg (to 1697).

1689 Peter the Great tsar of Russia (to 1725).

c.1690 Socket bayonet in general use.

1694 Foundation of the first national bank: the Bank of England.

1700 Great Northern War (to 1721).

1701 War of the Spanish Succession (to 1714).

1704 Battle of Blenheim.

1706 Battles of Ramillies and Turin.

1709 Battles of Malplaquet and Poltava.

1740 War of the Austrian Succession (to 1748). Reign of Frederick II of Prussia (to 1786).

1744 Carnatic wars in India between European powers and Indian allies (to 1754).

1756 Seven Years War (to 1763).

1757 Battles of Leuthen and Plassey.

1775 War of American Independence (to 1783).

1789 French Revolution.

1792 French revolutionary wars (to 1802).

1794 Semaphore telegraph developed.

1798 Nelson defeats French fleet at battle of the Nile.

1799 Napoleon becomes ruler of France.

1803 Napoleonic wars (to 1815).

1805 Battles of Austerlitz and Trafalgar. First torpedo.

1807 Peninsular War (to 1814). First successful steamboat voyage.

1812 Napoleon's invasion of Russia.

1815 Final defeat of Napoleon at Waterloo; Congress of Vienna.

1825 First railway line opened.

1827 Invention of the 'needlegun'.

1833 Electric telegraph developed.

1848 Revolutions in Paris, Vienna, Venice, Berlin, Milan, and Parma.

1853 Crimean War (to 1856).

1859 First 'ironclad' frigate built.

1861 American Civil War (to 1865).

1862 Richard Gatling develops first viable manually powered machine gun.

1863 Battle of Gettysburg. Lincoln's emancipation proclamation.

1866 Austro-Prussian War.

1870 Franco-Prussian War (to 1871); Napoleon III deposed.

1876 Invention of the telephone.

1879 Zulu War.

1881 Boers granted independence by British.

1882 British conquest of Egypt.

1884 Hiram Maxim invents automatic machine gun.

1885 First naval submarines built.

1887 First successful automobiles.

1894 Sino-Japanese War (to 1895).

1895 Invention of wireless telegraph.

1896 British conquest of Sudan (to 1898).

1899 Boer War (to 1902).

1903 First airplane flight.

1904 Russo-Japanese War (to 1905).

1905 First Russian Revolution.

1906 British launch the battleship *Dreadnought*.

1914 *28 June* Assassination of Archduke Ferdinand of Austria.
28 July Austria declares war on Serbia; World War I begins.
4 August German invasion of Belgium begins.
5–10 September Battle of the Marne; furthest German westward advance until 1918.
November Ottoman empire enters the war.

1915 *April* British assault on the Dardanelles.
May Italy enters war.

1916 First use of the tank in battle.
February–June Battle of Verdun

July–November Battle of the Somme.
August Romania enters the war.

1917 First use of aircraft for strategic bombing.
February Germany resumes unrestricted submarine warfare.
February Republican revolution in Russia.
April United States declares war on Germany.
October Bolshevik revolution ends Russian republic.
December Romania defeated by Germany.

1918 *March* German 'Michael' offensive in the west begins.
March Peace of Brest-Litovsk between Russia and Germany.
July Allied counter-offensive begins.
October Ottoman empire makes peace.
November Austria and Germany sign armistice; cease-fire on the Western Front.

1919 Treaty of Versailles.

1920 France begins construction of the Maginot line.

1926 Liquid-fuel rocket launched.

1929 New York Stock Market crash.

1933 Hitler becomes Chancellor of Germany and begins rearming.

1935 Radar used to detect aircraft.
Mussolini invades and annexes Ethiopia (to 1936).

1936 German remilitarization of the Rhineland.
Spanish Civil War (to 1939).

1937 Stalin begins military purges.

1938 German invasion of Austria.
Dismemberment of Czechoslovakia (to 1939).

1939 First helicopter flight; test-flight of turbo-jet airplane.
March German annexation of Czechoslovakia.
August Russo-German non-aggression pact (to 1941).
1 September Germany invades Poland.
3 September Britain and France declare war on Germany.

1940 *April* German invasion of Denmark and Norway.

May Germans attack in the west: Belgium and The Netherlands surrender; first use of paratroops in battle (Netherlands)
Churchill becomes British prime minister.
June Mussolini declares war on the allies; France surrenders.
September Japan, Germany, and Italy sign alliance treaty.

1941 *March* Anglo-American lend-lease programme begins.
April Russo-Japanese non-aggression pact (to 1945).
June Germans attack Russia.
7 December Japanese bomb Pearl Harbor.
11 December Germany and Italy declare war on United States.

1942 *May* Battle of the Coral Sea.
June Battle of Midway.
October Battle of El Alamein begins; first launch of V-1 missile.
November Anglo-American landing in North Africa.
November Atomic chain reaction achieved.

1943 *February* German forces at Stalingrad surrender.
July Battle of Kursk; Allies land in Sicily.
September Allies land on Italian mainland.

1944 First combat use of jet aircraft.
6 June Normandy landings.
22 June Soviet 'Operation Bagration': battle for White Russia.
July Assassination attempt on Hitler.
December Battle of the Bulge.

1945 *February* Yalta conference.
March Tokyo destroyed by bombing.
April Okinawa invaded.
28 April Mussolini hanged.
30 April Hitler commits suicide.
8 May Germany's unconditional surrender.
June United Nations charter approved.
6 August Atomic bomb dropped on Hiroshima.
8 August Russians attack Japanese positions in Manchuria.
9 August Second atomic bomb dropped on Nagasaki provokes Japan's unconditional surrender.

1946 First workable computer
developed.
Ho Chi Minh attacks French in
North Vietnam (to 1955).

1947 India wins independence.

1948 *May* Formation of the state of
Israel; first Arab–Israeli War.

1949 Soviet Union develops atomic
bomb.
North Atlantic Treaty signed–
beginning of NATO.
Communist People's Republic of
China proclaimed under
Mao Tse-Tung.

1950 *June* North Korea invades South
Korea; Korean war begins.
September MacArthur counter-
attacks.
October Chinese intervene on the
side of North Korea.

1953 *March* Stalin dies.
July Korean armistice signed.

1954 First atomic-powered submarine
launched.
May French defeated at Dien Bien
Phu in northern Vietnam.
July Geneva Peace Accords
establish two Vietnams.
November Algerian war begins
(to 1962).

1956 Second Arab–Israeli War; abortive
Suez landings.

1957 Soviet Union launches first man-
made satellite.

1958 Charles de Gaulle becomes
President of France (to 1969).

1960 Development of intercontinental
ballistic missiles begins.

1962 France concedes Algerian
independence.

1965 United States sends increasing aid
to South Vietnam (to 1973).

1967 Third Arab–Israeli War.

1968 North Vietnamese launch Tet
Offensive.

1972 First use of laser-guided bombs
('smart bombs').

1973 Americans withdraw from Vietnam.

1973 Fourth Arab–Israeli War.

1979 Russian forces invade Afghanistan
(to 1989)

1980 Deployment of cruise missiles
begins.
Iran–Iraq War (to 1988).

1981 Ronald Reagan president of the
United States (to 1989).

1982 Falklands War.

1989 George H. W. Bush becomes
president of the United States
(to 1993);
Russia withdraws from
Afghanistan, leaving chaos

1990 Iraq seizes Kuwait provoking Gulf
War (to 1991).

1991 Gulf War sees first combat use of
cruise missiles.
Croatia and Slovenia declare
independence from Yugoslavia,
provoking civil war (to 1992)

1992 United Nations forces intervene in
Somalia (to 1994)
Civil War breaks out in Bosnia (to
1996)

1993 Bill Clinton becomes president of
the United States (to 2001)
Russia invades Chechnya to
restore control (to 1996)

1996 Osama Bin Ladin moves from
Sudan to Afghanistan

1998 War breaks out in Kosovo (to 1999)
India and Pakistan successfully test
nuclear weapons.

1999 Russian forces invade Chechnya
again

2001 George W. Bush becomes
president of the United States;
Osama Bin Ladin masterminds
9/11 attacks on the United States;
US-led coalition invades
Afghanistan

2003 US-led coalition invades Iraq

2004 Struggles for Fallujah and Mosul
show limits of US-led Coalition's
ability to control Iraq.

2006 Israel invades Lebanon to root out
Hezbollah fighters but fails.

2007 President Bush announces a troop
'surge' to regain the initiative in
Iraq; North Korea carries out
nuclear test; Israel uses Suter
technology to disable Syrian early
warning defence system.

Glossary

A

amok combat military engagement in Indonesia in which a few warriors decide the outcome of a battle by a single desperate charge.

armada a fleet of warships.

armistice suspension of hostilities, truce.

army group the headquarters used to control armies, particularly during World War II by the British, Americans, and Germans. These multi-army, multicorps, and multi-divisional headquarters were essential to provide operational-level direction in the conduct of major campaigns.

arquebus fifteenth-and sixteenth-century hand-held firearm smaller than a musket.

artillery (especially cannons, field guns) weapons for firing missiles.

attack in depth attack which disrupts defences, causing systematic collapse. attrition continued attacks designed to wear down an opponent.

Axis powers Nazi Germany and Fascist Italy in alliance from 1936, joined by Japan in 1940, then by Hungary, Romania, Bulgaria, Slovakia, and Croatia.

B

B52 bomber the American bomber designed in the 1950s and built into the 1960s to execute a strategic nuclear war against the Soviet Union; enormously effective in the conventional wars against North Vietnam and Iraq.

ballistic missile missile guided on its ascent but with a free-falling descent.

ballistics the science of weapons trajectories.

Bar Lev Line a line of fortifications built by Israel along the Suez Canal after the Six Day Arab–Israeli War in 1967 to protect its hold on the Sinai peninsula; notably ineffective in the Yom Kippur Arab–Israeli War of 1973.

bastion quadrilateral projection from a defensive wall or fortification.

battalion body of soldiers made up of several companies.

battlecruiser armoured, fast warship displacing 25,000–35,000 tons.

battleship largest and most heavily armed of naval vessels.

bayonet pointed blade that fits onto the muzzle end of a rifle or musket, for use in hand-to-hand combat.

BEF (British Expeditionary Force) units of the British army in France at the outset of World Wars I and II.

Bf 109 the main German fighter aircraft of World War II, designed by Messerschmitt.

blockade closing off a strategic site such as a harbour or supply route.

bombard an early large-calibre gunpowder cannon.

Bomber Command RAF command, led by Sir Arthur Harris, that conducted Britain's strategic bombing campaign against Germany in World War II.

brevet major general a temporary rank with full command authority during the American Civil War; after the conflict Union officers reverted to their regular army rank.

brigade group of regiments or battalions.

brigadier officer in charge of a brigade.

broadside all the guns on one side of a warship firing in unison.

burg medieval fortress or walled town.

C

caisson large watertight chest for ammunition or other supplies.

calibre diameter of the bore of a gun or of a shell or bullet.

cantle the raised back of a saddle.

caravel large sailing galleon of the fifteenth and sixteenth centuries.

carbine light firearm with a short barrel, used by cavalry.

carrack large Mediterranean sailing galleon of the fourteenth and fifteenth centuries.

casus belli justification for war.

catapult engine of war for throwing projectiles (see also torsion catapult).

cattie a Chinese measure of weight of about one and a third pounds.

cavalry mounted soldiers.

centurion the leader of a century.

century the basic building block of the Roman legion (60–70 men).

CIA Central Intelligence Agency, established in 1947 with responsibility for all United States foreign intelligence operations.

chassepot a bolt-action French rifle of the late nineteenth century.

chasseur French infantryman or cavalryman trained to move swiftly.

chasseur à pied a soldier of the French light infantry.

chevauchée a raid on horseback.

chevaux-de-frises defensive poles with rows of pointed metal spikes protruding outwards at right angles, used in trench warfare before the introduction of barbed wire.

cohort after the late second century BC, the chief tactical and administrative unit of the Roman legion, comprising three maniples – about 480 men.

Combined Bomber Offensive a plan for combined strategic bombing favoured by the Allied high command in World War II, but with which Sir Arthur Harris refused to co-operate; designed to integrate the efforts of RAF Bomber Command and the US Eighth and Fifteenth Air Forces.

Comintern the Communist (Third) International, an association of communist parties dominated by the Soviet Union and dissolved by Stalin in 1943 as a gesture of good will towards non-communist allies in World War II.

commission the warrant which confers authority on an officer.

cluster bomb bomb which releases several smaller bombs on impact.

commando unit a military unit dedicated for raids into enemy territory.

company a unit of soldiers consisting of two or more platoons.

condottiere the leader of a band of mercenary soldiers.

conscription compulsory enrolment in the armed forces.

corned gunpowder gunpowder prepared in small granules, to prevent its components from separating (invented in Europe c.1430).

corps typically two or more divisions forming a tactical unit.

cruise missile highly accurate computer-guided missile that follows the terrain on pre-planned routes to the target; highly successful in the Gulf War of 1991.

cuirassier heavily armed French cavalry soldier wearing a cuirass (armoured breastplate).

culverin small, narrow-bore cannon, able to fire small shot at great distance.

D

defence in depth a network of interdependent defensive strongpoints, increasingly densely placed the further an attacker advances.

depth charge explosive anti-submarine charge dropped in sea.

division a tactical unit of three to five brigades with a headquarters.

dragoon heavily armed mounted soldier; in the sixteenth century, a mounted soldier trained to fight on foot.

dreadnought a large battleship on the model of HMS *Dreadnought* (1906) armed with big guns of a uniform calibre.

drill the exercise in unison of military skills and formations.

Dromon standard Byzantine warship with two banks of rowers.

F

falconet small artillery piece.

feint a feigned attack.

fief land given in return for military service.

firestorm a fire encompassing a large section of a bombed city in which the conflagration fans itself by creating a vacuum which draws in air.

flak shrapnel from bursting antiaircraft shells.

flintlock musket firearm which uses a flint to ignite the charge.

FLN (*Front de Libération Nationale*) the Algerian National Liberation Front, which waged a war to oust France from Algeria in 1954–62.

flower wars ritual conflict between the Aztecs and their neighbours in the valley of Mexico in the fifteenth and early sixteenth centuries aimed at securing captives for enslavement or sacrifice.

free-fire zone (Vietnam War) zone cleared of most South Vietnamese population and declared to be an area where all human movement was presumed hostile.

frigate the vessel next lower in size to a ship of the line.

full-rigged ship a large wooden sailing ship with three or four masts carrying a combination of square sails to provide motive power and triangular ('lateen') sails to assist lateral movement (first developed in fifteenth-century Europe).

G

galeass a sixteenth-century oared vessel larger and heavier than a galley.

galley long, low warship with single deck, propelled by both oars and a sail.

garrison the troops stationed in a military installation.

gladius the short, thrusting sword of the Romans, with a strong, firm blade sharpened on both edges.

grapeshot a cluster of iron balls which scatter when they are fired.

grapnel a grappling iron, small metal anchor with metal claws.

greave an armoured shin pad worn by Greek and Roman infantry.

guerrilla a member of an irregular militia using harassing tactics.

H

halberd a long-shafted weapon topped with an axe head and a spike, used in the fifteenth and sixteenth centuries.

Harrier jet vertical-take-off-and-landing fighter aircraft used by British forces in the Falklands War and US marines in the Gulf War.

hastati 'spearmen' – the first line of maniples in the Roman legion, armed with javelins and the gladius.

hegemony the dominance of one nation over others.

Hellcat F6F fighter American naval fighter aircraft of World War II that won air superiority in the Pacific over its Japanese opponents.

hetairoi 'companion cavalry' – an elite body of aristocratic Macedonians of the fourth century BC, heavily armed on strong mounts.

Ho Chi Minh Trail (so called by Americans after the leader of North Vietnam) a road built through Laos and Cambodia by North Vietnam to facilitate infiltration of South Vietnam.

hoplite a warrior-farmer of classical Greece, practised in phalanx fighting.

howitzer a short cannon firing shells at a steep angle, with sharp ascent and descent.

Hurricane one of two fighters built for the RAF in the late 1930s that proved crucial in winning the Battle of Britain (see also Spitfire).

hypaspists 'shield bearers' – in the fourth century BC, the Macedonian infantry which occupied the centre of the line and usually followed behind the cavalry.

I

impi a body of Zulu warriors making up a military formation.

infantry soldiers fighting on foot.

intelligence information about an enemy or potential conflict, collected for the sake of military advantage.

J

Jäger Prussian light infantry.

javelin light slender spear.

K

kamikaze 'divine wind'– a member of a World War II Japanese suicide air attack corps which crashed its bomb-laden aircraft into US navy ships.

keep a stronghold or fortified tower.

Kriegsmarine the German navy in World War II.

L

lance steel-tipped wooden pole held pointed at adversaries in combat on horseback.

Landwehr Prussian militia of all men aged seventeen to forty not enrolled in other military service.

legion major unit of the Roman army, consisting of 5,000 to 6,000 soldiers and divided into ten cohorts.

line ahead naval combat formation in which all warships engage the enemy arranged in a line one behind the other.

logistics the task of moving and supplying armies.

Luftwaffe the German air force.

M

machine gun a gun capable of firing bullets rapidly and continuously.

MACV (Military Assistance Command Vietnam) – the command group for American forces in Vietnam.

'Magic' code-name for Japanese naval signals intercepted and decoded by the United States during World War II.

Maginot Line a system of fortifications built by the French to prevent the Germans from invading France, but outflanked in 1940.

man-at-arms a heavily armed, usually mounted soldier of the late middle ages.

maniple a small tactical subunit (a 'handful'), comprising two centuries, first

of the Roman phalanx and eventually of the Roman legion.

marines naval troops trained and equipped to fight their way ashore.

matchlock musket gun fired by a slowburning match which is positioned over a hole in the breach.

mêlée tactics a series of ship-to-ship battles (cf. the 'line ahead').

mercenary a soldier fighting for pay alone.

militia a military force made up of citizens called into service, or liable to be called into service.

minié bullet lead bullet, hollowed at the bottom, allowing the explosive charge to push out the flanges causing a tight fit in a rifled barrel, giving spin and direction, thus increasing accuracy.

mortar a short artillery piece which fires bombs or heavy shells.

musket heavy, smooth-bore, long-barrelled firearm, fired from the shoulder; common from sixteenth to the nineteenth centuries.

N

NATO (North Atlantic Treaty Organization) a joint anti-Soviet defence force established in 1949 by the United States, Britain, Canada, France, Belgium, The Netherlands, Luxembourg, Denmark, Norway, Iceland, Italy, and Portugal, with the addition of Greece and Turkey in 1952 and of West Germany in 1954.

NCO non-commissioned officer, e.g. sergeant, corporal, bombadier.

needlegun breach-loading rifle that allowed fast reloading, first adopted by the Prussian army.

O

OAS (*Organisation de l'Armée Secrète*) a terrorist organization dedicated to keeping Algeria French.

onager a one-armed catapult, powered by the tortion of twisted hair or rope, capable of throwing an 8-pound stone 500 yards (used in ancient and medieval warfare).

ordre mince the Prussian shallow line formations imitated by French infantry in the eighteenth century.

ordre profonde the deep column formations used by French infantry in the eighteenth century.

P

panoply a full set of armour.

panzer division a German armoured division.

pezetairoi 'foot companions' – Macedonian professional infantry of the fourth century BC.

phalangite a member of a phalanx.

phalanx a solid column of foot soldiers, especially when armed with pikes.

pike a large, often unwieldy, wooden shaft with an iron or steel point, used by foot soldiers.

pilum the Roman javelin.

pistol a small handgun.

platoon a small body of soldiers.

polis the city-state of ancient Greece.

principes the second line of maniples in the Roman legion, armed with the *gladius* and javelins.

Pyrrhic victory a victory gained at too high a cost (named after the victory of Pyrrhus, king of Epirus, over the Romans at Heraclea).

Q

quartermaster the staff-officer responsible for transporting, quartering, and supplying the troops.

R

RAF (Royal Air Force) the airborne forces of Great Britain.

redoubt a small defended position.

regiment large army unit under the command of a colonel.

Reichswehr the German army (1920s).

rifled musket a musket with spiralled grooves cut into the barrel to give the bullet spin and thus better direction.

S

salient an outward-pointing angle in a military front.

sapper a soldier who digs trenches or tunnels to give access to the enemy, undermine defences, or lay mines.

SAS (Special Air Services Regiment) a British unit formed by Colonel David Sterling in 1941 that emphasized stealth, surprise, intelligence gathering, and attacks on enemy rear areas.

satrap the governor of a province of Persia in ancient times.

schiltron a cluster of spearmen in Scottish medieval combat.

scutum the curved, rectangular Roman shield.

sepoy an Indian soldier trained to fight in European fashion (seventeenth to nineteenth centuries).

ship of the line man-of-war large enough to take its place in line of battle.

sortie a raid.

Spitfire the main British fighter aircraft of World War II.

SS (*die Schutzstaffel* – 'defence corps') Nazi elite corps.

stealth bomber aircraft that uses complex technologies, in terms of design, computers, special materials, and routing, to render enemy radar systems ineffective.

storm troops elite German combat troops trained in 1917–18; the term was applied later to the para-military units of the Nazi party (1920s–30s).

Strategic Bombing Survey an extensive analysis of the effectiveness during World War II of Allied strategic bombing on the German war economy.

T

tercios permanent infantry regiments in Spanish service, first created in 1534.

thetes the landless poor of the Greek city-states.

torpedo a weapon which propels itself through water, after release from an aircraft, ship or submarine, and explodes on impact.

torsion catapult a catapult which propels its missiles by the force created when ropes or other materials untwist.

trace italienne fortifications designed in geometrical form with quadrilateral bastions projecting from the line of the walls at regular intervals; invented in Italy, where it became known as 'the modern style', c.1500.

trebuchet medieval stone thrower.

triplex acies conventional Roman battlefield order consisting of three successive lines of ten maniples, each comprising two centuries of 70–80 men.

trirari 'third liners' – the third line of maniples in the Roman legion, armed with spears.

trireme Greek or Roman galley with three tiers of oars; capable of high speed and equipped for ramming.

trunnions pivots on which a cannon can be tilted.

U

U-boat (*Unterseeboot*) a German submarine.

'Ultra' code-name for the Allied intelligence in World War II based on decrypted German high-level message traffic.

USAF United States Air Force.

V

V-1 German World War II flying bomb.

V-2 German World War II rocket.

velites light-armed skirmishers (including troops and horsemen) of the Roman legion.

Viet Cong derogatory name for the Viet Minh.

Viet Minh communist military force which fought a guerrilla war against the French in Vietnam in the 1950s.

W

Waffen SS (the armed SS) elite divisions raised and trained by Heinrich Himmler's SS; highly effective on the battlefield but instigators of innumerable atrocities due to their fanatical contempt for their opponents.

Wagenburgen mobile fortresses made from farm wagons, used in the fifteenth century by the Hussites of Bohemia.

Wehrmacht the German armed forces.

Z

'Zero' fighter Japanese fighter aircraft at the beginning of World War II whose range and flying capabilities provided a surprise for the Allies.

Bibliography

For the convenience of readers, most of the items suggested below are in English. Works considered to be of special interest or importance are starred with an asterisk.

Among the many general histories of war, six works stand out: H. Delbrück, *History of the Art of War within the Framework of Political History* (4 vols, Westport, 1975–85); J. F. C. Fuller, *A Military History of the Western World* (2 vols, New York, 1957); J. Keegan, *A History of Warfare* (New York, 1993); W. H. McNeill, *The Pursuit of Power. Technology, Armed Force and Society since AD 1000* (Oxford, 1983); R. L. O'Connell, *Of Arms and Men. A History of War, Weapons and Aggression* (Oxford, 1989); and A. Vagts, *A History of Militarism* (London, 1959). In addition, M. Howard, *War in European History* (Oxford, 1976) performs the near miracle of covering his chosen subject in 143 pages.

General works on the causes of war also abound. E. Luard, *War in International Society. A Study in International Sociology* (New York, 1986) is one of the most ambitious; G. Blainey, *The Causes of Wars* (London, 1976) one of the most readable (although it really considers only the period since 1700). R. I. Rotberg and T. K. Rabb, *The Origins and Prevention of Major Wars* (Cambridge, 1988) contains a wide range of essays that examine general theories as well as specific examples.

Foremost among considerations of how to prepare for and wage wars come E. N. Luttwak, *Strategy. The Logic of War and Peace* (Cambridge, Mass., 1987); P. Paret, ed., *Makers of Modern Strategy from Machiavelli to the Nuclear Age* (Princeton, 1986); and W. Murray, A. Bernstein and M. Knox, eds, *The Making of Strategy. Rulers, States and War* (Cambridge, 1994). E. Cohen offers an excellent consideration of the challenges war presents to those in control in *Supreme Command* (New York 2002), and J. Keegan an unrivalled picture of the challenges combat presents to those directly involved in *The Face of Battle. A Study of Agincourt, Waterloo and the Somme* (London, 1976). Finally, the various attempts to impose some limits to war in the West are studied by the various contributors to M. E. Howard, G. Andreopoulos, and M. R Shulman, eds, *The Laws of War. Constraints on Warfare in the Western World* (New Haven, 1994).

The military implications of technology, although of prime importance to the western way of war, scarcely attracted attention until 1945; and even then outstanding works on the subject only began to appear in the 1980s. Pride of place belongs to the trilogy of Daniel R. Headrick, which examines the contribution of technology to western expansion – *The Tools of Empire. Technology and European Imperialism in the Nineteenth Century* (Oxford, 1981); *The Tentacles of Progress. Technology and Transfer in the Age of Imperialism, 1850–1940* (Oxford, 1988); and *The Invisible Weapon: Telecommunications and International Politics, 1851–1945* (Oxford, 1992). See also the general survey of M. van Creveld, *Technology and War from 2000 bc to the Present* (New York, 1989), which (despite its title) deals primarily with Europe.

On the role of navies and seapower, see the broad surveys of J. Glete, *Navies and Nations. Warships, Navies and State Building in Europe and America, 1500–1860* (2 vols, Stockholm, 1993); C. S. Gray, *The Leverage of Seapower. The Strategic Advantage of Navies in War* (New York, 1992); and G. Modelski and W. R. Thompson, *Seapower in Global Politics* (London, 1988). Finally, on the crucial importance of paying for war (a constant theme of this book) see L. Neal, *War Finance* (3 vols, Aldershot, 1994).

Works that deal with war in one or more of the discrete chronological periods covered by this volume are discussed by each contributor; nevertheless, two books by Jeremy Black range widely over the last five centuries: *War and the World. Military Power and the Fate of Continents, 1450–2000* (New Haven, 1998) and *War: Past, Present and Future* (Stroud, 2000).

Chapter 1. Genesis of the Infantry

No comprehensive account of Near Eastern warfare exists, although the illustrated survey of Y. Yadin, *The Art of Warfare in Biblical Lands in the Light of Archaeological Study* (2 vols, London, 1963), is both accessible and readable. A. Ferrill, *The Origins of War* (New York, 1985) includes general chapters for the non-specialist on fighting in the ancient Near East and Egypt.

The field of Greek military history has expanded enormously in the last twenty years, mostly as a result of continuing publication of W. K. Pritchett's monumental work, **The Greek State at War* (5 parts, Berkeley, 1971–91), and his accompanying *Studies in Ancient Greek Topography* (8 vols, Berkeley, 1965–93), which deal with battlefields and campaign routes in Greece. Greek warfare before the fifth century BC is the subject of P. Greenhalgh's sober *Early Greek Warfare: Horsemen and Chariots in the Homeric and Archaic Ages* (Cambridge, 1973); and of G. Ahlberg, *Fighting on Land and Sea in Greek Geometric Art* (Stockholm, 1971); and **J. Latacz, Kampfparänese, Kampfdarstellung und Kampfwirklichkeit in der Ilias, bei Kallinos und Tyrtaios* (Munich, 1977).

Reliable and readable accounts of tactics, strategy, and the evolution of hoplite war may be found in **F. Adcock, The Greek and Macedonian Art of War* (Berkeley, 1957); P. Ducrey, *Warfare in Ancient Greece* (New York, 1986); Y. Garlan, *War in the Ancient World* (New York, 1975); and especially **J. K. Anderson, Military Theory and Practice in the Age of Xenophon* (Berkeley, 1970). Some interesting artistic recreations of Greek warfare, as well as valuable maps and charts, are found in the surveys of J. Hackett, ed., *A History of War in the Ancient World* (London, 1989); J. Warry, *Warfare in the Classical World* (New York, 1980); and P. Connolly, *Greece and Rome at War* (London, 1981).

The environment and experience of hoplite fighting are covered by **V. D. Hanson, The Western Way of War. Infantry Battle in Classical Greece* (New York, 1989); and V. D. Hanson, ed., *Hoplites: The Ancient Greek Battle Experience* (London, 1991). Social and economic problems of Greek warfare concern V. D. Hanson, *Warfare and Agriculture in Classical Greece* (Pisa, 1983); J. P. Vernant, ed., *Problèmes de la guerre en Grèce ancienne* (Paris, 1968); and Y. Garlan, *Recherches de poliorcétique grecque* (Paris, 1974). The study of Greek arms and armour rests still on the work of A. Snodgrass, *Early Greek Armour and Weapons* (Edinburgh, 1964) *and Arms and Armour of the Greeks* (Ithaca, 1967). Excellent works on the regionalism and specialization in Greek warfare include J. Lazenby, *The Spartan Army* (Westminster, 1985); G. Bugh, *The Horsemen of Athens* (Princeton, 1988); and J. Best, *Thracian Peltastsand their Influence on Greek Warfare* (Groningen, 1969). D. Kagan, *New History of the Peloponnesian War* (4 vols, Ithaca, 1969–87) has brief, though fine, accounts of the major land and sea battles between 431 and 404 BC.

Chapter 2. From Phalanx to Legion

No comprehensive survey exists for the long and complicated story of Hellenistic warfare, but the general outlines can be pieced together through a variety of specialized studies. *W.W. Tarn, *Hellenistic Military and Naval Developments* (Cambridge, 1930) offers a dated, but still valuable overview. More comprehensive is the first volume of H. Delbrück, *Warfare in Antiquity* (Westport, 1975); J. Kromayer and G. Veith, *Heerwesen und Kriegführung der Griechen und Römer* (Munich, 1928); and *H. Launey, *Recherches sur les armées hellenistiques* (Paris, 1949).

Among the scores of biographies of Alexander the Great that discuss his military record in detail, N. G. L. Hammond's *Alexander the Great: King, Commander, and Statesman* (London, 1981) reveals the author's lifetime mastery of Greek military history. J. F. C. Fuller, *The Generalship of Alexander the Great* (London, 1960); D. Engels, *Alexander the Great and the Logistics of the Macedonian Army* (Berkeley, 1978); and a series of articles by A. M. Devine (in the journals *Phoenix* [1983, 1986] and *Ancient World* [1985, 1986, 1987]) cover precise campaigns and battles.

The growing practice of hiring armies is the subject of G. T. Griffith, *Mercenaries of the Hellenistic World* (Cambridge, 1935); and H. W. Parke, *Greek Mercenary Soldiers* (Oxford, 1933). Fortifications and the massive walls of Hellenistic cities are covered well by A. W. Lawrence, *Greek Aims in Fortification* (Oxford, 1979); and F. E. Winter, *Greek Fortifications* (Toronto, 1971). F. W. Marsden reviews the growing evolution of catapults and siegecraft in his two-volume *Greek and Roman Artillery* (Oxford, 1969–71). B. Bar-Kochava, *The Seleucid Army* (Cambridge, 1976), is the sole specialized account devoted to the armies of the Successors. Both E. L. Wheeler, *Stratagem and the Vocabulary of Military Trickery* (Leiden, 1988); and D. Whitehead, *Aineias*

the Tactician: How to Survive Under Siege (Oxford, 1990), discuss the growing genre of Greek military science.

The early Roman army has a massive bibliography. General accounts accessible to the non-specialist include F. E. Adcock, *The Roman Art of War under the Republic* (Oxford, 1940); E. Gabba, *Republican Rome, the Army, and the Allies* (Oxford, 1976); L. Keppie, *The Making of the Roman Army* (Totowa, 1984); and H. M. D. Parker, *The Roman Legions* (Oxford 1971). Crucial questions of manpower and recruitment under the republic are discussed in P. A. Brunt's monumental *Italian Manpower, 225 BC–AD 14* (Oxford, 1971); L. Keppie, *Colonisation and Veteran Settlement in Italy, 47–14 BC* (London, 1980); and C. Nicolet, *The World of the Citizen in Republican Rome* (London, 1983). J. A. Brisson, ed., *Problèmes de la guerre à, Rome* (Paris, 1969); J. Suolahti, *The Junior Officers of the Roman Army in the Republican Period* (Helsinki, 1955); and P. Couissin, *Les armes romaines* (Paris, 1926) cover legion organization and formation under the republic.

Chapter 3. The Roman Way of War

Standard treatments of the imperial legions are numerous. Perhaps most accessible for the non-specialist are G. Webster, *The Roman Imperial Army* (3rd edn, London, 1985); G. R. Watson, *The Roman Soldier* (London, 1983); and M. Grant, *Armies of the Caesars* (New York, 1974). Larger and more controversial issues of imperial strategy and the role of military power are discussed by *E. Luttwak, *The Grand Strategy of the Roman Empire* (Baltimore, 1976); A. Ferrill, *The Fall of the Roman Empire: The Military Explanation* (London, 1986), B. Isaac, *The Limits of Empire: The Roman Army in the east* (Oxford, 1990); and *C. R Whittaker, *Frontiers of the Roman Empire* (Baltimore, 1994). E. Wheeler surveys these various approaches to Roman grand strategy in *The Journal of Military History*, lvii (1993), 7–41 and 215–40.

The growing problem of keeping the legions manned, and the actual conditions of such lengthy professional service are covered by E. Birley, *The Roman Army. Papers 1929–1986* (Amsterdam, 1988); R. Davies, *Service in the Roman Army* (New York, 1989); and J. C. Mann, *Legionary Recruitment and Veteran Settlement during the Principate* (London, 1983). For later problems between civilian and legionary, see R. MacMullen,

Soldier and Civilian in the Later Roman Empire (Cambridge, Mass., 1963). Roman military equipment and infrastructure became increasingly complex under the Empire: see A. Johnson, *Roman Forts* (London, 1983); H. R Robinson, *The Armour of Imperial Rome* (London, 1975); M. Bishop and J. Coulston, *Roman Military Equipment* (London, 1993); and V. A. Maxfield, *The Military Decorations of the Roman Army* (London, 1981). On non-legionary forces see G. L. Cheesman, *The Auxilia of the Roman Imperial Army* (Oxford, 1914); P. A. Holder, *Studies in the Auxilia of the Roman Army from Augustus to Trajan* (Oxford, 1980); and more recently, D. B. Saddington, *The Development of the Roman Auxiliary Forces from Caesar to Vespasian* (49 BC–AD 79) (Harare, 1982).

Numerous excellent accounts examine Rome's various wars with a variety of determined adversaries. Begin with J. F. Lazenby, *Hannibal's War* (Warminster, 1978); G. Webster, *The Roman Invasion of Britain* (London, 1980), M. Fentress, *Numidia and the Roman Army* (Oxford, 1979); and I. Rossi, *Trajan's Column and the Dacian Wars* (London, 1971). For Roman ships and navies, consult L. Casson, *The Ancient Mariners* (London, 1959) and *Ships and Seamanship in the Ancient World* (Princeton, 1971); J. Rougé, *La marine dans l'antiquité* (Paris, 1975); and especially C. G. Starr, *The Roman Imperial Navy* (New York, 1941). On the subject of ancient banked naval craft in general, *J. S. Morrison and R. T. Williams, *Greek Oared Ships 900–322 BC* (Cambridge, 1968), is indispensable.

Chapter 4. On Roman Ramparts

Readers can put a modicum of confidence in two general medieval military histories. First Philippe Contamine, *War in the Middle Ages* (Oxford, 1984), represents research done by Europe's leading medieval military historian (albeit during the later 1970s, making it thus a decade and a half behind the research front). A revised French edition, containing an updated *apparatus criticus*, was published in 1992. Second, J.-F. Verbruggen, *The Art of War in Western Europe during the Middle Ages, from the Eighth Century to 1340* (Amsterdam–New York, 1977), offers an excellent synthesis but represents research completed before 1954 and unfortunately does not include the footnotes of the original Dutch edition.

A substantial group of important and relatively new books on specific topics have greatly modified the traditional views set out in Contamine. *J. Bradbury, *The Medieval Siege* (Woodbridge, 1992) and R. Rogers, *Latin Siege Warfare in the Twelfth Century* (Oxford, 1992), read in conjunction with B. S. Bachrach, 'Medieval Siege Warfare: A Reconnaissance', *Journal of Military History*, lviii (1994), demonstrate the need for a fundamental rethinking of the manner in which medieval military history has been treated. The pioneering work of K. R. DeVries, *Medieval Military Technology* (Peterborough, 1992) also supports a rethinking of the field. Basic to a reinterpretation of medieval military demography is *K.-F. Werner, 'Heeresorganisation und Kriegsführung im deutschen Königreich des 10. und 11. Jahrhunderts', in *Settimane di Studio del Centra Italiano di studi sull'alto Medioevo* (2 vols, Spoleto, 1968), 791–843.

The interpretations developed in this chapter for the pre-crusade era rest upon *B. S. Bachrach, *Merovingian Military Organization, 481–751* (Minneapolis, 1972); *Armies and Politics in the Early Medieval West* (London, 1993); and *The Anatomy of a Little War: A Diplomatic and Military History of the Gundovald Affair (568–586)* (Boulder, 1994). For the eleventh century and after, see the brilliant articles of J. Gillingham: 'Richard I and the Science of War in the Middle Ages', in J. Gillingham and J. C. Holt, eds, *War and Government in the Middle Ages. Essays in Honour of J. O. Prestwich* (Woodbridge, 1984), 78–91; 'William the Bastard at War', in C. Harper-Bill, C. Holdsworth, and J. L. Nelson, eds, *Studies in Medieval History Presented to R. Allen Brown* (Woodbridge, 1989), 141–58; and *'War and Chivalry in the *History of William the Marshall'* in P. R. Cross and S. D. Lloyd, eds, *Thirteenth Century England,* (Woodbridge, 1990), 1–13.

For England the basic works remain *C. Warren Hollister, *Anglo-Saxon Military Organization* (Oxford, 1962) and *The Military Organization of Norman England* (Oxford, 1965); while R. Abels, *Lordship and Military Obligation in Anglo-Saxon England* (Berkeley, 1988), provides some interesting reinterpretations; and J. H. Beeler, *Warfare in England, 1066–1189* (Ithaca, 1971), is encyclopaedic. Regarding Spain see James Powers, *A Society Organized for War: the Iberian Municipal Militias in the Central Middle Ages, 1000–1284* (Berkeley, 1988);

and for Germany, L. Auer, *Studien zum Heer der Ottonen und der ersten Salier (919–1056),* (Bonn, 1985).

Concerning the crusades *R. C. Smail, *Crusading Warfare 1097–1193* (Cambridge, 1956); and C. Marshall, *Warfare in the Latin East, 1192–1291* (Cambridge, 1992) are basic and should be supplemented by D. C. Nicolle, *Arms and Armour of the Crusading Era, 1050–1350,* (2 vols, New York, 1988), which is a magisterial work of reference that goes well beyond the crusades themselves. Byzantium is well served by many technical works, such as J. Haldon, *Byzantine Praetorians* (Bonn, 1984); M. C. Bartusis, *The Late Byzantine Army: Arms and Society, 1204–1453* (Philadelphia, 1992); and J. R. Partington, *A History of Greek Fire and Gunpowder* (Cambridge, 1980).

R. H. C. Davis, *The Medieval Warhorse* (London, 1989), though seriously flawed, is nevertheless useful. C. Gillmore, 'Practical Chivalry: The Training of Horses for Tournaments and Warfare', *Studies in Medieval and Renaissance History*, n. s. xiii (1992), 7–29, is fundamental to understanding mounted warfare; and J. Bradbury, *The Medieval Archer* (New York, 1985), is crucial to the study of missile weapons. On naval matters, see R W. Unger, *The Ship in the Medieval Economy, 600–1600* (London, 1980); A. R Lewis and T. J. Runyan, *European Naval and Maritime History, 300–1500* (Bloomington, 1985); John H. Pryor, *Geography, Technology, and War. Studies in the Maritime History of the Mediterranean, 649–1571* (Cambridge, 1988); and J. Hayward, *Dark Age Naval Power: A Reassessment of Frankish and Anglo-Saxon Seafaring Activity* (London, 1991). All include useful bibliographies.

A plethora of useful information on fortifications may be found in *J.-F. Finó, *Fortresses de la France médiévale* (3rd edn, Paris, 1977); R. A. Brown, *English Castles* (3rd edn, London, 1976); and C. L. Salch, *Dictionnaire des châteaux et des fortifications du Moyen Age en France* (Strasbourg, 1979). However, this subject is very poorly conceptualized from the perspective of both military history and the history of warfare: compare B. S. Bachrach (with R Aris), 'Military Technology and Garrison Organization: Some Observations on Anglo-Saxon Military Thinking in Light of the Burghal Hidage', *Technology and Culture*, xxxi (1990); 1–17, and the brief review article by B. S. Bachrach in *Albion*, xxiv (1992), 301–4.

Chapter 5. New Weapons, New Tactics

Apart from the general studies of Verbruggen and Contamine noted in the bibliography for Chapter 4, *P. Contamine, *Guerre, Etat et société à la fin du moyen age. Etudes sur les armées des rois de France, 1337–1494* (Paris: The Hague, 1972) remains a fundamental work on military organization in late medieval France; while his collected papers, *La France aux XIVe et XVe siècles. Hommes, mentalités, guerre et paix* (London, 1981) contain much that is useful for the study of war in this period. For England, H. J. Hewitt, *The Organization of War under Edward III, 1338–62* (Manchester–New York, 1966) is much slighter but, with its emphasis on logistics, adopts a modern approach to the study of war. M. G. A. Vale, *War and Chivalry. Warfare and Aristocratic Culture in England, France and Burgundy at the End of the Middle Ages* (London, 1981) emphasizes and defends the role of the nobility in war, while his essay, 'New Techniques and Old Ideals: the Impact of Artillery on War and Chivalry at the End of the Hundred Years War', in C. T. Allmand, ed., *War, Literature and Politics in the Late Middle Ages* (Liverpool, 1976), 57–72, discusses the use and impact of artillery. B. H. St. J. O'Neil, *Castles and Cannon* (Oxford, 1960) relates the development of cannon to architectural developments. K. A. Fowler, ed., *The Hundred Years War* (London, 1971) is a useful collection of essays by a number of scholars, including C. F. Richmond, whose 'The Keeping of the Seas during the Hundred Years War: 1422–1440', *History*, xlix (1964), 283–98, discusses the contribution and limitations of naval warfare within the limits of the period. *C. J. Rogers, 'The Military Revolutions of the Hundred Years' War', *Journal of Military History*, lvii (1993), 241–78, is an important contribution to the debate regarding late medieval military developments. For the diffusion of the most popular military manual, see C. Allmand, 'The *De Re Militari* of Vegetius in the Middle Ages and the Renaissance', in C. Saunders, F. Le Saux, and N. Thomas, eds., *Writing War. Medieval Literary Responses to Warfare* (Woodbridge & Rochester, NY, 2004), 15–28.

Chapter 6. The Gunpowder Revolution

The military changes that occurred in Europe in the years around 1500 have excited great attention. See *G. Parker, *The*

Military Revolution. Military Innovation and the Rise of the West, 1500–1800 (Cambridge, 1988; revised edn, 2000); and C. J. Rogers, ed., *The Military Revolution Debate* (Boulder, 1995). Other important works on military change at this time include C. Cresti, A. Fara and D. Lamberini, eds, *Architettura militare nell' Europa del XVI secolo* (Siena, 1988); A. Guillerm, *La pierre et le vent. Fortifications et marine en Occident* (Paris, 1985); J. R. Hale, Renaissance War Studies (London, 1984); and *S. Pepper and N. Adams, Firearms and Fortifications. Military Architecture and Siege Warfare in Sixteenth-Century Siena* (Chicago, 1986). More recently, our understanding of siege warfare has been transformed by J. M. Ostwald. See also two more books edited by Jeremy Black, *War in the Early Modern World* (London, 1999) – a collection that (unusually) lives up to its title by including chapters on warfare around the globe – and *The Cambridge Illustrated Atlas of Warfare. Renaissance to Revolution, 1492–1792* (Cambridge, 1996), which contains four sections on Europe and two on the wider world.

Chapter 7. Ships of the Line

*C. M. Cipolla produced a path-breaking study three decades ago – *Guns and Sails in the Early Phase of European Expansion 1400–1700* (London, 1965) – which is still fresh and informative. A. Guillerm, *La pierre et le vent,* and G. Parker, *The Military Revolution,* both contain relevant sections, but pride of place belongs to the ambitious comparative study of J. Glete, *Navies and Nations* (see page 415). On the development of Mediterranean warfare, two books stand out: *J. F. Guilmartin, Jr, *Gunpowder and Galleys. Changing Technology and Mediterranean Warfare at Sea in the Sixteenth Century* (Cambridge, revised edn., 2003); and J. H. Pryor, *Geography, Technology and War. Studies in the Maritime History of the Mediterranean, 649–1571* (Cambridge, 1988). For the development of the English navy, see D. M. Loades, *The Tudor Navy. An Administrative, Political and Military History* (London, 1992); B. Capp, *Cromwell's Navy. The Fleet and the English Revolution, 1649–1660* (Oxford, 1989); and, above all, N. A. M. Rodger, *A Naval History of Britain* (2 vols. to date, London, 1997–2004): vol. 1 covers 660–1649 and vol. 2 covers 1649–1815. On Spanish naval power see R. A. Stradling, *The Armada of Flanders. Spanish Maritime Policy*

and European War, 1568–1668 (Cambridge, 1992); and C. J. M. Martin and G. Parker, *The Spanish Armada* (2nd edn., Manchester, 1999). On later conflicts, see G. Symcox, *The Crisis of French Sea-Power 1688–1697* (The Hague, 1974); J. Pritchard, 'From Shipwright to Naval Constructor: the Professionalization of Eighteenth-Century French Naval Shipbuilders', *Technology and Culture,* xxviii (1987), 1–25; and *J. Ehrman, *The Navy in the War of William III 1689–97. Its State and Direction* (Cambridge, 1953).

Chapter 8. Conquest of the Americas

The dramatic story of the Spaniards' lightning conquests in the New World inspired the imagination of the great nineteenth-century narrative historian William H. Prescott whose *Conquest of Mexico* (1843) and *Conquest of Peru* (1847) set standards that endured for over a century. *J. Hemming, *The Conquest of the Incas* (New York, 1970) attained a new level; and H. Thomas, *The Conquest of Mexico* (London, 1992) comes close. Cortés's accounts of his campaigns have been superbly translated by A. Pagden as *Letters from Mexico* (New Haven, 1986); and the narrative of his captain Bernal Díaz del Castillo appeared as *The Conquest of New Spain* (Baltimore, 1963).

For Peru, the second volume of Garcilaso de la Vega's *Royal Commentaries of the Incas* (1617; Austin, 1966) offers a Spanish captain's half-caste son's version of events. The best tactical study of Spanish warfare against the Incas is J. F. Guilmartin. Jr. 'The Cutting Edge: an Analysis of the Spanish Invasion and Overthrow of the Inca Empire, 1532–1549,' in K. Andrien and R. Adorno, eds, *Transatlantic Encounters* (Berkeley, 1991). *I. Clendinnen's *Ambivalent Conquests: Maya and Spaniard in Yucatán, 1517–1570* (Cambridge, 1987) provides the best English-language history of the conquest of the Yucatan.

Several sixteenth-century Spanish religious leaders criticized the brutality of warfare in the New World. Friar Bartolomé de Las Casas, *The Devastation of the Indies* (1552, Baltimore, 1992) indicted military abuses. Other sixteenth-century priests assisted native scribes to create counter-narratives, or write pictorial accounts called codices, showing the extent of the devastation: Friar Bernardino de Sahagún helped to produce one such text, known as *The Florentine Codex* (12 vols, Santa Fe, 1950–82);

Friar Diego Durán produced another – *Historia de las Indias,* (2 vols, Mexico, 1967). King Philip II of Spain considered such accounts subversive, however, and neither critique was published until the twentieth century. M. León-Portilla's *The Broken Spears* (Boston, 1962) summarizes some of this literature in an accessible format. *R. Hassig's *Aztec Warfare* (Norman, 1988) studies indigenous warfare using the information assembled by critical clerics. For Brazil, J. Hemming's *Red Gold: The Conquest of the Brazilian Indians* (Cambridge, 1978) is excellent.

For English North America, a flawed but readable comparative account is D. Leach, *Flintlock and Tomahawk* (New York, 1966), while P. Malone's *Skulking Way of War* (Lanham, 1991) offers an excellent account of indigenous adaptation to European technology. The Dutch military experience in North America has been relatively neglected, since much of the existing material on early wars with natives was assembled by anti-war factions. The opponents of war were translated by F. Jameson in *Narratives of New Netherland* (New York, 1909), while engineering details of the original fortress on Manhattan appear in A. J. F. Laer, *Documents Relating to New Netherland* (San Marino, 1924).

Writing on French warfare in the New World has tended to focus on Canada, to the neglect of the Caribbean region, but see G. Havard and C. Vidal, *Histoire de l'Amérique Française* (Paris, 2003) and P. Boucher, *Cannibal Encounters* (Baltimore, 1992). For Drake in the Caribbean, the volumes published by the Hakluyt Society are unsurpassed: K. R. Andrews, ed., *The Last Voyage of Drake and Hawkins* (Cambridge, 1972; 2nd ser. cxlii), and M. F. Keeler, ed., *Sir Francis Drake's West Indian Voyage, 1585–1587* (London, 1981; 2nd ser. cxlviii).

Chapter 9. Dynastic War

The classic study of C. W. C. Oman, *A History of the Art of War in the Sixteenth Century* (London, 1937) still provides the most detailed account of individual military events, although its approach is now outdated. For more challenging overviews, albeit with less factual detail, see: *M. S. Anderson, *War and Society in Europe, 1620–1789* (London, 1988); *J. R. Hale, *War and Society in Renaissance Europe, 1450–1620* (London, 1985); Hale, *Renaissance War*

Studies (London, 1984); and F. Tallett, *War and Society in Early Modern Europe, 1495–1715* (London, 1992).

One of the most exciting and important new areas of investigation in this period is logistics: see M. van Crevelt, *Supplying War. Logistics from Wallenstein to Patton* (Cambridge, 1977); the swingeing attack and new perspectives in J. A. Lynn, ed., *Feeding Mars: Logistics in Western Warfare from the Middle Ages to the Present* (Boulder, 1993); and G. Parker, *The Army of Flanders and the Spanish Road. The Logistics of Victory and Defeat in the Low Countries' Wars 1567–1659* (Cambridge, 1972; revised edn, 2004). The importance of changing technology in warfare is stressed by the contributors to J. A. Lynn, ed., *Tools of War. Instruments, Ideas and Institutions of Warfare 1445–1871* (Urbana, 1989).

Warfare in Italy is best approached through the meticulous case-studies of M. Mallett and J. R. Hale, *The Military Organization of a Renaissance State: Venice, c. 1400–1617* (Cambridge, 1984); and Pepper and Adams, *Firearms and Fortifications* (see the bibliography for chapter 6). Early modern French warfare has fared somewhat less well, perhaps because the reigning 'Annales' school of history tends to deprecate the importance of war. See, however, F. Lot, *Recherches sur les effectifs des armées françaises des guerres d'Italie aux guerres de religion, 1494–1562* (Paris, 1962); and P. Contamine, ed., *Histoire militaire de la France. i. Des origines à 1715* (Paris, 1992). For Spain, see above all I. A. A. Thompson, *War and Government in Habsburg Spain, 1560–1620* (London, 1976). On Spain's struggle for European hegemony, see G. Parker, *The Grand Strategy of Philip II* (New Haven, 1998); Parker, *Spain and the Netherlands, 1559–1659* (London, 1979; revised edn, 1991); and Parker, *The Dutch Revolt* (London, 1977; revised edn, Harmondsworth, 1985). The Thirty Years War has been covered by (among others) G. Parker, *The Thirty Years' War* (London, revised edn., 1997), and H. Langer, *The Thirty Years' War* (Poole, 1980: particularly strong on the social history of the war). For the wars in the British Isles see the standard survey of J. P. Kenyon, *The Civil Wars of England* (London, 1998); and the rich analysis of *C. Carlton, *Going to the Wars. The Experience of the British Civil Wars, 1638–51* (London, 1992) – perhaps the closest

approximation to the early modern 'face of battle' to appear so far.

Chapter 10. States in Conflict

For general works on war and society in early modern Europe see the bibliography for Chapter 9. In recent years the military forces of Louis XIV have received a good deal of attention. The most complete discussion of the French army in the seventeenth century is provided by J. A. Lynn, *Giant of the Grand Siècle: The French Army, 1610–1715* (New York, 1997). The discussion of military administration in this book has already been supplemented and superseded by D. Parrott, *Richelieu's Army: War, Government and Society in France, 1624–1642* (Cambridge, 2001) and G. Rowlands, *The Dynastic State and the Army under Louis XIV: Royal Service and Private Interest, 1661–1701* (Cambridge, 2002). The classics, L. André, *Michel Le Tellier* (Paris, 1906) and C. Rousset, *Histoire de Louvois*, 4 vols. (Paris, 1862–64), are still well worth reading, as is A. Corvisier, *Louvois* (Paris, 1983). Concerning the navy, nothing equals D. Dessert, *La Royale: Vaisseaux et marins du Roi-Soleil* (Paris, 1996).

See J. A. Lynn, *The Wars of Louis XIV, 1667–1714* (London, 1999), for a general treatment of the wars and campaigns. P. Sonnino, *Louis XIV and the Origins of the Dutch War* (Cambridge, 1989) provides an interesting view of the Sun King's policy. Biography proves a useful and popular mode for discussing war and foreign policy. See, for example J. Bérenger, *Turenne* (Paris, 1987); and C. C. Sturgill, *Marshall Villars and the War of the Spanish Succession* (Lexington, 1965). S. Baxter describes the life and work of Louis's most inveterate foe in *William III and the Defense of European Liberty, 1650–1702* (New York, 1966). The last of Louis's conflicts, the War of the Spanish Succession, provided the theatre for the greatest of English captains, the duke of Marlborough, and not surprisingly his exploits have received a great deal of attention from British authors: see Winston Churchill (his descendent), *Marlborough: his life and times* (6 vols, London, 1933); *D. Chandler, *Marlborough as a Military Commander* (London, 1973); and *The Art of War in the Age of Marlborough* (London, 1976). On the army, see R. E. Scouller, *The Armies of Queen Anne* (Oxford, 1966).

On the rise of Russia as a military power see *C. Duffy, *Russia's Military Way to the West* (London, 1981); and on the great tsar himself, see V. O. Klyuchevsky, *Peter the Great* (New York, 1958). Concerning emergent Prussia, see G. Ritter, *Frederick the Great: a Historical Profile,* tr. P. Paret (Berkeley, 1968); and C. Duffy, *The Military Life of Frederick the Great* (New York, 1986). The same prolific author describes Frederick's Austrian opponents in *The Army of Maria Theresa* (Newton Abbot, 1977). On the British army in the eighteenth century see J. A. Houlding, *Fit for Service: the Training of the British Army 1715–1795* (Oxford, 1981). The most complete statistical study of the French enlisted ranks is A. Corvisier, *L'armée française de la fin du XVIIIe siècle au ministère de Choiseul: le soldat,* (2 vols (Paris, 1964). L. Kennett provides a good study of military administration in *The French Armies in the Seven Years' War* (Durham, NC, 1967).

On supply, see *G. Perjés, 'Army Provisioning, Logistics and Strategy in the Second Half of the Seventeenth Century', *Acta Historica Academiae Scientiarum Hungaricae*, xvi (1970); as well as the works by van Creveld and Lynn discussed on page 000 above. The important subject of fortifications has received a fine survey treatment in three works by C. Duffy; for the period covered here see *The Fortress in the Age of Vauban and Frederick the Great, 1660–1789, Siege Warfare,* ii (London, 1985). On warfare in North America, see the short introduction *H. H. Peckham, *The Colonial Wars, 1698–1762* (Chicago, 1964); and the authoritative G. S. Graham, *Empire of the North Atlantic: the Maritime Struggle for North America* (Toronto, 1958). Philip Mason offers a readable account of the conflicts in India through the campaigns of Arthur Wellesley in *A Matter of Honour: and Account of the Indian Army, its Officers and Men* (London, 1974). This Anglocentric view must be tempered by other perspectives. See P. Barua, 'Military Developments in India, 1760–1850', *Journal of Military History,* lviii (1994), 599–614, on the campaigns and politics of the conquest. On the creation of sepoy armies see J. A. Lynn, *Battle: A History of Combat and Culture,* revised edition (Boulder: 2005), chapter. 5, 'Victories of the Conquered: The Native Character of the Sepoy, 1740–1805', and C. Wickremesekera, *'Best Black Troops in the World': British Perceptions and the Making of the Sepoy 1746–1805* (Manohar, 2002).

Chapter 11. Nations in Arms

The finest survey of international relations during the period covered by this chapter is P. W. Schroeder, *The Transformation of European politics, 1763–1848* (Oxford, 1994). The American War of Independence is covered in fine fashion by P. Mackesy, *The War for America, 1775–1783* (Cambridge, Mass., 1965); and *D. Higginbotham, *The War of American Independence: Military Attitudes, Policies, and Practice, 1763–1789* (New York, 1971). C. Royster charts changing popular feelings toward the war once it began in *A Revolutionary People at War: the Continental Army and American Character, 1775–1783* (Chapel Hill, 1979). On American strategy during the war see the excellent chapters in *R Weigley, *The American Way of War* (New York, 1973). Novel insights come from J. Shy, 'Logistical Crisis and the American Revolution: an Hypothesis', in J. A. Lynn, ed., *Feeding Mars: Logistics in Western Warfare from the Middle Ages to the Present* (Boulder, 1993).

A recent work describes the French aspects of the era, *J. Delmas, ed. *Histoire militaire de France, ii, De 1715 à 1871* (Paris, 1992). On the reform period that preceded the Revolution see: S. Wilkinson, *The French Army before Napoleon* (Oxford, 1915); R. Quimby, *The Background of Napoleonic Warfare* (New York, 1957), a book whose primary virtue is that it is in English; and J. Colin, *L'infanterie au XVIIIe siècle: la tactique* (Paris, 1907) a more original and better work from which Quimby borrowed much. The magisterial work on the French army during the Revolution is *J.-P. Bertaud, *The Army of the French Revolution: from Citizen Soldiers to Instruments of Power,* tr. R. R. Palmer (Princeton, 1988).

S. F. Scott, *The Response of the Royal Army to the French Revolution* (Oxford, 1978) discusses the composition, actions, and fate of the old royal army until its official dissolution in 1793. On warfare see G. Rothenberg, *The Art of Warfare in the Age of Napoleon* (Bloomington, 1978), an excellent short introduction to the entire period. On revolutionary combat style there is J. A. Lynn, *The Bayonets of the Republic: Motivation and Tactics in the Army of Revolutionary France, 1791–94* (1984, revised edn., Boulder, 1996). The Napoleonic Wars have inspired countless volumes. J. Tulard, *Napoleon: the Myth of the Saviour* (London, 1984) is a modern biography by a noted specialist. The classic by D.

Chandler, *The Campaigns of Napoleon* (New York, 1966), remains a highly valuable account of Napoleonic tactics and operations. This should be supplemented by the more critical Owen Connelly, *Blundering to Glory: Napoleon's Military Campaigns* (Wilmington, 1988), and the more recent C. J. Esdaile, *The Wars of Napoleon* (London, 1996). On the fatal Spanish disaster see D. Gates, *The Spanish Ulcer: a History of the Peninsular War* (1986). A. W. Palmer deals with the Emperor's greatest debacle in *Napoleon in Russia* (New York, 1967).

For additional works on Austrian and German military reforms see: G. Rothenberg, *Napoleon's Great Adversaries: the Archduke Charles and the Austrian Army, 1792–1814* (Bloomington, 1982); W. O. Shanahan, *Prussian Military Reforms, 1786–1813* (New York, 1945); and *P. Paret, *Yorck and the Era of Prussian Reform* (Berkeley, 1966). E. Longford recounts the life of Napoleon's nemesis in *Wellington* (2 vols, New York, 1969–72). Britain's triumph at sea is covered in C. D. Hall, *British Strategy in the Napoleonic War, 1803–1815* (Manchester, 1992). D. Walder, *Nelson: a Biography* (New York, 1978) details the life of Britain's most famous admiral, and D. Howarth describes his greatest victory in *Trafalgar: the Nelson Touch* (London, 1969).

Chapter 12. The Industrialization of War

Not surprisingly a wide literature deals with the topics covered by this chapter. W. McElwee, *The Art Of War, Waterloo to Mons* (Bloomington, 1974) provides a general survey of the period. For the Crimean War see C. Hibbert, *The Destruction of Lord Raglan* (London, 1961) and C. Woodham Smith, *The Reason Why* (London, 1965). G. Craig, *The Battle of Königgrätz* (Philadelphia, 1964) provides a compelling depiction of the decisive battle of the Seven Weeks War. D. Showalter, *Railroads and Rifles: Soldiers, Technology, and the Unification of Germany* (Hamden, 1975) brilliantly covers the impact of technology on the Prussians; while M. Howard, *The Franco-Prussian War* (London, 1961) remains a standard against which one can judge good military history.

The best single-volume history of the American Civil War for both readability and scholarship is *J. M. McPherson, *Battle Cry of Freedom, The Civil War Era* (Oxford, 1988). There are also two excellent three-volume histories of the war: B. Catton, *The

Centennial History of the Civil War* (Garden City, New York, 1961); and S. Foote, *The Civil War, A Narrative* (New York, 1958). Of the war's many memoirs, those by Ulysses S. Grant, *Personal Memoirs of U.S. Grant* (New York, 1984), stand out; Mark Twain described them, with only slight exaggeration, as the finest literary work in English in the nineteenth century. Finally, one should not forget M. Shaara, *The Killer Angels* (New York, 1974), a brilliant fictional reconstruction of the battle of Gettysburg which tells us more about the war than most histories.

Chapter 13. Towards World War

A number of interesting works assess the professionalization of European armies before World War I. B. Bond, *The Victorian Army and the Staff College, 1854–1914* (London, 1972) recounts the difficulties that such efforts encountered in Britain. For the evolution of the French army after the catastrophic defeat of 1870–71, see D. B. Ralston, *The Army of the Republic: The Place of the Military in the Political Evolution of France: 1871–1914* (Cambridge, Mass., 1967). G. Ritter, *The Sword and the Scepter, The Problem of Militarism in Germany* (2 vols, Miami, 1970) covers the German side in magisterial fashion. For background on the Russian experience see W. C. Fuller, Jr, *Civil-Military Conflict in Imperial Russia, 1881–1914* (Princeton, 1985). D. Walder, *The Short Victorious War, The Russo-Japanese Conflict, 1904–1905* (London, 1973), is a clear, readable account. The best works on the colonial wars of the European powers are D. R. Morris, *The Washing of the Spears, A History of the Rise of the Zulu Nation under Shaka and Its Fall in the Zulu War of 1879* (New York, 1965); and T. Pakenham, *The Boer War* (New York, 1979).

The literature on the origins of World War I is reaching unmanageable proportions. *L. Albertini, *The Origins of the War of 1914* (3 vols, New York, 1952) will remain the standard work on the outbreak of the war. G. Ritter, *The Schlieffen Plan: Critique of a Myth* (New York, 1958) unravels the mistaken assumptions of the German general staff. For an examination of the origins of the German planning process, see A. Bucholz, *Moltke, Schlieffen and Prussian War Planning* (New York, 1991). On British planning for war see J. Gooch, *The Plans of War, The General Staff and British Military Strategy, 1900–1916* (New York, 1974); for the general background to prewar planning see P. Kennedy, ed., *The War Plans of the Great Powers, 1880–1914* (London, 1979). S. R. Williamson, Jr, *The Politics of Grand Strategy. Britain and France Prepare for War, 1904–1914* (Cambridge, Mass., 1969) provides a striking account of the combined planning by the two powers.

Chapter 14. The West at War

The most comprehensive study of World War I remains C. R. M. F. Cruttwell, *A History of the Great War, 1914–1918* (Oxford, 1934), and a superior work is only now in production: Hew Strachan, *The First World War. Volume I: To Arms* (Oxford, 2004). Two more volumes will soon appear. Winston Churchill, *The World Crisis* (New York, 1930) at times smacks of special pleading, but is written with such brilliant style as to reward any reader. L. Woodward, *Great Britain and the War of 1914–1918* (Boston, 1967) stands as the best survey of a single nation's experience in the war. For the war from the perspective of the main Central Powers, see H. H. Herwig, *The First World War: Germany and Austria-Hungary, 1914–1918* (New York, 1997). J. H. Morrow, Jr., *German Air Power In World War I* (Lincoln, 1982) dispels the myth of airpower's ineffectiveness in the Great War and places the war in the air in economic perspective. F. Fischer, *Germany's Aims in the First World War* (English translation, New York, 1967) is controversial only among those who still swallow the disinformation campaign waged by the Germans after 1919. *J. M. Winter, *The Experience of World War I* (Oxford, 1989), provides an evocative survey in words, pictures, and diagrams.

Worthwhile monographs on individual episodes of the war abound. B. Tuchman, *The Guns of August* (New York, 1962), despite an egregious and grossly unfair attack on Clausewitz, still offers an interesting account of military operations in the first month of the war. T. Lupfer, *The Dynamics of Doctrine: The Changes in German Tactical Doctrine During World War I* (Leavenworth, 1981) broke new ground in rethinking the tactical dynamics of the war, while two works by Timothy Travers have fundamentally altered the picture of the British army on the Western Front: *The Killing Ground. The British Army, the Western Front, and the Emergence of Modern Warfare, 1900–1918* (London, 1987); and *How the War Was Won. Command and Technology in the British Army on the Western

Front, 1917–1918* (London, 1992). M. Middlebrook, *The First Day on the Somme, 1 July 1916* (New York, 1972) provides a stark look at that battle from the perspective of those who suffered the most, the front-line soldiers. A. Horne, *The Price of Glory, Verdun, 1916* (New York, 1962) is equally good on the horrors of that operation.

A. J. Marder, *From The Dreadnought to Scapa Flow* (6 vols, London, 1961) is a masterful account of the naval war from the British perspective. H. Herwig, *The 'Luxury' Fleet. The Imperial German Navy, 1888–1918* (London, 1980) provides a lively account of the bizarre activities of the German navy. On the air war see J. H. Morrow, Jr, *The Great War in the Air. Military Aviation from 1909 to 1921* (Washington, 1993).

The many novels and memoirs that appeared after the war represent one of the great movements in twentieth century literature, yet one that is for the most part ignored or misinterpreted by literary scholars and critics in the United States. Arguably the best novel based on the experiences of the front-line soldier is F. Manning, *The Middle Parts of Fortune, Somme and Ancre 1916* (London, 1929), while G. Chapman, *A Passionate Prodigality, Fragments of Autobiography* (London, 1933) provides perhaps the finest and most honest autobiographical experience of the war. C. S. Forrester, *The General* (London, 1936) is a devastating portrait of bad military leadership. For the terrible impact of the deaths of British soldiers on those whom they loved, V. Brittain, *Testament of Youth. An Autobiographical Study of the Years, 1900–1925* (London, 1933) offers a haunting portrait of the death of a generation. The English poetry of the war is accessible in a number of places: a good place to start is J. Silkin, ed., *The Penguin Book of First World War Poetry* (London, 1979). Finally, one should not forget that the Germans had a fundamentally different reaction to the war: E. Jünger, *Storm of Steel* (London, 1929) is an enthusiastic first-hand account of war by the winner of a *Pour le Mérite* for heroism, a soldier wounded innumerable times, and an individual who thought it had all been wonderful.

Chapter 15. The World in Conflict and Chapter 16. The World at War

If the literature on World War I is massive, that on World War II is so vast as to be totally unmanageable. *G. Weinberg, *A

World at Arms. A Global History of World War II* (Cambridge, 1994) is as close to a comprehensive strategic and political history of the war as we are ever likely to get. For an account focusing on the operational conduct of the war, see *A. R. Millett and W. Murray, *A War to Be Won: Fighting the Second World War* (Cambridge, Massachusetts, 2000). *R. Spector, *The Eagle Against the Sun. The American War with Japan* (New York, 1984) provides an outstanding survey of the war in the Pacific. G. Weinberg, *The Foreign Policy of Nazi Germany* (2 vols, Chicago, 1970–80) provide the background for understanding the origins of the war.

The monographic literature still floods the market. Among the best: M. Knox, *Mussolini Unleashed. 1939–1941, Politics and Strategy in Fascist Italy's Last War* (Cambridge, 1982) underlines the mendacious incompetence of the Italian regime and military; C. Sydnor, *Soldiers of Destruction. The Totenkopf Division* (Princeton, 1977) suggests the connection between ideology and the conduct of the war on the Eastern Front; R. Paxton, *Parades and Politics at Vichy* (Princeton, 1966) examines the French military's reaction to defeat; C. Thorne, *Allies of a Kind. The United States, Britain, and the War against Japan, 1941–1945* (Oxford, 1978) provides an in-depth examination of the workings of the Anglo-American alliance in the Pacific. R. J. Overy, *The Air War, 1939–1945* (New York, 1982), remains the best general account of the war in the air; *Overy, *Why the Allies Won* (New York, 1995) is a penetrating analysis that ranges from strategic planning and resource mobilization to operational contingencies. Some of the finest campaign histories of the war are D. M. Glantz and J. House, *When Titans Clashed: How the Red Army Stopped Hitler* (Lawrence, Kansas: 1995); R. B. Frank, *Guadalcanal* (New York, 1990); D. Graham and S. Bidwell, *Tug of War: The Battle for Italy: 1943–45* (New York, 1986); and E. J. Drea, *MacArthur's ULTRA: Codebreaking and the War against Japan, 1942–1945* (Lawrence, Kansas, 1992). R. S. Rush, *Hell in Hürtgen Forest: An American Infantry Regiment's Ordeal and Triumph* (Lawrence, Kansas, 2001), dispels the myth of American tactical inferiority on the ground through a brilliant combination of the records left by the opposing German and Allied units. R. B. Frank, *Downfall* (New York, 1995) traces Japan's defeat in detail and definitively puts to rest the notion that Japan's leaders entertained notions of surrender before atomic bombs fell on Hirioshima and Nagasaki.

It is worth noting that the official histories of the war achieved a higher standard of accuracy and honesty than those of World War I. The best of these efforts in English is the study of the strategic bombing campaign: C. Webster and N. Frankland, *The Strategic Air Offensive Against Germany* (4 vols, London, 1994). Eleven volumes of the official German history of the war, *Das Deutsche Reich und der Zweite Weltkrieg* have now been published, and Oxford University Press has published six of them in English translation. A product of the Federal Republic of Germany's Military History Office, this undertaking (organized by topics and theatres rather than in a single chronological sequence) is of particular importance in underlining the degree to which criminal ideology underlay the Wehrmacht's participation in the war, particularly on the Eastern front. Other significant works along this line are C. Streit, *Keine Kameraden. Die Wehrmacht und die sowjetischen Kriegsgefangenen, 1941–1945* (Stuttgart, 1978); and in English *O. Bartov, *Hitler's Army. Soldiers, Nazis, and War in the Third Reich* (Oxford, 1991); and *C. R. Browning, *Ordinary Men. Reserve Police Battalion 101 and the Final Solution in Poland* (New York, 1992). This new wave of historical research has underlined what most historians have generally suspected: the complete unreliability and intellectual dishonesty, even by the standards of the genre, of post-war memoirs by German generals.

Finally, the discovery of the crucial role of intelligence in Allied victory constitutes one of the major historio-graphical developments of the late 1970s. Three of the best of these books not only involve careful analysis of the historical record but were written by actual participants in intelligence: R. Bennett, *Ultra in the West. The Normandy Campaign, 1944–1945* (New York, 1979); P. Beesley, *Very Special Intelligence. The Story of the Admiralty's Operational Intelligence Centre, 1939–1945* (Garden City, 1977); and *R V. Jones, *Most Secret War. British Scientific Intelligence, 1939–1945* (London, 1978). Finally, *D. Glantz, *Soviet Military Deception in the Second World War* (London, 1989) examines how Soviet deception played a crucial role in the Soviet victories on the Eastern Front.

Chapter 17. The Post-War World

Quality works on the military history of the post-World War II period have appeared in greater numbers over the past decade. On the French experience in Vietnam Bernard Fall's works still remain of special note: *Street Without Joy. Insurgency in Indochina, 1946–1963* (Harrisburg, 1964); *Hell in a Very Small place. The Siege of Dien Bien Phu* (New York, 1967); and *The Two Vietnams, A Political and Military Analysis* (New York, 1963). S. Karnow, *Vietnam. A History* (New York, 1983) provides a general overview of the French and American experiences. On the French experience in Algeria, *A. Horne, *A Savage War of Peace. Algeria, 1954–1962* (London, 1977) represents a powerful work of literature as well as of history. There are also two very good films about that conflict: *The Battle of Algiers* and *The Lost Command*. Among accounts of Britain's many colonial wars, M. Hastings and S. Jenkins, *The Battle for the Falklands* (New York, 1983) is particularly worthwhile because of its interweaving of the political and strategic background with the conduct of operations. I. L. Janis, *Groupthink: Psychological Studies of Policy Decisions and Fiascoes* (New York, 1983) includes a detailed comparison of how the Kennedy administration handled the two crises over Cuba.

Not surprisingly America's 'limited' wars have also attracted considerable interest from historians; but the most important war in terms of its strategic impact, the Korean War, has received the least attention. T. R. Fehrenbach, *This Kind of War* (New York, 1964) is still the best general history of that conflict. Because of its damage to America's image of itself, the Vietnam War has attracted more interest. Some of the most interesting monographs are: A. F. Krepinevich, Jr, *The Army and Vietnam* (Baltimore, 1986); R. H. Spector, *Advice and Support. The Early Years of the US Army in Vietnam, 1941–1960* (London, 1985); and *After Tet. The Bloodiest Year in Vietnam* (New York, 1993); and F. Snepp, *Decent Interval. An Insider's Account of Saigon's Indecent End Told by the CIA's Chief Strategy Analyst in Vietnam* (New York, 1977). But the Vietnam experience has also resulted in some of the best literature and writing – fiction and non-fiction – by Americans in this century. See in particular: J. Webb, *Fields of Fire* (New York, 1978); F. Downs, Jr, *The Killing Zone. My Life in the Vietnam War* (New York, 1978) and *Aftermath. A Soldier's Return from Vietnam* (New York, 1984); and J. R. McDonough, *Platoon Leader* (New York, 1985).

Of the many books on conflict in the Middle East E. Hammel, *Six Days in June. How Israel Won the 1967 Arab-Israeli War* (New York, 1993) covers that war in an interesting fashion, while C. Herzog, *The Arab-Israeli Wars. War and Peace in the Middle East from the War of Independence through Lebanon* (New York, 1984) provides an insider's perspective. On the 'decline of war' in the late twentieth century, see the provocative and stimulating analysis of *J. Mueller, *The Remnants of War* (Ithaca, 2004). On America's military leadership since 1945, see the savage criticisms in Chapter 6 of E. Cohen, *Supreme Command: Soldiers, Statesmen and Leadership in Wartime* (New York, 2002) – and also his penetrating insights into the wartime leadership styles of Lincoln, Clemenceau, Churchill, and Ben-Gurion. On the First Gulf War, Cohen edited the penetrating five-volume *Gulf War Airpower Survey* (Washington, DC, 1993), in which a talented team of experts relentlessly analyze the successes and failures of Coalition air campaign. A plethora of books deal with that war, including the memoirs of the theatre commander (H. N. Schwartzkopf, *It Doesn't Take a Hero* [New York, 1992]) and of the Chairman of the Joint Chiefs of Staff (C. Powell with J. E. Persico, *My American Journey* [New York, 1995]). Perhaps the best-informed account is M. R. Gordon and B. E. Trainor, *The Generals' War: The Inside Story of Conflict in the Gulf* (Boston, 1995). On the Balkan wars, see the accounts by the leading civilian and militant participants, respectively: R. Holbrooke, *To End a War* (New York, 1998) and W. K. Clark, *Waging Modern War: Bosnia, Kosovo and the Future of Combat* (New York, 2001). Alas there is nothing on these conflicts like the magnificent account, filled with evidence from both 'sides', of the events leading up to and immediately following the attacks of 11 September 2001, *The 9/11 Commission Report* (Washington, 2004), which sets a new standard in the reporting and analysis of recent conflicts. On the second Gulf War, see M. R. Gordon and B. E. Trainor, *Cobra II: The Inside Story of the Invasion and Occupation of Iraq* (New York, 2006); G. Packer, *The Assassins' Gate: America in Iraq* (New York, 2005); and P. Mansoor, *Baghdad at Sunrise: A Brigade Commander's War in Iraq* (New Haven, 2008).

The Contributors

Christopher Allmand graduated from Oriel College, Oxford, in 1958 and was awarded the degree of DPhil in 1963. He is principally interested in the history of late medieval Europe, and taught this period at the University College of North Wales, Bangor, before moving, in 1967, to the University of Liverpool, where he is currently Professor Emeritus of Medieval History. He has edited *Society at War. The Experience of England and France during the Hundred Years War* (1973); *War, Literature and Politics in the Late Middle Ages* (1976); *English Suits before the Parlement of Paris, 1420–1436* (with C. A. J. Armstrong, 1982); and *Power, Culture, and Religion in France, c.1350–c.1550* (1989). He is the author of *Lancastrian Normandy, 1415–1450. The History of a Medieval Occupation* (1983); *The Hundred Years War. England and France at War, c.1300–c.1450* (1988), translated into three languages); and Henry V (1992). He is also editor of the final volume (*The Fifteenth Century*) of the *New Cambridge Medieval History*.

He would like to express his thanks to the editor of this book for the help and advice given him while he was preparing his contribution.

Upon completing his primary and secondary education in the New York City public schools, **Bernard S. Bachrach** attended Queens College, City University of New York, from which he graduated with honours in 1961 while majoring in history and minoring in classics. He earned an MA in 1962 and a PhD in 1966 in history at the University of California, Berkeley, under the direction of Bryce D. Lyon and F. L. Ganshof, and did post-graduate work in paleography and diplomatics with Jacques Boussard (Ecole des Hautes Etudes, Paris and the Centre for Medieval Studies at Poitiers). After a year as lecturer at Queens College, he taught at the University of Minnesota as assistant, associate (from 1971), and finally (from 1975) full professor of history. In 1993 Professor Bachrach won the Committee for Excellence in Education's Distinguished Teaching Award at the University of Minnesota. Professor Bachrach has been moderately active in service to the academic community. He served as the editor of the *International Medieval Bibliography* (1967–68); co-founded and co-edits the semi-annual journal *Medieval Prosopography* (since 1980); served on the editorial boards of the University of Minnesota Monographs in the Humanities (1976–81), The Speculum Anniversary Monograph Series (1985–88, chair 1987–88); and the journal *War in History*. He served as an elected member of the board of governors, Haskins Society (1982–89), and on the Medieval Academy Committee for Liaison with the American Historical Association (1986–88, acting Chair 1987–88). In 1989 he was appointed Cornelius Loew Lecturer, Western Michigan University; in 1991 he lectured at the University of Stockholm and Uppsala University and served as Consultant to the Medieval Studies Centre at the University of Stockholm. In 1986 Professor Bachrach was elected a fellow of the Medieval Academy of America. Professor Bachrach has focused largely upon the period prior to the First Crusade and has some 300 scholarly publications to his credit including eighty articles and thirteen books. The latter include: *Merovingian Military Organization 481–751* (1972), *A history of the Alans in the West* (1973), *Early Medieval Jewish Policy in*

Western Europe (1977), *Fulk Nerra: The Neo-Roman Consul (987–1040)* (1993), *Early Carolingian Warfare: Prelude to Empire* (2001); *Warfare and Military Organization in Pre-Crusade Europe* (2002); and *The Normans and the Adversaries: Studies in Honor of C. Warren Hollister*, co-edited with Richard Abels (2001). Variorum Press has published a collection of his articles, *Armies and Politics in the Early Medieval West* (1993).

Victor Davis Hanson was educated at the University of California, Santa Cruz, the American School of Classical Studies, Athens, and Stanford University, where he received his PhD in 1980. The author of *Warfare and Agriculture in Classical Greece* (1983) and the editor of *Hoplites: The Ancient Greek Battle Experience* (1991), he has also written some thirty articles and book reviews on Greek social and economic history. His *Western Way of War* (1989) has now appeared in seven editions and translations; a book on ancient agrarian and military life, *The Other Greeks*, appeared in 1995, followed by *Carnage and Culture* (2001) and *Ripples of Battle* (2003). In 1992 the American Philological Association presented him with an Award for Excellence in the Teaching of Classics, for his efforts between 1984 and 1990 to create an undergraduate classical languages programme at California State University, Fresno. Currently he is Senior Fellow at the Hoover Institution, Stanford University, and lives on his family's small farm, with his wife, Cara, and their three children, who are the sixth continuous generation to live in the same house.

He would like to thank Kathleen Much, resident editor at the Center for Advanced Study in the Behavioral Sciences, Stanford University, and Geoffrey Parker, general editor, who both read over earlier drafts, and made numerous corrections. The National Endowment for the Humanities, along with Stanford's Center for Advanced Study in the Behavioral Sciences, provided financial support for the 1992–93 academic year away from his teaching duties. The kindness of those institutions allowed him to write these chapters.

John A. Lynn earned his BA at the University of Illinois at Urbana-Champaign, his MA at the University of California at Davis, and his PhD at UCLA in 1973. After teaching at Indiana University and the University of Maine, he returned to Illinois in 1978, ever to remain at his alma mater, where he won the 'Campus Award for Excellence in Undergraduate Teaching' in 2001. His research interests include a broad range of military history, including early modern Europe and South Asia, along with the nature of military change and the relationship of culture and military practice. His major publications include *Battle: A History of Combat and Culture* (2003 and 2004), *The Wars of Louis XIV, 1667–1714* (1999), *Giant of the Grand Siècle: The French Army, 1610–1715* (1997), *The Bayonets of the Republic: Motivation and Tactics in the Army of Revolutionary France, 1791–94*, revised edition (1984 and 1996), and two edited collections, *Feeding Mars: Logistics in Western Warfare from the Middle Ages to the Present* (1993) and *The Tools of War: Ideas, Instruments, and Institutions of Warfare, 1445–1871* (1990).

He would like to thank Geoffrey Parker for the chance to contribute to this volume and for his editorial comments. He would also like to express his gratitude for the long-term support he has received from the College of Liberal Arts and Sciences at the University of Illinois, and particularly to Deans Larry Faulkner and Jesse Delia.

Williamson Murray is Professor Emeritus of European military history at Ohio State University and a Senior Fellow at the Institute of Defense Analysis. He received his BA, MA, and PhD from Yale University. He served in the United States Air Force for five years and completed his reserve obligations in 1992 as a Lieutenant Colonel. He is the author of a number of books including *The Changes in the European Balance of Power, 1938–1939, The Path to Ruin* (1984); *Luftwaffe* (1985); *German Military Effectiveness* (1992); *The Air War in the Persian Gulf* (1995); *Air War, 1914–1945* (1999); *A War to Be Won: Fighting the Second World War* (2000), with Allan R. Millet; and *The Iraq War: A Military History* (2003), with Major General Robert Scales, Jr. He also co-edited numerous collections, including *Military Innovations in the Interwar Period* (1996) with Allan R. Millet, and *The Dynamics of Military Revolution, 1300–2050* (2001), with MacGregor Knox.

Geoffrey Parker, born in Nottingham, England, and educated at Christ's College, Cambridge (BA 1965; MA and PhD 1968; LittD 1981), taught at St Andrews University (1972–79 and 1980–86), the University of British Columbia (1979–80), the University of Illinois at Urbana-Champaign (1986–93, serving as department chair 1989–91), and Yale (1993–96), before becoming Andreas Dorpalen Professor of History at the Ohio State University in 1997. He has written and edited thirty-four books, including *The Army of Flanders and the Spanish Road 1567–1659. The Logistics of Spanish Victory and Defeat in the Low Countries' Wars* (1972); *The Dutch Revolt* (1977); *The Thirty Years' War* (with nine co-authors, 1984); *The Spanish Armada* (with Colin Martin, 1988); *The Military Revolution 1500–1800. Military Innovation and the Rise of the West* (1988), and *The Grand Strategy of Philip II* (1998). He is also the author of over 80 articles.

He is grateful to Sandra Bolzenius, Robert Cowley, Kenneth Duncan, Mark Grimsley, Jane Hathaway, Peter Mansoor, Peter Richards, Keith Roberts, Leif Torkelsen and his fellow-authors for helpful suggestions and comments.

Patricia Seed is Professor of History at the University of California–Irvine and author of the Bolton Prize–winning *To Love, Honor, and Obey in Colonial Mexico: Conflicts over Marriage Choice, 1564–1821* (1988). She has published two of three volumes on the comparative history of European colonization of the Americas: *Ceremonies of Possession in Europe's Conquest of the New World* (1994) and *American Pentimento: The Invention of Indians and the Pursuit of Riches* (2001), which won the American Historical Association's Prize in Atlantic History. A planned third volume will deal with the conquest of the Americas. Presently she is working in digital humanities projects (supported by the ACLS and NEH) on the history of mapping the Atlantic coasts.

She is grateful to Sam Watson, a graduate student in the Rice University history department for research assistance, to Ira Gruber for reading it over, to Stuart Schwartz for loaning books unavailable locally, and to Geoffrey Parker for his invaluable editorial advice.

Notes

Greek and Roman passages are cited by their manuscript numbers and can be easily identified by those citations in nearly all modern English translations.

Introduction The Western Way of War

2 Sun Tzu, *The Art of War*, ed. S. B. Griffith (Oxford, 1963) 77. **2** Baron A. H.
Jomini, *The Art of War* ed. G. H. Mendell and W. P. Craighill (Westport, 1977) 47.
5 Carl von Clausewitz, *On War*, ed. Michael Howard and Peter Paret (Princeton,
1984) 228, 258. **5** Quotation from J. L. Axtell, *The European and the Indian. Essays
in the Ethnohistory of Colonial North America* (Oxford, 1981) 140; and W. Rodney, *A
History of the Upper Guinea Coast 1545–1800* (Oxford, 1970) 237. **7–8** Quoted by
John Brewer, *The Sinews of Power. War, Money and the English State, 1688–1783*
(Cambridge, MA, 1988) 187. **8** Quotation from Brewer, *The Sinews of Power*, 91.
9 J. P. Coen to the Directors of the Dutch East India Company, 27 December 1614,
from Java, quoted in H. T. Colenbrander, *Jan Pieterszoon Coen. Levenbeschrijving*
(The Hague, 1934) 64.

Chapter 1 Genesis of the Infantry

12 D. D. Luckenbill, *Ancient Records of Assyria and Babylonia* (Chicago, 1926) I, 84,
#243. **13** *Joshua* 6.20–1. **14** Phocylides, *Poetry fragment*,4. **14** Alcaeus,
Fragment 28a (cf. Thucydides, *The Peloponnesian War* 7.77.7). **15** Xenophon,
Oeconomicus (*On Estate Management*) 5.14. **15–16** Plutarch, *Life of Lycurgus*,
22.2–3. **16** Xenophon, *History of Greece* 6.4.11. **16** Xenophon, *Anabasis* (*March
up Country*) 3.2.18; cf. 3.2.27–8. **16** Archilochus, *Poetry Fragment* 114.
16 Tyrtaeus, *Poetry Fragment* 11.31–4. **18** Thucydides, *The Peloponnesian War*
4.96.4. **18** Thucydides, *The Peloponnesian War* 7.44.8. **18–19** Xenophon,
Memorabilia (*Memoirs*) 3.1.6. **20** Strabo, *Geography* 10.448. **20** Plutarch,
Moralia (*Moral Works*) 234 E44. **20** Polybius, *History of Rome* 13.3.2– 6 **20**
Thucydides, *The Peloponnesian War* 1.15. **21** Aeschylus, *Persians* 49–50. **22–3**
Herodotus, *The Persian Wars* 7.9.2 **25** Plato, *Laws* 707C. **26** Aeschylus, *Persians*
814–816, 1001–3, 240. **26** Plutarch, *Moralia* 214 A72 and 216 F 3. **27** Aristotle,
Politics 3.1279b 3–5. **27–8** Thucydides, *The Peloponnesian War* 2.16. **28**
Thucydides, *The Peloponnesian War* 2.87. **29** Xenophon, *History of Greece* 4.3.19.

Chapter 2 From Phalanx to Legion

32 Demosthenes, 9 (*Third Philippic*) 47–9. 32 Xenophon, *Ways and Means* 2.3–4.
33 Xenophon, *Ways and Means* 5.13. **34** Xenophon, *History of Greece* 7.5.27.
34 Isocrates 8 (*On the Peace*) 55. **34** Scholiast to Demosthenes 2 (*Second Olynthiac*)
17. **37** Iphicrates quoted in Plutarch, *Life of Pelopidas* 2.1. 37 Onasander, *On the
General* 28.1. **37** Sophocles, *Antigone* 670. 37 Polybius, *History of Rome* 18.30.9–10.
37 Polybius, *History of Rome* 18.31.5– 6. **38–9** Mnesimachus, comic fragment 7 (cf.
Athenaeus 10.421b). 39 Demos-thenes 11 (*Letter Against Philip*) 22. **39** Demosthenes
9 (*Third Philippic*) 49–51. **39** *Inscriptiones Graecae* (*Greek Inscriptions*) II.2 5226; cf.
Palatine Anthology 7.245. **40** Antiochus quoted in Xenophon, *History of Greece*
7.1.38. **40** Agesilaus quoted in Xenophon, *Life of Agesilaus* 7.5–6. **41** Frontinus,
Stratagems 4.1.6. **42** Polyaenus, *Stratagems* 4.2.10. **43** Antigonus Gonatas quoted
in Stobaeus, *Anthology* 4.13.46. **43** Plutarch, *Life of Aemilius* 19.3. **44** Pyrrhus
quoted in Frontinus, *Stratagems* 4.1.3. **44** Polybius, *History of Rome* 18.32.3–4.
44 Polybius, *History of Rome* 18.32.9–11. **45** Livy, *History of Rome* 42.34.
45 Polybius, *History of Rome* 15.15.7. **45** (Caption) Livy, *History of Rome* 31.34.4.
46 Livy, *History of Rome* 8.8.

Chapter 3 The Roman Way of War

50 Tacitus, *Annals* 1.35. 50 Scriptores Historiae Augustae, *Life of Probus* 9.3–5. **51**
Appian, *Civil Wars* 1.7. **53** Vegetius, *Concerning Military Matters* (*Epitoma rei mili-
taris*) 1.6. **53** Severus Alexander quoted in Scriptores Historiae Augustae, *Life of
Severus Alexander* 52.3. **54** Frontinus, *Stratagems* 4.1.7; cf. Festus 149M. **55**
Valerius Maximus, 2.3.2. **56** Suetonius, *Life of Julius Caesar* 37. **57** Dio Cassius,
Roman History 74.11.2–6 and 78.36.1–3. 58 Fronto, *Letters, Lucius Verius* 19 (*Ad
Verum* 2.1.19). **58** Hadrian quoted in Fronto, *Letters*, P4 11 (2.208). **58** C. C.
Edgar, A. E. R. Boak, J. G. Winter *et al., Papyrus in the University of Michigan*

Collection (Ann Arbor, 1931) 466. 18–32. 59 Josephus, *Jewish War* 3.102–7. 59
Vegetius, *Concerning Military Matters* 1.1.

Chapter 4 On Roman Ramparts

65–6 Scriptores Historiae Augustae, *Life of Severus Alexander* 58, 4–5. **66** (Box,
column 1) *Ammiani Marcellini rerum Gestarum*,2 vols ed. C. U. Clark (Berlin, 1910,
1915) 21.16.7. **66** (Box, column 2) *De procinctu Romanae militiae*, ed. E. Dümmler,
in *Zeitschrift für deutsches Altertum*,15 (1872) ch. 12. **66–7** (Box) Nithard, *Histoire
des fils de Louis le Pieux*, ed. and trans. Ph. Lauer (Paris, 1926) bk 3, ch. 6.
67 *Theodosiani Libri cum constitutionibus Sirmondianis et Leges Novellae*, ed. T.
Mommsen and P. Meyer (Berlin, 1905) 2 vols *CTh*, VII, 13.16. **68** *CTh. Nov. Val.*
V.1. **68** Pacatus, II. 22 in *XII Panegyrici Latini*, ed. E. Baehrens (Leipzig, 1874).
72–4 Gregory of Tours, *Historiarum libri X*, bk II, ch. 32, ed. Bruno Krusch and
Wilhelm Levison, *Scriptores rerum Merovingicarum: Monumenta Germaniae historica*,
(Hannover, 1951) 1.1. **73** *Mappae clavicula: A Little Key to the World of Medieval
Techniques*, ed. and trans. Cyril Stanley Smith and John G. Hawthorne
(Philadelphia, 1975) ch. 270. **78** *Die Sachsengeschichte des Widukind von Korvei*, I,
35, ed. H.-E. Lohmann and P. Hirsch, *Scriptores Rerum Germanicarum*
(Hannover,1935). **85** *Reginonis Abbatis Prumiensis Chronicon*, an. 882, ed. F.
Kurze, *Scriptores in usum scholarum: Monumenta Germaniae historica*, (Hannover,
1870). **86** *Annales qui dicuntur Einhardi*, an. 782, ed. F. Kurze, *Scriptores in usum
scholarum: Monumenta Germaniae historica*, (Hannover, 1895).

Chapter 5 New Weapons, New Tactics

93–4 Thomas Gray, *Scalacronica*, ed. J. Stevenson (Edinburgh: Maitland Club,
1836) 142. The testimony of Gray, an English knight captured by the Scots and
writing in captivity, concerning the connection between Courtrai and Bannockburn
is of exceptional interest. My thanks to Clifford J. Rogers for bringing it to my attention. **95–6** Quoted by R. Boutrouche, 'The Devastation of Rural Areas During the
Hundred Years' War and the Agricultural Recovery of France' in P. S. Lewis, ed., *The
Recovery of France in the Fifteenth Century* (London, 1972) 26. **100** Jean Froissart,
Chroniques, ed. Kervijn de Lettenhove, III, 196. **100–1** *Chronicon Galfridi le Baker
de Swynebroke*, ed. E. M. Thompson (Oxford, 1889) 68. **105** Cited in R. Vaughan,
Charles the Bold (London, 1973) 163.

Chapter 6 The Gunpowder Revolution

106 R. Barret, *The Theorike and Practike of Modern Warres, Discoursed in Dialogue*
(London, 1598) 2–3. **106** R. Williams, *A Briefe Discourse of Warre* in J. X. Evans,
ed., *The Works of Sir Roger Williams* (Oxford, 1972) 33. **106** F. W. Brie, ed., *The
Brut, or the Chronicles of England* (London, 1906) part i, 281–2. **107** Quo-tations
from C. J. Rogers, 'The military revolutions of the Hundred Years' War', *Journal of
Military History*, LVII (1993) 265. **109** J. Hogan, ed., *Letters and Papers Relating
to the Irish Rebellion between 1642–1646* (Dublin, 1936) 73: Lords Justices in
Dublin to the English Parliament, 8 July 1642. **109** Laparelli quoted by V.
Schmidtchen, *Kriegswesen im späten Mittelalter. Technik, Taktik, Theorie* (Weinheim,
1990) 206. **110** Andreas Bernaldez, *Memorias del reinado de los Reyes Católicos*,
cited by W. F. Cook, 'The cannon conquest of Nasrid Spain and the end of the
Reconquista', *Journal of Military History*, LVII (1993) 43. **110** Francesco
Guicciardini, *The History of Italy* (ed. J. R. Hale, New York, 1964) 153–4. **110** N.
Machiavelli, *Discourses on the First Decade of Titus Livy* (written 1519, published
1531) bk II ch. 17. **112** Report on the need to fortify Bologna, quoted in R. J.
Tuttle, 'Against Fortifications: the Defence of Renaissance Bologna', *Journal of the
Society of Architectural Historians*, XLI (1982) 198. **112** Fourquevaux, *Instructions
sur le faict de la guerre* (Paris, 1548) fo. 85. **115** Carl von Clausewitz, *On War*,
ed. M. Howard and P. Paret, 2nd edn (Princeton, 1984) 487, 596. **115** *Nueva
colección de documentos inéditos para la historia de España*, V (Madrid, 1894) 368:
Don Luis de Requeséns to Philip II, 6 October 1574. **115** British Library,
Additional Ms 28, 388 fos 70v–71, Requeséns to Don Gaspar de Quiroga, August
1575. 116 Sir William Cecil quoted by S. Adams, 'Tactics or politics? "The military

revolution" and the Hapsburg hegemony' in J. A. Lynn, ed., *Tools of War. Instruments, Ideas, and Institutions of Warfare, 1445–1871* (Urbana 1990) 46.

Chapter 7 Ships of the Line

120 Inscription quoted in Joseph Needham, Ho Pin-Yu, Lu Gwei-Djen and Wang Ling, *Science and Civilisation in China*, V, part vii: *Military Technology; the Gunpowder Epic* (Cambridge, 1986) 297.   **120** R. C. Temple, ed., *The Travels of Peter Mundy*, III, part i (London, 1919: Hakluyt Society, 2nd series, XLV) 198, 203.   **120** Kervijn de Lettenhove, ed., *Oeuvres de Jean Froissart*, V (Brussels, 1873) 259 n. 9, 265. This version of Froissart's chronicle dates from around 1400, so his assertions about events half a century before may be suspect. However, the fact that he considered 'canons et couleuvrines' to be 'necessary' for a ship's defence in 1400 is highly significant. (My thanks go to Clifford J. Rogers for this point.)   **120** K. R. DeVries, 'A 1445 Reference to Shipboard Artillery', *Technology and Culture*, XXXI (1990) 818–29.   **121** Quotation from G. Parker, *The Military Revolution. Military Innovation and the Rise of the West 1500–1800* (Cambridge, 1988) 89. **122** *Colección de Documentos Inéditos para la Historia de España*, III, 25, Don García de Toledo to Don John, 13 September 1571; Girolamo Diedo, an eye-witness, quoted in M. Lesure, *Lépante: la crise de l'empire ottomane* (Paris, 1972) 141f. **125** *Instructions* issued by King Manuel of Portugal in February 1500, in W. B. Greenlee, ed., *The Voyage of Pedro Alvares Cabral to Brazil and India* (London, 1938: Hakluyt Society, 2nd series, LXXXI) 183.   **125** Fernando Oliveira, *A arte da guerra do mar* (Lisbon, 1555: reprinted Lisbon, 1983) fo. xlviii.   **126** S. and E. Usherwood, *The Counter-Armada, 1596. The 'Journall' of the Mary Rose* (London, 1983) 77.   **127** J. S. Corbett, *Fighting Instructions 1530–1816* (London, 1905: Navy Records Society, XXIX) 100.   **128** Lord Torrington's speech at his Court Martial in November 1690, quoted in J. Ehrman, *The Navy in the War of William III 1689–1697. Its State and Direction* (London, 1953) 350.   **130** G. Correa, *Lendas da India*, I.i (Coimbra, 1922) 329–32.   **131** João Ribeiro, *Fatalidade historica da Ilha de Ceilão*, quoted by C. R. Boxer, *Portuguese Conquest and Commerce in Southern Asia, 1500–1750* (London, 1985) ch. 11, 11.

Chapter 8 The Conquest of the Americas

132 *The Diario of Christopher Columbus's First Voyage to America 1492–1493*, abstracted by Fray Bartolomé de Las Casas, trans. Oliver Dunn and James E. Kelley, Jr. (Norman, Oklahoma, 1989) 67.   **133** *The Diario*, 285–7. Turkish bows were hardened with cattle horn. There are no large horned animals indigenous to the Americas, hence the bow's hardness was as foreign to the natives as iron.   **134** H. J. Biggar, ed., *The Voyages of Jacques Cartier* (Ottawa, 1924) 135.   **134** René Laudonnière, *L'Histoire notable de la Floride située ès Indes Occidentales* (1586;Paris, 1958) 113–14.   **141** *The Diario*, 75.   **141** Jean de Forest quoted in Jean-Marcel Hurault, *Français et Indiens en Guayane* (Paris, 1972) 73.   **142** Additional instructions to Verhulst, April 1625 in *Documents Relating to New Netherland 1624–1626 in the Henry E. Huntington Library*, trans. and ed. A. J. F. Van Laer (San Marino, 1924) 93–4.   **145** Excerpted in Alexander Brown, ed. *Genesis of the American Nation*, 2 vols (Boston, 1890) I, 165.

Chapter 9 Dynastic Warfare

146 Blaise de Monluc, *Commentaires*, ed. J. Giono (Paris 1964) bk 10; Roger Boyle, earl of Orrery, *Treatise on the Art of War* (London, 1677) 15.   **147** Testi quoted in J. M. Brown and J. H. Elliott, *A Palace for a King. The Buen Retiro and the Court of Philip IV* (New Haven, 1980) 255.   **149** Sieur de Fourquevaux, *Instructions sur le faict de la guerre* (Paris, 1548) fo. 6.   **150** *Colección de documentos inéditos para la historia de España*, LXXIV, 433–6 (a history of the Low Countries' Wars by Alonso Vázquez); Carlos Coloma, *Las guerras de los estados baxos* (Antwerp 1635: *Biblioteca de Autores Españoles* edition, Madrid, 1948) 20. Both men were eye-witnesses. **151** Quotation on dress in a manuscript of 1610 cited in F. Deleito y Piñuela, *El declinar de la Monarquía Española* (2nd edn, Madrid, 1947) 177; on the duke of Alba and on dressing in black, see Martín de Eguiluz, *Milicia, discurso y regla militar* (Madrid, 1592) fos. 68–9v.   **151** G. Davies, ed., 'The Autobiography of Thomas Raymond', *Camden Society Publications*, third series XXVII (1917) 40.   **151** S. Reid, *Scots Armies of the Civil War 1639–1652* (Leigh-on-Sea, 1982) 18.   **152** Orrery, *Treatise*, 29.   **152** Hopton to Prince Rupert, September 1643, and John Strachan to

Lord Percy, 9 March 1644, quoted in M. D. G. Wanklyn, 'The King's Armies in the West of England 1642–6' (Manchester University MA thesis, 1966) 95, 98. **153** Archivio di Stato, Parma, *Carteggio Farnesiane* 109 [*Paesi Bassi* 4], unfol., Don Sancho de Londoño to the duke of Parma, 21 November 1568.   **153** *Colección de documentos inéditos para la historia de España*, lxxv, 236–40: Alba to Gabriel de Zayas, 8 July 1573. See similar laments from 1574–75 on page 115.   **157** The opinion of a member of Tilly's council of war (December 1631) cited by S. Riezler, *Geschichte Bayerns*, V (Munich, 1890) 395–6.   **158** Sir James Turner, *Pallas Armata. Military Essayes of the Ancient Graecian, Roman and Modern Art of War* (London, 1683) 237.   **159** Armand-Jean Duplessis, Cardinal Richelieu, *Testament politique* (1637–42: Amsterdam, 1688) 296.   **159** Calvinist pastors in C. A. Campan, ed., *Bergues sur le Soom assiégée* (Brussels, 1867, reprinting an original tract of 1623) 247.   **159** Royalist officer quoted in C. Carlton, *Going to the Wars. The Experience of the British Civil Wars 1638–1651* (London, 1992) 207. **160** Instituto de Valencia de Don Juan, Envío 51 fo. 1, Mateo Vázquez (who was also a royal chaplain) to Philip II, 8 February 1591.   **162** W. Beech, *More Sulphur for Basing: or, God Will fearfully Annoy and Make Quick Riddance of his Implacable Enemies, Surely, Sorely, Suddenly* (London, 1645).   **162** Archivo General de Simancas *Estado* 547/3, Philip II to the duke of Alba, 14 September 1571. **162** Archivo General de Simancas *Estado K*, royal apostil on a letter from Don Juan de Idiáquez to Don Bernardino de Mendoza, 27 April 1586.   **162** Bibliothèque publique et universitaire, Geneva, *Ms Favre* 30/73v, Philip II to Don Luis de Requeséns, 20 October 1573.   **162** *Documentos inéditos para la historia de España*, II (Madrid, 1943) 140: count of Gondomar to Philip III, 28 March 1619. **162** Gerhardt and Locke quoted in T. K. Rabb, *The Struggle for Stability in Early Modern Europe* (Oxford,1975) 119f; the peasant Bible in G.Parker, *The Thirty Years' War* (London, 1984) 179.

Chapter 10 States in Conflict

166 From Paul Sonnino, *Louis XIV and the origins of the Dutch War* (Cambridge, 1989) 172.   **166** Archives de Guerre, Service Historique de l'Armée de Terre, Vincennes, France, A^{1}1041, #303, Louis to Marshal Catinat, 21 July 1691. **168** Behr quoted in Christopher Duffy, *The Fortress in the Age of Vauban and Frederick the Great, 1660–1789* (London, 1985) 13–14. See also the views of Lord Orrery on page 152.   **168** Louis in a memoir printed in Camille Rousset, *Histoire de Louvois*, I (Paris, 1862) 517.   **169** Carl von Clausewitz quoted in Jean Bérenger, *Turenne* (Paris, 1987) 514.   **171** Kara Mustafa quoted in Duffy, *The Fortress*, 233. **173** Peter quoted in Christopher Duffy, *Russia's Military Way to the West* (London, 1981) 24.   **175** Robert Parker quoted in David Chandler, *Marlborough as a Military Commander* (London, 1973) 149.   **177** Saint Germain quoted in M. Delarue, 'L'éducation politique à l'armée du Rhin, 1793–1794,' M'emoire de maîtrise, Université de Paris-Nanterre, 1967–68.   **178** Frederick quoted in *Frederick the Great on the Art of War*, ed. Jay Luvaas (New York, 1966) 74; and J. F. C. Fuller, *A Military History of the Western World*, II (New York, 1957) 196.   **179** Bruce Lenman, 'The Transition to European Military Ascendency in India, 1600–1800,' in John A. Lynn, ed., *Tools of War: Instruments, Ideas, and Institutions of Warfare, 1445–1871* (Urbana, Illinois, 1990) 116.   **181** Directors quoted in Geoffrey Parker, *The Military Revolution* (Cambridge, 1988) 133.   **182–3** Napoleon quoted in Fuller, *Military History*, 213–14.   **183** Colonel Horace St Paul, quoted by J. M. Black, *European Warfare, 1660–1815* (London, 1994) 65.

Chapter 11 Nations in Arms

187 Public Record Office, London, *Colonial Office* 5/236, p. 28, Howe to Secretary of War, 20 December 1776.   **188** Public Record Office, *Colonial Office* 5/236, pp. 8–21, Howe to Secretary of War, 30 November 1776.   **188** Public Record Office, *Colonial Office* 5/236, pp. 55–61, Howe to Secretary of War, 2 April 1777.   **190** Greene quoted in Russell F. Weigley, *The American Way of War* (Bloomington, 1977) 31. **190** Greene and Mao in Weigley, *The American Way of War*, 36.   **190–1** Voltaire, *Oeuvres*, ed. M. Beuchot, XXVII (Paris, 1829) 306.   **192** Guibert, *Ecrits militaires, 1772–1790* (Paris, 1977) 57.   **192** Maurice de Saxe, 'My Reveries on the Art of War,' trans. T. R. Phillips, in *Roots of Strategy*, ed. T. R. Phillips (Harrisburg, 1940) 201. **193** Law of 23 August 1793 in J. Mandival and E. Laurent, eds, *Archives parlemen-*

taires, 1re s erie, LXXII, (Paris, 1907) 688. **195** Goethe quoted in J. F. C. Fuller, *A Military History of the Western World*, II (New York, 1957) 369. **196–7** Napoleon quoted in David Chandler, *The Campaigns of Napoleon* (New York, 1966) 53. Historians question whether he actually delivered this address or merely concocted it later. In either case, it illustrates his attitudes. **201** Napoleon in Chandler, *Campaigns*, 149. **201** Bulletin de la Grande Armée, 18 October 1805, in Napoleon, *Correspondance de Napoléon 1re*, XI (Paris, 1863) 336, no. 9392. **201** Translated from a passage quoted in Claude Manceron, *Austerlitz* (Paris, 1960) 90–1. Dates given according to the revolutionary calendar have been presented in the Gregorian calendar. **203** Frederick quoted in Fuller, *Military History*, 197. **204** Pelet in Gunther Rothenberg, *The Art of War in the Age of Napoleon* (Bloomington, 1978) 157. **204** Napoleon's proclamation of 7 September 1812 in Chandler, *Campaigns*, 799. **205** Scharnhorst quoted in Rothenberg, *The Art of War in the Age of Napoleon*, 190. **206** Order in Gordon A. Craig, *The Politics of the Prussian Army, 1640–1945* (Oxford, 1955) 43. **210** Nelson letter to Lady Hamilton, in Fuller, *Military History*, 389.

Chapter 12 The Industrialization of War

225 Lt. Gen. U.S. Grant, *Personal Memoirs of U.S. Grant* (New York, 1982) 191. **226** Lincoln quoted in James M. McPherson, *Battle Cry of Freedom, The Civil War Era* (New York, 1988) 585. **228–9** Grant, *Personal Memoirs of U.S. Grant*, 366. **230** Shelby Foote, *The Civil War, A Narrative*, III, *Red River to Appomattox* (New York, 1974) 295. **231** Sherman quoted in Walter L. Fleming, *Civil War and Reconstruction* (New York, 1905) 76. **232** Grant quoted in McPherson, *Battle Cry of Freedom*, 778. **232** Sheridan quoted in Michael Howard, *The Franco-Prussian War, The German Invasion of France, 1870–1871* (New York, 1969) 380. **234** Bismarck quoted in Stanley Chodorow and MacGregor Knox, *The Mainstream of Civilization* (New York, 1989) 745.

Chapter 13 Towards Total War

246 Sheridan quoted in Robert Debs Heinl, Jr., *Dictionary of Military and Naval Quotations* (Annapolis, 1966) 155. **256–7** Winston Churchill, *The World Crisis* (Toronto, 1931) 6. **265** Bethmann-Hollweg quoted in Sir Llewellyn Woodward, *Great Britain and the War of 1914–1918* (Boston, 1967) p. 24. **265** Grey quoted in Heinl, *Dictionary of Military and Naval Quotations*, p. 363.

Chapter 14 The West at War

269 Barbara W. Tuchman, *The Guns of August* (New York, 1962) 415. **276** Churchill quoted in Alan Moorehead, *Gallipoli* (New York, 1956) 157. **277** Pétain quoted in Alistair Horne, *The Price of Glory, Verdun 1916* (New York, 1962) 156–7. **277** Quoted in Horne, *The Price of Glory*, 279–80. **277–8** Quoted in Horne, *The Price of Glory*, 188. **279** Quoted in A. H. Farrar-Hockley, *The Somme* (London, 1970) 139. **280** Erich Ludendorff, *Ludendorff's Own Story, August 1914–November 1918* (New York, 1919) 24, 324. **283** Ludendorff quoted in Holger H. Herwig, *Politics of Frustration, The United States in German Naval Planning, 1889–1941* (Boston, 1976) 125. **286–7** Leon Wolff, *In Flanders Fields, The 1917 Campaign* (New York, 1963) 361. 290 Quoted in Holger Herwig, 'The Dynamics of Necessity: German Military Policy during the First World War,' in *German Military Effectiveness*, I, ed. Allan R. Millett and Williamson Murray (London, 1988) 99. **296** Rupert Brooke in Jon Silkin, *The Penguin Book of First World War Poetry* (London, 1979) 81–2. **296** Siegfried Sassoon, *The War Poems of Siegfried Sassoon* (London, 1919) 40.

Chapter 15 The World in Conflict

304 Hitler quoted in *Akten zur deutschen auswärtige Politik (1936–41)*, series D, 22 August 1939. **309** Guderian quoted in Robert Doughty, *The Breaking Point, Sedan and the Fall of France, 1940* (Hamden, Connecticut, 1990) 1. **316** John Erickson, *The Soviet High Command* (London, 1962) 587. 316 Franz Halder, *Kriegstagebuch*, entry for 3 July 1941. **317** Halder, *Kriegstagebuch*, entry for 11 August 1941.

Chapter 16 The World at War

322 Anthony Verrier, *The Bomber Offensive* (London, 1968). 333 *Time Magazine*, 8 December 1941, 15. **337–8** Allan R. Millett, *Semper Fidelis, The History of the United States Marine Corps* (New York, 1980) 430. **339** Winston Churchill, *Blood, Sweat and Tears* (New York, 1941) 314.

Chapter 17 The Post-War World

344 Bradley quoted in Russell F. Weigley, *The American Way of War, A History of United States Military Strategy and Policy* (Bloomington, Ind., 1973) 390. **345** MacArthur quoted in Weigley, *The American Way of War*, 391. **351** Dean Rusk, *As I Saw It* (New York, 1990), 208–10. **352** (Caption) William C. Westmoreland, *A Soldier Reports* (New York, 1976) 364. **353** *Time Magazine*, 22 October 1965, 28. **353** (Caption) James Fallows, 'Vietnam – the Class War', *The National Observer*, 21 February 1976. **362** Saddam Hussein quoted by Jim Hoagland, *Washington Post*, 13 September 1990, A33. The full name of the president of Iraq between 1979 and 2003 is Saddam Hussein 'Abd al-Majid al-Tikriti. 'Saddam' is a self-bestowed title meaning in Arabic 'the stubborn one' or 'he who confronts'. 'Hussein' is not a surname (in the Western sense) but rather his father's given personal name, while 'Abd al-Majid' is his grandfather's name and 'Al-Tikriti' means he was born and raised in (or near) Tikrit. Since neither 'Saddam' nor 'Hussein' alone seems adequate, this book refers to him by both names. **365** M. Bowden, *Black Hawk Down. A Story of Modern War* (New York, 1999), based on Bowden's dispatches for *The Philadelphia Inquirer*; *Black Hawk Down*, a film directed by Ridley Scott (2002); *Delta Force V: Black Hawk Down*, a computer game by Novalogic (2003). **369** Of the 161 persons indicted by the ICTY for war crimes, only four – including Ratko Mladic and the Bosnian Serb leader Radovan Karadzic – remained at large in November 2007. **372** 'Military Report on Mesopotamia (Iraq)' 1922, quoted in J. M. Black, *War, Past, Present and Future* (Stroud, 2000), 24. **373** *The 9/11 Commission Report* (Washington, D.C., 2004), 72–3, stresses the complacency engendered by the ease with which the FBI apprehended some of the 1993 WTC plotters. On p. 316, however, they note that the Port Authority, responsible for security in the WTC, greatly improved evacuation procedures in the wake of the attack: whereas in 1993 it took four hours to evacuate the building, in 2001 almost all those not trapped or physically incapable of escaping managed to leave the complex in under one hour. **374** *The 9/11 Commission Report*, 60, quoting testimony from Jamal Ahmed al-Fadl in the trial *US vs Bin Laden* in 2001. **374** *The 9/11 Commission Report*, 47, quoting 'Text of World Islamic Front's statement urging Jihad against Jews and Crusaders' (23 Feb. 1998) and 'Hunting Bin Laden' (PBS *Frontline* broadcast, May 1998.) **375** *The 9/11 Commission Report*, 118, quoting an *Economist* editorial 'Punish and be damned' of 29 Aug. 1998, and the outrage this caused National Security Adviser Sandy Berger. **375** The current estimate of 3,023 persons murdered in the 9/11 attacks refers only to those who can be *proved* to have died in or around the WTC and the Pentagon, or on the four hijacked planes. The total number who died will never be known because the US government – unlike the Spanish government after the attacks on 11 March 2004 – never took steps to ascertain how many illegal immigrants in the WTC had been killed. **376** *The 9/11 Commission Report*, 337, quoting the president's speech on 20 Sep. 2001. **376** *The 9/11 Commission Report*, 333–4, quoting National Security Presidential Directive 9 (25 Oct. 2001). **377** Lord Hutton, *Report of the Inquiry into the Circumstances Surrounding the Death of Dr David Kelly CMG* (London, 2004), para 9. **378** Although extensive materials are now available on how President Bush reached his decision to invade Iraq, many more records remain classified – and the president intends them to remain classified for the foreseeable future ('Presidential Records Act Executive Order', EO 13,233, dated 1 November 2001). These classified records may shed new light on his decision. **379** McNamara, the longest-serving secretary of defense in US history (1961–8), after serving in the Air Force, worked in Ford Motor Company for fifteen years until he became its president. Rumsfeld, the second-longest-serving secretary (1975–7 and 2001–6), after serving as a navy pilot, worked in business for more than twenty years, including eleven as CEO of major companies. **380** George Packer, *The Assassins' Gate: America in Iraq* (New York, 2005) 139. **380** US Congressional Transcripts: Senate Armed Services Committee, 25 Feb. 2003, testimony of General Eric K. Shinseki; and House Budget Committee, 27 Feb. 2003, testimony of Deputy Secretary of Defense Paul Wolfowitz. It is notable that Wolfowitz (like Vice-President Cheney) had avoided military service entirely through student draft deferments and that Rumsfeld (like President Bush) had never been under fire.   **380** Since the text of *National Security Presidential Directive* 24, dated 20 January 2003 and entitled 'Post-War Iraq Reconstruction', remains classified, its contents can only be deduced from subsequent events.   **381** Packer, *Assassins' Gate,* 191, quoting Garner, and 195, quoting Hughes. www.cpa-iraq.org/regulations contains facsimiles of all documents signed by Paul Bremer as administrator of the CPA, starting with Regulation 1 (its act of creation) and Order 1 (De-Ba'athification) both of 16 May 2003, and Order 2 ('Dissolution of Entities') of 23 May 2003. Order 13, on 22 April 2004, creating the 'Central Criminal Court of Iraq', which would try and condemn to death Saddam and his lieutenants, used the new language.   **383** Details from an intercepted al-Qaeda strategic paper in Robert A. Pape, *Dying to Win. The Strategic Logic of Suicide Terrorism* (New York, 2005) 55–57.   **383** R. S. Chari, 'The 2004 Spanish Election: Terrorism as a Catalyst for Change?', *West European Politics,* XXVII (2004) 954–963, table on p. 958, shows that two and a half million more votes were cast in the election of 2004 than in that of 2000, with a turnout of more than 77 percent, as opposed to almost 70 percent. He suggests that those who abstained in 2000, plus first-time voters, overwhelmingly supported the Socialists in 2004, raising their tally from less than 8 million to almost 11 million. (Votes for the PP only dropped from 10.3 to 9.6 million.)   **386** The ORB report may be viewed at www.opinion.co.uk/Newsroom_details.aspx?NewsId=78. Results are based on face-to-face interviews conducted 12–19 August 2007 amongst what ORB claimed was a 'nationally representative sample' of 1,720 adults aged eighteen or older throughout fifteen of Iraq's eighteen provinces (only 1,499 agreed to answer the question on household deaths). Karbala and al-Anbar provinces were excluded for security reasons; Irbil was excluded because the authorities refused the field team a permit.   **407** *The 9/11 Commission Report,* 333–4, quoting National Security Presidential Directive 9 (25 Oct. 2001). The full text of the directive is still classified.

Epilogue The Future of Western Warfare
393 L. Freedman, *The Revolution in Strategic Affairs* (Oxford: Oxford University Press, 1998), 11; C. S. Gray, *The American Revolution in Military Affairs: an Interim Assessment* (London, 1997), 14; A. W. Marshall, Director of the Office of Net Assessment, 'Statement prepared for the Subcommittee on Acquisition and Technology, Senate Armed Service Committee' [USA], 5 May 1995. (I am grateful to Mr. Marshall for sending me a copy of his important remarks.)   **393** Francis Bacon, *Novum Organum* (London, 1620), book I, aphorism CXIII.   **394** Robert K. Merton, "Singletons and Multiples in Scientific Discovery," *Proceedings of the American Philosophical Society,* CV (1961), 470–86. On Japan's 'singleton' experiment with the countermarch, see G. Parker, 'From the House of Orange to the House of Bush: 400 years of Revolutions in Military Affairs', in J. A. Lynn, ed., *Acta of the XXVIII International Conference of Military History* (Wheaton, IL, 2003), 40–71.   **394** Andrew F. Krepinevich, 'Cavalry to Computer. The Pattern of Military Revolution', *The National Interest* (Fall, 1994), 39.   **396** J. Mueller, *The Remnants of War* (Ithaca, 2004), 114, quoting Brian Hall, *The Impossible Country: a Journey through the Last Days of Yugoslavia* (New York, 1994).   **396** Grivas quoted in R. Asprey, *War in the Shadows: the Guerrilla in History,* vol 2 (New York, 1975) 992.   **397** R. Larson, *The British Army and the Theory of Armoured Warfare 1918–1940* (Newark, 1984) 34.   **400** Mueller, *Remnants,*1. See also the figure on p. 87 showing the declining frequency of war, 1946–2003.   **401** E. Cohen, *Supreme Command: soldiers, statesmen and leadership in wartime* (New York, 2002), 203.   **401** John Hampden, 'Some considerations about the most proper way of raising money in the present conjuncture', in *Cobbett's Parliamentary History of England,* vol. 5 (London, 1809), Appendix VI, col. liv.   **402** Cohen, *Supreme Command,* 185, 198, 209.   **402** W. Erfurth, *Der Vernichtungssieg. Eine Studie über das Zusammen-wirken getrennter Heeresteile* (Berlin: Mittler & Sohn, 1939), 58–76; US Department of State, *Foreign Relations of the United States, 1961–63. XI Cuban Missile Crisis* (Washington DC, 1988), 26–8, 'Report of conversation with Ambassador Dobrynin on Saturday, October 13 [1962]'; R. F. Kennedy, *Thirteen Days: a Memoir of the Cuban Missile Crisis* (New York: Norton, 1969), 105. JFK also quoted the lessons he drew from Tuchman's book in a conversation with his brother on 23 October 1962 (ibid., 40.)   **403** Cohen, *Supreme Command,* 98, 128.

Picture acknowledgements

Every effort has been made to obtain permission to use copyright material; the publishers apologise for any errors or omissions and would welcome these being brought to their attention.

Key: T TOP, C CENTRE, B BOTTOM, L LEFT, R RIGHT; **BN** BIBLIOTHEQUE NATIONALE, PARIS; **BAL** BRIDGEMAN ART LIBRARY, LONDON; **CMD** C M DIXON; **ETA** E T ARCHIVE; **HD** HULTON-DEUTSCH COLLECTION; **IWM** IMPERIAL WAR MUSEUM, LONDON; **MC** THE MANSELL COLLECTION; **NMM** NATIONAL MARITIME MUSEUM, LONDON; **PC** PRIVATE COLLECTION; **PN** PETER NEWARK'S MILITARY PICTURES; **TP** TOPHAM PICTUREPOINT.

i IWM CO 2246; **ii, iii** Anne S K Brown Military Collection, Brown University Library, Providence R.I.; **viii–ix** PN; 3 TP; 4 PC; 6 NASM, Smithsonian Institution; 7 Los Alamos National Laboratory; 10–11 CMD; 13 Bibliothèque de l'Institut de France, Paris/Bulloz; 14t Ecole Française d'Archéologie, Athens; 14b Scala; 16 PN; 17 Hirmer Fotoarchiv; 18 The Louvre, Paris/Photo RMN; 19 British Museum; 21 Foto della Soprintendenza Archeologica per l'Etruria Méridionale; 24–5 Paul Lipke/Trireme Trust USA; 25t Werner Forman Archive; 26, 27 MC; 29 Graeco-Roman Museum of Alexandria; 30t Vatican Museums and Galleries, Rome/BAL; 30b The Louvre, Paris/Photo RMN; 30–1 Sonia Halliday; 31r André Held; 32–3 W K Pritchett; 35 Henri Stierlin, Geneva; 37 National Archeological Museum of Athens; 38 Archeological Museum of Thessaloniki; 39 Ancient Art and Architecture Collection; 40 CMD; 43 Staatliche Museen zu Berlin – Preussischer Kulturbesitz Antikensammlung. Photo: Karin Marz; 45 Photo Alinari; 49 MC; 51, 53 CMD; 55 ETA; 56t CMD; 56c,56b MC; 58 Zefa; 59 CMD; 61 MC; 62–3 Sonia Halliday; 66 Bodleian Library, University of Oxford, MS Canon Misc378 folio 145; 67 Photo AKG London; 68 Scala; 69 Ashmolean Museum Oxford; 70 Sonia Halliday; 72 Biblioteca Capitolane Modena; 74tl Robert Harding; 74r Nordam-Ullitz and Balslev; 75 Treuchtlingen (Stadt Verkehrsamt); 76 CMD; 78–9 Sonia Halliday; 80 Dieter Barz; 82 Musée de la Tapisserie, Bayeux/Giraudon /BAL; 83 Michael Holford; 85 BN, Ms NAL 1390 fol. 57v; 86–7 Michael Holford; 89 A F Kersting; 90–1 Sonia Halliday; 92 ETA; 93 By courtesy of the Board of Trustees of the Victoria and Albert Museum; 94 Duomo, Florence/Scala; 95 BN/BAL; 97 PN; 98, 101 The British Library; 102 BN/Explorer Archives; 106 Needham Research Institute, Cambridge; 107 ETA; 108 Historic Scotland Photo Library; 110, 111 ETA; 114 Bibliothèque Royale Albert ler, Brussels, J Blaeu Tonneel der Steden, III 94.530 E 1 RP; 118–19 Spink & Son Ltd, London/BAL; 120 Bodleian Library, University of Oxford, MS Rawlinson A.315 plate no. 29; 122 NMM; 124 University of Nottingham; 125 HD; 126 ETA; 127 NMM/BAL; 128–9 NMM; 131t Gemeente Dordrecht Dienst Kunsten; 131b NMM/BAL; 132 Historia de las Indios de Nueva España – MAS; 133 Biblioteca Medicea Laurenziana; 134 MEPL; 137 South American Pictures; 138–9 Robert Harding; 143 MEPL/Explorer; 145 Ancient Art and Architecture Collection; 146 Heller: Battle of Pavia/Photo:National Museum, SKM, Stockholm; 148 The Wellcome Institute Library, London; 149 Parker: The Military Revolution, (Cambridge University Press 1988); 150 Rijksmuseum, Amsterdam; 151 Johnny van Haeften Gallery, London/BAL; 152 Austrian National Tourist Office; 154 Anne S K Brown Military Collection, Brown University Library, Providence R.I.; 156, 157 PC; 158t Geoffrey Parker; 158b The Royal Collection © Her Majesty Queen Elizabeth II; 161, 163 PC; 164 Versailles/Lauros-Giraudon; 167 Versailles/ Photo RMN – G Blot; 168 Paris, Collection Particulière/Giraudon; 169 J Feuillie/© CMNHS/SPADEM; 170–1, 171r Historisches Museum auf Stadt Wien; 173 Hermitage, St Petersburg/BAL; 174 Reproduced by kind permission of his Grace the Duke of Marlborough; 177 Photo AKG London; 179 Anne S K Brown Military Collection, Brown University Library, Providence R.I.; 180 Royal Armouries; 184 HD; 186 Historical Society of Pennsylvania, USA/BAL; 187 The Union League of Philadelphia; 189 MEPL; 191 Cowpens National Battlefield, National Parks Service; 193 Bulloz; 194 Musée de Versailles/Photo RMN; 195b Musée de Versailles/Reunion; 195t Musée de Versailles/Giraudon; 197 Bulloz; 198–9 The Metropolitan Museum of Art, Gift of Henry Hilton, 1887 (87.20.1); 202l Versailles/Giraudon; 202r Versailles/Bulloz; 203 Bulloz; 204 MC; 206l Copyright Photo Musée de l'Armée, Paris; 206–7, 207r By courtesy of the Board of Trustees of the Victoria & Albert Museum; 208 The Royal Collection © Her Majesty Queen Elizabeth II; 210 Crown Estate/Institute of Directors, London/BAL; 214–15 IWM H(AM) 1671; 216 MEPL; 218–19 The Royal Collection © Her Majesty Queen Elizabeth II; 220 PN; 223 Antietam National Battlefield, National Parks Service; 224, 225 Massachusetts Commandery Military Order of the Loyal Legion and the US Army Military History Institute; 226 Pejepscot Historical Society/Geoffrey C Ward:The Civil War (The Bodley Head 1991) © American Documentaries Inc; 228, 231 PN; 232 MEPL; 234 Photo AKG London; 236 PN; 238–9, 241, 243, 244 HD; 245, 246 PN; 247 Robert Harding; 248 Courtesy of the Director, National Army Museum, London; 250 Australian War Memorial A05311; 251 Africana Museum, Johannesburg/BAL; 252 HD; 257 Robert K Massie: Dreadnought (Jonathan Cape 1992); 259 Wyllie Gallery, London/ BAL; 261 HD; 262 Photo AKG London; 265 MEPL; 266 Courtesy of the Director, National Army Museum, London; 269, 272 IWM Q70075, Q 30859; 273 David King Collection; 275 HD; 276 Popperfoto; 277, 278–9, 280 IWM Q23783, Q70169, Q4055; 283 MEPL; 284, 286 IWM Q6024, CO 2246; 287 Australian War Memorial E01497; 289 IWM Q6425; 292 Range/Bettman; 294 HD; 295 IWM; 297 IWM Q33682; 299, 302 HD; 304 John Watney; 307, 309 PC; 310 HD; 311 PN; 312, 315 TP; 316 PC; 317 David King Collection; 318–19 TP; 320 IWM HU 5154; 321 Novosti; 322 MEPL/Signal; 323 MEPL/Explorer; 325 IWM NYF4307; 328 Novosti; 329 IWM series 1–16 CL–1; 331 Popperfoto; 332 HD; 333 IWM HU 2675; 334 TP; 335 US Navy Art Collection Washington DC /The Naval Historical Foundation; 336 HD; 337 IWM IND 4545; 338 Anne S K Brown Military Collection, Brown University Library, Providence R I; 339 Science Photo Library; 340 Range/Beltmann; 341 HD; 342 David King Collection; 344 TP; 345, 346 HD; 350 John Philby/Camera Press, London; 351 Popperfoto; 352 HD; 353 Associated Press; 355, 358, 359 Rex; 360 Popperfoto; 361 Camera Press, London; 362 Ian Black/Rex; 369 Paula Allen. This image appears in the traveling documentary photographic exhibit, "The Betrayal of Srebrenica: The Ten-Year Commemoration," conceptualized and produced by Lisa DiCaprio. 373 Two frames from "Operation Near Shatoi", a video posted on www.cihad.net; 384 Peter Mansoor; 385 Ashley Gilbertson/Aurora Photos; 387 Steven Boylan.

Index

A

Abrams, Creighton (American general, Vietnam War) 355
Abu Ghraib 383
Achilles as hoplite 30
Actium, battle of (31 BC) 399
Adrianople: battle of (AD 378) 65; most fought-over town in history 399
Aelian (*Tactics*) 4–5, 154, 391–2
Aemilius Paulus (Roman general) 43
Aeneas the Tactician 29
Aeschylus on the Persian wars 21, 26
Aetius (Roman general) 64, 65
Afghanistan, wars in 371, 374–8, 384, 387–8, 396; *see also* al-Qaeda; Laden, Osama bin
Agesilaus (Spartan general) 26, 40
aggression in the western military tradition 5, 9, 40, 48, 136, 390–2
Agilulf, king of the Lombards 68
Agincourt, battle of (1415) 95
agrarian warfare: bronze-age 12; hoplite 14–19, 24, 26, 31, 32; Roman militias 50, 51, 55
air attacks: World War I 294; Spanish Civil War 303; World War II 310–11, 325–6, 336, 337, 338–9; Six Day War 358; Vietnam War 352, 354, 355, 356; Yom Kippur War 359; Falklands War 360, 361; Gulf War 362–3
Air Corps Tactical School (USA) 301
airborne forces 308, 346, 347, 357, 360
aircraft carriers: American (1930s) 302; American (World War II) 334–5; Japanese (World War II) 334
air defence: British (1930s) 301; German (World War II) 325, 326; Egyptian (Yom Kippur War) 359; Iraqi (Gulf War) 362–3; Syrian, 371–2,400
Aire-sur-la-Lys besieged (1641) 151
Aisne offensive (1918) 292
Aix-la-Chapelle, treaty of (1748) 181
Ajax as hoplite 30
Alans 66, 68
Alba, duke of 151, 153, 154
'Alberich' (German withdrawal, 1917) 284
Alberti, Leon Battista, on angled defences 110
Alexander the Great 39–40, 42–3, 75, 105, 200, 203
Alexius (east Roman emperor) 86
Alfonso X of Castile (*Siete Partidas*) 105

Alfred the Great 76–7, 80
Algerian War (1954–62) 348
Algonkians 134, 140
Aljubarrota, battle of (1385) 92
Allerheim, battle of (1645) 158
Alma, battle of (1854) 219
Almagro, Diego de (Spanish conquistador) 140
Al-Qaeda 374–88
Al-Sadr, Muqtada 385–6
Alvarez de Toledo, Don Fernándo – *see* Alba
Ambrones 50
Ambrose, Archbishop of Milan (penance of Theodosius) 389
American Civil War 220–33
American War of Independence (1775–81) 186–91
Americas conquered 132–45
Amherst, Jeffrey (British general) 184
Amiens: treaty of (1802) 211; battle of (1918) 293
Amir al-Khattab 373
Ammianus Marcellinus on Constantius 66
Anastasius (east Roman emperor) 69–70
Adrianople: battle of (378) 65; most fought-over city in history 372
Angevin castles 80–1
angled bastions 110, 112–13, 114, 171
Anglo-Dutch wars 120, 127, 128–9, 399
Anglo-Saxon military organization 76–7, 80
Anna Comnena on Frankish cavalry 86
Antelope hit by Exocet missile (1982) 360
Antietam, battle of (1862) 223, 224
Antigonus Gonatas (Macedonian general) 43
Antioch taken by crusaders (1098) 84
Antipater (Macedonian general) 43
anti-war sentiment – *see* criticism of war
Antonine wall 74
Antwerp: defences (1560s) 112, 116; World War I 270; World War II 330, 331
Anzac (Australian and New Zealand army corps), Dardanelles campaign (1915) 275–6
Anzio landing (1944) 323
Apache resistance (1880s) 247
Apollo as hoplite 30
Appian: on Cannae 49; on rise of *latifundia* 51
Appomattox, Lee's surrender (1865) 232

aqulia (Roman eagle insignia) 55
Aquileia town walls 65
Arab–Israeli wars: 1948–49 357; 1956 (Suez Crisis) 357; 1967 (Six Day War) 357–8; 1973 (Yom Kippur War) 359
archery 2, 19, 20, 34, 82, 83, 93, 95, 99, 104, 109
Archilochus on commanders 16
Ardennes: German invasion route (1940) 306–7; German counter-attack (1944) 331
Aridius (Gallo-Roman magnate) 72–4
Aristophanes (war criticism) 389
Aristotle on decline of the hoplite 25, 27
Arkan 395
Armada: Spanish (1588) 124, 125, 126, 149, 399; Dutch (1688) 124
armour 14, 15–17, 37, 84, 92, 109, 134–6, 181
armoured warfare: British experiments (1920s–30s) 299; German development (1930s) 299; World War II 307, 315, 327, 330; Six Day War 358; Yom Kippur War 359, 360, 361; Iraq, 378–88
arms manufacture 152, 242, 272, 321–2, 325, 390–1
arms race, naval: 17th c. 227–8; before World War I 258
Army of Northern Virginia (American Civil War) 226
Army of the Potomac (American Civil War) 222
Army of Tennessee (American Civil War) 229
Arnhem, battle of (1944) 330
arquebuses 109, 132, 133, 144, 154
arrows 92, 95, 132, 135, 140
Artemis as hoplite 30
artificial limbs in the 1500s 148
artillery: gunpowder revolution 96–7, 102, 106–17; naval (late middle ages) 120–1, 122, 125–6, 130–1; Spanish New-World conquests 133–4; naval (16th c.) 127–9, 137, 167, 192, 195; naval (Napoleonic wars) 209–11; Paris siege (1870–71) 240; Russo-Japanese War (1904–05) 252; World War I 273; Verdun (1916) 276; the Somme (1916) 279; Flanders (1917) 285; Passchendaele (1917) 286; Kursk (1943) 327; Korean War (1950–53) 345
artillery fortresses 110, 112–13, 115–16

On the Art of Building (Leon Battista Alberti, 1440s) 110
The Art of War at Sea (Fernando Oliveira, 1555) 125
Aspern-Essling, battle of (1809) 205
Assaye, battle of (1803) 212
Assize of Arms (England, 1181) 104
Assyrian warfare 12–13
Atahualpa (Inca ruler) 138
Athena as hoplite 30, 31
Athenians 19, 21, 22, 23, 24, 25, 26–7, 32, 38–9
Atlanta, battle of (1864) 231
Atlantic, battle of (World War II) 324
atomic weapons 7, 338–9, 341, 366, 371, 394–5
atrocities, Thirty Years War 161; *see also* war crimes
attack in depth (World War I) 287–8, 290
Attila the Hun 64, 73
Augustus Caesar 56, 57, 58
Austerlitz, battle of (1805) 200, 202–3
Austrian Succession, War of (1740–48) 178, 181, 183
Austro-Prussian War (1866) 235
Avars 68
Ayamores 140
Aznar, José María 377, 384
Aztecs 133, 134, 136, 140, 144

B

B-17 bomber 325
B-24 bomber 326
B-29 bomber 339
B-52 bomber 356
Bacon, Francis 393–4
Badoglio, Marshal Pietro (Italian leader 1943–44) 323
Baghdad 381–3, 384, 385–6
'Bagration' (Soviet offensive, 1944) 328
Balaclava, battle of (1854) 219
Balkan Wars 268–269, 330, 367–70
Balkans campaign: Italian (1940) 311; German (1941) 313
Bank of England 8, 180, 212
Banks, Nathaniel Prentiss (Union general) 229
Bannockburn, battle of (1314) 93, 94, 391
'Barbarossa' (German invasion of the Soviet Union, 1941) 314–19
Bar Lev line breached (1973) 359
Barcelona taken in 801 72
Barret, Robert (*The Theory and Practice of Modern Wars*, 1598) 106

Barwick, Humphrey (English military writer) 154

bastions 112–13, 114, 116, 171

battalion attack column (revolutionary France) 194

battering rams: trireme 24; medieval 73

battle doctrine: hoplite 15–20; Macedonian 38; Roman 45–7; British (World War I) 285, 287, 289; French (World War I) 284, 290; German (World War I) 280–1, 287, 290; British (after World War I) 300; French (after World War I) 300; German (1924) 299

battle-leaders, hoplite 16

Bayeux tapestry 83

bayonets 167

Bazaine, François Achille, (French marshal in the Franco-Prussian War) 238

Beachy Head, battle of (1690) 128

Beatty, Sir David (World War I admiral) 282

Beck, Ludwig (chief of the German general staff, 1930s) 299

Bede, the Venerable, on Hadrian's Wall 74

Behr, Johann, on decline of the field battle 168

Belfast in action, Korean War 345

Belgium invaded: (1914) 267; (1940) 307

Belgrade bombed (1941) 313

Belgrano torpedoed (1982) 360

Belisarius (Byzantine general) 70

Bellisfortis (Conrad Kyeser of Eischstätt, 1402) 110

De bello gallico (Julius Caesar) 105

Benedek, Ludwig von (Austrian general) 235–6

Bentinck, Hans Willem 124

Bergen-op-Zoom besieged (1622) 159

Berlichingen, Götz von (military entrepreneur, 16th c.) 148

Berlin: bombed (1943) 325; taken (1945) 332

Berlin Decree (1806) 203

Bernhardi, Theodor von (German general) 242

Berwick-upon-Tweed besieged (1333) 106

Bf-109 (Messerschmitt) fighter aircraft 311

Biak, battle of (1944) 335–6

Bicocca, battle of (1522) 153

biological weapons 371

Bismarck, Otto von (Prussian statesman) 234–5, 236, 241

Black Hole of Calcutta 185

Black Prince 96

Black Week (Boer War) 249

Blackhawk helicopters 365

Blair, Tony (British Prime Minister) 377

Blenheim, battle of (1704) 174, 175

blind bombing system, (World War II) 311

Bloch, Ivan (*Is War Impossible?* 1899) 262

blockades: Calais (1346–47) 102; Napoleonic wars 203; American Civil War 222, 230; Heligoland bight (World War I) 282; Anglo-French (1939) 305

Blücher, Gebhard Leberecht von (Prussian general, Napoleonic wars) 208

Blücher, World War I German battlecruiser 282

Blücher, World War II German heavy cruiser 306

Bock, Fedor von (German general, World War II) 305, 308–9, 318

Boer uprising (1880–81) 246

Boer War (1889–1902) 249–52

Boeotia plain (Greek battleground) 39, 399

Bohemia, Hussite revolt 92, 97, 99

Bologna defences (1381) 110

Bolshevik Revolution (1917) 287

bombards 106–9, 121

bombing: 1930s doctrine 301; Spanish Civil War 303; battle of Britain (1940) 310–11; Pearl Harbor (1941) 332, 333; Germany (World War II) 325–6, 331; Japan (1945) 339; Vietnam 352, 355, 356; Balkan wars, 367–70, 396; Gulf wars 361–3, 378, 396

Bomber Command (Royal Air Force, World War II) 325

Bonaparte: Joseph 204; Napoleon – *see* Napoleon

Borodino, battle of (1812) 204

Bosnia, civil wars (1990s) 365–6, 367–71, 395–6

Bosnian rebellion (1876) 247

Boston besieged (1775–76) 187

Boulogne taken by Germans (1940) 309

Bourges taken by Pepin 1 (762) 72

bows 2, 19, 92, 109, 132, 135

Boyle, Roger, earl of Orrery 146, 152

Bradley, Omar (chairman of the American joint chiefs of staff, Korean War) 344

Bragg, Braxton (Confederate general) 228

Braun, Werner von, decorated 6

Breeds hill (battle of Bunker hill) 187

Breitenfeld, battle of (1631) 151, 156–8

Bremer, L. Paul 382–5

Brest-Litovsk, peace of (1918) 288

Brétigny, treaty of (1360) 96

Britain, battle of (1940) 310

British Expeditionary Force: in Entente Cordiale 259; World War I 268, 269, 273, 278–9,

285–6, 289, 293; World War II 308, 309

broadsides 120, 124–5, 128, 130, 209

bronze weapons 12–14, 16–17, 121, 133–4

Brooke, Sir Alan, chairman of the Chiefs of Staff 402

Brooke, Rupert (World War I poet) 296

Brunswick, duke of (Prussian general, French revolutionary wars) 195

Brussels taken: (1914) 266; (1940) 309

Brussilov, Alexei (Russian general, World War I) 281

Budapest, battle of (1944) 329

Bueil, Jean de (*Le jouvencel*, 1466) 103

Buell, Carlos (Union general) 224

Bulgaria: Germany ally (1941) 313; surrender to Soviets (1944) 329

Bulge, battle of (1944) 331

Bull Run: first battle of (1861) 222; second battle of (1862) 223

Buller, Redvers (British general, Boer War) 250

Bülow, Karl von (German general, World War I) 268, 269

Bunker hill, battle of (1775) 187

bureaucracy of war 42, 49, 57, 58, 60, 147

Burghal Hidage 77

Burgoyne, John (British general, War of American Independence) 188

burgs, Anglo-Saxon 77, 80

Burma: occupied by Japan (1942–43) 333; recaptured by Britain (1944–45) 336

Burnside, Ambrose (Union general) 224

Bush, George H. W. (US President) 364

Bush, George W. (US President) 376–88, 401

Butler, Benjamin Franklin (Union general) 229

Buxar, battle of (1764) 185

Byng, John (British admiral) 209

Byzantine warfare 69–70, 78–80, 84, 86–7

C

cadet schools (France, 1700s) 192

Cadiz raid (1596) 126

Caesar, Julius (Roman general) 4, 52, 56, 105

Cairo (Union riverboat) 224

Calais blockaded (1346–47) 102

caltrops 86

Camberley staff college 243

Cambodia invaded: by Americans (1970) 355; by Vietnamese (1978) 356

Cambrai, battle of (1917) 287

Camden, battle of (1780) 189

camp followers 159

Camperdown, battle of (1797) 209, 399

Campo Formio, treaty of (1797) 197

Cannae, battle of (216 BC) 48–9, 60, 155, 263, 402

cannon – *see* artillery

Canturino, battle of (1363) 94

Cap Colonna, battle of (982) 84

Cape St Vincent, battle of (1797) 209, 210

Capet, Hugh, king of France 80

Capital ships 120, 123–31

Caporetto, battle of (1917) 288

caravels 130, 131

Carcassonne: raided (1355) 96; town walls 89

Carlos II of Spain 175

Carnatic War: first (1744–48) 181; second (1749–54) 181

Carnot, Lazare (military leader, French revolutionary wars) 195

Carolingian dynasty 71–2, 74–5

carracks 130, 131

Carrhae, battle of (53 BC) 47, 56, 60

Cartier, Jacques, on Algonkians 134

Casablanca meeting (1943) 323

Cassel, battle of (1328) 93

castles 80, 81, 83, 86–7

casualties, civilian: Boer War 251; Belgium (1914) 268; Rotterdam (1940) 308; Belgrade (1941) 313; Hamburg (1943) 325; Dresden (1945) 331; Japan (1945) 339; Leningrad (World War II) 317; Algerian War 348; Vietnam War 353; 20th-c. civil wars 303; Gulf wars 386–8

casualties, military: hoplite 17; Macedonian phalanx 36; Roman legion 60, 61; native American (16th–17th centuries) 141–2; Napoleonic wars 208; French (1915) 273; Verdun (1916) 278; the Somme (1916) 280; Passchendaele (1917) 287; British (1918) 293; German (1918) 293; Italian (World War I) 276; World War I 295; Stalingrad (1942–43) 321; Soviet (World War II) 341; Okinawa landing (1945) 338; 20th-c. Gulf wars, 386–8; *see also* civilian casualties

catapults 34, 73, 106

The Cavalry Commander (Xenophon) 29

cavalry: Greek 27; Macedonian 34, 37, 39, 40, 41, 44; Roman 52, 66; medieval: 66–7, 81, 82, 83, 84–7, 88–91, 92, 93, 94, 95–6, 98–99; conquistadors 143;

16th–17th centuries 147, 152, 156; Louis XIV's 166, 167; Napoleonic 198; charge of the Light Brigade (1854) 220; battle of Omdurman (1896) 244; World War I 266

Central Intelligence Agency (CIA): estimates of Soviet strength (1980s) 342; Vietnam 356

centre-of-gravity concept (Clausewitz) 115

Centurion tank 359

centurions 46, 61

century (Roman legion) 46, 52

Chaeroneia, battle of (338 BC) 38–9, 399

chain-mail armour 92

Chalabi, Ahmed 380, 382

challenge-and-response dynamic 5–6

Châlons, battle of (AD 451) 64, 66

Chamberlain, Joshua (Union general) 226

Chamberlain, Neville (British prime minister, 1937–40) 304

Champagne offensive (1915) 273

Chancellorsville, battle of (1863) 226

Charlemagne 71–2, 74

Charles, Archduke (Austrian general, Napoleonic wars) 205

Charles I of England 127, 151

Charles II of England 168

Charles V, Holy Roman emperor 113, 116–17, 121, 150, 159

Charles VII of France 97, 105, 107

Charles VIII of France 152, 153, 160

Charles XII of Sweden 172, 173

Charles the Bald 72

Charles the Bold of Burgundy 99, 104, 105, 109, 116, 147

Charles of Lorraine 182

Charles Martel 71, 72

Charleston, battle of (1766) 189

chassepot rifle 237

Château-Thierry, battle of (1918) 292

Chattanooga besieged (1863) 228

Chechen Wars (1990s) 366–7, 372–4, 383

Chelmsford, Baron Frederick Augustus Thesiger (British general, Zulu War) 245

chemical weapons 371

Cherbourg: besieged by Henry V 96; taken by Americans (1944) 330

chevauchée 95, 96

chevaux-de-frise 225

Chickamauga, battle of (1863) 228

China: siege warfare 390; gunpowder weapons 106; early artillery at sea 120; attacked by Japanese (1937)

chivalry 88–91, 99

Christine de Pisan (Les Faits d'Armes et de Chevalerie, 1409) 105, 107

Churchill, John – see Marlborough

Churchill, Winston: on outbreak of World War I 256; on battleship numbers 258; on World War I stalemate 273; Dardanelles campaign (1915) 274, 276, 294; World War II 307, 310, 323, 402–3

CIA – see Central Intelligence Agency

Cimbri 50

city walls 35, 64, 65, 89, 110, 112–14, 116, 170–1

civil war 369–70, 371; American 220–33; Spanish 303; Lebanese 365; Yugoslav 367–70

Civitavecchia defences (1515) 110

Clark, Mark (American general, World War II) 324

Clausewitz, Carl von (On War) 5, 115, 169, 257, 262, 361

Clemenceau, Georges (French premier, World War I) 285, 400, 402

Clinton, Bill (US President) 365, 367, 372

Clinton, Sir Henry (British general, War of American Independence) 188–9

Clive, Robert (East India Company soldier) 179, 181, 185

Clovis (Merovingian king) 72, 390

clubs, South American weapons 134–5, 140

Coalition Provisional Authority (Iraq) 382–5

Coen, Jan Pieterzoon, on trade and war in 17th-c. Asia 9

Cohen, Eliot A. 401, 402

cohorts (Roman legion) 52–3

Colbert, Jean Baptiste 165–6

Cold War 340, 342, 362, 397–8

Collingwood, Cuthbert (British admiral at Trafalgar) 210, 211

Collins, General Lawton (US army chief of staff, Korean War) 341

Cologne bombed (1942) 325

colonial empires 178, 180, 187, 208, 211, 244, 333, 340, 348

colours, regimental 150–1

Columbus, Christopher on Caribbeans 132

Combined Bomber Offensive (World War II) 325, 326, 340

commandos: Boer 249, 250; German, in Soviet Union 314

commercial advantage: motive for war 176, 178–82; power-base for war 208, 211–13

commissars (French Revolution) 194

commissions purchased 166, 192

Committee of Public Safety (French Revolution) 195

Compagnie des Indes 185

compagnies d'ordonnance 105

companion cavalry (Macedon) 34, 38, 41

computer revolution (1980s) 342, 393

concentration camps (Boer War) 251

Concerning military matters – see Vegetius

Concord, battle of (1775) 187

Condé, Louis Prince de (Louis XIV's general) 168, 169

condotta (late-medieval military contract) 103

Conduct of the Defensive Battle (1916) 281

Congress of Vienna (1815) 216

conquistadors 131–45

Conrad von Hötzendorf, Franz (Austrian general, World War I) 271

conscription 68, 193, 198; and drill 367; French (Algerian War) 348; American (Vietnam War) 353

Constantine (Roman emperor) 59–60

Constantinople: Roman walls 62–3; defended by Byzantine fleet 78–9; sacked by crusaders (1204) 80; besieged (1453) 109; Russian threat (1877) 217

Constantius (east Roman emperor) 66

containment-of-communism policy 342

Continental System (Napoleon) 203, 204

Continentals (War of American Independence) 187, 191

convoys (battle of the Atlantic, World War II) 324, 325

copper weapons in the New World 134

Coral Sea, battle of (1942) 334

Corinthian warfare 14, 16, 24

Corinth, Mississippi, Halleck's advance on (1862) 225

'corned' powder 108

Cornwallis, Charles (British general, War of American Independence) 189, 190

Coroneia, battle of (447 BC) 25; (394 BC) 28

corps system introduced 198, 205

Cortés, Hernán (conquistador) 133–4, 140

costs of war 6–7, 24, 33, 92, 116, 121, 123, 124, 129, 166, 387–8, 397, 401

cotton armour 134, 135, 141

Courtrai, battle of (1312) 93, 391

Cowpens, battle of (1781) 189, 190–1

Crassus (Roman general) 47, 55–6, 60

Craterus (Macedonian general) 43

Crazy Horse (Sioux leader) 246

Crécy, battle of (1346) 94, 96, 109

credit mobilized for war 7–8, 165, 180, 212, 401

Crete invaded (1941) 313

Crimean War (1854–55) 217

criticism of war 349, 353–4, 378–9, 389–90

Croatia 367–9

Cronje, Piet (Boer commander) 250

crossbows 82–3, 92, 93, 109, 132, 135

cross-Channel invasion plans for 1943 322

crownworks 113

crusaders 84, 86

Cuban Missile Crisis (1962) 350–2, 379–80, 402

culverins 109, 120, 121

Cunaxa, battle of (401 BC) 40

Custer, George Armstrong (American cavalry commander, Indian wars) 246

Cuzco besieged (1536–37) 136, 137, 141, 143

Cyprus taken by Turks (1570–71) 122, 123

Cyrus II (Persian emperor) 40

Czechoslovakian crisis (1938) 304

D

Daladier, Edouard (French premier) 304

Damian of Tarsus 79

Danewirke 74

Danish War (1864) 234

Dardanelles campaign (1915) 274

Darius I (Persian emperor) 21, 22

Daun, Leopold von (Austrian marshal, Seven Years War) 183

Davout, Louis Nicolas (French marshal, Napoleonic wars) 200, 201, 202, 203

De Gaulle, Charles (French president, 1958–69) 349

De Nobilitatibus, sapientiis et prudentiis regum (Walter de Milamete, 1326–27) 107

De Regimine Principum (Giles of Rome, 13th c.) 105

defence in depth: Roman 59–60, 64; medieval 77, 78, 81, 87; German (1917–18) 281, 284, 288, 290; British (World War I) 289; see also fortifications

Delium, battle of (424 BC) 18

Demosthenes: on old-fashioned warfare 32; on Philip of Macedon 39

Denain, battle of (1712) 176

Desert Storm – see Operation Desert Storm

desertion 147, 177, 191, 196, 293

deterrence of Soviet aggression 342

Devolution, War of (1667–68) 168

Diem, Ngo Dinh (South Vietnamese dictator) 350

Dien Bien Phu, battle of (1954) 346, 347, 348
Dieppe raid (1942) 329
Dijon defences (1417) 110
Dio Cassius (Roman historian) 57
Diocletian (Roman emperor) 59, 65
Dipaea, battle of (471 BC) 26
Directory (French Revolution) 196–7
disability pensions for Elizabethan sailors 149
discipline 3, 401–2; hoplite 18; late medieval 103–4; Prussian 177–8; Roman 46–7, 59, 60; German storm troops (1918) 291
disease in conquest of the Americas 143
Dithmarschen, battle of (1319) 94
Djerba, battle of (1560) 122
Dogger Bank, battle of (1915) 282
Don John of Austria (16th-c. Spanish general) 122
Dönitz, Admiral Karl (U-boats commander, World War II) 324–5
Dordrecht (Dutch East India Company ship) 131
Dornberger, General Walter, decorated 6
Dorylaeum, battle of (1097) 86
Douhet, Giulio (Italian general, 1930s) 301
Dowding, Sir Hugh (commander-in-chief, Fighter Command, 1936–40) 301, 310
draft: Vietnam War 353; *see also* conscription
dragoons 66, 167
Drake, Sir Francis, Caribbean raid (1585–86) 145
Dreadnought: English capital ship (16th c.) 126; British battleship (1906) 258
dreadnoughts 243, 258
Dresden bombed (1945) 331
dress, military 149, 151–2, 220
dressing stations 61, 284
drill: western military tradition 3, 391–2; medieval cavalry practice 66; musketry 154–5; War of American Independence 188; French revolutionary wars 194
drill books 154, 155, 183, 191, 194, 205
dromons 78–9
Dudley, Thomas (English colonial leader) 155
Dumouriez, Charles (French general, revolutionary wars) 195
Duncan, Adam (British Admiral, Napoleonic wars) 209
Dunkirk (evacuation of British Expeditionary Force, 1940) 309

Dupleix, Joseph (governor of French India, 1741–54) 179, 181
Dutch Armada (1688) 124
Dutch Revolt 115–16, 153–4
'Dynamo' (evacuation of British Expeditionary Force, 1940) 310

E
East India Company, Dutch, 131
East India Company, English 179, 181, 185, 211–12
Eastern Front: World War I 270–2, 273–6, 281, 287–8; World War II 304–7, 311–321, 327–9, 330
east Roman empire – *see* Byzantine warfare
economic power: British (Napoleonic wars) 208, 211–13; Union (American Civil War) 221; late 19th c. 242–3; World War I 272, 280, 281, 295; World War II 362; after World War II 340, 342
Edict of Emancipation (Prussia 1807) 206
Edirne – *see* Adrianople
Education of Cyrus (Xenophon) 29
Edward I of England 6, 88, 93, 100
Edward II of England 93
Edward III of England 96, 100
Eisenhower, General Dwight: (commander of Normandy invasion, 1944) 329, 330; American president (1952–60) 345, 350
El Alamein: (1942) 321; (1942) 322
electronic warfare 393
elephants 43, 44, 181
Elizabeth, empress of Russia 183
Emancipation Proclamation (USA 1862) 224
Eniwetok, battle of (1944) 335
Entente Cordiale (1904) 258
epidemics in conquest of the Americas 143–4
Eritrea invaded (1940) 312
Essai général de tactique (Jacques de Guibert, 1772) 191, 192
Essex class aircraft carriers 334
ETA (Basque separatist organization, Spain) 384, 398
Ethiopia invaded (1935) 302
ethnic cleansing 367–70, 372
Etruscan phalanx, 44
Eugene of Savoy (Austrian general, 17th c.) 163, 175, 176
Eumenes (Macedonian general) 43
Euripides (war criticism) 389
Exercise of Arms (Jacob de Gheyn, 1607) 154–5
extermination camps 331

F
F-117 bombers 363
F6F 'Hellcat' fighter aircraft 335

Falaise besieged by Henry V 96
Falkenhayn, Erich von (chief of German general staff, World War I) 270, 273, 274, 276, 278, 280, 281
Falklands War (1982) 360, 392, 397
Fall, Bernard (expert on Vietnam) 352, 354
Fayttes of Armes and of Chyvalrye (William Caxton, 1490) 105
Ferdinand, Archduke Franz, assassinated (1914) 261
feudal military obligation 88, 90, 98, 103
Fighter Command (RAF) 311
finance 8, 147, 165, 166, 180, 212, 387–8, 397, 401
firearms 99, 106, 109, 132, 152–3, 167
firepower: battle of Hastings 82; gunpowder revolution 106–17; battle of Lepanto 122; musketry 155–8; Russo-Japanese War 256; World War I 266, 276–7, 279–80, 282–3, 285–72, 290, 292; World War II 316, 327–8; Korean War 345; French in Vietnam 347; Americans in Vietnam 352, 353, 354, 355; in Gulf Wars, 361–3, 380–8
fireships (17th c. China) 120
Firespit II tank 289
First Carnatic War (1774–48) 181
Fisher, Sir John (British first sea lord, 1904–10, 1914–15) 258
Five Forks, battle of (1865) 229, 232
Flanders campaign (1917) 285
Flavius Merobaudes (Roman general) 65
Fleurus, battle of (1794) 196
FLN (*Front de Libération Nationale*) Algerian National Liberation Front 348–9
Foch, Ferdinand (Allied supreme commander, 1918) 291
foot-companions, Macedonian 34
foot soldiers – *see* infantry
foraging 166, 199, 201, 204
Forest, Jean de (17th-c. soldier) on Indian casualties in Guyana 141
Fornovo, battle of (1495) 152–3
Fort Amsterdam 145
Fort Donelson taken by Grant (1862) 224
Fort Douaumont battles (1916) 277, 278
Fort Eben Emael taken (1940) 308
Fort Fisher taken by Union forces (1865) 232
Fort Henry taken (1862) 224
Fort Vaux battles (1916) 278
fortifications 365; Greek 35; Roman 59–60; 62–3, 64–5;

medieval 74, 76, 77, 78, 80–81, 83, 86–88, 89; gunpowder 96–16; New World 137–9, 144, 145; Vauban's 168–9; World War I 267, 276–8
Francesco Laparelli (16th-c. military architect) 112
Franco, Francisco (Spanish military dictator) 303, 396
Franco-Burgundian wars 99
Franco-Prussian War (1870–71) 236–40
François Kellermann (French general, revolutionary wars) 195
Franklin, battle of (1864) 231
Franks 65, 71–5, 85, 86
Frederick I of Prussia 177
Frederick II, the Great, of Prussia 176–8, 182–3, 203
Frederick William I of Prussia 177
Frederick William of Brandenburg 177
free companies (late medieval Italy) 94
free-fire zones (Vietnam War) 353
French and Indian War (1754–63) 184
French Revolution 186, 192–7
French, Sir John (commander of the British Expeditionary Force, 1914–15) 273
Friedensturm offensive (1918) 292
frigates 129
Fritsch, Werner von (commander-in-chief of the German army, 1933) 299
Froissart, Jean (chronicler of Hundred Years War) 100 120
Frontinus on Macedonian logistics 41
Fronto on idle legionaries 58
Fulk Nerra (987–1040), count of the Angevins 80, 81
Fuller, J.F.C. (British military commentator) 300
Full-rigged ship 123

G
galeasses 122
Galicia campaign: (1914) 271; (1915) 273
galleys 102, 120–3, 173
Gallipoli campaign (1915) 274–6
Gamelin, Maurice (commander-in-chief of the French army, 1939–40) 300, 308, 309
Garner, Jay 381–2
gas warfare 2; Ethiopia (1935) 303
Gatacre, Sir William (British general, Boer War) 249
Gates, Horatio (patriot general, War of American Independence) 188–9
Gaugamela, battle of (331 BC) 40
Gaul, Caesar's campaigns (58–51 BC) 56

Gaza Strip 371

Gaza taken by Alexander (332 BC) 42

Geneva Peace Accords (1954) 348, 350

Geoffrey Greymantle, count of the Angevins 80

Geoffrey Plantagenet, count of Anjou 4, 81

German High Seas Fleet (World War I) 282–3, 294

German navy, World War II 310, 324

German unification 233–6

'Germany first' (American World War II strategy) 322

Geronimo, Apache leader (1880s) 247

Gersdorff, Hans von (Manual of Military Surgery, 1517) 148

Gettysburg, battle of (1863) 221, 227

Gheyn, Jacob de (The Exercise of Arms, 1607) 154, 155

Giap, Vo Nguyen (Viet Minh military commander) 347

gladius (Roman sword) 45, 46, 47, 55

glider-borne infantry 308

Glorious First of June, battle of (1794) 208, 210

Gneisenau, August von (Prussian officer) 242

Goethe, Johann Wolfgang von, on the battle of Valmy 195

Golan heights: taken by Israel (1967) 358; defended by Israel (1973) 360

Goldwater, Senator Barry (American presidential candidate, 1964) 352

Goose Green, battle of (1982) 360

Goths – see Visigoths

Gough, Hubert (British general, World War I) 285, 290

Gracedieu (English warship, 1418) 123

Granada taken by Castile (1492) 99, 105, 108, 110

Grand Alliance against Louis XIV 174

grand strategy: late Roman 64; Charlemagne's 74–5; Schlieffen plan (Germany) 262–4; 'Plan XVII' (France) 268; Imperial Defence Plan (Japan) 332

Grande Armée, Napoleon's 200–1

Grandson, battle of (1476) 99

Granicus, battle of (334 BC) 40–1

Grant, John, on Indian rulers' armies (1749) 179

Grant, Ulysses S. (Union general) 5, 224–6, 227–32

Gravelotte, battle of (1870) 239

Graziani, Rudolfo (Italian general, World War II) 311

Great Company of Montréal d'Albarno 94

Great Harry (English warship, 1512) 124

Great Michael (Scottish warship, 1511) 124

Great Northern War (1700–21) 163, 172–3

Greece: hoplite warfare 14–20, 31–2, 32–3; Persian wars 20–26; Peloponnesian War 27–8; Macedonian warfare 34–44; attacked by Italy (1940) 311; invaded by Germany (1941) 313

Greek fire 73, 78–9

Greene, Nathanael (patriot general, War of American Independence) 189, 190–1

Grenada invaded (1983) 361

Gribeauval, Jean Vacquette de (French artillery system reformer, 1770s) 192

Grivas, George (Cypriot guerrilla leader) 396

Grozny – see Chechen Wars

Guadalcanal, battle of (1942) 334

Guantánamo 383

Guderian, Heinz (German general, World War II) 308, 309, 316, 317, 318

Guernica bombed (1937) 303

guerrilla warfare: Robert the Bruce (14th c.) 92; War of American Independence 190; Spain (Napoleonic wars) 204; American Civil War 222; Franco-Prussian war 240; South Africa (Boer War) 250; Yugoslavia (World War II) 313; Vietnam (1945–73) 347, 351; Malaya (1948–54) 349–50; Cyprus (1950s) 369; Algeria (1954–62) 348–9; Aghanistan (1980s) 370; Iraq 383–8

Guibert, Jacques de (Essai général de tactique, 1772) 191, 192

Gulf of Tonkin Resolution (1964) 353

Gulf War (1991) 342, 362, 365, 368, 372

Gulf War (2003–) 378–88

Gumbinnen, battle of (1914) 271

gunports 124, 126

gunpowder weapons 2, 96–7, 106–17, 120–1, 148, 367

Guns of August (Barbara Tuchman) 402

Guntram of Burgundy 69

Gustavus Adolphus of Sweden 115, 155, 156, 157, 158, 159, 163

H

Habsburg hegemony 117

Hadrian (Roman emperor) 58

Hadrian's wall 59, 74

Haider Ali (ruler of Mysore, 1759–82) 211, 212

Haig, Sir Douglas (commander, British Expeditionary Force, 1916–18) 278, 279, 285–7, 289–94

halberds 93

Halder, Franz (German general World War II) 307, 316, 317, 319

Halicarnassus taken by Alexander (334 BC) 42

Halleck, Henry (Union general) 226

Hamas 371

Hamburg bombed (1943) 325

Hamilton, Alexander (17th-c. Scottish mercenary) 149

Hamilton, Sir Ian (British general leading Gallipoli expedition) 256, 275, 276

Hampden, John, on taxes and war (1692) 401

Hancock, Winfield Scott (Union general, American Civil War) 220

Hannibal (Carthaginian general) 4, 48–9, 105

Hans Staden (True History and Description of a Journey to America, 1557) 125

Harfleur in the Hundred Years War 96, 102, 103, 107

Harkins, Paul (American general, Vietnam War) 351

Harlech castle 6

Harold II of England 80, 82–3

Harper's Ferry, battle of (1862) 223

Harrier jet fighter aircraft 361

Harris, Arthur (commander-in-chief of Bomber Command, RAF, 1942–45) 301, 325

Harvard Crimson on drafting students 353

hasta (Roman lance) 54

hastati (Roman legion first line) 46, 53

Hastings, battle of (1066) 80, 82–3, 84

Hawkwood, Sir John (14-c. free-company commander in Italy) 94

'hedgehogs' (German fortified areas on the Eastern Front, World War II) 320

Hedingham castle 83

Heinmot Tooyalaket (Chief Joseph of the Nez Percé) 246

helicopters: Algerian War 349; Vietnam War 350

'Hellcat' fighter aircraft 335

Henry II of England 81

Henry IV of England 98

Henry V of England 95–6, 99–101, 123

Henry VIII of England 124, 126

Henry the Fowler, king of Germany 78, 86

hetairoi (aristocratic Macedonian cavalry) 34

Hezbollah 371–2

Hindenburg plan 295

Hindenburg, Paul von (German general and statesman) 271, 273, 274, 280, 283, 294, 295

Hipper, Franz von (German admiral, World War I) 282

Hiroshima bombed (1945) 339, 340

History of the Peloponnesian War (Thucydides) 4, 27–8

Hitler, Adolf: World War I soldier 270; chancellor of Germany 298, 302; rearmament 299; Czechoslovakian crisis 304; Western Front (1940) 305, 309; Eastern Front 314, 315, 317, 327, 328; Western Front (1944) 329, 330; suicide 332; 401

Hitlerjügend Waffen SS division 329

Hittite warfare 12

Ho Chi Minh (Vietnamese revolutionary) 346, 347, 350, 351, 352

Ho Chi Minh Trail 350

Hoffman, Max von (German general staff officer) 256, 271

Hohenlinden, battle of (1800) 197

Homer 389

Honorius (Roman emperor) 67

Hood, John Bell (Confederate general) 230

Hooker, Joseph (Union general) 226

Hope, James (military engineer and American Civil War artist) 223

hoplite warfare 14–20, 25, 30–1, 32–3, 36, 38

Hopton, Sir Ralph (royalist commander, English Civil War) 152

hornworks 113

horses in warfare: On Horsemanship, Xenophon) 29; horse transports, Norman 79, 82; horse artillery (French revolutionary wars) 195; see also cavalry; chivalry

Howe, Sir William (British general, War of American Independence) 187, 188, 189, 208, 210

Huaitará, battle of (1536) 137

Hundred Days, Napoleon's (1815) 208

Hundred Years War (1337–1453) 94, 100, 102, 104, 107, 120

Hung Wu (first Ming emperor of China) 120

Huns 64

Hurons 140

Hussein, Saddam – see Saddam Hussein

Hussites 97, 100

Hutu killers 365–6, 395

Hydaspes, battle of (326 BC) 40

hypaspists ('shield bearers' – Macedonian light infantry) 34, 41

Hysiae, battle of (669 BC) 29

I

ICTY (International Criminal Tribunal for the Former Yugoslavia) 369–70
Imperial Defence Plan (Japan) 332
Imphal, battle of (1944) 337
impis (Zulu formations) 245
Incas 136–9, 140, 143
incendiaries, medieval 73, 78–9
Inchon landing (1950) 344
Indefatigable (British battlecruiser, World War I) 282
indentures (late-medieval military contracts) 103
Independence-class light aircraft carriers 334, 335
India, Europeans in 130, 179, 181
India (nuclear power) 379
Indian resistance in conquest of the Americas 134–44, 181–2
Indian wars (American west) 246–7
Indo-China: colonized by French 346; occupied by Japanese (1940–41) 333; after World War II 346–8, 350–5
Indonesia occupied by Japan (1942) 333
industrial power: 19th c. 212, 221, 234, 242; World War I 272, 281, 294, 295; World War II 321, 332, 365–6; Cold War 340–2
infantry: bronze-age 12–13; Greek phalanx 10–11, 14–20, 30–1, 33–4; Macedonian phalanx 34–7, 43–4; Roman legion 44–9, 51–5, 58–9, 60–1; medieval primacy 84–7, 91, 93–4, 99–100; lines and columns 152, 154–7, 166, 190–1, 194, 198; *see also*: marines; trench warfare
infrastructure: Macedonian 41; Roman 50, 60–1, 64; southern, destroyed by Union troops (American Civil War) 232
Inkerman, battle of (1854) 220
innovation in western warfare 2, 6–7, 393–5
insignia 55, 66, 150–2
inspection of troops, late medieval 104
intelligence: Byzantine 79; Boer 250; battle of Jutland (1916) 282–3; 'Ultra' (World War II) 311, 313, 318, 330; 'Magic' (World War II) 334, 336; Luftwaffe's in battle of Britain 310; British in Crete (1941) 313; battle of the Altantic (World War II) 324; CIA in Vietnam 356; satellite 400
internment (Boer War) 251
Intifada 371
Iphicrates (Athenian general) 37
Ipsus, battle of (301 BC) 43
Iran–Iraq War (1979–88) 362, 397

Iraq war 362–5, 372–3, 377–88; *see also* Saddam Hussein
Irish Republican Army (UK) 372, 377, 398
iron weapons in conquest of the Americas 132, 133, 140–2
Iroquois 140, 141
Is War Impossible? (Ivan Bloch, 1899) 262
Isandhlwana, battle of (1879) 245
Isocrates' criticism of commanders 34
Israel 357–8, 359, 371–2
Issus, battle of (333 BC) 40
Italian Somaliland invaded (1940) 312
Italian-style defence 112
Iwo Jima landing (1945) 337, 338

J

Jackson, Thomas 'Stonewall' (Confederate general) 223
James II of England 163
James II of Scotland 109
James peninsula expedition (1862) 222
Jankow, battle of (1645) 156, 158
javelins 45, 55, 134
Jellicoe, Sir John (British admiral, World War I) 282
Jena-Auerstadt, battle of (1806) 199, 205
Jericho 13, 390
Jerusalem taken (1099) 84
Jervis, John (British Admiral, Napoleonic wars) 209, 210
Joffre, Joseph (French general, World War I) 268, 269, 284, 294
John III of Poland (Jan Sobieski) 170
John of Austria, Don – *see* Don John of Austria
John of Nassau-Siegen 155
Johnson, Lyndon (American president, 1963–69) 351, 352, 353, 354
Johnston, Albert Sydney (Confederate general) 224
Joseph (Heinmot Tooyalaket, chief of the Nez Percé) 246
Josephus on Roman military preparedness 59
Jourdan law (France, 1798) 198
jousts 84, 104
Julian (Roman emperor) 65
Julianus (Roman general) 57
junks, Chinese military (17th c.) 120
Justinian (east Roman emperor) 70–1
Jutland, battle of (1916) 120, 282–3, 399

K

Kalkhin Gol, battle of (1939) 332
kamikaze attacks (World War II) 335, 337
Karbala 385

Karremans, Ton 367–8
Kashmir dispute (2002) 397
Kasserine Pass, battle of (1942) 323
Kellermann, François (French general, revolutionary wars) 194–5
Kemal, Mustafa (Turkish officer, World War I) 275
Kennedy, John F (American president, 1961–63) 350–2, 379–80, 402
Kharkov battles (1942–3) 320, 321, 328
Kharzai, Hamid (Afghan president) 376
Khe Sanh besieged (1968) 354
Kiggell, Launcelot (British general, World War I) 286
Kim Il-Sung (North Korean dictator) 342, 343
Kimberley: besieged (1899) 249; relieved (1900) 250
King George's War (1743–48) 181
King Philip's War (1675–76) 142
King William's War (1689–97) 130, 174
Kitchener, Horatio (British general): Sudanese campaign 244; Boer War 250
KLA – *see* Kosovo Liberation Army
Kluck, Alexander von (German general, World War I) 268, 269
knights 88, 90, 93, 94, 95, 152–3
Königgrätz, battle of (1866) 235
Korea: seized by Japan (1905) 253; occupied by Soviet and US forces (1945) 342; (2006) 388
Korean War (1950–53) 341–2
Kosovo 365–6, 370, 372
Kosovo Liberation Army (KLA) 370
Kriegsakademie (Prussian war college) 233
Kriegsmarine – *see* German navy, World War II
Krupp armaments 242
Kuropatkin, Alexei (Russian general, Russo-Japanese War) 254, 255
Kursk, battle of (1943) 327
Kutusov, Mikhail (Russian general, Napoleonic wars) 200, 204, 205
Kuwait 362–4; *see also* Saddam Hussein
Kwajalein, battle of (1944) 335
Kyeser, Conrad, of Eichstätt (*Bellisfortis*) 110
Kyushu (1945 landing plan) 338

L

Laden, Osama Bin 374–7
Ladysmith: besieged (1899) 249; relieved (1900) 250
Laffargue, Captain André (French tactician, World War I) 278, 284
Lamentations of Germany (1638) 161

lances 54, 66, 67, 84, 143
Lanrezac, Charles (French general, 1914) 268
Laos invaded by Vietnam (1978) 356
La Rochelle, battle of (1372) 102
latifundia (Roman agricultural estates) 51
Laudonnière, René, on Timucua Indians 134
Lawrence, Stringer (East India Company soldier) 179
laws of war 4, 22, 160–3
League of Augsburg, War of (1688–97) 174
Le Jouvencel (Jean de Bueil, 1466) 103
Le munitionnaire des armées de France (François Nodot, 1697) 165
Le Tellier, Michel (Louis XIV's secretary of state for war) 164
Leavenworth staff college 243
Lebanese Civil War 365, 371–2, 398
Le Baker, Geoffrey, on the battle of Sluys (1340) 100–1
Lechfeld, battle of the (955) 85
Lee, Robert E. (Confederate general) 5, 223, 224, 226, 227, 229, 230, 232
legions, Roman 44–9, 50–61
Leipzig, battle of (1813) 207
Lenin, Vladimir Ilyich (Russian revolutionary) 287, 288
Leningrad besieged (1941–44) 317, 328
Leo of Tripoli (Muslim admiral) 79
Leon Battista Alberti (*On the Art of Building*) 110
Leopold of Austria 94
Lepanto, battle of (1571) 122, 376, 399
Les Faits d'Armes et de Chevalerie (Christine de Pisan) 105
lettres de retenue (late medieval military contracts) 103
Leuctra, battle of (371 BC) 28
Leuthen, battle of (1757) 182–3
levées en masse: French Revolution 193; Franco-Prussian War 240
Lexington, battle of (1765) 187
Lexington (American aircraft carrier) 302
Leyte Gulf, battle of (1944) 336
Liaoyang, battle of (1904) 254
Libya invaded (1940) 312
Liddell Hart, B. H. (British military commentator) 300
Liège taken by Germans (1914) 268
Light Brigade, charge of (1854) 220
Lincoln, Abraham (American president, 1861–65) 221, 222, 224, 226, 228, 229, 231, 232
Lindisfarne stone 76
line ahead naval formation 120, 125, 127–9, 130, 209

line formations for infantry 152, 154, 155, 156, 167, 177, 194

Little Rock (Liberty ship launched 1944) 366

Livy: on the Macedonian phalanx 36, 45; on Cannae 49

Lloyd George, David (British prime minister, 1916–22) 283, 287, 294

Loches castle 80

Locke, John, on excesses of war 162

logistics 365; Macedonian 41–2, 44; Charlemagne's canal project 74; battle of Hastings 82; Louis XIV's 165, 166, 168; Napoleon's 199, 200, 201; Schlieffen plan 264, 267, 269; Eastern Front (1941) 314, 317, 318, 319; Normandy landing (1944) 331

Lombard kingdom 68, 71

London: bombed in World War II 311; target of V-weapons (1944–45) 327

Londoño, Don Sancho de (Spanish soldier, Dutch Revolt) 153

longbows 92–3, 106

Longstreet, James (Confederate general) 223

Loos, battle of (1915) 273

Lothair I, emperor of the West 4, 72

Lothair II, emperor of the West 66

Louis XI of France 105

Louis XIV of France 114, 124, 128, 163–9, 171, 174–6, 180

Louis XV of France 184

Louis XVI of France 192

Louis the German 72

Louis the Pious 72

Louisbourg taken: (1745) 181; (1758) 184

Louvain bombarded (1914) 268

Louvois, François Le Tellier, Marquis de (Louis XIV's war minister) 164–5, 169

Lucullus (Roman general) 56

Ludendorff, Erich von (German general and strategist): army spending (1912) 260; war plans (1913) 264; World War I 268, 271, 273, 274, 280, 283, 284, 287, 288–9, 291–2, 293, 294, 295

Ludendorff bridge taken (1945) 332

Luftwaffe (German air force): 1930s 301, 303; Dunkirk evacuation 309; battle of Britain (1940) 310–11; Belgrade bombing (1941) 313; invasion of Crete (1941) 313; North Africa 322; air defence 326

Lusitania sunk (1915) 283

Lutzen, battle of (1632) 158, 159

Lysimachus (Macedonian general) 43

Lysistrata (Aristophanes) 389

M

MacArthur, General Douglas: American commander in the Pacific (World War II) 334, 336; commander-in-chief of United Nations forces in Korea 341, 343, 345

Macedonian warfare 34–44, 367

Machiavelli, Niccolò: on artillery 110; on towns as artillery fortresses 112

Mackensen, August von (German general World War I) 273, 274

MacMahon, Patrice Maurice (French marshal, Franco Prussian War) 238

MACV (Military Assistance Command Vietnam) 352, 355

Madrid, bomb explosions in (2004) 384

Mafeking besieged (1899) 249

Magdeburg sacked (1631) 161

Magersfontein battles (1899–1900) 249, 250

'Magic' intelligence (World War II) 334, 336

Maginot line 298, 307, 308

Mago (Carthaginian general) 48

Magyars 85, 86

Mahan, Alfred Thayer (naval power theorist) 257

the Mahdi, (Mohammed Ahmed, Sudanese fundamentalist ruler, 1883–85) 244

Malakoff stormed by French (1855) 220

Malaya: taken by Japan (1941–42) 333; communist insurgency (1948–54) 349–50

Malplaquet, battle of (1709) 176

Malta, battle of (1565) 122

Malvern Hill, battle of (1862) 223

Manchuria: taken by Japan (1931) 332; occupied by Soviet Union (1945) 339

Manco (Inca leader) 138, 140

Manhattan defences (17th c.) 145

Manhattan Project 6

maniples (Roman legion) 45, 47, 52, 53

manoeuvres sur les derrières 199, 201

Manstein, Erich von (German general, World War II) 307, 316, 320, 321, 327

Mantineia, battle of (362 BC) 28, 32, 33, 391

manuals of warfare 4, 5, 29, 64, 66, 73, 87, 102, 104, 110, 154, 183, 194, 155

Mao Tse-tung (Chinese revolutionary) 190, 347

Mappae Clavicula (8th-c. technical treatise) 73

Mapuche Indians 141

Maratha War, second (1803–05) 212

Marathon, battle of (480 BC) 21, 22

Mardonius (Persian general) 22–3

Marengo, battle of (1800) 197

Maria Theresa, empress of Austria 178, 182

Marianas air battle (1944) 336

Marignano, battle of (1515) 153

marines: Greek 42; Byzantine 79; United States 337, 338, 344, 354

Marius, Gaius (Roman general) 52–4

'Marius's mules' 54, 61

'Market Garden' (Montgomery's advance on Arnhem, 1944) 330

Marlborough, John Churchill, duke of (British general) 174–6

Marne, battle of (1914) 269

Marne counter-offensive (1918) 293

Marne offensive (1918) 292

Marshall, General George C., on Thucydides 4

Marshall Plan 341

Mars-la-Tour, battle of (1870) 239

Marston Moor, battle of (1644) 152

Mary Rose (16th-c. English warship) 126

Masséna, André (French marshal, Napoleonic wars) 200

Massu, Jacques (French paratroop general, Algerian War) 349

Maurice of Nassau (Dutch leader) 4, 154–6, 158, 393–4, 402

McClellan, George (Union general) 222

McNamara, Robert Strange (American secretary of defence, Vietnam War) 351, 352, 353, 356, 380

Meade, George (Union general) 227

Mechelen: defences (1360s) 110; hospital for Spanish soldiers 149

medicine, military: 16th c. 148; 20th c. 280, 284, 296–7

medieval warfare 66–110

mêlée naval tactics 209–11

men-at-arms 93, 99

mercantilism 176

mercenaries 16, 27, 30, 34, 40, 41, 43, 44, 68, 82, 94, 98, 103, 147, 149, 172, 173

merchant shipping: World War I 283; Allied (World War II) 324, 325, 365; Japanese (World War II) 336

Messines ridge, battle of (1917) 285

Metellus (Roman general) 56

Methuen, Paul (British general, Boer War) 249

Metz: besieged (1552) 113, 117; French encircled (1870) 240

Meuse-Argonne, battle of (1918) 294

Mexico – see Tenochtitlán

'Michael' offensive (1918) 290–1

Middle Service Class cavalry (17th-c. Russia) 172

Midway, battle of (1942) 334

Milamete, Walter de (*De Nobilitatibus, sapientiis et prudentiis regum*, 1326–27) 107

Milanese military organization 88, 105

military academies – see war colleges

Military Assistance Command Vietnam (MACV) 352, 355

militias: Greek 32; Roman 68, 70; medieval 69, 80, 82, 94; War of American Independence 187, 191; French Revolution 193; Prussian 207; Confederate 221; Boer 249; Iraqi 385–7

Milosevic, Slobodan (Serb leader) 367–70, 372, 373

minié bullets 218

Mithridates 50, 55, 56

Mladic, Ratko 367–8

Mnesimachus (*Philip*, c.350 BC) 38

Mohacs, battle of (1687) 171

Mohawks 132

Moltke, Helmuth, Count von (chief of the Prussian, then German, general staff, 1858–88) 4, 233, 235, 236, 238, 239, 240, 262

Moltke, Helmuth, the younger (chief of the German general staff, 1906–14) 261, 264, 265, 268, 271

Monluc, Blaise de, on siegecraft 146

Monro, Robert (17th-c. Scottish colonel): on distance marched 151; *Monro His Expedition with the Worthy Scots Regiment Called Mackays*, London (1637) 160

Mons, battle of (1914) 268

Mons-en-Pévèle, battle of (1304) 93

Mons Meg (15th-c. bombard) 108, 109

Montcalm, Marquis Louis Joseph de (18th-c. French general) 184

Montezuma (Aztec emperor) 133, 134

Montgomery, Viscount Bernard Law: British Eighth Army commander, North Africa 322; Normandy ground-forces commander (1944) 329, 330, 332

Montréal d'Albarno (leader of the 'Great Company' in 14th-c. Italy) 94

Morant, 'Breaker' (Boer war soldier) 250

Morat, battle of (1476) 99
Moreau, Jean (French general, Revolutionary wars) 197
Morgan, Daniel (patriot general, War of American Independence) 189, 190, 191
Morgarten, battle of (1315) 94
Moscow, battle of (1941) 317, 318–19
Mueller, John (political scientist) 400
Mühlberg, battle of (1547) 153
Mukden, battle of (1905) 255
Munda, battle of (45 BC) 56
Mundy, Peter (English traveller, 17th-c. China) 120
Munro, Hector (East India Company soldier) 185
Mursa, battle of (AD 351) 66
musketry 2, 144, 147, 152, 154, 155, 156, 157–8, 166–7, 179
Mussolini, Benito (Italian dictator) 298, 304, 311, 323
mustard gas: World War I 2; Ethiopia (1935) 303
muster and review (Hundred Years War) 104
mutinies: Spanish (1573) 154; British (1797) 209; French (1917) 284
My Lai massacre (1967) 352
Mysore War, third (1789–92) 212

N
Nagasaki bombed (1945) 339
Naher defences 64
Namur besieged (1692) 167
Nancy, battle of (1477) 99
Naples, citizen army 105
Napoleon Bonaparte 182, 186, 195–205, 207–8, 213
Napoleon III, emperor of France 4, 237, 240
Narses (Byzantine general) 70
Narva besieged (1700) 172
Narvik, battle of (1940) 306
Nasser, Gamal Abdel (Egyptian president, 1954–70) 357
National Guard (French Revolution) 193
nationalism: Algerian 348; French 186, 193, 205; German 234; Hungarian 216–7; Malay 350; Serbian 260, 261; Vietnamese 346
NATO (North Atlantic Treaty Organization) 341, 370, 377–8
Naupactus, battle of (Peloponnesian War) 399
naval air forces: 1930s 302; World War II 325, 336
naval warfare 371–2; Greek 23, 24–5, 42; Roman 55; Byzantine 78–9; medieval 100–103; armed with gunpowder weapons 120–131; Peter the Great 173; Napoleonic wars

197, 208–11; American Civil War 224, 230; Russo-Japanese War 253, 256; dreadnought arms race 257–8; World War I 282–3; World War II 302, 324–5, 334, 335, 336–7; Falklands War 360, 361
needlegun 234, 235, 237
Neerwinden, battle of (1693) 175
Nelson, Horatio (British admiral, Napoleonic wars) 197, 208–11
Nemea, battle of (394 BC) 28
New Amsterdam defences 145
'new formation regiments' (Russia, 17th century) 172
New Guinea campaign (World War II) 334
New World conquests 132–45
New York taken by Howe (1776) 187
Nez Percé resistance (1870s) 246
Nieuwpoort, battle of (1600) 155, 156, 394
Nijmegen, treaty of (1678) 168–9
Nile, battle of the (1798) 197, 209
9/11 attacks 374–6, 399; see also al-Qaeda; Laden, Osama Bin
Nimitz, Admiral Chester (American naval commander in the Pacific, World War II) 334, 335, 336
Nivelle, Robert (French general, World War I) 278, 284
Nivelle offensive (1917) 284
Nixon, Richard M. (American president, 1968–75) 355, 356
Nodot, François (*Le munitionnaire des armées de France* 1697) 165
Normans 79, 82–3, 86
Normandy invasion (1944) 329–30
North African campaign (1942–43) 323
North Atlantic Treaty Organization – see NATO
Northern Ireland 372, 377, 398
Northern Virginia, Army of (American Civil War) 226
Nördlingen, battle of (1634) 115, 158
nuclear weapons 6, 340, 341, 342, 345, 397
Nuremberg bombed (1944) 325

O
OAS (Organisation de l'Armée Secrète) 349
obsidian weapons 135
Octavian – see Augustus Caesar
Oeconomicus (Xenophon) 15, 29
offensive doctrine, German (World War I) 287, 288, 290
officers: Roman 47, 61; English naval (17th c.) 130; French (17th c.) 165; Russian (17th c.) 172; Prussian (18th c.) 178, 206; French (18th c.) 192; French revolutionary, 193–4;

208; American Civil War 220, 221, 229; Prussian (19th c.) 233; German 242–3, 259; British 243, 252, 300; Soviet 315
oil: German shortages (World War II) 305, 320; Japanese shortages (World War II) 333; Organization of Petroleum Exporting Countries (OPEC) 361
Oinophyta, battle of (457 BC) 26
Okinawa landings (1945) 337, 338
Oliveira, Fernando (*The Art of War at Sea*, 1555) 125
Ollantaytambo besieged 137, 138
Olympias, reconstructed trireme 24–5
'Olympic' (invasion plan for Japan, 1945) 338
Omaha beach (Normandy landings, 1944) 329
Omdurman, battle of (1896) 244
On the Art of Building (Leon Battista Alberti, 1440s) 110
On War (Carl von Clausewitz) 5, 115, 169, 257, 262, 361
onagers, 73
Onasander, on Macedonian phalanx 37
Operation Desert Storm 362–5
Operation Iraqi Freedom 380–8
ordre mince 191
ordre mixte 191, 198
ordre profond 190
Organization of Petroleum Exporting Countries (OPEC) 361
Ostrogoths 65, 69, 70
Otto I, the Great, emperor of the West 85
Otto II, emperor of the West 84

P
P-51 'Mustang' 326
Paardeberg, battle of (1900) 250
Pacific war (World War II) 332–9
Packer, George 381
Pactus Drepanius on Theodosius 68
Pakistan (nuclear power) 397
panzer divisions developed (1930s) 299–300
paratroops: Western Front (1940) 308; Crete (1941) 313; Dien Bien Phu 346, 347; Suez crisis 357; Falklands War 360
Parcos, battle of (1536) 137
Paré, Ambroise (16th-c. military doctor) 149
Paris, treaty of (1783) 190
Paris besieged (1870) 240
Paris Peace Accords (1973) 356
Parker, Captain Robert, on Louis XIV 175
Passchendaele, battle of (1917) 286
Paullu (Inca leader) 140
Paulus, Friedrich (German general, World War II) 321

Pavia: taken by Charlemagne (774) 72; battle of (1525) 152, 153
Pearl Harbor bombed (1941) 332, 333
Peloponnesian War (431–404 BC) 18, 19, 25, 26, 27–8, 392
Peninsular War (1807–14) 211
Peñón de Vélez, battle of (1564) 123
Pepin I (Carolingian king) 71, 72
Pequot War (1638–39) 141
Perdiccas (Macedonian general) 43
Persian Gulf – see Gulf Wars
Persian wars (490, 480–478 BC) 20–6
personal armed followings, medieval 68, 69, 72, 77, 80
Pertinax (Roman emperor) 57
Perugia arsenal (1364) 109
Pétain, Philippe (French general World War I) 277, 285, 291, 293, 310
Peter I, the Great, of Russia 172–3
Peter III of Russia 183
Petersburg, battle of (1865) 225, 232
Petraeus, David 386–7
Petrarch on English raiding in France 95
Pett, Phineas (naval architect to Charles I of England) 127
pezetairoi ('foot companions', Macedonian heavy infantry) 34
phalanx warfare 10–11, 14–20, 30–1, 34–9, 40–1, 44, 85, 156
Pharnaces defeated by Caesar (47 BC) 56
Pharsalia, battle of (48 BC) 56
Philadelphia, battle of (1777) 188
Philip II of Macedon 34, 37–40
Philip II of Spain 115–16, 121, 126, 147, 154, 160, 161, 162
Philip IV (the Fair) of France 88, 100
Philip VI of France 100
Philip of Anjou 175
Philip the Bold, duke of Burgundy 105
Philip the Good, duke of Burgundy 99
Philippines: taken by Japan (1941) 333; invaded by Americans (1944) 336
Phocylides on the city-state 14
Pickens, Andrew (patriot general, War of American Independence) 189
Pickett, George (Confederate general) 227
pikes: Macedonian 17, 36, 37, 41, 43; medieval 66, 93, 97, 99, 109; 16th c. 146, 152, 154; 17th c. 156–7, 166
pilum (Roman javelin) 45, 46; improved by Marius 55
Pizarro brothers (conquistadors) 137, 140, 141
Plains of Abraham, battle of (1758) 184–5

Plan XVII (French World War I plan) 268
Plassey, battle of (1757) 185
Plataea, battle of (479 BC) 23, 25, 399
Plate armour 92, 93, 98–9
Plato on Salamis 25
Plevna besieged (1877) 247
Plumer, Sir Herbert (British general, World War I) 285, 286, 291
Poitiers, battle of (1356) 94, 95
Polaris submarines 342
Poltava besieged (1709) 173
Polyaenus on Macedonian logistics 42
Polybius: on hoplites 20; on the Macedonian phalanx 37, 44; on the Roman *gladius* 45
Pompey (Roman general) 56, 57, 105
Pondichery: besieged (1746) 181; surrendered (1760) 185
Pope, John (Union general) 223
Port Arthur besieged (1904) 252, 254
Portuguese naval warfare (15th–16th centuries) 123, 125, 127, 130–1
Potomac, Army of (American Civil War) 222
'pressed' men in the English navy 130
Prevesa, battle of (1538) 122
Prince of Wales sunk (1941) 333
Prince Royal (British warship, 1610) 126
Princeton, battle of (1777) 186, 187
principes (second line in Roman legion) 46, 53
prisoners of war: Russian (1914) 273; German (1918) 293; Soviet (World War II) 317; Canadian (1944) 329
Probus (Roman emperor) 50
professionalization: Roman legion 50, 52–5; medieval 103–4; 17th c. 146–52; 18th c. 178, 192, 194; 19th c. 206, 233, 242
Ptolemy (Macedonian general, ruler of Egypt) 43
Ptolemy IV of Egypt 42
Punic wars 50; *see also* Cannae
Pusan enveloped (1950) 343–4
Pydna, battle of (168 BC) 43
Pyramids, battle of the (1798) 197
Pyrrhus, king of the Epirus 44

Q
Quebec taken by Wolfe (1758) 184–5
Queen Anne's War – *see* War of the Spanish Succession
Queen Mary (British ship, World War I) 282
quinqueremes 42

R
Rabanus Maurus (epitome of Vegetius's *Concerning Military Matters*) 66
radar early warning systems 301, 310, 363
RAF – *see* Royal Air Force
railways: American Civil War 224; Prussia 216, 233; Sudan (1896) 244; Trans-Siberian 253
rams 5, 24, 73, 121
Ramillies, battle of (1706) 176
Rangoon captured (1945) 336
ravelins 171
Rawlinson, Sir Henry (British general, World War I) 279, 280, 285
Razdelnaya Station, battle of (1944) 328
Raznjatovic, Zeljko ('Arkan') 395
Reagan, Ronald (American president, 1981–89) 361, 365
rearmament, German (1933) 302, 303
recruitment: Roman legions 52–3, 58, 60, 65–8; medieval 69, 76–7, 80, 82, 89, 99, 103; *see also* conscription; *levées en masse*
Red River Valley campaign (1951) 346–7, 350
Redoutable (British ship at Trafalgar) 211
Regensburg bombed (1944) 326
Regino of Prüm on untrained levies 84
Reichswehr (German army in the 1920s) 299
Reinsurance Treaty (1887) 257
religious wars 160–3
Remagen bridge taken (1945) 332
Rennenkampf, Paul (Russian general, World War I) 270, 271
reparation payments, German 298
Representatives on Mission (French Revolution) 193, 194
Repulse sunk (1941) 333
Requeséns, Don Luis de (16th-c. Spanish general) 115
reserve system, Prussian 237
'Reunions' (Louis XIV's 1681 and 1684 acquisitions) 169, 174
Revolution in Military Affairs (RMA) 393–5
Rhee, Syngman (South Korean leader) 342
Rheims: in Hundred Years War 96; German offensive (1918) 292
Rhodes taken by Turks (1522) 123
Riade, battle of (933) 86
Richelieu, Cardinal, on provisions 159
Ridgway, Matthew B. (American general, Korean War) 344
rifled muskets 218, 219, 220, 225
Rimpler, George (17th-c. engineer) 170

RMA – *see* Revolution in Military Affairs
Robert Bruce (Robert I of Scotland) 92, 93, 391
Rochambeau, Jean-Baptiste (French commander, War of American Independence) 189
Rodríguez Zapatero, José Luis 384
'Rolling Thunder' (American bombing campaign against Vietnam, 1965) 352
Roman warfare 44–68
Romano-German armies 68–70
Rome sacked (AD 455) 112
Rommel, Erwin: German officer, World War I 288; panzer commander (1940) 308; Afrika Korps commander 312, 321, 323; Inspector of Coastal Defences (1943) 329
Roosebeek, battle of (1382) 93
Roosevelt, Franklin: Assistant Secretary of the US Navy (World War I) 293; American president (World War II) 310, 322, 333, 334, 340
Rorke's Drift, battle of (1879) 245
Rosecrans, William Starke (Union general) 228
Rossbach, battle of (1757) 182–3
Rotterdam bombed (1940) 308
Rouen besieged (1415) 96, 103
rowers 26, 30, 42, 78
Royal Air Force: battle of Britain (1940) 310–11; Crete (1941) 313; Falklands War (1982) 361; Gulf war (1991) 363; *see also* Bomber Command
Royal Navy: early modern 124, 125–6, 127–30; 18th c. 179, 180, 208; staff college (1911) 243; World War I 282; 1930s 302; World War II 324
Royal Oak (British ship, World War I) 283
Ruhr: occupied by France (1923) 298; bombed (1943) 325
Rumsfeld, Donald H. 380–6, 402
Rundstedt, Gerd von (German general, World War II) 305, 329
Rupert of the Rhine 151
Rupprecht of Bavaria 268, 289
Russo-Japanese non-aggression pact (1941) 333, 339
Russo-Japanese War (1904–05) 252, 255
Rwanda 365–6, 395

S
Sacred Band (Thebes) 38, 39
Sacsahuaman besieged (1536) 137
Sadat, Anwar (Egyptian president, 1970–81) 358
Saddam Hussein 364–5, 372, 377–82

sails 78, 123, 127, 129
Saint-Mihiel offensive (1918) 293
Saipan, battle of (1944) 336
Salamis, battle of (480 BC) 23, 25
Salerno, battle of (1943) 323
Samarra 386
Samsonov, Alexander (Russian general, World War I) 270, 271
San Lorenzo (Spanish Armada galeass) 121
San Martín (Spanish Armada galleon) 125
San Stefano, treaty of (1878) 247
Sarajevo 367–9
Saratoga (American aircraft carrier) 302
Saratoga, battle of (1777) 188
Sargon II of Assyria 12, 13
Sarmatians 68
Sassoon, Siegfried (World War I poet) 296, 389
satellites 400
Savannah taken by British (1778) 189
Savo Island, battle of (1942) 334
Saxe, Maurice de, on good officers 192
Saxe-Weimar, Bernard of (17th c. mercenary entrepreneur) 149
Scharnhorst, Gerhard von (Prussian army reformer) 205, 206, 242
Scheer, Reinhard (German admiral, World War I) 282
Schilling, Diebold, of Bern (*Chronicle*, 1483) 110
Schleswig-Holstein seized by Prussia and Austria (1864) 234
Schlieffen, count Alfred von (German strategist) 4, 262, 270, 402
Schlieffen plan 259, 262–3, 267–9, 308
Schola Militaris (Siegen, Germany, 1616) 155
Schweinfurt bombed (1944) 326
Scipio (Roman general) 49
Scottish navy 124
scutum (Roman shield) 45, 47
'Sealion' (German plan to invade Britain, 1940) 310
search-and-destroy missions (Vietnam War) 352
Sebastopol besieged (1854–05) 217, 219
Second Carnatic War (1749–54) 181
Second Maratha War (1803–05) 212
Sedan, battle of (1870) 239
Seeckt, Hans von (German commander-in-chief 1920s) 298, 299
Ségur law (France, 1781) 192
Seleucus (Macedonian general) 43
Seoul: taken by Japan (1904) 253; in Korean War (1950–51) 344
sepoys 179, 181, 185, 211

Serbia 260–1, 264, 274, 367–70
Sertorius (Roman general) 55
Seven Years War (1756–63) 182–5
Severus Alexander (Roman emperor) 53, 65
Sha-Ho, battle of (1904) 254
Shaka (Zulu leader) 245
Sheridan, Philip (Union general) 231, 246
Sherman, William T. (Union general) 230–1
Shigemitsu, Mamoru (Japanese foreign minister, 1945) 340
Shiloh, battle of (1862) 224
Shinseki, Eric 380–1, 402
short-war scenario 256, 262, 263, 264
Shrewsbury, battle of (1403) 98
Sicily invaded (1943) 323
Sidi Barrani, battle of (1940) 312
siege warfare 365; Greek 20, 27–8, 29, 34; Macedonian 42, 43; medieval 66, 73, 76, 84, 87–8, 89, 96–7, 106–16; 16th c. 146, 147, 154; 17th c. 151, 160–1, 167, 168–9
Siegfried Line breached (1918) 293
Siete Partidas (Alfonso X of Castile) 105
Sigismund (Holy Roman emperor) 100
Singapore taken by Japan (1942) 333
Sioux resistance (1870s) 246
Six Day War (1967) 358
skirmishing 19, 26, 27, 30, 31, 46, 187, 194, 205
Slim, Field Marshal the Viscount William (British commander in Burma, World War II) 336, 337
Sluys, battle of (1340) 100, 399
Smolensk, battle of, (1812) 204
Social War (90–89 BC) 55
Sobieski, Jan (John III of Poland) 170
Somalia peace-keeping mission (1992–94) 365, 373
Somme, battle of, 1916 278–80
sonar 302
Soult, Nicolas (French marshal, Napoleonic wars) 196, 200, 203
South Korea 343, 395
Sovereign of the Seas (English warship, 1637) 126
Soviet-German non-aggression pact (1939) 304, 315
space-based capabilities 342
Spanish Armada – see Armada
Spanish Civil War (1936–39) 303, 396
Spanish High Seas fleet 126
Spanish Succession, War of (1701–14) 174, 175, 181
Spartans 23, 25, 26, 27, 28, 32, 33, 40

Special Air Services Regiment (SAS) 350
Speer, Albert (German armaments minister, World War II) 322, 325
Spickern, battle of (1870) 238
spingards 133
Spion Kop, battle of (1900) 250–1
Spitfire fighter aircraft 309, 310
Spottsylvania, battle of (1864) 229
Spurius Ligustinus (Roman legionary) 45
Srebrenica 367–70, 373
St Germain, count of, on common soldiers 177
St James's Day Fight (1666) 128
St Quentin, battle of (1557) 153
staff colleges 243
staff system: Prussian 233, 237; Union army 220; German model 243
Stalin, Josef (Soviet leader): military purges (1930s) 300, 305; World War II 315, 317, 321, 328; Cold War 340–1, 343, 345
Stalingrad, battle of (1942–43) 320–1
standardized arms 152
Standish, Miles, English colonial leader 155
Statute of Winchester (England, 1285) 104
stealth aircraft 362, 363
steam-powered navies 218
Steuben, August von (Prussian officer in Washington's Continental army, War of American Independence) 188
stirrups 2, 67, 84
storm troops (German elite divisions, World War I) 288, 291, 293
Stratagemata (Sextus Julius Frontinus) 105
Strategic Bombing Survey (World War II) 326
Streltsy (Russian infantry) 172
submarines 302; battle of the Atlantic (World War II) 324, 325; American (World War II) 336; nuclear 342
successors to Alexander the Great 42, 43–4
Sudan, US Cruise missile firing on 374
Suez Crisis (1956) 357
suicide missions in war 359, 360, 374–6, 383–8, 398
Sulla (Roman general) 55
Sulpicianus (Roman general) 57
Sun-Tzu (Chinese theorist) 2
Supply lines 166, 168, 199, 201, 204
surveillance systems 400
Svensksund, battle of (1790) 123
Swiss pikemen 97, 98, 99

swords, 44, 45, 46, 132
syphilis (Spanish army in the Netherlands) 149
Syracuse campaign (415–413 BC) 28, 392
Syria 357–9, 371–2
Szigeth besieged (1566) 114

T
T-54 tank 358
Tacitus (war criticism) 389
Taginae, battle of (552) 70
Tainos Indians 132
Taliban 374–6, 396; *see also* al-Qaeda; Laden, Osama Bin
Tallard, comte Camille de (French commander at Blenheim) 175
Tapia, Gonzalo de (conquistador) 137
Tanagra, battle of (457 BC) 26
tank warfare: World War I 287, 289, 293; World War II 315, 319, 327–8; Yom Kippur War 361; *see also* armoured warfare
Tannenberg, battle of (1914) 271, 294
Tarawa, battle of (1943) 335
taxation and war 8, 61, 103, 116, 180, 212, 373
technology of war 2, 217, 225, 233, 237, 242, 266, 299, 340, 342, 363, 367–8
Tel-el-Kebir, battle of (1882) 244
telegraph communications: Crimean War 218; mobilization in 1914 265
Tennessee, Army of (American Civil War) 229
ten-year rule (British war planning) 371
Tenochtitlán besieged (1521) 133, 135, 140
tercios (permanent regiments) 150, 154
terrorism 357, 358, 371
Testi, Fulvio, on soldiers 147
Tet offensive (1968) 353, 354
Thapsus, battle of (46 BC) 56
Thatcher, Margaret (British prime minister, Falklands War) 360
Thebans 27, 28, 38–9
Themistocles (Athenian admiral) 23, 25
Theodoric the Great (Ostrogothic king) 65
Theodosian walls (Constantinople) 63–4
Theodosius I 68, 389
Thermopylae, battle of (480 BC) 25
Third Coalition against Napoleon (1805) 200, 213
Third Mysore War (1789–92) 212
Thirteen Years War (1654–67) 172
Thirty Years War (1618–48) 148–9, 155–6, 158, 160–3, 177
Thomas, George (Union general) 228

Thucydides (*History of the Peloponnesian War*) 2, 18, 20, 27–8, 391
Ticinus, battle of (218 BC) 48
Tigers (Bosnian Serb Group) 395
Tiglath-Pileser (Assyrian king) 12
Tilly, Jan Tserklaes, count of (first commander of the Catholic army, Thirty Years War) 156, 157, 161
Tilsit, treaty of (1807) 203, 206
Timucua Indians 134
Tippoo, Sultan of Mysore 212
Tirpitz, Alfred von (German admiral, World War I) 257, 258
Tlaxcalans 140
tokens of allegiance 151, 158
Tokugawa shoguns 252, 253
Tokyo bombed (1945) 339
Tora Bora mountains 376, 396
Tornado aircraft 363
torsion catapults 34, 73
Toulon, battle of (1793) 195
Tourcoing, battle of (1794) 195
trace italienne (angled defences) 112–15
Trafalgar, battle of (1805) 209–11
training 50, 59–60, 98, 147, 155, 178, 221
Trasimene, battle of (217 BC) 48
Trebia, battle of (218 BC) 48
trebuchets 87, 96, 106, 107
trench warfare: 16th–17th centuries 113, 147, 154, 171; American Civil War 225; World War I 270, 280, 286, 287
Trenchard, Viscount Hugh Montague (chief of the British air service staff, 1919–29) 301
Trenton, battle of (1776) 186, 187
triarii (third line, Roman legion) 46, 52, 53, 54
Tricameron, battle of (535) 70
triplex acies (Roman battlefield order) 46, 52, 53
triremes 24, 25–6
Trojan Women (Euripides) 389
Truman, Harry S. (American president, 1945–53) 341, 343, 344, 345
trunnions 97, 109
Truppenführung (German doctrinal manual, 1924) 299
Tsushima Straits, battle of (1905) 256
Tuchman, Barbara (*Guns of August*) 402
Tugela river battles (1899–1900) 250
Tunis battles (16th c.) 123
Tupac Amaru (Inca leader) 138
Tupi warriors 135, 140
Turenne, Henri de la Tour d'Auvergne, vicomte de (17th-c. French general) 168, 169
Turnhout, battle of (1597) 155, 156
Tutsis minority 365–6, 395

'Typhoon' (German advance on Moscow, 1941) 317–18
Tyre taken by Alexander (332 BC) 42
Tyrtaeus, on hoplite warfare 16

U

U-boats 283, 285, 302, 324, 325
Ulm manoeuvre, Napoleon's (1805) 200, 201
'Ultra' intelligence (World War II) 311, 313, 318, 330
Umezu, General Yoshijiro (Japanese army chief of staff, 1945) 340
uniforms 150, 151, 152, 221
United Nations forces: Korean War (1950–53) 343; Sinai (1956) 357; Somalia (1993–4) 365; Yugoslavia (1990s) 367–70
United States Air Force strategic bombing of Germany (World War II) 325, 326; nuclear deterrence 342; Vietnam War 352, 355–6; Iraq 380–8
'Uranus' (Stalingrad counter-attack, 1942) 321

V

V-1 and V-2 weapons (World War II) 6, 326, 327
Vaal Kranz, battle of (1900) 250
Valentinian (Roman emperor) 68
Valerius Maximus on Marius 55
Valmy, battle of (1792) 194, 195
Valutino, battle of (1812) 204
Vandals 65, 69, 70
Varus's legions destroyed (AD 9) 56, 60
Vauban, Sébastien le Prestre de (Louis XIV's engineer) 113–14, 167, 168–9, 174, 195
Vegetius (Concerning Military Matters) 4, 53, 59, 64, 66, 87, 105, 392
velites (Roman skirmishes) 46, 54
Venetian warfare 79, 100, 105, 112, 121, 123
Verdun: treaty of (843) 72, 75–6; battle of (1916) 276, 277, 284
Versailles, treaty of (1918) 298
Vespasian (Roman emperor) 59
Vicksburg, siege of (1863) 226, 227–8
Victory (Nelson's flagship) 127, 210, 211
Vienna, siege of (1683) 170–1; taken by Napoleon (1805) 200
Viet Cong (Viet Minh) 346, 347, 348, 351
Vietnam: colonized by France 346; occupied (1945) 347; French war with Viet Minh 346–8; American intervention (1965–73) 350; attacked by China (1979) 356
Vietnam-War protesters 353
Vikings 76, 77, 82

Vilcabamba (Inca stronghold) 138
Villars, Claude de (18th-c. French general) 176
Villeneuve, Pierre (French admiral, Napoleonic wars) 210
Virginia Capes, battle of (1813) 189
Visigoths 65, 68, 69, 70, 71
Vitoria, battle of (1813) 204
volley fire 154–5, 178, 394
Voltaire on French attack style 190

W

Wagenburgen (Hussite fortified wagons) 97
Wagram, battle of (1809) 205
Wall Street: 17th-c. fortifications 145; financial crisis (1929) 298
walled towns: medieval 68, 69, 89; after gunpowder revolution 112, 114, 116
Wallenstein, Albert of (17th-c. mercenary entrepreneur) 149, 158
Wallhausen, Johann Jakob von (director, Schola Militaris) 155
war, criticism of – see criticism of war
war colleges: French (École supérieur de guerre) 300; Prussian 206, 233
war crimes: German (World War II) 331, 339; Italian (World War II) 339; Japanese (World War II) 336, 339; Yugoslavia (1990s) 369–70; American (Iraq) 383
war junks 120
War of 1812 (1812–14) 211
War of American Independence (1775–83) 187–91
War of the Austrian Succession (1740–48) 178, 181, 183
War of Devolution (1688–97) 168
War of the League of Augsburg (1688–97) 130, 174
war reporting 372–4, 383
War of the Spanish Succession (1701–14) 174, 175, 181
Warsaw uprising (1944) 328
Wartgelt (mercenary retainer) 148
Washington, George (patriot commander, War of American Independence) 4, 186, 187, 188, 189, 190
Watergate affair (1972–75) 356
Waterloo, battle of 207–8
Ways and Means (Xenophon) 32
Weapons of Mass Destruction (Iraq's) 378, 382
Weissenburg, battle of (1870) 238
Wellington, Arthur Wellesley, duke of 204, 207–8, 212
West Bank taken by Israel (1967) 358

Western Front: World War I 267–70, 273, 276–87, 289–94; World War II 306–11, 325–6, 329–32
Westmoreland, William (American general, Vietnam War) 352, 354
Weygand, Maxime (French general, World War II) 309
White Company (15th-c. mercenaries) 94
White Mountain, battle of (1620) 156
Widukind on Henry the Fowler's garrisons 78
Wiener Neustadt military academy 183
Wilderness, battle of (1864) 229
Wilhelm I of Prussia 234
Wilhelm II of Germany 257, 264, 271
William I of England, the Conqueror 82–3, 84, 85, 87
William III, ruler of the Dutch Republic, king of England, Scotland, and Ireland 124, 128, 129, 175
William III's War (1689–97) 130, 174
William Louis of Nassau 154, 155, 394, 402
William of Orange – see William III
Wilson, Woodrow (American president, World War I) 283
Wingate, Orde (British commander, World War II) 356
Winthrop, John, English colonial leader 155
Wolfe, James (18th-c. British general) 184–5
Wolfowitz, Paul 380–1, 402
Wolseley, Sir Garnet (British general at Tel-el-Kebir, 1882) 244
women's role in war 272, 295
World Trade Center, attack on 374, 376, 384, 399
World War I 256–97
World War II 304–49

X

Xenophon (Greek historian and military theorist) 15, 16, 18, 28, 29, 32, 33
Xerxes (Persian emperor) 21, 23, 25

Y

Yalu river: battle of (1904) 254; in Korean War 344
Yamashita, Tomoyuki (Japanese general, World War II) 336
Yardley, George (Governor of Virginia, 1616–17) 158
Yeltsin, Boris 366, 373
Yom Kippur War (1973) 359–61
Yorktown besieged (1781) 190
Yugoslavia 367–70

Z

Zama, battle of (202 BC) 49
Zaire 370
Zela, battle of (47 BC) 56
'Zero' (Japanese fighter aircraft in World War II) 334, 335
'Zitadelle' (German offensive against Kursk salient, 1943) 327
Zhukov, Georgi (Soviet general, World War II) 318, 320, 332
Zizka, John (Hussite general) 97
Zulu War (1877) 244